C#

Joseph Mayo

SAMS

Unleashed

C# Unleashed

International Standard Book Number: 0-672-32122-x

Library of Congress Catalog Card Number: 00-111066

Printed in the United States of America

First Printing: November 2001

04 03 02 01 4 3 2 1

Trademarks

All terms mentioned in this book that are known to be trademarks or service marks have been appropriately capitalized. Sams Publishing cannot attest to the accuracy of this information. Use of a term in this book should not be regarded as affecting the validity of any trademark or service mark.

Warning and Disclaimer

Every effort has been made to make this book as complete and as accurate as possible, but no warranty or fitness is implied. The information provided is on an "as is" basis. The author and the publisher shall have neither liability nor responsibility to any person or entity with respect to any loss or damages arising from the information contained in this book or from the use of programs accompanying it.

Publisher
Paul Boger

Executive Editor
Shelley Kronzek

Development Editor
Susan Hobbs

Managing Editor
Charlotte Clapp

Project Editors
Elizabeth Finney
Leah Kirkpatrick

Copy Editor
Maryann Steinhart

Indexer
D&G Limited, LLC

Proofreader
D&G Limited, LLC

Technical Editors
Kevin Burton
Bill Craun

Team Coordinator
Pamalee Nelson

Media Developer
Dan Scherf

Interior Designer
Gary Adair

Cover Designer
Aren Howell

Page Layout
D&G Limited, LLC

Contents at a Glance

Introduction **1**

Part I C# Basics 9

1 The C# Environment **11**

2 Getting Started with C# **19**

3 Writing C# Expressions **47**

4 Using Statements and Loops to Control Program Flow **69**

5 Debugging and Pre-Processing **91**

Part II Object and Component Programming with C# 107

6 Object and Component Concepts **109**

7 Working with Classes **129**

8 Designing Object-Oriented Programs **177**

9 Overloading Class Members and Operators **219**

10 Handling Exceptions and Errors **237**

11 Delegates and Events **255**

12 Organizing Code with Namespaces **277**

13 Creating `structs` **289**

14 Implementing Interfaces **301**

15 Performing Conversions **329**

Part III Using Class Libraries with C# 341

16 Presenting Graphical User Interfaces **343**

17 File I/O and Serialization **381**

18 XML **407**

19 Database Programming with ADO.NET **417**

20 Writing Web Applications with ASP.NET **439**

21 Remoting **459**

22 Web Services **483**

Part IV Extreme C# 495

23 Multi-Threading **497**

24 Browsing the Network Libraries **503**

25 String Manipulation **515**

26 C# Collections **545**

27 Attributes **567**

28 Reflection **581**

29 Localization and Resources **595**

30 Unsafe Code and `PInvoke` **619**

31 Runtime Debugging **635**

32 Performance Monitoring **647**

33 Integrating C# with COM **679**

Part V The C# Environment 693

34 Garbage Collection **695**

35 Cross-Language Programming with C# **711**

36 The Common Language Runtime **725**

37 Versioning and Assemblies **733**

38 Securing Code **745**

Part VI Appendixes 759

A Compiling Programs **761**

B The .NET Frameworks Class Library **767**

C Online Resources **773**

Index 775

Contents

Introduction 1

Part I C# Basics 9

1 The C# Environment 11

The Common Language Infrastructure (CLI) 12
Standardization 15
The .NET Architecture 16
  Common Language Runtime (CLR) 16
  Libraries 16
  Languages 17
Where C# Fits In 17
Summary 17

2 Getting Started with C# 19

Writing a Simple C# Program 20
Comments 22
  Multi-Line Comments 22
  Single-Line Comments 23
  XML Documentation Comments 23
Identifiers and Keywords 24
  Identifiers 24
  Keywords 26
Style 26
Preparing a Program To Run 27
Basic C# Types 28
  Variable Declarations 29
  The Simple Types 29
  Struct Types 34
  Reference Types 34
  Enumeration Types 35
  String Type 36

Definite Assignment 37
Basic Conversions 38
Arrays 40
Single-dimension Arrays 40
N-Dimensional Arrays 42
Jagged Arrays 42
Interacting with Programs 43
Summary 46

3 Writing C# Expressions 47

Unary Operators 48
The Plus Operator 48
The Minus Operator 49
The Increment Operator 49
The Decrement Operator 50
The Logical Complement Operator 50
The Bitwise Complement Operator 50
Binary Operators 51
Arithmetic Operators 51
Relational Operators 53
Logical Operators 55
Assignment Operators 58
The Ternary Operator 59
Other Operators 60
The `is` Operator 60
The `as` Operator 60
The `sizeof()` Operator 60
The `typeof()` Operator 60
The `checked()` Operator 61
The `unchecked()` Operator 61
Enumeration Expressions 61
Array Expressions 63
Statements 65
Blocks 65
Labels 66
Declarations 66
Operator Precedence and Associativity 66
Summary 68

4 Using Statements and Loops to Control Program Flow 69

`if` Statements 70
Simple `if` 70
`if-then-else` 71
`if-else if-else` 71

`switch` Statements 73
C# Loops 76
`while` Loops 77
`do` Loops 78
`for` Loops 79
`foreach` Loops 80
`goto` Statements 81
`break` Statements 83
`continue` Statements 84
`return` Statements 84
Summary 88

5 Debugging and Pre-Processing 91

Pre-Processing Directives 92
Define Directive 92
Conditionals 92
Errors 93
Line Numbers 94
Comments 94
Debugging C# Programs 94
The Debugging Approach 95
Using the Debugger To Find a Program Error 96
Attaching to Processes 101
Summary 106

Part II Object and Component Programming with C# 107

6 Object and Component Concepts 109

What Is an Object? 110
Object Classification 112
Object Hierarchies 113
Abstraction 114
Objects within Objects 115
Objects with Different Behaviors 116
Component Interfaces 120
Component Properties 123
Component Events 125
Summary 128

7 Working with Classes 129

Class Members 130
Instance and Static Members 131
Use of Accessibility Modifiers 131
Fields 132

Field Initialization 132
Definite Assignment 133
Constant Fields 134
`readonly` Fields 135
XML Comments 135
Constructors 135
Instance Constructors 136
Static Constructors 141
Destructors 142
Methods 143
Instance Methods 144
Method Signature 144
Method Body 147
Local Fields 147
Method Parameters 148
Static Methods 155
XML Comments 156
Properties 156
Property Accessors 157
Transparent Access 159
Static Properties 160
Late Bound Object Creation 161
XML Comments 162
Indexers 162
XML Comments 164
Full XML Comments 165
Summary 176

8 Designing Object-Oriented Programs 177

Inheritance 178
Base Classes 178
Abstract Classes 180
Calling Base Class Members 188
Hiding Base Class Members 191
Versioning 193
Sealed Classes 197
Encapsulating Object Internals 198
Data Hiding 198
Modifiers Supporting Encapsulation 199
Other Encapsulation Strategies 199
Relationship of Encapsulation to Inheritance 200

Polymorphism 200
Implementing Polymorphism 201
Hiding Again 206
Most-Derived Implementations 210
Polymorphic Properties 213
Polymorphic Indexers 215
Summary 217

9 Overloading Class Members and Operators 219

Overloading Methods 220
Overloading Indexers 223
Overloading Operators 227
Resolving Overloaded Members 234
Summary 235

10 Handling Exceptions and Errors 237

`try/catch` Blocks 238
`finally` Blocks 240
Predefined Exception Classes 241
Handling Exceptions 241
Handling Multiple Exceptions 242
Handling and Passing Exceptions 243
Recovering from Exceptions 246
Designing Your Own Exceptions 249
`checked` and `unchecked` Statements 251
Summary 253

11 Delegates and Events 255

Delegates 256
Defining Delegates 256
Creating Delegate Method Handlers 257
Hooking Up Delegates and Handlers 257
Invoking Methods through Delegates 258
Multi-Cast Delegates 258
Delegate Equality 261
Events 262
Defining Event Handlers 262
Registering for Events 264
Implementing Events 265
Firing Events 267
Modifying Event Add/Remove Methods 269
Summary 275

12 Organizing Code with Namespaces 277

Why Namespaces? 278
Organizing Code 278
Avoiding Conflict 279
Namespace Directives 280
The `using` Directive 280
The `alias` Directive 281
Creating Namespaces 282
Namespace Members 286
Scope and Visibility 286
Summary 288

13 Creating `structs` 289

Identifying the `class/struct` Relationship 290
Value Versus Reference 291
Inheritance 292
Other Differences 293
Trade-Offs 293
Type System Unification 294
The Pre-Defined Types as `structs` 294
Boxing and Unboxing 295
Designing a New Value Type 295
Summary 298

14 Implementing Interfaces 301

Abstract Class Versus Interface 302
Interface Members 302
Methods 303
Properties 303
Indexers 304
Events 304
Implicit Implementation 304
Single Class Interface Implementation 305
Simulating Polymorphic Behavior 309
Explicit Implementation 315
Mapping 321
Inheritance 324
Summary 327

15 Performing Conversions 329

Implicit Versus Explicit Conversions 330
Value Type Conversions 335
Reference Type Conversions 338
Summary 339

Part III Using Class Libraries with C# 341

16 Presenting Graphical User Interfaces 343

Windows 344
Controls 348
N-Tier Architecture 351
Menus 373
Summary 379

17 File I/O and Serialization 381

Files and Directories 382
Streams 391
  Reading and Writing with Streams 391
  Implementing a Cryptographic Stream 395
Serialization 398
  Automatic Serialization 398
  Custom Serialization 401
Summary 406

18 XML 407

Writing 408
Reading 411
Summary 416

19 Database Programming with ADO.NET 417

Making Connections 418
Viewing Data 420
Manipulating Data 425
Calling Stored Procedures 429
Retrieving DataSets 435
Summary 438

20 Writing Web Applications with ASP.NET 439

A Simple Web Page 440
Controls 441
  Server Controls 441
  HTML Controls 442
  Validation Controls 443
Making a Web Form 443
  A Simple Web Form 444
  Manipulating Web Form Controls 448
Code-Behind Web Pages 452
Summary 457

21 Remoting 459

Basic Remoting 460
Remoting Server 461
Remoting Client 463
Remoting Setup 465
Proxys 471
Channels 475
Lifetime Management 478
Summary 481

22 Web Services 483

Web Service Basics 484
Web Service Technologies 484
A Basic Web Service 485
Viewing Web Service Info 486
Using Web Services 490
Summary 493

Part IV Extreme C# 495

23 Multi-Threading 497

Creating New Threads 498
Synchronization 499
Summary 502

24 Browsing the Network Libraries 503

Implementing Sockets 504
A Socket Server 504
A Socket Client 507
Compiling and Running Server and Client 511
Working with HTTP 512
Summary 514

25 String Manipulation 515

The `String` Class 516
static Methods 517
Instance Methods 522
Properties and Indexers 532
The `StringBuilder` Class 533
Instance Methods 533
Properties and Indexers 538
`String` Formatting 540
Numeric Formatting 540
Picture Formatting 541

Regular Expressions 541
Summary 543

26 C# Collections 545

Pre-Existing Collections 546
The `ArrayList` Collection 546
The `BitArray` Collection 547
The `Hashtable` Collection 549
The `Queue` Collection 549
The `SortedList` Collection 550
The `Stack` Collection 551
Collection Interfaces 552
Creating a Collection 553
A List Collection 553
Using the `SiteList` Collection 563
Summary 565

27 Attributes 567

Using Attributes 568
Using a Single Attribute 568
Using Multiple Attributes 569
Using Attribute Parameters 570
Positional Parameters 571
Named Parameters 571
Using Attribute Targets 572
Creating Your Own Attributes 574
The `AttributeUsage` Attribute 574
Getting Attributes from a Class 578
Summary 579

28 Reflection 581

Discovering Program Information 582
Dynamically Activating Code 588
`Reflection.Emit` 590
Summary 594

29 Localization and Resources 595

Resource Files 596
Creating a Resource File 596
Writing a Resource File 599
Reading a Resource File 600
Converting a Resource File 601
Creating Graphical Resources 603

Multiple Locales 609
Implementing Multiple Locales 610
Finding Resources 616
Summary 617

30 Unsafe Code and `PInvoke` 619

Unsafe Code 620
What Do You Mean My Code Is Unsafe? 620
The Power of Pointers 621
The `sizeof()` Operator 625
The `stackalloc` Operator 626
The `fixed` Statement 628
Platform Invoke 631
Summary 633

31 Runtime Debugging 635

Simple Debugging 636
Conditional Debugging 638
Runtime Tracing 641
Making Assertions 643
Summary 644

32 Performance Monitoring 647

Accessing Built-in Performance Counters 648
Implementing Timers 656
Building a Customized Performance Counter 657
Analyzing Performance with Sampling 668
Summary 677

33 Integrating C# with COM 679

Communicating with COM from .NET 680
Early-Bound COM Component Calls 680
Late-Bound COM Component Calls 682
Exposing a .NET Component as a COM Component 683
Introduction to .NET Support for COM+ Services 685
Transactions 687
JIT Activation 688
Object Pooling 689
Other Services 690
Summary 690

Part V The C# Environment 693

34 Garbage Collection 695

Automatic Memory Management 696
Inside the Garbage Collector 697
Garbage Collector Optimization 698
Finalizing Your Code Properly 699
The Problems with Destructors 699
The Dispose Pattern 700
The `using` Statement 701
Controlling Garbage Collection 703
Controlling Objects 703
Weak References 705
Summary 709

35 Cross-Language Programming with C# 711

The Common Type System (CTS) 712
The Common Language Specification (CLS) 713
Tips for Making Your Code CLS-Compatible 713
General 714
Naming 715
Types 715
Methods 716
Indexers and Properties 717
Events 717
Pointers 718
Interfaces 718
Inheritance 718
Arrays 719
Enums 719
Attributes 720
Assemblies 720
Writing a Cross-Language Program 721
Summary 724

36 The Common Language Runtime 725

Managed Execution 726
Creating Source Code 727
Compiling to Intermediate Code 727
Compiling to Native Code 727
Executing the Program 728
Metadata 728
Uses of Metadata 729

Managed Services 729
Exception Handling 729
Automatic Lifetime Management 730
Interoperability 730
Security 730
Profiling and Debugging 730
Summary 730

37 Versioning and Assemblies 733

Inside Assemblies 734
Manifests 735
Attributes 735
Assembly Features 738
Identity 738
Scope 738
Versioning 738
Security 739
Configuration 740
Startup Configuration 741
Runtime Configuration 741
Deployment 743
Summary 744

38 Securing Code 745

Code-Based Security 746
Evidence 746
Permissions 747
Code Groups 747
Security Policy Levels 749
Permission Requests 750
Implementing Security Policy 753
Role-Based Security 755
Security Utilities 757
Summary 758

Part VI Appendixes 759

A Compiling Programs 761

Assemblies 762
Debug 762
Miscellaneous 763
Optimization 764
Output 764

Preprocessing 765
Resources 765

B The .NET Frameworks Class Libraries 767

C Online Resources 773

C# Sites 774
.NET Sites 774

Index 775

About the Author

Joe Mayo is a pioneer within the C# community. Joe created the C# Station Web site shortly after this new language was introduced. His very popular C# Tutorials are accessed by Web developers and Web sites throughout the world. Joe is a seasoned developer with more than 15 years of robust experience. Over the years, he has programmed in a variety of languages including assembler, C, C++, VBA, and Forte 4GL. His database experience encompasses Paradox, Dbase III, MS Access, and Oracle. Frameworks include MFC and Motif. He has programmed several operating systems including VAX VMS, RSX-11, UNIX, and several versions of MS-DOS and MS Windows. He has developed applications in standalone mode for desktops, client-server on LANs, and n-tier applications on LANs and WANs. Joe opened a Web site titled C# Station in late June 2000. He is currently a software engineer for Qwest Communications.

Dedication

To my beautiful wife, Maytinee

You are the vision, the light
guiding my way

Your strength and support
enable perseverance

Mother of our children and best friend
I love and thank you dearly

—Joe Mayo

Acknowledgments

Although my name appears on the cover of this book, work of such magnitude could never have occurred without the valuable contributions of many people. To the people at Sams Publishing, Microsoft, and friends and family I am eternally grateful.

I'd first like to thank Shelley Kronzek, Executive Editor, for finding me and offering this wonderful opportunity. Her leadership is inspiring. Susan Hobbs, Development Editor, was totally awesome, keeping me on focus and organized. Maryann Steinhart, Copy Editor, made my writing look great. Other people at Sams Publishing I'd like to recognize include Katie Robinson, Leah Kirkpatrick, Elizabeth Finney, Pamalee Nelson, and Laurie McGuire. Thanks also to all the editors, indexers, printers, production, and other people at Sams who have contributed to this book.

Special thanks goes to Kevin Burton and Bill Craun, technical editors. Their technical expertise and advice was absolutely top-notch. They provided detailed pointers, and their perspectives made a significant difference. Thanks to Keith Olsen, Charles Tonklinson, Cedric, and Christoph Wille for reviewing my early work.

Thanks to all the people at Microsoft who set up author seminars and training. They are transforming the way we do computing and leading the industry in a move of historic proportions—an initiative deserving of much praise. Special thanks to Eric Gunnerson for taking time out of his extremely busy schedule to review my chapters.

This first book is a significant milestone in my life. As such, I must recognize those people who contributed to my success. In many ways, they define who I am.

Thanks to family members: Maytinee Mayo, Joseph A. Mayo Jr., Jennifer A. Mayo, Kamonchon Ahantric, Lacee and June Mayo, Bob Mayo, Margina Mayo, Richard Mayo, Gary Mayo, Mike Mayo, Tony Gravagno, Tim and Kirby Hoffman, Richard and Barbara Bickerstaff, Bobbie Jo Burns, David Burns, Mistie Lea Bickerstaff, Cecil Sr. and Margaret Sloan, Cecil Jr. and Jean Sloan, Lou and Rose Weiner, Mary and Ron Monette, Jack Freeman Sr., and Bill Freeman.

Thanks to friends and professional associates: Evelyn Black, Harry G. Hall, Arthur E. Richardson, Carl S. Markussen, Judson Meyer, Hoover McCoy, Bill Morris, Gary Meyer, Tim Leuers, Angela Dees-Prebula, Bob Jangraw, Jean-Paul Massart, Jeff and Stephanie Manners, Eddie Alicea, Gary and Gloria Lefebvre, Bob Turbyfill, and Dick Van Bennekom, Barry Patterson, Otis Solomon, and Brian Allen.

Tell Us What You Think!

As the reader of this book, *you* are our most important critic and commentator. We value your opinion and want to know what we're doing right, what we could do better, what areas you'd like to see us publish in, and any other words of wisdom you're willing to pass our way.

As an Executive Editor for Sams, I welcome your comments. You can fax, e-mail, or write me directly to let me know what you did or didn't like about this book—as well as what we can do to make our books stronger.

Please note that I cannot help you with technical problems related to the topic of this book, and that due to the high volume of mail I receive, I might not be able to reply to every message.

When you write, please be sure to include this book's title and author as well as your name and phone or fax number. I will carefully review your comments and share them with the author and editors who worked on the book.

Fax: 317-581-4770

Email: `feedback@samspublishing.com`

Mail: Shelley Kronzek
Executive Editor
Sams
201 West 103rd Street
Indianapolis, IN 46290 USA

Introduction

Welcome to *C# Unleashed*, a programmer's guide and reference to the C# (pronounced "see sharp") programming language. C# is a brand-new object-oriented programming (OOP) language that emphasizes a component-based approach to software development.

While component-based programming has been with us, in one form or another, for a few years now, the vision of what C# enables promises to take us to the next level in software development. This is the new paradigm shift toward XML Web Services—the view of software as a service, disconnected, stateless, and conforming to international open standards.

Software as a service is the vision of the next generation of computing systems. For example, C# is well suited for building Web services, reusable components on the Internet that conform to open standards. Software development is no longer constrained to the monolithic architectures we have been developing over the last several years. Web services enable applications to use distributed services over the Web, which simplify development and promote a greater scale of software reuse. C# is a major player in the Web services arena, promoting the vision of software as a service.

This book not only teaches the C# language itself, but its goal is to show how C# could be used to develop software as a service. Looking at the evolution of software, it's evident how we've reached this point in time. For many years, programs were written as monolithic applications with a single purpose. Through research and experience, we realized the benefits of modularization, which eventually led to object-oriented methods. This gave us large-scale re-use and maintainability. Client/server and networking technology evolved naturally as collaboration and communication became business requirements. Enter the Internet and Web technology, providing distributed, stateless, and secure software technologies, including applets and other Web page objects. The next evolutionary step is where C# fits in: automating the Internet.

Why This Book Is for You

If you've developed software in any other computer programming language, you will be able to understand the contents of this book with no trouble. You already know how to make logical decisions and construct iterative code. You also understand variables and basic number systems like hexadecimal. Honestly, ambitious beginners could do well with this book if they're motivated.

Having developed software for several years, I stepped back into some old shoes many times during writing this book. A common question I'd ask myself was, "What if I just spent the last two years programming Y2K fixes in COBOL?" or "What if I was a PROLOG programmer doing scientific research for a number of years?" Would someone working with language X understand a certain explanation or example? When the answer was positive, I felt confident that I had given you fair consideration.

This is a book written for every programmer. Although it has notes for a couple of the larger potential groups of readers, C++ and Java programmers, it considers all programmers. It's basic enough for you to see every aspect of C# that's possible, yet it's sufficiently advanced to provide insight into the modern enterprise-level tasks you deal with every day. I hope this book leaves you with a sense that you now have a valuable new tool in your backpack to develop the Web services and distributed solutions that are ultimately our destiny.

Organization and Goals

C# Unleashed is all about writing code in the C# programming language. Many of the advanced topics could fill books of their own, but the primary focus is not to teach the details of the advanced topics, although some areas do have significant depth. The goal within each of the chapters is to show how C# is used to perform a given task. Even in the more theoretical chapters, the focus is on how each topic applies to writing code in C#.

This book is divided into six major parts. It begins with the simpler material and those items strictly related to the C# language itself. Later, the book moves into C#-related areas, showing how to use libraries. Then it covers more advanced topics, showing how to develop code for various technologies using C#.

Part I: C# Basics

Part I provides the most basic elements of C# language syntax. It begins by introducing the environment C# operates in and then showing how to create a couple simple C# programs. The different C# types and how they're used to create expressions and statements are covered. There is a chapter on controlling program flow with branching and iteration. After enough material has been covered so that the reader understands a moderately sophisticated program, there is a chapter on how to debug C# programs.

- **Chapter 1** C# does not operate in a typical environment where programs are compiled directly to machine code. It runs in a virtual execution system that manages how the code runs. There are several technologies that enable this environment to operate the way it does. C# is also being submitted as an open standard. The material is purposely brief, so you can quickly dive into the main purpose of the book, writing C# code.

- **Chapter 2** The basics of C# include how to build a simple program, basic syntax, and information on C# types. C# syntax and types are much like those of its C and C++ parent languages.
- **Chapter 3** Central to computing in any language is the ability to manipulate data with expressions. C# includes an entire suite of unary, binary, and ternary expressions. Highlights include forming expressions, operator precedence, and working with enum and array types.
- **Chapter 4** Rounding out basics of the C# language are several constructs allowing control of program flow. Besides the traditional `if` and `select` statements and `while` and `for` loops, there is an explanation of the new `foreach` loop. I even touch upon the infamous `goto` statement.
- **Chapter 5** Advanced programmers, please bear with me. I sincerely believe that debugging is so important, especially to intermediate programmers, that there is an entire chapter dedicated to it. There is also an introductory section on pre-processing directives.

Part II: Object and Component Programming with C#

Part II covers object and component programming in C#. For some, this is one of the toughest things to learn, so I start at a very basic level and then go into more depth. In fact, there is a set of three entire chapters dedicated exclusively to object and component programming concepts. The rest of the chapters in this part deal with other types of C# objects and how to use the object-oriented features of C#.

- **Chapter 6** A large part of programming with C# is understanding object-oriented programming (OOP). If you're an OOP purist, count to 10. This is a chapter focused on programmers coming from functional, logical, or procedural paradigms. Many people learning OOP will scratch their heads for a while before they get the "Ah-ha!" experience. This material is designed to help "Ah-ha!" come a little more quickly.
- **Chapter 7** One of the most used objects in C# is the class. This chapter's focus is on the mechanics of creating a class and its members, including constructors, destructors, fields, methods, properties, and indexers. There is also an entire program demonstrating how XML comments are used.
- **Chapter 8** Classes define objects that, in turn, have object-oriented behavior. Discussion and examples drill down into how object-oriented programming is performed with classes.

- **Chapter 9** Method and operator overloading in C# is similar to C and C++ but has nuances that make it unique. There are several examples that explain how to overload members and operators and show some of the new constraints and safeguards.
- **Chapter 10** C# has extensive error handling and exception support. Pertinent items discussed include exception handling with `try/catch/finally` blocks, exception creation and management, and exception recovery.
- **Chapter 11** Events and delegates are closely related and provide support for late-bound method invocation. This chapter presents the delegate object first and then shows how it is used with the event class member.
- **Chapter 12** Namespaces were briefly introduced earlier in the book, but now they are discussed in detail, including namespace declaration and how to use namespaces to organize code and avoid identifier naming conflicts.
- **Chapter 13** A struct is another C# object type. It's similar to a class in mechanics but possesses different semantics. Since a struct contains many of the same members as a class, this chapter focuses on the unique features of a struct and its difference from the class type.
- **Chapter 14** Interface-based programming is superior in exposing the public contract an object exposes to potential clients. This chapter presents thorough and detailed information on how to implement interfaces in a C# program.
- **Chapter 15** C# is a very strongly typed language. The discussion focuses on how to maintain type safety, while still being able to make conversions between user-defined types.

Part III: Using Class Libraries with C#

Part III introduces several of the class libraries available to C#.

- **Chapter 16** Although the new vision is Web services, there is still a large audience for desktop graphical user interface (GUI) applications. The Windows Forms library is presented with emphasis on showing how to create a simple user interface with Windows Forms controls.
- **Chapter 17** An entire chapter is devoted to file input/output (I/O), explaining how C# is used to write to and read from files. There is also a discussion about streams.
- **Chapter 18** XML is integrated thoroughly with the base class libraries, underlying its importance in future applications. Examples concentrate on using existing libraries with C# to manipulate XML data.

- **Chapter 19** The primary means of programming databases with C# is through ADO.NET. The examples show how to use many of the ADO.NET classes for traditional and Web-based database access.
- **Chapter 20** The discussion of ASP.NET brings Web software development into focus. ASP.NET Web pages can be developed with code written in C#. Examples include how to program controls and Web programs with C# code.
- **Chapter 21** Remoting is an extensible distributed object programming technology. C# is excellently suited for developing programs using remoting technology. This chapter not only shows how to program remote objects, but also how to employ the technology's extensibility features.
- **Chapter 22** Building Web services with C# is extremely easy. Examples use the existing ASP.NET infrastructure and .NET utilities to show how simple it is to develop a Web service.

Part IV: Extreme C#

Part IV gives those advanced topics for extreme performance and enterprise programming projects.

- **Chapter 23** Modern programming languages support multithreading and so does C#. This chapter includes examples of how to create a multithreaded program and how to implement thread synchronization.
- **Chapter 24** The base class library includes classes supporting Internet communications. This chapter presents methods of communicating via TCP/IP sockets as well as how to use classes that implement the HTTP protocol. There are examples of HTTP Web and SMTP e-mail programming.
- **Chapter 25** Much of the information manipulation performed in programming deals with text data. This entire chapter is dedicated to string manipulation with C#, including the `String` and `StringBuilder` classes, string formatting, and regular expressions.
- **Chapter 26** When the array type isn't enough for an application's data structure requirements, there are collections. Examples show how to use several collections in the base class library as well as how to create a custom collection with code implementing the required interfaces.
- **Chapter 27** Attributes are the part of the C# language that allow you to add declarative functionality to a program. Attribute usage is explained, as well as how to create custom attributes.

- **Chapter 28** C# has a capability called reflection that enables a program to examine information about itself. The examples show how to perform reflection as well as how to dynamically build programs that can be run from memory or saved to an executable file.
- **Chapter 29** Localization is the process of making a program present information for different cultures. There are examples of how to localize programs for multiple cultures.
- **Chapter 30** In practical terms, there will be many projects that want to reuse existing native libraries, interact with operating system code, and perform low-level operations. This chapter shows how to accomplish these things in C#.
- **Chapter 31** Complex systems need mechanisms to detect runtime problems. Examples in this chapter show how to perform runtime debugging and tracing with pertinent elements of the base class libraries.
- **Chapter 32** Another important runtime task is the ability to capture application performance data. Performance counters are used to gather statistics, which help in analyzing how an application performs at runtime under specified conditions.
- **Chapter 33** There are a lot of COM and COM+ programmers out there. Programs in this chapter show how to call COM from C# and how to call C# from COM. The base class libraries include enterprise service classes enabling C# programs to use COM+ services. Examples show how to perform tasks using COM+ services such as transactions, object pooling, and others.

Part V: The C# Environment

Part V goes into depth on the C# environment.

- **Chapter 34** Memory for C# programs is managed by a high-performance garbage collector. Discussions illustrate how the garbage collector works and why it's efficient. There are examples that demonstrate how to interact with the garbage collector and different ways to work with objects to help control their clean-up.
- **Chapter 35** The environment C# operates in supports cross-language programming. There are examples of how to create code in different languages and compile them into the same program. The section on the Common Language Specification (CLS) illuminates the specific areas of the CLS that affect C# programs.
- **Chapter 36** To understand how C# programs run and the meaning of managed code, you must have an understanding of the theory behind the CLR. Much of the information has already been described as a natural part of other C# language elements, but this material enhances and solidifies what is known.

- **Chapter 37** C# programs are deployed as assemblies, so it's important to understand what assemblies are and how to work with them. This chapter shows what assemblies are made of and covers the various attributes that define them.
- **Chapter 38** The book wraps up with security. The material covers the elements of code-based security and how they interact to protect a system from code. Other sections show how to implement code-based and role-based security with both code and attributes.

Part VI: Appendixes

Part VI consists of supplementary material on compiling programs, an overview of .NET Class Library components, and some other resources that may be of interest.

- **Appendix A** Examples of various compiler options are provided in this appendix.
- **Appendix B** This appendix provides an overview of the .NET libraries.
- **Appendix C** This index of selected C# and .NET Web sites is helpful.

C# Basics

PART I

IN THIS PART

1 The C# Environment *11*

2 Getting Started with C# *19*

3 Writing C# Expressions *47*

4 Using Statements and Loops to Control Program Flow *69*

5 De-Bugging and Pre-Processing *91*

CHAPTER 1

The C# Environment

In This Chapter

- The Common Language Infrastructure (CLI) *12*
- Standardization *15*
- The .NET Architecture *16*
- Where C# Fits In *17*

This chapter provides an overview of the environment in which C# operates. This is important for a couple reasons. While learning C#, a familiar question may reappear as to what functionality belongs to the libraries and what capabilities are built into the language. This question is addressed in this chapter to help evaluate what capabilities are available to meet requirements.

Another good reason to understand the C# environment relates to standardization. There will be a need for some software engineers to develop cross-platform applications. With a good understanding of what elements of an environment contribute to a standard installation, cross-platform development can proceed in a much smoother fashion.

The Common Language Infrastructure (CLI)

The primary purpose of the Common Language Infrastructure (CLI) is to facilitate the creation and execution of distributed components and services. It accomplishes this by enabling programs written in different languages to operate together, giving programs the capability to describe themselves, and providing the execution environment to support multiple platforms. The CLI is composed of the following four major sections:

- Common Type System (CTS)
- Common Language Specification (CLS)
- Metadata
- Virtual Execution System (VES)

The CTS was designed to support common data types from a wide variety of programming languages. This opens the door for many languages to join the CLI. In addition, the CTS supports concepts such as type safety, which produces more robust programs and better security.

The CLS is a sub-specification of the CTS. Its purpose is to enhance the communication between programs written in other languages. When a program or class declares it is CLS-compliant, that means it can be reliably used in a cross-language environment. The CLI has a set of libraries called the Base Class Library (BCL). The entire BCL is CLS-compliant.

Metadata provides the capability for code to be self-describing. This is a powerful concept, enabling components to expose their capabilities for use in various tools. Metadata also allows program capabilities to be dynamically implemented through runtime method calls. This is used for any late bound requirements and for software development tools.

Through the CTS, CLS, and metadata, the CLI is able to support a robust Virtual Execution System (VES). Services provided by the VES include managed code execution and security. The VES operates on Common Intermediate Language (CIL) code produced by CLI-compliant compilers.

Note

Managed code refers to the way the VES handles memory allocation and code execution. The VES has full control over managed code in order to provide security. Managed code is compiled to an intermediate language, CIL, where it can be verified by the VES. Traditional languages such as C and C++ are considered unmanaged because they compile to machine code and have only those controls a programmer establishes in the code.

All C# code is managed code.

An often-confused concept is the difference between managed code and unsafe code. C# has a way of allowing programmers to use certain language elements that are considered unsafe. These are language elements such as pointers and memory allocation on the stack. One of the primary advantages of unsafe code is to interface with APIs that require pointers in their parameters or within a structure. Although there is potential to do unsafe things in unsafe code, even unsafe code is managed.

Base Class Libraries

The CLI's Base Class Library (BCL), an entire suite of libraries, is designed to support multiple languages. The level of CLI compliance is defined by what subset of these libraries is implemented. So far, there are three BCL Profiles proposed for the ECMA standard: the kernel profile, the compact profile, and the complete profile. An implementation can include more, but not less, support for official compliance certification. Figure 1.1 shows the relationship between the libraries. At the center is the kernel profile. The compact profile includes all its libraries in addition to what's in the kernel profile. Likewise, the complete profile includes itself and all other libraries.

Note

Currently there are plans to ship four languages with .NET. These languages are Visual Basic.NET, Visual C++.NET, Visual Jscript.NET, and (the one near and dear to my heart) Visual C#.NET. Currently there are approximately 50 other ISVs that are considering porting languages to the .NET platform.

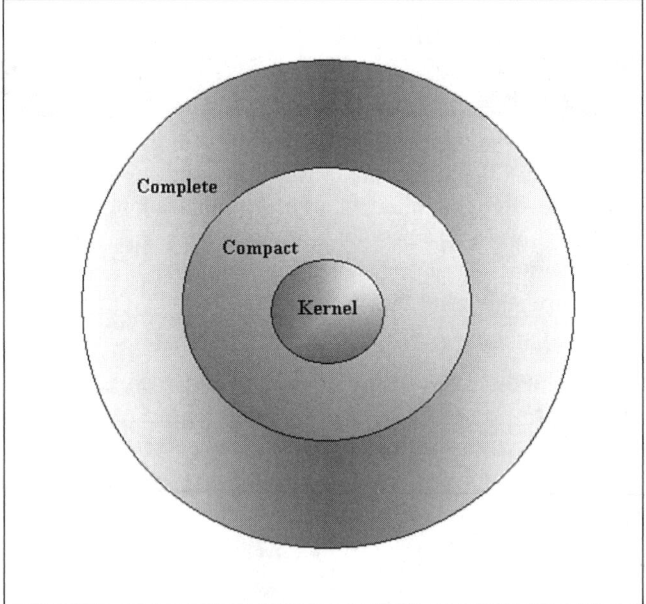

FIGURE 1.1
CLI profiles.

The Kernel Profile

The kernel profile is the minimal amount of library support an implementation can provide to call itself CLI-compliant. This is the smallest footprint that can still support C# and a VES.

The Compact Profile

The compact profile is specified primarily for small implementations such as embedded devices. It typically would be used in resource-constrained environments.

The Complete Profile

The complete profile includes all 25 packages of the CLI. This is a fairly complete suite of libraries, enabling support for a diverse range of services. A typical environment for this profile would be those intended for desktop or server deployment.

Appendix B, "The .NET Frameworks Class Libraries," contains an overview of libraries available and details the profiles they are part of.

Standardization

On October 31, 2000, Hewlett-Packard, Intel, and Microsoft jointly submitted C# and the CLI to the European Computer Manufacturers Association (ECMA) for standardization. The purpose of this was to establish a standard for future implementations of C# and the CLI.

This is significant because historically speaking, most languages are created, released, and available for years before standardization occurs. Then after multiple incompatible versions have been implemented, vendors play catch-up to mitigate the effects of non-standard portions of their implementations. Furthermore, applications written with nonstandard implementations break and need modification to comply with the new standards-based compilers upon release. In a rare historical occurrence, this is an opportunity to have a language open to a public standards organization (such as ECMA) from the beginning, creating an optimistic outlook for a new entry in cross-environment program compatibility.

Of significant note is the recent mass adoption of the Java programming language/ environment. Although this is not a public standard, it still proves the interest in a standardized environment with a philosophy of "write once, run anywhere." I believe there is great potential for the C# programming language and CLI environment to achieve these goals also. Standardization increases the probability of cross-environment adoption of a common standard.

The primary focus in standardizing the CLI and C# is for cross-language compatibility—so that anyone can write a component in any .NET-compatible language and that same component may be reused in any other .NET-compatible language. The term reuse relates to any object-oriented employment of a component to include inheritance, containment and encapsulation, and polymorphism.

The CLI also promotes standardization by implementing common Internet protocols and standards into its core libraries. The technologies of HTTP, SOAP, and XML are well known and accepted. They enable CLI applications such as Web services to interoperate in a platform-neutral manner with Web services created with any other technology. The CLI is simply a specification of a framework that enables developers to create standards-compatible components that interoperate with any other standards-compatible component implementations.

The .NET Architecture

The .NET (pronounced "dot net") architecture is Microsoft's implementation of the CLI, plus several packages to support user interfaces, data and XML, Web services, and a base class library. The .NET architecture is broken into three primary subsets: Common Language Runtime, Libraries, and Languages. Figure 1.2 shows the .NET architecture.

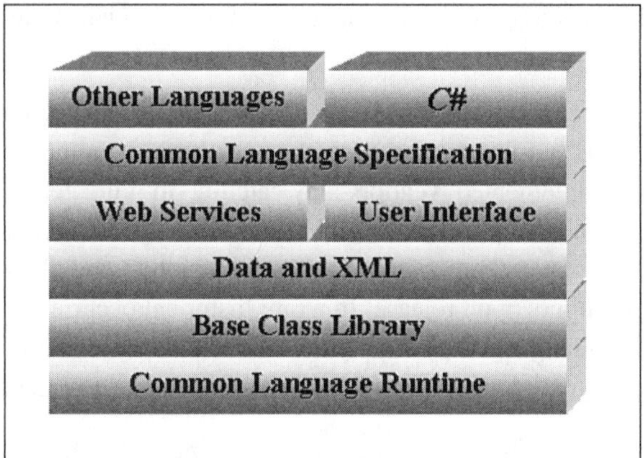

FIGURE 1.2
The .NET architecture.

Common Language Runtime (CLR)

The Common Language Runtime (CLR) is synonymous with the Virtual Execution System (VES) in the Common Language Infrastructure (CLI) specification. The primary goals of the CLR are to simplify development of applications, provide an execution environment that is robust and secure, make deployment and management easier, and support multiple languages.

Libraries

The .NET libraries have much more functionality than the CLI specification. Extra enhancements include ASP.NET (Web application programming tools), Windows Forms (interface to the Windows operating system), and ADO.NET (database connectivity tools). The goals of the .NET libraries were to use common Web standards as their foundation, unify disparate application models, enhance simplicity, and make the entire framework factored and extensible.

Languages

The .NET Framework software development kit ships with four programming languages: C++, Visual Basic, JScript, and C#. Many more third-party companies have begun work on additional .NET-compatible languages. What makes the .NET support for languages so unique is that all languages are first-class players. The goal is to make them work interchangeably. While this is mostly true, there are differences between languages and the user must ultimately decide which language best suits his needs. This book will show how to use C# in filling a very wide range of development requirements.

Where C# Fits In

Traditionally, languages and their libraries have been referred to as single entities. Programmers knew they were separate, but since the library only worked with that language, there was no harm in saying certain functionality was a part of a certain language.

With C# this is different. The libraries belong to the CLI. The language itself is very simple and it uses the CLI libraries. These are the same libraries used by other CLI-compliant languages. Therefore, they can't be considered specifically C# libraries.

C# played a significant part in the development of the .NET Framework libraries. Of course, there are other library modules written with two other CLI-compliant languages: Visual Basic.NET and Managed C++. This means that while programming in C# and using CLI libraries, the classes being used are very likely written in other languages. Since this is totally transparent, it should be of no concern. However, it does prove that the cross-language philosophy of the CLI specification does indeed work.

Summary

This chapter introduced the Common Language Infrastructure (CLI). The CLI consists of a Common Type System (CTS), a Common Language Specification (CLS), metadata, and a Virtual Execution System (VES).

The significance of standardization and how it could benefit the software development community was discussed.

I also talked about the .NET Architecture. The software in this book was developed with .NET.

Finally, there was a discussion on where C# fits into the CLI. C# is a new object-oriented language, designed from the ground up to support the component concepts intrinsic to the CLI. The C# programming language played a major role in the development of the .NET Frameworks.

CHAPTER 2

Getting Started with C#

IN THIS CHAPTER

- Writing a Simple C# Program *20*
- Comments *22*
- Identifiers and Keywords *24*
- Style *26*
- Preparing a Program To Run *27*
- Basic C# Types *28*
- Definite Assignment *37*
- Basic Conversions *38*
- Arrays *40*
- Interacting with Programs *43*

This chapter starts by creating a simple, minimal C# program that will give you a feel for what C# looks like and will be a stepping-stone to more features. This chapter includes instructions on how to compile this program. When needed, additional compilation features will be presented. Appendix A has a detailed list of compilation options.

This chapter also provides coverage of the C# data types. It tells about the various types C# provides. There will be plenty of examples of declarations and the kinds of data that can be stored. It also covers the relationship between types and how to make conversions. The chapter will finish by showing various ways to provide input and output for programs.

Writing a Simple C# Program

Let's dig in. For this first program, Listing 2.1 shows the near-minimal amount of code necessary to write a C# program. When it executes, it will print the words "Howdy, Partner!" to the console.

LISTING 2.1 A Simple C# Program

```
 1: /*
 2:  * FileName:  HowdyParner.cs
 3:  * Author:    Joe Mayo
 4:  */
 5:
 6: // Program start class
 7: public class HowdyPartner
 8: {
 9:         // Main begins program execution
10:     public static void Main()
11:     {
12:                 // Write to console
13:         System.Console.WriteLine("Howdy, Partner!");
14:     }
15: }
```

Line 7 of Listing 2.1 shows a `class` declaration. Classes are what C# uses to declare or define objects. They describe the attributes and behavior of an object. An object is anything that has attributes and behavior. While classes are definitions, objects are the actual entities that exist when the program runs. There can normally be many objects based upon a single class declaration. Objects are the building blocks of the C# programming language. C# is an object-oriented programming language; therefore, it has a starting object. That's what this class represents—the starting object of this program.

For C++ Programmers

The `Main()` method is located inside of a class instead of by itself. Also, the method's first letter is capitalized.

For Java Programmers

C# is case sensitive. The first letter of the `Main()` method is capitalized. Also, the C# `Main()` method can declare return types of both `int` and `void`.

The identifier, or name, of a class follows the class keyword. This class is called `HowdyPartner`. Classes can have almost any name, but whatever the name, it should be meaningful. Details of identifiers and keywords are described in a couple more sections.

Left and right braces indicate the beginning and ending, respectively, of a block. In Listing 2.1, the beginning of the class block starts on line 8 after the `HowdyPartner` identifier, and the end of the class block is on line 15, by itself. In C#, it's common to begin and end portions of programs with curly braces.

There's a method declaration on line 10. This is the `Main()` method. Every program has a `Main()` method that is the starting point for the program. When the program begins, this is the first method called.

There are a couple identifiers in front of the `Main()` method. C# `Main()` methods always have a `static` modifier. In C# there are two types of objects—static and instance. Instance objects are formally declared, and there can be many of the same type with different attributes. However, there can be only a single copy of a static object in existence for a given program. The only way to execute a method without an instance of its containing object is if that method is static. Since no instance of the starting class exists as an object when the program starts, a static method must be called. This is why the `Main()` method is static.

The other identifier is `void`. This is actually the `Main()` method's return value. Return values are useful for returning program status to a calling program or utility when a program exits. When void is specified, the method does not return a value. In this case, the `Main()` method does not return a value. Besides returning a void, the `Main()` method could return an integer.

Within the body of the `Main()` method on line 13 is a single statement that causes the words "Howdy, Partner!" to be written to the console screen. The statement `System.Console.WriteLine("Howdy, Partner!")` writes text to the console screen. Figure 2.1 shows the output.

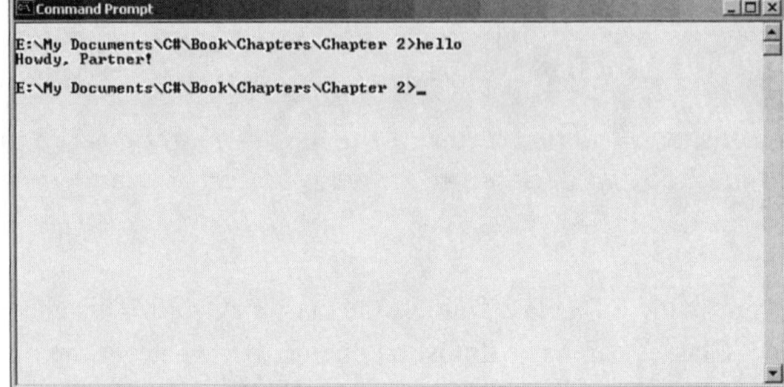
Command Prompt
E:\My Documents\C#\Book\Chapters\Chapter 2>hello
Howdy, Partner!
E:\My Documents\C#\Book\Chapters\Chapter 2>_

FIGURE 2.1
Output from the HowdyPartner program.

Comments

There are three types of commenting syntax in C#—multi-line, single-line, and XML.

Multi-Line Comments

Multi-line comments have one or more lines of narrative within a set of comment delimiters. These comment delimiters are the begin comment `/*`and end comment `*/` markers. Anything between these two markers is considered a comment. The compiler ignores comments when reading the source code. Lines 1 through 4 of Listing 2.1 show a multi-line comment:

```
1: /*
2:  * FileName:  HowdyParner.cs
3:  * Author:    Joe Mayo
4:  */
```

Some languages allow embedded multi-line comments, but C# does not. Consider the following example:

```
/*
   Filename:   HowdyPartner.cs
   Author:        Joe Mayo
     /*
           Initial Implementation:   04/01/01
           Change 1:                 05/15/01
           Change 2:                 06/10/01
     */
*/
```

The begin comment on line 1 starts a multi-line comment. The second begin comment on line 4 is ignored in C# as just a couple characters within the comment. The end comment on line 8 matches with the begin comment on line 1. Finally, the end comment on line 9 causes the compiler to report a syntax error because it doesn't match a begin comment.

Single-Line Comments

Single-line comments allow narrative on only one line at a time. They begin with the double forward slash marker, //. The single-line comment can begin in any column of a given line. It ends at a new line or carriage return. Lines 6, 9, and 12 of Listing 2.1 show single-line comments:


```
 6: // Program start class
 7: public class HowdyPartner
 8: {
 9:     // Main begins program execution
10:     public static void Main()
11:     {
12:         // Write to console
13:         System.Console.WriteLine("Howdy, Partner!");
```

Single-line comments may contain other single-line comments. Since they're all on the same line, subsequent comments will be treated as comment text.

XML Documentation Comments

XML documentation comments start with a triple slash, ///. Comments are enclosed in XML tags. The .NET C# compiler has an option that reads the XML documentation comments and generates XML documentation from them. This XML documentation can be extracted to a separate XML file, and then XML style sheets can be applied to the XML file to produce fancy code documentation for viewing in a browser. Table 2.1 shows all valid XML documentation tags.

TABLE 2.1 XML Documentation Tags

<c>	<code>	<example>	<exception>
<list>	<param>	<paramref>	<permission>
<remarks>	<returns>	<see>	<seealso>
<summary>	<value>		

To provide a summary of an item, use the <summary> tag. The following shows what one might look like for a Main() method.

```
/// <summary>
///     Prints "Howdy, Partner" to the console.
/// </summary>
```

Documentation comments can be extremely useful in keeping documentation up to date. How many programmers do you know who conscientiously update their documentation all the time? Seriously, when meeting a tight deadline, documentation is the first thing to go. Now there's help. While in the code, it's easy to update the comments, and the resulting XML file is easy to generate. The following line of code extracts documentation comments from the `HowdyPartner.cs` file and creates an XML document named `HowdyPartner.xml`.

```
csc /doc:HowdyPartner.xml HowdyPartner.cs
```

For C++ Programmers

C# has XML documentation comments that can be extracted to separate XML files. Once in an XML file, XML style sheets can be applied to produce fancy code documentation for viewing in a browser.

Identifiers and Keywords

Identifiers are names of various program elements in the code that uniquely identify an element. They are the names of things like variables or fields. They're specified by the programmer and should have names that indicate their purpose.

Keywords are reserved words in the C# language. Since they're reserved, they can't be used as identifiers. Examples of keywords are `class`, `public`, or `void`—they are the names of permanent language elements.

Identifiers

Identifiers are names used to identify code elements. The class name `HowdyPartner` on line 7 of Listing 2.1 is an example of an identifier. Identifiers should be meaningful for their intended purpose. For example, the HowdyPartner program prints the words "Howdy, Partner!" to the console.

The C# character set conforms to Unicode 3.0, Technical Report 15, Annex 7. Unicode is a 16-bit character format designed to represent the many character sets from all languages worldwide. Any Unicode character can be specified with a Unicode escape sequence, \u or \U, followed by four hex digits. For example, the Unicode escape sequence \u0043\u0023 represents the characters C#.

The decision to make the C# character set conform to Unicode standards is significant. The most prevalent character set among languages has been the American Standard Code for Information Interchange (ASCII). The primary limitation of ASCII is its 8-bit character size. This doesn't accommodate multi-byte character sets for various international languages. Languages, such as Java, were designed with the Unicode character set built-in. As the world becomes smaller, international considerations must become larger.

Identifiers can have nearly any name, but a few restrictions apply. Here are some rules to follow when creating identifiers:

- Use non-formatting Unicode characters in any part of an identifier.
- Identifiers can begin with an allowed Unicode character or an underline.
- Begin an identifier with an @ symbol. This allows use of keywords as identifiers.

Normally, it's not permitted to use keywords as identifiers unless they're prefixed by an @ symbol. Give serious consideration before using the @ symbol, because it can obfuscate code and make it confusing to read later on. There are always exceptions, but if there is a unique requirement, proceed with caution. Here are a few examples of legal C# identifiers:

```
currentBid

_token

@override

\u0043sharp
```

Now for a few examples of invalid identifiers:

```
1twothree       // error - first letter is a number

decimal         // error - reserved word

\u0027format    // error - Unicode formatting character
```

The first line is invalid because its first character is a number, which is not allowed. The first character of an identifier must be either a letter character or an underscore. The second identifier is invalid because it is a keyword. C# keywords are reserved and cannot be used as identifiers. The exception is when the keyword is prefixed with the "@" character. The third line is invalid because the first character is a Unicode formatting character. Unicode formatting characters are not allowed in any part of an identifier.

Keywords

Keywords are words reserved by the system and have special predefined meanings when writing C# programs. The `class` keyword, for instance, is used to define a C# class. Another example is the `void` keyword, which means that a method does not return a value. These are words that are part of the language itself. Usage of keywords in any context other than what they are defined for in the C# language is likely to make code unreadable. This is the primary reason why keywords are reserved. They are meant to be used only for constructs that are part of the language. You can see examples of keywords in Listing 2.1: `class` on line 7 and `static` and `void` on line 10. Valid keywords are listed in Table 2.2.

TABLE 2.2 Complete List of C# Keywords

abstract	as	base	bool	break
byte	case	catch	char	checked
class	const	continue	decimal	default
delegate	do	double	else	enum
event	explicit	extern	false	finally
fixed	float	for	foreach	goto
if	implicit	in	int	interface
internal	is	lock	long	namespace
new	null	object	operator	out
override	params	private	protected	public
readonly	ref	return	sbyte	sealed
short	sizeof	stackalloc	static	string
struct	switch	this	throw	true
try	typeof	uint	ulong	unchecked
unsafe	ushort	using	virtual	void
while				

Style

Style is the manner or mode of expression in a program. It is distinct from the meaning of the code. Proper utilization of style elements can contribute significantly to understandability by programmers attempting to ascertain the semantics of an algorithm. These style elements include whitespace, placement of language elements, and naming conventions.

Whitespace characters separate language elements such as identifiers and keywords. These characters include newline, tab, form feed, and control-Z characters. A program may have any amount of whitespace between language elements. The compiler will ignore any extra whitespace. Effective use of whitespace goes a long way toward making programs readable.

A consistent naming convention can also make code easier to read. There are essentially two forms of naming conventions in C#. The first is *pascal casing*, where the first letter of each word in a name is capitalized, such as `HelloWorld`, `DotProduct`, or `AmortizationSchedule`. This is normally used in all instances except for parameters and private fields of classes. In the case of private class fields and method parameters, use *camel casing,* where the first letter of the first word is lowercase and the first letter of subsequent words is capitalized, such as `bookTitle`, `employeeName`, or `totalCompensation`. Again, keeping consistent standards makes code easier to read when going through it at a later date.

Tip

Seriously consider the practicality of the naming convention used. If it makes sense, do it. But don't hold on to old practices, unless there's a good reason to do so. Recent style guidance by Microsoft and others suggests that a variable name should reflect its semantics more so than type.

Preparing a Program To Run

The programs in this book were compiled with the Microsoft C# command-line compiler from the .NET Frameworks SDK. For a simple program such as the HowdyPartner program in Listing 2.1, use the following command line:

```
csc HowdyPartner.cs
```

The C# compiler name is `csc` and `HowdyPartner.cs` is the name of the program. This will create an executable program named `HowdyParner.exe` in the directory in which you executed the command. Figure 2.2 shows the output from the C# compiler when invoked with the example command line.

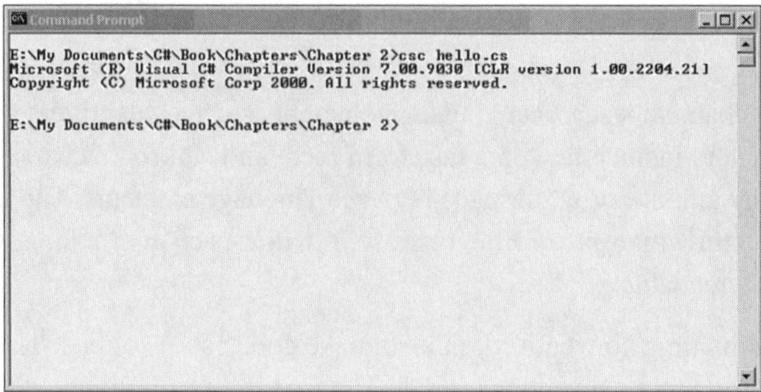

FIGURE 2.2
Compiling a simple program.

Compile multiple files by adding each file to the command line with space separation between files. By default, the output file name will be the same as the first file on the command line. When changing the name of an output file, use the `/out:` option as in the following command line example:

```
csc /out:HowdyPartner.exe HowdyPartner.cs
```

This produces the program `HowdyPartner.exe`.

Another useful command-line option is `/help`, which provides a quick listing of other useful command line options.

Basic C# Types

A `type` is the organization and format of information. For instance, an `integer` type is limited to 32 bits. It has a least significant bit, bit #0, which could be zero or one, and 30 more bits designating its magnitude. The most significant bit of an `integer`, the 31st, designates its sign as either positive or negative. `Integers` are positive or negative whole numbers. Another example is the `float` type, which conforms to IEEE 754 format and represents rational numbers. These are two different types. They have different formats and are generally used for different purposes. For example, `integers` can't be used for fractional representations, and `floats` can't be used very meaningfully in many situations as whole numbers. Some languages are weakly typed, and there are times when the interpretation of types in these weakly typed languages will cause program errors.

C# is a strongly typed language. This essentially means the compiler and runtime system does a good job of verifying the type consistency of expressions. All variables have a type. The type produced by an expression is always either defined by the C# language or is a user-defined type. C# provides a mechanism for converting one type to another.

While discussing each type, this section also shows how to declare a `literal` of each type. `Literals` are values that can't be changed. They can't be referenced, either. They occupy the memory space where they're used. While it's possible to copy the value of a `literal` into a variable and then change the variable, this does not change the value of the original literal.

Variable Declarations

`Variables` are programming elements that can change during program execution. They're used as storage to hold information at any stage of computation. As a program executes, certain `variables` will change to support the goals of an algorithm. Every `variable` has a `type`, and this section will show how to specify a `variable's type`. The syntax of a `variable` definition always conforms to the following pattern:

```
Type Identifier [Initializer];
```

In this example `Type` is a placeholder, representing one of the types listed in this section or a user-defined type. Every variable must have a `Type` part in its declaration. Similarly, every variable declaration must have an identifier or name. Declarations may optionally include an initializer to set the value of a variable when it is created. The `type` of the value used to initialize a variable must be compatible with the type that the variable is declared as.

The Simple Types

The simple types consist of `Boolean` and `Numeric` types. The `Numeric` types are further subdivided into `Integral` and `Floating Point`.

The Boolean Type

There's only a single Boolean type named `bool`. A `bool` can have a value of either `true` or `false`. The values `true` and `false` are also the only literal values you can use for a `bool`. Here's an example of a `bool` declaration:

```
bool isProfitable = true;
```

> **Note**
>
> The `bool` type does not accept integer values such as `0`, `1`, or `-1`. The keywords `true` and `false` are built into the C# language and are the only allowable values.

For C++ Programmers

There is no casting conversion between int and bool types. To accomplish a similar effect, a bool result can be obtained with the equality operator. For example, (x == 0) would evaluate to true when the integer type x is equal to 0.

The Integral Types

The Integral types are further subdivided into eight types plus a character type: sbyte, byte, short, ushort, int, uint, long, ulong, and char. All of the Integral types except char have signed and unsigned forms. All Integral type literals can be expressed in hexadecimal notation by prefixing "0x" to a series of hexadecimal numbers 0 thru F. The exception is the char.

A char holds a single Unicode character. Some examples of char variable declarations include

```
char middleInitial;          \\ uninitialized

char yesNo = 'Y';

char studentGrade = '\u005A';     \\ Unicode 'Z'

char studentGrade = '\x0041';     \\ Unicode 'A'
```

As shown previously, Unicode escape character notation requires four hexadecimal digits, prefixed by \u or \U. The digits are left padded with zeros to make the digit part four characters wide. A char may also be specified in hexadecimal notation by prefixing \x to between 1 and 4 hexadecimal digits.

For C++ Programmers

Notice the difference between the size of the C# char (16 bits) and the normal C++ char on a PC (8 bits). The C# char is similar to the C++ wchar_t (16 bits).

There are also special escape sequences representing characters. They're used for alert, special formatting, and building strings to avoid ambiguity. The following list shows the valid C# escape sequences:

```
\'     Single Quote

\"     Double Quote
```

`\\`	Backslash
`\0`	Null
`\a`	Bell
`\b`	Backspace
`\f`	Form Feed
`\n`	Newline (linefeed)
`\r`	Carriage Return
`\t`	Horizontal Tab
`\v`	Vertical Tab

A `byte` is an unsigned type that can hold 8 bits of data. Its range is from `0` to `255`. An `sbyte` is a signed byte with a range of `-128` to `127`. This is how you declare byte variables:

```
byte age = 25;

sbyte normalizedTolerance = -1;
```

The `short` type is signed and holds 16 bits. It can hold a range from `-32768` to `32767`. The unsigned short, `ushort`, holds a range of `0` to `65535`. Here are a couple examples:

```
ushort numberOfJellyBeans = 62873;

short temperatureFarenheit = -36;
```

The integer type is signed and has a size of 32 bits. The signed type, `int`, has a range of `-2147483648` to `2147483647`. The `uint` is unsigned and has a range of `0` to `4294967295`. Unsigned integers may optionally have a `u` or `U` suffix. Examples follow:

```
uint nationalPopulation = 4139276850;     // also 4139276850u or 4139276850U

int tradeDeficit = -2058293762;
```

A `long` type is signed and holds 64 bits with a range of `-9223372036854775808` to `9223372036854775807`. A `ulong` is unsigned with a range of `0` to `18446744073709551615`. Unsigned long literals may have suffixes with the combination of uppercase or lowercase characters `UL`. Their declarations can be expressed like this:

```
ulong lightYearsFromEarth = 72038289347236792;
                            //  also 72038289347236792ul
                            //    or 72038289347236792UL
                            //    or 72038289347236792uL
                            //    or 72038289347236792Lu
                            //    or 72038289347236792LU
                            //    or 72038289347236792lU
```

```
long negativeVariance = -1636409717646593274;
                        // also -1636409717646593274l
                        //   or -1636409717646593274L
```

Each of the types presented to this point have a unique size and range. Table 2.3 provides a summary and quick reference of the size and range of each Integral type.

TABLE 2.3 The Integral Types

Type	*Size (in bits)*	*Range*
`char`	16	0 to 65535
`sbyte`	8	-128 to 127
`byte`	8	0 to 255
`short`	16	-32768 to 32767
`ushort`	16	0 to 65535
`int`	32	-2147483648 to 2147483647
`uint`	32	0 to 4294967295
`long`	64	-9223372036854775808 to 9223372036854775807
`ulong`	64	0 to 18446744073709551615

For C++ Programmers

There is no native equivalent in C++ for the byte. However, there are ways of producing the same effect with typedef's signed and unsigned `char`s. Also, a C++ long is 32 bits, whereas a C# long is 64 bits.

For Java Programmers

There are no unsigned types in Java, but there are in C#.

The Floating Point Types

C# provides two floating point types—`float` and `double`—and a new type called `decimal`. The floating point types conform to IEEE 754 specifications.

Floating point literals may optionally be specified with exponential notation. This allows specification of very large numbers with the least amount of space necessary to write them. The tradeoff between exponential and normal notation is size versus precision. The general form of exponential syntax is

```
N.Ne±P
```

where `N` is some decimal digit, `e` can be uppercase or lowercase, and `P` is the number of decimal places. The ± indicates a `+`, a `-`, or neither, which is the same as `+`. This is standard scientific notation.

The `float` type can hold a range of around 1.5×10^{-45} to 3.4×10^{38}. It has a 7-digit precision. To designate a floating point literal as a `float`, add an `F` or `f` suffix. A `float` literal can be written with or without exponential notation as follows:

```
float profits       = 36592.73;    // also 36592.73F
                                   //   or 36592.73f
float atomicWeight = 1.54e-15;
float warpSpeed     = 3.21E3;
```

A `double` has a range of about 5.0×10^{-324} to 1.7×10^{308} and a precision of 15 to 16 digits. `Double` literals may have the suffix `D` or `d`. It, too, may have literals expressed with or without exponential notation:

```
double vectorMagnitude    = 8.2e127;
double accumulatedVolume = 7982365.83658341;
                         // also 7982365.83658341D
                         //   or 7982365.83658341d
```

A new type, not seen in any other language, is the `decimal` type. The `decimal` type has 28 or 29 digits of precision and can range from 1.0×10^{-28} to about 7.9×10^{28}. `Decimal` literals can be specified with an `M` or `m` suffix. The tradeoff between `decimal` and `double` is precision versus range. The `decimal` is the best choice when precision is required, but choose a `double` for the greatest range. The `decimal` type is well suited for financial calculations as shown in the following example:

```
decimal annualSales = 99873582948769876589348317.95;
```

Tip

Use the C# `decimal` type for greater precision in financial calculations.

Table 2.4 provides a quick lookup of the floating point types.

TABLE 2.4 The Floating Point Types

Type	*Size (bits)*	*Precision*	*Range*
`float`	32	7 digits	1.5×10^{-45} to 3.4×10^{38}
`double`	64	15–16 digits	5.0×10^{-324} to 1.7×10^{308}
`decimal`	128	28–29 decimal places	1.0×10^{-28} to 7.9×10^{28}

A final word on literal suffixes: There are common suffixes for each literal type. Suffixes ensure that the literal is the intended type. This is good for documentation. However, the primary benefit is ensuring that your expressions are evaluated correctly; that is, the compiler interprets `float` and `decimal` literals without suffixes as a `double` when evaluating an expression. To avoid the associated errors, use an appropriate literal suffix.

Struct Types

A `struct` is a value type. All of the types presented thus far fall into the value type category. Value types are variables that directly hold their data. They are allocated on the stack, which makes them very efficient for storing and retrieving information. Structs are containers that can hold a collection of other items. They provide a method for programmers to create their own value types.

Reference Types

There are four reference types in C#: classes, interfaces, delegates, and arrays. Reference types are library or user-defined types that are allocated on the heap. Being allocated on the heap means that reference types use more system resources. They are managed by a built-in garbage collector, which also manages their lifetimes. Classes may contain many other C# language members. They also define unique types.

Interfaces are used to expose the public attributes and behavior of classes. They have no implementations themselves. Whenever a class specifies an interface, a programmer knows, by the definition of that interface, that the class supports certain attributes and behavior. This way, a number of different classes can implement the same interface and be used in the same basic manner, but provide their own unique behavior.

Delegates provide a type-safe way to dynamically reference class methods. When the exact method to implement won't be known until runtime, a delegate can be used to accept a reference to a method. Then whatever method is assigned to the delegate at runtime can be executed by calling the delegate to which the method was assigned. This is type safe, because a method must conform to the type specified in the delegate declaration before it is assigned to a delegate.

Arrays provide a method of storing multiple items of a specific type. Their interface represents a linear collection of data that can be referenced in sequence. Their power extends to providing specialized methods for managing their data. A C# array is a useful method of storing many items of the same type of data in a linear form.

Enumeration Types

The `enum` type is a list of constant values. Elements of an enum are expressed in words rather than numbers, which makes it convenient for understanding the meaning of the value being used. Here's an example:

```
enum Months { Jan, Feb, Mar, Apr, May, Jun, Jul, Aug, Sep, Oct, Nov, Dec };
```

For Java Programmers

Java does not have an equivalent to `enum`.

By default, the first element of an `enum` starts with `0`, unless specified otherwise. Subsequent elements have a value one greater than their predecessor, unless they also have a designated value. In the following example, `Mon` has the value `1`; `Tue` is `2`; `Wed` is `3`; `Thu` is `4`; and `Fri` is `5`. Then after `Sat` is changed to `10`, `Sun` becomes `11`.

```
enum Weekday { Mon = 1, Tue, Wed, Thu, Fri, Sat = 10, Sun };
```

The type of `enum` elements may be `byte`, `short`, `int`, or `long`. Specify this with a colon and type specification after the name. Here's an example:

```
enum Month: byte
{
    January,
    February,
    March,
    April,
    May,
    June,
    July,
    August,
    September,
    October,
```

```
    November,
    December
};
```

For C++ Programmers

In C#, enums can be specified as `byte`, `short`, `int`, or `long`, but in C++ they are `int`.

String Type

The `string` type is a C# primary type. Its value is represented by a string of Unicode characters. There are two types of string literals. The first type may be any valid set of characters between two double quotes, including character escape sequences.

```
string thankYou = "Grazie!\a"; // Grazie! <ding>
string hello    = "Sa-waht dee\tkrahp!";
                                // Sa-waht dee<tab>krahp!

string kewl = "Das ist\nzehr\ngut!"; // Das ist
                                     // zehr
                                     // gut!
```

For C++ Programmers

A C++ `string` was originally the same as a normal C string, a pointer to a null-terminated array of characters. With the introduction of Standard C++, a C++ `string` now refers to the Standard Template Library (STL) string type. A C# `string` is a built-in type, and its representation is transparent.

The second type is a `verbatim string literal`. It's made by prefixing a string with an `@`. The difference between `verbatim string literals` and normal string literals is that the character escape sequences are not processed but are interpreted as is. Since the double quote escape sequence won't work, use two quotes side-by-side to include a single quote in a string. Verbatim string literals may span multiple lines, if needed. The following examples show various forms of the `verbatim string literals`.

```
string whoSaid = @"He said, ""She said.""";
                // He said, "She said."

string beerPlease = @"Een \'Duvel\', alstublieft!";
                   // Een \'Duvel\', alstublieft!
```

```
string gettysburg = @"Four score and seven years ago
our fathers brought forth upon this continent
a new nation, conceived in liberty
and dedicated to the principle
that all people are considered equal...";
```

For C++ and Java Programmers

C# includes a special type of string literal called the verbatim string literal. It's useful for avoiding escape sequences in file paths and similar situations where decorations detract from the readability of the string literal.

Definite Assignment

Definite assignment is a rule simply stating every variable must have a value before it's read from. The process of assigning a value to a variable for the first time is known as initialization. Once the initialization process has taken place, a variable is considered initialized. If the initialization process has not yet taken place, a variable is considered to be uninitialized. Initialization ensures that variables have valid values when expressions are evaluated. Uninitialized variables are unassigned variables. If a program attempts to read from an unassigned variable, the compiler will generate an error.

For C++ Programmers

C++ programs are allowed to read data from uninitialized variables. C# detects uninitialized variables at compile time and returns an error.

Default initialization rules depend upon where a variable is declared in a program. For the purposes of default initialization, there are two types of variables—local variables and class variables. Variables are initialized based upon whether they're class variables or local variables.

Local variables are uninitialized. Local variables are those variables declared within a method or other language element defined by a block. Blocks are language elements that denote the beginning and end of a C# language construct. In the case of methods, blocks denote the beginning and end of a method. Methods are C# language constructs allowing programmers to organize their code into groups. If a variable is declared within a method, it is considered to be a local variable.

This is different from class variables, which are declared as class members. Class members can be nearly any C# type or language element. Variables and methods are class members. Class variables are initialized to default values if a program's code does not explicitly initialize them. Table 2.6 lists each type's default values.

TABLE 2.6 Default Values of C# Types

Type	*Default Value*
`bool`	`False`
`char`	`\u0000`
`sbyte`	`0`
`byte`	`0`
`short`	`0`
`ushort`	`0`
`int`	`0`
`uint`	`0`
`long`	`0`
`ulong`	`0`
`float`	`0.0f`
`double`	`0.0d`
`decimal`	`0.0m`

Basic Conversions

Conversions allow moving the value of one variable into another. There are two types of conversions: `explicit` and `implicit`. `Implicit` conversions happen without intervention. Table 2.7 shows the legal `implicit` conversions for C# simple types. In addition, the `integer` literal 0 (zero) can be implicitly converted to an `enum`. There are no implicit conversions to the `char` type.

TABLE 2.7 Legal Implicit Conversions for Simple C# Types

Type	*Allowable Conversions*
`bool`	none
`char`	`ushort`, `int`, `uint`, `long`, `ulong`, `float`, `double`, `decimal`

TABLE 2.7 continued

Type	*Allowable Conversions*
`sbyte`	`short`, `int`, `long`, `float`, `double`, `decimal`
`byte`	`short`, `ushort`, `int`, `uint`, `long`, `ulong`, `float`, `double`, `decimal`
`short`	`int`, `long`, `float`, `double`, `decimal`
`ushort`	`int`, `uint`, `long`, `ulong`, `float`, `double`, `decimal`
`int`	`long`, `float`, `double`, `decimal`
`uint`	`long`, `ulong`, `float`, `double`, `decimal`
`long`	`float`, `double`, `decimal`
`ulong`	`float`, `double`, `decimal`
`float`	`double`
`double`	none
`decimal`	none

Special syntax to perform implicit conversions is unnecessary because the system will recognize them when they occur. A basic consideration about `implicit` conversion with simple types is whether the destination type will be big enough to hold the source type without loss of data. If not, use an `explicit` conversion. Any conversion not listed in Table 2.7 requires an `explicit` conversion.

An `explicit` conversion is necessary when there's the possibility of data loss or that an error can occur. To implement this, insert a `cast` operator in front of the source expression. A `cast` operator is simply the name of the type being converted to inside of parentheses. Here are a few examples:

```
byte floor = 5;
int level = floor; // implicit - no cast necessary

double maxWeight = 53.751;
float upperLimit = (float) maxWeight;
                  // smaller type - cast required

ushort distance  =  32768;
short milesToGo = distance;
                  // error - possibility of data loss

short milesToGo = (short) distance;
                  // data loss - milesToGo = -32768
```

Reference types and structures also can be converted. The rules for determining whether a conversion is `implicit` or `explicit` are still the same. `Explicit` conversions could possibly cause loss of data or generate an error, but `implicit` conversions won't. Conversions for reference types require methods to perform the transfer of data from one type to another. These methods use the `explicit` and `implicit` keywords to mark the method appropriately. `Explicit` conversions from a reference type or structure require a cast, the same as the built-in types do.

Arrays

Arrays are collection classes, built into C#. Arrays are a useful construct for organizing data. They provide matrix support and, even further, multidimensional support. As a collection, an array allows going beyond simple storage of data and provides fundamental discovery and manipulation of that data. Array methods are discussed in the next chapter. This chapter shows declaration and instantiation of single-dimension, multidimension, and jagged arrays.

For C++ Programmers

A C++ array is a pointer to a contiguous block of memory that is manipulated with pointers or indexes to store and retrieve data. C# arrays are objects with built-in functionality for operations such as sorting and determining length. C# array declarations place the brackets after the type rather than after the identifier.

For Java Programmers

Java allows the option of placing the brackets after the type or after the identifier. C# permits placement of the brackets only after the type.

Single-Dimension Arrays

Single-dimension arrays provide the capability to store and manipulate a list of items. Every element is of the same type. This is how such an array should be declared:

```
Type[] Array-Identifier [initializer] ;
```

The array identifier is any valid identifier. It should be meaningful for the purpose of the array. The optional initializer allocates memory for the array.

Tip

Once a C# array has been initialized, it can't change its size. If dynamic resizing of an array is needed, use one of the collection classes.

Here are some examples of single-dimensional array declarations:

```
// uninitialized declaration
MyClass[] myArray;
byte[] inputBuffer = new byte[2048];

// creates an array of 3 strings
string[] countStrings = { "eins", "zwei", "drei" };
```

Arrays may be declared with no initialization. Remember, an array must be initialized before it's used. It may be initialized with an integer type value inside the brackets of the initializer, as the following example shows:

```
// creates an array of 3 strings
string[] countStrings
      = new string[3] { "eins", "zwei", "drei" };
```

Another way to initialize an array is by leaving the space in the brackets of the initializer blank and then following the initializer brackets with an initializer list in braces. The array initializer list is a comma-separated list of values of the array type. The size of the array becomes the number of elements in the initializer list. If an integer value is added to the initializer brackets and there is an initializer list in the same array initializer, make sure the integer value in the initializer brackets is greater than or equal to number of elements in the initializer list. Take a look at this code sample:

```
// error
string[] countStrings
      = new string[3] { "eins", "zwei", "drei", "vier" };
```

The initializer in this code fails with an error because the allocated size of the `countStrings` array is only 3, but the number of strings in the list is 4. The number of strings in the list can't exceed the allocated size.

Tip

Don't specify a size when using an initializer list on an array. Later, it will be easier to add an item to the list and avoid the mistake of not incrementing the number.

N-Dimensional Arrays

Multidimensional arrays are similar in declaration and initialization to single-dimensional arrays with a few exceptions. For every new dimension included, add a comma to brackets of the array declaration. During initialization, add an integer value to each of the dimensions specified in the declaration. Here are a couple examples:

```
long [ , ] determinant = new long[4, 4];
int [ , , ] stateSpace = new int[2, 5, 4];
bool [ , ] exclusiveOr
        = new bool[2, 2] { {false, true}, {true, false} };
```

Remember, the integer values in the initializer brackets are optional when including an initializer list.

Jagged Arrays

Jagged arrays allow creation of multidimensional arrays without the requirement of making every element of every dimension the same size. If an application has data that doesn't cover the entire range of possible values, this may be an option. It may also open the opportunity to save memory space. Here are some examples:

```
decimal[][] monthlyVariations = new decimal[12][];

monthlyVariations[(int)Months.Jan] = new decimal[31];
monthlyVariations[(int)Months.Feb] = new decimal[28];
    .
    .
    .
monthlyVariations[(int)Months.Dec] = new decimal[31];
```

For C++ Programmers

The `enum` type does not convert implicitly to an integer. It must be cast to an int to be used in arrays.

Using constant values from the `Months` enum example, this shows how `monthlyVariations` has a different number of entries for each month. When creating a jagged array, first establish the size of the first dimension. Here, it's `12` to correspond to the months in the year. Once the first dimension is created, make each element of the second dimension any size needed. Continue for as many dimensions as required.

Array assignments are done by identifying the index of the array element to which a value will be assigned. Here are a few examples:

```
int[] month = new int[12];
month[(int)Months.Jan] = 31;

double[,] affineTransform = new double[4, 4];
affineTransform[0, 2] = 1/Math.Sin(37.59);

string[][] electoralMembers = new string[50][];
.
.
.
electoralMembers[10] = new string[25];
electoralMembers[10][3] = "Smith";
```


Interacting with Programs

One of the things done with many programs is user interaction at runtime. You can do this on the command line. This knowledge may be useful if there's a need to create a command-line utility. Listing 2.2 shows an example of interacting with a program via the command line.

LISTING 2.2 An Interactive Program

```
/*
   Filename:  HelloName.cs
   Author:    Joe Mayo
*/

using System;    // use the System namespace

class HelloName
{
    static void Main()
    {
        string name;    // holds user's name

        // Ask for input
        Console.Write("What is your name?:  ");

        // Get user's input
        name = Console.ReadLine();

        // Print greeting to console
        Console.WriteLine("Hello, {0}!  ", name);
    }
}
```

One of the first differences from Listing 2.1 in Listing 2.2 is the `using System;` statement on line 6. This indicates class and method names in this file can be written without putting the namespace name `System` in front. On lines 15, 18, and 21, `System` is not in front of these statements anymore. The class name is changed to `HelloName` because it provides a better idea of the purpose of the class. Its starting method is `Main()`, and this name will never change.

Within the `Main()` method is the first variable on line 11. It has an identifier called `name`, and it is a `string` type.

Line 15 prints a message to the screen, asking the user for input. This particular command, `Console.Write()`, differs from `Console.WriteLine()` in that it prints the message to the screen and leaves the carat on the same line. In this case, it produces the desired effect of having the user type on the same line as the question being asked.

The `Console.ReadLine()` statement on line 18 causes the system to wait for the user to type some series of characters and press the Enter or Return key. Pressing Enter or Return causes the system to generate a newline character. The series of characters can be any valid `string` except for the newline. Once a newline is encountered, the `ReadLine()` method returns all the characters entered on the command line except for the newline. The assignment operator, `=`, puts that string of characters into the name variable.

On line 21, the string the user entered displays on the screen with the `Console.WriteLine()` method. Both the `Console.Write()` and `Console.WriteLine()` methods allow formatting of `strings`. The `Console.WriteLine()` method on Line 21 of Listing 2.2 takes a single parameter, `{0}`, inside its string argument, `"Hello, {0}!"`. The second argument in `Console.WriteLine()` is the `string` variable name. When the program executes this statement, it replaces the parameter `{0}` with the value of the variable name. Figure 2.3 shows the output of this program.

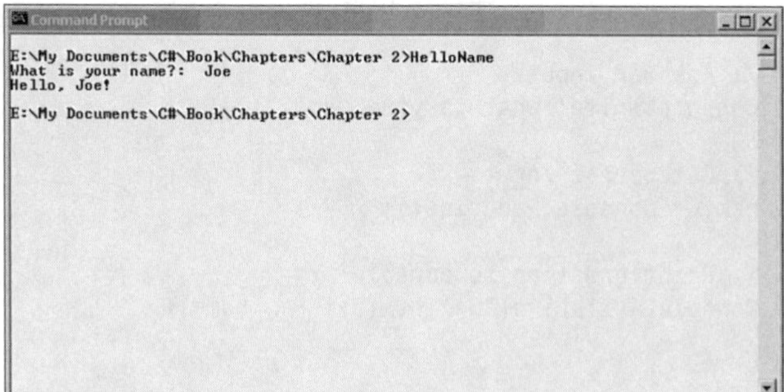
Command Prompt
E:\My Documents\C#\Book\Chapters\Chapter 2>HelloName
What is your name?: Joe
Hello, Joe!
E:\My Documents\C#\Book\Chapters\Chapter 2>

FIGURE 2.3
Output from Listing 2.2.

Programs can run with command-line parameters. This is useful when implementing a certain configuration with a script or desktop shortcut. Listing 2.3 has an example of accepting command-line arguments.

LISTING 2.3 Accepting Command-Line Arguments

```
 1: /*
 2:    Filename:   HelloCmdLine.cs
 3:    Author:     Joe Mayo
 4: */
 5:
 6: using System;
 7:
 8: // Program start class
 9: class HelloCmdLine
10: {
11:       // Accept command line arguments
12:       public static void Main(string[] args)
13:       {
14:          // Write to console
15:          Console.WriteLine("Hello, {0}!", args[0]);
16:       }
17: }
```


The first difference from Listing 2.2 is on line 12 where the `Main()` method has a parameter. This parameter is an array type named `args` that can hold a list of `string` types. The system populates this `array` from the entries added in the command line following the program name.

On line 15, is a `Console.WriteLine()` statement, similar to the one in Listing 2.2. It accepts an argument of `args[0]`. This argument, `args[0]`, holds the first element of the `args` array. Subsequent arguments would be in `args[1]`, `args[2]`, …, `args[n]`. This program replaces the `{0}` parameter with the value of `args[0]` when it prints to the console. Figure 2.4 shows how to use this program.

For C++ Programmers

C++ command-line entries are passed with two variables to main, `argc` (a count of variables) and `argv` (an array of pointers to strings holding command-line input). This is accomplished in C# with a single array variable, `args`, with built-in functions to determine the number of strings in the array.

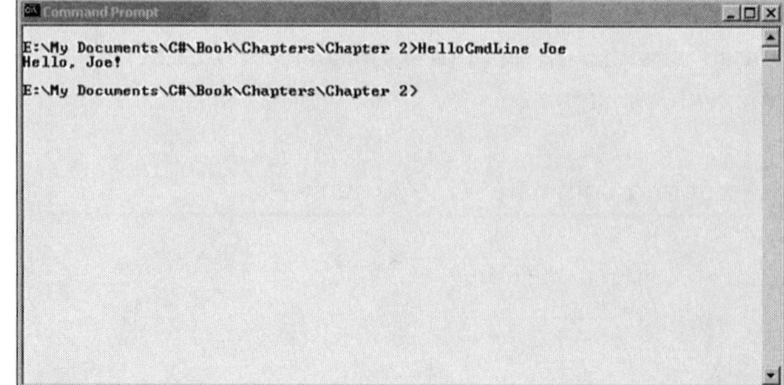
Command Prompt
E:\My Documents\C#\Book\Chapters\Chapter 2>HelloCmdLine Joe
Hello, Joe!
E:\My Documents\C#\Book\Chapters\Chapter 2>

FIGURE 2.4
Demonstration of command-line input for Listing 2.3.

Summary

This chapter presented the basic elements of writing a simple C# program. This included a minimal C# program that defined a class, a `Main()` method, and wrote a greeting to the screen.

Three types of commenting syntax were discussed: single-line, multiline, and XML documentation comments. Identifiers (user-defined names given to variables and various program elements the user defines), and keywords (reserved words used for the names of C# language elements) were defined. Ways to use whitespace and naming conventions to help make code easier to read and consistent with expected standards were also discussed.

The various C# types and literal values they can accept were explained. These include the `bool`, `integral`, floating point, and `decimal` types. Structs, reference types, enums, and arrays were introduced. How to perform basic conversions was explained, as was the difference between implicit and explicit conversions.

This chapter finished up with demonstrations on how to interact with programs via the console and via the command line during start-up. C# offers a plethora of built-in types to help make programs more expressive. The sections of this chapter presented the basics of the C# language. This essential bit of knowledge will help in preparing to build C# expressions.

Writing C# Expressions

In This Chapter

- Unary Operators 48
- Binary Operators 51
- The Ternary Operator 59
- Other Operators 60
- Enumeration Expressions 61
- Array Expressions 63
- Statements 65
- Blocks 65
- Labels 66
- Declarations 66
- Operator Precedence and Associativity 66

CHAPTER

C# provides a complete set of language elements for writing expressions. An expression is a set of language elements combined to perform a meaningful computation. This chapter provides guidance in building C# expressions.

This chapter demonstrates expressions created with each of C#'s built-in operators. All aspects of operators are covered in order to provide an understanding of their effects.

There are four types of operators—unary, binary, ternary, and a few others that don't fit into a category. Unary operators affect a single expression. Binary operators require two expressions to produce a result. The ternary operator has three expressions. The others can only be explained by reading each of their descriptions.

For C++ and Java Programmers

C# operators and their precedence are the same. No surprises here at all. If desired, you could skip this section without missing anything.

Unary Operators

As previously stated, unary operators affect a single expression. In many instances, the unary operators enable operations with simpler syntax than a comparable binary operation. The unary operators include + (plus), - (minus), ++ (increment), -- (decrement), ! (logical negation), and ~ (bitwise complement).

Note

Mathematical operations on floating-point types are performed according to IEEE 754 arithmetic.

The Plus Operator

The plus operator (+) has no effect on the expression it's used with. Why would a language have an operator that has no effect? For consistency. Most C# operators have a logical complement. Since there is a minus operator, its logical complement is the plus operator. The + operator is available to explicitly document code. Here are a couple examples:

```
int negative = -1;
int positive = 1;
int result;
```

```
result = +negative;    // result = -1
result = +positive;    // result = 1
```

The Minus Operator

The minus operator (-) allows negation of a variable's value. In integer and decimal types, the result is the number subtracted from zero. For floating-point types, the - operator inverts the sign of the number. When a value is NaN (not a number), the result is still NaN. Here are some examples:

```
int     negInt = -1;
decimal posDec =  1;
float   negFlt = -1.1f;
double nanDbl = Double.NaN;
int     resInt;
decimal resDec;
float   resFlt;
double  resDbl;

resInt = -negInt;  // resInt = 1
resDec = -posDec;  // resDec = -1
resFlt = -negFlt;  // resFlt = 1.1
resDbl = -nanDbl;  // resDbl = NaN
```


The Increment Operator

The increment operator (++) allows incrementing the value of a variable by 1. The timing of the effect of this operator depends upon which side of the expression it's on.

Here's a post-increment example:

```
int count;
int index = 6;

count = index++;  // count = 6, index = 7
```

In this example, the ++ operator comes after the expression index. That's why it's called a post-increment operator. The assignment takes place and then index is incremented. Since the assignment occurs first, the value of index is placed into count, making it equal 6. Then index is incremented to become 7.

Here's an example of a pre-increment operator:

```
int count;
int index = 6;

count = ++index;  // count = 7, index = 7
```

This time the ++ operator comes before the expression `index`. This is why it's called the pre-increment operator. `Index` is incremented before the assignment occurs. Since `index` is incremented first, its value becomes 7. Next, the assignment occurs to make the value of count equal 7.

The Decrement Operator

The decrement operator (`--`) allows decrementing the value of a variable. The timing of the effect of this operator again depends upon which side of the expression it is on. Here's a post-decrement example:

```
int count;
int index = 6;

count = index--;   // count = 6, index = 5
```

In this example, the `--` operator comes after the expression `index`, and that's why it's called a post-decrement operator. The assignment takes place and then `index` is decremented. Since the assignment occurs first, the value of `index` is placed into `count`, making it equal 6. Then `index` is decremented to become 5.

Here's an example of a pre-decrement operator:

```
int count;
int index = 6;

count = --index; // count = 5, index = 5
```

This time the `--` operator comes before the expression `index`, which is why it's called the pre-decrement operator. `Index` is decremented before the assignment occurs. Since `index` is decremented first, its value becomes 5, and then the assignment occurs to make the value of `count` equal 5.

The Logical Complement Operator

A logical complement operator (`!`) serves to invert the result of a Boolean expression. The Boolean expression evaluating to `true` will be `false`. Likewise, the Boolean expression evaluating to `false` will be `true`. Here are a couple examples:

```
bool bexpr   = true;
bool bresult = !bexpr;     // bresult = false
bresult      = !bresult;   // bresult = true
```

The Bitwise Complement Operator

A bitwise complement operator (~) inverts the binary representation of an expression. All 1 bits are turned to 0. Likewise, all 0 bits are turned to 1. Here's an example:

```
byte bitComp = 15;              // bitComp =  15 = 00001111b
byte bresult = (byte) ~bitComp; // bresult = 240 = 11110000b
```

Binary Operators

Binary operators are those operators that work with two operands. For example, a common binary expression would be a + b—the addition operator (+) surrounded by two operands. The binary operators are further subdivided into arithmetic, relational, logical, and assignment operators.

Arithmetic Operators

This is the first group of binary operators, those supporting arithmetic expressions. Arithmetic expressions are composed of two expressions with an arithmetic operator between them. This includes all the typical mathematical operators as expected in algebra.

The Multiplication Operator

The multiplication operator (*) evaluates two expressions and returns their product. Here's an example:

```
int expr1 = 3;
int expr2 = 7;
int product;

product = expr1 * expr2;  // product = 21
```

The Division Operator

The division operator (/), as its name indicates, performs mathematical division. It takes a dividend expression and divides it by a divisor expression to produce a quotient. Here's an example:

```
int dividend = 45;
int divisor = 5;
int quotient;

quotient = dividend / divisor;  // quotient = 9
```

Notice the use of integers in this expression. Had the result been a fractional number, it would have been truncated to produce the integer result.

The Remainder Operator

The remainder operator (%) returns the remainder of a division operation between a dividend and divisor. A common use of this operator is to create equations that produce a remainder that falls within a specified range. Here's an example:

```
int dividend = 33;
int divisor = 10;
int remainder;

remainder = dividend % divisor;  // remainder = 3
```

No matter what, as long as the divisor stays at 10, the remainder will always be between 0 and 9.

The Addition Operator

The addition operator (+) performs standard mathematical addition by adding one number to another. Here's an example:

```
int one = 1;
int two;

two = one + one;  // two = 2
```

The Subtraction Operator

The subtraction operator (-) performs standard mathematical subtraction by subtracting the value of one expression from another. Here's an example:

```
decimal debt    = 537.50m;
decimal payment = 250.00m;
decimal balance;

balance = debt - payment;  // balance = 287.50
```

The Left Shift Operator

To shift the bits of a number to the left, use the left shift operator (<<). The effect of this operation is that all bits move to the left a specified number of times. High-order bits are lost. Lower order bits are zero filled. This operator may be used on the int, uint, long, and ulong data types. Here's an example.

```
uint intMax = 4294967295; // 11111111111111111111111111111111b
uint byteMask;
byteMask    = intMax << 8; // 11111111111111111111111100000000b
```

The Right Shift Operator

The right shift operator (>>) shifts the bits of a number to the right. By providing a number to operate on and the number of digits, every bit shifts to the right by the number of digits specified. Only use the right shift operator on `int`, `uint`, `long`, and `ulong` data types. The `uint`, `ulong`, positive `int`, and positive `long` types shift zeros from the left. The negative `int` and negative `long` types keep a `1` in the sign bit position and fill the next position to the right with a `0`. Here are some examples:

```
uint intMax = 4294967295; // 11111111111111111111111111111111b
uint shortMask;
shortMask = intMax >> 16; // 00000000000000001111111111111111b

int intMax = -1;          // 11111111111111111111111111111111b
int shortMask;
shortMask = intMax >> 16; // 10000000000000001111111111111111b
```

For Java Programmers

C# doesn't have a right shift with zero extension operator (>>>).

Relational Operators

Relational operators are used to make a comparison between two expressions. The primary difference between relational operators and arithmetic operators is that relational operators return a bool type rather than a number. Another difference is that arithmetic operators are applicable to certain C# types whereas relational operators can be used on every possible C# type, whether built-in or not. Floating-point types are evaluated according to IEEE 754. The results of a relational expression are either `true` or `false`.

The Equal Operator

To see if two expressions are the same, use the equal operator (==). The equal operator works the same for integral, floating-point, decimal, and enum types. It simply compares the two expressions and returns a bool result. Here's an example:

```
bool bresult;
decimal debit  = 1500.00m;
decimal credit = 1395.50m;

bresult = debit == credit;  // bresult = false
```

When comparing floating-point types, `+0.0` and `-0.0` are considered equal. If either floating-point number is NaN (not a number), equal returns `false`.

The Not Equal Operator

The not equal operator (`!=`) is the opposite of the equal operator for all types, with a slight variation for floating-point types only. If one of the floating-point numbers is NAN (not a number), not equal returns true.

There are two forms of not equal applicable to expressions. The first is the normal not equal operator (`!=`). The other is a negation of the equal operator `!(a==b)`. Normally, these two forms always evaluate to the same value. The exception occurs when evaluating floating-point expressions where one or both expressions evaluate to NaN and the relational operator in the negation of an expression is <, >, <=, or >=. The `a > b` form evaluates to `false`, but the `!(a<=b)` evaluates to `true`. Here are some examples:

```
bool bresult;
decimal debit  = 1500.00m;
decimal credit = 1395.50m;

bresult = debit != credit;     // bresult = true
bresult = !(debit == credit); // bresult = true
```

The Less Than Operator

If it's necessary to find out if one value is smaller than another, use the less than operator (<). The expression on the left is being evaluated and the expression on the right is the basis of comparison. When the expression on the left is a lower value than the expression on the right, the result is `true`. Otherwise, the result is `false`. Here's an example:

```
short redBeads   = 2;
short whiteBeads = 23;
bool bresult;

bresult = redBeads < whiteBeads; // bresult=true, work harder
```

The Greater Than Operator

If it's necessary to know that a certain value is larger than another, use the greater than operator (>). It compares the expression on the left to the basis expression on the right. When the expression on the left is a higher value than the expression on the right, the result is `true`. Otherwise, the result is `false`. Here's an example:

```
short redBeads   = 13;
short whiteBeads = 12;
bool bresult;

bresult = redBeads > whiteBeads; // bresult=true, good job!
```

The Less Than or Equal Operator

Sometimes it's necessary to know if a number is either lower than or equal to another number. That's what the less than or equal operator (<=) is for. The expression on the left is compared to the expression on the right. When the expression on the left is either the same value as or less than the one on the right, less than or equal returns `true`. This operator is the opposite of the greater than operator, which means that `!(a>b)` would produce the same results. The exception is when there's a floating-point expression evaluating to NaN, in which case the result is always `true`. Here's an example of the less than or equal operator:

```
float limit     = 4.0f;
float currValue = 3.86724f;
bool Bresult;

bresult = currValue <= limit; // bresult = true
```

The Greater Than or Equal Operator

As its name implies, the greater than or equal operator (>=) checks a value to see if it's greater than or equal to another. When the expression to the left of the operator is the same as or more than the expression on the right, greater than or equal returns `true`. The greater than or equal operator is the opposite of the less than operator. Here's an example:

```
double rightAngle = 90.0d;
double myAngle    = 96.0d;
bool isAbtuse;

isAbtuse = myAngle >= rightAngle; // Yes, myAngle is abtuse
```

Logical Operators

Logical operators perform Boolean logic on two expressions. There are three types of logical operators in C#: bitwise, Boolean, and conditional.

The bitwise logical operators perform Boolean logic on corresponding bits of two integral expressions. Valid integral types are the signed and unsigned int and long types. They return a compatible integral result with each bit conforming to the Boolean evaluation.

Boolean logical operators perform Boolean logic upon two Boolean expressions. The expression on the left is evaluated, and then the expression on the right is evaluated. Finally, the two expressions are evaluated together in the context of the Boolean logical operator between them. They return a bool result corresponding to the type of operator used.

The conditional logical operators operate much the same way as the Boolean logical operators with one exception in behavior: Once the first expression is evaluated and found to satisfy the results of the entire expression, the second expression is not evaluated. This is efficient because it doesn't make sense to continue evaluating an expression when the result is already known.

The Bitwise AND Operator

The bitwise AND operator (`&`) compares corresponding bits of two integrals and returns a result with corresponding bits set to 1 when both integrals have 1 bits. When either or both integrals have a 0 bit, the corresponding result bit is 0. Here's an example:

```
byte oddMask  = 1;  // 00000001b
byte someByte = 85; // 01010101b
bool isEven;

isEven = (oddMask & someByte) == 0; //(oddMask & someByte) = 1
```

The Bitwise Inclusive OR Operator

The bitwise inclusive OR operator (`|`) compares corresponding bits of two integrals and returns a result with corresponding bits set to 1 if either of the integrals have 1 bits in that position. When both integrals have a 0 in corresponding positions, the result is zero in that position. Here's an example:

```
byte option1 = 1; // 00000001b
byte option2 = 2; // 00000010b
byte totalOptions;

totalOptions = (byte) (option1 | option2); // 00000011b
```

The Bitwise Exclusive OR Operator

The bitwise exclusive OR operator (`^`) compares corresponding bits of two integrals and returns a result with corresponding bits set to `1` if only one of the integrals has a `1` bit and the other integral has a `0` bit in that position. When both integral bits are `1` or when both are `0`, the result's corresponding bit is `0`. Here's an example:

```
byte invertMask = 255; // 11111111b
byte someByte   = 240; // 11110000b
byte inverse;

inverse = (byte)(someByte ^ invertMask); //inversion=00001111b
```

The Boolean AND Operator

The Boolean AND operator (&) evaluates two Boolean expressions and returns true when both expressions evaluate to `true`. Otherwise, the result is `false`. The result of each expression evaluated must return a bool result. Here's an example:

```
bool inStock = false;
decimal price = 18.95m;
bool buy;

buy = inStock & (price < 20.00m); // buy = false
```

The Boolean Inclusive OR Operator

The Boolean inclusive OR operator (`|`) evaluates the results of two Boolean expressions and returns `true` if either of the expressions returns `true`. When both expressions are false, the result of the Boolean inclusive OR evaluation is false. Both expressions evaluated must return a bool type value. Here's an example:

```
int mileage = 2305;
int months = 4;
bool changeOil;

changeOil = mileage > 3000 | months > 3; // changeOil = true
```

The Boolean Exclusive OR Operator

The Boolean exclusive OR operator (^) evaluates the results of two Boolean expressions and returns true if only one of the expressions returns true. When both expressions are true or both expressions are false, the result of the Boolean exclusive OR expression is false. In other words, the expressions must be different. Here's an example:

```
bool availFlag = false;
bool toggle    = true;
bool available;

available = availFlag ^ toggle; // available = true
```


The Conditional AND Operator

The conditional AND operator (&&) is similar to the Boolean AND operator in that it evaluates two expressions and returns true when both expressions are true. It is different when the first expression evaluates to false. Since both expressions must be true, it's automatically assumed that if the first expression evaluates to false, the entire expression is false. Therefore, the conditional AND operator returns false and does not evaluate the second expression. When the first expression is true, the conditional AND operator goes ahead and evaluates the second expression. Here's an example:

```
bool inStock   = false;
decimal price = 18.95m;
bool buy;

buy = inStock && (price < 20.00m); // buy = false
```

Notice that price < 20 will never be evaluated.

The Conditional OR Operator

The conditional OR operator (||) is similar to the Boolean inclusive OR operator (|) in that it evaluates two expressions and returns true when either expression is true. The difference is when the first expression evaluates to true. Since either expression can be true to prove that the overall expression is true, the operator automatically assumes that the entire expression is true when it finds the first expression is true. Therefore, the conditional OR operator returns `true` without evaluating the second expression. When the first expression is `false`, the conditional OR operator goes ahead and evaluates the second expression. Here's an example:

```
int mileage = 4305;
int months = 4;
bool changeOil;

changeOil = mileage > 3000 || months > 3; // changeOil = true
```

Notice that because `mileage > 3000` is true, `months > 3` will never be evaluated.

Side Effects

Watch out for side effects with conditional Boolean operations. Side effects occur when your program depends on the expression on the right of the conditional logical operator being evaluated. If the expression on the right is not evaluated, this could cause a hard-to-find bug. The conditional logical operators are also called *short circuit* operators. Take a look at this example:

```
decimal totalSpending = 3692.48m;
decimal avgSpending;

bool onBudget = totalSpending > 4000.00m
    && totalSpending < calcAvg();
```

Notice that the second half of the expression was not evaluated. If `calcAvg()` was supposed to change the value of a class field for later processing, there would be an error.

Warning

When using conditional AND and conditional OR operators, make sure a program does not depend upon evaluation of the right-hand side of the expression, because it may not be evaluated. Such side effects are likely to cause bugs.

Assignment Operators

This chapter has already demonstrated plenty of examples of the simple assignment operator in action. This section explains the compound operators and what can be expected from them. Basically, the concept is simple. A compound operator is a combination of the assignment operator and an arithmetic operator, bitwise logical operator, or Boolean logical operator. Here's an example:

```
int total = 7;
total += 3; // total = 10
```

This is the same as saying: `total = total + 3`. Table 3.1 shows a list of the available compound assignment operators.

TABLE 3.1 Compound Assignment Operators

Operator	*Function*
`*=`	Multiplication
`/=`	Division
`%=`	Remainder
`+=`	Addition
`-=`	Subtraction
`<<=`	Left Shift
`>>=`	Right Shift
`&=`	AND
`^=`	Exclusive OR
`|=`	Inclusive OR

The Ternary Operator

The ternary operator contains three expressions, thus the name *ternary*. The first expression must be a Boolean expression. When the first expression evaluates to `true`, the value of the second expression is returned. When the first expression evaluates to `false`, the value of the third expression is returned. This is a concise and short method of making a decision and returning a choice based upon the result of the decision. The ternary operator is often called the conditional operator. Here's an example:

```
long democratVotes   = 1753829380624;
long republicanVotes = 1753829380713;

string headline = democratVotes != republicanVotes ?
                  "We Finally Have a Winner!" : recount();
```

Other Operators

C# has some operators that can't be categorized as easily as the other types. These include the `is`, `as`, `sizeof()`, `typeof()`, `checked()`, and `unchecked()` operators. The following sections explain each operator.

The `is` Operator

The `is` operator checks a variable to see if it's a given type. If so, it returns `true`. Otherwise, it returns `false`. Here's an example.

```
int i = 0;
bool isTest = i is int; // isTest = true
```

The `as` Operator

The `as` operator attempts to perform a conversion on a reference type. The following example tries to convert the integer i into a string. If the conversion were successful, the object variable `obj` would hold a reference to a string object. When the conversion from an `as` operator fails, it assigns `null` to the receiving reference. That's the case in this example where `obj` becomes `null` because `i` is an integer, not a string:

```
int i = 0;
object obj = i as string;
Console.WriteLine("i {0} a string.",
    obj == null ? "is not" : "is" ); // i is not a string.
```

The `sizeof()` Operator

C# provides a facility to perform low-level functions through a construct known as `unsafe` code. The `sizeof()` operator works only in `unsafe` code. The operator takes a type and returns the type's size in bytes. Here's an example:

```
unsafe
{
    int intSize = sizeof(int); // intSize = 4
}
```

The `typeof()` Operator

The `typeof()` operator returns a `Type` object. The `Type` class holds type information about a value or reference type. The `typeof()` operator is used in various places in C# to discover information about reference and value types. The following example gets type information on the `int` type:

```
Type myType = typeof(int);
Console.WriteLine(
    "The int type: {0}", myType ); // The int type: Int32
```

The checked() Operator

The `checked()` operator detects overflow conditions in certain operations. The following example causes a system error by attempting to assign a value to a short variable that it can't hold:

```
short val1 = 20000, val2 = 20000;
short myShort = checked((short)(val1 + val2)); // error
```

The unchecked() Operator

If it is necessary to ignore this error and accept the results regardless of overflow conditions, use the `unchecked()` operator as in this example:

```
short val1 = 20000, val2 = 20000;
short myShort =
    unchecked((short)(val1 + val2)); // error ignored
```


Tip

Use the `/checked[+|-]` command line option when the majority of program code should be checked (`/checked+`) or unchecked (`/checked-`). Then all that needs to be done inside the code is to annotate the exceptions with the `checked()` and `unchecked()` operators.

Enumeration Expressions

The elements of enumeration expressions evaluate the same as their underlying types. In addition to using normal operators, there are additional methods that can be performed with an `enum` type. An `Enum` class is used to obtain the majority of functionality shown in this section. Where the `Enum` class is being used, the capitalized `Enum` class name prefixes the method call. The examples in this section refer to the following enum:

```
enum Weekday { Mon = 1, Tue, Wed, Thu, Fri, Sat = 10, Sun };
```

For C++ Programmers

C# enums have much more functionality than C++ enums.

As a typed value, the enum must be assigned to a variable of its type. For example, the underlying representation of a Weekday enum may default to an integral value, but it's still a Weekday type. The following line shows the declaration and initialization of an enum variable:

```
Weekday w = Weekday.Mon;
```

During a `Console.WriteLine()` method call, enum values are printed with their names rather than their underlying integral values. Here's an example:

```
Console.WriteLine("WeekDay: {0}", w); // WeekDay: Mon
```

The `Format()` method returns the string representation of an enum value, as shown here:

```
Console.WriteLine("Format: {0}", w.Format()); // Format: Mon
```

To go in the opposite direction and convert a string to an enum, use the `FromString()` method. The arguments it accepts are the enum type, the string representation of the value to be converted, and a Boolean condition to verify case. The following example uses the `typeof()` operator to get the enum type. The string to be converted is Tue, and the method is case-sensitive.

```
Console.WriteLine("FromString: {0}",
    Enum.FromString(typeof(EnumTest.Weekday),
    "Tue", true));                          // FromString: Tue
```

To get the name of an enum variable, use the `GetName()` method. The following example shows the `GetName()` method accepting the enum type and an instance of that enum type and returning its name as a string.

```
w = EnumTest.Weekday.Wed;
Console.WriteLine("GetName: {0}",
    Enum.GetName(typeof(EnumTest.Weekday), w)); // GetName: Wed
```

If there is a need to get the string representations of all the members of an enum, use the `GetNames()` method—plural of the previous method. The following example shows an array being filled with the names. The method call only needs the enum type.

```
string[] weekDays = new string[7];
weekDays = Enum.GetNames(typeof(EnumTest.Weekday));

Console.WriteLine("Day 1: {0}", weekDays[0]); // Day 1: Mon
Console.WriteLine("Day 2: {0}", weekDays[1]); // Day 2: Tue
Console.WriteLine("Day 3: {0}", weekDays[2]); // Day 3: Wed
Console.WriteLine("Day 4: {0}", weekDays[3]); // Day 4: Thu
Console.WriteLine("Day 5: {0}", weekDays[4]); // Day 5: Fri
Console.WriteLine("Day 6: {0}", weekDays[5]); // Day 6: Sat
Console.WriteLine("Day 7: {0}", weekDays[6]); // Day 7: Sun
```

A corresponding method to get the values of an enum is the `GetValues()` method. The following example shows the `GetValues()` method accepting an enum type and returning an array of objects. Notice that the array is of type objects. In C#, all types are also object types. Therefore, any type can be assigned to the object type.

```
object[] weekDayVals = new object[7];
weekDayVals = Enum.GetValues(typeof(EnumTest.Weekday));

Console.WriteLine("Day 1: {0}", weekDayVals[0]); // Day 1: Mon
Console.WriteLine("Day 2: {0}", weekDayVals[1]); // Day 2: Tue
Console.WriteLine("Day 3: {0}", weekDayVals[2]); // Day 3: Wed
Console.WriteLine("Day 4: {0}", weekDayVals[3]); // Day 4: Thu
Console.WriteLine("Day 5: {0}", weekDayVals[4]); // Day 5: Fri
Console.WriteLine("Day 6: {0}", weekDayVals[5]); // Day 6: Sat
Console.WriteLine("Day 7: {0}", weekDayVals[6]); // Day 7: Sun
```

To find out the underlying type of an enum, use the `GetUnderlyingType()` method. It accepts an enum type argument, and the return value is the integral type of the enum's underlying type. Here's an example:

```
Console.WriteLine("Underlying Type: {0}",
    Enum.GetUnderlyingType(
        typeof(EnumTest.Weekday))); // Underlying Type: Int32
```


When it's necessary to determine if an enum value is defined, use the `IsDefined()` method. It accepts an enum type and an enum value and returns a Boolean true if the value is defined in the enum. Otherwise, it returns false. Here's an example:

```
w = EnumTest.Weekday.Thu;
Console.WriteLine("Thu is Defined: {0}",
    Enum.IsDefined(typeof(EnumTest.Weekday), w));
    // Thu is Defined: True
```

To obtain an enum type that is set to a specific value, use the `ToObject()` method. The following example shows the method accepting an enum type and an integer, and returning an enum of the requested type with the value corresponding to the integer.

```
Console.WriteLine("Get Friday: {0}",
    Enum.ToObject(typeof(EnumTest.Weekday), 5));
    // Get Friday: Fri
```

Array Expressions

Besides being an efficient storage construct, arrays have additional functionality that helps make programs more expressive and powerful. The following example shows one such capability:

```
string[] weekDays = new string[7];
Console.WriteLine("Number of Days: {0}",
    weekDays.Length); // Number of Days: 7
```

For C++ Programmers

From the perspective of traditional built-into-the-language arrays, C++ arrays are simply a pointer to a block of memory. This refers to the C++ arrays derived from its C language ancestry. C# arrays have much more functionality.

The C++ `STL` array class is similar to the C# `ArrayList` collection class. Both are library classes.

The previous example showed the array's Length property. The array type has many more methods and properties, as shown in Table 3.2.

TABLE 3.2 C# Array Members

Method/Property	*Description*
`AsList`	Returns an `Ilist` representation of the array
`BinarySearch`	Finds a value in a one-dimensional array using a binary search
`Clear`	Cleans out a range of array values by setting them to `0` or `null`
`Copy`	Copies a range of array elements to another array
`CreateInstance`	Creates a new instance of an array
`IndexOf`	Finds the first occurrence of a value and returns its index
`LastIndexOf`	Finds the last occurrence of a value and returns its index
`Reverse`	Reverses the elements of a one-dimensional array
`Sort`	Sorts a one-dimensional array
`IsReadOnly`	Returns `true` if read-only
`IsSynchronized`	Returns `true` if synchronized
`Length`	Returns the number of elements in all dimensions
`Rank`	Returns the number of dimensions
`SyncRoot`	Returns array synchronization object
`Clone`	Performs a shallow copy
`CopyTo`	Copies from one array to another

TABLE 3.2 continued

Method/Property	*Description*
`Equals`	Compares array references for equality
`GetEnumerator`	Returns an `IEnumerator` of a one-dimensional array
`GetHashCode`	Returns a unique identifier
`GetLength`	Returns the number of elements in specified dimension
`GetLowerBound`	Returns the lower bound of a dimension
`GetType`	Returns the Type object
`GetUpperBound`	Returns the upper bound of a dimension
`GetValue`	Returns values from specified elements
`Initialize`	Calls the default constructor of each element
`SetValue`	Sets values of specified elements
`ToString`	Returns a string representation

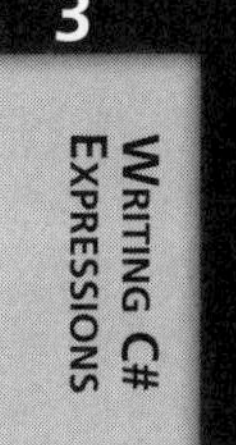

Statements

Statements in C# are single entities that cause a change in the program's current state. They're commonly associated with some type of assignment statement, changing the value of a variable. A statement ends with a semicolon (;). Leave one out and the compiler will issue a prompt notification. Statements may span multiple lines, which could help make your code more readable, as the following example shows:

```
decimal closingCosts = loanOrigination
           + appraisal
           + titleSearch
           + insuranceAdvance
           + taxAdvance
           + points
           + realtorCommission
           + whateverElseTheyCanRipYouOffFor;
```

Had the statement been placed on one line, it would have either continued off the right side of the page or wrapped around in an inconvenient location. This way, each item is visible, lined up nicely, and easier to understand.

Blocks

Setting off code in blocks clearly delimits the beginning and ending of a unit of work and establishes scope. Begin a block of code with a left-hand brace ({), and end it with a right-hand brace (}). Blocks are required to specify the boundaries of many language elements such as classes, interfaces, structures, properties, indexers, events, and methods.

Labels

Labels are program elements that simply identify a location in a program. Their only practical use is to support the `goto` statement. The `goto` statement allows program control to jump to the place where a label is defined. A label is any valid identifier followed by a colon (not a semicolon). Here are two examples:

```
loop:        // a label named "loop"

jumphere:    // a label named "jumphere"
```

Declarations

Declarations enable definition and announcement of the existence and nature of program data. There are two forms of declaration in C#: simple declaration and declaration with initialization. A simple declaration takes the following form:

```
<type> <identifier>;
```

The `type` may be any C# or user-defined type. The `identifier` is any valid identifier as defined in Chapter 2, "Getting Started with C#."

A declaration with initialization looks like this:

```
<type> <identifier> = <expression>;
```

The `type` and `identifier` are the same as the previous example. The equal sign takes the evaluated expression on its right and loads it into the variable declared on the left. The expression can be any valid C# statement evaluating to the type of variable specified by type. The declaration is a statement followed by a semicolon.

Operator Precedence and Associativity

When evaluating C# expressions, there are certain rules to ensure the outcome of the evaluation. These rules are governed by precedence and associativity and preserve the semantics of all C# expressions. Precedence refers to the order in which operations should be evaluated. Sub-expressions with higher operator precedence are evaluated first.

There are two types of associativity: left and right. Operators with left associativity are evaluated from left to right. When an operator has right associativity, its expression is evaluated from right to left. For example, the assignment operator is right associative. Therefore, the expression to its right is evaluated before the assignment operation is invoked. Table 3.3 shows the C# operators, their precedence, and associativity.

Certain operators have precedence over others to guarantee the certainty and integrity of computations. One effective rule of thumb when using most operators is to remember their algebraic precedence. Here's an example:

```
int result;
result = 5 + 3 * 9;  // result = 32
```

This computes `3 * 9 = 27 + 5 = 32`. To alter the order of operations use parentheses, which have a higher precedence:

```
result = (5 + 3) * 9;  // result = 72
```

This time, 5 and 3 were added to get 8 and then multiplied by 9 to get 72. See Table 3.3 for a listing of operator precedence and associativity. Operators in top rows have precedence over operators in lower rows. Operators on the left in each row have higher precedence over operators to the right in the same row.

TABLE 3.3 Operator Precedence and Associativity

Operators	*Associativity*
`(x)`, `x.y`, `f(x)`, `a[x]`, `x++`, `x--`, `new`, `typeof`, `sizeof`, `checked`, `unchecked`	Left
+ (unary), - (unary), ~, `++x`, `--x`, `(T)x`	Left
*, / %	Left
+ (arithmetic), - (arithmetic)	Left
<<, >>	Left
<, >, <=, >=, `is`, `as`	Left
==, !=	Left
&	Left
^	Left
|	Left
&&	Left
||	Left
?:	Right
=, *=, /=, %=, +=, -=, <<=, >>=, &=, ^=, |=	Right

Summary

This chapter covered the various C# operators—unary, arithmetic, relational operators, and other operators—and provided examples of how to use them.

The unary operators include plus, minus, increment, decrement, logical complement, and bitwise complement operators. Binary operators include the arithmetic, logical, relational and assignment operators. There is a single ternary operator that produces conditional results. C# has a few other operators that don't fit into the any of those categories; they include the `is`, `as`, `typeof`, `sizeof`, `checked`, and `unchecked` operators.

The enum and array types have additional functions that make programs more expressive and powerful. I included several examples of enums and a table of array methods and properties.

This chapter also described statements, blocks, labels, and declarations, and included a section about operator precedence and associativity.

Having mastered the material in this chapter, it's simple to move into logical manipulation of program flow.

CHAPTER 4

Using Statements and Loops to Control Program Flow

In This Chapter

- `if` Statements *70*
- `switch` Statements *73*
- C# Loops *76*
- `goto` Statements *81*
- `break` Statements *83*
- `continue` Statements *84*
- `return` Statements *84*

This chapter provides the information needed to make logical decisions, iteratively execute a sequence of instructions, and modify the normal flow of control in programs. Although there is much more to C#, this chapter provides ample tools necessary to create useful, sophisticated programs.

For C++ and Java Programmers

Many of the statements in this chapter contain a Boolean expression for decision-making capability. A C++ program can interpret positive integers as `true` values; it does not work that way in C#. In C# the Boolean expression must return a `true` or `false` Boolean value. It does interpret an integral value as being `true` or `false`.

`if` Statements

`if` statements allow evaluation of an expression and, depending on the truth of the evaluation, the capability to branch to a specified sequence of logic. C# provides three forms of `if` statements: simple `if`, `if-then-else`, and `if-else if-else`.

Simple `if`

A simple `if` statement takes the following form:

```
if (Boolean expression)
[{]
    true condition statement(s)
[}]
```

As expected, the Boolean expression must evaluate to either `true` or `false`. When the Boolean expression is `true`, the program performs the following true condition statements:

```
if (args.Length == 1)
{
  Console.WriteLine("What is your pleasure, {0}?", args[0] );
}
```

Warning

The curly braces are optional if there's only one action. It's usually a good practice to add them anyway. Their omission has been known to cause unexpected bugs.

if-then-else

The simple `if` statement only guarantees you can perform certain actions on a `true` condition. It's either done or it's not. To handle both the `true` and `false` conditions, use the `if-then-else` statement. It has the following form:

```
if (Boolean expression)
[{]
    true condition statement(s)
[}]
else
[{]
    false condition statement(s)
[}]
```

This statement behaves the same as the simple `if`, except when the Boolean expression evaluates to `false`. Then the `false` condition statements in the `else` part are executed. Here's an example:

```
if (args.Length == 0)
{
  Console.WriteLine("What is your pleasure, Master?");
}
else
{
  Console.WriteLine("What is your pleasure, {0}?", args[0]);
}
```

if-else if-else

Sometimes it's necessary to evaluate multiple conditions to determine what actions to take. In this case, use the `if-else if-else` statement. Here's its general form:

```
if (Boolean expression)
[{]
    true condition statement(s)
[}]
else if (Boolean expression)
[{]
    true condition statement(s)
[}]
    .
    .
    .
else if (Boolean expression)
[{]
    true condition statement(s)
[}]
else
```

```
[{]
    false condition statement(s)
[}]
```

In a sequential order, each statement, beginning with `if` and continuing through each `else if`, is evaluated until one of their Boolean expressions evaluates to `true`. The dots indicate possible multiple `else if` blocks. There can be any number of `else if` blocks required.

Once one of the Boolean expressions evaluates to `true`, the `true` condition statements for that `if` or `else if` are executed, and then flow of control transfers to the first statement following the entire `if-else if-else` structure.

If none of the Boolean expressions evaluates to `true`, the `false` condition statement(s) of the `else` section is executed. Here's an example:

```
if (args.Length == 0)
{
  Console.WriteLine("What is your pleasure, Master?");
}
else if (args.Length == 1)
{
  Console.WriteLine("What is your pleasure, {0}?", args[0]);
}
else
{
  Console.WriteLine("Too many arguments!\a");
}
```

It's permissible to include any valid statement inside an `if`, `else if`, or `else` statement block. If necessary, add another `if` statement. Here's an example:

```
if (args.Length == 0)
{
    Console.WriteLine("What is your pleasure, Master?");
}
else if (args.Length == 1)
{
  if (args[0] == "Joe")
    Console.WriteLine(
        "What is your pleasure, {0}?", "Master");
  else
    Console.WriteLine(
        "What is your pleasure, {0}?", args[0]);
}
else
{
  Console.WriteLine("Too many arguments!\a");
}
```

`if` statements excel at decisions involving evaluation of dynamic runtime calculations and relational expressions. The following example shows how to evaluate a wide range of values:

```
if (waterTemp <= 0)
{
  Console.WriteLine("Solid");
}
else if (waterTemp > 0 & waterTemp < 100)
{
  Console.WriteLine("Liquid");
}
else
{
  Console.WriteLine("Gas");
}
```

switch Statements

When there are many conditions to evaluate, the `if-else if-else` statement can become complex and verbose. A much cleaner solution for some situations is the `switch` statement. The `switch` statement allows testing any integral value or string against multiple values. When the test produces a match, all statements associated with that match are executed. Here's the basic form of a `switch` statement:

```
switch(integral or string expression)
{
    case <literal-1>:
        statement(s)
        break;
        .
        .
        .
    case <literal-n>:
        statement(s)
        break;
    [default:
        statement(s)]
}
```


For C++ Programmers

C++ accepts only integer values in a `switch` statement. C# accepts strings and enums as well as integers.

Also, C++ permits case fall-through. C# does not. Break statements are mandatory in C# unless two cases are combined with no statements between them.

For Java Programmers

Java accepts integer values in a `switch` statement. C# accepts strings as well as integers.

Also, Java permits case fall-through. C# does not. Break statements are mandatory in C# unless two cases are combined with no statements between them.

The integral, enum, or string expression is compared against each `case` statement's literal value. Add as many `case` statements as necessary. When there's a match, those statements following the matching `case` are executed. Here's an example:

```
switch (choice)
{
  case "A":
    Console.WriteLine("Add Site");
    break;
  case "S":
    Console.WriteLine("Sort List");
    break;
  case "R":
    Console.WriteLine("Show Report");
    break;
  case "Q":
    Console.WriteLine("GoodBye");
    break;
  default:
    Console.WriteLine("Huh??");
    break;
}
```

The `break` statement is mandatory. One `case` can't drop through to another `case` after executing its statements. There are a couple of slight exceptions to this rule. One exception is grouping `case` statements together, as this example shows:

```
switch (choice)
{
  case "a":
  case "A":
    Console.WriteLine("Add Site");
    break;
  case "s":
  case "S":
    Console.WriteLine("Sort List");
    break;
```

```
  case "r":
  case "R":
    Console.WriteLine("Show Report");
    break;
  case "q":
  case "Q":
    Console.WriteLine("GoodBye");
    break;
  default:
    Console.WriteLine("Huh??");
    break;
}
```

This example shows an exception to the restriction against `case` fall-through. The `case` for all initial capped and lowercased letters are grouped together with one immediately following the other. The top `case` falls through to the next `case` when there are no statements between the two `cases`. The other exception is by using a `goto` statement:

```
switch (choice)
{
  case "A":
    Console.WriteLine("Add Site");
    break;
  case "S":
    Console.WriteLine("Sort List");
    break;
  case "R":
    Console.WriteLine("Show Report");
    break;
  case "V":
    Console.WriteLine("View Sorted Report");
    // Sort First
    goto case "R";
  case "Q":
    Console.WriteLine("GoodBye");
    break;
  default:
    Console.WriteLine("Huh??");
    break;
}
```

This example shows the second exception to the restriction against case fall-through. It uses a `goto` statement to execute another `case`. It doesn't matter whether the `goto case` is the next in line or somewhere else in the `switch` statement. Program control still transfers to the `case` specified in the `goto` statement. When none of the cases match, control transfers to the default case.

Warning

Although the `default case` in a `switch` statement is optional, it should normally be included. Its absence has been known to create subtle bugs that occur when none of the `cases` match.

The `default case` in a `switch` statement is optional. When there is no `default case`, program control transfers to the next statement following the ending curly brace of the `switch` statement. The following example shows a `switch` statement without a `default case`.

```
switch (calculation)
{
  case 1:
    // perform calculation #1
    break;
  case 2:
    // Perform calculation #2
    break;
  case 3:
    // Perform calculation #3
    break;
}
```

In the preceding code, three calculations can be performed as a result of a deliberate choice. If no choice was made, the user would expect some default calculation to take place. Clearly, this would not happen. The result is a bug whose consequences depend upon the severity of not performing the default action.

Tip

`Switch` statements are very efficient with conditions requiring equality relations and very small numbers of ranges. For anything more sophisticated, evaluation wise, go with the `if` statement.

C# Loops

It's often necessary to perform a sequence of logic multiple times in a program. For example, there might be a list of some items where each item needs the same processing. This processing is performed with language constructs called loops. In C# there are four types of loops—the `while` loop, the `do` loop, the `for` loop, and the `foreach` loop. Each has its own benefits for certain tasks.

`while` Loops

If it's necessary to continually execute a group of statements while a condition is `true`, use the `while` loop. The general form of the `while` loop is as follows:

```
While (Boolean expression)
[{]
    true condition statement(s)
[}]
```

When the Boolean expression evaluates to `true`, the `true` condition statements are executed. The following example shows how a `while` loop can be used.

```
string doAgain = "Y";
int count = 0;
string[] siteName = new string[10];

while (doAgain == "Y")
{
  Console.Write("Please Enter Site Name: ");
  siteName[count++] = Console.ReadLine();

  Console.Write("Add Another?: ");
  doAgain = Console.ReadLine();
}
```

A sneaky bug to watch out for with all loops is the empty statement bug. The following code is for illustrative purposes only, so don't try it:

```
string doAgain = "Y";

while (doAgain == "Y"); // loop forever
{
  // this is never executed
}
```

Since curly braces are optional, the semicolon after the Boolean expression represents the true condition statement. Thus, every time the Boolean expression evaluates to `true`, the empty statement is executed and the Boolean statement is evaluated again—ad infinitum.

The reason the curly braces don't cause a bug is because they represent a block, which is legal syntax in C#.

Warning

A single semicolon is interpreted as a statement. A common mistake is to put a semicolon after a loop statement, which causes subsequent loop statements to execute only one time. These are hard-to-find errors.

do Loops

`while` loops evaluate an expression before executing the statements in a block. However, it may be necessary to execute the statements at least one time. This is what the `do` loop allows. Here's its general form:

```
do {
    Statement(s)
} while (Boolean expression);
```

The statements execute, and then the Boolean expression is evaluated. If the Boolean expression evaluates to `true`, the statements are executed again. Otherwise, control passes to the statement following the entire `do` loop. The following is an example of a `do` loop in action.

```
do
{
  Console.WriteLine("");
  Console.WriteLine("A - Add Site");
  Console.WriteLine("S - Sort List");
  Console.WriteLine("R - Show Report\n");

  Console.WriteLine("Q - Quit\n");

  Console.Write("Please Choose (A/S/R/Q): ");

  choice = Console.ReadLine();

  switch (choice)
  {
    case "a":
    case "A":
      Console.WriteLine("Add Site");
      break;
    case "s":
    case "S":
      Console.WriteLine("Sort List");
      break;
    case "r":
    case "R":
      Console.WriteLine("Show Report");
```

```
        break;
      case "q":
      case "Q":
        Console.WriteLine("GoodBye");
        break;
      default:
        Console.WriteLine("Huh??");
        break;
    }

} while ((choice = choice.ToUpper()) != "Q");
```

This code snippet prints a menu and then asks the user for input. For this purpose, it is logical to use a do loop, because the menu has to print at least one time. If this were to be done with another type of loop, some artificial condition would have needed to be set just to get the first iteration.

for Loops

for loops are good for when the number of times to execute a group of statements is known beforehand. Here's its general syntax:

```
for (initializer; Boolean expression; modifier)
[{]
    statement(s)
[}]
```

The initializer is executed one time only, when the for loop begins. After the initializer executes, the Boolean expression is evaluated. The Boolean expression must evaluate to true for the statement(s) to be executed. Once the statement(s) have executed, the modifier executes, and then the Boolean expression is evaluated again. The statement(s) continue to be executed until the Boolean expression evaluates to false, after which control transfers to the statement following the for loop. The following example illustrates how to implement a for loop.

```
int n = siteName.Length-2;
int j, k;
string save;

for (k=n-1; k >= 0; k--)
{
  j = k + 1;
  save = siteName[k];
  siteName[n+1] = save;

  while ( String.Compare(save, siteName[j]) > 0 )
  {
    siteName[j-1] = siteName[j];
```

```
    j++;
  }
  siteName[j-1] = save;
}
```

The insertion sort in this code shows how a `for` loop is used in a realistic scenario. Often, `for` loops begin at 0 and are incremented until a predetermined number of iterations have passed. This particular example starts at the end of the array and moves backward, decrementing each step. When `k` reaches `0`, the loop ends.

For C++ Programmers

In Standard C++, `for` Loop initializer declarations define a new scope for a variable with the same name in its enclosing block. In C# this would be flagged as an error, because a variable in the `for` loop initializer is not allowed to hide a variable with the same name in an enclosing block.

When programming in C#, there is a full set of libraries from which to choose pre-made functions. The Boolean condition of the `while` loop shows the `String.Compare()` method. In this particular instance, the program checks to see if `save` is greater than `siteName[j]`. If so, the Boolean result is `true`.

foreach Loops

The `foreach` loop is excellent for iterating through collections. Here's its syntax:

```
foreach (type identifier in collection)
[{]
    statement(s)
[}]
```

The type can be any C# or user-defined type. The identifier is the variable name you want to use. The collection is any C# collection object.

For C++ Programmers

C++ does not have a `foreach` loop.

Upon entering the `foreach` loop the identifier variable is set with an item from collection. Then the statement(s) are executed and control transfers back to get another item from the collection. When all items in the `collection` have been extracted, control transfers to the statement following the `foreach` loop.

Here's an example that iterates through the `siteName` array, printing each entry to the console.

```
foreach(string site in siteName)
{
  Console.WriteLine("\t{0}", site);
}
```

Had this been done with another loop, the program would have taken more effort. Then there's always the possibility of corrupting a counter. The `foreach` loop is a clean and simple way to iterate through an array.

The `foreach` loop was specially designed to work with collections. There are several collections in the System libraries, and `Array` is a built-in collection.

goto Statements

The `goto` statement allows unconditional branching to another program section. The form of the `goto` statement is as follows:

```
goto label;
```

The destination is marked by a `label`. Legal destinations include the current level of the `goto` statement or outside of the current loop.

For C++ Programmers

C++ `goto` statements can transfer control to anywhere in a program. C# `goto` statements must always jump at the same level or higher out of its enclosing block.

For Java Programmers

Java does not have a goto statement. In C#, the `goto` statement has restrictions that make it similar to a Java labeled `break` statement.

The following code shows how a `goto` statement could be used.

```
do {
  // some processing
  while (/* some Boolean condition */)
  {
```

```
    // some processing
    for (int i=0; i < someValue; i++)
    {
      if (/* some Boolean condition */)
      {
        goto quickExit;
      }
    }
  }
} while (/* some Boolean condition */);

quickExit:
```

This example displays a potential scenario where the code is deeply nested in processing. If a certain condition causes the end of processing to occur in the middle of that loop, the program has to make several less-than-graceful checks to get out. The example shows how using a `goto` might be helpful in making a clean exit from a tricky situation. It may even make the code easier to read, instead of trying to design a clumsy workaround. Again, the decision to use a `goto` is based on the requirements a project needs to meet.

A `goto` may never jump into a loop. Here's an example that should help you visualize just how illogical such an attempt might be:

```
// error
while (/* some Boolean condition */)
{
  // some processing
  innerLoop:
  // more processing
}

goto innerLoop;
```

It's normally desirable to have some type of initialization and control while executing a loop. This scenario could easily violate the integrity of any loop, which is why it is not allowed.

Note

Much has been said about the value of the `goto` statement in computer programming. Arguments range from recommending that it be eliminated to using it as an essential tool to get out of a hard spot. Although many people have been able to program without the `goto` for years, there's always the possibility that someone may still find it necessary. Just be careful with its use and make sure programs are maintainable.

break Statements

The `switch` statement mentioned previously showed one way to use the `break` statement. It allowed program control to jump out of the `switch` statement. Similarly, the `break` statement allows jumping out of any decision or loop. Its destination is always the first statement following the decision or loop. The following example shows two ways to break out of a loop:

```
string doAgain = "Y";

while (doAgain == "Y")
{
  Console.Write("Please Enter Site Name: ");
  siteName[count++] = Console.ReadLine();

  Console.Write("Add Another?: ");
  doAgain = Console.ReadLine();

  if (count >= 5)
  {
    break;
  }
}
```

Normally, a user presses Y to continue or types anything else to leave. However, an array is a specified size, and it wouldn't be nice to attempt to overflow its bounds because this would cause an error. The `if` statement is present to guard against this happening. When the number of entries in the array exceeds its max capacity, the program breaks out of the loop with the `break` statement. The `break` statement only goes to the next level below its enclosing loop.

For Java Programmers

Java has a labeled break statement, but C# does not. In C#, whenever a jump to a label is needed, use the `goto` statement.

Gee, if it was necessary to jump more than one level out, it might make sense to use a `goto` statement. The question is, "What would be more difficult to understand: extra logic to control exit out of multiple layers of loops, or a clean jump to the end of the outermost loop?"

continue Statements

`continue` statements are used in loops. They allow a program to jump immediately to the Boolean expression of the loop. Here's a program snippet that shows how to use a `continue` statement to discontinue processing during a given iteration:

```
foreach(string site in siteName)
{
  if (response.ToUpper() == "Y" &&
    site != null &&
    site.IndexOf(filter) == -1)
  {
    continue;
  }

  Console.WriteLine("\t{0}", site);
}
```

This example checks the current array entry against a predefined filter. The `IndexOf()` method, a predefined string function, returns a `-1` if the value of `filter` does not exist in the site string. When the value is `-1`, the `continue` statement is invoked. This sends program control back to the top of the `foreach` loop for another iteration.

> **For Java Programmers**
>
> Java has a labeled `continue` statement, but C# does not.

Had the `continue` statement not been used, this program would need alternate or additional logic to avoid executing the `Console.WriteLine()` statement. With the `continue` statement, the program explicitly expresses its intent. The `continue` statement increases the efficiency and understandability of a program by avoiding execution of unnecessary logic.

return Statements

`return` statements allow jumping out of a method or, in the case of the `Main()` method, the program. The following example shows how the `return` statement is used in the `Main()` method:

```
public static int Main(string[] args)
{
  // other program statements
```

```
  return 0;
}
```

The `Main()` method has a return type of `int`, as specified by the `int` declaration in front of the word "`Main`." If the `return` value were `void`, there would be two choices: Don't use the `return` statement, or just use the statement `return;` with no value. Since the example returns an `int`, the `return` statement must return an integer value. Therefore, when this program runs without problems and ends, it returns a value of `0` on the command line.

All methods have return types and have the same `return` statement options as shown previously. The difference is that the value is returned to the statement making the method call. Listing 4.1 contains examples of most of the concepts covered in this chapter.

LISTING 4.1 Program Flow Control Example

```
using System;

/// <summary>
///  This class allows a user to enter
///  and print a list of web sites.
/// </summary>
public class WebSites1
{
  // Program entry
  public static int Main(string[] args)
  {
    string[] siteName = new string[6];
    string phrase = "What is your pleasure";
    string choice;
    int count = 0;

    // If there was a cmd line arg, use it.
    if (args.Length == 0)
    {
      Console.WriteLine("{0}, Master?", phrase );
    }
    else
    {
      Console.WriteLine("{0}, {1}?", phrase, args[0]);
    }

    do
    {
      // Print menu.
      Console.WriteLine("");
      Console.WriteLine("A - Add Site");
```

LISTING 4.1 continued

```
      Console.WriteLine("S - Sort List");
      Console.WriteLine("R - Show Report\n");

      Console.WriteLine("Q - Quit\n");

      Console.Write("Please Choose (A/S/R/Q): ");

      choice = Console.ReadLine();

      // Figure out what user wanted.
      switch (choice)
      {
        // Add a site
        case "a":
        case "A":
          Console.WriteLine("\nAdding Site\n");
          string doAgain = "Y";

          // Keep it up as long as user wants
          while (doAgain.ToUpper() == "Y")
          {
            Console.Write(
              "Please Enter Site Name: ");
            siteName[count++]
              = Console.ReadLine();

            Console.Write("Add Another?: ");
            doAgain = Console.ReadLine();

            // There can only be 5 items
            if (count >= 5)
            {
              break;
            }
          }
          break;
        // Sort the site list
        case "s":
        case "S":
          Console.WriteLine("Sorting List...");

          int n = siteName.Length-2;
          int j, k;
          string save;

          // Insertion sort, start at end & move up
          for (k=n-1; k >= 0; k--)
          {
            j = k + 1;
```

LISTING 4.1 continued

```
            save = siteName[k];
            // Sentinel makes inner
            //  loop more efficient
            siteName[n+1] = save;

            // Insert siteName[k] into
            //  its sorted position
            while ( String.Compare(
                save, siteName[j]) > 0 )
            {
              siteName[j-1] = siteName[j];
              j++;
            }
            siteName[j-1] = save;
          }
          // clean out sentinel so it's not printed
          siteName[siteName.Length-1] = null;

          Console.WriteLine("Done sorting.");

          break;
        // Print a report
        case "r":
        case "R":
          string filter = "";
          string response = "";

          // If user wants to filter,
          //  get filter string
          Console.Write(
            "Would you like a Filter? ");
          response = Console.ReadLine();

          if (response.ToUpper() == "Y")
          {
            Console.Write(
              "\nPlease enter a filter: ");
            filter = Console.ReadLine();
          }

          Console.WriteLine("");
          Console.WriteLine("Site Report");
          Console.WriteLine("");

          // Process every entry in siteName
          foreach(string site in siteName)
          {
            // Execute filter
            if (response.ToUpper() == "Y" &&
```

LISTING 4.1 continued

```
              site != null &&
              site.IndexOf(filter) == -1)
            {
              continue;
            }

            // Print non-filtered items
            Console.WriteLine("\t{0}", site);
          }

          break;
        // Exit Program
        case "q":
        case "Q":
          Console.WriteLine("GoodBye");
          break;
        // User entered bad data
        default:
          Console.WriteLine("Huh??");
          break;
      } // end switch

    // Keep going until user wants to quit
    } while ((choice=choice.ToUpper()) != "Q");

    return 0;
  }
}
```

Listing 4.1 shows how to use most of the branching and looping statements in a working program. It has `if` and `switch` statements; `while`, `do`, `for`, and `foreach` loops; and `break`, `continue`, and `return` statements.

Summary

This chapter covered all of the C# language constructs for decision making, looping, and jumping. For decision making, it showed `if` and `switch` statements and when to use each. The three forms of the `if` statement are `if`, `if-else`, and `if-else if-else`. `if` and `switch` statements support branching to different logic, based on a decision.

The four loop types— the `while` loop, the `do` loop, the `for` loop, and the `foreach` loop— were demonstrated. Loops permit repetition of logic sequences.

Branching statements and how each should be used were discussed. These branching statements included the `goto` statement, the `break` statement, the `continue` statement, and the `return` statement. Branching statements cause the flow of logic in a program to jump to another place in the code.

All the topics in this chapter were pulled together in Listing 4.1. Please experiment to see what else can be done with this program. Now that you're able to create working programs of sufficient complexity, it's time to learn how to filter through that complexity by using a debugger.

CHAPTER 5

Debugging and Pre-Processing

IN THIS CHAPTER

- Pre-Processing Directives *92*
- Debugging C# Programs *94*

This chapter shows the C# pre-processing directives. Pre-processing, as the name suggests, occurs before a program is actually compiled. It provides the ability to manage the development environment through conditional compilation of source code.

This chapter also covers how to debug C# programs. It introduces plausible bugs into a program that would reasonably require use of a debugger. Effective debugging strategies that are sure to prevent headaches and promote better use of time also are discussed.

Pre-Processing Directives

Pre-processing provides the capability to make conditional compilation decisions before a program is compiled. One of the most frequent uses of pre-processing is to create debug versions of code. This lets the same code exist in the same program and support both development and release versions. Another possible use of pre-processing is to support multiple libraries or platform dependencies. The categories of pre-processing directives cover definitions, conditionals, errors, line numbers, and comments.

Define Directive

The define directive allows declaration of the existence of an identifier. These identifiers don't have a value; they either exist or they don't. Using `#define` makes the value exist:

```
#define CLIBUILD
```

To eliminate the existence of an identifier, use the `#undef` pre-processing directive:

```
#undef DOTNETBUILD
```

The `#define` and `#undef` directives must be used at the beginning of a source file. Their placement must be prior to any lines of code. They cannot be embedded within lines of code.

> **For C++ Programmers**
>
> Although C++ permits creation of macros with the `#define` directive, C# does not. The `#define` directive in C# simply states that an identifier exists or is defined.

Conditionals

The conditional pre-processing directives allow decisions to be made based upon the conditions specified in the directive. If a condition is true, then code pertaining to the true condition is included in the code. Otherwise, the true condition code is not included. This section explains how to use the conditional pre-processing directives.

To make a decision, use the `#if` directive. The `#if` directive accepts an expression. The expression is often an identifier that has been defined with a `#define` directive. If this identifier is defined, then the expression evaluates to true. Otherwise, the expression evaluates to false. When the `if` statement evaluates to a true condition, all code between the `#if` directive and the `#end if` directive is included in the program. The `#end if` directive indicates the end of code that belongs to the `#if` directive:

```
#if DOTNETBUILD
using System.Winforms;
#endif
```

For complete decision-making capability use the `#elif` and `#else` directives. When the `#if` statement returns false, lines following it are ignored during compilation and the `#elif` directives are evaluated. When none of the previous directives returns true, the code following the `#else` directive is included during compilation. Pre-processing decision control and inclusion of source code ends at the `#endif` directive:

```
#if DOTNETBUILD
#define WINFORMS
using System.Winforms;
#elif CLIBUILD
using Some.Graphics.Package;
#else
using Some.Text.Package;
#endif
```

Pre-processing decisions can become more sophisticated through the use of several operators. Identifiers can be separated with the following operators to create a desired Boolean expression:

`!`	`Not`
`==`	`Equal`
`!=`	`Not Equal`
`&&`	`AND`
`||`	`OR`

Errors

Sometimes illogical conditions may occur during pre-processing. The most common scenario is when two conflicting identifiers are defined. C# provides a way to handle these problems. Use the `#error` directive to notify the user when illogical conditions occur. The `#error` directive is used to send a message to the output, explaining what the error is:

```
#if DOTNETBUILD && CLIBUILD
#error Can't define "DOTNETBUILD" and "CLIBUILD" together
```

For more minor notifications, use the `#warning` directive:

```
#if RELEASE && TRACE
#warning TRACE turned on in RELEASE build
```

Line Numbers

The `#line` directive permits altering the line number and output file name. This can be used by the compiler for error and warning messages:

```
#line 50 "ErrorInfo.log"
```

The `#line` directive can be useful in pre-processing programs where one or more lines are automatically inserted or removed. Using this directive allows the automated tool to keep line numbering in sync with the original source file. This enables users to see where the error or warning occurred in the original source file.

Comments

Multi-line comments that begin or end on the same line as a pre-processing directive are not compiled; however, single-line comments are acceptable. As expected, pre-processing directives within a comment are not compiled. Here are a few examples of pre-processing directives with comments on the same line:

```
/* illegal */ #if DEBUG

#if RELEASE /* illegal */

#if TRIAL // Okay
```

The first line is illegal because it has a multi-line comment on the same line. The second line is illegal for the same reason. The third line is okay because single line comments are acceptable on the same line after the pre-processing directive.

Debugging C# Programs

Debugging is the process of finding errors in a program. During development, debugging is useful for checking code and verifying it works properly. Also, if an algorithm isn't working properly during development, it's necessary to find and resolve the problems.

Debugging is useful during testing because it provides another level of verification that code is producing the results expected. After a program has been released, debugging provides a means to recreate and detect the errors that were reported in a program. Debugging helps find errors in code.

This section discusses various aspects of debugging. It begins by suggesting an approach to debugging. A well-planned approach helps the debugging process proceed in a smoother fashion than just jumping in. This section shows how to use the .NET Framework SDK debugger to find a program error. A discussion on attaching to processes and using more advanced techniques of finding errors is included.

The Debugging Approach

Many times programmers approach a bug in a haphazard fashion. They start messing with this and that to see what the effects are. Maybe they get lucky after a while and find the bug. If the bug is simple and obvious, no problem. However, when the bug is well hidden and subtle, this behavior is not the most effective use of time.

When a problem with a program arises, an organized approach definitely makes the task easier. Here are a few simple tips to consider:

- Step back and get a clear understanding of the problem. What is the program doing? Why is it wrong? What is the desired behavior? This helps establish a goal of what to accomplish. It also provides the first clues as to what the problem may be.

> **Note**
>
> This process assumes operator and hardware errors have been eliminated as possibilities.

- Ascertain the reproducibility of the bug. When did the bug first appear? How often does it happen? Under what conditions does it happen? If the bug appears in an unpredictable manner, debugging is more difficult. Making the bug happen in a predictable manner is extremely useful—it exposes conditions causing the bug. These conditions provide more clues as to where the real bug may be. Many times the observed bug is merely a symptom of deeper problems.
- Make note of where in the program the bug occurs. At what point in time was the program operating properly? At what point is the bug observed? This helps begin isolating where in the code should be searched. By knowing the last good operating conditions and when the error occurred, the search space is more focused.

Once the bug has been identified, it is reproducible, and its program area is known, the hunt is on.

Using the Debugger To Find a Program Error

You can use the .NET Frameworks SDK debugger to find an error in a program. It takes a step-by-step approach to showing the sequence of events that could occur in a typical debugging session. Listing 5.2 contains the program that, as suspected, has bugs in it. Type the program exactly as is, bugs and all. Go ahead—and compile and run it. Use the makefile in Listing 5.1.

LISTING 5.1 makefile for `MathSequence.cs`

```
csc /optimize- /debug+ MathSequence.cs
```

LISTING 5.2 Source Code for `MathSequence.cs`

```
using System;

/// <summary>
///  This program prints a couple mathematical sequences.
/// </summary>
public class MathSequences
{
  public static void Main()
  {
     string input;
     int index;
     int number;
     int choice;
     int count = 0;

     do
     {
       // Print menu.
       Console.WriteLine("\nMath Sequences\n");
       Console.WriteLine("1 - Fibonacci");
       Console.WriteLine("2 - Squares");

       Console.WriteLine("3 - Exit\n");

       Console.Write("Please Choose (1, 2, or 3): ");

       input = Console.ReadLine();
       choice = Int32.Parse(input);

       // Figure out what user wanted.
```

LISTING 5.2 continued

```
      switch (choice)
      {
        // Print Fibonacci Sequence
        case 1:
          int temp;
          int lastnum;
          int fibnum;

          Console.WriteLine(
            "\nFibonacci Sequence\n");

          Console.Write("How many numbers? ");
          input = Console.ReadLine();
          number = Int32.Parse(input);

          for (index=0, lastnum=0, fibnum=1;
            index < number;
            index++);
          {
            temp = fibnum;
            fibnum += lastnum;
            lastnum = temp;

            Console.WriteLine("{0}: {1}",
              index+1, fibnum );
          }

          break;
        // Print Squared numbers sequence
        case 2:
          // point of int overflow
          const int maxSquare = 46352;

          Console.WriteLine(
            "Squared Number Sequence");

          Console.Write("How many numbers? ");
          input = Console.ReadLine();
          number = Int32.Parse(input);
          for (index=0;
            index < number && index < maxSquare;
            index++)
          {
            Console.WriteLine("{0}: {1}",
              index+1, index*index );
          }
          if (number >= maxSquare)
          {
            Console.WriteLine(
```

LISTING 5.2 continued

```
   "Overflow: Enter a number less than {0}!",
       maxSquare);
     }
     break;
    // Exit Program
    case 3:
     Console.WriteLine("\nGoodBye\n");
     break;
    // User entered bad data
    default:
     Console.WriteLine(
      "No, no , no - That just won't do!");
     break;
   } // end switch

  // Keep going until user wants to quit
  } while (choice != 3);

  return;
 }
}
```

Notice the `/optimize-` and `/debug+` options in Listing 5.1. These turn optimization off and debugging on. Use these options to effectively debug a program. Debugging doesn't work without the `/debug+` option. Now perform the following tasks:

1. At the main menu, select 1 for Fibonacci report. This option is for printing out a sequence of Fibonacci numbers.
2. Observe the output. It's the number entered plus 1, a semicolon, and the number 1. The expected output was the number of lines corresponding to the number entered, with the next Fibonacci number on each subsequent line. This is a bug. The program must be fixed to obtain the expected output.
3. Reproduce the problem. This is simple; just select 1 from the menu again. In real life, reproducing the problem is often not this easy.
4. During the reproduction step it is observed that the problem happens at the time the Fibonacci report is executed. Again, a trivial observation, but it does tell where in the program to start looking.
5. Now start the debugger. The .NET Framework SDK debugger should be located in `C:\Program Files\Microsoft.NET\FrameworkSDK\GuiDebug\DbgUrt.exe`. Substitute drive C: with the appropriate drive letter.

6. From the Debug menu, select Program To Debug to open the program selection dialog box. In the dialog box that pops up, locate the `MathSequences.exe` file and click the OK button. Then open the file `MathSequences.cs`. Figure 5.1 shows the screen.

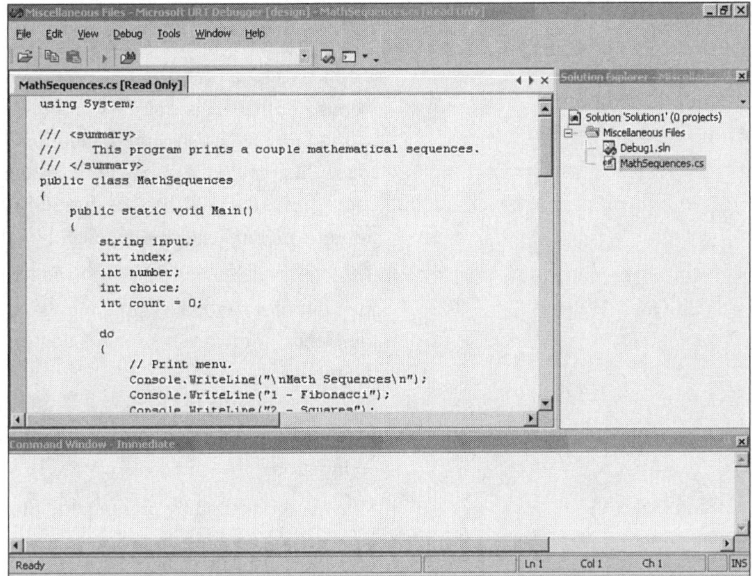

FIGURE 5.1
The .NET SDK debugger.

7. Set a breakpoint as close as possible to the place before the problem occurred. A breakpoint is the place to stop the program's execution so you can begin analyzing the program in its current state. The problem occurs when menu option 1 is selected. Therefore, find that place in the program to set the breakpoint. This is at Line 39.
8. To set the breakpoint, click on the left margin of line 39 and a red dot appears. This indicates a breakpoint on that line. Now run the program by pressing the blue triangle (start) button on the toolbar.
9. When the console window appears, a menu is printed. Select menu option 1 to reproduce the problem. The program stops at the breakpoint.

Now it's possible to step through the program and observe its behavior in a controlled manner. The easiest way to step through programs is to click the relevant buttons on the button bar. The buttons supporting the procedures described in Table 5.1 are on the right side of the button bar. If this is the first time running for `DbgUrt.exe`, the buttons can be found by clicking the >> symbols on the far right side of the Debug Toolbar. From then on, the buttons appear on the normal button bar, where they are easy to find. Table 5.1 shows the various methods of navigating.

TABLE 5.1 Commands To Step Through Code

Action	*Description*
Step In	Step into a method by pressing the Step Into button on the Debug Toolbar. This transfers program control into the method on the current highlighted line in the debugger. Since there are no methods in this program, this is of no concern right now. When the currently highlighted line is not on a method call, the statement on that line is executed and control passes to the next logical place in the program.
Step Out	Step out of a method by pressing the Step Out button on the Debug Toolbar. This returns control to the place where the method was called. If control is at the top level of a program, pressing the Step Out button causes the program to resume running as normal and in many cases, run to completion.
Step Over	Step over a method by pressing the Step Over button on the Debug Toolbar. This executes the method and transfers control to the next logical place in the program. This works well when a breakpoint is set earlier than normal and it's necessary to move through a program quickly. It's also another technique for isolating where a bug occurs.

Use Step In or Step Over for this program. The effects are the same because there are no methods. Just don't use Step Out. Now perform the following procedure:

1. Go ahead and step. The highlighted line is now Line 41.
2. Now observe the variables to see their values. To do this, open the watch window by selecting the Debug menu, Window submenu, and then the Watch menu item. This displays a watch window below the source code display window. To add a variable to the `watch` window, double-click to select it. Press the right mouse button for a context menu and select the Add Watch menu item. Do this for the following int variables: `number`, `index`, `temp`, `lastnum`, and `fibnum`. Alternatively, each variable can be highlighted then dragged and dropped into the watch window.

3. Step until the program asks for the number of numbers to generate. Enter the number 5, and step until the program reaches the `for` loop. Watch the variables in the watch window with each step.
4. The current line is a `for` loop and the `index` variable is zero. Take another step. What's this? Look at the value of `index`. It's changed to `5`.
5. Step a few more times. The body of the `for` loop is executed line-by-line, and then control moves to the `break` statement past the body of the `for` loop.

Take a better look at the line with the `for` loop statement. It appears to look like any other `for` loop. `index`, `lastNum`, and `figNum` were initialized to `0`, `0`, and `1` respectively. The value of the `index` should be less than 5, the `index` is being incremented, and the statement is terminated with a semicolon. Hmmmm…a semicolon? `for` loops don't have semicolons.

Remove the semicolon, recompile, and run (or debug, if preferred). Notice the bug is fixed and the output prints as expected.

What happened was that the `for` loop interpreted the semicolon as its program statement. Since curly braces are optional, the semicolon was the only statement that belonged to the `for` loop. Therefore, the loop iterated on nothing, then transferred control to the following block with the instructions. This block printed out the line "5: 1" similar to what it should on its first run, executed the `break` statement, and then moved on to show the menu again.

This particular problem may have been flagged as a compiler warning. However, when multiple files are being compiled at the same time, a warning can scroll off the screen without being noticed. Also, compiler warnings may be turned off. Therefore, another lesson to learn is to look at compiler warnings. Sometimes they are important.

Tip

Always try to have a logical explanation of what the bug was. Be suspect of bugs that seem to mysteriously go away without rationale. More often than not, these illusive problems will reappear at a later stage in development where their effects have more impact.

Attaching to Processes

Sometimes it may be necessary to begin a debugging session while a program is running. Perhaps there might be a daemon process acting up. This would be a good reason to attach to an existing process.

The next scenario uses the second menu item of the Math Sequences program from Listing 5.2. This part of the program prints a sequence of square numbers from 0 to whatever number the user enters.

Imagine that a user submits a bug with the program that needs to be investigated. He selected menu option number 2, for a Square Number Sequence. His requirements were to obtain the square of 50,000, so that's what he entered at the prompt. The program ran, but gave him the wrong number and an error.

To get started, run the program in Listing 5.2. Remember to turn optimization off and debugging on when compiling, otherwise the program can't be debugged. Select option number 2 from the menu for printing a Sequence of Squares. Enter "50000" at the prompt and press the Enter key. The program runs and ends with the error message `Overflow: Enter a number less than 46352!` Figure 5.2 shows the program output.

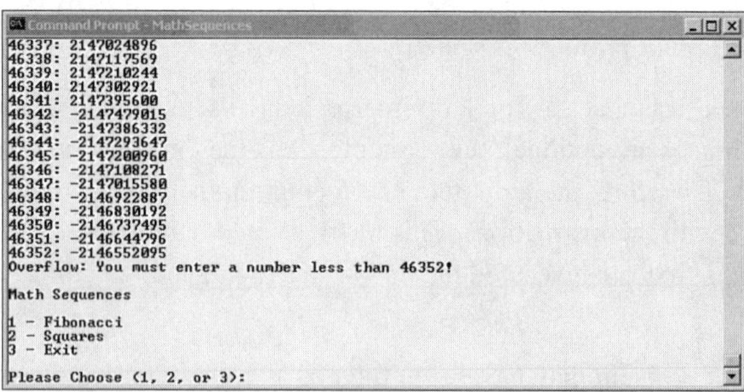

FIGURE 5.2
`MathSequence.exe` *program output.*

Observing the output, it's evident there's some type of error checking applied; however, it doesn't seem to be working as effectively as it should. The output shows numbers being calculated appropriately and suddenly going negative. Since the program is still running, it is easy to attach to its process and see what's happening inside. To attach to this process, follow these steps:

1. Start `DbgUrt.exe`. Select Debug Processes from the Debug menu. The Processes screen, shown in Figure 5.3, appears.
2. Select the `MathSequences.exe` process from the Available Processes list, and click the Attach button. The Attach to Process dialog box pops up. It provides an option of what type of program to attach.
3. Make sure the Common Language Runtime entry is checked, then click the OK button. The `MathSequences.exe` process then appears in the Debugged Processes.
4. The `MathSequences.exe` process is now attached for debugging. Click the Close button to return to the debugger screen.

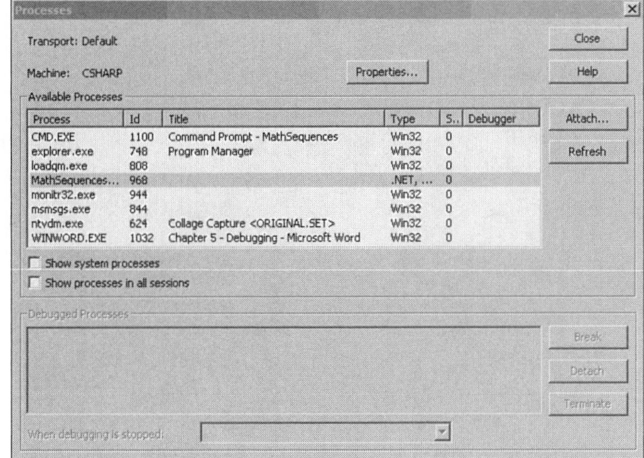

FIGURE 5.3
Processes dialog box for attaching processes.

Now it's necessary to create a breakpoint in the program to stop execution and examine what's happening. This breakpoint is different than the one used in the Fibonacci example because the number of iterations needed to recreate the problem is much greater. The strategy for this program is to execute a specified number of iterations, and then examine what happens when the calculations get messed up. This means the program must run until a predefined number of iterations has passed, and then it must stop. Fortunately, the SDK Debugger provides this capability. The following steps show how to run a program through a loop for a specified number of iterations:

1. Make sure the `MathSequences.cs` file is loaded in the debugger.
2. Scroll down to Line 76, where the `Console.Writeline` statement is.
3. Create a breakpoint by clicking in the left margin of Line 76.
4. Right-click the highlighted code on the breakpoint line.
5. Select the Breakpoint Properties option from the context menu. The Breakpoint Properties dialog box, shown in Figure 5.4, appears.
6. Click the Hit Count button. The Breakpoint Hit Count dialog box, shown in Figure 5.5, appears.
7. From the When the Breakpoint Is Hit: drop-down list, select Break When the Hit Count Is Greater Than or Equal To.
8. In the text field to the right, type the number **`46340`**.
9. Click the Reset Hit Count button to make sure it's set to `0`.

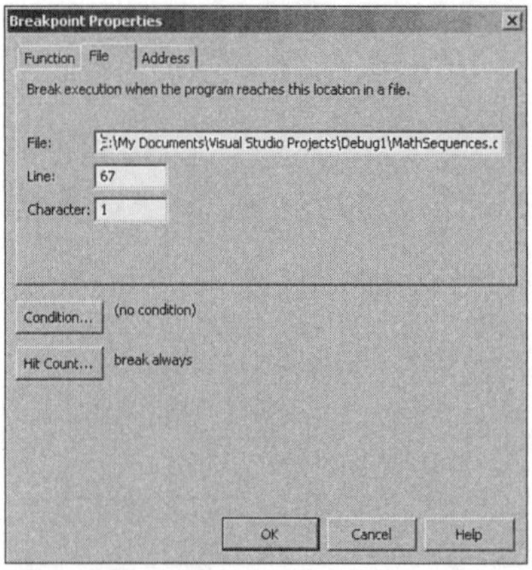

FIGURE 5.4
The Breakpoint Properties dialog box.

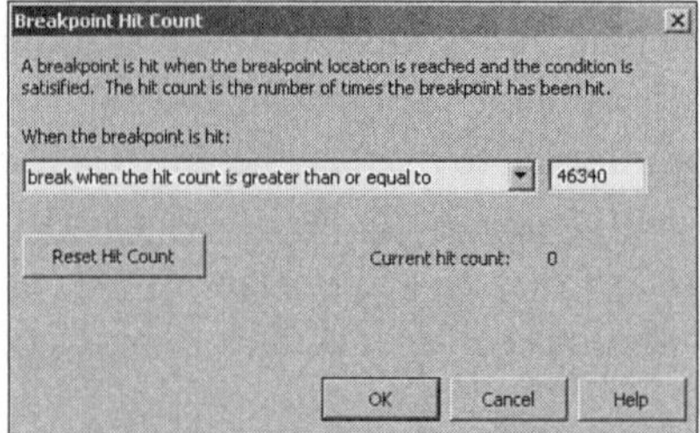

FIGURE 5.5
The Breakpoint Hit Count dialog box

10. Click the OK button to return to the Breakpoint Properties dialog. Observe from the text to the right of the Hit Count button that the breakpoint is now set for when the hit count is greater than or equal to `46340`. This means that when the program arrives at Line 75 for the 46,340th time, it stops there on the breakpoint.
11. Click the OK button to accept the breakpoint parameters.

> **Note**
>
> The number 46340 is used for the breakpoint because it's the last valid square to be calculated before an overflow condition occurs on the int type.

12. Return to the console window where the program is running and select option number 2 from the menu for printing a Sequence of Squares. Enter **`50000`** at the prompt and press the Enter key. The program will break when the number reaches 46340.

> **Note**
>
> Now is a good time to reflect upon the amount of time this procedure just saved. It would have been a bear to have stepped through over 46 thousand individual iterations.

13. Once the program reaches the breakpoint, add the `index` variable to the watch window.
14. Below the index variable in the watch window, add a new line: `index*index`. The variable `index` is `46339` and the `index*index` is `2147302921`.
15. Perform the step operation two more times. `index` is `46340` and `index*index` is `2147395600`. This is normal.
16. Perform the step operation two more times. `index` is `46341` and "`index*index`" is `-2147479015`. This is clearly where the program is going awry. The `index` variable is never able to reach `46341`.

Looking at Listing 5.2, it's apparent that preventing overflow was a part of this program's design. The `for` loop on Line 65 checks to make sure the program doesn't make a calculation when `index` reaches the `maxSquare` variable. Additionally, the `if` statement on Line 78 checks to see if `number` is greater than or equal to `maxSquare`. If so, it prints an error message to the console. The problem is that the program didn't stop before the error occurred.

Take a closer look at `maxSquare`. It's defined on Line 62 as a constant integer with a value of 46352. This is not the correct value. Earlier investigation revealed an overflow condition on an integer occurred at 46341. Therefore, to fix this problem simply change the value of `maxSquares` to 46341. This will stop the program before it prints out incorrect values.

It's easy to see how this bug happened. Perhaps the developer added the overflow checks after the program was written. He might have seen the overflow occurring in the output at 46342. This is because the line number is printed as `index+1`. To compound this oversight, a typo was made when creating the `maxSquares` constant integer initialization by transposing a 4 with a 5 in the tens position. Scenarios like this are why some bugs are so hard to find. Many times, it's not just a single bug, but a series of mistakes made together. To totally fix a problem, a professional developer takes a fair stab at finding the reason(s) why a bug occurred and fixes the whole problem.

This scenario, its causes, and resolution hint at a process-related approach to reducing the number of bugs in a program. C# provides language constructs for the designer to use when considering error conditions in programs.

Summary

This chapter covered the Pre-Processing directives. You learned just enough to get started and begin thinking about how to use them. The purpose of these directives is for conditional compilation and communication during the compilation process.

The pre-processing directives discussed include the `#define`, `#undef`, `#if`, `#elif`, `#else`, `#endif`, `#error`, `#warning`, and `#line`. There was also mention of using pre-processing directives with comments.

Programmers should approach debugging in a process-driven, methodical manner. That, with a touch of creativity and a bit of psychological analysis, will aid in finding the toughest bugs.

A decent tool, such as the .Net Frameworks SDK Debugger, can be useful in finding bugs. Two debugging examples demonstrated different techniques for finding bugs. The first was a straightforward explanation of how to set an explicit breakpoint on a line of code. The second debugging example explained how to attach to a process. It also showed how to set a conditional breakpoint.

Once breakpoints were set, you looked at methods of examining the state of the program to determine what the errors were.

Part I of this book introduced basic concepts of the C# programming language. It showed how to create simple programs, the various C# types and expressions, control flow statements, and debugging techniques. Now it's time to go beyond the procedural elements and learn about the object-oriented aspects of developing software with C#.

Object and Component Programming with C#

PART II

IN THIS PART

6 Object and Component Concepts *109*

7 Working With Classes *129*

8 Designing Object-Oriented Programs *177*

9 Overloading Class Members and Operators *219*

10 Handling Exceptions and Errors *237*

11 Delegates and Events *255*

12 Oganizing Code with Namespaces *277*

13 Creating `structs` *289*

14 Implementing Interfaces *301*

15 Performing Conversions *329*

CHAPTER

Object and Component Concepts

IN THIS CHAPTER

- What Is an Object? *110*
- Object Classification *112*
- Object Hierarchies *113*
- Abstraction *114*
- Objects within Objects *115*
- Objects with Different Behaviors *116*
- Component Interfaces *120*
- Component Properties *123*
- Component Events *125*

For some people, understanding object and component concepts may be one of the most challenging parts of the C# language to learn. It's not really difficult—it's just plain different, and it takes a little time to warm up. While getting started, try to visualize the concepts presented here. They may come in handy for comparison with later chapters.

Some programmers may already have object-oriented experience, but not necessarily understand component programming. This chapter discusses component concepts in a simplistic manner. Although other component technologies such as COM and Java Beans have wide acceptance, components are not necessarily part of the languages used to implement them. In C#, components are a first-class concept. Having a grasp of component programming is essential to building modern distributed applications.

What Is an Object?

Thinking about objects is easy at first if they're visualized in a concrete and physical manner. For instance, look around the house. There are several well-known objects such as chairs, TVs, and computers.

These objects have varying degrees of sophistication. This is evident by how they appear and what they do. A couple more appropriate object-oriented terms for "appearance" and "what they do" would be, respectively, attributes and behavior. The following paragraphs examine the attributes and behavior of these three objects.

Chairs are high on attributes but low on behavior. Some of their attributes are legs, seat, and back. Being a little more specific, each attribute can be used to describe the chair. Number of legs could be an integer between 3 to 5. Seat can be a string describing the type of material, such as cushioned or hard wood. Back may be a Boolean for true or false, depending on whether the chair had a back or not. These are three simple attributes, but they tell a lot about what kind of chair it is.

Behavior for a chair may be a little more challenging to describe. Depending on the purpose of the chair, it could possibly recline, swivel, or rock. These are distinct behaviors of each chair. Behaviors occur on the basis of some action. When people sit in a chair, they invoke whatever behavior that chair is capable of.

Identifying TV attributes could give screen size, manufacturer, and stereo sound. Just as we did with the chair, these attributes can map to variables more fully describing the TV. TVs have more behavior than chairs: They turn on and off, switch channels, and play sound. These behaviors are invoked by human interaction.

Computers have many attributes and are very high on behavior. Considering the immense collection of attributes and boundless behavior of a computer, it is an extremely complex object. Figure 6.1 shows a diagram of the three objects—TV, chair, and computer—with their appropriate attributes and behaviors.

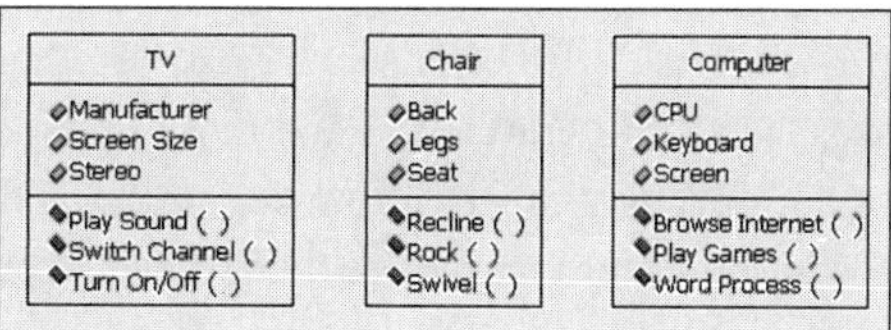

FIGURE 6.1
TV, Chair, and Computer object diagram.

In general, objects can be described completely by their attributes and behavior. (We're not talking about components yet, thus leaving discussion of interfaces, properties, and events until later in this chapter.) Objects don't have to be physical entities. They can be anything imaginable. A useful analogy may be that an object is similar to a noun. If it can be described with attributes and/or behavior, it can be an object.

In a more abstract sense, time can be an object. It has hours, minutes, and seconds for attributes and passing for behavior. Going a little deeper, "emotion" could be an object having sullen or happy attributes and running wild or well controlled as behavior. The sky is the limit when creating objects.

In C#, objects are represented using the "class" language type. Within a class, attributes are the same thing as "fields." To implement behavior, C# uses a "method." The following example shows how C# is used in general to create an object definition:

```
class Time
{
    int hours;
    int minutes;
    int seconds;

    void PassTime()
    {
        // implementation of behavior
    }
}

class Emotion
{
    bool happy;
    bool sullen;

    void RunWild()
    {
        // implementation of behavior
    }
```

```
    void BeControlled()
    {
        // implementation of behavior
    }
}
```

This example shows two classes, `Time` and `Emotion`. Each class is indicated with the word "`class`" before the class name. Curly braces show beginning and ending of classes and methods. Fields have types and the field name. Methods have a return type, the method name, and an implementation.

Objects can be anything that meets a project's requirements. They possess all the flexibility required to make a program as descriptive as it needs to be. That being said, it's normally useful to ensure that object definitions make sense for their intended purpose. Developing proper abstractions contributes immensely to well-engineered software.

Object Classification

It's helpful to divide objects into groups. Considering the way things are classified, this makes sense. Geologists classify rocks, artists classify art forms, and biologists classify animals. This makes the objects to be dealt with more manageable and applicable to the work being accomplished.

Take animals, for example. A biologist may classify them into birds, mammals and reptiles. Birds would have attributes such as beaks and wings; mammals, hair and warm blood; and reptiles, scales and cold blood. Behavior-wise, birds fly, mammals feed their young with milk, and reptiles walk funny.

These are major object categories, and it's often advantageous to further subcategorize. This can be accomplished by adding a new string attribute called subcategory. Then, when classifying a new sub-type of bird, load the subcategory with something like ostrich, robin, or duck. It's even possible to add other new attributes to be modified depending on the value of the subcategory just described. If adding extra attributes for subcategorization is simple, it may be all that's necessary for the classification requirements of a task. The following example shows how this might be done in C#:

```
class Bird
{
    string beakDescription;
    int wingSpan;
    string typeOfBird = "ostrich";

    void Fly()
    {
        // implementation of behavior
```

```
    }
}
```

This example shows a typical class, except that it has a field to help with classification: the `typeOfBird` string, which is set to `ostrich`. This helps differentiate this class from others that may have this field set to `robin` or `duck`.

Object Hierarchies

The previous method of adding attributes may be acceptable for simple classification, but it just doesn't scale well for future growth. Say the requirements specified numerous levels of classification. Adding new attributes to represent new subcategories, plus any other attributes supporting each subcategory, can greatly increase the complexity of a project.

What's happening with subcategories is that a natural hierarchy is being created. Object-oriented programming provides the methodology to manage natural hierarchies. If the project specifies the categorization of animals, it may be logical to place an animal object at the top of the hierarchy. At the next level would be birds, mammals, and reptiles. Under birds would be ostriches, robins, and ducks. This process would continue until the required hierarchy was built.

In object-oriented programming, the concept holding these objects together in a natural hierarchy is called inheritance. For the animal classification task, there's a top-level object called animal. Animal is a very general term. It has to be, because all the objects with all their differences must fit into the animal category to be a part of the animal hierarchy.

Animal may have only a single attribute, such as living. To be an animal, rather than a star or a rock, it has different behavior, such as breathing oxygen and eating. Furthermore, every object under animal must have at least the same attributes as animal for it to fit naturally into the hierarchy.

The difference between animal and the rest of the objects is that the objects below animal must add attributes and/or behavior. The attributes and/or behavior of lower objects must be more specific than the attributes and behavior of animal. This indicates a consistent concept for each level up or down the hierarchy. Going up the hierarchy yields more generalization in objects and, conversely, going down the hierarchy yields more specialization in objects.

Lower, or child, objects in the hierarchy inherit attributes and behavior from higher, or parent, objects in the hierarchy. This creates an "is a" relationship between child and parent. A bird is an animal. Likewise, ostriches and ducks are birds as well as animals.

The simplicity of inheritance comes from how the inheritance hierarchy is built. Child objects specify their parent objects in their description. Therefore, all that is required is to put new attributes and behavior in each child object. This eliminates the complexity, from the previous section on classification, of figuring out what attributes and behaviors go with what subcategory. Figure 6.2 shows what a hierarchy of objects looks like.

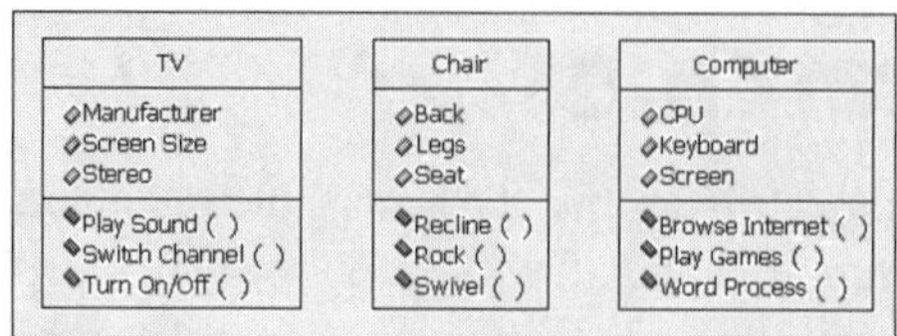

FIGURE 6.2
The animal hierarchy.

Besides making a classification more organized and easier to understand, inheritance also saves work. Every time an object is added to the hierarchy, it automatically has the attributes and behavior of all its parents. There's no need to re-specify all these things again, because of the assumption of inheritance. Another way to think about this is that inheritance provides a way to re-use existing attributes and behavior.

By using inheritance in the classification system, biologists have the opportunity to spend more time doing what they enjoy the most—watching animals—and less time maintaining the supporting classification system. Likewise, a software professional has more time to devote to business logic without the hassle of complex software maintenance.

Abstraction

This is a good time to make a point about abstraction. Some objects are pure abstractions and others are real things. For example, something called an animal does not exist. It's merely a description of a class of objects. Furthermore, there is no physical entity that is only a bird. These things are only classifications and there are no tangible instances of them.

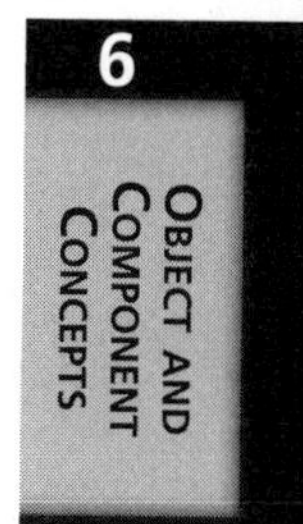

On the other hand, there definitely is a thing called a duck. It has physical characteristics such as webbed feet and a bill. It looks like a duck, walks like a duck, and quacks like a duck. Therefore, it must be an instance of a duck.

These things cannot be said about "animal" and "bird," which merely exist to add a useful classification mechanism to a hierarchy. Although there cannot be instances of animals and birds, they are still very important. They give the hierarchy structure and provide a basis of attributes and behavior for all objects beneath them. Well-defined abstractions such as animal and bird are extremely useful to classification hierarchies. The following example shows how abstractions are implemented in C#:

```
abstract class Animal
{
    // abstract definitions and implementations
}

class Bird : Animal
{
    // class implementation
}
```

The class at the top is marked with an abstract modifier to indicate that it is abstract. Because abstractions don't exist, C# prevents instances of abstract classes from being created. The second class, `Bird`, shows that it inherits from the abstract `Animal` class by putting a colon and `Animal` after its class name.

Objects within Objects

Hierarchies are one way to establish relationships between objects. However, there are other methods by which objects relate and express real-life scenarios. One very common way to relate objects is by having objects within objects.

A more common term for the "object within object" concept is encapsulation. Effective use of encapsulation reduces complexity by exposing only the amount of detail necessary to understand an object. For instance, the aerial capabilities of birds may be extremely fascinating. Biologists may study wings, feathers, and bone structures for a deeper understanding. On the other hand, there may not be much interest in studying a digestive system. Therefore, a biologist may not have the desire to examine the operation of a gizzard. Just knowing that it's there and that it works is all the information needed. Through the concept of encapsulation, detail is divulged as needed to meet the requirements of the task at hand.

Think of the bird objects discussed so far. Birds have beaks and wings. A wing is an object itself, having a forewing, backwing, and feathers. It has behavior: flapping and folding. The key word here is "having." These are things a bird possesses and they are part of the bird. There is a natural "has a" relationship between and object and those items it possesses. The following example shows how encapsulation could be implemented in C#:

```
class Wing
{
    int forewingSize;
    int backwingSize;

    void Flap()
    {
        // implementation
    }
    void Fold()
    {
        // implementation
    }
}

class Bird : Animal
{
    int beakSize;
    Wing wings;

    void Fly()
    {
        // implementation
    }
}
```

This example has two classes, `Bird` and `Wing`. The `Wing` class has its own fields and methods. Inside the `Bird` class is a `Wing` declaration with the name `wings`. This sets up the containment relationship where "a `bird` has `wings`." The only thing necessary from an abstract perspective is that we know the `bird` has `wings`. The attributes and behavior of the `wings` are controlled by the `Wing` class itself.

Objects with Different Behaviors

Sometimes it's appropriate to classify each object in a group as belonging to the same group, but still allow each object to maintain its own behavior. When speaking of each object, it would be useful to group them into the same category; yet it is also practical for each object to have its own identity as required—same but different.

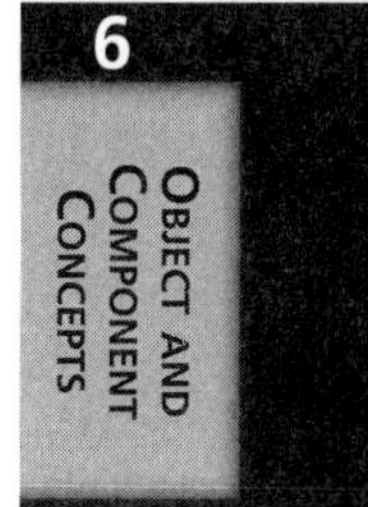

For instance, a pigeon, a robin, and a seagull are objects relating to the bird group. A biologist wants to conduct a behavioral experiment with these three birds. So one day the biologist grabs the birds and puts them in a specially built birdcage where each bird has its own compartment. The cage may be similar to a pigeon coop, but it can't be a pigeon coop because another bird may not fit in the small space. This means the special cage has to be generally selected to hold most birds. The cage can be called a flying-bird cage. Since all of the birds selected by the biologist are flying birds, they fit well into this cage. As you can see, it was necessary to classify birds into the same category to meet the requirements of the task. The following example shows how such a relationship could be implemented in C#:

```
abstract class FlyingBird : Bird
{
    // class implementation
}

class Pigeon : FlyingBird
{
    // class implementation
}

class Robin : FlyingBird
{
    // class implementation
}

class Seagull : FlyingBird
{
    // class implementation
}

class Experiment
{
    public static void Main()
    {
        FlyingBird[] flyingBirdCage = new FlyingBird[3];

        flyingBirdCage[0] = new Pigeon();
        flyingBirdCage[1] = new Robin();
        flyingBirdCage[2] = new Seagull();
    }
}
```

This code creates four new classes. The first is the `FlyingBird` class, which is derived from `Bird`. Since not all birds fly, though they may try, this class is only for the ones that do. The next three classes, `Pigeon`, `Robin`, and `Seagull`, are derived from the `FlyingBird` class. The last class is `Experiment`, where the `Main()` method is. Within the

`Main()` method, which begins the program, is an array declaration named `flyingBirdCage` of type `FlyingBird`. This is a special array, only for objects of type `FlyingBird`. Since the `Pigeon`, `Robin`, and `Seagull` classes are also of type `FlyingBird`, they can be put into the `flyingBirdCage` array. This is what happens in the `Main()` method of the `Experiment` class.

Next the biologist loads the flying-bird cage in the back of a truck and drives out into the country. During the trip, all that matters is that each bird is a flying bird in a flying-bird cage. This simple idea is what led the biologist to figure out how to meet the task requirements.

Imagine what would happen if the biologist didn't have a flying-bird cage. Perhaps the alternative would have been to construct multiple cages of multiple sizes, specialized for each type of bird. When the biologist had to put a different type of bird in a cage, that bird may not have fit into one of the existing cages because of the over-specialization of each cage. Furthermore, it would be a lot more work carrying around multiple cages instead of one. Here's how such a kludge would be implemented in C#:

```
class Experiment
{
    public static void Main()
    {
        Pigeon pigeonCage = new Pigeon();

        Robin robinCage = new Robin();

        Seagull seagullCage = new Seagull();
    }
}
```

This example shows separate containers for holding each of the three types of birds. Sure, there may be one less declaration by eliminating the array, but think about the follow-on logic necessary to access and manipulate three separate containers. To be more specific, think about which arrangement would be easier to use with a `foreach` loop: a common array or separate objects.

Once out in the country, the experiment continues. The biologist wants to see what happens when each flying bird is let loose. On the trip into the country, the only thing that mattered was that these were flying birds in a flying-bird cage, and the birds were not going anywhere until the biologist decided otherwise. Now the biologist expects different behavior from each flying bird. This is because even though each bird was in a cage and each was regarded as a flying bird, each compartment in the cage held a different type of flying bird.

To get the experiment under way, the biologist frees each bird and observes its behavior. It's assumed that the birds will fly, being flying birds, but the way they fly is different. The pigeon heads straight home, because that's what pigeons do. The seagull looks for the ocean, its natural habitat. Finally, the robin heads straight for the nearest shady tree. The biologist has manipulated the birds in such a way to accomplish a task in the most effective manner possible.

The task of making each bird perform the same action, flying, although each is a different type of bird, is similar in concept to polymorphism. *Polymorphism* is the ability to make different things, or objects, perform the same task. Listing 6.1 shows how polymorphism is implemented in C#.

LISTING 6.1 Demonstration of Polymorphism with C#

```
using System;

class FlyingBird
{
    public virtual void Fly()
    {
        Console.WriteLine("This shouldn't be called!");
    }
}

class Pigeon : FlyingBird
{
    public override void Fly()
    {
        Console.WriteLine("Pigeon: Flying Home");
    }
}

class Robin : FlyingBird
{
    public override void Fly()
    {
        Console.WriteLine("Robin: Finding a Shady Tree");
    }
}

class Seagull : FlyingBird
{
    public override void Fly()
    {
        Console.WriteLine("Seagull: Searching for Water");
    }
}
```

LISTING 6.1 continued

```
class Experiment
{
    public static void Main()
    {
        FlyingBird[] flyingBirdCage = new FlyingBird[3];

        flyingBirdCage[0] = new Pigeon();
        flyingBirdCage[1] = new Robin();
        flyingBirdCage[2] = new Seagull();

        foreach(FlyingBird bird in flyingBirdCage)
        {
            bird.Fly();
        }
    }
}
```

In Listing 6.1, there are three classes—`Pigeon`, `Robin`, and `Seagull`—that inherit from the `FlyingBird` class. Each of these classes has a `Fly()` method. The differences between the `Fly()` methods are the modifiers and implementation. The `FlyingBird` class adds the virtual modifier and the three derived classes have an override modifier. There is a `foreach` loop in the `Main()` method that calls the `Fly()` method of each bird in the `flyingBirdCage` array. Because the `Fly()` method in each of the derived classes is marked with the override modifier, the `Fly()` method of each individual bird is called. Without virtual and override modifiers, the `Fly()` method of the `FlyingBird` class would have been called because that is the type of object in the `flyingBirdCage` array.

This manipulation of object classification or same-but-different behavior can be referred to as polymorphism. It provides the capability of grouping any type of object into a more generalized object for any purpose. At the same time, that object is allowed to change into many different types of behaviors as needed. Polymorphism can be a very powerful and useful tool in accomplishing complex tasks.

Component Interfaces

Interaction with objects requires some stimulus to invoke their behavior. In an inheritance hierarchy, the interaction is similar as you move down the hierarchy. For example, if there was an electrical appliance hierarchy, it could have child objects of clock, radio, and microwave. Each of these objects has the behavior of running on electrical power. Therefore, this behavior could be invoked by a power connection.

The run-through-power-connection behavior is expected behavior that is relied upon to accomplish the task we need done in the most efficient manner. If one of these objects operated in another way, it would lead the operator to be confused or believe something was wrong. Common behavior helps tasks be performed much easier, and makes for more efficient operations by eliminating uncertainty. This common behavior is more properly termed an interface.

Inheritance is an immediately appealing and natural way to establish interfaces to objects. However, it doesn't apply in many cases. For instance, what if a task required the construction of a clock radio. It isn't logical to put the common behavior of both the clock and the radio into the electrical appliance object. Such a situation would require a microwave to also be a radio. This may not be desired.

Another way to fix the clock radio problem is by creating a new class under electrical appliances called clockradio. This is logical in that it doesn't set unreasonable requirements on other classes in the hierarchy. However, it causes other problems. First, the behavior of clock is duplicated in both the clock object and the clockradio object, and the radio behavior is duplicated in a similar manner. Second, this sets off an explosion of new classes for any generic capability needed across multiple classes where inheritance relationships may be illogical. Figure 6.3 shows what this hybrid hierarchy would look like.

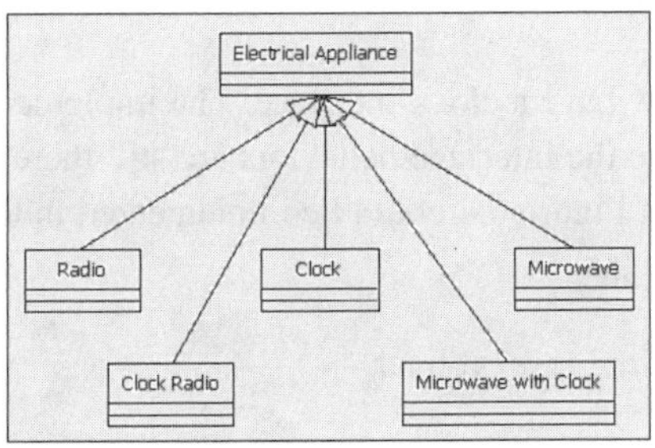

FIGURE 6.3
Hybrid object hierarchy.

Restating that second point, the duplication continues if another task required development of a microwave with a clock. An inheritance hierarchy can get unruly when too many new levels are inserted where behavior spans objects across the hierarchy rather than via the inheritance mechanism.

Additionally, the inheritance hierarchy can become polluted with unnatural hybrids of behavior. This makes interpretation of the hierarchy itself more complex. Fortunately, the concept of interface in component programming reaches beyond inheritance.

Interfaces, more often than not, are separate entities from the inheritance hierarchy. They can be applied to any object, making the statement of that object exhibiting the behavior of the interface.

Going back to the clock radio object, if a clock was an interface instead of a normal object, it could be applied to any type of object. In this case, the clock interface would be applied to the radio. The radio is still a radio, but now it has clock behavior.

The clock radio can display time, ring an alarm, and have its alarm turned off. The actual behavior depends on how the radio handles it. However, the point is that the clock radio has the interface of a clock and the clock behavior can be invoked as specified by the clock interface. There are no surprises. Figure 6.4 shows the new interface relationship.

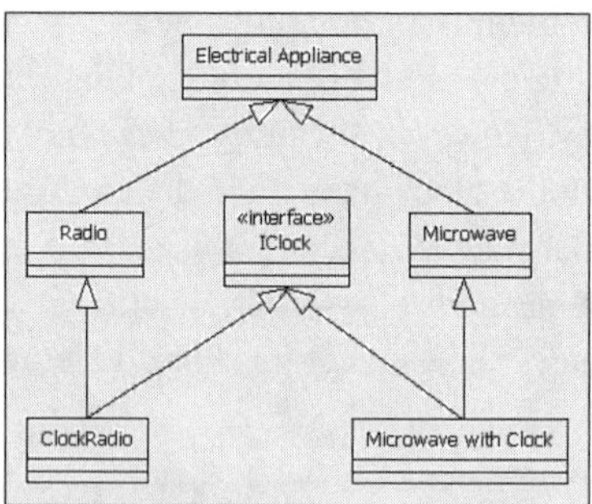

FIGURE 6.4
Interface diagram.

Similarly, the microwave can now have a clock interface. The implementation of this interface is of no concern because the interface behaviors are still there. The following example shows how the model in Figure 6.4 could be implemented in C#:

```
abstract class ElectricalAppliance
{
    // class definitions and implementations
}

class Radio : ElectricalAppliance
{
    // class implementation
}

class Microwave : ElectricalAppliance
{
    // class implementation
}

interface IClock
{
```

```
    // class implementation
}

class ClockRadio : IClock
{
    // class implementation
}

class MicrowaveWithClock : IClock
{
    // class implementation
}
```

This example shows a hierarchical relationship using interface and normal inheritance in C#. The `ElectricalAppliance` class serves as the base class for the `Radio` and `Microwave` classes. Both the `ClockRadio` and `MicrowaveWithClock` inherit respectively from the `Radio` and `Microwave` classes. They also inherit behavior definition from the `IClock` interface. Unlike the `Radio` and `Microwave` classes, which implement inheritable behavior, the `IClock` interface specifies the behavior that derived classes must implement. It does not implement any behavior.

What is gained by implementing this interface inheritance relationship is that all objects with clock behavior implement the same type of behavior. This was not guaranteed when all classes derived from the ElectricalAppliance class. It would have been easy for each class to modify its clock-like behavior with different method signatures. The `IClock` interface solves this problem by ensuring that other classes using the `IClock`-derived classes can call `IClock` methods on these classes. This is a guarantee of clock-like behavior.

Interfaces represent a contract. They are commonly held truths of how to interact with an object. As mentioned earlier, this is a powerful concept, reducing complexity between objects attributable to expected communication.

Component Properties

If an object's attributes were as simple as a switch that could have only two states, on or off, then that would be nearly everything required to describe an object. However, that is not the case, and more sophistication is needed to manage the complex objects of today.

This is why components have properties in addition to attributes. Properties provide underlying logic to manage the state of an object through attributes. You can think of properties as attributes on steroids.

In ancient times, sundials were the primary means of keeping time. They were simple: a couple pieces of stone, and the guarantee that the sun would revolve around the earth once a day. The stones were attributes and, since they didn't move and they were part of the sundial, there was no problem in letting people see the stones.

Later on people became impatient at the fact that the sundial wouldn't work at night. So they decided to build clocks. These first clocks probably had many gears and moving parts that had to be manipulated every so often to get them to run. All these attributes of a clock must have been fascinating at first, but they certainly became unsightly after a while. So the clockmakers put the gears inside a box, and put the hands and windup key outside. The clock hands and windup key were properties.

The clockmakers encapsulated the attributes on the inside of the box. No one needed to see the gears unless he was a clockmaker. This made the clock understandable and accessible to everyone. Now, if the clockmaker wants to change the type of gears inside the clock to make it work better, everyone can still use the clock because the properties are still the same.

Although clocks have evolved in sophistication through the years, the concept of a clock has remained the same. Even the clock radio possesses the same properties as any other clock. It has a time and an alarm as properties that can be set. Most of us don't need to know the underlying electronics making these properties work. The following example shows how these properties could be implemented in C#:

```
class Clock
{
    private int hours;
    private int minutes;
    private int seconds;

    private void UpdateTime()
    {
        // underlying implementation
    }

    public int HourHand
    {
        get
        {
            UpdateTime();
            return hours;
        }
        set
        {
            // set implementation
        }
```

```
        }
        public int MinuteHand
        {
            get
            {
                UpdateTime();
                return minutes;
            }
            set
            {
                // set implementation
            }
        }
        public int SecondHand
        {
            get
            {
                UpdateTime();
                return seconds;
            }
            set
            {
                // set implementation
            }
        }
    }
```

This example shows the properties of the `Clock` class: `Hours`, `Minutes`, and `Seconds`. When each of these properties is read, the get portion of the property executes. Effectively, the `UpdateTime()` method is called and the appropriate value is returned to the calling program. The calling program only knows about the public properties. Everything else is private, including the `UpdateTime()` method. There is no reason for any of the users of the class to know the internal time representation, nor the specific implementation of how the time is updated. Properties are a first-class concept that makes a component more usable to a wider variety of other entities requiring its services.

Component Events

Stuff happens to people every day. They deal with it whether they're prepared or not. Being prepared is the most desirable way to handle unplanned happenings. This is the real world and it needs real-time software to manage planned and unplanned events. Components have the capability to generate events based upon multiple criteria. The criteria could be the passing of time, the accumulation of certain conditions, or some other event triggering this one. Getting back to the clock thing, the clock generates events based on certain criteria. When time passes, the hands move. When a time is reached, the alarm goes off. Events are occurrences caused by specific conditions, resulting in an action when the truth of those conditions is met.

Events don't mean much unless some action is taken when they occur. They must be handled. For instance, when time passes, the clock has a handler that moves the hands, indicating the change in time. When the alarm goes off, a person wakes up and switches it off. These are all ways to handle an event.

How events are handled depends entirely upon the requirements of the task. For example, simply flipping the switch of the alarm is usually sufficient. However, events can be mishandled. If the alarm is ignored, someone may be late to work. On the other hand, if the alarm goes off and someone grabs the clock off the nightstand, hurls it at the wall on the other side of the room, and smashes it to pieces, the goal of handling the event in the immediate term would be met, but the overall result may be overkill. Planning for event handling is important because it makes for better-behaved programs. The following example is a program fragment, showing how events could be implemented in C#.

```
class Timer
{
    // other event related code...

    public event Tick;
}

class Clock
{
    private int hours;
    private int minutes;
    private int seconds;

    public Clock()
    {
        Timer timeEvent = new Timer();

        TimeEvent.Tick += new TimeEventHandler(UpdateTime());
    }

    private void UpdateTime()
    {
        // underlying implementation
    }

    public int HourHand
    {
        get
        {
            return hours;
        }
```

```
            set
            {
                // set implementation
            }
        }
        public int MinuteHand
        {
            get
            {
                return minutes;
            }
            set
            {
                // set implementation
            }
        }
        public int SecondHand
        {
            get
            {
                return seconds;
            }
            set
            {
                // set implementation
            }
        }
    }
```

This example shows two classes, `Timer` and `Clock`. When the `Clock` class is created, the `Clock` constructor is called. This creates an object called `timeEvent`, which is of type `Timer`. Next the `UpdateTimer()` method is added to the `Tick` event of the `Timer` class. Assuming that all the event-related code has been implemented, the `Tick` event fires on regular intervals and calls the `UpdateTimer()` method that is attached to it. Now notice that the `UpdateTimer()` method has been taken out of the get sections of each of the properties in the `Clock` class. This is because the `UpdateTimer()` method is being called automatically every time the `Tick` event of the `Timer` class fires, and the time will always be up-to-date whenever one of the properties is read.

Those entities that need to handle an event must make themselves known to the component capable of initializing the event. The component itself is responsible for generating the event. Remember the clock: when a person plugs it in and sets the alarm, the clock takes care of the rest. The person is then free to do whatever he needs to and just handles the event properly when it happens.

Summary

Objects are organized by categorization and classification. This provides a means of keeping them organized for more efficient utilization. A common way to organize objects is through hierarchies. This chapter showed how hierarchies are formed, and also explained the concepts of inheritance, generalization, and specialization.

Hierarchies are built by using varying degrees of abstraction. This chapter discussed abstraction and how to apply it, and also explained why some objects are pure abstractions as opposed to concrete instances of objects.

Object-oriented software employs containment and encapsulation. You saw how to achieve this by having objects within objects. Encapsulation is used to expose only those attributes and behaviors that should be seen by other objects and to hide the rest.

This chapter also showed how objects that belong to the same classification structure can implement different behaviors with a similar operation. By using an object higher in the hierarchy, behaviors of lower-level objects can be invoked at runtime. This is called polymorphism.

Component concepts such as events, interfaces, and properties were discussed. An interface provides a contract other classes can use to call well-defined methods on classes implementing that interface. Properties enable components to expose public interfaces without exposing the underlying implementation of class functionality. Events are a component concept allowing external users of a class to be notified when a specified occurrence transpires. On that occurrence, the event fires, notifying all registered listeners and giving them the opportunity to react to the event.

With a good understanding of object and component concepts, you're now be ready for the next chapter, which presents one of the most important language features for creating objects: the class.

CHAPTER 7

Working with Classes

In This Chapter

- Class Members *130*
- Instance and Static Members *131*
- Use of Accessibility Modifiers *131*
- Fields *132*
- Constructors *135*
- Destructors *142*
- Methods *143*
- Properties *156*
- Indexers *162*
- Full XML Comments *165*

This chapter provides information for working with classes. It also includes significant coverage of class members, where practical. The chapter looks at class members to provide an understanding of their roles and how they describe attributes and behavior and contribute to the definition of a class as a whole. Many class members have been shown in previous chapters, but this chapter goes into more detail, explaining what each member is and how to use it.

Some class members are so significant that they need their own chapters. In those cases, the concepts are introduced and the exact chapter number is given where the member is covered in more depth.

Class Members

Classes are essentially object definitions, providing applicable information on the data and behavior of the objects you declare and instantiate in your programs. Classes should be self-contained with a single purpose in mind. All included members should be compatible and interact effectively to support that purpose.

Remember how objects were described in the last chapter: they have attributes and behavior that define what they are. Classes define objects; they tell what attributes and behaviors an object will have. Here's a simple class skeleton:

```
class WebSite
{
        // constructors

        // destructors

        // fields

        // methods

        // properties

        // indexers

        // events

        // delegates

        // enumerations

        // classes
}
```

In this example, the class key word tells that this is a class. `WebSites` is the name of the class, and the class members are contained within the braces.

The following sections provide details of each class member. These include fields, constructors, destructors, methods, properties, indexers, and events.

Instance and Static Members

Each member of a class can be classified in one of two ways: instance member or static member. When a copy of a class is created, it is considered instantiated. At that point in time, that class exists as a sole entity, with its own set of attributes and behavior. If a second instance of that class were created, it would have a separate set of data from that of the first class instance. This continues ad infinitum for as long as new instances are created. This is the normal course of action for classes, unless one or more class members are labeled as static.

By using the static key word with a class member, only a single copy of that member can exist at any given time, regardless of how many copies of a class are instantiated. As shown in multiple upcoming sections, static class members are useful for specific purposes.

Use of Accessibility Modifiers

C# provides facilities for full control over who can see and use classes and class members. This is done through class accessibility modifiers. Proper use of accessibility modifiers can protect the implementation of code and help to provide a clean interface.

For instance, a class may have a private field and provide a public accessor to external users, who have no need to know the nature of that field or how you use it. Furthermore, this practice enables the option to change the nature of that field later on, without causing the external user's code to break.

Accessibility modifiers also allow management of user interfaces. They can be used to expose certain class members to users who assist them in using a class more efficiently, and they hide the parts a user may not care about. This reduces the clutter when reviewing the documentation for a class's public interface.

Class members default to private accessibility when no accessibility modifier is specified. Table 7.1 provides a list of C# accessibility modifiers.

TABLE 7.1 Accessibility Modifiers

Accessibility Modifier	*Can Be Seen by*
Private	Members of the same class only
Protected	Members of the same class and derived classes
Internal	Members of the same program
Protected internal	Members of the same program or derived classes
Public	Any member—open accessibility

Fields

Fields comprise the primary "data" portion of a class. They are synonymous with attributes, describing the features of a class. Their types could be primary types, user defined structures, or other classes. Although fields represent information about a class, can also be thought of as self-contained objects, each with their own behavior.

Field Initialization

Fields can be initialized during declaration or afterward, depending on style and/or the nature of requirements. There are pros and cons each way.

For example, a conservative approach may be to ensure that all fields have default values, which would lead to initialization of fields at declaration or soon thereafter. This is safe and perhaps it also helps plan design more thoroughly by thinking about the nature of the data up front. Here's an example of a field declaration:

```
string siteName    = "Computer Security Mega-Site";
```

The field declaration and initialization can happen on the same line. However, this isn't an absolute requirement. Fields can be declared on one line and then initialized later, as the following example shows:

```
string url;

// somewhere in the code
url = "http://www.comp_sec-mega_site.com";
```

If desired, multiple fields can be declared on the same line. They must be separated by commas. This can even include declaration of one or more of the fields, as the following example shows:

```
String siteName, url, description = "Computer Security Information";
```

All three of those fields are strings. The description field is initialized with a literal string. The other fields are still uninitialized. They could have been initialized in the same manner as the description field.

Fields can be initialized with the same value at the same time. This happens by taking advantage of the right associative nature of the equals operator.

```
SiteName = url = description = "Not Specified";
```

Another possibility is that a field may be an encapsulated class declaration and the implementation is designed to create many instances of this field in a large data structure. Furthermore, suppose the field wasn't required for use in every instance. It would save time and memory to not instantiating this field until it was ready to be used. Here's an example of instantiating a class object:

```
SortedList sites = new SortedList();
```

The sites field is of type `SortedList`. Since `SortedList` is a class, or reference, it must be instantiated. References are instantiated by using the `new` operator. This example uses the `new` operator to create a new instance of `SortedList`. When references are instantiated, memory for them is allocated on the heap. The `new` operator initiates the memory allocation process and returns a reference to that memory. Therefore, the `sites` field becomes a reference to the memory allocated on the heap for an instance of the `SortedList` class. The instantiation process is covered in more detail in the "Constructors" section of this chapter.

Definite Assignment

The C# programming language has field utilization rules falling under the title of "Definite Assignment," which governs when a field must be initialized. In a nutshell, definite assignment means a field can't be used or read from unless it's been given a valid value to work with.

During applicable discussion, this chapter explains when definite assignment rules kick in. This is simply a guide to help reduce the errors in code. Rest assured, the compiler reports immediately when a definite assignment rule has been broken. Here's an example showing improper use of a local field (a field defined in a method):

```
public int someMethod()
{
     int count;

    // error
    int next = count + 1;

    return next;
}
```

The local field count was never initialized. To prevent unpredictable behavior, this example code produces a compile time error.

Instance fields, which are defined as being a class member, are always initialized to their default values. See Table 2.6 in Chapter 2 for a listing of default values.

For C++ Programmers

C++ allows use of the current value of a field at any time, regardless of whether it's been initialized. Sometimes this is necessary for situations where a function is expected to accept a pointer parameter and the function will assign a valid value to that pointer before returning. The "Methods" section of this chapter shows how this is not a limitation for C#.

Constant Fields

When it's known up front what the value of a field is going to be and that value won't change, use constants. A constant field is guaranteed not to change during program execution. It can be read as many times as needed. However, don't write to them or try to change them in any way.

Constants are efficient. Their values are known at compile time. This enables certain optimizations unavailable to other types of fields. By definition, constants are also static. Here's an example:

```
const string http = "http://";
```

This example shows a constant string declaration, initialized with a literal string. Constants are initialized with literal representations. This was a good selection for a constant because it's something that doesn't change. Think about the way addresses are sometimes entered into Web browsers: a user just types part of the address, assuming that the Internet protocol will conform to World Wide Web standards. An easy way to accommodate this perceived usage is to have a constant field specifying the HTTP protocol as a default prefix to any Web address.

Integral constants could be implemented with the constant key word, but it's often much more convenient to implement them as enumerations. Using enumerations also promotes a more strongly typed implementation. Chapter 3 discusses enumerations in more detail.

readonly Fields

readonly fields are similar to constant fields in that they can't be modified after initialization. The biggest difference between the two is when they're initialized: constants are initialized during compilation, and readonly fields are initialized during runtime. There are good reasons for this, including flexibility and providing more functionality for users.

Sometimes the value of a variable is unknown until runtime. The value may depend on several conditions and program logic. readonly fields are initialized during class creation. Their values could depend entirely on how a user decides to initialize a class. Class initialization with constructors is described in more detail in the section on "Constructors."

In the following example, currentDate is initialized with the date at the time the field is created.

```
public static readonly string
currentDate = new DateTime().ToString();
```

Since the creation date of an object is something that can't possibly be known at compile time, the readonly modifier is the most appropriate way to approach this case. This particular field is labeled with a static modifier, but that doesn't necessarily have to be. The static modifier could be left out if there was a need for every instance of an object to have its own unique date/time stamp.

Sometimes a readonly field may be a reference type. Reference types must be instantiated at runtime, so there's no way to know the compile-time value of this field. You must use readonly fields for reference types.

XML Comments

Use the <summary> tag when applying XML comments to fields. Here's an example:

```
/// <summary>
///    Used as a prefix for URLs submitted
///    without protocol prefixes
/// </summary>
const string http = "http://";
```

Constructors

The primary purpose of a constructor is to initialize an object. Initialization consists of setting the initial state of class fields. Because of definite assignment rules, it's often desirable to initialize your fields in constructors. This section shows how to gain full control over field initialization.

There are two categories of constructors: static and instance. Each category defines what fields can be initialized and the sequence of initialization. If need be, both types of constructors can be used in a single class. Just be careful to design your class properly. Using both types of constructors in the same class could be an indication of a class possibly supporting multiple roles—which may complicate a design.

Instance Constructors

The purpose of instance constructors is to initialize instance fields. Instance constructors are convenient because they provide a centralized place to instantiate class fields. A class doesn't have to be searched for the field anywhere else to see if it was initialized during declaration or subsequently manipulated through another class member. Instance constructors also enable the ability to dynamically alter the initial values of fields, based on arguments passed to the constructor when the instance of a class is created. Constructors are only invoked on instantiation and can't be called by other programs later. This is a good thing, because it preserves the integrity of a class.

Static fields shouldn't be accessed within constructors, because that could possibly create redundant code to execute every time a new instance is created or leave a class in an inconsistent state when subsequent static methods, if any, are invoked. A good rule of thumb is to keep static field initialization in static constructors, and instance field initialization in instance constructors.

Declare constructors with the same name as the class of which they are members. It's permissible to include zero or more parameters for users to pass initialization information. Constructors don't have return values. Here's an example of a constructor signature:

```
public class WebSite
{

    string siteName;
    string url;
    string description;

    public WebSite(string newSite,
                   string newURL,
                   string newDesc)
    {
        siteName    = newSite;
        url         = newURL;
        description = newDesc;
    }
}
```

In this example, the constructor name is the same as the class name. It has three parameters that have values that become whatever a caller submits as arguments whenever the class is instantiated. The parameters are the types specified in front of the parameter name. Parameters are covered in greater detail in the "Methods" section of this chapter.

Constructors do not have a return value. Since their purpose is to instantiate an object, it would be bad form to try to accomplish anything else through a constructor.

Sometimes it's a pain in other languages when trying to figure out new names for the same thing. It just makes sense to use a meaningful name and then have a convention specifying which object is being referred to. That's what the `this` key word can be used for, as shown in the following example:

```
public class WebSite
{

    string siteName;
    string url;
    string description;

    public WebSite(string siteName,
                   string url,
                   string description)
    {
        this.siteName    = siteName;
        this.url         = url;
        this.description = description;
    }
}
```

In this example, the constructor parameters have the same name as the class fields. To avoid ambiguity, the `this` key word is used. The `this` keyword refers to the current instance of a class. In the example, `this.siteName` refers to the class field `siteName`. Within the constructor, `siteName` (without the `this` key word) refers to the parameter `siteName`.

Note

The `this` key word can't be used in static classes because it would be illogical. There is no such thing as a static instance.

When the constructor in the example executes, it instantiates class fields with the values of the parameters. This is a common method of instantiating class fields. Objects are customized by specifying unique arguments during their instantiation. Here's an example of object instantiation:

```
WebSite mySite = new WebSite(
                   "Computer Security Mega-Site",
                   "http://www.comp_sec-mega_site.com",
                   "Computer Security Information");
```

This example instantiates a new object of class type `WebSite`. Its name is `mySite` and its three parameters are set to the three literal string arguments in the parameter list.

Classes are not limited to a single constructor. They can have more. In this way classes can be even more customized and flexible. The following example shows multiple constructors for the `WebSite` class:

```
public class WebSite
{

    string siteName;
    string url;
    string description;

    // Constructors
    public WebSite()
        : this("No Site", "no.url", "No Description") {}

    public WebSite(string newSite)
        : this(newSite, "no.url", "No Description") {}

    public WebSite(string newSite, string newURL)
        : this(newSite, newURL, "No Description") {}

    public WebSite(string newSite,
                   string newURL,
                   string newDesc)
    {
        siteName    = newSite;
        url         = newURL;
        description = newDesc;
    }
}
```

This example shows multiple constructors. They are primarily differentiated by the number of parameters they accept. The last constructor with the three parameters is familiar, because it's identical to a previous example. The most notable difference between all the other constructors and the one with three parameters is that the other constructors have no implementation.

The first three constructors also have a different declaration. After the constructor name is a colon and the key word `this`. The `this` keyword refers to the current instance of an object. When used with a constructor declaration, the `this` keyword calls another constructor of the current instance.

Note

This type of initialization is unlike C++ initialization and only applies to a base class. For example, the following code is illegal:

```
Public WebSite(string newSite,
               String newURL,
               String newDesc) :
    SiteName(newSite),
    url(newURL),
    description(newDesc)
{
}
```

The first three constructors have three parameters in their parameter list. The effect is that the last constructor with three parameters is called. Since none of the other constructors have three parameters of their own, they supply all the information they have available and then add a default value to the argument they don't have a value for.

Each of the first three constructors could have its own implementations. However, this is risky, and any time it becomes necessary to modify an object's initialization, all of the constructors would have to be modified. This could lead to bugs, not to mention unnecessary work. By using the `this` keyword in every constructor to call a single constructor that implements the object initialization, a class becomes more robust and easier to maintain.

In class initialization there is a defined order of initialization as follows:

1. Class field initializers. This guarantees they can be initialized before one of the constructors try to access them.
2. Other constructors called with the `this` operator.
3. Statements within the constructor's block.

For C++ and Java Programmers

C++ and Java have default parameter values to provide the flexibility necessary to allow users to instantiate an object in multiple ways. C# does not have default values, but the same effect is accomplished by using multiple constructors and calling them with the default values.

Multiple constructors provide a flexible way to instantiate a class, depending on an application's needs. It can also contribute to making a class more reusable.

If desired, an object can be declared with no constructors at all—this does not mean that the object doesn't have a constructor, because C# implicitly defines a default constructor. This allows an object to be instantiated, regardless of whether it has a constructor or not. Default constructors have no parameters.

If a class declares one or more constructors, a default constructor is not created automatically. Therefore, it's usually a good idea to include a parameterless constructor, just in case someone tries to instantiate a class with no parameters. A parameterless constructor can also come in handy with automated tools.

A relevant problem existed in the Java community when using one of the popular development tools. A FAQ had developed from multiple people experiencing a problem with graphical components in the IDE called Red Beans. This was caused by programmers building graphical components without a default or parameterless constructor. Since the tool, seeking the parameterless constructor, couldn't instantiate the graphical component properly, it displayed in the IDE as a red panel, thus the name Red Bean.

Normally, constructors are declared with public access, but sometimes it's necessary to declare a private constructor. A single private constructor can prevent the class from being derived from or instantiated. This is useful if all of a class's members are static, because it would be illogical to try to instantiate an object of this class type.

Here's an example of a class where the constructor is private and the methods are static:

```
public class MortgageCalculations
{
    private MortgageCalculations() {}

    public static decimal MonthlyPayment(
        decimal rate,
        decimal price,
         int years)
    {
```

```
        // implementation
    }
    public static decimal TotalInterest(
         decimal rate,
         decimal price,
         int years)
    {
        // implementation
    }
    public static void PrintSchedule(
         decimal rate,
         decimal price,
         int years)
    {
        // implementation
    }
}
```

The class in this example has no state. Its methods are well-known functions that can be used by many different programs. There is no reason to instantiate a class for calling these methods. Therefore, it is useful to prevent instantiation of this class with a private constructor.

Static Constructors

Static constructors are invoked when a class is loaded. Since classes are loaded only once during the lifetime of a program's execution, static constructors are only invoked once each time your program runs.

Static constructors can access only static fields. There are two reasons for this. First, classes are loaded before any instance of an object can be created. It stands to reason, then, that instance fields may not have been initialized at that point in time. Certainly, the instance constructor, which is invoked when an object is instantiated, hasn't been invoked yet. It may never be invoked. Therefore, there shouldn't be any attempts to access uninstantiated fields. Such behavior would violate definite assignment and cause funny things to happen to the code (or not so funny, depending on one's perspective).

Second, the purpose of instance fields is just as their name implies, for a specific instance. Static fields are applicable to the class, regardless of instance. That is the purpose of static fields. Therefore, trying to access instance fields in a static constructor would be illogical. Here's an example of a static constructor:

```
public class Randomizer
{
    private static int seed;

    static Randomizer()
```

```
    {
        DateTime myDateTime = DateTime.Now;
        seed = myDateTime.GetHashCode();
    }
}
```

Static constructors start with the key word `static`. They do not return a value. The static constructor name is the same as the class name. It always has an empty parameter list. Since it's never instantiated, parameters wouldn't make sense.

Static constructors cannot be called by programs. They're only invoked when a class is loaded. There is no specified sequence of operations for when a static constructor is invoked, but there are a few conditions that can be relied upon:

- The class is loaded before the first instance is created.
- The class is loaded prior to accessing static members.
- The class is loaded ahead of any derived types.
- The class is loaded only once per program execution.

Note

The reason the class loading process is not more specific is because the C# specification doesn't restrict any implementations of the language in this area. Vendors are free to design their class loaders as they deem necessary.

For Java Programmers

Java has static initializers that are analogous to static constructors. The primary difference is that C# static constructors have a name that is the same as their class, and an empty parameter list.

Destructors

The purpose of destructors is to implement finalization code when an object goes out of scope or is destroyed. Because of the way the CLR garbage collector handles objects, there is the distinct possibility of a destructor not being called. Furthermore, there is no precise time after which your object is destroyed that a destructor is called. Here's an example of a destructor:

```
public class WebSite
{

    string siteName;
    string url;
    string description;

    public WebSite(string newSite,
                   string newURL,
                   string newDesc)
    {
        siteName    = newSite;
        url         = newURL;
        description = newDesc;
    }

    ~WebSite() {}
}
```


The destructor in the example shows a typical implementation. All destructors begin with the tilde (~) symbol. Their names are the same as their enclosing class name. Their parameter lists are empty. They do not return a value—destructors cannot be called by functions, so return values wouldn't make sense.

For Java Programmers

The Java equivalent of a destructor is the `Finalize()` method. Its behavior in light of garbage collection is similar.

Using a destructor to clean up class resources increases the risk of resource depletion, system corruption, or deadlock. The basic rule is this: Don't depend on a destructor to release critical resources being held by a class.

For C++ Programmers

C++ destructors are guaranteed to be called directly when an object goes out of scope or is destroyed. However, this is not the case in C#.

Methods

Methods embody a significant portion of a class's behavior. They are the primary mechanism whereby messages may be passed between objects. Each method within a class should be designed with a single purpose in mind. Furthermore, the purpose of the method should contribute to the role of the class and interact cohesively with other class members to support class goals.

Methods may be declared as either instance or static class members. Instance methods belong to the object instance of which they are a part. Static methods are invoked without an instance.

Instance Methods

Each object instance has its own separate method instances. Instance methods must be invoked on an instance of a class. Once this has happened, the method has access to all of the object's instance and static members.

Method Signature

Methods have signatures that distinguish them from other class members. Here's the basic format of a method:

```
[modifiers] returnType MethodName([parameter list])
{
    [statements]
}
```

Modifiers are optional and can be any of the access specifiers shown in the "Fields" section of this chapter. Table 7.2 shows the available method modifiers and their descriptions.

TABLE 7.2 Method Modifiers

Method Modifier	*Meaning/Reference*
`abstract`	Method signature only, no implementation.
`extern`	Method signature for external method.
`internal`	Program accessibility.
`new`	Hides a base class method of the same name.
`override`	Overrides implementation of the same method, declared virtual, in a base class when that virtual base class method is invoked through a base class reference.
`private`	Same class accessibility only.
`protected`	Same class or derived class accessibility only.
`static`	Does not belong to a class instance.

TABLE 7.2 continued

Method Modifier	*Meaning/Reference*
`virtual`	Allows derived class methods to be defined as override and be invoked when this method is called through a reference to its enclosing class.

The `returnType` value can be any valid primary or reference type (or void). The `MethodName` is any valid C# identifier. A method may specify zero or more parameters to be used as input and/or output parameters. Following the method parameter is the method body. Here's a method example:

```
public class WebSite
{
    const string http      = "http://";


    // other code removed...

    public string ValidateUrl(string url)
    {
        if (!(url.StartsWith(http)))
        {
           return http + url;
        }

        return url;
    }
}
```

This example shows a method named `ValidateUrl()`. It's a `public` method and therefore can be invoked by another member of any other class. `ValidateUrl()` has a single parameter named `url` that accepts a string argument. Within the body of the `ValidateUrl`() method, a check is made to see if the beginning of the given `url` matches the value of the constant `http`. The method `StartsWith()` is a built-in string method that checks the beginning of a string for a specified value. When the Boolean expression of the `if` statement returns `true`, the `url` is appended to "http://" and returned. If not, the `url` itself is returned unchanged. The return value must be of type string, as specified in the method signature ahead of the method name `ValidateUrl()`. The following example shows how this method could be called:

```
string myUrl;

WebSite mySite = new WebSite(
                    "Computer Security Mega-Site",
```

```
                        "http://www.comp_sec-mega_site.com",
                        "Computer Security Information");

myUrl = mySite.ValidateUrl("www.comp_sec-mega_site.com");
```

This example invokes an instance method from another class. First an instance of the method's enclosing class is created. Then that instance is used to call the method with the necessary arguments. The dot (`.`) operator separates the class name from the method name. A string field named `myUrl` is declared and used to accept the return value from the method. Since the method signature specifies a string type for a return type, the field used to accept the return value must also be a string. The assignment operator (=) loads the return value from the method into the `myUrl` field.

That example is a bit contrived, but it is intended to show how a method is called from another class. To be more realistic, this particular method is really intended to be used inside the class itself. Here's an example:

```
public class WebSite
{
    const string http       = "http://";

    string siteName;
    string url;
    string description;

    public WebSite(string siteName,
                   string url,
                   string description)
    {
        this.siteName    = siteName;
        this.url         = ValidateUrl(url);
        this.description = description;
    }

    protected string ValidateUrl(string url)
    {
        if (!(url.StartsWith(http)))
        {
           return http + url;
        }

        return url;
    }
}
```

In this example, the `ValidateUrl()` method is used in the class constructor. Since it's a class member, there's no need to prefix the method call with a class instance—just call same class members directly. The method modifier for the `ValidateUrl()` method has been changed from public to protected. That's because this method isn't meant to be used by other classes. However, its protected status considers the possibility of derived classes using it in their constructors. Derived classes will be covered in more detail in Chapter 8, where the subject of class inheritance is discussed.

Method Body

The method body is where a method's logic is specified. Any compilation of sequential statements, decision making, and looping constructs may be used within the body of a method. From within the method body, it's possible to use an enclosing class's members, and call methods on objects that are accessible. Here's an example of a simple method body:

```
public string getSiteName()
{
    return siteName;
}
```

The example shows a method used as an accessor to obtain the value of the siteName field. Here's another example using parameters:

```
public void setSiteName(string siteName)
{
    this.siteName = siteName;
}
```

This example accepts a string parameter named siteName. Using the this operator, it assigns the value of the parameter siteName to the class field siteName. In this method there is no reason to return a value, therefore the return type is void. The void return type can be used with any method that doesn't return a value.

Local Fields

Methods may declare their own local fields. This is useful when working data is needed only for the purpose of that method. Allocated on the stack, these local variables normally go away once the method has executed. For references, the reference itself may be allocated on the stack, but the actual object is allocated on the heap and is marked for deletion by the garbage collector when the method ends.

So what happens when you use a local field with the same identifier as a class field? Simple, you prefix the class field name with a this operator. This distinguishes between the class field and the local field. Use the normal field name, without enhancements, to access the local field. Here's an example:

```
public class WebSite
{
```

```
    const string http       = "http://";

    string fullUrl;

    protected string ValidateUrl(string url)
    {
        string fullUrl;

        if (!(url.StartsWith(http)))
        {
           fullUrl = http + url;
           this.fullUrl = fullUrl;

           return fullUrl;
        }

        return url;
    }
}
```

This example has a `fullUrl` class member field. Its `ValidateUrl()` method also has a `fullUrl` local field. To distinguish between the two, the `this` operator is used to assign the value of the local `fullUrl` to the class field `fullUrl`.

Method Parameters

Method parameters are the mechanism by which the type of variables a method accepts as arguments from callers is specified. There may be zero or more parameters, as many as needed, in a method parameter list. A lower number of parameters is usually better. Although there are no hard rules, carefully consider usability of a method when passing parameters. There are four kinds of parameters to work with: value, reference, output, and params. The kind is normally specified in front of each parameter type declaration.

Value Parameters

When it's necessary to pass a parameter by value, use a value parameter.

Normally, a parameter kind defaults to value when its kind is not specified in the parameter declaration. If the parameter is already a reference, then its kind is reference. Also, when an array is passed in, its kind defaults to `params`.

Value parameters provide a local copy of themselves to the method. This means that the method may read and write to them as much as needed, but the original copy from the caller is not changed. An argument passed into a method must be the same type as the specified parameter, or must be implicitly convertible to that type. Value parameters must be definitely assigned before being passed as an argument. Here's an example:

```
public class WebSite
{
    const string http = "http://";

    public string ValidateUrl(string url)
    {
        if (!(url.StartsWith(http)))
        {
           url = http + url;
           Console.WriteLine("Within ValidateUrl: {0}", url);
        }

        return url;
    }
}

public class test
{
    public static void Main()
    {
        string url = "www.newsite.com";

        WebSite mySite = new WebSite();

        Console.WriteLine("Before ValidateUrl: {0}", url);

        mySite.ValidateUrl(url);

        Console.WriteLine("After ValidateUrl: {0}", url);
    }
}
```

And here's the output:

```
Before ValidateUrl: www.newsite.com
Within ValidateUrl: http://www.newsite.com
After ValidateUrl: www.newsite.com
```

In this example, the `WebSite` class defines the method `ValidateUrl()`, which modifies the parameter `url` when it is passed in without the `http` prefix. The test driver shows that the `url` passed in is not modified after the `ValidateUrl()` method executes. Within the `ValidateUrl()` method, the `url` parameter is a local copy because it was passed by value, which is the default when no parameter kind is specified.

Reference Parameters

Reference parameters can be thought of as `in/out` parameters. Modifying a `ref` parameter within the body of a method also changes the original variable passed in as an argument. `ref` parameters must be definitely assigned before passing them to a method.

Here's an example:

```
public class WebSite
{
    const string http = "http://";

    public string ValidateUrl(ref string url)
    {
        if (!(url.StartsWith(http)))
        {
           url = http + url;
           Console.WriteLine("Within ValidateUrl: {0}", url);
        }

        return url;
    }
}

public class test
{
    public static void Main()
    {
        string url = "www.newsite.com";

        WebSite mySite = new WebSite();

        Console.WriteLine("Before ValidateUrl: {0}", url);

        mySite.ValidateUrl(ref url);

        Console.WriteLine("After ValidateUrl: {0}", url);
    }
}
```

And here's the output:

```
Before ValidateUrl: www.newsite.com
Within ValidateUrl: http://www.newsite.com
After ValidateUrl: http://www.newsite.com
```

In this example, the `ValidateUrl()` method accepts a string `url` with a `ref` modifier. When `ValidateUrl()` changes `url`, it also changes the original `url` that was passed in because of the `ref` modifier. The `ref` modifier passes a reference to an object, and although it is a copy of the reference that is passed to the method, both references point to the same object. This is how modifications persist through method invocations using `ref` modifiers.

Output Parameters

Another way to return information from a method is via `out` parameters. The `out` parameter doesn't need to be definitely assigned going in, but it must be definitely assigned before the method returns. Even if a variable is definitely assigned before a method call, it is considered unassigned once inside the method call. Therefore, any attempt to access the `out` variable within the method prior to its initialization renders a compile-time error. Since there's a requirement to assign the parameter prior to leaving the method, anything that may have been put in the `out` object before the method call will be gone. It is replaced with the data put into it during method execution. Here's an example:


```
public class WebSite
{
    const string http = "http://";

    public string ValidateUrl(string inUrl, out string outUrl)
    {
        outUrl = inUrl;
        if (!(inUrl.StartsWith(http)))
        {
           outUrl = http + inUrl;
           Console.WriteLine("Within ValidateUrl: {0}", outUrl);
        }

        return outUrl;
    }
}

public class test
{
    public static void Main()
    {
        string inUrl = "www.newsite.com";
        string outUrl;

        WebSite mySite = new WebSite();

        mySite.ValidateUrl(inUrl, out outUrl);

        Console.WriteLine("After ValidateUrl:  {0}", outUrl);
    }
}
```

And here's the output:

```
Within ValidateUrl: http://www.newsite.com
After ValidateUrl: http://www.newsite.com
```

This example shows the `ValidateUrl()` method modified to take two parameters. The first is a value parameter, which has been covered. The second is an `out` parameter. The `outUrl` field is not initialized prior to passing it as an argument to the `ValidateUrl()` method. It doesn't need to be, because its purpose is to be used as an `out` parameter in the `ValidateUrl()` method. That's where it will be modified. It would be an error to try to read the `outUrl` field prior to invocation of `ValidateUrl()` because it is uninitialized. The `outUrl` field must be assigned before the method returns. Failure to do so causes a compile-time error. Once the `ValidateUrl()` method completes, the `outUrl` field is set to a valid value.

Of course, it is possible to assign a value to the `outUrl` field and use it. However, as soon as it is passed as an out parameter to the `ValidateUrl()` method, it loses its value and becomes unassigned within the method. Besides, it is illogical to use a variable for two different purposes. It introduces the risk of making the code too complicated. Give each field its own purpose to keep a program understandable and maintainable.

`params` Parameters

`params` parameters permit passing a single dimension or jagged array into a method, and must be the last parameter in a method's parameter list. The argument passed in may be either an array or a list of values that could be converted to an array. A `params` parameter is good way to pass multiple values to a method when it's unknown up front how many values will be passed. Here's an example of passing an array:

```
public class WebSite
{
    const string http      = "http://";

    string siteName;
    string url;
    string description;

    public WebSite(params string[] siteInfo)
    {
        siteName    = siteInfo[0];
        url         = siteInfo[1];
        description = siteInfo[2];

        Console.WriteLine("Site Name:   {0}", siteName);
        Console.WriteLine("URL:         {0}", url);
        Console.WriteLine("Description: {0}", description);
    }
}

public class test
{
```

```
    public static void Main()
    {
        string[] siteInfo = new string[3]
            {
                "A New Site",
                "www.newsite.com",
                "The Newest Site on the Web"
            };

        WebSite mySite = new WebSite(siteInfo);
    }
}
```

And here's the output:

```
Site Name:    A New Site
URL:          www.newsite.com
Description:  The Newest Site on the Web
```

This example creates a single dimension array and passes it as a parameter. It's also possible to pass a list of parameters with the same type as the array. These parameters are gathered up and put into a single-dimension array by the system and passed to the method as a single-dimension array `params` parameter. Here's an example:

```
public class WebSite
{
    const string http      = "http://";

    string siteName;
    string url;
    string description;

    public WebSite(params string[] siteInfo)
    {
        siteName    = siteInfo[0];
        url         = siteInfo[1];
        description = siteInfo[2];

        Console.WriteLine("Site Name:   {0}", siteName);
        Console.WriteLine("URL:         {0}", url);
        Console.WriteLine("Description: {0}", description);
    }
}

public class test
{
    public static void Main()
    {
        WebSite mySite = new WebSite(
            "A New Site",
            "www.newsite.com",
```

```
            "The Newest Site on the Web");
    }
}
```

And here's the output:

```
Site Name:   A New Site
URL:         www.newsite.com
Description: The Newest Site on the Web
```

Although it's not possible to pass multidimensional arrays as `params` parameters, the same effect can be achieved by using jagged arrays. Here's an example:

```
using System;

public class WebSite
{
    const string http      = "http://";
    public WebSite(params string[][] siteInfo)
    {
        Console.WriteLine("Site Name:   {0}", siteInfo[0][0]);
        Console.WriteLine("URL:         {0}", siteInfo[0][1]);
        Console.WriteLine("Description: {0}", siteInfo[0][2]);
        Console.WriteLine();
        Console.WriteLine("Site Name:   {0}", siteInfo[1][0]);
        Console.WriteLine("URL:         {0}", siteInfo[1][1]);
        Console.WriteLine("Description: {0}", siteInfo[1][2]);
    }
}

public class test
{
    public static void Main()
    {
        string[][] siteInfo = new string[2][];
        siteInfo[0] = new string[]
        {
            "A New Site",
            "www.newsite.com",
            "The Newest Site on the Web"
        };

        siteInfo[1] = new string[]
        {
            "Some Other Site",
            "www.somesite.com",
            "Another Site on the Web"
        };

        WebSite mySite = new WebSite(siteInfo);
    }
}
```

And here's its output:

```
Site Name:    A New Site
URL:          www.newsite.com
Description:  The Newest Site on the Web

Site Name:    Some Other Site
URL:          www.somesite.com
Description:  Another Site on the Web
```

This example adds two sets of data to a jagged array and passes the jagged array to the WebSite class constructor. Using jagged arrays, a very large amount of structured data can be transferred via params parameters.

Static Methods

Static methods are not invoked on object instances. They're invoked with only the class definition itself. There can only be a single copy of a static method. Unlike instance methods, static methods can only operate on static members within the class in which they are defined. Static methods are useful for functions such as mathematical calculations, where the data used is not part of the class to which the static method belongs. The static method normally just takes input values, processes them, and returns a result. The following code is an example of a class with static methods:

```
public class MortgageCalculations
{
    private MortgageCalculations() {}

    public static decimal MonthlyPayment(
        decimal rate,
        decimal price,
         int years)
    {
        // implementation
    }
    public static decimal TotalInterest(
         decimal rate,
         decimal price,
         int years)
    {
        // implementation
    }
    public static void PrintSchedule(
         decimal rate,
         decimal price,
         int years)
    {
        // implementation
    }
}
```

Each of these static methods does not require an instance to run. They are invoked with the name of the class, rather than the name of an instance. Here's an example:

```
decimal myPayment = MortgageCalculations.MonthlyPayment(
                                          8.75m, 593000.00m, 30);
```

XML Comments

There are special XML comments related to methods. These are the `<param>` tag for parameters and the `<return>` tag for return values. Here's an example:

```
/// <summary>
/// Compares two Web Sites for equality
/// </summary>
/// <remarks>
/// Overrides Object.Equals() by comparing
/// <paramref name="evalString"/> to this site.
/// </remarks>
/// <param name="evalString">
/// Value compared against this object.
/// </param>
/// <returns>
///    <list>
///       <item> true:  Sites are equal.</item>
///       <item>false:  Sites are not equal.</item>
///    </list>
/// </returns>
public override bool Equals(object evalString)
{
    return this.ToString() == evalString.ToString();
}
```

In this example, the `<param>` tag is used to describe the purpose of the `evalString` parameter. It has an attribute called `name`, which is used to indicate the parameter's identifier.

The `<paramref>` tag is used to identify a parameter for special XML styling. Its syntax is similar to the `<param>` tag.

The `<returns>` tag is used to describe the return value of a method. Often it's convenient to use the `<list>` tag with a returns tag to classify the different types of return value.

Properties

Properties are class members that provide specialized access to class fields. They provide encapsulation for a class, so users are unaware of the underlying implementation required to access a class field. Their use is also transparent to the calling program.

For C++ Programmers

Properties are a new programming construct. In C++ you would use explicit get/set methods to encapsulate properties. These methods are called to access class attributes. However, in C# the property name is used as if it were a field itself.

For Java Programmers

Java formalized accessors through predefined signature patterns. However, they were still methods. C# properties are not methods. They provide the means to access a field by using the property as if it was the field itself.

Here's an example of a very simple property:

```
public string Description
{
    get
    {
        return description;
    }

    set
    {
        description = value;
    }
}
```

The example begins with a property modifier of `public`. Accessibility of properties is the same as of methods. The next item is the property type. This one is a string. The name of this property is `Description`. Notice that it's the same name as the class field `description`, only the first letter is uppercase. This is a common convention with properties. The private field name is lowercase and the property name is capitalized. This property has both a `get` and a `set` accessor.

Property Accessors

C# offers two types of accessors. The first is a `get` accessor to get the value of a property. The other is the `set` accessor to modify the value of a property. It makes no difference which is declared first.

A property doesn't have to include both get and set accessors. For example, if you want a property to be read-only, don't include a set accessor. A similar technique is appropriate for get accessors and write-only capability.

get Accessor

get accessors obtain the property value and return it to the caller. A property doesn't necessarily have a one-to-one correspondence with a class field. It could be a couple fields that could be concatenated into strings before returning. It could also have logic maintaining object state, other than a similarly named field, when a certain property is read. Here's an example:

```
public string SiteName
{
    get
    {
        siteCount++;
        return siteName;
    }
}
```

This property only has a get accessor. This is useful if the property represents a field corresponding to a key column in a database. Then it would be wise to make the property read-only. Before returning the value of siteName, it increments a siteCount field. This could be a static count, such as keeping track of how many people browsed this site's information.

set Accessor

set accessors change the value of a property. Similar to how the get accessor is used, a field may be modified directly or a calculation with modification of multiple fields could be performed. It's also a good opportunity to perform class state management. Here's an example that shows a set accessor manipulating the data assigned to the property:

```
public string URL
{
    get
    {
        return url;
    }

    set
    {
        url = ValidateUrl(value);
    }
}
```

The variable assigned to the property always has the name `value`. In this case, `value` is being transformed by the `ValidateUrl()` method, and the result is being placed in the `url` field.

Transparent Access

What's really great about C# properties is their transparent utilization. Simply use the name of the property as if it was the variable itself. This way, if there were a `public` field being used today, it could be converted to a property tomorrow with minimal effect on users' code.

One exception between properties and fields is that properties can't be passed as `ref` or `out` parameters in method calls. If there's a need to pass a property to a method, there are a few different choices to be made. It could be passed by `value`. In that case there would be no way to modify the property. The underlying field, if one exists, could be made public and passed instead. Another possibility is to copy the result of a property into a working variable before the call, for `ref` parameters, then assign the working variable back to the property after the method call. Regardless of the method used, the property no longer behaves the same as a field when used with methods. However, there definitely are workarounds to achieve the results needed.

If there is any possibility that the implementation of a field will be modified in the future, seriously consider making it a property up front. This minimizes impact for the users of a class. Here's an example of a constructor using properties:

```
public class WebSite
{
    string description;

    public string Description
    {
        get
        {
            return description;
        }

        set
        {
            description = value;
        }
    }

// other code
}

// within some other code
```

```
WebSite mySite = new WebSite("Great Site",
                             "www.great.com",
                             "You'll love it.");

// SiteDescription will equal "You'll love it."
string SiteDescription = mySite.Description;

// MySite.Description now equals "You'll Love It!"
mySite.Description = "You'll Love It!";
```

This example shows how easy it is to read from and write to a property. The fact that it's a property is totally transparent to the user.

Static Properties

There aren't any surprises here. Static properties operate with the same rules as static methods. Just remember, you need to access only static members of the class. Here's an example of how to use a static property:

```
public class MortgageCalculations
{
    private decimal rate;

    public static decimal InterestRate
    {
        get
        {
            return rate;
        }

        set
        {
            rate = value;
        }
    }
}

// within some other class
MortgageCalculations.InterestRate = 9.53m;
```

The example assumes there is only a single rate at any given time with which to calculate mortgages. Therefore, it's set as a static property for all users to use the same value. The property has the `static` modifier to show it is static. The name of the class is used with the dot (`.`) operator to set the property.

Late Bound Object Creation

Properties are useful in delaying object creation until an object is needed at runtime. What if a recent study showed that FTP sites were not viewed as often as Web sites, and that the people interested in FTP sites didn't view Web sites as often, and vise versa. This scenario would open the door to an opportunity for optimization of how sites were handled in the code. Using properties, creation of the objects managing these two types of sites could be delayed until needed. Here's an example:

```
Public class SiteManager
{
    private WebSiteManager myWebSites;
    private FTPSiteManager myFTPSites;

    public WebSiteManager MyWebSites
    {
        get
        {
            if (myWebSites == null)
            {
                myWebSites = new WebSiteManager();
            }
            return myWebSites;
        }
    }
    public FTPSiteManager MyFTPSites
    {
        get
        {
            if (myFTPSites == null)
            {
                myFTPSites = new FTPSiteManager();
            }
            return myFTPSites;
        }
    }
}

// code in another class
SiteManager Sites = new SiteManager();
Console.WriteLine("Please choose site type (Web or FTP):  ");
string choice = ReadLine();

if (choice == "Web")
{
    Sites.MyWebSites.DisplaySites();
}
else if (choice == "FTP)
```

```
{
    Sites.MyFTPSites.DisplaySites();
}
```

In this example, the `if` statement in the `get` accessor of each property checks to see if the object has been created yet. If not, the appropriate object is created and returned. This prevents reallocation of the object every time it's needed. It also saves processing time for object creation and uses less memory by not allocating objects that are not being used. This could also be built upon to manage an object's lifetime and free the memory when the object was no longer being used. Perhaps setting a timer in the `get` accessor or some other mechanism could support lifetime management.

XML Comments

Properties have their own special XML documentation tag: the `<value>` tag. Here's an example:

```
/// <value>
/// Sets and gets Web Site Description.
/// </value>
/// <remarks>
/// Sets and gets the value of
/// <see cref="description"/> field.
/// </remarks>
public string Description
{
    get
    {
        return description;
    }
    set
    {
        description = value;
    }
}
```

In the example, the `<value>` tag is used to document the behavior of the property. Notice there is no `<summary>` tag. The `<value>` tag replaces the `<summary>` tag on properties.

Indexers

Indexers allow you to access members of a class similar to the way arrays are used. A useful comparison may be to view their implementation as a cross between an array, property, and method.

For C++ Programmers

C++ doesn't have indexers, but the same effect can be achieved by overloading the square bracket operator.

For Java Programmers

Java doesn't have indexers.

Indexers behave like arrays in that they use the square bracket syntax to access their members. The .NET collection classes use indexers to accomplish the same goals. Their elements are accessed by index.

Indexers are implemented like properties because they have `get` and `set` accessors, following the same syntax. Given an index, they obtain and return an appropriate value with a `get` accessor. Similarly, they `set` the value corresponding to the index with the value passed into the indexer.

Indexers also have a parameter list, just like methods. The parameter list is delimited by brackets, but it serves the same purpose. The only difference is that they can't be passed `ref` or `out` parameters. (The "Methods" section earlier in the chapter described the kinds of C# parameters.) Normally, indexers are used with integers so a class can provide array-like operations. Here's an example:

```
using System;
using System.Collections;

public class WebSite
{
  // WebSite implementation
}

public class SiteList {

    SortedList sites;

    public SiteList()
    {
        sites      = new SortedList();
    }

    public WebSite this[int index]
    {
```

```
        get
        {
            if (index > sites.Count)
                return (WebSite)null;

            return (WebSite) sites.GetByIndex(index);
        }

        set
        {
            if ( index < 10 )
                sites[index] = value;
        }
    }
}

// code in another class

SiteList sites = new SiteList();

// add a new entry to sites
sites[0] = new WebSite("Joe",
                       "http://www.mysite.com",
                       "Great Site!");

// prints "Joe, http://www.mysite.com, Great Site!"
Console.WriteLine("Site: {0}", sites[0].ToString());
```

The indexer in the example accepts an integer argument. The `get` accessor guards against any attempt to retrieve out-of-range values. The `set` accessor guarantees that no more than 10 sites will be stored in the list.

Utilization of this indexer looks and feels just like an array. At the end of the example there is an assignment of a `WebSite` to the `sites` object using the indexer. Next, that same item is referenced through the indexer, which returns an instance of `WebSite`. The `ToString()` method of the `WebSite` instance is invoked to obtain a string representation of the `WebSite` instance data.

To get a gist of how indexers are beneficial, imagine what the last two lines in the example would have look like if only methods were used. Also, consider the fact that the underlying implementation can change with zero impact to calling code.

XML Comments

XML documentation for indexers is the same as it is for properties. See the "XML Comments" part of the "Properties" section earlier in this chapter for an example.

Full XML Comments

Listings 7.2 and 7.3 contain a full implementation of the concepts presented in this chapter. Both listings contain a full set of XML documentation comments. Remember the /doc command line switch to generate documentation. Compilation instructions are shown in Listing 7.1.

LISTING 7.1 Site Manager Make File

```
csc /target:library /doc:WebSites.xml WebSites.cs
csc /r:WebSites.dll /doc:SiteManager.xml SiteManager.cs
```


LISTING 7.2 WebSites Library with XML Documentation Comments

```
namespace WebSites
{
    using System;
    using System.Collections;

    /// <summary>
    ///    Describes a single web site.
    /// </summary>
    /// <remarks>This class has the following members:
    ///   <para>Constructors:
    ///     <list>
    ///       <item>Default Constructor<see cref=
    ///             "WebSite()"/></item>
    ///       <item>Single Parameter Constructor<see cref=
    ///             "WebSite(string)"/></item>
    ///       <item>Double Parameter Constructor<see cref=
    ///             "WebSite(string, string)"/></item>
    ///       <item>Triple Parameter Constructor<see cref=
    ///             "WebSite(string, string, string)"/></item>
    ///     </list>
    ///   </para>
    ///   <para> Methods:
    ///     <list>
    ///      <item>ValidateUrl<see cref="ValidateUrl"/></item>
    ///      <item>ToString<see cref="ToString"/></item>
    ///      <item>Equals<see cref="Equals"/></item>
    ///      <item>GetHashCode<see cref="GetHashCode"/></item>
    ///     </list>
    ///   </para>
    ///   <para>Properties:
    ///     <list>
    ///      <item>SiteName<see cref="SiteName"/></item>
```

LISTING 7.2 continued

```
///     <item>URL<see cref="URL"/></item>
///     <item>Description<see cref="Description"/></item>
///    </list>
///   </para>
/// </remarks>
public class WebSite
{
    const string http      = "http://";

    public static readonly string
        currentDate = new DateTime().ToString();

    string siteName;
    string url;
    string description;

    // Constructors

    /// <summary>
    /// Default Constructor
    /// </summary>
    /// <remarks>
    /// Invokes another constructor with 3
    /// default parameters
    /// </remarks>
    public WebSite()
        : this("No Site", "no.url", "No Description") {}

    /// <summary>
    /// Single String Constructor
    /// </summary>
    /// <remarks>
    /// Invokes another constructor with 3
    /// default parameters
    /// </remarks>
    public WebSite(string newSite)
        : this(newSite, "no.url", "No Description") {}

    /// <summary>
    /// Double String Constructor
    /// </summary>
    /// <remarks>
    /// Invokes another constructor with 3
    /// default parameters
    /// </remarks>
    public WebSite(string newSite, string newURL)
        : this(newSite, newURL, "No Description") {}

    /// <summary>
```

LISTING 7.2 continued

```
        /// Three String Constructor
        /// </summary>
        /// <remarks>
        /// Provides full support for WebSite
        /// object initialization
        /// </remarks>
        public WebSite(string newSite,
                       string newURL,
                       string newDesc)
        {
            SiteName    = newSite;
            URL         = newURL;
            Description = newDesc;
        }

        /// <summary>
        /// Generates String Representation of Web Site
        /// </summary>
        /// <remarks>
        /// Creates a SiteName, URL, and Description comma
        /// separated string.  Overrides Object.ToString()
        /// </remarks>
        /// <returns>
        /// <para>Comma separated string</para>
        /// </returns>
        public override string ToString()
        {
            return siteName + ", " + url + ", " + description;
        }

        /// <summary>
        /// Compares two Web Sites for equality
        /// </summary>
        /// <remarks>
        /// Overrides Object.Equals() by comparing
        /// <paramref name="evalString"/> to this site.
        /// </remarks>
        /// <param name="evalString">
        /// Value compared against this object.
        /// </param>
        /// <returns>
        ///    <list>
        ///       <item> true:  Sites are equal.</item>
        ///       <item>false:  Sites are not equal.</item>
        ///    </list>
        /// </returns>
        public override bool Equals(object evalString)
        {
            return this.ToString() == evalString.ToString();
```

LISTING 7.2 continued

```
        }

        /// <summary>
        /// Gets a Hash Code
        /// </summary>
        /// <remarks>
        /// Overrides Object.GetHashCode();
        /// </remarks>
        /// <returns>
        ///    <para>integer hash code.</para>
        /// </returns>
        public override int GetHashCode()
        {
            return this.ToString().GetHashCode();
        }

        /// <summary>
        /// Checks URL prefix
        /// </summary>
        /// <remarks>
        /// "http://" prefix prepended when absent.
        /// </remarks>
        /// <param name="url">
        /// URL to check.
        /// </param>
        /// <returns>
        ///    <para>String with "http://" prefix.</para>
        /// </returns>
        protected string ValidateUrl(string url)
        {
            if (!(url.StartsWith(http)))
            {
                return http + url;
            }

            return url;
        }

        /// <value>
        /// Sets and gets Web Site Name.
        /// </value>
        /// <remarks>
        /// Sets and gets the value of
        /// <see cref="siteName"/> field.
        /// </remarks>
        public string SiteName
        {
            get
            {
```

LISTING 7.2 continued

```
                return siteName;
            }
            set
            {
                siteName = value;
            }
        }

        /// <value>
        /// Sets and gets the URL for the Web Site.
        /// </value>
        /// <remarks>
        /// Sets and gets the value of
        /// <see cref="url"/> field.
        /// </remarks>
        public string URL
        {
            get
            {
                return url;
            }
            set
            {
                url = ValidateUrl(value);
            }
        }

        /// <value>
        /// Sets and gets Web Site Description.
        /// </value>
        /// <remarks>
        /// Sets and gets the value of
        /// <see cref="description"/> field.
        /// </remarks>
        public string Description
        {
            get
            {
                return description;
            }
            set
            {
                description = value;
            }
        }

        /// <summary>
        /// Destructor
        /// </summary>
```

LISTING 7.2 continued

```
        /// <remarks>
        /// No Implementation
        /// </remarks>
        ~WebSite() {}
    }

    /// <summary>
    ///    This object holds a collection of sites.
    /// </summary>
    public class SiteList
    {
        /// <summary>
        /// Declared as a <see cref="SortedList"/>
        /// Collection Class.
        /// </summary>
        /// <seealso cref="System.Collections"/>
        SortedList sites;

        /// <summary>
        /// Default Constructor
        /// </summary>
        /// <remarks>
        /// Initializes <see cref="sites"/>
        /// </remarks>
        public SiteList()
        {
            sites = new SortedList();
        }

        /// <value>
        /// Gets the next valid index number to use.
        /// </value>
        /// <remarks>
        /// Gets the count of <see cref="sites"/> field.
        /// </remarks>
        public int NextIndex
        {
            get
            {
                return sites.Count;
            }
        }

        /// <value>
        /// Adds and retrieves Web Site at index.
        /// </value>
        /// <remarks>
        /// Sets and gets the value of
        /// <see cref="sites"/> field.
```

LISTING 7.2 continued

```
        /// </remarks>
        /// <param name="index">
        /// Position in collection to get or set Web Site.
        /// </param>
        public WebSite this[int index]
        {
            get
            {
                if (index > sites.Count)
                    return (WebSite)null;

                return (WebSite) sites.GetByIndex(index);
            }
            set
            {
                if ( index < 10 )
                    sites[index] = value;
            }
        }

        /// <summary>
        /// Deletes Web Site from sites
        /// </summary>
        /// <remarks>
        /// Removes the Web Site from the
        /// <see cref="sites"/>collection.
        /// </remarks>
        /// <param name="element">
        /// Index from where element will be deleted.
        /// </param>
        public void Remove(int element)
        {
            sites.RemoveAt(element);
        }

    }
}
```


LISTING 7.3 Site Manager Program with XML Documentation Comments

```
using System;
using WebSites;

/// <summary>
///     User Interface for managing Web Sites.
/// </summary>
/// <remarks>This class has the following members:
```

LISTING 7.3 continued

```
///    <para> Methods:
///       <list>AddSite<see cref="AddSite"/></list>
///       <list>DeleteSite<see cref="DeleteSite"/></list>
///       <list>ModifySite<see cref="ModifySite"/></list>
///       <list>ViewSites<see cref="ViewSites"/></list>
///       <list>DisplayShortList
///            <see cref="DisplayShortList"/></list>
///    </para>
/// </remarks>
class SiteManager
{
    /// <summary>
    /// Collection of WebSites.
    /// </summary>
    SiteList sites = new SiteList();

    /// <summary>
    /// Program Entry Point.
    /// </summary>
    /// <remarks>
    /// Loads Web Sites and begins program.
    /// </remarks>
    public static void Main()
    {
        SiteManager mgr = new SiteManager();

        mgr.sites = new SiteList();
        mgr.sites[mgr.sites.NextIndex] = new WebSite(
                              "Joe",
                              "http://www.mysite.com",
                              "Great Site.");
        mgr.sites[mgr.sites.NextIndex] = new WebSite(
                              "Don",
                              "http://www.dondotnet.com",
                              "Must See.");
        mgr.sites[mgr.sites.NextIndex] = new WebSite(
                              "Bob",
                              "www.bob.com",
                              "No http://");

        mgr.ShowMenu();
    }

    /// <summary>
    /// Shows Console Menu
    /// </summary>
    /// <remarks>
    /// Let's user make choice and performs action.
    /// </remarks>
```

LISTING 7.3 continued

```
    public void ShowMenu()
    {
        string choice;

        do
        {
            Console.WriteLine("Web Site Editor\n");

            Console.WriteLine("A - Add");
            Console.WriteLine("D - Delete");
            Console.WriteLine("M - Modify");
            Console.WriteLine("R - Report");
            Console.WriteLine("Q - Quit");

            Console.Write("\nPlease Choose:  ");

            choice = Console.ReadLine();

            switch (choice.ToUpper())
            {
                case "A":
                    AddSite();
                    break;
                case "D":
                    DeleteSite();
                    break;
                case "M":
                    ModifySite();
                    break;
                case "R":
                    ViewSites();
                    break;
                case "Q":
                    choice = "Q";
                    break;
                default:
                    Console.WriteLine(
    "({0})? Err...That's not what I expected.", choice);
            }
        } while (choice != "Q");
    }

    /// <summary>
    /// Adds a Web Site
    /// </summary>
    /// <remarks>
    /// Prompts user for info and adds site to collection.
    /// </remarks>
    private void AddSite()
```

LISTING 7.3 continued

```
    {
        string siteName;
        string url;
        string description;

        Console.Write("Please Enter Site Name: ");
        siteName = Console.ReadLine();

        Console.Write("Please Enter URL: ");
        url = Console.ReadLine();

        Console.Write("Please Enter Description: ");
        description = Console.ReadLine();

        sites[sites.NextIndex] = new WebSite(siteName,
                                             url,
                                             description);
    }

    /// <summary>
    /// Deletes Web Site
    /// </summary>
    /// <remarks>
    /// Prints sites, get's user's choice,
    /// and deletes Web Site from collection
    /// </remarks>
    private void DeleteSite()
    {
        string choice;

        do {
            Console.WriteLine("\nDeletion Menu\n");

            DisplayShortList();

            Console.Write(
                "\nPlease select an item to delete: ");

            choice = Console.ReadLine();

            if (choice == "Q" || choice == "q")
                break;

            if (choice.ToInt32() <= sites.NextIndex)
                sites.Remove(choice.ToInt32()-1);

        } while (true);
    }

```

LISTING 7.3 continued

```
    /// <summary>
    /// Modifies a Web Site
    /// </summary>
    /// <remarks>
    /// No Implementation Yet.
    /// </remarks>
    private void ModifySite()
    {
        Console.WriteLine("Modifying Sites.");
    }

    /// <summary>
    /// View Web Sites
    /// </summary>
    /// <remarks>
    /// Prints list of Web Sites to Console.
    /// </remarks>
    private void ViewSites()
    {
        Console.WriteLine("");
        for (int i=0; i < sites.NextIndex; i++)
        {
            Console.WriteLine("Site: {0}",
                              sites[i].ToString());
        }
        Console.WriteLine("");
    }

    /// <summary>
    /// View Numbered List
    /// </summary>
    /// <remarks>
    /// Used by the deletion operation to let user
    /// select specific Web Site to delete.
    /// </remarks>
    private void DisplayShortList()
    {
        for (int i=0; i < sites.NextIndex; i++)
        {
            Console.WriteLine("{0} - {1}",
                              i+1,
                              sites[i].ToString());
        }
        Console.WriteLine("Q - Quit (Back To Main Menu)");
    }
}
```

Summary

This chapter covered most class members. It showed how constructors initialize an object and it explained why destructors shouldn't be used, even though they're available. Other members include fields, methods, properties, and indexers. With each class member there was a discussion of how XML documentation comments can be applied to those class members.

Methods were covered in-depth. There were explanations about the four kinds of method parameters: value, `ref`, `out`, and `params`. With new language elements like indexers and properties, the role of methods in C# is scaled down as compared to other languages.

There were explanations of the class member modifiers. Accessibility is maintained with the private, protected, internal, and public modifiers. There were discussions, where applicable, on how the static modifier affects class members.

Listings 7.2 and 7.3 pull together the class concepts presented in this chapter. It is a full working program. It also contains full XML documentation from which to generate an XML file.

This chapter focused primarily on the composition, syntax, and structure of a C# class. The next chapter takes concepts presented in Chapter 6, combines them with the mechanics of this chapter, and produces a complete explanation of how to implement an object-oriented program in C#.

CHAPTER

Designing Object-Oriented Programs

In This Chapter

- **Inheritance** *178*
- **Encapsulating Object Internals** *198*
- **Polymorphism** *200*

C# is a modern object-oriented programming language. As such it has many new features to support object-oriented programming. The preceding chapter covered the proper syntax of classes and their members. This chapter takes you a step further. It builds upon what has already been presented to create object-oriented programs.

This chapter discusses inheritance, the capability to derive new classes from existing ones. It solidifies what has been presented about encapsulation. Then it examines the nuances of polymorphism, allowing classes to dynamically modify their runtime behavior. This chapter provides a basis for how to do detailed design of object-oriented programs with C# as an implementation language.

Inheritance

Inheritance is an object-oriented term relating to how one class, a derived class, can share the characteristics and behavior from another class, a base class. There should be a natural parent/child relationship between the base class and the derived class, respectively. This can be thought of as an "is a" relationship, because the derived class can be identified by both its class type and its base class type. Essentially, any base class members with protected or greater access also belong to a derived class.

The benefits gained by this are the ability to reuse the base class members and also to add members to the derived class. The derived class then becomes a specialization of the parent. This specialization can continue for as many levels as necessary, each new level derived from the base class above it. In the opposite direction, going up the inheritance hierarchy, there is more generalization at each new base class traversed. Regardless of how many levels between classes, the "is a" relationship holds.

Base Classes

Normal base classes may be instantiated themselves, or inherited. Derived classes inherit each base class member marked with protected or greater access. The derived class is specialized to provide more functionality, in addition to what its base class provides.

A derived class declares that it inherits from a base class by adding a colon (`:`) and the base class name after the derived class name. Here's an example:

```
public class Contact
{
    string name;
    string email;
    string address;

    public Contact()
    {
```

```
            // statements ...
        }

        public string Name
        {
            get
            {
                return name;
            }
            set
            {
                name = value;
            }
        }

        public string Email
        {
            get
            {
                return email;
            }
            set
            {
                email = value;
            }
        }

        public string Address
        {
            get
            {
                return address;
            }
            set
            {
                address = value;
            }
        }
    }

    public class Customer : Contact
    {
        string gender;
        decimal income;

        public Customer()
        {
            // statements ...
        }
    }
```

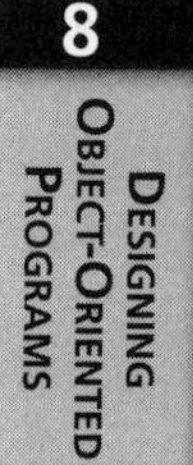

In the example, the `Contact` class is inherited by the `Customer` class. This means the `Customer` class possesses all the same members as its base class (`Contact`) in addition to its own. In this case, `Customer` has the properties `Name`, `Email`, and `Address`.

Since Customer is a specialization of Contact, it has its own unique members: gender and income.

Abstract Classes

Abstract classes are a special type of base classes. In addition to normal class members, they have abstract class members. These Abstract class members are methods and properties that are declared without an implementation. All classes derived directly from abstract classes must implement these abstract methods and properties.

Abstract classes can never be instantiated. This would be illogical, because of the members without implementations. So what good is a class that can't be instantiated? Lots! Abstract classes sit toward the top of a class hierarchy. They establish structure and meaning to code. They make frameworks easier to build. This is possible because abstract classes have information and behavior common to all derived classes in a framework. Take a look at the following example:

```
abstract public class Contact
{
    protected string name;

    public Contact()
    {
        // statements...
    }

    public abstract void generateReport();

    abstract public string Name
    {
        get;
        set;
    }}

public class Customer : Contact
{
    string gender;
    decimal income;
    int numberOfVisits;

    public Customer()
    {
        // statements
```

```
    }

    public override void generateReport()
    {
        // unique report
    }

    public override string Name
    {
        get
        {
            numberOfVisits++;
            return name;
        }
        set
        {
            name = value;
            numberOfVisits = 0;
        }
    }
}

public class SiteOwner : Contact
{
    int siteHits;
    string mySite;

    public SiteOwner()
    {
        // statements...
    }

    public override void generateReport()
    {
        // unique report
    }

    public override string Name
    {
        get
        {
            siteHits++;
            return name;
        }
        set
        {
            name = value;
            siteHits = 0;
        }
    }
}
```

This example has three classes. The first class, `Contact`, is now an abstract class. This is shown as the first modifier of its class declaration. `Contact` has two abstract members, and it has an abstract method named `generateReport()`. This method is declared with the abstract modifier in front of the method declaration. It has no implementation (no braces) and is terminated with a semicolon. The `Name` property is also declared abstract. The accessors of properties are terminated with semicolons.

The abstract base class `Contact` has two derived classes, `Customer` and `SiteOwner`. Both of these derived classes implement the abstract members of the `Contact` class. The `generateReport()` method in each derived class has an `override` modifier in its declaration. Likewise, the `Name` declaration contains an `override` modifier in both `Customer` and `SiteOwner`.

The `override` modifier for the overridden `generateReport()` method and `Name` property is mandatory. C# requires explicit declaration of intent when overriding methods. This feature promotes safe code by avoiding the accidental overriding of base class methods, which is what actually does happen in other languages. Leaving out the `override` modifier generates an error. Similarly, adding a `new` modifier also generates an error. Abstract methods must be overridden and cannot be hidden, which the `new` modifier or the lack of a modifier would be trying to do.

Notice the `name` field in the `Contact` class. It has a `protected` modifier. Remember, a `protected` modifier allows derived classes to access base class members. In this case, it enables the overridden `Name` property to access the `name` field in the `Contact` class.

The most famous of all abstract classes is the `Object` class. It may be referred to as `object` or `Object`, but it's still the same class. `Object` is the base class for all other classes in C#. It's also the default base class when a base class is not specified. The following class declarations produce the same exact results:

```
abstract public class Contact : Object
{
    // class members
}

abstract public class Contact
{
    // class members
}
```

`Object` is implicitly included as a base class if it is not already declared. Besides providing the abstract glue to hold together the C# class framework, `object` includes built-in functionality, some of which is useful for derived classes to implement. Table 8.1 lists each `object` method and its purpose.

TABLE 8.1 Object Class Methods

Method	*Purpose*
`Equals()`	Compares object references for equality.
`GetHashCode()`	Returns a hash code for an object.
`GetType()`	Returns the type of the object.
`ToString()`	Returns a string representation of an object.
`Finalize()`	Same as a destructor.
`MemberwiseClone()`	Performs shallow copy of an object.

All of the methods in Table 8.1 are public, except for `Finalize()` and `MemberwiseClone()`, which are protected. The `GetType()` and `MemberwiseClone()` methods may not be overridden, but all others may. Listing 8.1 shows an example of using object methods.

LISTING 8.1 Object Class Member Implementations in a Derived Class

```
using System;

public class WebSite
{
    public string SiteName;
    public string URL;
    public string Description;
    public WebSite()
    {
    }

    public WebSite( string strSiteName, string strURL, string strDescription )
    {
        SiteName    = strSiteName;
        URL         = strURL;
        Description = strDescription;
    }
}

abstract public class Contact
{
    protected string name;

    public Contact()
    {
        // initialization code...
    }
```

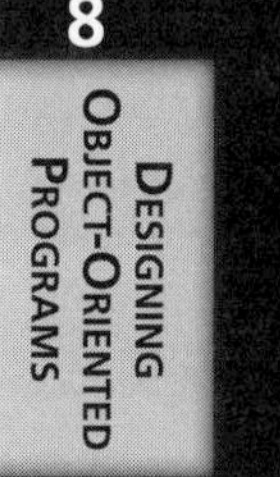

LISTING 8.1 continued

```
    public abstract string generateReport();

    abstract public string Name
    {
        get;
        set;
    }
}

public class SiteOwner : Contact
{
    int siteHits;
    WebSite mySite;

    public SiteOwner()
    {
        mySite = new WebSite();
        siteHits = 0;
    }

    public SiteOwner(string aName, WebSite aSite)
    {
        mySite = new WebSite(aSite.SiteName,
                             aSite.URL,
                             aSite.Description);

        Name = aName;
    }

    public override string generateReport()
    {
        return this.ToString();
    }

    public override string Name
    {
        get
        {
            siteHits++;
            return name;
        }
        set
        {
            name = value;
            siteHits = 0;
        }
    }
```

LISTING 8.1 continued

```
    public override string ToString()
    {
        return "["                +
               Name               +
               ", "               +
               siteHits.ToString() +
               "]";
    }

    public override bool Equals(Object anOwner)
    {
        return this.ToString().Equals(anOwner.ToString());
    }

    public override int GetHashCode()
    {
        return this.ToString().GetHashCode();
    }

    public SiteOwner Clone()
    {
        return (SiteOwner) this.MemberwiseClone();
    }
}

public class Test
{
    public Test() {}

    public static void Main()
    {
        WebSite mySite = new WebSite("Le Financier",
                                     "www.LeFinancier.com",
                                     "Fancy Financial Site");

        SiteOwner firstOwner  = new SiteOwner("Jack", mySite);
        SiteOwner secondOwner = firstOwner.Clone();

        Console.WriteLine("Report:    {0}",
            firstOwner.generateReport());
        Console.WriteLine("To String: {0}",
            firstOwner.ToString());
        Console.WriteLine("Hash Code: {0}",
            firstOwner.GetHashCode());

        Console.WriteLine("Report:    {0}",
            secondOwner.generateReport());
        Console.WriteLine("To String: {0}",
            secondOwner.ToString());
```

LISTING 8.1 continued

```
        Console.WriteLine("Hash Code: {0}",
            secondOwner.GetHashCode());

        Console.WriteLine(
            "1stOwner: {0} equals: {1} 2ndOwner: {2}.",
            firstOwner.Name,
            firstOwner.Equals(secondOwner),
            secondOwner.Name);

        Console.WriteLine(
            "2nd Equality Check: {0}",
            firstOwner.Equals(secondOwner));

        Console.WriteLine("Report:    {0}",
            firstOwner.generateReport());
        Console.WriteLine("To String: {0}",
            firstOwner.ToString());
        Console.WriteLine("Hash Code: {0}",
            firstOwner.GetHashCode());

        Console.WriteLine("Report:    {0}",
            secondOwner.generateReport());
        Console.WriteLine("To String: {0}",
            secondOwner.ToString());
        Console.WriteLine("Hash Code: {0}",
            secondOwner.GetHashCode());
    }
}
```

And here's its output:

```
Report:    [Jack, 1]
To String: [Jack, 2]
Hash Code: 179554879
Report:    [Jack, 1]
To String: [Jack, 2]
Hash Code: 179554879
1stOwner: Jack equals: False 2ndOwner: Jack.
2nd Equality Check: True
Report:    [Jack, 7]
To String: [Jack, 8]
Hash Code: 179555189
Report:    [Jack, 7]
To String: [Jack, 8]
Hash Code: 179555189
```

Listing 8.1 contains three classes to show implementation of `object` methods. The `Contact` class is the base class for the `SiteOwner` class. Although the `Contact` class possesses functionality and abstract definitions, it does not contain overridden methods from the `Object` class. The `SiteOwner` class does have the overridden methods from the `Object` class. This shows that a class doesn't have to inherit directly from a base class to override its members.

The `SiteOwner` class overrides three of Object's methods, `ToString()`, `Equals()`, and `GetHashCode()`. Each of these methods has the `override` modifier in its declaration. The `Object` class method definitions for these members are not invoked because the `Object` class method definitions are overridden by `SiteOwner`.

The `ToString()` method returns a string representation of an object's contents. This is often useful for debugging where the contents of an object are dumped to an error log file or perhaps to the console. In this case, `ToString()` concatenates `Name` and `siteHits` and formats them into a string to be returned to the calling program. This example uses the `ToString()` method extensively.

The `Equals()` method compares the current `SiteOwner`'s `ToString()` method to the value of the parameter's `ToString()` method. This comparison takes advantage of the built-in capabilities of the string type.

The `GetHashCode()` method executes the `ToString()` method of the current `SiteOwner` and uses that to get a hash code. A hash value is normally calculated from a key value that is not expected to change within an object. In this case, the process is simplified by using the string type's built-in `GetHashCode()` method. Hash codes are useful for any function requiring a unique integer value from a class. The most common use of this is with the `HashTable` collection class.

The `Clone()` method uses `Object`'s `MemberwiseClone()` method. The `Object` class's `MemberwiseClone()` method can't be overridden and has protected access. Therefore, other objects cannot call this method on an instance of `SiteOwner`. This is why this method call is wrapped in the `Clone()` method.

The output of this program is somewhat strange. The first comparison, where `firstOwner` is compared to `secondOwner`, fails. However, the second comparison, immediately after that, passes. What gives?

Fortunately, the `ToString()` printouts provide some clues. The second parameter of the `ToString()` method output increments from 1 to 2 in the first pair of printouts before the equality checks. After the equality checks, the numbers increment from 7 to 8. Going back to the `ToString()` method shows this second parameter is the `siteHits` field.

Further investigation reveals that the only place where the `siteHits` field is modified is in the `get` accessor of the `Name` property. This shows why the number is changing. Every time `ToString()` executes, it uses the `Name` property. This invokes the `get` accessor of `Name`, which increments `siteName`. Since, during processing of the `ToString()` method, the `get` accessor of `Name` executes before `siteHits` is read, the printout never shows `siteHits` as being 0.

So, to explain the printouts: `ToString()` is called twice for each object, `firstOwner` and `secondOwner`, incrementing `siteHits` twice. This leaves `siteHits` at 2 on both objects. In the equality check, `firstOwner.Name` is accessed, leaving `firstOwner.siteHits` at 3. Now, `secondOwner.siteHits` is still 2 because its `Name` property has not been accessed. Therefore, when the `Equals()` method is called, these two objects produce different strings and are, in fact, not equal. Finally, `secondOwner.Name` is accessed, incrementing its `siteHits` to 3. Now both objects produce the same strings, so when `Equals()` is called again on the next line it returns `true`. The rest of the printouts should be understandable after this explanation.

Warning

Properties can have side effects. In the `ToString()` method of this chapter, it seemed pretty slick to update the `siteHit` every time the `Name` property was read. Perhaps some motivation for this would be that every time a site was visited, the Site Owner's name would be referenced. This was a narrow view of how this class could be used. The choice to use the `Name` property in the `ToString()` method seemed natural, but the side effect of incrementing the `siteHits` field caused a potentially serious bug. When building a class, think about how properties will be used.

A couple of `Object` methods not shown here are `GetType()` and `Finalize()`. The `GetType()` method is shown later in the chapter, when polymorphism is discussed. The `Finalize()` method is normally never used in a class declaration. The destructor syntax is used instead. Destructors and Finalizers are the same thing. During compilation, C# converts all destructors to the `Finalize()` method, for compatibility with other languages conforming to Common Language Infrastructure (CLI) standards. This enables the garbage collector to work with `Finalize()` methods instead of language specific syntax.

Calling Base Class Members

Derived classes can access the members of their base class if those members have protected or greater access. Simply use the member name in the appropriate context, just as if that member were a part of the derived class itself. Here's an example:

```
abstract public class Contact
{
    private string address;
    private string city;
    private string state;
    private string zip;

    public string FullAddress()
    {
        string fullAddress =
            address + '\n' +
            city + ',' + state + ' ' + zip;

        return fullAddress;
    }
}

public class Customer : Contact
{
    public string GenerateReport()
    {
        string fullAddress = FullAddress();
        // do some other stuff...
        return fullAddress;
    }
}
```

In this example, the `GenerateReport()` method of the `Customer` class calls the `FullAddress()` method in its base class, `Contact`. All classes have full access to their own members without qualification. Qualification refers to using a class name with the dot operator to access a class member—`MyObject.SomeMethod()`, for instance. This shows that a derived class can access its base class members in the same manner as its own.

Base class constructors can be called from derived classes. To call a base class constructor, use the `base()` constructor reference. This is desirable when it's necessary to initialize a base class appropriately.

Here's an example that shows the derived class constructor with an address parameter:

```
abstract public class Contact
{
    private string address;

    public Contact(string address)
    {
        this.address = address;
    }
}
```

```
public class Customer : Contact
{
    public Customer(string address) : base(address)
    {
    }
}
```

In this code, the `Customer` class does not have an address, so it passes the parameter to its base class constructor by adding a colon and the base keyword with the parameter to its declaration. This calls the `Contact` constructor with the address parameter, where the `address` field in `Contact` is initialized.

Warning

Depending on the design of a class hierarchy, failure to initialize base class constructors may leave code in an inconsistent state.

The following example will not compile. It illustrates the effects of not including a default constructor in a class definition:

```
abstract public class Contact
{
    private string address;

    public Contact(string address)
    {
        this.address = address;
    }
}

public class Customer : Contact
{
    public Customer(string address)
    {
    }
}
```

In this example, the `Customer` constructor does not call the base class constructor. This is obviously a bug, since the `address` field will never be initialized.

When a class has no explicit constructor, the system assigns a default constructor. The default constructor automatically calls a default or parameterless base constructor. Here's an example of automatic default constructor generation that would occur for the preceding example:

```
public Customer() : Contact()
{
}
```

When a class does not declare any constructors, the code in this example is automatically generated. The default base class constructor is called implicitly when no derived class constructors are defined. Once a derived class constructor is defined, whether or not it has parameters, a default constructor will not be automatically defined, as the preceding code showed.

Hiding Base Class Members

Sometimes derived class members have the same name as a corresponding base class member. In this case, the derived member is said to be "hiding" the base class member. When hiding occurs, the derived member is masking the functionality of the base class member. Users of the derived class won't be able to see the hidden member; they'll see only the derived class member. The following code shows how hiding a base class member works. If you're compiling this example now, please disregard the compiler warning, which I explain at the start of the next section, "Versioning."

```
abstract public class Contact
{
    private string address;
    private string city;
    private string state;
    private string zip;

    public string FullAddress()
    {
        string fullAddress =
            address + '\n' +
            city + ',' + state + ' ' + zip;

        return fullAddress;
    }
}

public class SiteOwner : Contact
{
    public string FullAddress()
    {
        string fullAddress;

        // create an address...
        return fullAddress;
    }
}
```

In this example, both SiteOwner and its base class, Contact, have a method named FullAddress(). The FullAddress() method in the SiteOwner class hides the FullAddress() method in the Contact class. This means that when an instance of a SiteOwner class is invoked with a call to the FullAddress() method, it is the SiteOwner class FullAddress() method that is called, not the FullAddress() method of the Contact class.

Although a base class member may be hidden, the derived class can still access it. It does this through the base identifier. Sometimes this is desirable. It is often useful to take advantage of the base class functionality and then add to it with the derived class code. The next example shows how to refer to a base class method from the derived class. If compiling this code now, please disregard the warnings, which I explain at the start of the next section, "Versioning."

```
abstract public class Contact
{
    private string address;
    private string city;
    private string state;
    private string zip;

    public string FullAddress()
    {
        string fullAddress =
            address + '\n' +
            city + ',' + state + ' ' + zip;

        return fullAddress;
    }
}

public class SiteOwner : Contact
{
    public string FullAddress()
    {
        string fullAddress = base.FullAddress();

        // do some other stuff...
        return fullAddress;
    }
}
```

In this particular example, the FullAddress() method of the Contact class is called from within the FullAddress() method of the SiteOwner class. This is accomplished with a base class reference. This provides another way to reuse code and add on to it with customized behavior.

Versioning

Versioning, in the context of inheritance, is a C# mechanism that allows modification of classes (creating new versions) without accidentally changing the meaning of the code. Hiding a base class member with the methods previously described generates a warning message from the compiler. This is because of the C# versioning policy. It's designed to eliminate a class of problems associated with modifications to base classes.

Warning

Often these warning messages scroll off the screen or are overlooked during compilation in an IDE. These overlooked warnings could be early indications of a bug.

Here's the scenario: A developer creates a class that inherits from a third-party library. For the purposes of this discussion, we assume that the `Contact` class represents the third-party library. Here's the example:

```
public class Contact
{
    // does not include FullAddress() method
}

public class SiteOwner : Contact
{
    public string FullAddress()
    {
        string fullAddress = mySite.ToString();

        return fullAddress;
    }
}
```

In this example, the `FullAddress()` method does not exist in the base class. There is no problem yet. Later on, the creators of the third-party library update their code. Part of this update includes a new member in a base class with the exact same name as the derived class:

```
public class Contact
{
    private string address;
    private string city;
    private string state;
    private string zip;
```

```
    public string FullAddress()
    {
        string fullAddress =
            address + '\n' +
            city + ',' + state + ' ' + zip;

        return fullAddress;
    }
}

public class SiteOwner : Contact
{
    public string FullAddress()
    {
        string fullAddress = mySite.ToString();

        return fullAddress;
    }
}
```

In this code, the base class method `FullAddress()` contains different functionality than the derived class method. In other languages, this scenario would break the code because of implicit polymorphism. (Polymorphism is discussed later in this chapter.) However, this does not break any code in C# because when the `FullAddress()` method is called on `SiteOwner`, it is still the `SiteOwner` class method that gets called.

This scenario generates a warning message. One way to eliminate the warning message is to place a `new` modifier in front of the derived class method name, as the following example shows:

```
using System;

public class WebSite
{
    public string SiteName;
    public string URL;
    public string Description;

    public WebSite()
    {
    }

    public WebSite( string strSiteName, string strURL, string strDescription )
    {
        SiteName    = strSiteName;
        URL         = strURL;
        Description = strDescription;
    }
```

```
    public override string ToString()
    {
        return SiteName + ", " +
               URL      + ", " +
               Description;
    }
}


public class Contact
{
    public string address;
    public string city;
    public string state;
    public string zip;

    public string FullAddress()
    {
        string fullAddress =
            address + '\n' +
            city + ',' + state + ' ' + zip;

        return fullAddress;
    }
}

public class SiteOwner : Contact
{
    int     siteHits;
    string  name;
    WebSite mySite;

    public SiteOwner()
    {
        mySite = new WebSite();
        siteHits = 0;
    }

    public SiteOwner(string aName, WebSite aSite)
    {
        mySite = new WebSite(aSite.SiteName,
                             aSite.URL,
                             aSite.Description);

        Name = aName;
    }

    new public string FullAddress()
    {
        string fullAddress = mySite.ToString();
```

```
        return fullAddress;
    }

    public string Name
    {
        get
        {
            siteHits++;
            return name;
        }
        set
        {
            name = value;
            siteHits = 0;
        }
    }
}

public class Test
{
    public static void Main()
    {
        WebSite mySite = new WebSite("Le Financier",
                                     "www.LeFinancier.com",
                                     "Fancy Financial Site");

        SiteOwner anOwner = new SiteOwner("John Doe", mySite);
        string address;

        anOwner.address = "123 Lane Lane";
        anOwner.city    = "Some Town";
        anOwner.state   = "HI";
        anOwner.zip     = "45678";

        address = anOwner.FullAddress();  // Different Results
        Console.WriteLine("Address: \n{0}\n", address);

    }
}
```

Here's the output:

```
Address:
Le Financier, www.LeFinancier.com, Fancy Financial Site
```

This has the effect of explicitly letting the compiler know the developer's intent. Placing the `new` modifier in front of the derived class member states that the developers know there is a base class method with the same name, and they definitely want to hide that member. This prevents breakage of existing code that depends on the implementation of the derived class member. With C#, the method in the derived class is called when an object of the derived class type is used. Likewise, the method in the base class is called when an object of the Base class type is called. Another problem this presents is that the base class may present some desirable new features that wouldn't be available through the derived class.

To use these new features requires one of a few different workarounds. One option would be to rename the derived class member, which would allow programs to use a base class method through a derived class member. The drawback to this option would be if there were other classes relying upon the implementation of the derived class member with the same name. This scenario will break code and, for this reason, is considered extremely bad form.

Another option is to define a new method in the derived class that called the base class method. This allows users of the derived class to have the new functionality of the base class, yet retain their existing functionality with the derived class. While this would work, there are maintainability concerns for the derived class.

Sealed Classes

Sealed classes are classes that can't be derived from. To prevent other classes from inheriting from a class, make it a sealed class. There are a couple good reasons to create sealed classes, including optimization and security.

Sealing a class avoids the system overhead associated with virtual methods. (The "Polymorphism" section later in this chapter has in-depth discussion of virtual methods.) This allows the compiler to perform certain optimizations that are otherwise unavailable with normal classes.

Another good reason to seal a class is for security. Inheritance, by its very nature, dictates a certain amount of protected access to the internals of a potential base class. Sealing a class does away with the possibility of corruption by derived classes. A good example of a sealed class is the String class. The following example shows how to create a sealed class:

```
public sealed class CustomerStats
{
    string gender;
    decimal income;
    int numberOfVisits;

    public CustomerStats()
    {
    }
}
```

```
public class CustomerInfo : CustomerStats // error
{
}

public class Customer
{
    CustomerStats myStats;  // okay
}
```

This example generates a compiler error. Since the CustomerStats class is sealed, it can't be inherited by the CustomerInfo class. The CustomerStats class was meant to be used as an encapsulated object in another class. This is shown by the declaration of a CustomerStats object in the Customer class.

Encapsulating Object Internals

Encapsulation is an object-oriented concept associated with hiding the internals of a class from the outside world. C# has several mechanisms for supporting encapsulation. Some, such as properties and indexers, are new concepts we haven't seen implemented in languages before. There are several reasons to take advantage of C#'s built-in mechanisms for managing encapsulation:

- Good encapsulation reduces coupling. By using only those class members exposed, users can write code with less dependency on that class.
- Internal implementation of a class can freely change. This reduces the possibility of breaking someone else's code.
- A class has a much cleaner interface. Users only see those members that are exposed, which reduces the amount of understanding they need to use a class. It simplifies reuse.

Data Hiding

One of the most useful forms of encapsulation is data hiding. Most of the time, users shouldn't have access to the internal data of a class. Class data represents the state of an object. A class normally has full control of its own state to guarantee its consistent behavior. Anytime access to data is opened, the potential of someone else wreaking havoc with the operation of that class increases.

There are times when it's logical and necessary to expose class data—especially if it's necessary to expose constants, enumerations, and read-only fields. Perhaps a design goal is to increase the efficiency of data access for a field that's accessed frequently. The decisions made depend on the requirements. However, give serious consideration to proper encapsulation of class information.

Modifiers Supporting Encapsulation

Manage class encapsulation with appropriate use of C# access modifiers, which specify who can access class members. They also control the method of access:

- Private access is the most restrictive. This allows members, only within a class, to access another member marked as private. Anyone outside the class cannot access this member. They won't even know it's there without source code or documentation telling them otherwise. Private access is useful because it allows modification of a private member implementation without anyone knowing.
- Protected access is a little less restrictive than private. Users may know the member is in a class, but they can't access protected members directly. The only way to use a protected member is through inheritance. A derived class has full access to protected base class members. This is regardless of the depth of the hierarchy. The protected member need not be in the derived class's immediate base class. Protected access is good for optimization when a derived class needs frequent access to base class information.
- Internal access is for use only in the program or project where the data resides. If data only has particular relevancy in the context of a single program, this access is useful. This type of modifier would be used for in-house projects where a given class member was used by other teams on the same project. Other programs or user code would have no idea that this internal class member existed.
- Protected Internal is a combination of protected and internal modifiers. It's a little bit more open than straight internal, allowing all members of a program to access the member. Additionally, derived classes of base classes in a program with protected internal members can access those members if they are either other program members or external user code. This access is useful for third-party libraries where users need access to protected members, with the added convenience that in-house developers would have free utilization of that class member without restriction.
- Public access is the least restrictive of all. It lets anyone and everyone have access to class members without restriction. Public access is necessary to publish the interface of a class. It is through these members that communication with a class is accomplished. Great care should be taken to ensure that only those members contributing to effective use of an interface to a class are made public.

Other Encapsulation Strategies

The purpose of properties and indexers is to encapsulate the details of a class and provide a public interface to users of the class. See Chapter 7, "Working with Classes," for a detailed description of properties and indexers. Since one of their purposes is encapsulation, it's wise to use them as much as practical.

Relationship of Encapsulation to Inheritance

Encapsulation implies containment, where one object is inside of another. This is the "has a" relationship. An object inside another object is a field of its containing object.

When speaking of inheritance, it's useful to think of the "is a" relationship, where a class is a part of the classification hierarchy associated with its parent class.

Inheritance and containment are two different concepts, but one can be used improperly in place of the other. This text has repeatedly spoken of the "natural" inheritance hierarchy that is implemented between objects. Studies have shown inheritance is sometimes used where it doesn't necessarily make sense. For a good discussion, see *C++ Programming Style*, Tom Cargill, 1992, Addison-Wesley. Inheritance is good when applied naturally and is a good fit for the problem.

An alternative to inheritance is containment. By encapsulating one object within another, a class can control what behavior is used by derived classes. If need be, it can provide access to each member of the contained object through its own methods. In contrast, all class members in a base class, accessible to a derived class, are also accessible to further derivation. The efforts required to restrict base class access through a derived class would be tedious and error prone. Containment helps encapsulate the contained object's members.

Another factor to consider is that C# has only single inheritance. This means it can inherit functionality only from a single base class. Therefore, if a class already inherits from a base class, containment is the only way to reuse pre-canned functionality.

For C++ Programmers

C++ has multiple inheritance, whereas C# allows only single inheritance.

Polymorphism

Earlier sections of this chapter covered abstract classes, including the ultimate abstract class, `object`. It showed how to implement overrides of virtual classes in the `object` class. This section goes further by explaining how virtual classes are overridden, why, and what good it is. This capability enables an object-oriented programming concept known as polymorphism.

Implementing Polymorphism

To begin, it's useful to get an appreciation of the problem polymorphism solves. The key factor is the ability to dynamically invoke methods in a class based on their type. Essentially, a program would have a group of objects, examine the type of each one, and execute the appropriate method. Here's an example:

```
using System;

public class WebSite
{
    public string SiteName;
    public string URL;
    public string Description;

    public WebSite()
    {
    }

    public WebSite( string strSiteName, string strURL, string strDescription )
    {
        SiteName    = strSiteName;
        URL         = strURL;
        Description = strDescription;
    }

    public override string ToString()
    {
        return SiteName + ", " +
               URL      + ", " +
               Description;
    }
}

abstract public class Contact
{
    public virtual string UpdateNotify()
    {
        return "Web Site Change Notification";
    }
}

public class Customer : Contact
{
    public new string UpdateNotify()
    {
        return @"
This is to let you know your
favorite site, Financial Times,
has been updated with new links";
```

```
    }
}

public class SiteOwner : Contact
{
    WebSite mySite;

    public SiteOwner(string aName, WebSite aSite)
    {
        mySite = new WebSite(aSite.SiteName,
                             aSite.URL,
                             aSite.Description);
    }

    public new string UpdateNotify()
    {
        return @"
This is to let you know your site, " + "\n" +
mySite.SiteName + @", has been added as
a link to Financial Times.";
    }
}

public class Test
{
    public static void Main()
    {
        WebSite leFin = new WebSite("Le Financier",
                                    "www.LeFinancier.com",
                                    "Fancy Financial Site");

        Contact[] Contacts = new Contact[2];

        Contacts[0] = new SiteOwner("Pierre Doe", leFin);
        Contacts[1] = new Customer();

        foreach (Contact poc in Contacts)
        {
            if (poc is SiteOwner)
            {
                Console.WriteLine("Message: {0}\n",
                 ((SiteOwner)poc).UpdateNotify());
            }
            else
            {
                Console.WriteLine("Message: {0}\n",
                 ((Customer)poc).UpdateNotify());
            }
        }
    }
}
```

In this example, the `Main()` method of the `Test` class creates an array of `Contact` objects. It puts a `SiteOwner` object and a `Customer` object in the array. Each of these classes has an `UpdateNotify()` method, and the point of this program is to call the `UpdateNotify()` method belonging to each object.

The `foreach` loop checks the type of each object with the `is` operator. Depending on the type, the `poc` object is cast to that type and used in the `Console.WriteLine()` method. Here's another technique that could be used in the preceding `foreach` loop:

```
foreach (Contact poc in Contacts)
{
    SiteOwner anOwner = poc as SiteOwner;

    if (anOwner != null)
    {
        Console.WriteLine("Message: {0}\n",
                          anOwner.UpdateNotify());
    }
    else
    {
        Console.WriteLine("Message: {0}\n",
                         ((Customer)poc).UpdateNotify());
    }
}
```

This example uses the `as` operator. The `as` operator does an assignment of one object to another object when the type on the right side of the `as` operator is the same as the object on its left. Otherwise, the `as` operator returns `null`. This is more efficient than the `is` operator because the `is` operator required a type check and an assignment in two separate steps. In that last code example, the `if` statement only needs to check whether the value is not `null` and to execute the `SiteOwner` class `UpdateNotify()` method when this condition is `true`. Otherwise, the `UpdateNotify()` method of the `Customer` class is executed. Although the cast is necessary for `Customer` objects, using `as` is still more efficient because half of the objects don't need a cast.

Tip

Use the `as` operator for greater efficiency when iterating through a list of objects requiring type checks and casting. Use the `is` operator when a single object is being type checked or when casting is not necessary.

The preceding examples accomplish the task of dynamically invoking object methods. However, there is a more efficient and elegant way to accomplish the same thing. This method is called polymorphism. Polymorphism is efficient because C# rather than explicit coding is managing this process. It's also more elegant because there is less code, which makes for a simpler implementation.

Polymorphism is the capability of a program to carry out dynamic operations by implementing methods of multiple derived classes through a common base class reference. Another definition of polymorphism is the ability to treat different objects the same way. This means that the runtime type of an object determines its behavior rather than the compile-time type of its reference. Chapter 6, "Object and Component Concepts," discussed polymorphic behavior at a simplified and abstract level. It may help to review Chapter 6 and visualize those concepts before proceeding.

It's sometimes necessary to manipulate a collection of objects with multiple object types. A common task is to iterate through these objects performing some type of similar operation. Since the object types are different, it usually isn't possible to perform the same operation on each one. However, it would be convenient to request the same type of operation with specialized behavior for each object type. This is accomplished through polymorphism in a very efficient manner.

Imagine a scenario where a Web site creates notifications to multiple contacts about updates. There are different types of `Contacts` that require different types of notifications, but they are all `Contacts`. This example makes the assumption that `Contact` is a well-defined and natural abstraction for this purpose.

There are two types of `Contacts` interested in Web site updates: `Customer` and `SiteOwner`. While both types of `Contacts` are interested in updates, the actual message generated to each will be different, because each of their particular interests is different. Polymorphism is a useful tool to solve this problem. Take a look at the following example:

```
using System;

abstract public class Contact
{
    public virtual string UpdateNotify()
    {
        return "Web Site Change Notification";
    }
}

public class Customer : Contact
{
    public override string UpdateNotify()
    {
        return @"
This is to let you know your
favorite site, Financial Times,
```

```
has been updated with new links";
    }
}

public class SiteOwner : Contact
{
    string siteName;

    public SiteOwner(string sName)
    {
        siteName = sName;
    }

    public override string UpdateNotify()
    {
        return @"
This is to let you know your site, " + "\n" +
siteName + @", has been added as
a link to Financial Times.";
    }
}
```

This example shows three primary classes: `Contact`, `Customer`, and `SiteOwner`. `Contact` is the abstract base class for the other two, providing a virtual `UpdateNotify()` method. Both `Customer` and `SiteOwner` override the `Contact` class `UpdateNotify()` method.

Virtual methods are those base class methods that enable polymorphism to work. They use the `virtual` modifier to indicate that they can be overridden by derived classes. The difference between abstract methods and virtual methods is that virtual methods have implementations, and abstract methods don't. Abstract methods are implicitly virtual, and they must be overridden. Virtual methods don't have to be overridden.

The `override` keyword indicates that a derived class method can be invoked at runtime, instead of the virtual base class method. The key points are

- The object reference is a base class type, declaring the virtual method.
- The runtime object is of the derived type with the overriding method.

The following code snippet shows polymorphism at work:

```
public class Test
{
    public static void Main()
    {
        Contact[] Contacts = new Contact[2];

        Contacts[0] = new SiteOwner("Le Financier");
        Contacts[1] = new Customer();
```

```
        foreach (Contact poc in Contacts)
        {
            Console.WriteLine("Message: {0}\n",
                              poc.UpdateNotify());
        }
    }
}
```

And here's the output:

```
Message:
This is to let you know your site,
Le Financier, has been added as
a link to Financial Times.

Message:
This is to let you know your
favorite site, Financial Times,
has been updated with new links
```

This example shows a simple implementation using polymorphism. The program declares the array `Contacts` (plural) of type `Contact`. This is the first key point, the fact that the `Contacts` array possesses base class references to a virtual method. Also, `Contact` is the compile-time type of each `Contacts` array object.

Next, the program assigns objects of type `SiteOwner` and `Customer` to the `Contacts` array elements. This is the second key point, the fact that the runtime type of the object is a derived class with an override on a base class virtual method.

At runtime, the `foreach` loop uses the `UpdateNotify()` method of each `Contacts` array object. Although the compile-time type of each object is `Contact`, the `Contact` class virtual `UpdateNotify()` method is not executed. Instead, the overridden `UpdateNotify()` method of each derived class is executed.

Hiding Again

Now let's look at some scenarios with polymorphism-related modifiers and versioning. Using an `override` modifier in a derived class where there is no corresponding virtual method in a base class yields an error as in the following example:

```
abstract public class Contact
{
    public virtual string UpdateNotify()
    {
        return "Web Site Change Notification";
    }
}
```

```
public class Customer : Contact
{
    public override string SendMail() {}// error

    public override string UpdateNotify(int number) {}// error
}
```

This code produces an error during compilation. This is because the `SendMail()` method is declared with an `override` modifier, and there is not a corresponding virtual method to be overridden.

The same error occurs with the `UpdateNotify()` method in the `Customer` class. However, the reason is somewhat different. The `UpdateNotify()` method in the `Customer` class has a parameter, but the `UpdateNotify()` method of the `Contact` class doesn't have any parameters. Since there is a signature mismatch, polymorphism can't occur, and compilation generates an error. Remember, a method's signature consists of its name, number of parameters, and type of each parameter.

A virtual modifier by itself presents no problem at all. It's normal to label a method with a virtual modifier to indicate its availability for polymorphism to potential derived classes. This way any future classes may inherit from the class and override its virtual method.

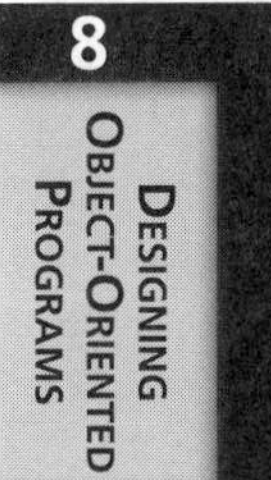

When a derived class adds a normal method, with no modifiers, with the same signature of a base class virtual method, it generates a compile-time warning. This is the same behavior as described earlier with hiding. If you compile the following code, it generates a compiler warning:

```
abstract public class Contact
{
    public virtual string UpdateNotify()
    {
        return "Web Site Change Notification";
    }
}

public class Customer : Contact
{
    public string UpdateNotify()
    {
        return @"
This is to let you know your
favorite site, Financial Times,
has been updated with new links";
    }
}
```

There are two ways to correct this example. One is to add an `override` modifier to the derived class method:

```
public override string UpdateNotify() {...}
```

The other way is to add the `new` modifier to the derived class method. This hides the base class virtual method. Since the derived class hides the base class virtual method, any further derivations from the original derived class are not able to see the original base class virtual method. Here's an example:

```
public new string UpdateNotify() {...}
```

Earlier, there was an example of the `UpdateNotify()` method where each derived class overrode the virtual `UpdateNotify()` method in the `Contact` class. Here's an example of what happens when a virtual method is not overridden:

```
using System;

abstract public class Contact
{
    public virtual string UpdateNotify()
    {
        return "Web Site Change Notification";
    }
}

public class Customer : Contact
{
    public new string UpdateNotify()
    {
        return @"
This is to let you know your
favorite site, Financial Times,
has been updated with new links";
    }
}

public class SiteOwner : Contact
{
    string siteName;

    public SiteOwner(string sName)
    {
        siteName = sName;
    }

    public override string UpdateNotify()
    {
        return @"
```

```
This is to let you know your site, " + "\n" +
siteName + @", has been added as
a link to Financial Times.";
    }
}

public class Test
{
    public static void Main()
    {
        Contact[] Contacts = new Contact[2];

        Contacts[0] = new SiteOwner("Le Financier");
        Contacts[1] = new Customer();

        foreach (Contact poc in Contacts)
        {
            Console.WriteLine("Message: {0}\n",
                              poc.UpdateNotify());
        }
    }
}
```

And here's the output:

```
Message:
This is to let you know your site,
Le Financier, has been added as
a link to Financial Times.

Message: Web Site Change Notification
```


This example shows what happens when virtual methods are not overridden. The `UpdateNotify()` method of the `Customer` class has a `new` modifier but does not have an `override` modifier. When the `foreach` loop of the `Main()` method of the `Test` class executes, it operates on `Contact` references to objects of type `Customer` and `SiteOwner`.

Viewing the output, the `UpdateNotify()` method of the `SiteOwner` class executes first. Since it overrides the virtual `UpdateNotify()` method of the `Contact` class, its method is executed. Next, the `UpdateNotify()` method of the `Contact` class executes. This time the `UpdateNotify()` method of the `Customer` class isn't executed, because the `Customer` class does not override the virtual `UpdateNotify()` method of the `Contact` class. When the runtime type of an object does not override a method of a virtual base class, the virtual method in the base class executes.

Most-Derived Implementations

The most derived implementation of a method is the lowest class in a hierarchy, down to the current class, that holds an implementation of a virtual method. The examples presented thus far have a base class and a derived class. To determine the most derived implementation, see whether the current object being referred to has an overridden implementation of a virtual method. If so, it is the most derived implementation. Otherwise, check the immediate base class of the current class, continuing up the hierarchy until an overriding method is found or the original virtual method itself is found. When there is only a single virtual method with no overrides in derived classes, then that virtual method is the most derived implementation. Here's an example that helps demonstrate how this works:

```
using System;

abstract public class Contact
{
    public virtual string UpdateNotify()
    {
        return "Web Site Change Notification";
    }
}

public class Customer : Contact
{
    public new string UpdateNotify()
    {
        return @"
This is to let you know your
favorite site, Financial Times,
has been updated with new links";
    }
}

public class SiteOwner : Contact
{
    string siteName;

    public SiteOwner(string sName)
    {
        siteName = sName;
    }

    public override string UpdateNotify()
    {
        return @"
This is to let you know your site, " + "\n" +
siteName + @", has been added as
```

```
a link to Financial Times.";
    }
}

public class PayingSiteOwner : SiteOwner
{
    public PayingSiteOwner(string ownerName)
         : base(ownerName)
    {
        // Initializers
    }

    public new string UpdateNotify()
    {
        return @"
This is to let you know your bill
is coming due.  We award early
payment with a 5% discount.";
    }
}


public class Test
{
    public static void Main()
    {
        Contact[] Contacts = new Contact[3];

        Contacts[0] = new SiteOwner("Le Financier");
        Contacts[1] = new Customer();
        Contacts[2] = new PayingSiteOwner("Rip Uoff");

        foreach (Contact poc in Contacts)
        {
            Console.WriteLine("Message: {0}\n",
                              poc.UpdateNotify());
        }
    }
}
```

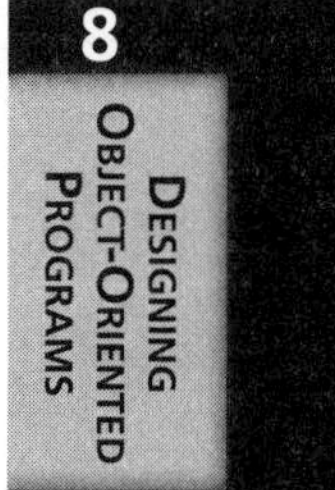

And here's the output:

```
Message:
This is to let you know your site,
Le Financier, has been added as
a link to Financial Times.

Message: Web Site Change Notification

Message:
This is to let you know your site,
```

```
Rip Uoff, has been added as
a link to Financial Times.
```

The PayingSiteOwner class inherits SiteOwner, which in turn inherits Contact. The PayingSiteOwner class has an UpdateNotify() method that hides inherited UpdateNotify() methods. The SiteOwner class has an UpdateNotify() method that overrides the virtual UpdateNotify() method in the Contact class.

In the Main() method of the Test class is the declaration of both the SiteOwner and PayingSiteOwner classes. They are assigned to a Contact class reference. When the foreach loop executes, it calls the UpdateNotify() methods of each object in the array. Looking at the output, there are three outputs from UpdateNotify() methods. The first is from the overriding method in SiteOwner. The second is from the Contact class, which isn't overridden by the derived Customer class. The third entry is also from the SiteOwner class.

The reason for the third entry is because the UpdateNotify() method of the SiteOwner class is the most derived implementation of the UpdateNotify() method. Although the runtime object of the third entry is of the PayingSiteOwner class type, its UpdateNotify() method does not override the parent class UpdateNotify() method.

Since the object reference is a Contact class type, it searches for the most derived implementation of the virtual UpdateNotify() method. The search begins with the PayingSiteOwner class, where it doesn't find an override. Next, the base class of PayingSiteOwner, SiteOwner, is searched. A valid override exists there, so that is the method that gets executed.

If the example code was changed to

```
public class PayingSiteOwner : SiteOwner
{
    public PayingSiteOwner(string ownerName)
        : base(ownerName)
    {
        // Initializers
    }

    public override string UpdateNotify()
    {
        return @"
This is to let you know your bill
is coming due.  We award early
payment with a 5% discount.";
    }
}
```

The output would be

```
Message:
This is to let you know your site,
Le Financier, has been added as
a link to Financial Times.

Message: Web Site Change Notification

Message:
This is to let you know your bill
is coming due.  We award early
payment with a 5% discount.
```

The modifier on the `UpdateNotify()` method of the `PayingSiteOwner` class was changed from `new` to `override`. This made the `UpdateNotify()` method of the `PayingSiteOwner` class the most derived implementation, resulting in it being executed as the third entry of the output.

Polymorphic Properties

C# permits polymorphism with property accessors. The same rules applied to methods also apply to properties. Here's an example.

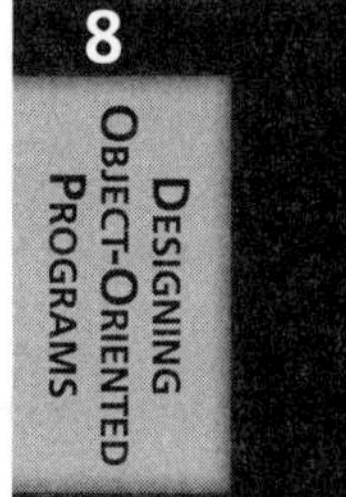


```
using System;

public class SiteStats
{
    public int numberOfVisits = 0;
}

abstract public class Contact
{
    protected string name;

    public virtual string Name
    {
        get
        {
            return name;
        }
        set
        {
            name = value;
        }
    }
}
```

```
public class Customer : Contact
{
    SiteStats myStats = new SiteStats();

    public override string Name
    {
        get
        {
            myStats.numberOfVisits++;
            Console.WriteLine("Number of visits: {0}",
                              myStats.numberOfVisits);

            return name;
        }
        set
        {
            base.Name = value;
            myStats.numberOfVisits = 0;
            Console.WriteLine("Name: {0}", Name);
        }
    }
}

public class Test
{
    public static void Main()
    {
        Contact myContact = new Customer();
        myContact.Name = "George";
    }
}
```

And here's the output:

```
Number of visits: 1
Name: George
```

In this example, the `Contact` class declares the `Name` property with a virtual modifier. The `Customer` class overrides each of the `Name` property accessors. The `set` accessor of the `Customer` class `Name` property calls the `set` accessor of the `Contact` class `Name` property by using the `base` keyword.

The reason the output reflects access to both the `get` and `set` accessors can be seen in the `set` accessor of the `Customer` class `Name` property. It uses the `Name` property as an argument to the `Console.WriteLine()` method call. This causes a `get` to be performed using that class `Name` property. The `get` does its own `Console.WriteLine()` method, which results in the first line of output. The `Console.WriteLine()` method of the `set` accessor executes, producing the second line in the output.

Warning

C# allows both the get and set accessors of a property to reference the same property. Beware of creating circularities where the get accessor causes the set accessor to be called and vice versa. This results in an endless loop.

Polymorphic Indexers

C# permits polymorphism with indexer accessors. The same rules applied to methods and properties also apply to indexers. Here's an example:

```
using System;
using System.Collections;

public class SiteList
{
    protected SortedList sites;

    public SiteList()
    {
        sites = new SortedList();
    }

    public int NextIndex
    {
        get {
            return sites.Count;
        }
    }

    public virtual string this[int index]
    {
        get
        {
            return (string) sites.GetByIndex(index);
        }
        set
        {
            sites[index] = value;
        }
    }
}

public class FinancialSiteList : SiteList
{
    public override string this[int index]
    {
```

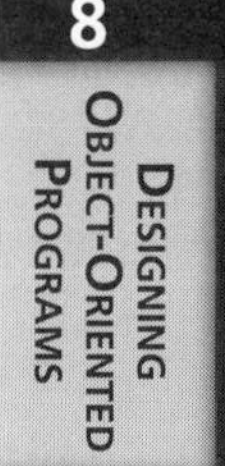

```
        get
        {
            Console.WriteLine("FinancialSiteList Indexer Get");
            if (index > sites.Count)
                return (string)null;

            return base[index];
        }
        set
        {
            Console.WriteLine("FinancialSiteList Indexer Set");
            base[index] = value;
        }
    }
}

class SiteManager
{
    SiteList sites = new SiteList();

    public static void Main()
    {
        SiteManager mgr = new SiteManager();

        mgr.sites = new FinancialSiteList();

        mgr.sites[mgr.sites.NextIndex] = "Great Site!";

        Console.WriteLine("Site: {0}",
            mgr.sites[0].ToString());
    }
}
```

And here's the output:

```
FinancialSiteList Indexer Set
FinancialSiteList Indexer Get
Site: Great Site!
```

In this example, the `SiteList` class declares its indexer as virtual. The `FinancialSiteList` indexer overrides the indexer of its base class, `SiteList`. The `FinancialSiteList` indexer accessors call the `SiteList` indexer accessors by using the `base` keyword with the index value.

The `Main()` method of the `SiteManager` class creates an object of type `FinancialSiteList` and assigns it to the `sites` field of the `mgr` object. The `sites` field is a `SiteList` class type. Then it assigns a string to the `sites` object. Because the `FinancialSiteList` indexer accessors override the `SiteList` indexer, the `FinancialSiteList` indexer `set` accessor is executed.

Viewing the output shows that the `Console.WriteLine()` method in the `FinancialSiteList` `set` accessor executed first. After the string is assigned to `sites`, the `Main()` method of `SiteManager` executes a `Console.WriteLine()` call. Because of polymorphism, this calls the `get` accessor of the `FinancialSiteList` class, which prints out the second line of output. Finally, the last line is printed from the `Main()` method of the `SiteManager` class.

Summary

In the first part of this chapter, I discussed inheritance. Issues associated with inheritance include base classes, abstract base classes, accessing base class members, hiding base class members, versioning, and sealed classes.

The next part covered encapsulation. Relevant encapsulation topics included data hiding, modifiers supporting encapsulation, encapsulation strategies using indexers and properties, and the relationship of encapsulation to inheritance.

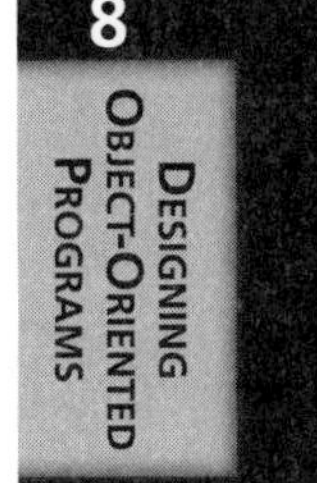

Finally, the subject of polymorphism was explained. This section included strategies on how to implement polymorphism, the use of hiding in a polymorphic context, determining the most derived implementation of a virtual method, polymorphism with properties, and polymorphism with indexers.

This chapter touched upon the ability of classes to have multiple members with the same name when it presented constructor overloading. This is not all that C# can do with overloading, and you'll see why in the next chapter, "Overloading Class Members and Operators."

CHAPTER

Overloading Class Members and Operators

In This Chapter

- Overloading Methods 220
- Overloading Indexers 223
- Overloading Operators 227
- Resolving Overloaded Members 234

Overloading is the capability of a program to define more than one member of the same name within the same class. The only difference among multiple overloaded members is that they have different argument types, a different number of arguments, or both. Overloaded members may not differ by return type alone, as this would cause ambiguity by not knowing which method should be called.

Of special note is the difference between overloading and overriding. Although their names may sound the same, they are very distinct concepts. In overriding, a derived class implements functionality, which can replace a base class member of the same name at runtime. It's a method of enabling polymorphism in programs. However, overloading has nothing to do with polymorphism. It exists to provide flexibility to users of a class, so they can call methods in a convenient and intuitive manner.

This chapter covers several ways to implement overloading in C#. These include overloading methods, properties, indexers, and operators. Finishing up the chapter is a section on resolving overloaded members, explaining how C# figures out what is the right method to call.

Overloading Methods

This section discusses method overloading, which is the ability to have multiple methods with the same name. Methods are overloaded by varying the number and type of parameters they accept. Listing 9.1 shows an example of method overloading.

LISTING 9.1 Overloading Methods

```
using System;

public class Budget
{
    enum Month {
                    Jan, Feb, Mar, Apr, May, Jun,
                    Jul, Aug, Sep, Oct, Nov, Dec
               }

    enum Category {
                    Food, Home, Jeans, Fun
                  }

    decimal[,] myBudget = new decimal[4, 12];

    public void Initialize(decimal[] initVals)
    {
        for (Category c=Category.Food; c <= Category.Fun; c++)
        {
```

LISTING 9.1 continued

```
            for (Month m=Month.Jan; m <= Month.Dec; m++)
            {
                myBudget[(int)c, (int)m] = initVals[(int)m];
            }
        }
    }

    public void Initialize(decimal initVal)
    {
        for (Category c=Category.Food; c <= Category.Fun; c++)
        {
            for (Month m=Month.Jan; m <= Month.Dec; m++)
            {
                myBudget[(int)c, (int)m] = initVal;
            }
        }
    }

    public void PrintBudget()
    {
        Console.WriteLine("\n\nMY BUD - Annual Budget\n");

        Console.Write("       ");
        for (Month m=Month.Jan; m <= Month.Dec; m++)
        {
            Console.Write("{0,6}", Enum.GetName(
                                   typeof(Month), m));
        }

        Console.WriteLine();
        for (Category c=Category.Food; c <= Category.Fun; c++)
        {
            Console.Write("\n{0,-7}", Enum.GetName(
                                   typeof(Category), c));
            for (Month m=Month.Jan; m <= Month.Dec; m++)
            {
                Console.Write("{0,4}  ",
                              myBudget[(int)c, (int)m]);
            }
        }
    }
}

public class BudgetTester
{
    public static int Main(string[] args)
    {
        Budget bud = new Budget();
```

LISTING 9.1 continued

```
        decimal[] monthlyInit = new decimal[]
            {
                5.55m, 3.22m, 9.73m, 2.24m, 1.89m, 4.67m,
                6.10m, 9.32m, 7.59m, 3.56m, 1.28m, 4.30m
            };

        bud.Initialize(0.0m);

        bud.PrintBudget();

        bud.Initialize(monthlyInit);

        bud.PrintBudget();

        return 0;
    }
}
```

> **For C++ Programmers**
>
> C++ has default parameters, but C# doesn't. To accomplish the same thing, use method overloading where a method with fewer parameters will call an overloaded member with the extra parameter(s).

Listing 9.1 shows the shell of a program that is meant to help keep track of an annual budget. It keeps track of four budget categories for a 12-month period. Its current functionality includes two forms of initialization and the ability to print a report of the current budget.

This program has the `Initialize()` method overloaded. It has two definitions. The first method accepts an array of decimal values. It's assumed that the array will have 12 values, one for each month of the year. Within each category, each month's value of the `initVals` array replaces the corresponding month's value of the `myBudget` array.

The second method accepts a single `decimal` value. This is the `intVal` decimal parameter that is used to initialize every month of every category in the `myBudget` array with the same value.

The `BudgetTester` class tests each of the `Initialize()` methods of the `Budget` class. Its `Main()` method performs two actions. First, it creates a new `Budget` object and initializes the `monthlyInit` array with 12 values. Each of the `monthlyInit` values corresponds to a month of the year. The `Main()` method's second task is to initialize the `Budget` object with a constant value.

The `Main()` method calls the `Initialize()` method of the `Budget` class with a single decimal literal of `0.0m`. This causes every element in the `myBudget` array of the `Budget` class to be initialized to zero. Next the `PrintBudget()` method of the `Budget` class is invoked, printing the results to the console.

The next statement in `Main()` calls the `Initialize()` method of the `Budget` class. Only this time, it passes the `monthlyInit` array to the method. This causes each month in each category to be set to the corresponding month value in the `monthlyInit` array. The `PrintBudget()` method of the `Budget` class is called again to print the new values. Figure 9.1 shows the two `PrintBudget()` method invocations.

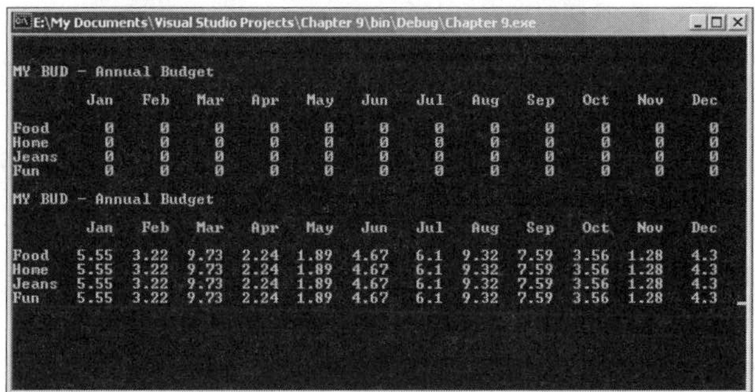

FIGURE 9.1
Annual budget report results from overloaded methods.

Overloading Indexers

Indexers are overloaded similar to methods. By providing different numbers and types of parameters, indexers can be very flexible. Listing 9.2 shows an example of indexer overloading.

LISTING 9.2 Overloading Indexers

```
using System;

public enum Month {
                        Jan, Feb, Mar, Apr, May, Jun,
                        Jul, Aug, Sep, Oct, Nov, Dec
                  }

public enum Category {
                        Food, Home, Jeans, Fun
                     }
```

LISTING 9.2 continued

```
public class Budget
{
    decimal[,] myBudget = new decimal[4, 12];

    public void Initialize(decimal[] initVals)
    {
        for (Category c=Category.Food; c <= Category.Fun; c++)
        {
            for (Month m=Month.Jan; m <= Month.Dec; m++)
            {
                myBudget[(int)c, (int)m] = initVals[(int)m];
            }
        }
    }

    public void Initialize(decimal initVal)
    {
        for (Category c=Category.Food; c <= Category.Fun; c++)
        {
            for (Month m=Month.Jan; m <= Month.Dec; m++)
            {
                myBudget[(int)c, (int)m] = initVal;
            }
        }
    }

    public decimal this[int cat, int mon]
    {
        get
        {
            return myBudget[cat, mon];
        }
        set
        {
            myBudget[cat, mon] = value;
        }
    }

    public decimal this[Category cat, Month mon]
    {
        get
        {
            return myBudget[(int)cat, (int)mon];
        }
        set
        {
            myBudget[(int)cat, (int)mon] = value;
        }
    }
```

LISTING 9.2 continued

```
    public decimal this[string cat, string mon]
    {
        get
        {
            return myBudget[
                     (int)Enum.Parse(typeof(Category),
                                          cat, true),
                     (int)Enum.Parse(typeof(Month),
                                          mon, true)
                           ];
        }
        set
        {
            myBudget[
                 (int)Enum.Parse(typeof(Category),
                                      cat, true),
                 (int)Enum.Parse(typeof(Month),
                                      mon, true)
                    ] = value;
        }
    }

    public void PrintBudget()
    {
        Console.WriteLine("\n\nMY BUD - Annual Budget\n");

        Console.Write("      ");
        for (Month m=Month.Jan; m <= Month.Dec; m++)
        {
            Console.Write("{0,6}", Enum.GetName(
                                  typeof(Month), m));
        }

        Console.WriteLine();
        for (Category c=Category.Food; c <= Category.Fun; c++)
        {
            Console.Write("\n{0,-7}", Enum.GetName(
                                  typeof(Category), c));
            for (Month m=Month.Jan; m <= Month.Dec; m++)
            {
                Console.Write("{0,4}  ",
                              myBudget[(int)c, (int)m]);
            }
        }
    }
}

public class BudgetTester
{
```

LISTING 9.2 continued

```
    public static int Main(string[] args)
    {
        Budget bud = new Budget();

        bud.Initialize(0.0m);

        bud[Category.Food, Month.Jan] = 9.95m;

        bud["Jeans", "Jan"]           = 5.73m;

        bud[3, 0]                     = 3.17m;

        bud.PrintBudget();

        return 0;
    }
}
```

For C++ Programmers

C++ allows overloading the [] operator, but C# doesn't. The same thing can be accomplished in C# by using indexers.

Listing 9.2 shows new additions to the `Budget` and `BudgetTester` classes. The added functionality includes a way to directly modify specific categories in specific months. This is done through indexers.

This program has three overloaded indexers. The first indexer in the `Budget` class accepts a traditional set of integers to indicate the category row and month column. These integers are used to directly get and set members of the `myBudget` array.

The second indexer accepts a Category enum for the row and a `Month` enum for the column. Within the `get` and `set` method, each value is converted to an `int` before being used in the `myBudget` array.

The third indexer accepts a pair of strings. The first string is used to select the category row and the second string is used to select the month column. The allowable strings must correspond to legal equivalents in the `Category` and `Month` enums. The strings are converted into their equivalent enum values by using the `Enum.FromString()` method, which produces `Category` and `Month` enums. Once each enum is created, it is converted to an `int` and used to index rows and columns in the `myBudget` array.

The `BudgetTester` class shows how to use these indexers. Within the `Main()` method of the `BudgetTester` class, the `Initialize` method of the `Budget` class is called with the value `0.0m`. This initializes the `myBudget` array of the Budget class to all have decimal zeros.

In the `Main()` method, the first indexer called accepts the `Category.Food` and `Month.Jan` enums. This sets the Food row and Jan column of the `myBudget` array value to `9.95`.

The next indexer called in the `Main()` method accepts the strings `Jeans` and `Jan` as values. This is passed to the indexer in the `Budget` class that accepts two strings. As explained earlier, these strings are converted to enum and then to `int` before indexing into the `myBudget` array. This sets the Jeans row and Jan column of the myBudget array to 5.73.

The final indexer invoked in the `Main()` method calls the indexer in the `Budget` class with traditional integer values. The corresponding row and column in the `myBudget` array are accessed directly without conversion. This sets the Fun row and Jan column of the `myBudget` array to `3.17`. Figure 9.2 shows the individual rows and columns that were set.

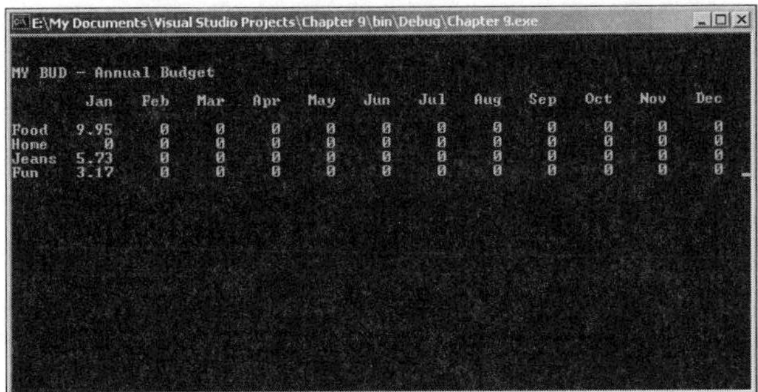

FIGURE 9.2
Rows and columns set by overloaded indexers.

Overloading Operators

Operator overloading is the capability to redefine C# operators. Overloaded operators apply to the class in which they are defined. Not all operators can be overloaded. Also, there are restrictions placed on when certain operators can be overloaded, such as requiring `==` and `!=` to be defined together. This section discusses how to overload operators and the rules governing their creation.

For Java Programmers

Java doesn't have operator overload support, but C# provides comprehensive support.

Overloaded unary operators require an argument of the same type of class or struct they are defined in. The following unary operators can be overloaded:

`+`	`++`
`-`	`--`
`!`	`true`
`~`	`false`

Note

The prefix and postfix (++) and (--) operators can't be overloaded separately.

When overloading binary operators, one parameter must be of the class or struct in which they are defined. The other parameter can be any type. Here's the list of binary operators that can be overloaded:

`+`	`%`	`<<`	`>`
`-`	`&`	`>>`	`<`
`*`	`|`	`==`	`>=`
`/`	`^`	`!=`	`<=`

The following list includes operators that are not overloadable:

`.`	`&&`	`sizeof`	`checked`
`f()`	`||`	`typeof`	`unchecked`
`[]`	`?:`	`as`	`->`
`=`	`new`	`is`	

Note

The conditional logical operators can't be overloaded, but they are evaluated using `&` and `|`, which can be overloaded.

Compound operators can't be explicitly overloaded. However, when a binary operator is overloaded, its corresponding compound operator assumes the same overloaded behavior. For example, when binary + is overloaded, += is also overloaded.

For C++ Programmers

C# forces the developer to match up the == and !=, > and <, and the >= and <= operators. C++ has no such restriction. This is to promote semantic consistency among these operators.

Such rules maintain the consistency of overloading behavior. In that spirit are other rules governing operator overloading. Any time the == operator is overloaded, the != operator must also be overloaded and vice versa. The same holds true for the > and < operators as well as the >= and <= operators. Listing 9.3 shows an example of operator overloading.

LISTING 9.3 Overloading Operators

```
using System;

public enum Month {
                        Jan, Feb, Mar, Apr, May, Jun,
                        Jul, Aug, Sep, Oct, Nov, Dec
                  }

public enum Category {
                        Food, Home, Jeans, Fun
                     }

public class Budget
{
    static decimal increment = 0.1m;

    decimal[,] myBudget = new decimal[4, 12];

    public void Initialize(decimal[] initVals)
    {
        for (Category c=Category.Food; c <= Category.Fun; c++)
        {
            for (Month m=Month.Jan; m <= Month.Dec; m++)
            {
                myBudget[(int)c, (int)m] = initVals[(int)m];
            }
        }
    }

    public void Initialize(decimal initVal)
    {
        for (Category c=Category.Food; c <= Category.Fun; c++)
        {
            for (Month m=Month.Jan; m <= Month.Dec; m++)
```

LISTING 9.3 continued

```
            {
                myBudget[(int)c, (int)m] = initVal;
            }
        }
    }

    public decimal this[int cat, int mon]
    {
        get
        {
            return myBudget[cat, mon];
        }
        set
        {
            myBudget[cat, mon] = value;
        }
    }

    public decimal this[Category cat, Month mon]
    {
        get
        {
            return myBudget[(int)cat, (int)mon];
        }
        set
        {
            myBudget[(int)cat, (int)mon] = value;
        }
    }

    public decimal this[string cat, string mon]
    {
        get
        {
            return myBudget[
                 (int)Enum.Parse(typeof(Category),
                                      cat, true),
                 (int)Enum.Parse(typeof(Month),
                                      mon, true)
                           ];
        }
        set
        {
            myBudget[
                 (int)Enum.Parse(typeof(Category),
                                      cat, true),
                 (int)Enum.Parse(typeof(Month),
                                      mon, true)
                   ] = value;
```

LISTING 9.3 continued

```
        }
    }

    public static Budget operator+(Budget oldBud, decimal amount)
    {
        Budget newBud = new Budget();

        for (Category c=Category.Food; c <= Category.Fun; c++)
        {
            for (Month m=Month.Jan; m <= Month.Dec; m++)
            {
                newBud[c, m] = oldBud[c, m] + amount;
            }
        }
        return newBud;
    }

    public static Budget operator++(Budget oldBud)
    {
        Budget newBud = new Budget();

        for (Category c=Category.Food; c <= Category.Fun; c++)
        {
            for (Month m=Month.Jan; m <= Month.Dec; m++)
            {
                newBud[c, m] = oldBud[c, m] + Increment;
            }
        }
        return newBud;
    }

    public static decimal Increment
    {
        get
        {
            return increment;
        }
        set
        {
            increment = value;
        }
    }

    public void PrintBudget()
    {
        Console.WriteLine("\n\nMY BUD - Annual Budget\n");

        Console.Write("      ");
        for (Month m=Month.Jan; m <= Month.Dec; m++)
```

LISTING 9.3 continued

```
        {
            Console.Write("{0,6}", Enum.GetName(typeof(Month), m));
        }

        Console.WriteLine();
        for (Category c=Category.Food; c <= Category.Fun; c++)
        {
            Console.Write("\n{0,-7}", Enum.GetName(typeof(Category), c));
            for (Month m=Month.Jan; m <= Month.Dec; m++)
            {
                Console.Write("{0,4}  ", myBudget[(int)c, (int)m]);
            }
        }
    }
}

public class BudgetTester
{
    public static int Main(string[] args)
    {
        Budget bud = new Budget();

        decimal[] monthlyInit = new decimal[]
            {
                5.55m, 3.22m, 9.73m, 2.24m, 1.89m, 4.67m,
                6.10m, 9.32m, 7.59m, 3.56m, 1.28m, 4.30m
            };

        bud.Initialize(0.0m);

        bud.PrintBudget();

        bud += 0.5m;

        bud.PrintBudget();

        Budget.Increment = 0.95m;

        bud++;

        bud.PrintBudget();

        return 0;
    }
}
```

Note

User-defined operators are always invoked before system-defined operators.

The program in Listing 9.3 can be used to increment the values of a budget. It has demonstrations of two types of operator overloading. These are unary and binary operator overloads. Each overloaded operator uses the `operator` keyword in its definition.

The first overloaded operator is the binary addition operator (+) in the `Budget` class. This is a public static function, accepting a parameter of type `Budget` class and another parameter of type decimal. This function creates a new instance of the `Budget` class. Then it takes each value of the input `Budget` object, adds the input `amount`, and assigns that value to the newly created `Budget` object. When complete, the new `Budget` object is returned to the caller.

The other overloaded operator is the unary increment (++) operator. It is a static function that takes an input parameter of type `Budget` class. This function creates a new instance of the `Budget` class. Then it uses a predefined `Increment` property and adds its value to each element of the input `Budget` object. The `sum` is then assigned to the corresponding value of the new `Budget` object. When complete, the new `Budget` object is returned to the caller.

The functionality for the two operators, just discussed, is demonstrated in the `Main()` method of the `BudgetTester` class. `Main()` first initializes all the budget elements of the `myBudget` array in the `Budget` class to `0.0m`. The `Budget` class is printed to show the initial values of zero in every cell.

Next the binary addition operator (+) is used to increment the `Budget` object, `bud`, by `0.5m`. This calls the overloaded binary addition operator (+) in the `Budget` class, which increments each element of its `myBudget` array. Notice that the program uses the compound addition operator (+=), which shows that the compound operators are overloaded automatically in the same class where their respective binary operators are defined.

Figure 9.3 shows the output from the operator-overloading program.

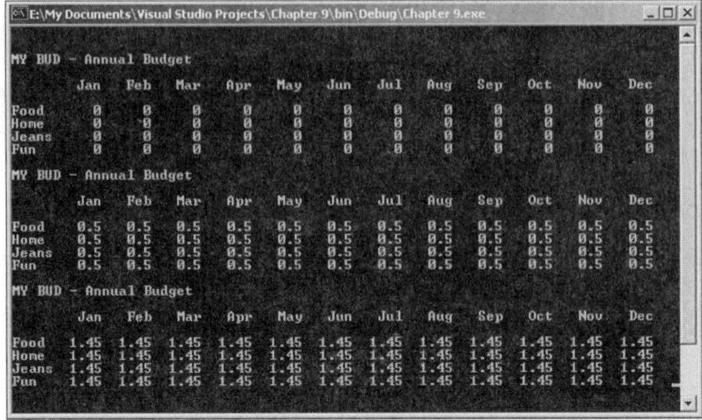

FIGURE 9.3
Array elements incremented by overloaded operators.

Resolving Overloaded Members

C# employs a deliberate mechanism to determine which overloaded class member is called in a program. Understanding these rules assists in building overloaded class members that are robust enough to meet requirements. Here are a few guidelines to help determine which overloaded method, indexer, or operator is executed. They are also the sequence of steps the compiler uses to resolve overloaded members.

1. Clearly, if there is an exact match, then that member is selected.
2. The candidate list of members is evaluated for a best match. Identifying the best match involves a couple of steps. Basically, one member is better than another if there is an implicit conversion of parameters to that member and not to the others. Here's an example:

   ```
   int myVal = 0;
   bud.someMethod(myVal);
   ```

   Now suppose the two following overloaded methods exist:

   ```
   public void someMethod(string myValue)
   {
       Console.WriteLine("In someMethod(string).");
   }
   ```

   and

   ```
   public void someMethod(long myValue)
   {
       Console.WriteLine("In someMethod(long).");
   }
   ```

   Since the parameter of the first overloaded method is a string, it won't be called. However, the int in the original method call is implicitly convertible to long. Therefore, the overloaded `someMethod(long myVal)` method is called.

Another scenario is when the argument of a calling member is implicitly convertible to multiple overloaded members. In this case, an implicit conversion can be made to the member with the closest conversion. Here's an example:

```
ushort myVal = 0;

bud.someMethod(myVal);
```

Now suppose the two following overloaded methods exist:

```
public void someMethod(uint myValue)
{
    Console.WriteLine("In someMethod(uint).");
}
```

and

```
public void someMethod(long myValue)
{
    Console.WriteLine("In someMethod(long).");
}
```

In this case, the calling method is passing an unsigned short argument. Here the implicit conversion from ushort to uint is shorter than to long. Therefore the `someMethod(uint myValue)` method is called.

3. When methods have multiple parameters, as long as the conversion of a single argument from a calling method is better in one overloaded method than any others, that overloaded method with the better parameter match is automatically better than the other methods. If there are two or more methods with equal conversion matches, the next parameter is evaluated to find the better overloaded method(s). This continues until one method comes out on top.
4. If there is no best match, the call is considered ambiguous and results in an error.

Summary

This chapter discussed various methods of overloading in C#, and the difference between overriding and overloading.

The first section discussed overloading of methods. It explained how to vary the number and type of parameters to produce overloaded methods.

The next section covered indexers. It showed a few different ways to define indexers, making a class act like a two-dimensional array. Example indexers were overloaded so the class could be used in an intuitive and flexible manner, depending on requirements.

C# also allows operator overloading. I discussed which operators could and could not be overloaded, as well as the rules that require certain operators to be overloaded in pairs.

Finally, this chapter explained how overload resolution works. It is useful to be able to figure out which overloaded method will be called by a program, especially when there isn't an exact match. Understanding overload resolution should make overloaded member development simpler and more intuitive.

All the chapters of this book, so far, have presented programs that were simple and had little need for error checking. Don't be misled, because C# has extensive error-handling capabilities. This will be revealed in the next chapter, "Handling Exceptions and Errors."

CHAPTER 10

Handling Exceptions and Errors

In This Chapter

- `try/catch` Blocks 238
- `finally` Blocks 240
- Predefined Exception Classes 241
- Handling Exceptions 241
- Designing Your Own Exceptions 249
- `checked` and `unchecked` Statements 251

This chapter discusses C# support for error handling and exceptions. Error handling is the technique of successfully trapping expected and unexpected runtime errors. The goal is to be able to anticipate errors before they occur. This makes a program more robust and promotes graceful degradation.

In C#, error handling is built around *exceptions*. Exceptions are special occurrences in a program that indicate an error condition. When an error occurs, an exception is `thrown`. The program should be constructed, using error-handling techniques, to `catch` applicable exceptions and deal with them as appropriate.

In discussing error handling, this chapter includes the `try/catch` block, the `throw` clause, the `finally` block, and error-recovery techniques. To provide an understanding of exceptions, this chapter covers predefined exception classes and shows how to create a new exception. `checked` and `unchecked` statements are also discussed.

try/catch Blocks

To get a real appreciation for C# exception handling, consider the error-handling methods used in procedural programming languages with no built-in exception handling mechanism. For example, look at the following C programming language error-handling routine:

```
int someMethod();
...
int result;
result = someMethod();
if (result != 0) {
    // do some error handling
}
```

In this example there's a prototype of `someMethod()`, showing that it returns an `int`. Under the prototype is code that would normally be part of a routine. The result variable captures the return value from `someMethod()`. Then the program checks the return to see whether it's nonzero. If so, there must have been an error, and it is handled right there.

This is the way C does error handling. The problem with this approach is that every method call must have its own error handler. The real problem is noticed in algorithms with several method calls. This clutters the code and makes it more difficult to develop as well as maintain. C# has error-handling mechanisms that avoid the difficulties with this approach.

The `try/catch` block is the primary mechanism of C# exception handling. This permits separation of error handling from the normal flow of an algorithm. Essentially, the algorithm is more understandable because its actions relate primarily toward the goal of a method, rather than with the complex mixture of error handling. Here's the basic syntax of the try/catch block:

```
try
{
    // some algorithm
}
catch (Exception e)
{
    // exception handling code
}
```

The try portion of the try/catch block holds the algorithm supporting the goal of a method. If there is an error in the code, that error may be propagated to the catch portion of the try/catch block. The error that causes control to jump into a catch block is called an exception. The catch block is where exceptions are handled. Listing 10.1 shows an example of using try/catch blocks:

LISTING 10.1 A Simple Exception: Exceptions.cs

```
using System;

public class Exceptions
{
    public static int Main(string[] args)
    {
        byte[] myStream = new byte[3];

        try
        {
            for (byte b=0; b < 10; b++)
            {
                Console.WriteLine("Byte {0}: {1}", b+1, b);
                myStream[b] = b;
            }
        }
        catch (Exception e)
        {
            Console.WriteLine("{0}", e.Message);
        }

        return 0;
    }
}
```

And here's the output:

```
Byte 1: 0
Byte 2: 1
```

```
Byte 3: 2
Byte 4: 3
An exception of type System.IndexOutOfRangeException was thrown.
```

This example shows a try/catch block in action. Prior to the try block, the program declares a three-element array of bytes named myStream. Within the try block there is a for loop, set to add 10 bytes to the myStream array. It prints out the byte number and then the value. Then it assigns the byte value to the myStream array.

This works well until the fourth iteration of the for loop. Because the myStream array can hold only three bytes, trying to add a fourth is an error. This generates an exception, causing program control to jump into the catch block. Within the catch block there's a Console.WriteLine() method that prints the exception message to the console.

finally Blocks

Many times a program ends when an exception occurs. This is okay if that's part of the design, but sometimes there are system resources that need to be released. This is the purpose of the finally block. It performs any necessary cleanup chores prior to program exit. The finally block is guaranteed to be executed before a method exits. Listing 10.2 shows an example of how to use it:

LISTING 10.2 The finally Block: Exceptions2.cs

```
using System;
using System.IO;

public class Exceptions
{
    public static int Main(string[] args)
    {
        byte[] myStream = new byte[3];
        StreamWriter sw = new StreamWriter("exceptions.txt");

        try
        {
            for (byte b=0; b < 10; b++)
            {
                sw.WriteLine("Byte {0}: {1}", b+1, b);
                myStream[b] = b;
            }
        }
        catch (Exception e)
        {
            Console.WriteLine("{0}", e.Message);
        }
```

LISTING 10.2 continued

```
        finally
        {
            sw.WriteLine("Close");
            sw.Close();
        }

        return 0;
    }
}
```

In this example, the exception occurred, printing the exception message to the console. Then control transferred to the `finally` block. Within the `finally` block, the word `Close` is written to the file, and the file itself is closed. If this code was not in the `finally` block—that is, after the closing curly brace of the finally block—it would not have been executed after the exception was generated.

The `finally` block is executed regardless of whether there is an exception or not. To check this, change the condition in the for loop in the try block to "`i < 3`" and run the program again. The `finally` block still executes. This is evident by the word "`Close`" being written as the last line of the `exceptions.txt` file.

Predefined Exception Classes

The framework libraries have several predefined exception classes to choose from. These classes are designed for the most common and generic type of exceptions that occur.

Previous examples in this chapter showed the `System.Exception` class being used in `catch` clauses. It is the most generic exception that can be generated. All other exception classes inherit from the `System.Exception` class.

Handling Exceptions

While setting up `try/catch/finally` blocks and catching the generic exception is better than not catching errors at all, there are various methods of handling errors to make code more robust. This section shows how to handle errors in a couple different ways, including handling multiple exception types, handling and passing on exceptions, and recovering from exceptions.

Handling Multiple Exceptions

Previous examples showed how to catch the generic exception, `System.Exception`. Generic error handling isn't adequate in most situations. That's why C# provides the ability to specify multiple exception handlers for a single `try` block.

This works by placing additional `catch` blocks below the `try` block. `catch` blocks should be ordered by specificity of the exception they handle. Failure to do so results in a compiler error. Listing 10.3 shows a program with multiple `catch` blocks:

LISTING 10.3 Multiple `catch` Blocks: `Exceptions3.cs`

```
using System;
using System.IO;

public class Exceptions
{
    public static int Main(string[] args)
    {
        int mySize = 3;
        byte[] myStream = new byte[mySize];
        int iterations = 5;

        StreamWriter sw = new StreamWriter("exceptions.txt");

        try
        {
            for (byte b=0; b < iterations; b++)
            {
                sw.WriteLine("Byte {0}: {1}", b+1, b);
                myStream[b] = b;
            }
        }
        catch (IndexOutOfRangeException iore)
        {
            Console.WriteLine(
                "Index Out of Range Exception: {0}",
                iore.Message);
        }
        catch (Exception e)
        {
            Console.WriteLine("Exception: {0}", e.Message);
        }
        finally
        {
            sw.WriteLine("Close");
            sw.Close();
        }
```

LISTING 10.3 continued

```
        return 0;
    }
}
```

The example shows two `catch` blocks. The `catch` block with the `IndexOutOfRangeException` handler is more specific than the `catch` block with the `Exception` handler. Therefore, when this program executes, an exception is generated that invokes the `catch` block for the `IndexOutOfRangeException`. Had the error been another type of exception, the `catch` block for the `Exception` handler would have been executed.

Handling and Passing Exceptions

One method of handling exceptions is to pass the exception to the calling program. This is done using the `throw` clause. The throw clause raises a new exception and passes it to the next enclosing try/catch block, which is normally the calling program. Listing 10.4 shows how to use the `throw` clause to pass an exception to the calling program.

LISTING 10.4 Passing Exceptions: `Exceptions4.cs`

```
using System;
using System.IO;

public class ExceptionTester
{
    public static int Main(string[] args)
    {
        ExceptionTester myExceptionMaker = new ExceptionTester();

        try
        {
            myExceptionMaker.GenerateException();
        }
        catch (Exception e)
        {
            Console.WriteLine("\nNow processing Main() Exception:");
            while (e != null)
            {
                Console.WriteLine("\tInner: {0}", e.Message);
                e = e.InnerException;
            }
        }
        finally
        {
```

LISTING 10.4 continued

```
            Console.WriteLine("Finally from Main()");
        }

        return 0;
    }

    void GenerateException()
    {
        int mySize = 3;
        byte[] myStream = new byte[mySize];
        int iterations = 5;
        StreamWriter sw = new StreamWriter("exceptions.txt");

        try
        {
            for (byte b=0; b < iterations; b++)
            {
                sw.WriteLine("Byte {0}: {1}", b+1, b);
                myStream[b] = b;
            }
        }
        catch (IndexOutOfRangeException iore)
        {
            Console.WriteLine(
"\nIndex Out of Range Exception from GenerateException: {0}",
iore.Message);

            throw new Exception(
"Thrown from GenerateException.",
iore);
        }
        catch (Exception e)
        {
            Console.WriteLine(
"\nException from GenerateException: {0}", e.Message);
        }
        finally
        {
            Console.WriteLine("Finally from GenerateException.");
            sw.WriteLine("Close");
            sw.Close();
        }
    }
}
```

Here's the code's output:

```
Index Out of Range Exception from GenerateException: An exception of type
 System.IndexOutOfRangeException was thrown.
Finally from GenerateException.

Now processing Main() Exception:
        Inner: Thrown from GenerateException.
        Inner: An exception of type System.IndexOutOfRangeException was thrown.
Finally from Main()
```

The `Main()` method instantiates an `ExceptionTester` object and, within a `try` block, calls its `GenerateException()` method. In the `GenerateException()` method, within a `try` block, there is a `for` loop that causes an `IndexOutOfRangeException`.

This causes the `catch` block that handles the `IndexOutOfRangeException` to be executed. Notice the multiple `catch` blocks. It's usually a good practice to include the generic `Exception` `catch` block, just in case any unforeseen exceptions occur.

Within the `catch` block that handles the `IndexOutOfRangeException`, there is a `Console.WriteLine()` method call to print a message to the screen. Next is the `throw` clause, which throws a new exception. The first argument of this new exception is a unique message that is the `Message` property. The second argument is the exception object that causes this `catch` block to be executed.

This second argument becomes the `InnerException` of the new exception. `InnerExceptions` are useful for creating exception chains that show what exceptions have been generated in a program. If an exception is purposely thrown for multiple layers, each time adding the original exception as the `InnerException`, it could have a long exception chain.

When the exception is thrown, it propagates to the calling program, which is the `Main()` method. Since the `GenerateException()` method was called inside a `try/catch` block, the thrown exception is caught within `Main()`. This causes control to pass to the `catch` block in `Main()`. Within that `catch` block, the `Message` property of each exception in the exception chain is printed to the console. This is made possible by calling the `InnerException` property of each exception to obtain the next exception in the chain.

The output of this program shows some interesting facts about the sequence of events in exception handling. The first line is from the `Console.WriteLine()` method of the `catch` block that handles the `IndexOutOfRangeException` in the `GenerateException()` method. Notice that the `finally` block of the `GenerateException()` method executes before the `catch` block in the `Main()` method executes. Next, the `catch` block in the `Main()` method executes, printing the `Message` property from each exception in the exception chain. The last line shows the `finally` block of the `Main()` method executing.

Recovering from Exceptions

Many times, allowing a program to crash with an exception is an unacceptable method of dealing with errors. In a production environment, it's imperative that a program deal with exceptions by degrading gracefully and recovering, if possible, on its own. This section shows one way to recover from an exception. Listing 10.5 shows how to recover from an exception, perform corrective measures, and keep on processing.

LISTING 10.5 Recovering from Exceptions: `ExceptionTester.cs`

```
using System;
using System.IO;

public class ExceptionTester
{
    public static int Main(string[] args)
    {
        ExceptionTester myExceptionMaker =
            new ExceptionTester();

        try
        {
            myExceptionMaker.GenerateException();
        }
        catch (Exception e)
        {
            Console.WriteLine(
                "\nNow processing Main() Exception:");
            while (e != null)
            {
                Console.WriteLine("\tInner: {0}", e.Message);
                e = e.InnerException;
            }
        }
        finally
        {
            Console.WriteLine("Finally from Main()");
        }

        return 0;
    }

    void GenerateException()
    {
```

LISTING 10.5 continued

```
        int mySize = 3;
        byte[] myStream = new byte[mySize];
        int iterations = 5;

        do
        {
            StreamWriter sw =
                new StreamWriter("exceptions.txt");

            try
            {
                for (byte b=0; b < iterations; b++)
                {
                    sw.WriteLine("Byte {0}: {1}", b+1, b);
                    myStream[b] = b;
                }
                break;
            }
            catch (IndexOutOfRangeException iore)
            {
                Console.WriteLine(
"\nIndex Out of Range Exception from GenerateException: {0}",
iore.Message);
                iterations—;
            }
            catch (Exception e)
            {
                Console.WriteLine(
"\nException from GenerateException: {0}", e.Message);
            }
            finally
            {
                Console.WriteLine(
                    "Finally from GenerateException.");
                sw.WriteLine("Close");
                sw.Close();
            }
        } while (true);
    }
}
```

Here's the code's output:

```
Index Out of Range Exception from GenerateException:
➥An exception of type System
.IndexOutOfRangeException was thrown.
Finally from GenerateException.
```

```
Index Out of Range Exception from GenerateException:
➥An exception of type System
.IndexOutOfRangeException was thrown.
Finally from GenerateException.
Finally from GenerateException.
Finally from Main()
```

The `Main()` method calls the `GenerateException()` method. Within the `try` block of the `GenerateException()` method, a `for` loop executes until an exception is raised. This exception is generated because the iterations field is set to `5`, but the `myStream` array size is set to `3`.

Within the `catch` block that handles the `IndexOutOfRangeException`, the iterations field is decremented. This is an error correction technique because the program knows that the iterations field controls the number of items placed into the `myStream` array. A program may not always know the exact cause of a problem, but if it's constructed properly, it can adjust itself toward an acceptable mode of operation or continue in a degraded state.

This is what happens after the first exception. The `iteration` field is decremented from 5 to 4 and continues in a degraded state. The program continues because of the `do` loop enclosing the `try/catch/finally` block. The `while` condition is set to `true`, causing it to loop until some condition causes the program to break out of the loop.

This causes the logic in the `try` block to execute again, raise another exception, and decrement the `iterations` field from 4 to 3. The loop keeps the program from crashing again, and the `try` block is executed once more, but this time the program is no longer in a degraded state.

The program is in a stable state because the `iterations` field is set to the size of the array. This causes the `for` loop to execute successfully. Once this happens, control passes to the `break` statement following the `for` loop, which allows program control to pass out of the `do` loop. The program has fully recovered and can now complete as normal.

The output shows results of the sequence of events just described. The first two lines show the exception generated and the `finally` block being executed as the result of the `iterations` field set at 5. The next two lines show the same exception generation and `finally` block from the `iterations` field set at 4. After the `iterations` field is set to 3, the fifth line is created by the `finally` block of the `GenerateException()` method. Control then passes to the `finally` block of the `Main()` method, as evidenced by the last output line.

Designing Your Own Exceptions

A program is not limited to the predefined C# exceptions. It's possible to create unique exceptions, tailored to a specific application. This section shows how to design your own exception. Listing 10.6 shows how to create a new exception and how to use it.

LISTING 10.6 Designing an Exception: `NewException.cs`

```
using System;
using System.IO;

public class TooManyItemsException : Exception
{
    public TooManyItemsException() : base(@"

**TooManyItemsException**  You added too many items
to this container.  Try specifying a smaller number
or increasing the container size.

")
    {
    }
}

public class ExceptionTester
{
    public static int Main(string[] args)
    {
        ExceptionTester myExceptionMaker = new ExceptionTester();

        try
        {
            myExceptionMaker.GenerateException(5);
        }
        catch (Exception e)
        {
            Console.WriteLine("\nMessage: {0}", e.Message);
        }
        finally
        {
            Console.WriteLine("Finally from Main()");
        }

        return 0;
    }

    void GenerateException(int iterations)
    {
        int mySize = 3;
```

LISTING 10.6 continued

```
        byte[] myStream = new byte[mySize];
        StreamWriter sw = new StreamWriter("exceptions.txt");

        try
        {
            if (iterations > myStream.Length)
            {
                throw new TooManyItemsException();
            }

            for (byte b=0; b < iterations; b++)
            {
                sw.WriteLine("Byte {0}: {1}", b+1, b);
                myStream[b] = b;
            }
        }
        finally
        {
            Console.WriteLine("Finally from GenerateException.");
            sw.WriteLine("Close");
            sw.Close();
        }
    }
}
```

Here's the code's output:

```
Finally from GenerateException.

Message:

**TooManyItemsException**  You added too many items
to this container.  Try specifying a smaller number
or increasing the container size.

Finally from Main()
```

The first class, `TooManyItemsException`, is the new exception class. It inherits from `Exception`. During initialization of `TooManyItemsException` it would have been nice to set the `Message` property of `Exception`. However, that isn't possible because its `Message` property is read-only. Therefore, the `TooManyItemsException` class uses base class initialization by calling the base class constructor that accepts a string. This effectively updates the `Message` property with the desired string. This is how a new exception class can be constructed.

This class is used in the `GenerateException()` method of the `ExceptionTester` class. The `GenerateException()` method tests the value of the `iterations` argument that was passed in during invocation in the `Main()` method. If that value is larger than the `myStream` array's length, then the `TooManyItemsException` is thrown.

Notice that the `GenerateException()` method doesn't have a `catch` block after its `try` block. This is permissible and purely a matter of style. In this case the program uses a `try/finally` block where the `finally` block guarantees closing the file resource regardless of whether the exception is thrown or not.

The `Main()` method catches the exception and prints its `Message` property. The output is as may be expected. When `TooManyItemsException` is thrown, the `finally` block of the `GenerateException()` method executes. The exception prints in the `catch` block of the `Main()` method. Last, the `finally` block of the `Main()` method executes.

checked and unchecked Statements

C# has built-in expressions for checking the overflow context of arithmetic operations and conversions. These are `checked` and `unchecked` statements. `checked` statements watch expressions for evidence of overflow. When overflow occurs, the system raises an exception. Listing 10.7 shows how the `checked` statement causes an `OverflowException` to be generated.'

LISTING 10.7 `checked` Statements: `checked.cs`

```
using System;

public class ExceptionTester
{
    public static int Main(string[] args)
    {
        int prior = 250000000;
        int after = 150000000;
        int total;

        try
        {
            checked
            {
                total = prior * after;
            }
        }
        catch (OverflowException oe)
        {
            Console.WriteLine("\nOverflow Message: {0}",
```

LISTING 10.7 continued

```
                                    oe.Message);
        }
        catch (Exception e)
        {
            Console.WriteLine("\nMessage: {0}", e.Message);
        }
        finally
        {
            Console.WriteLine("Finally from Main()");
        }

        return 0;
    }
}
```

In the `try` block of the `Main()` method there is a `checked` statement around an arithmetic equation that causes an overflow. When the overflow occurs, this generates an exception, causing program control to branch to the `catch` block that handles an `OverflowException`.

Expressions can also be enclosed in `unchecked` statements. This allows the overflow to proceed, undetected. There are likely to be occasions when this type of behavior is desired. Listing 10.8 shows how to use the `unchecked` statement to prevent overflow exceptions.

LISTING 10.8 `unchecked` Statements: `unchecked.cs`

```
using System;

public class ExceptionTester
{
    public static int Main(string[] args)
    {

        try
        {
            unchecked
            {
                int absShortMask = (int)0xFFFF0000;
            }
        }
        catch (OverflowException oe)
        {
            Console.WriteLine("\nOverflow Message: {0}", oe.Message);
        }
        catch (Exception e)
```

LISTING 10.8 continued

```
        {
            Console.WriteLine("\nMessage: {0}", e.Message);
        }
        finally
        {
            Console.WriteLine("\nFinally from Main()");
        }

        return 0;
    }
}
```

In the `try` block of the `Main()` method there is an `unchecked` statement containing an arithmetic operation that causes an overflow condition. Since it is `unchecked`, no exceptions are generated, and the program proceeds as normal.

In the preceding example, it was useful to assign the bit pattern to the `absShortMask` variable. Subsequent possible operations could have been to get the absolute value of a short expression, implicitly cast to an integer, by using a bitwise exclusive or operation.

A program is always running in a `checked` or `unchecked` state. During runtime, the checking context for nonconstant expressions is determined by the environment in which your program is running. The default for the C# compiler in the Microsoft .NET Frameworks SDK is `unchecked`. Constant expressions are always in a `checked` context. Here's an example:

```
Total = 25000000 * 15000000;    // generates an exception
```

To turn `checked` and `unchecked` on or off for an entire program, C# has a `checked/unchecked` compiler switch. Here's an example of turning on the `checked` context:

```
csc /checked+ myprogram.cs
```

To compile code in an `unchecked` context you would use a "`-`" with the `checked` switch:

```
csc /checked- myprogram.cs
```

Summary

This chapter presented C# exceptions and exception handling. The first section introduced `try/catch` blocks. It showed how to use `try/catch` blocks to wrap up code where a possible exception may occur and to handle the exception when it occurs.

A section on the `finally` block explained how to make sure certain operations are always carried out, regardless of whether or not an exception occurs. The example showed how to release a system resource when an exception occurs.

I also talked about the predefined exception classes. I explained how they fit into a hierarchical organization.

This chapter also went in-depth to show various ways of handling exceptions, including how to handle multiple exceptions, handling and passing on exceptions to callers, and how to recover from exceptions.

Sometimes the predefined exceptions won't meet a program's requirements. This chapter showed how to create a new exception that met the unique requirements of an example program. It also showed how to determine which predefined exception to inherit and how to throw an exception.

Finally, this chapter covered the `checked` and `unchecked` statements. It showed how to control overflow exception checking for arithmetic operations and conversions. It also explained a situation where generating an overflow condition may be desirable and how to achieve that goal without generating an exception.

This chapter explained how to control program flow when unforeseen circumstances arrive. Chapter 11, "Delegates and Events," shows how to gain even greater control of program flow.

Delegates and Events

IN THIS CHAPTER

- **Delegates** ***256***
- **Events** ***262***

The C# programming language contains constructs called delegates and events, which enable late-bound operations such as method invocation and call-back procedures. Late-bound operations are characterized by their ability to occur during runtime, rather than when the program is initially compiled. This chapter introduces C# delegates and events. These language constructs enable programs to implement callback procedures and other dynamic functionality. This capability is popular in many graphical user interface systems in use today. This chapter also shows how events are implemented in C#.

Delegates

A C# delegate is a type-safe method reference. With delegates, a program can dynamically call different methods at runtime. The primary purpose of delegates is to establish an infrastructure to support events. Events are simply specialized delegates. They enable programs to create callback methods and register those methods with events in a publish/subscribe notification pattern. This section shows how to create delegates.

Defining Delegates

A delegate defines the signature and return type of a method. It also creates a new type to which a method must conform before it may be assigned to a delegate. Once a method has been assigned to a delegate, it is called when the delegate is invoked. Here's how a delegate signature is defined shows the syntax of creating a delegate:

```
[modifiers] delegate <delegate name>([parameter list]);
```

Modifiers and parameters are optional. Here's an example of a delegate declaration with the first line showing how to define a delegate:

```
delegate decimal Calculation(decimal val1, decimal val2);

Calculation MyCalc;
```

It has public accessibility, returns a decimal, and accepts two decimal parameters. Its type name is `Calculation`. The next line shows how to create an instance of a new delegate. This example shows a delegate called `MyCalc`, which is of type `Calculation`.

For C++ Programmers

Delegates are similar to function pointers in C++, except that they are type-safe, object-oriented, and secure. C# allows delegates to refer to both instance and static methods. When referring to instance methods, delegates encapsulate both the object reference and its method.

Creating Delegate Method Handlers

To use a delegate, there must be a delegate method handler. This is a method that adheres to the delegate signature and return type and implements some functionality. The parameter list must be the same and it must return the same type. Here's an example that conforms to the signature and return type requirements of a delegate:

```
delegate decimal Calculation(decimal val1, decimal val2);

Calculation MyCalc;
...
public decimal add(decimal add1, decimal add2)
{
    return add1 + add2;
}
```

This example accepts two decimal parameters, operates on them, and returns a decimal value. It is ready to be used as a delegate method handler.

Hooking Up Delegates and Handlers

For a delegate method handler to be invoked, it must be assigned to a delegate object. This delegate method handler must conform to the signature and return type of the underlying delegate type of the delegate to which it is being assigned. The following example assigns the add method to the MyCalc delegate by creating a new instance of the DelegateExample delegate type and including the add method handler in the parameter list.

```
delegate decimal Calculation(decimal val1, decimal val2);

Calculation MyCalc;
...
DelegateExample del = new DelegateExample();
del.MyCalc = new Calculation(del.add);
```

A delegate also accepts a method group, a group of overloaded methods. The following example shows the `add()` method overloaded to accept an array of decimals.

```
public decimal add(decimal[] addList)
{
    decimal total = 0;

    foreach( decimal number in addList )
    {
        total += number;
    }

    return total;
}
```

When the add() method group is assigned to the MyCalc delegate, it determines which method matches its signature and return type. The matching method is assigned to the delegate.

Invoking Methods through Delegates

A delegate method handler is invoked by making a method call on the delegate itself. This effectively causes the delegate method handler to invoke with the designated input parameters as if it were invoked directly by the program. The next example shows a delegate being called as if it were a method:

```
decimal result = MyCalc(5.35m, 9.71m); // result = 15.06m
```

What's really happening underneath is that the add() delegate method handler is being called with the parameters passed to the MyCalc delegate.

Multi-Cast Delegates

A multi-cast delegate is a single delegate made up of two or more other delegates. It's created by adding one delegate to another with the add (+) operator. Similarly, individual delegates may be removed from a multi-cast delegate by using the remove (-) operator. Multiple delegates may be added to a multi-cast delegate.

Tip

Double-check method return types to make sure they are void before assigning them to a multi-cast delegate.

Multi-cast delegates have a couple restrictions beyond single method delegates. They must have a return type of void and they can't have any out parameters in their parameter lists. When the multi-cast delegate is invoked, each individual delegate that has been added is invoked in the order in which it was added. Listing 11.1 shows how to implement multi-cast delegates.

LISTING 11.1 Creating a socket server: MultiCast.cs

```
using System;

public delegate void Calculation(decimal val1,
                                 decimal val2,
                                 ref decimal result);
```

LISTING 11.1 continued

```
public class DelegateExample
{
    Calculation MyCalc1;
    Calculation MyCalc2;

    public void Add(decimal add1, decimal add2, ref decimal result)
    {
        result = add1 + add2;
        Console.WriteLine("add({0}, {1}) = {2}",
                          add1, add2, result);
        return;
    }

    public void Sub(decimal sub1, decimal sub2, ref decimal result)
    {
        result = sub1 - sub2;
        Console.WriteLine("sub({0}, {1}) = {2}",
                          sub1, sub2, result);
        return;
    }

    public decimal add(decimal[] addList)
    {
        decimal total = 0;

        foreach( decimal number in addList )
        {
            total += number;
        }

        return total;
    }

    public static int Main(string[] args)
    {
        decimal result = 0.0m;
        DelegateExample del = new DelegateExample();

        del.MyCalc1 = new Calculation(del.Add);
        del.MyCalc2 = new Calculation(del.Sub);

        del.MyCalc1(5.35m, 9.71m, ref result);
        del.MyCalc2(8.39m, 1.75m, ref result);

        Console.WriteLine();

        Calculation MultiCalc = del.MyCalc1;
        MultiCalc += del.MyCalc2;
```

LISTING 11.1 continued

```
        MultiCalc(7.43m, 5.19m, ref result);

        Console.WriteLine();
        Console.WriteLine("MultiCalc(7.43m, 5.19m) = {0}",
                          result);

        return 0;
    }
}
```

And here's the output:

```
add(5.35, 9.71) = 15.06
sub(8.39, 1.75) = 6.64

add(7.43, 5.19) = 12.62
sub(7.43, 5.19) = 2.24

MultiCalc(7.43m, 5.19m) = 2.24
```

In this implementation of a multi-cast delegate, the delegate to be used is the `Calculation` delegate. It conforms to multi-cast restrictions by having a return type of `void` and no `out` parameters. It accepts two `value` decimal type parameters and a `ref` decimal type parameter. The `ref` parameter shows that it is possible to have a method return a value, a workaround for not having an `out` parameter.

Within the `DelegateExample` class there are a couple `Calculation` delegate fields. These are used to create a multi-cast delegate. There are also a couple methods, `Add()` and `Sub()`, conforming to the `Calculation` delegate signature and return type. They are used as delegate method handlers.

After initializing the result field and creating a new instance of the `DelegateExample` class in the `Main()` method, the two `Calculation` delegate fields, `MyCalc1` and `MyCalc2`, are instantiated. `MyCalc1` holds the `Add()` delegate method handler and `MyCalc2` holds the `Sub()` delegate method handler. These two delegates are invoked, resulting in the first two lines of output.

Next, the multi-cast `Calculation` delegate, `MultiCalc` is created. This occurs by first making `MultiCalc` equal `MyCalc1`. Then `MyCalc2` is added with the compound addition operator. This also could have been written as follows:

```
Calculation MultiCalc = del.MyCalc1 + del.MyCalc2;
```

The third and fourth lines of the output show invocation of the multi-cast delegate `MultiCalc`. Each delegate is invoked in the order it was added. They both operate with the same input values. Remember the `ref` decimal result parameter? This was to avoid the limitation of not having a return type or an `out` parameter. The last line of output shows what this parameter is after the multi-cast delegate is invoked. It is the value of the last delegate in the multi-cast delegate to be invoked. This illustrates the reason why multi-cast delegates don't return values and don't have `out` parameters. It just doesn't normally make sense, since each method's output can't be used anyway. However, if you can find a practical reason for needing the output of the last delegate of a multi-cast delegate, use a `ref` parameter.

Delegate Equality

Sometimes an application may have a need to evaluate the equality of single or multi-cast delegates. A possible application for this in single delegates might be to make sure that a certain method is only invoked one time. Such an ambiguous situation could evolve as a result of multiple delegates being dynamically instantiated at different times or places in a program.

Another potential application of equality checking on delegates could arise with multi-cast delegates. The individual delegates of a multi-cast delegate are placed and invoked in a specific sequence. If an application had to rely upon the sequence of individual delegates in a multi-cast delegate being different, the equality or inequality operator would be handy.

If two delegates reference the same method or one delegate references the other, the equal operator returns `true`. When two delegates contain separate functions, the equal operator evaluates to `false`, as shown in the following example:

```
bool equal = del.MyCalc1 == del.MyCalc2; // equal is false
```

Assume `del.MyCalc1` and `del.MyCalc2` are from the example in the previous section on multi-cast delegates. Each of these delegates has different delegate method handlers. Therefore this equation assigns the Boolean value `false` to the equal field. If the not equal (`!=`) operator had been used instead, it would have returned `true`.

For two multi-cast delegates to be considered equal, they must have the same number of delegates. Additionally, delegates in corresponding positions of each multi-cast delegate must be equal. For example, assume `MyCalc1` and `MyCalc2` are multi-cast delegates. If the sequence of delegates added to `MyCalc1` are `Add()` + `Sub()` + `Add()`, then the same sequence, `Add()` + `Sub()` + `Add()` must also be added to `MyCalc2`. However, if instead the sequence of `Add()` + `Add()` + `Add()` were added to `MyCalc2`, then `MyCalc1` and `MyCalc2` would not be equal because the second delegate in each sequence are not equal. Similar to single delegates, the not equal (`!=`) operator is opposite of equal.

Events

An event is a C# language element that indicates a certain, user-defined, occurrence. It is a mechanism that initiates a dynamic form of communication between program elements. Rather than a procedural flow of control from one part of a program to another, events are the way to establish connection between program occurrences and resulting actions during runtime processing.

Events are used to notify interested listeners of various occurrences during a program's lifetime. They're used in C# components to provide a callback functionality in programs. This produces a level of efficiency not available in many languages where switch statements and object-hierarchy searching are the norm for invoking dynamic functionality.

Events derive their power from the publish/subscribe pattern they support. Effectively, certain objects publish their availability to generate certain types of events. With this knowledge, interested components subscribe to those events. When the event occurs, or fires, each subscribed component is notified of that event and supplied with applicable information.

Defining Event Handlers

Events are commonly used in graphical user interfaces (GUIs) for things like button clicks or menu selections. In those instances, the event is already defined and all that needs to be done is to register with the event. However, events can be defined and used anywhere for GUI or non-GUI purposes. Here are the elements that make up an event:

```
[modifiers] event type name;
```

This line shows optional modifiers, the same as methods, followed by the keyword, `event`. Next is the `type`. Since all events are based on delegates, the `type` must be a delegate type. Following the `type` is the `name` of the event. Listing 11.2 shows how to declare an event:

LISTING 11.2 Event Declaration: `MenuItem.cs`

```
using System;

public delegate void MenuHandler();

public class MenuItem
{
    public event MenuHandler MenuSelection;

    string text;
```

LISTING 11.2 continued

```
    public MenuItem(string text)
    {
        this.text = text;
    }

    public void Fire()
    {
        MenuSelection();
    }

    public string Text
    {
        get
        {
            return text;
        }
        set
        {
            text = value;
        }
    }
}
```

The `MenuItem` class defines an event named `MenuSelection`. The delegate type of this event is `MenuHandler`. The `MenuHandler` delegate is defined just before the `MenuItem` class declaration.

For C++ Programmers

C++ doesn't have events that are a part of its language specification. However, the C# events can be fairly compared to the event models in technologies such as XWindows, MS Windows, and the COM+ asynchronous event model.

For Java Programmers

Unlike Java events, which are invoked with adapters, C# events use delegates to accomplish the same task.

Registering for Events

Programs that want to be notified of when an event occurs register their interest with the event provider. In the last section, the `MenuItem` class was an event provider. Its event is public and it can also be considered an event publisher. Programs that register can be considered subscribers. This is the publisher/subscriber pattern. Listing 11.3 shows how to wire up subscribers to publishers.

LISTING 11.3 Event method handlers: `DelegatesAndEvents.cs`

```
using System;

public class DelegatesAndEvents
{
    public static int Main(string[] args)
    {
        // create main menu
        Menu myMenu = new Menu("Financial Sites");

        // create data object
        SiteManager sm = new SiteManager();

        // create menu items
        MenuItem addMenu = new MenuItem("Add");
        MenuItem delMenu = new MenuItem("Delete");
        MenuItem modMenu = new MenuItem("Modify");
        MenuItem seeMenu = new MenuItem("View");

        // add events
        addMenu.MenuSelection += new MenuHandler(sm.AddSite);
        delMenu.MenuSelection += new MenuHandler(sm.DeleteSite);
        modMenu.MenuSelection += new MenuHandler(sm.ModifySite);
        seeMenu.MenuSelection += new MenuHandler(sm.ViewSites);

        // populate menu with menu items
        myMenu.Add(addMenu);
        myMenu.Add(delMenu);
        myMenu.Add(modMenu);
        myMenu.Add(seeMenu);

    // invoke menu for user input
        myMenu.Run();

        return 0;
    }
}
```

There are four components in Listing 11.3: `DelegatesAndEvents`, `Menu`, `MenuItem`, and `SiteManager`.. The `DelegatesAndEvents` class is the main component. It sets up the other three components—a `Menu` component, `myMenu`, which takes care of user interface and user interaction; a `SiteManager` component, `sm`, that performs all the data manipulation for the program; and the `MenuItem` components, which represent choices that could be made with a program.

Once each object is created, the program begins connecting them. Since the `SiteManager` class contains the data manipulation, its methods are associated with `MenuItem` objects by assigning the `SiteManager` method to a new `MenuHandler` delegate. In the same call, the `MenuHandler` delegate is assigned to the `MenuSelection` of its corresponding `MenuItem`. For example, the first event registration takes the `AddSites()` method from the `sm` object, assigns it to a new `MenuHandler` delegate, and then adds that delegate to the `addMenu MenuItem`.

Attaching to an event is performed through the event add operator (+=). Similarly, the remove event operator (-=) is used to detach a subscriber from an event. Detachment prevents any subsequent notifications from the publisher object.

Each of these `MenuItems` is then added to the `myMenu Menu` object. Now the program has a `Menu` object with `MenuItems`, and each `MenuItem` has an associated method from `SiteManager`. To get the `Menu` to show on the screen and begin user interaction, the `Run()` method of the `myMenu` object is invoked. This ends the `DelegatesAndEvents` class role because when the `Run()` method of the `Menu` class completes, it returns to the `Main()` method, and the program ends immediately.

Implementing Events

The methods to implement an event must conform to the signature and return type of the event's delegate type. This way they can be assigned to the delegate before being added to the event. Listing 11.4 shows a class with event method implementations.

LISTING 11.4 Event method handlers: `SiteManager.cs`

```
using System;

public class SiteManager
{
    SiteList sites = new SiteList();

    public SiteManager()
    {
        this.sites = new SiteList();
```

LISTING 11.4 continued

```
        this.sites[this.sites.NextIndex]
            = new WebSite("Joe",
                          "http://www.mysite.com",
                          "Great Site!");
        this.sites[this.sites.NextIndex]
            = new WebSite("Don",
                          "http://www.dondotnet.com",
                          "okay.");
        this.sites[this.sites.NextIndex]
            = new WebSite("Bob",
                          "www.bob.com",
                          "No http://");
    }

    public void AddSite()
    {
        string siteName;
        string url;
        string description;

        Console.Write("Please Enter Site Name: ");
        siteName = Console.ReadLine();

        Console.Write("Please Enter URL: ");
        url = Console.ReadLine();

        Console.Write("Please Enter Description: ");
        description = Console.ReadLine();

        sites[sites.NextIndex] = new WebSite(siteName,
                                             url,
                                             description);
    }

    public void DeleteSite()
    {
        string choice;

        do
        {
            Console.WriteLine("\nDeletion Menu\n");
            DisplayShortList();

            Console.Write("\nPlease select an item to delete:  ");
            choice = Console.ReadLine();

            if (choice == "Q" || choice == "q")
                break;
```

LISTING 11.4 continued

```
            if (Int32.Parse(choice) <= sites.NextIndex)
                sites.Remove(Int32.Parse(choice)-1);

        } while (true);
    }

    public void ModifySite()
    {
        Console.WriteLine("Modifying Sites.");
    }

    public void ViewSites()
    {
        Console.WriteLine("");

        for (int i=0; i < sites.NextIndex; i++)
        {
            Console.WriteLine("Site: {0}", sites[i].ToString());
        }

        Console.WriteLine("");
    }

    private void DisplayShortList()
    {
        for (int i=0; i < sites.NextIndex; i++)
        {
            Console.WriteLine("{0} - {1}", i+1, sites[i].ToString());
        }

        Console.WriteLine("Q - Quit (Back To Main Menu)");
    }
}
```

These methods conform to the signature and return type of the `MenuHandler` delegate. They don't have parameters and return void, just as the `MenuHandler` delegate. For example, look at the `AddSites()` method. It's easily used as an event method because its signature and return type conform to the `MenuHandler` delegate signature and return type.

Firing Events

When events are invoked, they are also said to be fired. Events are fired from within the class that defines them. Outside of their class, they can only be used on the left side of an `add` or `remove` operation. The next example shows how to invoke or fire an event.

LISTING 11.5 Firing events: `Menu.cs`

```
using System;
using System.Collections;

public class Menu
{
    ArrayList menuItems = new ArrayList();
    string title;

    public Menu(string title)
    {
        this.title = title;
    }

    public void Add(MenuItem menu)
    {
        menuItems.Add(menu);
    }

    public void Run()
    {
        string choice;

        do
        {
            Console.WriteLine("{0}\n", title);

            foreach(MenuItem menu in menuItems)
            {
                Console.WriteLine("{0} - {1}", menuItems.IndexOf(menu),
menu.Text);
            }

            Console.WriteLine("Q - Quit");
            Console.Write("\nPlease Choose:  ");
            choice = Console.ReadLine();

            if (choice.ToUpper() != "Q")
            {
                ((MenuItem)menuItems[Int32.Parse(choice)]).Fire();
            }

        } while (choice != "Q");
    }
}
```

This example has an array of `MenuItem` objects, a constructor that initializes its title string, an `Add()` method, and a `Run()` method. The `Add()` method adds a new `MenuItem`

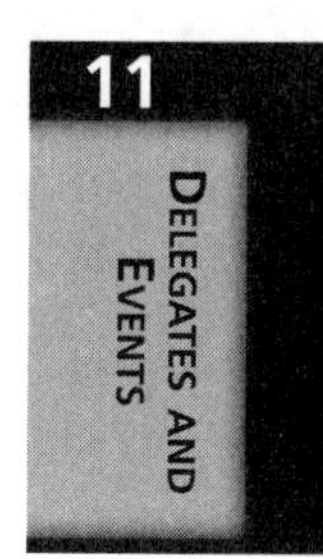

object to the menuItems ArrayList. The Run() method has a do loop that displays a menu, accepts user input, and fires the event corresponding to a user's selection.

The first task of the do loop in the Run() method is to print the menu title and then each menu item to the console. Each menu item is printed in a foreach loop that takes the Text property of each MenuItem object in the menuItem ArrayList. Each menu item is associated with its numeric position in the ArrayList.

Then the program waits for input from the user. When a menu item is selected, the program uses the input number to index into the menuItems ArrayList. This is done by using the ToInt() method of the string class. The menuItems ArrayList returns a reference to the MenuItem object matching what the user selected. Since an ArrayList collection accepts objects of type Object, each MenuItem is converted to type Object when it's inserted. Therefore, when pulling the MenuItem object from the menuItems ArrayList, it must be converted back to the MenuItem class type. The indexing and conversion are enclosed in parentheses to ensure that the sequence of operations is performed together. This produces a proper reference to an object of type MenuItem.

Using the dot operator, the Fire() method of the new MenuItem object is invoked. This is the same Fire() method that was shown in the "Defining Event Handlers" section earlier in this chapter. Here it is again for reference.

```
public void Fire()
{
    MenuSelection();
}
```

This example shows how to invoke an event. It must be a member of the class where the event is defined, because events can't be invoked directly. The Fire() method calls the MenuSelection event as if it were another method. Recall that a method was assigned to this event in the Main() method of the DelegatesAndEvents class. It is that method, assigned in the Main() method, which is invoked.

Modifying Event Add/Remove Methods

Adding and removing callback methods to and from events, respectively, is configurable. This technique is most appropriate when you have a large number of events, but only a few are hooked up at a time. This is accomplished by including add and remove accessors with an event declaration. Listing 11.6 is a modification of the MenuItem class from a previous example in this chapter.

LISTING 11.6 Event Accessors: `MenuItem2.cs`

```
using System;

public delegate void MenuHandler(object sender, EventArgs e);

public class MenuItem
{
    int    numberOfEvents;
    string text;

    private MenuHandler mh = null;

    public event MenuHandler MenuSelection
    {
        add
        {
            mh += value;
            numberOfEvents++;
        }
        remove
        {
            mh -= value;
            numberOfEvents--;
        }
    }

    public MenuItem(string text)
    {
        this.text = text;
        numberOfEvents = 0;
    }

    public void Fire()
    {
        OnMenuSelection();
    }

    protected void OnMenuSelection()
    {
        if (mh != null)
        {
            mh(this, null);
        }
    }

    public string Text
    {
        get
        {
            return text;
```

LISTING 11.6 continued

```
        }
        set
        {
            text = value;
        }
    }

    public int NumberOfEvents
    {
        get
        {
            return numberOfEvents;
        }
    }
}
```

The MenuSelection event of Listing 11.6 is different from events in previous listings. It has two accessors, add and remove. The add accessor adds the method, indicated by the value keyword, to the event, and then increments the numberOfEvents field. The remove accessor removes the method, indicated by the value keyword, from the event, and then decrements the numberOfEvents field. This modification could be useful if it were necessary to know how many subscribers there were to an event. To support this, the read-only property NumberOfEvents was added to the class.

Events may be treated much like indexers and properties in using the abstract, overrides, static, and virtual modifiers. Using the overrides modifier, the accessors of an event in a derived class may specialize the implementation of abstract and virtual base class events.

The SiteManager class in Listing 11.4 depends on the WebSite and SiteList classes in Listing 11.7. Therefore, Listing 11.7 is presented for completeness.

LISTING 11.7 The Rest of the Program: MenuItem2.cs

```
using System;
using System.Collections;

/// <summary>
///     Describes a single web site.
/// </summary>
public class WebSite
{
    const string http = "http://";
    public static readonly string currentDate
        = new DateTime().ToString();
```

LISTING 11.7 continued

```
    string siteName;
    string url;
    string description;

    public WebSite()
        : this("No Site", "no.url", "No Description") {}

    public WebSite(string newSite)
        : this(newSite, "no.url", "No Description") {}

    public WebSite(string newSite, string newURL)
        : this(newSite, newURL, "No Description") {}

    public WebSite(string newSite,
                   string newURL,
                   string newDesc)
    {
        SiteName    = newSite;
        URL         = newURL;
        Description = newDesc;
    }

    public override string ToString()
    {
        return siteName    +
               ", "        +
               url         +
               ", "        +
               description;
    }

    public override bool Equals(object evalString)
    {
        return this.ToString() == evalString.ToString();
    }

    public override int GetHashCode()
    {
        return this.ToString().GetHashCode();
    }

    protected string ValidateUrl(string url)
    {
        if (!(url.StartsWith(http)))
        {
            return http + url;
        }
        return url;
    }
```

LISTING 11.7 continued

```
    public string SiteName
    {
        get
        {
            return siteName;
        }
        set
        {
            siteName = value;
        }
    }

    public string URL
    {
        get
        {
            return url;
        }
        set
        {
            url = ValidateUrl(value);
        }
    }

    public string Description
    {
        get
        {
            return description;
        }
        set
        {
            description = value;
        }
    }

    ~WebSite() {}
}

/// <summary>
///     This object holds a collection of sites.
/// </summary>
public class SiteList
{
    protected SortedList sites;

    public SiteList()
    {
```

LISTING 11.7 continued

```
        sites = new SortedList();
    }

    public int NextIndex
    {
        get
        {
            return sites.Count;
        }
    }

    public WebSite this[int index]
    {
        get
        {
            if (index > sites.Count)
                return (WebSite)null;

            return (WebSite) sites.GetByIndex(index);
        }
        set
        {
            if ( index < 10 )
                sites[index] = value;
        }
    }

    public void Remove(int element)
    {
        sites.RemoveAt(element);
    }
}
```

Listing 11.7 doesn't add any new material to this chapter, but it does manage the underlying information for the program and make it more realistic. Therefore, it's here for your convenience. Listing 11.8 shows how to compile the listings in this chapter so they may be run as a program.

LISTING 11.8 Compilation Instructions for Chapter 11 Listings

```
csc WebSites.cs SiteManager.cs Menu.cs MenuItem.cs
➥DelegatesAndEvents.cs
```

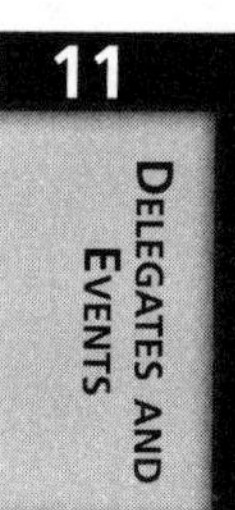

Summary

This chapter covered delegates and events. It explained how delegates provide the infrastructure for events. There was a section showing how to define a delegate. It showed how to define delegate method handlers and how to connect them to a delegate. This led to the purpose of delegates and a demonstration of how to invoke methods through delegates. The multi-cast delegate section showed how to invoke multiple delegates at the same time through a single delegate invocation. Delegates can be compared with the equal (==) and not equal (`!=`) operators.

The section covering events showed how to define event handlers using delegates. Then there was a section on how subscribers can register for events. Once registered, the subscriber is notified when those events are invoked. There was a section showing how to invoke or fire events. Finally, there was an example of how to customize events by implementing their `add` and `remove` accessors.

Organizing Code with Namespaces

IN THIS CHAPTER

- Why Namespaces? *278*
- Namespace Directives *280*
- Creating Namespaces *282*
- Namespace Members *286*
- Scope and Visibility *286*

Namespaces are such an ingrained part of C#; in fact, there is not way to avoid them. Every program written in C# uses the System namespace. All the libraries supporting C# are included in namespaces, which must be identified in a program before being used. The designers of C# thought namespaces were so important that they should design them into the language.

This chapter covers C# namespaces and provides information on scope and visibility issues affecting C# programs. Throughout this book, namespaces have been used consistently. In the `using System;` statement at the beginning of each program, the word "System" was a reference to the `System` namespace. This chapter explains why it was necessary to reference the System namespace in the simplest of programs.

The primary purpose of namespaces is to help organize code and reduce conflicts between names. The concepts are generally simple, but this chapter points out some strange situations that can occur with namespaces. There's also a section that deals with scope and visibility. C#'s scope and visibility rules are generally similar to other languages, but there are a few differences that need to be identified.

Why Namespaces?

Namespaces are language elements that help organize code and reduce conflicts between various identifiers in a program. By helping organize code, namespaces help programmers manage their projects more efficiently. Reducing conflict is perhaps the greatest strength of namespace. This allows reusable components from different companies to be used in the same program without the worry of ambiguity caused by multiple instances of the same identifier.

For Java Programmers

Namespaces are similar to Java packages with a single, significant difference. There are no built-in language rules forcing C# namespaces to conform to the directory placement of the files. C# namespaces are logical, rather than physical.

Organizing Code

Namespaces provide a logical organization for programs to exist. C# namespaces provide a hierarchical framework upon which to organize code. Starting with a top-level namespace, sub-namespaces are created to further categorize code, based upon its purpose.

> **Note**
>
> The CLR does not recognize that namespaces exist. For instance, it does not know that `Console` is a member of the System namespace. It thinks that System.Console is the name of the class.

The perfect example is how the base class library is organized. It begins at the `System` namespace. There are several classes at the `System` namespace level, such as `Console`, `DateTime`, and `Exception`. Consider the `System.Console.WriteLine()` method. `System` refers to the base class library namespace by the same name. `Console` is a class under the `System` namespace. `WriteLine()` is a method of the `Console` class within the `System` namespace.

There are also nested namespaces within the `System` namespace, such as the `System.Collections`, `System.Data`, and `System.Security` namespaces. This is along the lines of the hierarchical nature of namespaces. Using nested namespaces is good for categorizing code.

> **Note**
>
> The hierarchical organization of code into namespaces is a logical function only. It differs from object-oriented inheritance in that there are no language rules defining the hierarchical relationship. Namespaces can be used to organize code in any way the programmer desires.

Avoiding Conflict

Another service provided by namespaces is the capability to avoid naming conflicts between program elements. Class and method names often collide when using multiple libraries. This risk increases as programs get larger and include more third-party tools. For example, consider the following program that uses two different types of ArrayList.

```
System.Collections.ArrayList myArrayList;
SuperDuperWidgets.Collections.ArrayList thierArrayList;

// some type of initialization on myArrayList ...

foreach (widget myWidget in myArrayList)
{
    theirArrayList.Add(myWidget);
}
```

Check out the ArrayList declarations in the first two lines of code. The first line declares an ArrayList from the System.Collections namespace named myArrayList. The second line references a namespace from a fictitious company named Super Duper Widgets. Perhaps the ArrayList from the SuperDuperWidgets.Collections namespace provides some capability that isn't available in the ArrayList in the System.Collections namespace. This means that the two types of ArrayList must be present in the same program to copy from one to the other.

Without the namespace declaration in the first two lines, this would not be possible because the class names of both objects is ArrayList. That would cause a compiler error because the ArrayList class was defined twice, causing logical ambiguity in the program. Fortunately, namespaces solve this problem. They let the compiler know exactly which ArrayList is being used in each situation. Namespaces avoid conflict by introducing certainty into a program.

Namespace Directives

Namespace directives are C# language elements that allow a program to identify namespaces that are used in a program. They allow namespace members to be used without specifying a fully qualified name. When using the entire namespace hierarchy to make a method call, a program uses a method's fully qualified name. If every statement in every method used fully qualified names, a program would be very wordy, redundant, and perhaps more difficult to read. C# has two namespace directives: `using` and `alias`.

The `using` Directive

The `using` directive permits specification of a method call without the mandatory use of a fully qualified name. Here's an example of the `using` directive:

```
using System;

class HowdyPartner
{
    static void Main()
    {
        // Write to console
        Console.WriteLine("Howdy, Partner!");
    }
}
```

The first line in the example has the `using` directive. It states that the programs in this file can use any types within the `System` namespace without a fully qualified name. In other words, statements don't need the `System` prefix. This is evident in the `Main()`

method where the `Console.WriteLine()` method is invoked. `Console` is not a namespace. It is the name of a class that holds the static method, `WriteLine()`.

The benefits in clarity and of not needing to type in fully qualified names are apparent with the `using` directive approach. In cases where there is a possible conflict, the fully qualified name can be used where necessary. The next section discusses another way of avoiding conflict, with the `alias` directive.

The `alias` Directive

The `alias` directive allows a program to have another name for a namespace. This is commonly used to provide a shorthand notation to long namespace names. Besides aliasing namespaces, aliases can also be assigned other types of objects within a namespace. Aliases conform to the rules for any other C# identifier. The following example shows how difficult program readability can get when every member is fully qualified.

> **Tip**
>
> Check out the .NET Framework Reference in the .NET Framework SDK for a good picture of how the .NET Framework is laid out. It provides some familiarity with what is where.

```
public class AliasExample
{
    public static int Main(string[] args)
    {
        System.Security.Permissions.FileIOPermissionAccess
            fileAccess = new
        System.Security.Permissions.FileIOPermissionAccess();

        fileAccess =
 System.Security.Permissions.FileIOPermissionAccess.NoAccess;

        System.Console.WriteLine(
            "Level of File IO Access: {0}", fileAccess);

        return 0;
    }
}
```

How many programmers do you think would like to maintain several thousand lines of that? If you like it, then you can have it. I'm going to use the language constructs available to make life easier for me and others. There's absolutely no doubt about what is being executed, but I think we can use C# aliases to make this a bit more palatable. The following example shows how to implement a program with aliases.

```
using System;
using aFilePerm
    = System.Security.Permissions.FileIOPermissionAccess;

public class AliasExample
{
    public static int Main(string[] args)
    {
        aFilePerm fileAccess = new aFilePerm();

        fileAccess = aFilePerm.NoAccess;

        Console.WriteLine(
            "Level of File IO Access: {0}", fileAccess);

        return 0;
    }
}
```

The second line shows how to declare an alias. The `alias`, `aFilePerm`, becomes an `alias` for the enum named `System.Security.Permissions.FileIOPermissionAccess`. This shows that aliases aren't limited to only namespaces. Although the `alias` follows the `using System;` declaration, it must still use the word `System` when specifying the namespace.

Within the program, the `alias` `aFilePerm` is used everywhere the fully qualified name would have been. With a combination of the `using` directive and `alias`, this program has become much easier to read. The fact that the `alias` has a meaningful name also facilitates more self-documenting code.

For Java Programmers

C# allows programmers to define an alias for a namespace, which is generally a shorthand notation for a namespace. Java has no equivalent.

Creating Namespaces

Creating a namespace is easy. Just use the word namespace followed by the name. The contents of a namespace are enclosed in curly braces. The following example shows how to create a namespace and add a class to it.

```
namespace SAMS
{
    using System;
    using aFilePerm =
        System.Security.Permissions.FileIOPermissionAccess;

    public class FilePerm
    {
        aFilePerm fileAccess = new aFilePerm();

        public FilePerm()
        {
            fileAccess = aFilePerm.NoAccess;
        }

        public aFilePerm FileAccess
        {
            get
            {
                return fileAccess;
            }
            set
            {
                fileAccess = value;
            }
        }
    }
}
```

The first line shows that this code is in the `SAMS` namespace. The next example shows how to access this class from another class.

```
using System;
using aFilePerm = System.Security.Permissions.FileIOPermissionAccess;

public class AliasExample
{
    public static int Main(string[] args)
    {
        SAMS.FilePerm myFilePerm = new SAMS.FilePerm();

        aFilePerm fileAccess = myFilePerm.FileAccess;

        Console.WriteLine("Level of File IO Access: {0}",
                          fileAccess);

        return 0;
    }
}
```

This example shows how to access a class in another namespace. Within the `Main()` method there is a field named `myFilePerm` of type `FilePerm` within the `SAMS` namespace. This is declared with the fully qualified name of `SAMS.FilePerm`.

The `SAMS` namespace helps avoid conflicts with other classes that may be named `FilePerm`, but the namespace name is kind of short. Because the name is short and relatively common, its entirely possible for a name conflict to occur—for instance, there may be another namespace named `SAMS` in a third-party library. In fact if there were another book within the company using this namespace name, there would definitely be a conflict. Also, just using the name `SAMS` is too generic. It would help to organize this book's code with something more specific.

Nested namespaces are just the trick to meet both goals of organization and avoiding conflict. A nested namespace makes the category of code more specific and makes more sense. Also, deepening the hierarchy reduces the chance of conflicts. Here's a revised namespace:

```
namespace SAMS
    namespace Unleashed {
    // namespace members
    }
}
```

This shows more specialization in namespaces. However, what if there were a Visual C# Unleashed, ASP.NET Unleashed, or .NET Unleashed that used the `SAMS.Unleashed` namespace? It may be a good idea to go a tad bit further. Here's another revision:

```
namespace SAMS.Unleashed.csharp.Chapter12 {
    // namespace members
}
```

With this new namespace, it's highly unlikely that there will ever be a namespace conflict between code in this namespace and any third-party library. It's nested all the way to four levels to provide a safe degree of uniqueness. It's possible to specialize it even further, but there is such a thing as too far.

Notice that this example used a dot operator between namespace names, whereas the previous example actually reproduced the namespace syntax of the `Unleashed` namespace within the `SAMS` namespace. The first example could have been written just as well like this:

```
namespace SAMS.Unleashed
{
    // namespace members...
}
```

Either method is acceptable, and they both produce the same results. It depends on how a program is written as to which method should be used. The dot operator is quick and short and adapts well to the four-level namespace above. On the other hand, if there were two nested namespaces declared in the same file, it may be more convenient to use the more explicit notation. The following example is one way to specify that certain namespace members belong in specific nested namespaces.

```
namespace SAMS
{
    namespace Unleashed
    {
        // namespace members...
    }
    namespace TwentyOneDays
    {
        // namespace members...
    }
}
```


Some would find this more expressive. Regardless of how namespaces are declared, they are always accessed with the same type of fully qualified name. Here's a snippet of how that four-level nested namespace would be accessed:

```
// code to access namespace
        SAMS.Unleashed.csharp.Chapter12.FilePerm myFilePerm
            = new SAMS.Unleashed.csharp.Chapter12.FilePerm();
...
```

Namespaces are not bound to a single file or directory structure. They're logical, not physical. They can be divided among multiple files. The following examples show how the same namespace can be used in different files. Notice that they're not only in two different files, but they're also in two different directory names and at two different levels.

This code shows the contents of the file located at `C:\examples\chapter12.cs`:

```
namespace SAMS.Unleashed.csharp.Chapter12 {
    // namespace members
}
```

This code shows the contents of the file located at `C:\testcode\csharp\alias.cs`:

```
namespace SAMS.Unleashed.csharp.Chapter12 {
    // namespace members
}
```

While similar code is normally located in the same place, this shows the logical nature of namespaces.

Tip

Plan out namespaces ahead of time. Good organization avoids problems later. With a good hierarchy in place, new code can be easily developed to fit in logically with no problem.

Namespace Members

Namespaces are at the top of the food chain of the C# language element hierarchy. While namespaces may contain other namespaces, nothing else can encapsulate a namespace. Here's a list of all the C# language elements that go into namespaces:

- classes
- delegates
- enums
- interfaces
- structs
- namespaces
- `using` directives
- `alias` directives

Scope and Visibility

When discussing scope, this section refers to the parts of a program where an identifier refers to a specific declaration. Visibility refers to whether an identifier can be seen by other program elements. Now let's look at how these concepts are implemented in C#.

Besides required blocks, it's possible to place blocks within code, independent of supporting other language constructs. This could be useful if there was an iterative or recursive routine with local variables that weren't necessary for subsequent iterations or recursive calls. By isolating these variables and the data working on them within a block, a local scope can be established where those data items only exist within the scope of that block and aren't carried longer than necessary. This could help conserve system memory.

Visibility of a program's elements exists within their declaring block and within subordinate blocks. Within class, interface, and structure blocks, data may be declared anywhere and still be visible anywhere throughout the block. However, on methods, properties, and indexers, data must be declared before it is referenced. Otherwise, that data won't be visible.

Subordinate program elements may re-declare the visible program elements outside their local scope. Doing so effectively hides the enclosing block's corresponding program element. To access those corresponding program elements within the local scope of a block, use the this operator.

Within methods and property, indexer, and event accessors, program elements may be re-declared. However, re-declaration within an unnamed block or flow-control statement causes an error. Here's an example of both proper and improper re-declaration:


```
using System;
using aFilePerm
    = System.Security.Permissions.FileIOPermissionAccess;

public class AliasExample
{
    aFilePerm fileAccess;

    public AliasExample()
    {
        fileAccess = aFilePerm.AllAccess;
    }

    public static int Main(string[] args)
    {
        AliasExample myAlias = new AliasExample();

        myAlias.printFilePerm();

        return 0;
    }

    public void printFilePerm()
    {
        string fileAccess = this.fileAccess.ToString();

        // error - can't redeclare within method
        //if (this.fileAccess != aFilePerm.NoAccess)
        //{
        //    int fileAccess = (int)this.fileAccess;
        //}

        // error - can't redeclare within method
        //{
        //    int fileAccess = (int) this.fileAccess;
        //}
```

```
            Console.WriteLine("Level of File IO Access: {0}", fileAccess);
        }
    }
```

This code shows legal and illegal examples of class member re-declaration. At the class level, there is a member named `fileAccess` with a type defined by the `aFilePerm` alias. Within the scope of the `printFilePerm()` method, the visibility of the class member named `fileAccess` of alias type `aFilePerm` is effectively hidden by the declaration of the local string field also named `fileAccess`.

Any unqualified reference to `fileAccess` within the `printFilePerm()` method refers to the local string type `fileAccess`. In this case, the program needs access to the class level field `fileAccess`, so it uses the `this` keyword.

Two illegal redeclarations are marked out with comments. The first is within an `if` statement that re-declares the `fileAccess` name as an `int`. The second is in an unnamed block that tries to do the same thing. It may work in other languages, but not in C#.

Summary

This chapter covered the subject of namespaces, and included a brief discussion about scope and visibility. The namespaces discussion provided rationale for why namespaces are necessary, including organization and avoiding conflict.

There was a section on how to make abbreviated code references. It included examples of how to employ the `using` directive to avoid adding fully qualified names to every method call. The `alias` directive provides a way to use shorthand notation when executing class members.

Once namespaces were well explained, this chapter showed how to create them. This included nested namespaces and some tips on how to organize a namespace hierarchy. There was also a section that detailed the members of a namespace.

The final section of this chapter outlined a couple areas to keep in mind about scope and visibility. It showed an example of what to do and what not to do.

Previous chapters have discussed some of the namespace members, but there are more to cover. The next chapter is about another namespace member, the `struct`.

CHAPTER 13

Creating structs

In This Chapter

- Identifying the `class/struct` Relationship 290
- Type System Unification 294
- Designing a New Value Type 295

A `struct` is a C# object with value semantics. It's an object because it possesses class members, such as fields and methods, the same as a class. Value semantics refers to the way a `struct` is initialized and used, like the primitive types (int, `char`, `double`, and so on). One fact that hasn't been emphasized in earlier chapters is that the primitive types are also referred to as value types and have value semantics. This is because the primitive types are `structs`. This has important consequences because it means that everything in C# is an object, creating an environment of type system unification. It's even possible to create new value types by creating a new `struct`.

Identifying the class/struct Relationship

Although `classes` and `structs` are both objects, they serve separate purposes and it's good to know when to use each. The primary differences between the two types are in the area of value versus reference types and in their inheritance properties. There are also a couple other differences that are presented in this chapter. Before racking and stacking the differences, let's look at exactly what a `struct` is and what it looks like, as shown in the following example.

```
public struct Person
{
        string name;
        int    height;
        int    weight;

        public bool OverWeight()
        {
                // some theoretical calculation
                return false;
        }
}
```

Perhaps the `struct` in this code belongs to an application for dieticians. The `name`, `height`, and `weight` fields represent the information that may be of use to a dietician. Additionally, there is an `OverWeight()` method that could use the fields to provide the dietician with more sophisticated information about the person.

This `struct` looks just like a `class` with one notable feature: a `struct` keyword in place of where a `class` keyword would be. There will be more mechanical differences, as additional information is presented on `structs`, but this is the most significant.

This `struct` was designed to create a new data type, `Person`. As a new type, it can be reused in many other applications. Some people may ask, "If `classes` create new types and `structs` create new types, why have two object members in the same language that perform the same function?" There are significant differences, and the decision whether to use a `class` or a `struct` can usually be determined by matching the requirements of a program with the facts presented in this section.

Value Versus Reference

Structs are value types, and classes are reference types. A value type is one that is allocated on the stack or inline as a part of another object. The implementation that does exist supports manipulation of the object's data. A `struct` is often a small object that needs to be treated like a primitive type.

`classes` are reference types. When they are created, their memory is allocated on the heap. The nature of a `class` varies a great deal, but they're normally used for those implementations requiring more processing power. They have class members that support the role of attributes. However, a `class` would normally be used to implement a piece of business logic, rather than to support data related or primitive-like objects.

Stacks and Heaps

For an appreciation of `struct` efficiency consider the way they're allocated in `stack` memory versus versus `heap` memory (the `stack` and the `heap`). Figure 13.1 shows a simplified hypothetical memory layout. On the left is the `stack`; the top of the `stack` is indicated by a thick vertical bar. The rest of the rectangle, to the right of the thick vertical bar, is the `heap`.

Memory allocation, whether it is heap or stack, is generally simple and efficient. he process of managing and releasing that memory is where the greatest difference lies.

Memory on the heap is allocated in chunks as necessary. Over time, memory is released and reallocated, causing fragmentation and indicating a need for additional memory management. The resources employed to manage and release heap memory are other memory objects, keeping track of what's happening. Heap memory management is more efficient than secondary storage management, such as hard disk, but stack memory management is more efficient than heap memory management.

The efficiency of the stack derives from the way it's allocated, managed, and released. The stack begins on the far left of Figure 13.1. For each method that is called, a new entry is placed on the stack, causing it to grow incrementally to the right, toward the thick bar.

continues

A hardware stack pointer (represented by the letters SP and the arrow in Figure 13.1) normally controls the location of the next place to allocate memory. The types of items placed on the stack are indexer and method parameters and local fields of method bodies and various class member accessors. Each time a new value is pushed on the stack, SP is moved farther to the right by the size of the value's type. Conversely, when a value is popped from the stack, SP moves to the left.

Only the top (farthest to the right in Figure 13.1) item on the `stack` can be removed. This is a very simple mechanism that avoids the fragmentation problems inherent in `heap` memory management. The combination of hardware `stack` pointer, simple memory management, and release rules make the stack the most efficient memory structure in an operating system. A `struct` is a very efficient object because it is allocated on the `stack`.

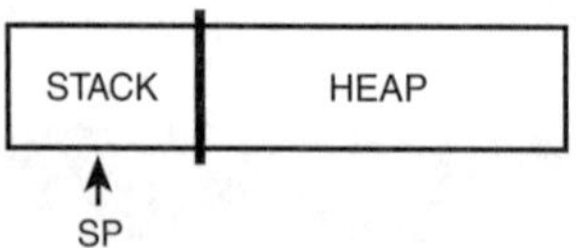

FIGURE 13.1
A simplified memory layout, showing the heap and the stack.

Inheritance

`structs` are much more limited than `classes` in the way of inheritance. They can't inherit from another `class` or `struct`. However, they can implement `interfaces`. They are also implicitly considered objects.

`structs` are implicitly `sealed`. Remember that a sealed `class` is one that can't be inherited from. Along the same lines, `structs` are `sealed`, but the `sealed` keyword doesn't have to be explicitly stated because it's implied.

On the other hand, `classes` are fully extendable; they can choose to inherit from any other `class` or `interface`. They can be inherited from, unless they are explicitly `sealed`. Both `classes` and `structs` are implicitly derived from the `object` type. A `class` may have base classes, but its ultimate base `class` is always be `object`.

Other Differences

Assignment between structs, from source struct to target struct, creates a new struct by copying from the source struct to the target struct. This differs significantly from classes, where only the reference is copied. There are no references and therefore no null fields. Furthermore, there are normal constructors, but default constructors cannot be explicitly defined. The default constructor of a struct is implicitly defined and its behavior is to zero out the struct's data members. Speaking of constructors, structs don't have destructors. Say that three times fast!

Trade-Offs

The trade-offs between structs and classes affect the efficiency of an application and its capability to perform certain types of operations. In deciding whether to make an object a struct or a class, consider their differences in relation to their roles as value versus reference and their inheritance properties.

As a value type, allocated on the stack, structs provide a significant opportunity to increase program efficiency. Objects on the stack are faster to allocate and de-allocate. A struct is a good choice for data-bound objects which don't require too much memory. The memory requirements should be considered based on the fact that the size of the memory available on the stack is more limited than memory available on the heap. If there is a chance of exhausting stack memory, be prepared to catch the StackOverflowException.

Since stack space is limited, it would be illogical to try to put everything there. The size of an object may not make stack allocation practical. It may also be useful to keep an object around for a while. These would be good reasons to create a class instead of a struct. For large objects with lots of logic, it would be better to create a class instead of a struct.

The object-oriented properties desired in an object have a bearing on whether it should be a class or struct. For instance, the need to encapsulate an aggregation of other objects points to the need for a class. Although structs can encapsulate, a large amount of encapsulation may make them an impractical solution, which follows the rationale of the previous paragraphs.

A struct would certainly provide adequate abstraction for a data type. However, if abstractions were necessary to form the framework of a multi-level object hierarchy, a class is the only way to perform such a task.

When considering the need for polymorphism, a `struct` is also limited. Since `class` and `struct` inheritance is not an option, the only thing available is polymorphism with `interfaces`. Although interface polymorphism is available with `structs`, there is no way to support a requirement for invoking a generic base class member implementation. A class-based polymorphic requirement, such as the need to invoke a base class implementation along with derived class overrides, is a clear indication of when a `class` would make a better choice. If polymorphism is not a requirement, then it's necessary to look at the other factors mentioned to determine whether an object type should be implemented as a struct.

Type System Unification

Type system unification is a concept where all types in C# are considered to be objects. The primitive types are value types, which are `structs`. Both `classes` and `structs` implicitly inherit from object. This leads to the conclusion that all types in C# are objects, which is type system unification. Value semantics enhances a program's ability to take advantage of efficiencies discussed earlier in this chapter. At the same time, all types have the inherent ability to support reference semantics in a clear and direct manner.

The Pre-Defined Types as `structs`

To further the concept of type system unification, C# pre-defined types are really `struct` typesAnd `structs` implicitly inherit from type `object`. The pre-defined types have formal `struct` definitions, which essentially makes them objects. Table 13.1 shows the pre-defined types and their `struct` equivalents.

TABLE 13.1 Simple Type/`struct` Comparison

Simple Type	*Corresponding* `struct`
`bool`	`System.Boolean`
`char`	`System.Char`
`sbyte`	`System.Sbyte`
`byte`	`System.Byte`
`short`	`System.Int16`
`ushort`	`System.UInt16`
`int`	`System.Int32`
`uint`	`System.UInt32`

TABLE 13.1 continued

Simple Type	*Corresponding* `struct`
`long`	`System.Int64`
`ulong`	`System.UInt64`
`float`	`System.Single`
`double`	`System.Double`
`decimal`	`System.Decimal`
`string`	`System.String`

Boxing and Unboxing

Type system unification also defines techniques called `boxing` and `unboxing`. This is where primary types and reference types can be used interchangeably.

`Boxing` is the process used to convert a primitive type to a reference type. To implement this, all you need to do is assign the primitive type to an object. You don't have to do anything special to make this happen, as it occurs implicitly during the assignment.

`Unboxing` is just the opposite. We already know the underlying type of an object that's been boxed. Therefore, all we need to do is cast the object back to its original primitive type while assigning it back to a field of its original primary type. The following example shows a `boxing` and `unboxing` operation on a built-in Boolean field.

```
bool profitable = true;
object madeMoney = profitable;
bool doneWell = (bool) madeMoney;
```

The first line establishes the Boolean field, initializing it to `true`.

The second line converts the Boolean field to an object type. This is the `boxing` operation. Now there is an object on the heap named `madeMoney` with the value `true`. Since it's now in a reference type, it can be used anywhere a reference type can be used.

The last line converts the object back to a Boolean. This is called `unboxing`. For `unboxing` to work, the value must be explicitly cast back to its original type. Any attempt to cast it to another type will raise a `System.InvalidCastException`.

Designing a New Value Type

C# allows a user to create their own structs. This is useful if there is a need for creating a new value type, an object with value semantics. Struct creation is much like designing a new class. There are differences and the following paragraphs will show what they are. The following example provides a general description of the syntax of creating a struct.

```
[modifiers] struct Name [: Interface [, Interfaces]]
{
        // non-default constructors
        // fields
        // methods
        // properties
        // indexers
        // events
        // delegates
        // enumerations
        // structs
}
```

A `struct`'s optional `modifiers` are the same as a class. Of course, the primary exceptions are that `structs` don't have `abstract` and `sealed` modifiers. They can't have a `protected` modifier, either. These restrictions stem from the fact that `structs` can't inherit or be inherited from.

The `struct` keyword identifies this as a `struct`. The name is a valid C# identifier. Although `structs` can't inherit `classes` or other `structs`, they can inherit `interfaces`. The preceding example shows that the syntax for inheriting `interfaces` is the same as class inheritance.

`struct` members are pretty much the same as `class` members with a couple significant exceptions. `structs` do not have default constructors nor do they have destructors. Here's an example of how to create a `struct`:

```
using System;

public struct Currency
{
    private double amount;

    public Currency(double amount)
    {
        this.amount = amount;
    }

    public override string ToString()
    {
        return String.Format("{0:C}", amount);
    }

    public static Currency operator+(Currency c1, Currency c2)
    {
        Currency cur = new Currency();
```

```
            cur.Amount = c1.Amount + c2.Amount;
            return cur;
        }

        public double Amount
        {
            get
            {
                return amount;
            }
            set
            {
                amount = value;
            }
        }
    }
```

The struct in this example is for holding money values or currency. Although it can't declare a default constructor, it has declared a constructor accepting a single parameter of type double.

Another interesting property is that structs can't inherit other classes or structs. However, they do implicitly inherit from object, since the object type is the ultimate base class of any other type. This is how the ToString() method of the object class can be overridden. The ToString() method returns a formatted string that shows the value in the form of money.

The addition (+) operator is overloaded to accept two Currency structs. It adds the amounts of the two Currency parameters, assigns the total to a new Currency struct, and returns the new struct. Overloaded operators are typical for new value types. This gives them semantics similar to the built-in types, and makes them more intuitive and easier to use.

The Amount property exists to encapsulate the underlying value of the struct. It's used to support members like the overloaded addition operator. This property is also a good idea because the implementation of the private amount field might turn into a decimal later, and this protects the struct and user code from breaking.

The actual implementation to use this struct is much like a class. The following example shows an implementation of using structs.

```
public class StructExample
{
    public static int Main(string[] args)
    {
        Currency myCurrency1 = new Currency(2.0);
        Currency myCurrency2 = new Currency(3.62);
```

```
            Currency myCurrency3 = myCurrency1 + myCurrency2;

            Console.WriteLine("Amount = {0}", myCurrency3);

            return 0;
        }
    }
```

This example shows how to instantiate and perform a couple of operations on the `Currency` class, shown a few paragraphs earlier.

The first two lines in the `Main()` method instantiate two `Currency` structs. This is the same syntax used for creating class objects. Although these instantiations used the existing single `double` type parameter constructor, each of them could have also used the default constructor. Although default constructors for a struct cannot be defined, they can still be used to initialize a `struct` by zeroing out the `struct's` data members. This would have created a `Currency` object initialized to `$0.00`.

The previous example shows how initialization of a `struct` can occur with the `new` operator. It's also a good way to initialize a `struct` with parameters. Without using a `new` operator, a `struct` must be manually initialized by explicitly assigning values to fields or properties or calling a method, as appropriate. Another reminder is that although the `new` operator was used, similar to `class` initialization, the `struct` object is still allocated on the stack, and not the heap.

The next line shows the addition operator being used with the two `Currency structs`. This invokes the overloaded addition (+) operator of the currency struct.

The next line prints the value of the `Currency struct myCurrency3` to the console. There are two interesting events occurring here. First, `myCurrency3` is being boxed for this operation. It's converted from type `Currency struct` to type `object`. Once it's converted to an `object`, the overridden `ToString()` method produces the formatted output of the `Currency struct`. This all happens through the graces of type system unification.

Summary

This chapter covered C# `struct` types. Primary topics covered were the relationship between classes and structures, type system unification, and designing a new type.

The section on the relationship between classes and `structs` discussed three general topics: the differences between value and reference types, `structs` being value and `classes` being reference; inheritance differences; and a few topics covering other miscellaneous differences between `classes` and `structs`.

The next section described type system unification. Its main topics were the pre-defined types and boxing/unboxing. The part on pre-defined types explained how all the built-in types in C# are really `structs`. The boxing/unboxing section showed the relationship between value types and object types by converting between the two.

Finally, there was a demonstration of how to create a struct type. It embodied all the properties of `structs` described in the first couple of sections. There was also an example driver program showing how to use that `struct`.

CHAPTER 14

Implementing Interfaces

In This Chapter

- Abstract Class Versus Interface *302*
- Interface Members *302*
- Implicit Implementation *304*
- Explicit Implementation *315*
- Mapping *321*
- Inheritance *324*

Interfaces are C# language elements that force a `class` or struct to implement a specified set of members. They also indicate to users of a class or struct that certain members are supported. This is somewhat of a contract between the user and implementer. Interfaces establish a set of expected standards that enhance class and struct reuse and polymorphism.

C# classes and structs support multiple interface inheritance. Factors associated with managing multiple interface inheritance include explicit interface implementation and interface mapping. Explicit interface implementation deals with determining which interface is being implemented and resolving ambiguity between multiple interfaces with identical member definitions. Interface mapping is the process of determining if and where an interface member is implemented.

Abstract Class Versus Interface

Interfaces are specifications defining the type of behaviors a class must implement. They are contracts a class uses to allow other classes to interact with it in a well-defined and anticipated manner. Interfaces define an explicit definition of how classes should interact.

Abstract classes are a unit of abstraction, whereas interfaces define further specification. Abstract class members may contain implementations. The exception is when an abstract class member has an abstract modifier. Derived classes must implement abstract class members with an abstract class modifier, but they don't have to implement any other method declared `virtual`. On the other hand, classes inheriting an interface must implement every interface member. Interface members have no implementation.

For C++ Programmers

Although C++ doesn't have a language element called an interface, the same effect can be simulated with abstract classes.

Interface Members

The definition of an interface is much like a class or struct. However, since an interface doesn't have an implementation, its members are defined differently. The following example shows how to declare an interface, and how an interface is structured.

```
[modifiers] interface IName [: Interface [, Interfaces]]
{
        // methods
        // properties
```

```
        // indexers
        // events
}
```

The modifiers may be `public`, `protected`, `protected internal`, internal, `private`, and `new`. Next is the keyword `interface` followed by the interface name, `IName`. A common convention is to make the first character of an interface name the letter `I`. The name must conform to the C# rules for identifiers. After the name is a colon and a comma-separated list of interfaces that this one inherits. The colon/inherited interface list is optional.

While classes have only single class inheritance, they have multiple interface inheritance. Along the same lines, structs and interfaces have multiple interface inheritance. Later sections of this chapter explain some of the issues involved with multiple interface inheritance.

Following the interface inheritance list is the interface body, which consists of the members enclosed in curly braces. Legal members are methods, properties, indexers, and events.

Interface members are assumed to be `public` and therefore, have no modifiers. Interface implementations must also be `public`. Since the purpose of interfaces is to define class members that are callable by another class, making them `public` is logical.

Methods

Interface methods are declared similar to normal methods. The difference is that they have no implementation. The following example shows an interface method:

```
string GetRating(string stock, out string provider) ;
```

Everything is the same as a normal method, except that it has a semicolon on the end in place of the implementation.

Properties

At first it may seem strange that a property could be an interface member, especially when the normal implementation of a property is associated with a field. Although fields can't be interface members, this doesn't prevent the use of properties, because the implementation of a property is independent of its specification.

Remember, one of the primary reasons for properties is to encapsulate implementation. Therefore, the fact that an interface doesn't have fields is not a limiting factor. For this reason, property specifications may be added to interfaces with no problem, as shown in the following example.

```
decimal PricePerTrade
{
get ;
set ;
}
```

This property example is structured similar to a regular property. However, the accessors don't have implementations. Instead, the `get` and `set` keywords are closed with a semicolon.

Indexers

Interface indexer specifications appear similar to normal indexers, but their accessor specifications are the same as property accessors, as shown in the following example:

```
decimal this[string StockName]
        {
            get ;
            set ;
        }
```

This example shows an indexer accepting a `string` argument and returning a `decimal` value. Its `get` and `set` accessors are closed with semicolons, similar to how property accessors are defined.

Events

There is no difference in the way interface events and normal events are declared. Here's an example:

```
public delegate void ChangeRegistrar(object sender,
                                     object evnt);
...
event ChangeRegistrar PriceChange ;
```

As you can see, the event has the exact same type of signature that goes in a normal class. No surprises.

Implicit Implementation

It is easy to implement a single interface on a class or struct. It simply requires declaration of the class or struct with interface inheritance and the implementation of those interface members. There are two views of implicit interface implementation. The first is the easiest: a single class implementing a single interface. The second uses interface polymorphism by implementing the same interface in two separate classes.

Single Class Interface Implementation

As I mentioned previously, it is easy for a class to implement a single interface. Implementation of an interface simply follows the rules set in previous sections. Listing 14.1 shows the full interface definition.

LISTING 14.1 The IBroker Interface Definition

```
using System;
using System.Collections;

public delegate void ChangeRegistrar(object sender,
                                     object evnt);

public interface IBroker
{
    string GetRating(string stock) ;

    decimal PricePerTrade
    {
        get ;
        set ;
    }

    decimal this[string StockName]
    {
        get ;
        set ;
    }

    event ChangeRegistrar PriceChange ;
}
```

The interface in Listing 14.1 represents a plausible set of class members that a stockbroker or financial company may want to expose to a client. The interface name begins with the conventional `I` in `IBroker`. It has four members—the `GetRating()` method, the `PricePerTrade` property, an indexer, and the `PriceChange` event. The delegate type of the `PriceChange` property, `ChangeRegistrar`, is defined also. As mentioned earlier, interface members do not have implementations. It is up to a class or struct to implement interface member declarations. Listing 14.2 shows a class that implements the `IBroker` interface, which is an object that represents a finance company. It has an overridden constructor to ensure that the `pricePerTrade` field is initialized properly.

LISTING 14.2 An Implementation of the `IBroker` Interface

```
public class FinanceCompany : IBroker
{
    Hashtable hash = new Hashtable();
    decimal pricePerTrade;

    public FinanceCompany() : this(10.50m)
    {
    }

    public FinanceCompany(decimal price)
    {
        pricePerTrade = price;
    }

    public string GetRating(string stock)
    {
        return "Buy";
    }

    public decimal PricePerTrade
    {
        get
        {
            return pricePerTrade;
        }
        set
        {
            pricePerTrade = value;
            PriceChange("FinanceBroker", value);
        }
    }

    public decimal this[string StockName]
    {
        get
        {
            return (decimal)hash[StockName];
        }
        set
        {
            hash.Add(StockName, value);
        }
    }

    public event ChangeRegistrar PriceChange;
}
```

As the listing shows, the private `pricePerTrade` field is encapsulated by the `PricePerTrade` property. The `get` accessor of the `PricePerTrade` property simply returns the current value of the `pricePerTrade` field. However, the `set` accessor provides more functionality. After setting the new value of the `pricePerTrade` field, it invokes the `PriceChange` event.

The `PriceChange` event is based on the `ChangeRegistrar` delegate, which specifies two object parameters. When the `PriceChange` event is invoked in the `set` accessor of the `PricePerTrade` property, it receives two arguments. The `string` argument is implicitly converted to `object`. The `decimal` value is boxed and passed as an object. Event declaration and implementation are normally as simple as shown in Listing 14.2. However, the event implementation can be much more sophisticated if there is a need to override its `add` and `remove` accessors.

The `GetRating()` method is implemented to always return the same value. In this context, the broker is always bullish, regardless of the real value of a stock. This is typical of the booming '90s.

The indexer implementation uses the `HashTable` collection for maintaining its data. Its `get` accessor returns the value of a stock using `Stockname` as a key. Since a `HashTable` stores its contents as objects, a cast is necessary to convert the value to `decimal`. The `set` accessor creates a new `Hashtable` entry by using the indexer string parameter as a key and the value passed in as the hash value.

Now there's a class that faithfully follows the contract of the `IBroker` interface. What's good about this is that any program can now use that class and automatically know that it has specific class members that can be used in a specific way. Listing 14.3 shows a program that uses a class that implements the `IBroker` interface.

LISTING 14.3 Implementation of Single Interface Inheritance

```
public class InterfaceTester
{
    public static int Main(string[] args)
    {
        FinanceCompany  finco = new FinanceCompany();
        InterfaceTester iftst = new InterfaceTester();

        finco.PriceChange += new ChangeRegistrar(
                             iftst.PricePerTradeChange);

        finco["ABC"] = 15.39m;
        finco["DEF"] = 37.51m;
```

LISTING 14.3 continued

```
        Console.WriteLine("ABC Price is {0}", finco["ABC"]);
        Console.WriteLine("DEF Price is {0}", finco["DEF"]);

        Console.WriteLine("");

        finco.PricePerTrade = 10.55m;

        Console.WriteLine("");

        string recommendation = finco.GetRating("ABC");

        Console.WriteLine(
"finco's recommendation for ABC is {0}", recommendation);

        return 0;
    }

    public void PricePerTradeChange(object sender,
                                    object evnt)
    {
        Console.WriteLine(
            "Trading price for {0} changed to {1}.",
             (string) sender, (decimal) evnt);
    }
}
```

And here's the output from Listing 14.3:

```
ABC Price is 15.39
DEF Price is 37.51

Trading price for FinanceBroker changed to 10.55.

finco's recommendation for ABC is Buy
```

Because the `FinanceCompany` class implements the `IBroker` interface, the program in Listing 14.3 knows what class members it can implement. The `Main()` method instantiates a `FinanceCompany` class (`finco`) and an `InterfaceTester` class (`iftst`).

The `InterfaceTester` class has an event handler method named `PricePerTradeChange()`. In the `Main()` method, the `InterfaceTester` class makes itself a subscriber to the `finco.PriceChange` event by assigning the `PricePerTradeChange()` event handler to that event.

Next, two stocks are added to `finco`. This is done by using a stock name as the indexer and giving it a `decimal` value. The assignment is verified with a couple `Console.WriteLine()` methods.

The `finco` object's `PricePerTrade` property is changed to `10.55m`. Within the `FinanceCompany` class, this invokes the `PriceChange` event, which calls the `PricePerTrade()` method of the `InterfaceTester` class. This shows how events are effective tools for obtaining status changes in an object. Finally, the `GetRating()` method of the `finco` object is invoked. Method calls are the most typical interface members.

The output follows the sequence of events in `Main()`. The first two lines show the stock values from the indexer. The third line is from the `PricePerTradeChange` event handler in the `InterfaceTester` class. The last line of output shows the results of requesting a stock rating from the `finco` object.

Simulating Polymorphic Behavior

Implementing an interface in a single class and using it is relatively easy, as described in the previous section. However, the real power of interfaces comes from being able to use them in multiple classes. Let's take a look at using interfaces to implement polymorphism in a program.

Let's combine the examples from the previous section in a test program. Listing 14.4 shows another implementation of the `IBroker` interface. It's a bit more complicated than the `FinanceCompany` class implementation of `IBroker` due to additional objects and extra class members with more logic.

LISTING 14.4 Another Implementation of the `IBroker` Interface

```
public enum StockRating
{
    Buy=0, Accumulate, Hold, Sell
}

public struct Stock
{
    private string      name;
    private decimal     price;
    private StockRating rating;

    public string Name
    {
        get
        {
            return Name;
        }
        set
        {
            name = value;
```

LISTING 14.4 continued

```
        }
    }

    public StockRating Rating
    {
        get
        {
            return rating;
        }
        set
        {
            rating = value;
        }
    }

    public decimal Price
    {
        get
        {
            return price;
        }
        set
        {
            price = value;
        }
    }
}

public class StockBroker : IBroker
{
    Hashtable stocks = new Hashtable();
    decimal pricePerTrade;
    string  brokerName;

    public StockBroker() : this(13.59m, "Anonymous")
    {
    }

    public StockBroker(decimal price)
             : this(price, "Anonymous")
    {
    }

    public StockBroker(decimal price, string brokerName)
    {
        pricePerTrade   = price;
        this.brokerName = brokerName;
    }
```

LISTING 14.4 continued

```
    public string GetRating(string stock)
    {
        Stock myStock = (Stock) stocks[stock];
        return Enum.GetName(typeof(StockRating),
                      myStock.Rating);
    }

    private StockRating AssignRating(Stock newStock)
    {
        Random myRand = new Random();
        int nextRating = myRand.Next(4);
        return (StockRating) Enum.ToObject(
                          typeof(StockRating),
                          nextRating);
    }

    public decimal PricePerTrade
    {
        get
        {
            return pricePerTrade;
        }
        set
        {
            pricePerTrade = value;
            PriceChange(brokerName, value);
        }
    }

    public decimal this[string StockName]
    {
        get
        {
            Stock myStock = (Stock)stocks[StockName];
            return myStock.Price;
        }
        set
        {
            Stock myStock  = new Stock();
            myStock.Name   = StockName;
            myStock.Price  = value;
            myStock.Rating = AssignRating(myStock);

            stocks.Add(StockName, myStock);
        }
    }

    public event ChangeRegistrar PriceChange;
}
```

There are two object types participating in the implementation of the StockBroker class: StockRating and Stock. The StockRating enum is used by the StockBroker class to define its rating system for individual stocks. The Stock struct defines a stock. It has three private fields, encapsulated by three corresponding properties. The name field is a string that holds the name of the stock. A stock's value is held in the decimal price field. The rating field holds a company's assessment of the value of a particular stock. Its type is the StockRating enum. The StockBroker class uses these two objects.

The StockBroker class implements the IBroker interface. It has three fields that support this implementation. The stocks field is a Hashtable that holds objects of type Stock struct. A StockBroker object manages the amount it charges for trades through the decimal pricePerTrade field. Its name is saved in the brokerName string field. To support its fields, the StockBroker class implements three overloaded constructors.

Stock objects are created in the StockBroker indexer. The set accessor creates a new Stock object. The name is assigned through the stock object Name property from the StockName indexer string parameter. The price is set with the indexer value by using the Price property of the stock object. When creating a rating, the AssignRating() method is used to obtain a StockRating enum value and assign that to the Rating property of the stock object. Using the HashTable Add() method, the stock is then added to the stocks collection.

The private AssignRating() method determines what type of rating each stock has by using the Random class. After instantiating the myRand object of type Random, it calls the Next() method and assigns the result to the nextRating int field. The Next() method of the myRand object accepts an int parameter, indicating upper bound of the result. This produces an int in the range of 0 to 4. This is also the corresponding range of values in the StockRating enum. This value is then translated into a valid StockRating enum value using the ToObject() method of the Enum class. This peculiar method of rating a stock is indicative of the Millennium generation .com companies trying to survive. They have no real management skill, yet their techniques are not quite as retro as those implemented in the FinanceCompany class.

To return a string type, the GetRating() method must first obtain the correct Stock object from the stocks collection. It does this by using the string parameter stock as an index for the stocks collection. Once it has the stock, it uses the GetName() method of the Enum class to translate the Rating property (which returns a StockRating type) from the stock object into a string.

The PricePerTrade property is the same as the one for the FinanceCompany class. Its get accessor simply returns the pricePerTrade decimal field. When setting the property, the set accessor assigns the new value to the pricePerTrade decimal field and then invokes the `PriceChange` property. Any subscribed classes are notified with the value of the `brokerName` field and the new `pricePerTrade` `decimal` field value.

Despite the increased complexity of the `StockBroker` `class` implementation over the `FinanceCompany` class, they are both used in the same way. They provide the same type of services because they implement the `IBroker` interface. Listing 14.5 shows a program that uses both of these classes, implementing polymorphic behavior to exploit the power of interfaces.

LISTING 14.5 Using Two Classes with the Same Interface

```
public class InterfaceTester
{
    public static int Main(string[] args)
    {
        string recommendation;
        ArrayList Brokers = new ArrayList();

        Brokers.Add(new FinanceCompany(7.32m));
        Brokers.Add(new StockBroker(11.51m, "Gofer Broke"));

        InterfaceTester iftst = new InterfaceTester();

        foreach(IBroker broker in Brokers)
        {
            broker.PriceChange += new ChangeRegistrar(
                                    iftst.PricePerTradeChange);

            broker["ABC"] = 15.39m;
            broker["DEF"] = 37.51m;

            Console.WriteLine("");
            Console.WriteLine("ABC Price is {0}", broker["ABC"]);
            Console.WriteLine("DEF Price is {0}", broker["DEF"]);

            Console.WriteLine("");

            broker.PricePerTrade = 10.55m;

            Console.WriteLine("");

            recommendation = broker.GetRating("ABC");

            Console.WriteLine(
            "Broker's recommendation for ABC is {0}",
            recommendation);
        }
```

LISTING 14.5 continued

```
        return 0;
    }

    public void PricePerTradeChange(object sender,
                                    object evnt)
    {
        Console.WriteLine(
            "Trading price for {0} changed to {1}.",
             (string) sender, (decimal) evnt);
    }
}
```

And here's the output:

```
ABC Price is 15.39
DEF Price is 37.51

Trading price for FinanceBroker changed to 10.55.

Broker's recommendation for ABC is Buy

ABC Price is 15.39
DEF Price is 37.51

Trading price for Gofer Broke changed to 10.55.

Broker's recommendation for ABC is Accumulate
```

Listing 14.5 shows how to implement polymorphism with interfaces. It does this by creating an instance of both the `FinanceCompany` and `StockBroker` classes and using each through the `IBroker` interface. The `Main()` method of the `IntefaceTester` class begins by declaring an `ArrayList` collection named `brokers`. Each of the `IBroker` derived classes is created and added to the `brokers` collection.

All of the primary implementation of the `Main()` method is enclosed in a `foreach` loop. Although both the `FinanceCompany` and `StockBroker` objects were instantiated and placed into the `broker` collection individually, they're extracted as `IBroker` objects in the `foreach` loop. Within the `foreach` loop, only the `IBroker` interface members are used on each object.

First, the `PricePerTradeChange()` event handler is added to the `PriceChange` event of each broker. Any time the `PricePerTrade` property of a broker changes, this event handler is called. It's interesting to note that this demonstrates how a single event handler can be used as a callback for multiple events. Each of these multiple events is the price change for each of the brokers.

Each `broker` object's stock list is initialized with the same values, and then these values are printed, which shows that the interface works the same for all `IBroker` objects, regardless of the `IBroker` derived object's underlying implementation.

Then, the `PricePerTrade` property of each broker is updated. This triggers each broker's `PriceChange` event and invokes the `PricePerTradeChange()` event handler of the `InterfaceTester` class. After that, the `GetRating()` method is called. This is more demonstration of the power of interfaces. Interface polymorphism works for all `IBroker` object members.

Since the first four lines of output are from the `FinanceCompany` class, they are the same as from the previous section. Then fifth and sixth lines show the stock prices. The seventh line is from the `PriceChange` event invocation, where it called the `PricePerTradeChange()` event handler. It prints out the name of the `StockBroker` company and the new trading price. The last line shows the recommendation from the `StockBroker` class. The recommendation is regenerated every time the program is run and therefore will most likely change between program executions.

Explicit Implementation

Sometimes it's necessary to explicitly declare which interface a class or struct member implements. One common reason for explicit implementation is when there is multiple interface inheritance and two or more `interfaces` declare a member with the same name. Another reason to use explicit interface implementation is to hide a specific implementation.

To perform explicit interface implementation, a class implements an interface member by using its fully qualified name. The implementation is not declared with modifiers, because they are implicitly hidden from an object of the implementing class. However, they are implicitly `visible` to objects of the explicit interface type. The examples in this chapter show how this occurs.

Disambiguation of interfaces occurs when a class inherits two or more interfaces that have members with the same signature. Normally, a class can just implement the interface member, regardless of which interface it is a part of. However, sometimes it may be necessary to specify the interface in a user class. For this reason, explicit implementation is necessary to specify which implementation serves which interface. Listing 14.6 shows the implementation of two interfaces that have some members in common.

LISTING 14.6 A Couple Interfaces with Identical Members

```
using System;
using System.Collections;

public delegate void ChangeRegistrar(object sender,
                                     object evnt);

public interface IBroker
{
    string GetRating(string stock) ;

    decimal PricePerTrade
    {
        get ;
        set ;
    }

    decimal this[string StockName]
    {
        get ;
        set ;
    }

    event ChangeRegistrar PriceChange ;
}

public interface IAdvisor
{
    string GetRating(string stock) ;

    decimal HourlyFees
    {
        get ;
        set ;
    }

    decimal this[string StockName]
    {
        get ;
        set ;
    }
}
```

The `IBroker` interface in this listing is the same as in previous sections. In the `IAdvisor` interface, the `GetRating()` method and indexer methods are the same as corresponding members in the `IBroker` interface.

Sometimes it may be necessary to hide the implementation of an interface so that the particular member is private to the implementing class and users won't know about it. Hiding interface implementations can occur regardless of whether there are one or more inherited interfaces.

Hiding interface members with explicit implementation is not like hiding an inherited method. The difference is that a conversion is required to reference the explicit interface member definition. It generally indicates that the interface is not of particular interest to a user of that class or struct. Listing 14.7 demonstrates explicit interface implementation.

LISTING 14.7 Explicit Interface Implementation

```
public class FinancialAdvisor : IBroker, IAdvisor
{
    Hashtable stocks = new Hashtable();
    decimal pricePerTrade;
    decimal fee;
    string  brokerName;

    public FinancialAdvisor()
            : this(13.59m, 11.73m, "Anonymous")
    {
    }

    public FinancialAdvisor(decimal tradePrice,
                            decimal fee,
                            string  brokerName)
    {
        pricePerTrade   = tradePrice;
        this.fee        = fee;
        this.brokerName = brokerName;
    }

    string IBroker.GetRating(string stock)
    {
        Stock myStock = (Stock) stocks[stock];
        return Enum.GetName(typeof(StockRating),
                           myStock.Rating);
    }

    string IAdvisor.GetRating(string stock)
    {
        Stock myStock = (Stock) stocks[stock];
        return Enum.GetName(typeof(StockRating),
                            (((int)++myStock.Rating)%5));
    }
```

LISTING 14.7 continued

```
    private StockRating AssignRating(Stock newStock)
    {
        Random myRand = new Random();
        int nextRating = myRand.Next(4);
        return (StockRating) Enum.ToObject(
                             typeof(StockRating),
                             nextRating);
    }

    decimal IAdvisor.HourlyFees
    {
        get
        {
            return fee;
        }
        set
        {
            fee = value;
        }
    }

    public decimal PricePerTrade
    {
        get
        {
            return pricePerTrade;
        }
        set
        {
            pricePerTrade = value;
            PriceChange(brokerName, value);
        }
    }

    public decimal this[string StockName]
    {
        get
        {
            Stock myStock = (Stock)stocks[StockName];
            return myStock.Price;
        }
        set
        {
            Stock myStock  = new Stock();
            myStock.Name   = StockName;
            myStock.Price  = value;
            myStock.Rating = AssignRating(myStock);
```

LISTING 14.7 continued

```
            stocks.Add(StockName, myStock);
        }
    }

    public event ChangeRegistrar PriceChange;
}
```

Listing 14.7 shows how to use explicit interface implementation to disambiguate the implementation of interface methods and the hiding of interface members. The code is very similar to the `StockBroker` class implementation with a few exceptions.

The `FinancialAdvisor` class inherits both the `IBroker` and `IAdvisor` interfaces. Commas separate multiple interface inheritance in class and struct declarations. This class has three explicit interface member implementations.

The `GetRating()` method has two explicit member implementations. The first is the explicit implementation of the `IBroker.GetRating()` method. It obtains the rating from the `Stock` object returned from the `stocks` collection.

The second explicit implementation is the `IAdvisor.GetRating()` method. It's similar to the `IBroker.GetRating()` method implementation, except that the `myStock.Rating` object is manipulated before being converted to a `string`. This manipulation consists of incrementing its value, casting it to an `int` type, and performing a modulus operation with the value `5` to keep it in the range of legal `StockRating` values.

The third explicit implementation is the `IAdvisor.HourlyFees` property. This property is essentially hidden to a `using` object of type `FinancialAdvisor`. This is how interface members are hidden.

The first two properties are also hidden to objects of type `FinancialAdvisor` class. However, they serve to disambiguate the implementation of that member to using classes. Listing 14.8 shows how these two members are used.

LISTING 14.8 Implementation of Explicit Interface Members

```
public class InterfaceTester
{
    public static int Main(string[] args)
    {
        string recommendation;
        FinancialAdvisor  finad = new FinancialAdvisor();
        InterfaceTester   iftst = new InterfaceTester();
```

LISTING 14.8 continued

```
        finad.PriceChange += new ChangeRegistrar(
                                iftst.PricePerTradeChange);

        finad["ABC"] = 15.39m;
        finad["DEF"] = 37.51m;

        Console.WriteLine("ABC Price is {0}", finad["ABC"]);
        Console.WriteLine("DEF Price is {0}", finad["DEF"]);

        Console.WriteLine("");

        finad.PricePerTrade = 10.55m;

        // HourlyFees property is hidden and won't compile
        //finad.HourlyFees    = 9.00m;

        Console.WriteLine("");

        recommendation = ((IBroker) finad).GetRating("ABC");

        Console.WriteLine(
            "(IBroker)finad's recommendation for ABC is {0}",
            recommendation);

        recommendation = ((IAdvisor)finad).GetRating("ABC");

        Console.WriteLine(
            "(IAdvisor)finad's recommendation for ABC is {0}",
            recommendation);

        return 0;
    }

    public void PricePerTradeChange(object sender,
                                    object evnt)
    {
        Console.WriteLine(
            "Trading price for {0} changed to {1}.",
             (string) sender, (decimal) evnt);
    }
}
```

Listing 14.8 shows how to use class members that were explicitly implemented to avoid disambiguation. It also has a commented member that shows how an error would be generated for an explicit implementation of an interface member for the purpose of hiding. The `Main()` method of the `InterfaceTester` class contains code that tests the `FinancialAdvisor` class implementation.

The `FinancialAdvisor` class is instantiated, the `PricePerTradeChange` event handler is added to the `PriceChange` event, and the stock values are instantiated similar to examples in previous sections. The first difference in this code is the commented section where there is an instruction to load the `HourlyFees` property of the finad object with a value. If this were uncommented, it would produce a compiler error because the code wouldn't recognize the `HourlyFees` property of the `FinancialAdvisor` class since that property is hidden through explicit interface implementation.

The next portion of code uses the `GetRating()` methods of the `FinancialAdvisor` class. The difference between the two calls is the object type used. Each is cast to a separate interface type. The object with the `IBroker` cast invokes the explicit implementation of `IBroker.GetRating()`. Similarly, the `IAdvisor` cast causes invocation of the `IAdvisor.GetRating()` explicit member implementation. This is how explicit implementation for disambiguation of interface implementation is used.

Tip

The example in Listing 14.8 made the assumption that the classes implemented the interfaces. In a production environment, it would be necessary to use the `is` and `as` operators to avoid the exception that could be raised.

Mapping

Mapping is the method used to determine where and if an interface member is implemented. Interface mapping is important because programmers need a way to figure out why they're getting program errors for not implementing an interface. Another scenario might be strange program behavior because of an interface member implemented somewhere other than the class that directly inherits from the interface. The solution method is to understand enough about interface mapping to determine if and where an interface member was implemented.

In all previous cases, mapping was easy to determine: it happened directly in the derived class that implemented that interface. Most interface implementation occurs that way. However, interface mapping allows alternate means of determining whether an interface has been implemented. Besides the directly derived class of the interface, an implementation could be in the parent class hierarchy of the class derived from the interface. This follows object-oriented principles where a derived class *is* an inherited class. Remember, when declaring inheritance relationships with both a class and interfaces, the class comes first in the list. Using the `IBroker` and `IAdvisor` interfaces from previous sections in this chapter, Listing 14.9 shows an example of how this could occur.

LISTING 14.9 Interface Mapping Example

```
public class StockBroker
{
    Hashtable stocks = new Hashtable();
    decimal pricePerTrade;
    string  brokerName;

    public StockBroker() : this(13.59m, "Anonymous")
    {
    }

    public StockBroker(decimal price)
                    : this(price, "Anonymous")
    {
    }

    public StockBroker(decimal price, string brokerName)
    {
        pricePerTrade = price;
        this.brokerName = brokerName;
    }

    public string GetRating(string stock)
    {
        Stock myStock = (Stock) stocks[stock];
        return Enum.GetName(typeof(StockRating),
                      myStock.Rating);
    }

    private StockRating AssignRating(Stock newStock)
    {
        Random myRand = new Random();
        int nextRating = myRand.Next(4);
        return (StockRating) Enum.ToObject(
                            typeof(StockRating),
                            nextRating);
    }

    public decimal PricePerTrade
    {
        get
        {
            return pricePerTrade;
        }
```

LISTING 14.9 continued

```
        set
        {
            pricePerTrade = value;
            PriceChange(brokerName, value);
        }
    }

    public decimal this[string StockName]
    {
        get
        {
            Stock myStock = (Stock)stocks[StockName];
            return myStock.Price;
        }
        set
        {
            Stock myStock  = new Stock();
            myStock.Name   = StockName;
            myStock.Price  = value;
            myStock.Rating = AssignRating(myStock);

            stocks.Add(StockName, myStock);
        }
    }

    public event ChangeRegistrar PriceChange;
}
```

Listing 14.9 is the same as the `StockBroker` class in previous sections of this chapter with one significant exception: it doesn't inherit the `IBroker` interface. If a class were to inherit from this class, it would inherit the entire implementation. The following example shows how the C# interface mapping strategy works to find the implementation of interface members.

```
public class Accountant : StockBroker, IBroker
{
    // no implementation
}
```

The `Accountant` class has absolutely no implementation. However, it does inherit from the `StockBroker` class and therefore possesses the implementation of the `StockBroker` class.

The `Accountant` class also inherits the `IBroker` interface. It has no implementation of its own, yet the preceding code compiles perfectly without error. This is because with C# interface mapping, the implementation of the `StockBroker` class is used to map to the implementation requirements of the IBroker interface. Of note is that the interface mapping would have worked even if the StockBroker class inherited the IBroker interface itself.

If the StockBroker class did not implement a given interface member, the Accountant class would then be required to implement that member. Remember, every member of an interface must be implemented.

Inheritance

Interfaces have the capability to inherit from each other. This makes it possible to create an abstract hierarchy of interfaces that support some domain. When interfaces inherit from each other, they inherit the contract of the interfaces above them. Also, interfaces can inherit multiply from other interfaces. The following example shows how one interface can inherit from another.

```
public interface IShareTrade
{
    decimal PricePerTrade
    {
        get ;
        set ;
    }

    event ChangeRegistrar PriceChange ;
}

public interface IBroker : IShareTrade
{
    string GetRating(string stock) ;

    decimal this[string StockName]
    {
        get ;
        set ;
    }
}
```

The IBroker interface inherits the PricePerTrade property declaration and the PriceChange event declaration from the IShareTrade interface. All combined, these are the same interface members from the IBroker interface of previous sections. Therefore, any class inheriting the IBroker interface will have the exact same set of interface members to implement, which is also the exact same contract. Listing 14.10 demonstrates that the contract of inherited interfaces is passed with derived interfaces to derived classes and structs for implementation.

LISTING 14.10 Interfaces Inheriting Other Interfaces

```
public class FinanceCompany : IBroker
{
    Hashtable hash = new Hashtable();
    decimal pricePerTrade;

    public FinanceCompany() : this(10.50m)
    {
    }

    public FinanceCompany(decimal price)
    {
        pricePerTrade = price;
    }

    public string GetRating(string stock)
    {
        return "Buy";
    }

    public decimal PricePerTrade
    {
        get
        {
            return pricePerTrade;
        }
        set
        {
            pricePerTrade = value;
            PriceChange("FinanceBroker", value);
        }
    }

    public decimal this[string StockName]
    {
        get
        {
            return (decimal)hash[StockName];
        }
        set
        {
            hash.Add(StockName, value);
        }
    }

    public event ChangeRegistrar PriceChange;
}

public class InterfaceTester
{
```

LISTING 14.10 continued

```
    public static int Main(string[] args)
    {
        FinanceCompany  finco = new FinanceCompany();
        InterfaceTester iftst = new InterfaceTester();

        finco.PriceChange += new ChangeRegistrar(
                                 iftst.PricePerTradeChange);

        finco["ABC"] = 15.39m;
        finco["DEF"] = 37.51m;

        Console.WriteLine("ABC Price is {0}", finco["ABC"]);
        Console.WriteLine("DEF Price is {0}", finco["DEF"]);

        Console.WriteLine("");

        finco.PricePerTrade = 10.55m;

        Console.WriteLine("");

        string recommendation = finco.GetRating("ABC");

        Console.WriteLine(
            "finco's recommendation for ABC is {0}",
            recommendation);

        return 0;
    }

    public void PricePerTradeChange(object sender,
                                    object evnt)
    {
        Console.WriteLine(
            "Trading price for {0} changed to {1}.",
             (string) sender, (decimal) evnt);
    }
}
```

In this listing, the `FinanceCompany` class and the `InterfaceTester` class that uses it are exactly the same as in previous sections of this chapter. If one of the `FinanceCompany` class members specified in either the `IStockTrade` or `IBroker` interfaces were omitted from the `FinanceCompany` class implementation, a compiler error would be generated. This proves that an implementing class must fulfill the contract of every interface in the interface inheritance hierarchy.

Summary

This chapter covered C# interfaces. It explained the differences between abstract classes and interfaces. Interfaces have four types of members: methods, properties, indexers, and events.

The section on implicit implementation showed how to implement single interface inheritance and how to implement multiple interfaces.

Next was a section on explicit interface implementation. It showed how to implement explicit interfaces. There are a couple reasons why explicit interface implementation is necessary: to disambiguate multiple definitions and to hide interface members.

Interface mapping was discussed. An example showed how to determine if and where an interface member is implemented.

Interfaces also support inheritance. This chapter showed how an interface can inherit from another interface. Then there was a class that inherited from the derived interface, implementing the contract of the entire interface hierarchy.

CHAPTER

Performing Conversions

In This Chapter

- Implicit Versus Explicit Conversions *330*
- Value Type Conversions *335*
- Reference Type Conversions *338*

Conversion refers to the capability to change an object from one type to another. This is a runtime versus compile-time feature. Conversions can be explicit or implicit; implicit conversions occur when automatic conversion is possible, and explicit conversions are invoked when there is a possibility of error or data loss.

C# has built-in conversions for the primitive data types. Programmers can also create their own conversions when designing a new class. This provides the capability to convert to and from a user-defined type and another user-defined or primitive type.

Implicit Versus Explicit Conversions

There are two types of conversions in C#, implicit and explicit. Implicit conversions happen automatically, without any special syntax or casting. For example, converting an `int` to a `long` can occur as a normal assignment operation as follows:

```
int  myInt  = 5;
long myLong = myInt;
```

This conversion occurs without problem because of two simple principles. First, the `long` is a 64-bit value and the `int` is a 32-bit value. The `int` can fit into the `long` with no problem. Second, no errors will occur. The semantics of an `int` value don't change when it's put into a `long` variable. It still represents the same thing—a whole number.

On the other hand, an explicit conversion is required when the same principles don't lead to a positive result. To be more specific, larger types moving to smaller types or anything that can possibly generate an error require an explicit conversion.

For instance, going in the opposite direction of the previous example, `long` to `int` requires an explicit conversion because it's possible for a `long` value to be larger than what can be represented by an `int` type. This forces the programmer to make a deliberate decision that could cause corruption of data. Here's an example of converting the `long` type to the `int` type:

```
long myLong = 5;
int  myInt  = (int)myLong;
```

The other reason to use an explicit conversion is to cover the possibility of an error or exception being thrown. Looking at a scenario with the simple types, imagine what would happen if one were to attempt putting a negative number into an unsigned type. Sure, the unsigned type may be large enough to accept the value, but the results are likely to be undesirable. It causes an error because the value loses its semantics on conversion. This is why an explicit conversion is required, to force a potentially erroneous conversion to occur. Here's an example of converting a signed value to an unsigned type:

```
int  mySigned = -1;
uint myUnsigned = (uint)mySigned;  // myUnsigned = 4294967295
```

Implicit conversion occurs in expressions, too. During evaluation of expressions of two or more variables, some values are automatically converted to a larger type and the result is of that larger type. Table 15.1 shows the types that convert automatically in expressions.

A little more freedom to perform implicit conversions is available with constant expressions. For instance, implicit conversion is allowed when assigning an `int` type to an `sbyte`, `byte`, `short`, `ushort`, `uint`, or `ulong`. Where, in this case, the constant `int` type is the source and the other types are the `target`, `implicit` conversion is allowed when the value of the source type is within the allowable range of the target type. Additionally, a constant `long` may be converted to type `ulong` when the constant long is positive.

TABLE 15.1 Automatic Expression Conversions

To	*From*
`int`	`sbyte`, `byte`, `short`, `ushort`
`double`	`float`

There are essentially two choices when dealing with the results of automatic promotion conversions. The first is to make sure the value returned by the expression is placed into a field of the resulting type of the expression. Here's an example:

```
ushort myShort1 = 3, myShort2 = 5;
int result = myShort1 + myShort2;
```

Tip

Explicit conversion enables the results of an arithmetic expression to be the same type as the expression members. Remember, arithmetic expressions where the integral type is smaller than `int` produce a result of type `int`. Similarly, arithmetic expressions where the types are `float` produce a result of type `double`.

This example has an arithmetic expression where two `ushort` fields are added together. The result is an `int`, which is placed into an `int` field. A compiler error would have been generated if an attempt were made to place the result of the arithmetic operation into a ushort type field. The alternative is to perform an explicit conversion back to the original types in the expression. Here's an example:

```
ushort myShort1 = 3, myShort2 = 5;
ushort result = (ushort)(myShort1 + myShort2);
```

This code example is able to copy the value returned by the arithmetic expression into a field of type `ushort`. This is possible because of the conversion operation `(ushort)`. Another way implicit conversion occurs is during the boxing process. The conversion of a value type to an object type happens implicitly. This is due to the principle of type system unification where everything is an object. Since value type is an object, it is implicitly converted to type object during boxing. Here's an example:

```
char myChar = 'x';
object objChar = myChar;
```

During boxing, implicit conversions are also allowed between a value type and an interface that the value type implements. The following example shows a struct named `Currency` that inherits the `IMoney` interface.

```
public interface IMoney
{
    // No Members
}

public struct Currency : IMoney
{
    // Currency Implementation
}

...

IMoney myMoney = new Currency(10.25d);
```

Interfaces aren't required to have members, so `IMoney` simply gives `Currency` an alias identity. Being a value type, `Currency` is being boxed to fit into the interface object `myMoney`.

The opposite occurs during the unboxing process. There is a requirement to explicitly convert the object back to the value type. This follows the principle that all conversions that could result in an error must be done explicitly. For instance, suppose a `char` type is boxed to an object. What if the program tried to unbox that `char` type to an `int`? It would cause an error:

```
char myChar = 'x';
object objChar = myChar;
//int myInt = (int)objChar; // InvalidCastException
```

The behavior of explicit conversion during the unboxing process is somewhat different than other explicit conversions. This is because a value can be unboxed only to its original type. The following example shows how implicit conversion can occur after an object is unboxed to its original type:

```
int myInt = 7;
object objInt = myInt;
long myLong = (int)objInt;
```

The `objInt` field is converted from an object to an `int` with the `(int)` cast. Then it is implicitly converted to `long` when assigning it to `myLong`. Explicit conversion can be used after an object is unboxed to its original type, as the following example shows:

```
float myFloat = 2.3f;
object objFloat = myFloat;
myLong = (long)(float)objFloat;
```

The `objFloat` field is unboxed to its original type, `float`. Then it is explicitly converted to type `long` with the `(long)` cast. The last couple of examples could have been written with separate statements to first unbox the object to a field of its original type and then perform an explicit conversion to assign that value to a field of another type. This just shows a couple shortcuts that may simplify a complex expression.

So why must an explicit conversion exist at all for the unboxing operation if the explicit conversion doesn't allow unboxing to another type? Simply for consistency with the principles of conversion and making sure programmers explicitly state their intent (which could be considered more or less as documentation).

There's only one allowable implicit enum conversion—to convert the integer value `0` (zero) to an enum. All other enum conversions are explicit. Here's an example.

```
enum CurrencyType
{
    Dollar, Euro, Franc, Lire, Yen
};

...

CurrencyType myCurrType = 0;  // myCurrType = Dollar
```

In this example, the zero (`0`) is implicitly converted to the `CurrencyType` enum. One thing to note with this example is that if `CurrencyType.Dollar` would have been declared as one (`1`), where `Dollar = 1`, then the assignment statement would have resulted in an error because the `0` would be considered an illegal value.

Conversions that are normally performed implicitly can also be performed explicitly. Performing an explicit conversion where an implicit conversion is possible does not change the results of the conversion that would have resulted from an implicit conversion alone. It's just allowed.

Various results can be obtained from the explicit conversion of a `double` to a `float` type. A `double` type is rounded when converted to a `float`. If the `double` is smaller than what can fit into a `float`, the resulting value is zero. When the `double` is larger, the result is positive or negative infinity. An explicit conversion of a `double` to a `float` where the value of the `double` is `NaN` results in a `float` that is also `NaN`. The following example shows these effects.

```
float myFloat;

double posInfinity =
            999999999999999999999999999999999999999.0;
myFloat = (float)posInfinity;  // myFloat = Infinity

double negInfinity =
            -999999999999999999999999999999999999999.0;
myFloat = (float)negInfinity;  // myFloat = -Infinity

double zeroDouble =
            0.0000000000000000000000000000000000000000000001;
myFloat = (float)zeroDouble;  // myFloat = 0

double myDouble = Double.NaN;
myFloat = (float)myDouble;   // myFloat = NaN
```

This example shows various conditions that result from explicit assignment of `double` type values to `float` type variables. The first couple of examples show how positive and negative `infinity` are produced when the `double` value is too large to fit into a `float` type variable. The next example shows how values that are too small result in zero when explicitly converted from a `double` to a `float`. The last example shows how an explicit conversion from `double`, with a value of `NaN` (Not a Number), to `float` causes a `float` value to become `NaN`.

Conversion of a `float` or `double` to a `decimal` type results in a rounded value up to the 28th decimal place. Values that are too small result in zero. If the value is too large for the decimal to represent, `infinity`, or `NaN`, an `OverflowException` is thrown. Converting the other way, from `decimal` to `double` or `float`, can result in loss of precision, but still won't throw an exception. The following example shows a few results of when `float` and `double` types are explicitly converted to the `decimal` type.

```
decimal myDecimal;

double posInfinity =
           9999999999999999999999999999999999999999.0;
double negInfinity =
           -9999999999999999999999999999999999999999.0;
double tooLarge = 999999999999999999999999999999.0;
double doubleNaN = Double.NaN;
double zeroDouble =
           0.0000000000000000000000000000000000000000000001;

//myDecimal = (decimal)posInfinity; // OverflowException
//myDecimal = (decimal)negInfinity; // OverflowException
//myDecimal = (decimal)tooLarge;    // OverflowException
//myDecimal = (decimal)double.NaN;  // OverflowException

myDecimal = (decimal)zeroDouble; // myDecimal = 0
```

The positive and negative `infinity` examples cause an `OverflowException` when an attempt is made to move the value of the `double` type into the `decimal` type variable.

Value Type Conversions

Conversions with simple types are easy. It's just a matter of putting a cast operator in front of the variable being converted from. For complex types, the expression syntax is the same. However, there's a lot of work going on behind the scenes to make sure complex type conversions happen properly. This section shows how to implement conversions on structs, complex value types.

A conversion definition can be either implicit or explicit. What is important is that one of the types being converted must be the same type as the enclosing class or struct. The following is the signature for defining a conversion operator.

```
public static convType operator toType(fromType typeName)
{
    // conversion code
}
```

The `public` and `static` modifiers are mandatory and must be included as shown. The `convType` can be either the keyword `implicit` or `explicit`. The `operator` keyword is mandatory. There are two types involved in a conversion, `toType` and `fromType`. One of these is the type of the enclosing class or struct. The other is the type being converted either to or from. The `fromType` is the source type and the `toType` is the destination or target type. The `typeName` is a user-defined identifier.

Listing 15.1 shows how to define `implicit` and `explicit` conversion operators for a struct.

LISTING 15.1 Implicit and Explicit Struct Conversions

```
using System;

public struct Currency
{
    private double amount;

    public Currency(double amount)
    {
        this.amount = amount;
    }

    public static implicit operator Currency(double dbl)
    {
        return new Currency(dbl);
    }

    public static explicit operator float(Currency curr)
    {
        return (float)curr.Amount;
    }

    public override string ToString()
    {
        return String.Format("{0:C}", amount);
    }

    public static Currency operator+(Currency c1, Currency c2)
    {
        Currency cur = new Currency();
        cur.Amount = c1.Amount + c2.Amount;
        return cur;
    }

    public double Amount
    {
        get
        {
            return amount;
        }
        set
        {
            amount = value;
        }
    }
}
```

LISTING 15.1 continued

```
public class Conversions
{
    public static int Main(string[] args)
    {
        Currency myCurrency;
        double   myDouble;
        float    myFloat;

        myCurrency = 9.3f;
        Console.WriteLine("myCurrency: {0}", myCurrency);

        myFloat = (float)myCurrency;
        Console.WriteLine("myFloat: {0}", myFloat);

        myDouble = (double)myCurrency;
        Console.WriteLine("myDouble: {0}", myDouble);

        return 0;
    }
}
```

And here's the output:

```
myCurrency: $9.30
myFloat: 9.3
myDouble: 9.30000019073486
```

Listing 15.1 contains both `explicit` and `implicit` conversion operators. The `implicit` conversion operator converts `double` to `Currency` and the `explicit` conversion operator converts `Currency` to `double`.

The code in the `Main()` method performs three conversions. The first conversion implicitly converts a `float` value, `9.3f`, to `Currency`. Although there is no conversion for `float` to `Currency` defined in the `Currency` struct, this is still possible because the `float` is implicitly converted to `double` according to built-in `implicit` conversion of primitive types. Once the `float` is converted to `double`, the `double` is implicitly converted to `Currency` via the Currency `struct's implicit double` to `Currency` conversion operator.

The second conversion shows how to copy a Currency value to a float. The cast to `float` first invokes the `explicit` conversion of `Currency` to `double` and then an `explicit` conversion from `double` to `float` occurs.

The third example invokes the `explicit` conversion of the `Currency` struct directly to convert `Currency` to `double`.

Reference Type Conversions

Reference type conversions are performed the same as value type conversions. However, there are more conversion options for reference types. The additional options are related to the class inheritance capabilities of reference types.

> **For C++ Programmers**
>
> C++ has conversion constructors that allow assignment of one type to another. These conversion constructors can contain an `explicit` modifier to force them to be normal instance constructors. Although C# doesn't have this feature, the same effect can be achieved by the use of `implicit` and `explicit` operator implementations within a class definition.

Conversions from a derived class to a base class are implicit. This comes from the fact that the derived class has an "is a" relationship with the base class. Anything that can be done with a derived class can also be done with its base class.

When converting from a base class to a derived class, an explicit conversion is required. Listing 15.2 shows how class conversion works.

LISTING 15.2 Implicit and Explicit Class Conversions

```
using System;

class BaseClass
{
    int baseField;

    public BaseClass(int bf)
    {
        baseField = bf;
    }
}

class DerivedClass : BaseClass
{
    int derivedField;

    public DerivedClass(int df, int bf) : base(bf)
    {
        derivedField = df;
    }
}
```

LISTING 15.2 continued

```
class ClassConversions
{
    static void Main(string[] args)
    {
        BaseClass    bc = new BaseClass(1);
        DerivedClass dc = new DerivedClass(2, 3);

        bc = dc;
        //dc = bc;  // compile time error
        dc = (DerivedClass)bc;
    }
}
```

The `Main()` method of Listing 15.2 performs conversions between a base class instance and a derived class instance. The first statement, converting the derived class instance, `dc`, to the base class instance, `bc`, works fine. Derived class to base class conversions are always implicit.

The next line is commented out because it generates a compile-time error. There is no implicit conversion from a base class instance to a derived class instance.

The last line uses an explicit conversion to assign the base class instance to the derived class instance. This illustrates why base class to derived class conversions must be explicit. In this case, the base class does not have a `derivedField` field. During the `explicit` conversion, the derived class instance only receives an object with a `baseField` field, which leaves the derived class in a potentially inconsistent state.

> **Note**
>
> One thing to be aware of when implementing conversions is to consider the inheritance relationship between classes. Trace any possible implementation against an object not in the class hierarchy to make sure that it supports potential destinations in that hierarchy.

Summary

This chapter covered conversions in C#. It explained the differences between implicit and explicit conversions in depth. There are several scenarios to consider when performing conversions with the simple types. This chapter discussed automatic conversions in expressions, boxing and unboxing conversions, and explicit conversions that raise exceptions.

Value type conversions involve converting data between structs. This chapter showed how to implement both `implicit` and `explicit` conversion operators. It also showed how to use those operators.

The final section was on reference type conversions. It provided some information unique to reference conversions and gave some tips on their implementation.

Using Class Libraries with C#

PART III

IN THIS PART

16 Presenting Graphical User Interfaces *343*

17 File I/O and Serialization *381*

18 XML *407*

19 Database Programming with ADO.NET *417*

20 Writing Web Applications with ASP.NET *439*

21 Remoting *459*

22 Web Services *483*

CHAPTER 16

Presenting Graphical User Interfaces

IN THIS CHAPTER

- Windows *344*
- Controls *348*
- N-Tier Architecture *351*
- Menus *373*

Windows Forms are the Graphical User Interface (GUI) libraries of the Microsoft .NET Frameworks. The Windows Forms library contains most of the graphical controls familiar to GUI programmers. All of the concepts learned in previous chapters are applied when doing GUI programming. Of special significance is the use of events to connect GUI controls, such as buttons, to the code that implements the program's behavior related to that control.

Windows Forms is not included in the proposed Common Language Infrastructure (CLI) submission to European Computer Manufacturers Association (ECMA). However, it is of such importance to development that its coverage is provided here. Specific emphasis is placed on how C# is used to produce GUIs, and the language constructs involved. The same C# language features are likely to be applied to any future GUI library implementations.

Examples in this chapter begin with the basic element of Windows Forms programming: the window. Then there is an introduction to the standard window controls such as buttons and text boxes. The menu, a common element of GUIs, is included.

Windows

The basic element of most GUI programming in Windows Forms is the window. Essentially, everything on a GUI screen—buttons, text boxes, and icons—are windows. Because of this, most of the windows and controls in the Windows Forms package have the same characteristics. For instance, they all have a `Text` property. How they use the property is up to the specific type of window.

Building a Windows Forms application is easy once a few basic concepts are understood. This section covers some of these concepts and provides a starting point from which to proceed. Listing 16.1 shows a relatively simple Windows Forms application. To compile the code in Listing 16.1, use the command line in Listing 16.2.

LISTING 16.1 A Simple Windows Forms Application

```
using System;
using System.Windows.Forms;
using System.ComponentModel;
using System.Drawing;

public class FirstForm : Form
{
    private Container components;
    private Label     howdyLabel;
```

LISTING 16.1 continued

```
    public FirstForm()
    {
        InitializeComponent();
    }

    private void InitializeComponent()
    {
        components = new Container ();
        howdyLabel = new Label ();

        howdyLabel.Location  = new Point (12, 116);
        howdyLabel.Text      = "Howdy, Partner!";
        howdyLabel.Size      = new Size (267, 40);
        howdyLabel.AutoSize  = true;
        howdyLabel.Font      = new Font (
            "Microsoft Sans Serif",
            26, System.
            Drawing.FontStyle.Bold);
        howdyLabel.TabIndex  = 0;
        howdyLabel.Anchor    = AnchorStyles.None;
        howdyLabel.TextAlign = ContentAlignment.MiddleCenter;

        Text = "First Form";
        Controls.Add (howdyLabel);
    }

    public static void Main()
    {
        Application.Run(new FirstForm());
    }
}
```

LISTING 16.2 Command Line for Listing 16.1

```
csc /r:System.Windows.Forms.DLL
➥/r:System.Drawing.DLL FirstForm.cs
```

Listing 16.2 contains a command line that can be used to compile the code from Listing 16.1. The command line references a few dynamic link libraries by using the `/r:` `<dllname>` option. The System.Windows.Forms.DLL and System.Drawing.DLL libraries contain all the routines required to present graphical components, such as forms and controls, on the screen.

At the top of the file are a few new namespaces to be familiar with. The most familiar is the `System` namespace, holding all the basic class libraries. The `System.Windows.Forms` namespace holds definitions of all the Windows Forms windows and controls. It also has other supporting types including interfaces, structs, delegates, and enumerations supporting the window types. The `System.ComponentModel` namespace contains several classes and interfaces (language as opposed to graphical interfaces) for providing generalized support of components. The `System.Drawing` namespace provides access to the operating system graphics functionality.

The first two class members of the `FirstForm` class are `components` and `howdyLabel`. The `components` field is a Container object from the `System.ComponentModel` namespace. This object doesn't participate in the graphical presentation of the program. However, it does do a lot of behind-the-scenes work to support timers, multithreading, and cleanup when the program ends. Its declaration and instantiation are mandatory. The other field, `howdyLabel`, is a Windows Forms Label Control. It is used in this program to display the "Howdy, Partner!" message in the window that is created.

The `FirstForm` constructor calls the `InitializeComponent()` method. The `InitializeComponent()` method creates and instantiates the Windows Forms Controls and Forms that make up the graphical interface of this program. It begins by instantiating the `components` and `howdyLabel` fields as objects. The following paragraphs explain the rest of this method.

The first group of statements initializes the `howdyLabel` label. Labels are well suited to presenting static text. That's exactly what `howdyLabel` does.

`Labels` have a `Location` property, keeping track of where the `Label` is placed on the screen. The `Location` property accepts a `Point` structure, which is a member of the `System.Drawing` namespace. The `Point` struct is used frequently in Windows Forms applications to specify X and Y screen coordinates. In the example, the `Location` of the `howdyLabel` is 12 pixels from the left and 116 pixels from the top of the main form. Here's how the `Location` property of the `howdyLabel label` is set:

```
howdyLabel.Location  = new Point (12, 116);
```

The static text of a `Label` is set through the `Text` property. The following statement sets the text of the `Label` to the string `"Howdy, Partner!:`

```
howdyLabel.Text      = "Howdy, Partner!";
```

A `Label` also has a `Size` property that takes a `Size` structure. In Listing 16.1, the size of `howdyLabel` is set to 267 pixels wide by 40 pixels high:

```
howdyLabel.Size      = new Size (267, 40);
```

The `AutoSize` property accepts a Boolean value, which tells whether a `Label` can automatically resize itself to accommodate its contents. For instance, in this program the actual size of the howdyLabel contents exceeds its set size from the previous statement, so the label must grow to fully show the entirety of its text. Here's how the AutoSize property of the howdyLabel label is set.

```
howdyLabel.AutoSize  = true;
```

A Label can change its typeface through the Font property. It accepts a Font object. The constructor for the Font object in the following statement accepts three parameters: the font name, the font size, and a font style. The font style is from the FontStyle enum in the System.Drawing namespace.

```
howdyLabel.Font      = new Font (
    "Microsoft Sans Serif",
    26,
    System.Drawing.FontStyle.Bold);
```

When there are multiple controls on a form, each control that can accept input can have its TabIndex property set. This permits the user to press the Tab key to move to the next control on the form, based on TabIndex. In this example, the TabIndex of howdyLabel is set to 0. This is for illustrative reasons only. The fact is that a Label can never be a tab stop because it doesn't normally accept user input. Furthermore, for this program, this is the only control on the form. There isn't any other control to tab to. Here's how the TabIndex property of the howdyLabel label is set:

```
howdyLabel.TabIndex  = 0;
```

Window layout in Windows Forms is done with the techniques of anchoring and docking. Docking specifies the location of the form that a control will reside in. Anchoring tells which side of a control will be attached to another control. These two techniques permit any type of layout a window design would need. The following code line states that howdyLabel will not be anchored. It uses the AnchorStyles enumeration to set the Anchor property.

```
howdyLabel.Anchor    = AnchorStyles.None;
```

The horizontal alignment of a Label may be set with the TextAlign property, which accepts a ContentAlignment enumeration. The following statement sets the horizontal alignment of howdyLabel to be centered between its left and right margins.

```
howdyLabel.TextAlign = ContentAlignment.MiddleCenter;
```

The next few statements perform initialization on the main form. Since FirstForm is a Form object, it is considered the main form.

```
Text = "First Form";
```

All forms and controls have `Text` properties. What they do with them is unique to each form or control. A `Form` object sets its title bar with the value of the `Text` property. This example sets the program's title bar to say "First Form."

```
Controls.Add (howdyLabel);
```

A form's `Controls` object holds a collection of all of its controls. When the form has to redraw itself, it iterates through this collection and sets itself up according to several factors, including the anchoring and docking properties of each control. This example adds `howdyLabel` to the `FirstForm` `Controls` collection object.

```
public static void Main()
{
    Application.Run(new FirstForm());
}
```

The `Main()` method simply gets the program running. It calls the static `Run()` method of the `Application` class. Its parameter is a new instance of the `FirstForm` class. When the `HowdyPartner` program runs, it looks like the window shown in Figure 16.1.

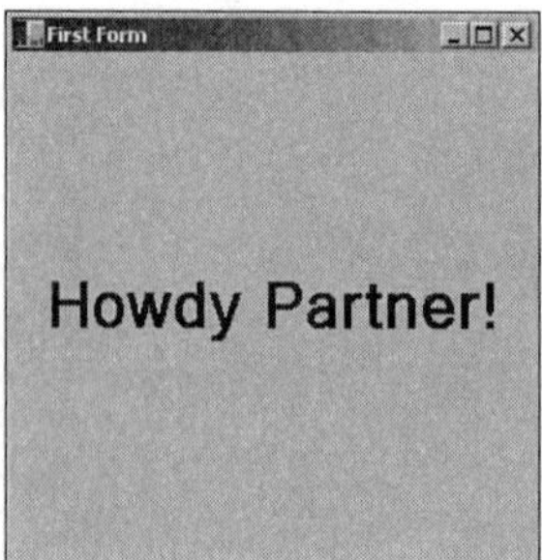

FIGURE 16.1
The HowdyPartner Windows Forms program.

Controls

A control is a specialized window with specific features and a unique purpose. These are things like buttons, labels, and lists. Table 16.1 introduces each of the standard Windows Forms controls and explains how they're used.

TABLE 16.1 Windows Forms Controls

Control	*How It's Used*
Button	Controls that can be clicked to perform some desired action.
CheckBox	Primarily used for displaying a binary state of an object. Clicking the CheckBox causes it to toggle between a checked and unchecked state.

TABLE 16.1 continued

Control	*How It's Used*
CheckListBox	ListBox with a column of CheckBoxes. These are superior to using normal ListBox semantics where multiple items are selected by using the Ctrl and Shift keys when selecting items. It allows users to select each item they want without worrying about losing all their choices if they forget to hold down the Ctrl or Shift key.
ComboBox	A drop-down list of choices that operates similar to the ListBox. The primary difference is that the ComboBox is more compact and efficient with screen real estate.
DataGrid	An extremely powerful control that permits a program to bind to a data source.
DateTimePicker	Provides a capability to select a date and time without typing.
DomainUpDown	Permits a user to scroll through a list of data items that can only be shown one at a time.
Form	The main window of an application, a dialog, or a multiple-document interface (MDI) child. It provides all the capabilities for hosting child controls.
GroupBox	Houses a group of other controls, often used to encapsulate a group of RadioButtons. It can help organize a form and has a customizable title.
Label	Used to display static text. Labels can also contain images. Although they can be programmed for more functionality, such as reacting to double-clicks, other control types are probably more appropriate for more complex tasks.
LinkLabel	The same as a Label, but it can contain an URL that can be clicked to invoke an Internet connection.
ListBox	Holds selectable lists of data items. When the viewable portion of the ListBox is filled, a scrollbar appears so all of its contained items may be selected.
ListView	Provides capabilities for multiple columns, column headers, column resizing, and list sorting. It can also be configured in four different display modes. More sophisticated than a ListBox. MessageBox Provides notifications to users on certain program events. It has a configurable message, title bar, icon, and button. MonthCalendar A visual calendar control.

TABLE 16.1 continued

Control	*How It's Used*
NumericUpDown	The same as a DomainUpDown with the restriction that its contents are numeric.
Panel	Blank forms with little or no decoration that are used primarily for organization and form layout.
PictureBox	Displays an image.
ProgressBar	Used to display the status of an ongoing operation. It has a graphical indicator, set by a program to show the percentage of task completion.
PropertyGrid	For user interface type applications, to set and display a list of properties associated with a certain component.
RadioButton	Mutually exclusive buttons that permit users to make a choice. Also called option buttons.
RichTextBox	An enhanced TextBox control that provides more control over its text. It has the capability of creating Rich Text Format (RTF) files.
ScrollBar	Often used to help position the current location in a document that's too large to fit onscreen or in whatever space is available.
Splitter	Permit a user to resize multiple portions of a workspace. When the splitter is moved, one portion of the workspace gets larger, and others become smaller.
StatusBar	Performs multiple functions. Primarily it's a place to notify users of a program's status or other forms of current information.
TabControl	User interfaces that appear like file folder tabs. When selected, they open a specific page where the tab and content match.
TextBox	Allows a user to type text. They can be single or multi-line and have many capabilities for text manipulation such as selection, cut, copy, and paste.
Timer	Nonvisual controls that raise events at specified intervals. They can be used for such things as reminders or auto-save operations.
ToolBar	Permits a user to invoke selected operations in a program; similar in functionality to Menus.

TABLE 16.1 continued

Control	*How It's Used*
ToolTip	Helpful messages that appear when a cursor hovers over a control for a specified amount of time.
TrackBar	Controls that provide a means to establish settings for a certain purpose. They are often handy in specifying the frequency or speed in which an operation should occur.
TrayIcon	Icons displayed on the icon tray of the window's task bar. They usually have different pictures to indicate the current state of a program.
TreeView	Displays items in a hierarchical fashion. It has a root node at the top of the tree and can have multiple branches and nodes. Traditionally it has collapsible branches and is coordinated with another control to display details of selected nodes.

It's evident from Table 16.1 that there is a plentiful supply of graphical components and controls available with Windows Forms. These can be combined to create relatively sophisticated applications. The next section shows how to use C# to build an application with a healthy subset of these components.

N-Tier Architecture

The Windows Forms system makes it easy to build n-tiered architectures. N-tiered architectures are those applications that are broken into multiple cooperating components. Although the various components, in the example programs, are compiled into the same program, they are logically separate and provide a framework for a more sophisticated distributed application.

The actual pattern employed, in the examples, is Model-View-Controller (MVC). The Windows Forms component is the View. There are a couple classes that are solely concerned with managing the data, which are the Model. A central object, referred to as the Controller, coordinates the View and Model portions. This section introduces where each portion of the program fits into the MVC pattern. Listing 16.3 shows the main form of an application named Cite Manager.

LISTING 16.3 Cite Manager—Main Form: `CiteManagerForm.cs`

```
using System;
using System.Drawing;
using System.ComponentModel;
using System.Windows.Forms;

public class CiteManagerForm : Form
{
    private SiteManager citeMgr;

    private Container components;
    private Button    addButton;
    private Button    deleteButton;
    private Button    modifyButton;
    private Button    viewButton;
    private Label     selectLabel;

    public CiteManagerForm()
    {
        InitializeComponent();

        citeMgr = new SiteManager();
    }

    public override void Dispose()
    {
        base.Dispose();
        components.Dispose();
    }

    private void InitializeComponent()
    {
        components   = new Container();
        addButton    = new Button();
        deleteButton = new Button();
        modifyButton = new Button();
        viewButton   = new Button();
        selectLabel  = new Label();

        addButton.Text     = "Add";
        addButton.Click   +=
            new EventHandler (addButton_Click);
        addButton.Location = new Point(94, 80);
        addButton.Size     = new Size(75, 23);
        addButton.TabIndex = 0;

        deleteButton.Text     = "Delete";
        deleteButton.Click   +=
            new EventHandler(deleteButton_Click);
        deleteButton.Location = new Point(94, 128);
        deleteButton.Size     = new Size(75, 23);
        deleteButton.TabIndex = 1;
```

LISTING 16.3 continued

```
        modifyButton.Text     = "Modify";
        modifyButton.Click   +=
            new EventHandler(modifyButton_Click);
        modifyButton.Location = new Point(94, 176);
        modifyButton.Size     = new Size(75, 23);
        modifyButton.TabIndex = 2;

        viewButton.Text     = "View";
        viewButton.Click   +=
            new EventHandler(viewButton_Click);
        viewButton.Location = new Point(94, 224);
        viewButton.Size     = new Size(75, 23);
        viewButton.TabIndex = 3;

        selectLabel.Text        = "Please Make a Selection:";
        selectLabel.Font        = new Font("Lucida Console",
                                           12,
                                           FontStyle.Italic);
        selectLabel.Location    = new Point(10, 32);
        selectLabel.Size        = new Size(246, 18);
        selectLabel.BorderStyle =
            System.Windows.Forms.BorderStyle.Fixed3D;
        selectLabel.AutoSize    = true;
        selectLabel.TabIndex    = 4;

        Text       = "Cite Manager";
        ClientSize = new Size (264, 273);
        Controls.Add(selectLabel);
        Controls.Add(modifyButton);
        Controls.Add(viewButton);
        Controls.Add(deleteButton);
        Controls.Add(addButton);
    }

    protected void deleteButton_Click (object sender,
                                       System.EventArgs e)
    {
        DeleteForm df = new DeleteForm(citeMgr);
        df.ShowDialog(this);
    }

    protected void modifyButton_Click (object sender,
                                       System.EventArgs e)
    {
        ModifyForm mf = new ModifyForm(citeMgr);

        mf.ShowDialog(this);
    }
    protected void viewButton_Click (object sender,
                                     System.EventArgs e)
```

LISTING 16.3 continued

```
    {
        ViewForm vf = new ViewForm(citeMgr);

        vf.ShowDialog(this);
    }

    protected void addButton_Click (object sender,
                                    System.EventArgs e)
    {
        AddForm af = new AddForm();

        DialogResult dlgRes = af.ShowDialog(this);

        switch (dlgRes)
        {
            case DialogResult.OK:
                citeMgr.AddSite(
                    af.sitenameTextbox.Text,
                    af.addressTextbox.Text,
                    af.descriptionTextbox.Text);
                break;
            case DialogResult.Cancel:
                // do nothing
                break;
            default:
                break;
        }
    }

    public static void Main(string[] args)
    {
        Application.Run(new CiteManagerForm());
    }
}
```

Listing 16.3 declares a `Form` class, `CiteManager`, with a `Label` and four `Button` controls. It also has a `SiteManager` object to manage the data associated with each site. The `CiteManager` constructor initializes the controls by calling the `InitializeComponents()` method. Then it instantiates the `cites` object as a `SiteManager`.

After instantiating the `Label` and `Button` objects, the `InitializeComponents()` method proceeds to initialize each of these controls. Initialization of all buttons is similar, so we'll concentrate on the `Add` button as typical of the others.

Most controls have a `Text` property. The `Add` button's text property is set to "`Add`". This is the text that shows up on the front of the button. The next line sets the `Add` button's

Click event. It uses the standard Windows Forms EventHandler delegate to encapsulate the event handler method. Every time the Add button is clicked, the addButton_Click() method is called. The Location property specifies where the upper left-hand corner of the button will be located on its parent form. It's set with a Point object. The Size property controls the width and height of a button. It's set with a Size object. Tab Indexes indicate the sequence of controls that get focus when the Tab key is pressed. When a form first starts up, Tab Index 0 gets the focus first. This is the Add button. If the Tab key is pressed again, focus transfers to the Delete button with Tab Index 1. Labels are meant to hold static information and are not operated on. Therefore, they won't receive focus, regardless of their Tab Index.

The Label control has a couple differences from the other controls on this form worth noting. First, its Font is set to something other than the default. This is done by instantiating a Font object. The three parameters to the Font constructor are the font name, size, and style. The style parameter is a member of the FontStyle enum. Most controls also have a border style. The Label's border style is set to Fixed3D by using the BorderStyle enum. This produces the sunken border effect on the label.

Finally, the CiteManager form's Text property is set to "Cite Manager". This changes the text in the main form's title bar. Every Form object has a Controls collection, which holds all of the form's controls and iterates through that list when laying out the form for display. Each Label and Button defined in this method is added to Controls by using the standard Collections Add() method syntax.

The deleteButton_click(), modifyButton_click(), and viewButton_click() methods are similar in operation. They instantiate their associated form objects and then call them. Each uses the ShowDialog() method. This pops up the appropriate form to be used as a modal dialog box. Alternatively, each of these forms could have been started with the Show() method. The difference is that the Show() method starts the form as an ordinary window, which doesn't have all the built-in functionality of a dialog box.

Note

Modal dialog boxes prevent interaction with any other part of a program while they are running. They must be dismissed before resuming operations on the rest of the program. On the other hand, Modeless dialog boxes permit users to interact with other parts of a program at the same time that the dialog is up and running. A good example of a modeless dialog box is the Find function of a word processor.

The addButton_click() method shows how to retrieve the results from a dialog box. It instantiates the AddForm object and calls the ShowDialog() method, just like the other event handler methods, but this retrieves the return value into a DialogResult field. The dlgRes field holds a DialogResult enum, which is used in a switch statement to determine the proper action to take. The only real action occurs when dlgRes equals DialogResult.OK. Then the program calls the AddSite() method of the citeMgr object to add a new site. The parameters for the AddSite() method call are obtained from the AddForm form. The AddForm form has three TextBox controls: sitenameTextbox, addressTextbox, and descriptionTextbox. The data is pulled out of each of these controls by calling their Text properties.

There is a method in the CiteManager class called Dispose(). The Windows Forms framework uses this to clean up system resources allocated during the session. This is the recommended method of cleaning up program resources.

The CiteManager class has the Main() method for this program. Its single task is to call the static Run() method of the System.Application class. The Run() method begins the program with a new instance of the CiteManager class. Figure 16.2 shows how the CiteManager form looks when run.

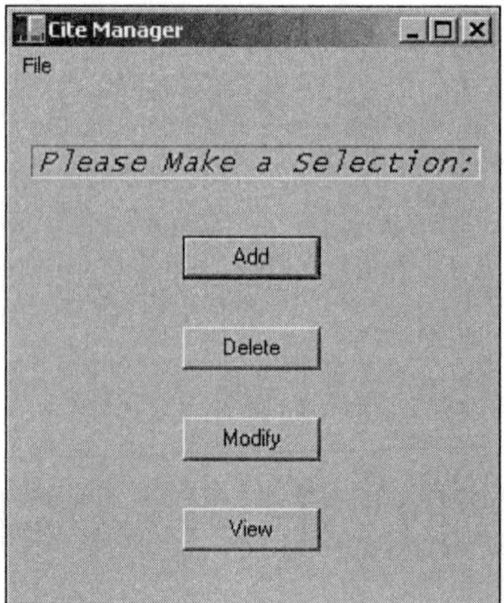

FIGURE 16.2
The Main screen of the Cite Manager program.

The SiteManager class is used extensively in this program. As the Controller component of this program, it coordinates input from the Windows Forms View components. The input is used to manage a collection of WebSite objects that are the primary data items, the Model component, of this program. Listings 16.4 and 16.5 show these classes and how they manage the data for the Cite Manager program.

LISTING 16.4 The Site Manager Class: `SiteManager.cs`

```
using System;
using WebSites;

public class SiteManager {
    SiteList sites = new SiteList();

    public SiteManager()
    {
        this.sites = new WebSites.SiteList();
        this.sites[this.sites.NextIndex] = new WebSite
             ("Joe", "http://www.mysite.com", "Great Site!");
        this.sites[this.sites.NextIndex] = new WebSite
             ("Don", "http://www.dondotnet.com", "okay.");
        this.sites[this.sites.NextIndex] = new WebSite
             ("Bob", "www.bob.com", "No http://");
    }

    public WebSite this[int index]
    {
        get
        {
            return sites[index];
        }
    }

    public int Count
    {
        get
        {
            return sites.NextIndex;
        }
    }

    public void AddSite(string siteName,
                        string url,
                        string description)
    {
        sites[sites.NextIndex] = new WebSite
             (siteName, url, description);
    }

    public void DeleteSite(int index)
    {
        if (index <= sites.NextIndex)
            sites.Remove(index);
    }

    public void ModifySite()
    {
```

LISTING 16.4 continued

```
        Console.WriteLine("Modifying Sites.");
    }
}
```

The `SiteManager` class in Listing 16.4 provides logic that properly manages the manipulation of data in the `sites` container. The implementation of this class is similar to classes by the same name in earlier chapters. Changes were made to support the requirements of this program. Listing 16.5 shows the classes of the `WebSites` namespace. These classes comprise the Model components of this program.

LISTING 16.5 The `WebSites` Namespace and Classes: `WebSites.cs`

```
namespace WebSites
{
    using System;
    using System.Collections;

    public class WebSite
    {
        const string http       = "http://";
        public static readonly string currentDate =
            new DateTime().ToString();
        string siteName;
        string url;
        string description;

        public WebSite()
            : this("No Site", "no.url", "No Description") {}

        public WebSite(string newSite)
            : this(newSite, "no.url", "No Description") {}

        public WebSite(string newSite, string newURL)
            : this(newSite, newURL, "No Description") {}

        public WebSite(string newSite,
                       string newURL,
                       string newDesc)
        {
            SiteName    = newSite;
            URL         = newURL;
            Description = newDesc;
        }

        public override string ToString()
        {
            return siteName + ", " +
```

LISTING 16.5 continued

```
                    url + ", " +
                description;
        }

        public override bool Equals(object evalString)
        {
            return this.ToString() == evalString.ToString();
        }

        public override int GetHashCode()
        {
            return this.ToString().GetHashCode();
        }

        protected string ValidateUrl(string url)
        {
            if (!(url.StartsWith(http)))
            {
                return http + url;
            }
            return url;
        }

        public string SiteName
        {
            get
            {
                return siteName;
            }
            set
            {
                siteName = value;
            }
        }

        public string URL
        {
            get
            {
                return url;
            }
            set
            {
                url = ValidateUrl(value);
            }
        }

        public string Description
        {
```

LISTING 16.5 continued

```
            get
            {
                return description;
            }
            set
            {
                description = value;
            }
        }
    }

    public class SiteList
    {
        protected ArrayList sites;

        public SiteList()
        {
            sites = new ArrayList();
        }

        public int NextIndex
        {
            get
            {
                return sites.Count;
            }
        }

        public WebSite this[int index]
        {
            get
            {
                if (index > sites.Count)
                    return (WebSite)null;

                return (WebSite) sites[index];
            }
            set
            {
                if ( index < 10 )
                    sites.Add(value);
            }
        }

        public void Remove(int element)
        {
            sites.RemoveAt(element);
        }
    }
}
```

Listing 16.5 shows the classes of the `WebSites` namespace. This namespace exists to provide specialized support for data relating to the definition of a Web site. It has a `SiteList` class, providing access to `WebSite` objects. The `WebSite` class is also a member of the `WebSites` namespace. It is used extensively in the Cite Managers program. The rest of this section shows the various Windows Forms that this program uses to manipulate `WebSite` data held in `SiteList` containers. Listing 16.6 shows how to add a new Web site to the program.

LISTING 16.6 A Windows Form for Adding a Web Site Listing: `AddForm.cs`

```
using System;
using System.Drawing;
using System.ComponentModel;
using System.Windows.Forms;

public class AddForm : Form
{
    private Container components;
    public  TextBox   descriptionTextbox;
    public  TextBox   addressTextbox;
    public  TextBox   sitenameTextbox;
    private Button    cancelButton;
    private Button    okButton;
    private Label     descriptionLabel;
    private Label     addressLabel;
    private Label     sitenameLabel;

    public AddForm()
    {
        InitializeComponent();
    }

    public override void Dispose()
    {
        base.Dispose();
        components.Dispose();
    }

    private void InitializeComponent()
    {
        components         = new Container();
        okButton           = new Button();
        cancelButton       = new Button();
        sitenameLabel      = new Label();
        addressLabel       = new Label();
        descriptionLabel   = new Label();
        sitenameTextbox    = new TextBox();
        addressTextbox     = new TextBox();
        descriptionTextbox = new TextBox();
```

LISTING 16.6 continued

```
        okButton.Text         = "OK";
        okButton.Location     = new Point(120, 168);
        okButton.Size         = new Size(75, 23);
        okButton.DialogResult = DialogResult.OK;
        okButton.TabIndex     = 6;

        cancelButton.Text         = "Cancel";
        cancelButton.Location     = new Point(256, 168);
        cancelButton.Size         = new Size(75, 23);
        cancelButton.DialogResult = DialogResult.Cancel;
        cancelButton.TabIndex     = 7;

        sitenameLabel.Text      = "Site Name:";
        sitenameLabel.Location  = new Point(24, 24);
        sitenameLabel.Size      = new Size(64, 20);
        sitenameLabel.TextAlign =
            ContentAlignment.MiddleRight;
        sitenameLabel.TabIndex  = 0;

        sitenameTextbox.Location = new Point(96, 24);
        sitenameTextbox.Size     = new Size(344, 20);
        sitenameTextbox.TabIndex = 3;

        addressLabel.Text      = "Address:";
        addressLabel.Location  = new Point(24, 72);
        addressLabel.Size      = new Size(64, 20);
        addressLabel.TextAlign =
            ContentAlignment.MiddleRight;
        addressLabel.TabIndex  = 1;

        addressTextbox.Location = new Point(96, 72);
        addressTextbox.Size     = new Size(344, 20);
        addressTextbox.TabIndex = 4;

        descriptionLabel.Text      = "Description:";
        descriptionLabel.Location  = new Point(24, 120);
        descriptionLabel.Size      = new Size(64, 20);
        descriptionLabel.TextAlign =
            ContentAlignment.MiddleRight;
        descriptionLabel.TabIndex  = 2;

        descriptionTextbox.Location = new Point(96, 120);
        descriptionTextbox.Size     = new Size(344, 20);
        descriptionTextbox.TabIndex = 5;

        Text       = "Add Form";
        ClientSize = new Size(464, 213);
        Controls.Add(descriptionTextbox);
        Controls.Add(addressTextbox);
```

LISTING 16.6 continued

```
            Controls.Add(sitenameTextbox);
            Controls.Add(cancelButton);
            Controls.Add(okButton);
            Controls.Add(descriptionLabel);
            Controls.Add(addressLabel);
            Controls.Add(sitenameLabel);
        }
}
```

This listing shows the Add form from the Cite Manager application. There are two significant new items to learn from this form. First is that this form has `TextBox` controls. The only properties being set on them are the `Location`, `Size`, and `TabIndex`. It's possible to set their `Text` property, but in this case it doesn't fit the purpose of the application. One way to explicitly blank out the text of a `TextBox` is by setting its Text property to `""`. Figure 16.3 shows what this form looks like.

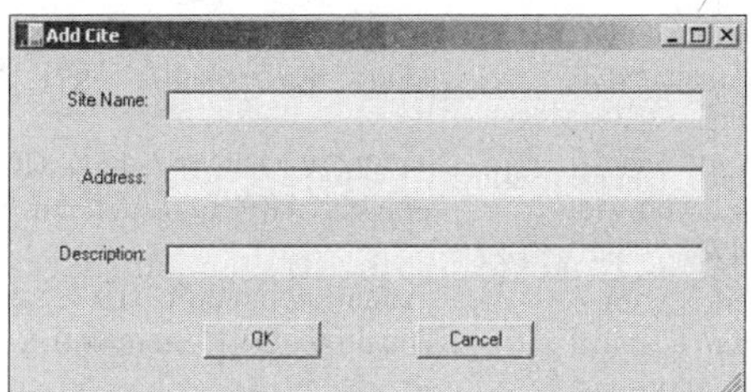

FIGURE 16.3
The Add Cite screen of the Cite Manager program.

The other interesting item on this form is the OK and Cancel buttons. They have their `DialogResult` properties set with `DialogResult.OK` and `DialogResult.Cancel` enums, respectively. This does several things. It establishes default behavior when the form is started with a `ShowDialog()` call. Pressing the Enter or Return key invokes the `OK` button. Similarly, pressing the Esc key invokes the `Cancel` button. When either button is clicked or its behavior is invoked, the dialog box closes and returns the `DialogResult` associated with that button. This is a lot of functionality that isn't available when the form is invoked with the `Show()` method.

Another interesting aspect of this form is that the `TextAlign` properties of the `Label` controls are set with the `ContentAlignment.MiddleRight` enum. This causes their text to have vertical alignment in the middle of the label and horizontal alignment on the right side of the label. Next is the `DeleteForm`, shown in Listing 16.7.

Listing 16.7 A Windows Form for Deleting a Web Site Listing: `DeleteForm.cs`

```
using System;
using System.Drawing;
using System.ComponentModel;
using System.Windows.Forms;

public class DeleteForm : Form
{
    SiteManager citeMgr;

    private Container components;
    private Panel     separator;
    private Button    okButton;
    private Button    cancelButton;
    private Button    deleteButton;
    private ListBox   deleteListbox;

    public DeleteForm(SiteManager citeMgr)
    {
        InitializeComponent();

        this.citeMgr = citeMgr;

        for (int i=0;i < this.citeMgr.Count; i++)
        {
            deleteListbox.Items.Insert(i, this.citeMgr[i].ToString());
        }
    }

    public override void Dispose()
    {
        base.Dispose();
        components.Dispose();
    }

    private void InitializeComponent()
    {
        components    = new Container();
        okButton      = new Button();
        cancelButton  = new Button();
        deleteButton  = new Button();
        deleteListbox = new ListBox();
        separator     = new Panel();

        okButton.Text         = "OK";
        okButton.Location     = new Point(40, 216);
        okButton.Size         = new Size(75, 23);
        okButton.DialogResult = DialogResult.OK;
        okButton.TabIndex     = 2;
```

LISTING 16.7 continued

```
        cancelButton.Text     = "Cancel";
        cancelButton.Location = new Point (176, 216);
        cancelButton.Size     = new Size (75, 23);
        cancelButton.TabIndex = 3;

        deleteButton.Text     = "Delete";
        deleteButton.Click   += new EventHandler (deleteButton_Click);
        deleteButton.Location = new Point(104, 152);
        deleteButton.Size     = new Size(75, 23);
        deleteButton.TabIndex = 1;

        deleteListbox.Location = new Point(8, 8);
        deleteListbox.Size     = new Size(280, 134);
        deleteListbox.TabIndex = 0;

        separator.BorderStyle = System.Windows.Forms.BorderStyle.Fixed3D;
        separator.Location    = new Point(8, 184);
        separator.Size        = new Size(280, 4);
        separator.TabIndex    = 4;

        Text       = "Delete Form";
        ClientSize = new Size (296, 261);

        Controls.Add(separator);
        Controls.Add(cancelButton);
        Controls.Add(okButton);
        Controls.Add(deleteButton);
        Controls.Add(deleteListbox);
    }

    protected void deleteButton_Click (object sender, System.EventArgs e)
    {
        citeMgr.DeleteSite(deleteListbox.SelectedIndex);
        deleteListbox.Items.Remove(deleteListbox.SelectedIndex);
        deleteListbox.Invalidate();
    }
}
```

Listing 16.7 shows the `DeleteForm` of the Cite Manager application. The new control on this form is the `ListBox`. The `DeleteForm` constructor loads the `deleteListbox` control by calling the `Insert()` method of its `Items` collection property. The first parameter is the zero-based position in the `ListBox` to locate the entry. The second parameter is the text to be displayed. This example uses the `ToString()` method of the `WebSite` object that is returned by the `citeMgr` indexer. The appearance of the DeleteForm is shown in Figure 16.4.

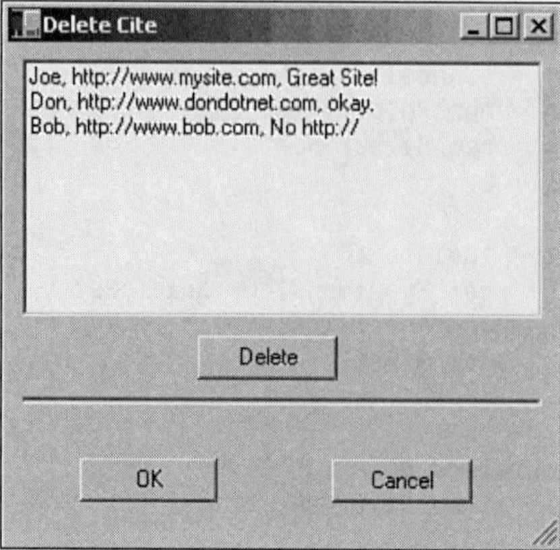

FIGURE 16.4
The Delete Cite screen of the Cite Manager program.

This example also uses a `Panel` as a separator. The straight-line effect is achieved by specifying a height of 3 when setting the `Size` property of the `separator` control. Another interesting item in this form is the omission of a setting for the `Cancel` button's `DialogResult` property. This causes nothing to happen when the `Cancel` button is clicked. If the `DialogResult` property had been set appropriately, such an action would close the dialog box and return with a `DialogResult.Cancel` enum value. Listing 16.8 shows implementation of the ComboBox and Group controls.

LISTING 16.8 A Windows Form for Modifying a Web Site Listing: `ModifyForm.cs`

```
using System;
using System.Drawing;
using System.ComponentModel;
using System.Windows.Forms;

public class ModifyForm : Form
{
    SiteManager citeMgr;

    private Container components;
    private Label     selectionLabel;
    private ComboBox  selectionCombobox;
    private Button    changeButton;
    private Label     sitenameLabel;
    private Label     addressLabel;
    private Label     descriptionLabel;
    private TextBox   sitenameTextbox;
    private TextBox   addressTextbox;
    private TextBox   descriptionTextbox;
    private GroupBox  groupBox;
    private Button    okButton;
    private Button    cancelButton;
```

LISTING 16.8 continued

```
    public ModifyForm(SiteManager citeMgr)
    {
        InitializeComponent();

        this.citeMgr = citeMgr;

        for (int i=0;i < this.citeMgr.Count; i++)
        {
            selectionCombobox.Items.Insert(i, this.citeMgr[i].ToString());
        }

        selectionCombobox.SelectedIndex = 0;
}

    public override void Dispose()
    {
        base.Dispose();
        components.Dispose();
    }

    private void InitializeComponent()
    {
        components          = new Container();
        selectionLabel      = new Label();
        selectionCombobox   = new ComboBox();
        changeButton        = new Button();
        sitenameLabel       = new Label();
        addressLabel        = new Label();
        descriptionLabel    = new Label();
        sitenameTextbox     = new TextBox();
        addressTextbox      = new TextBox();
        descriptionTextbox = new TextBox();
        groupBox           = new GroupBox();
        okButton            = new Button();
        cancelButton        = new Button();

        selectionLabel.Text      = "Select Cite:";
        selectionLabel.Location  = new Point(32, 24);
        selectionLabel.Size      = new Size(64, 21);
        selectionLabel.TextAlign = ContentAlignment.MiddleRight;
        selectionLabel.TabIndex  = 9;

        selectionCombobox.Text                        = "comboBox1";
        selectionCombobox.SelectedIndexChanged += new
➥_ EventHandler(selectionCombobox SelectedIndexChanged);
        selectionCombobox.Location                    = new Point(104, 24);
        selectionCombobox.Size                        = new Size(232, 21);
        selectionCombobox.TabIndex                    = 8;
```

Listing 16.8 continued

```
        changeButton.Text     = "Change";
        changeButton.Click   += new EventHandler(changeButton_Click);
        changeButton.Location = new Point(368, 24);
        changeButton.Size     = new Size(75, 23);
        changeButton.TabIndex = 10;

        sitenameLabel.Text      = "Site Name:";
        sitenameLabel.Location  = new Point(32, 80);
        sitenameLabel.Size      = new Size(64, 20);
        sitenameLabel.TextAlign = ContentAlignment.MiddleRight;
        sitenameLabel.TabIndex  = 0;

        addressLabel.Text      = "Address:";
        addressLabel.Location  = new Point(32, 128);
        addressLabel.Size      = new Size(64, 20);
        addressLabel.TextAlign = ContentAlignment.MiddleRight;
        addressLabel.TabIndex  = 1;

        descriptionLabel.Text      = "Description:";
        descriptionLabel.Location  = new Point(32, 176);
        descriptionLabel.Size      = new Size(64, 20);
        descriptionLabel.TextAlign = ContentAlignment.MiddleRight;
        descriptionLabel.TabIndex  = 2;

        sitenameTextbox.Location = new Point(104, 80);
        sitenameTextbox.Size     = new Size(344, 20);
        sitenameTextbox.TabIndex = 5;
        addressTextbox.Location = new Point(104, 128);
        addressTextbox.Size     = new Size(344, 20);
        addressTextbox.TabIndex = 6;

        descriptionTextbox.Location = new Point(104, 176);
        descriptionTextbox.Size     = new Size(344, 20);
        descriptionTextbox.TabIndex = 7;

        groupBox.Text     = "Modified Data";
        groupBox.Location = new Point(16, 56);
        groupBox.Size     = new Size(456, 152);
        groupBox.TabStop  = false;
        groupBox.TabIndex = 11;

        okButton.Text             = "OK";
        okButton.Location         = new Point(128, 224);
        okButton.Size             = new Size(75, 23);
        okButton.DialogResult     = DialogResult.OK;
        okButton.TabIndex         = 3;

        cancelButton.Text         = "Cancel";
        cancelButton.Location     = new Point(272, 224);
```

LISTING 16.8 continued

```
        cancelButton.Size         = new Size(75, 23);
        cancelButton.DialogResult = DialogResult.Cancel;
        cancelButton.TabIndex     = 4;

        Text       = "Modify Form";
        ClientSize = new System.Drawing.Size (488, 261);

        Controls.Add(changeButton);
        Controls.Add(selectionLabel);
        Controls.Add(selectionCombobox);
        Controls.Add(descriptionTextbox);
        Controls.Add(addressTextbox);
        Controls.Add(sitenameTextbox);
        Controls.Add(cancelButton);
        Controls.Add(okButton);
        Controls.Add(descriptionLabel);
        Controls.Add(addressLabel);
        Controls.Add(sitenameLabel);
        Controls.Add(groupBox);
    }

    protected void changeButton_Click (object sender, System.EventArgs e)
    {
        citeMgr.DeleteSite(selectionCombobox.SelectedIndex);
        citeMgr.AddSite(sitenameTextbox.Text, addressTextbox.Text,
➥_ descriptionTextbox.Text);
        selectionCombobox.Items[selectionCombobox.SelectedIndex] =
citeMgr[selectionCombobox.SelectedIndex].ToString();
    }

    protected void selectionCombobox_SelectedIndexChanged
➥_ (object sender, System.EventArgs e)
    {
        WebSites.WebSite cite = citeMgr[selectionCombobox.SelectedIndex];

        sitenameTextbox.Text    = cite.SiteName;
        addressTextbox.Text     = cite.URL;
        descriptionTextbox.Text = cite.Description;
    }
}
```

Listing 16.8 shows the `ModifyForm` of the `Cite Manager` application. Because of its interaction between controls and increased number of controls, this is probably the most complex of all the forms so far. This form enables a user to select a Web site from a `ComboBox` control (also known as drop-down list) and make changes to the entry. When the changes are complete, the user clicks the `Change` button. This makes the underlying changes to the data and then updates the `ComboBox`. Figure 16.5 shows what this form looks like.

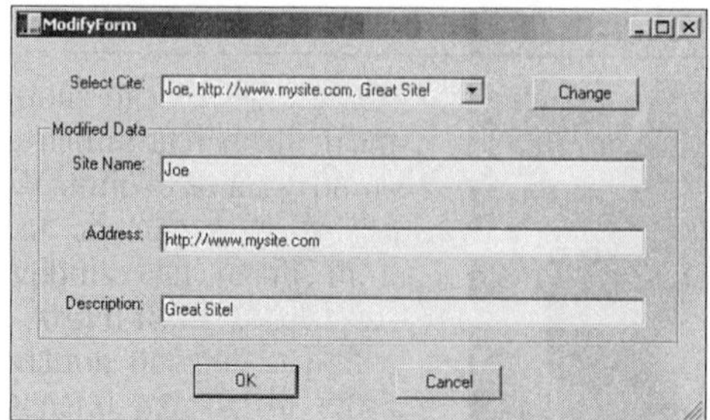

FIGURE 16.5
The ModifyForm screen of the Cite Manager program.

The two new controls on this form are the `ComboBox` and `GroupBox`. The `ComboBox`, `selectionCombobox`, is initialized in the constructor of the `ModifyForm` class. A `for` loop iterates through the `WebSite` objects of the `citeMgr` object. The `ComboBox` itself is loaded differently than a `ListBox` control. It uses the `Insert()` method of the `ComboBox Item` property. Next, it selects the first item in the list by setting the `SelectedIndex` property to zero.

The `selectionCombobox` has its `SelectedIndexChanged` event loaded with a delegate referring to the `selectionCombobox_SelectedIndexChanged()` event handler method. This method uses the current index from the `selectionCombobox` and maps it to the corresponding `WebSite` index in the `citeMgr` object. Then it updates the corresponding `TextBox` controls with the value from the selected `WebSite` object.

The `Change` button has its `Click` event loaded with a delegate referring to the `changeButton_Click` event handler method. This method uses the current index from the `selectionCombobox` and maps it to the corresponding `WebSite` index in the `citeMgr` object. This index is used to first delete the site, and then add it back to the `citeMgr` object. Then it updates the `selectionCombobox` control with the modified entry from the `citeMgr` object.

The `GroupBox` control surrounds the three `TextBox` controls and their `Labels`. This helps organize the form and make it more intuitive to users. A `GroupBox` control is commonly used to surround radio buttons and return the mutually exclusive value when queried. Other controls are initialized similar to that described in previous forms in this section. The last form, shown in Listing 16.9, is for viewing the available Web sites.

LISTING 16.9 A Windows Form for Viewing Web Site Listings: `ViewForm.cs`

```
using System;
using System.Drawing;
using System.ComponentModel;
using System.Windows.Forms;
```

LISTING 16.9 continued

```
public class ViewForm : Form
{
    private Container    components;
    private Button       cancelButton;
    private Button       okButton;
    private ColumnHeader nameColumnHeader;
    private ColumnHeader urlColumnHeader;
    private ColumnHeader descriptionColumnHeader;
    private ListView     viewListview;

    public ViewForm(SiteManager citeMgr)
    {
        string[] columns = new string[3];

        InitializeComponent();

        for (int i=0;i < citeMgr.Count; i++)
        {
            columns[0] = citeMgr[i].SiteName;
            columns[1] = citeMgr[i].URL;
            columns[2] = citeMgr[i].Description;

            ListViewItem list = new ListViewItem(columns);
            viewListview.Items.Add(list);
        }
    }

    public override void Dispose()
    {
        base.Dispose();
        components.Dispose();
    }

    private void InitializeComponent()
    {
        components              = new Container();
        okButton                = new Button();
        cancelButton            = new Button();
        nameColumnHeader        = new ColumnHeader();
        urlColumnHeader         = new ColumnHeader();
        descriptionColumnHeader = new ColumnHeader();
        viewListview            = new ListView();

        okButton.Text         = "OK";
        okButton.Location     = new Point(88, 224);
        okButton.Size         = new Size(75, 23);
        okButton.DialogResult = DialogResult.OK;
        okButton.TabIndex     = 1;
```

LISTING 16.9 continued

```
            nameColumnHeader.Text      = "Cite Name";
            nameColumnHeader.TextAlign = HorizontalAlignment.Left;
            nameColumnHeader.Width     = 87;

            urlColumnHeader.Text      = "Address";
            urlColumnHeader.TextAlign = HorizontalAlignment.Left;
            urlColumnHeader.Width     = 135;

            descriptionColumnHeader.Text      = "Description";
            descriptionColumnHeader.TextAlign = HorizontalAlignment.Left;
            descriptionColumnHeader.Width     = 255;

            cancelButton.Text         = "Cancel";
            cancelButton.Location     = new Point(232, 224);
            cancelButton.Size         = new Size(75, 23);
            cancelButton.DialogResult = DialogResult.Cancel;
            cancelButton.TabIndex     = 2;

            viewListview.Columns.AddRange(new ColumnHeader[3]
                {
                    nameColumnHeader,
                    urlColumnHeader,
                    descriptionColumnHeader
                }
            );
            viewListview.Location             = new Point(8, 8);
            viewListview.Size                 = new Size(368, 192);
            viewListview.Sorting              = SortOrder.Ascending;
            viewListview.View                 = View.Details;
            viewListview.GridLines            = true;
            viewListview.TabIndex             = 0;

            Text       = "View Form";
            ClientSize = new System.Drawing.Size(384, 273);

            Controls.Add (okButton);
            Controls.Add (cancelButton);
            Controls.Add (viewListview);
        }
}
```

The most important addition to this form is the `ListView` control, `viewListview`. Implementation of the `viewListview` control requires two important items, setting up columns and loading the data in the proper columns. Figure 16.6 shows what this form looks like.

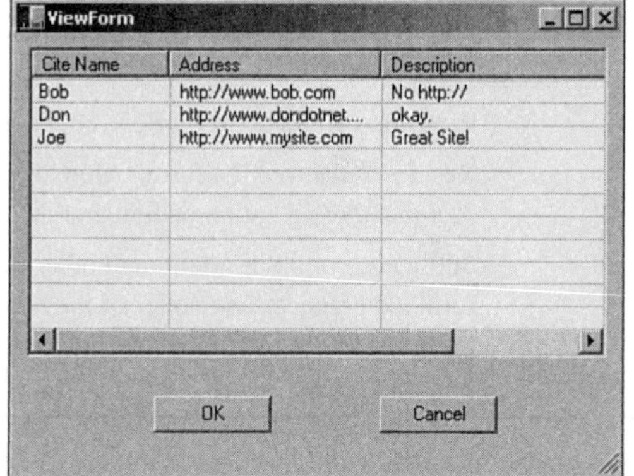

FIGURE 16.6
The ViewForm screen of the Cite Manager program.

Setting up columns requires creation of three `ColumnHeader` objects: `nameColumnHeader`, `urlColumnHeader`, and `descriptionColumnHeader`. They're declared and instantiated the same as all other controls. Initialization of each `ColumnHeader` object involves setting its `Text`, `TextAlignment`, and `Width` properties. These three items affect the appearance of the column header on the screen.

The data is loaded into the `viewListview` control in the `ViewForm` constructor. This process is different from what is used for both the `ListBox` and `ComboBox` controls. There is an array of three strings, `columns`, for holding each column of `WebSite` data. In the `for` loop the `columns` array is loaded with the `SiteName`, `URL`, and `Description` properties of the current `WebSite` object. The `columns` array is used to create a `ListViewItem` object. Then the `ListViewItem` object is added to the `Items` property of the `ListView` control, `viewListview`. Listing 16.10 has the command line to compile a complete program from the preceding files.

LISTING 16.10 Command Line for The Cite Manager Program

```
csc /out:citemgr.exe /r:System.Windows.Forms.DLL
➥/r:System.Drawing.DLL CiteManagerForm.cs
➥AddForm.cs DeleteForm.cs ModifyForm.cs
ÂViewForm.cs SiteManager.cs WebSites.cs
```

Menus

`Menus` are one of the primary means of selecting a program's available options. They're similar to controls, but their function is specialized to invoking selected features of a program. Table 16.2 shows how to create and use Windows Forms `Menus`.

TABLE 16.2 Windows Forms Menu Controls

Menu Control	*What It Does*
ContextMenu	Menus that are invoked by right-clicking a control.
MainMenu	Resides at the top of a form, below its title bar. It is the root menu of an entire menu hierarchy.
MenuItem	Sub-menus of a `MainMenu` and other `MenuItems`. They form the branches and nodes of the menu hierarchy. `MenuItems` are used to invoke some capability of a program.

As a part of any standard GUI implementations, `Menus` are very straightforward and easy to implement. They have a hierarchical structure that makes as much sense in development as in use. Listing 16.11 shows an example of how to implement menus. It's an enhancement of the `CiteManagerForm` class from previous sections.

LISTING 16.11 Cite Manager With Menus: `CiteManagerFormMenus.cs`

```
using System;
using System.Drawing;
using System.ComponentModel;
using System.Windows.Forms;

public class CiteManagerForm : Form
{
    private SiteManager citeMgr;

    private Container components;
    private Button    addButton;
    private Button    deleteButton;
    private Button    modifyButton;
    private Button    viewButton;
    private Label     selectLabel;

    private MainMenu  citeMgrMenu;
    private MenuItem  fileMenu;
    private MenuItem  fileOpenMenu;
    private MenuItem  fileSaveMenu;
    private MenuItem  fileSeparatorMenu;
    private MenuItem  fileExitMenu;

    public CiteManagerForm()
    {
        InitializeComponent();
        citeMgr = new SiteManager();
    }
```

LISTING 16.11 continued

```
    public override void Dispose()
    {
        base.Dispose();
        components.Dispose();
    }

    private void InitializeComponent()
    {
        components   = new Container();
        addButton    = new Button();
        deleteButton = new Button();
        modifyButton = new Button();
        viewButton   = new Button();
        selectLabel  = new Label();

        citeMgrMenu       = new MainMenu();
        fileMenu          = new MenuItem();
        fileOpenMenu      = new MenuItem();
        fileSaveMenu      = new MenuItem();
        fileSeparatorMenu = new MenuItem();
        fileExitMenu      = new MenuItem();

        addButton.Text     = "Add";
        addButton.Click   +=
            new EventHandler (addButton_Click);
        addButton.Location = new Point(94, 80);
        addButton.Size     = new Size(75, 23);
        addButton.TabIndex = 0;

        deleteButton.Text     = "Delete";
        deleteButton.Click   +=
            new EventHandler(deleteButton_Click);
        deleteButton.Location = new Point(94, 128);
        deleteButton.Size     = new Size(75, 23);
        deleteButton.TabIndex = 1;

        modifyButton.Text     = "Modify";
        modifyButton.Click   +=
            new EventHandler(modifyButton_Click);
        modifyButton.Location = new Point(94, 176);
        modifyButton.Size     = new Size(75, 23);
        modifyButton.TabIndex = 2;

        viewButton.Text     = "View";
        viewButton.Click   +=
            new EventHandler(viewButton_Click);
        viewButton.Location = new Point(94, 224);
        viewButton.Size     = new Size(75, 23);
        viewButton.TabIndex = 3;
```

LISTING 16.11 continued

```
        selectLabel.Text        = "Please Make a Selection:";
        selectLabel.Font        = new Font("Lucida Console",
                                           12,
                                           FontStyle.Italic);
        selectLabel.Location    = new Point(10, 32);
        selectLabel.Size        = new Size(246, 18);
        selectLabel.BorderStyle =
            System.Windows.Forms.BorderStyle.Fixed3D;
        selectLabel.AutoSize    = true;
        selectLabel.TabIndex    = 4;

        fileMenu.Text           = "&File";
        fileMenu.Index          = 0;

        fileOpenMenu.Text       = "&Open";
        fileOpenMenu.Click     +=
            new EventHandler (fileOpenMenu_Click);
        fileOpenMenu.Index      = 0;

        fileSaveMenu.Text       = "&Save";
        fileSaveMenu.Click     +=
            new EventHandler (fileSaveMenu_Click);
        fileSaveMenu.Index      = 1;

        fileSeparatorMenu.Text  = "-";
        fileSeparatorMenu.Index = 2;

        fileExitMenu.Text       = "E&xit";
        fileExitMenu.Click     +=
            new EventHandler (fileExitMenu_Click);
        fileExitMenu.Index      = 3;

        fileMenu.MenuItems.Add(fileOpenMenu);
        fileMenu.MenuItems.Add(fileSaveMenu);
        fileMenu.MenuItems.Add(fileSeparatorMenu);
        fileMenu.MenuItems.Add(fileExitMenu);

        citeMgrMenu.MenuItems.Add(fileMenu);

        Menu       = citeMgrMenu;
        Text       = "Cite Manager";
        ClientSize = new Size (264, 273);

        Controls.Add(selectLabel);
        Controls.Add(modifyButton);
        Controls.Add(viewButton);
        Controls.Add(deleteButton);
        Controls.Add(addButton);
    }
```

LISTING 16.11 continued

```
    protected void deleteButton_Click (object sender,
                                       System.EventArgs e)
    {
        DeleteForm df = new DeleteForm(citeMgr);

        df.ShowDialog(this);
    }

    protected void modifyButton_Click (object sender,
                                       System.EventArgs e)
    {
        ModifyForm mf = new ModifyForm(citeMgr);

        mf.ShowDialog(this);
    }

    protected void viewButton_Click (object sender,
                                     System.EventArgs e)
    {
        ViewForm vf = new ViewForm(citeMgr);
        vf.ShowDialog(this);
    }

    protected void addButton_Click (object sender,
                                    System.EventArgs e)
    {
        AddForm af = new AddForm();

        DialogResult dlgRes = af.ShowDialog(this);

        switch (dlgRes)
        {
            case DialogResult.OK:
                citeMgr.AddSite(
                    af.sitenameTextbox.Text,
                    af.addressTextbox.Text,
                    af.descriptionTextbox.Text);
                break;
            case DialogResult.Cancel:
                // do nothing
                break;
            default:
                break;
        }
    }

    protected void fileOpenMenu_Click (object sender,
                                       System.EventArgs e)
    {
```

LISTING 16.11 continued

```
        MessageBox.Show("File/Open Clicked",
                        "Menu Selection",
                        MessageBoxButtons.OK,
                        MessageBoxIcon.Information);
    }

    protected void fileSaveMenu_Click (object sender,
                                       System.EventArgs e)
    {
        MessageBox.Show("File/Save Clicked",
                        "Menu Selection",
                        MessageBoxButtons.OK,
                        MessageBoxIcon.Information);
    }

    protected void fileExitMenu_Click (object sender,
                                       System.EventArgs e)
    {
        DialogResult dlgRes = MessageBox.Show(
            "Are You Sure?",
            "Program Exiting",
            MessageBoxButtons.OKCancel,
            MessageBoxIcon.Warning);

        if (dlgRes == DialogResult.OK)
            Close();
    }

    public static void Main(string[] args)
    {
        Application.Run(new CiteManagerForm());
    }
}
```

Listing 16.11 can be compiled with previous listings by using the command line from Listing 16.12.

LISTING 16.12 Command Line for The Cite Manager Program

```
csc /out:citemgr.exe /r:System.Windows.Forms.DLL
➥/r:System.Drawing.DLL CiteManagerForm.cs
➥AddForm.cs DeleteForm.cs ModifyForm.cs
➥ViewForm.cs SiteManager.cs WebSites.cs
```

Listing 16.11 shows how to implement Windows Forms menus. Following the hierarchical organization of menus, the `citeMgrMenu` is defined as a `MainMenu`. The rest of the menus are defined as `MenuItems`.

Each MenuItem has a Text and Index property. The Text property sets the text that appears on screen. The & character in front of a letter in the text makes the following character a shortcut for the menu item. In the case of the File menu, the user can press the Alt+F keys to open the menu. The Index property is a zero-based position identifier for the menu. In this case, the first menu item in the File menu is the Open menu item at index 0. The last is the Exit menu item at index 3.

Menu items are tied to actions the same as Buttons. Just add an EventHandler delegate with an event handler method parameter to the menu item Click event. Each of the Open, Save, and Exit menu items has an event handler that invokes a Windows Forms MessageBox. The MessageBox has three parameters. The first is the text to be displayed in the MessageBox. The second is the text that goes into the MessageBox title bar. The second controls decoration of the MessageBox. The Open and Save MessageBox calls use the MessagBox.IconInformation constant. This is what shows the information icon when the MessageBox appears on screen. A MessageBox has an OK button by default. The Exit event handler method is a bit different. It has a couple OR'd constants as its third MessageBox parameter. This causes it to show a Warning icon and both an OK and a Cancel button. When the user clicks the OK button, the program calls the form's Close() method, which quits the application.

A menu hierarchy is built from the bottom up. The example shows the Open, Save, Separator, and Exit menu items being added to the File menu's MenuItems collection. The File menu is added to the MainMenu, citeMgrMenu. Then the form's Menu property is set with the citeMgrMenu.

Summary

This chapter showed how to use C# to build a graphical user interface (GUI). It used the .NET Windows Forms library classes to build the GUI. The first section explained the nature of the Windows Forms library and the basic components required to create a user interface.

The Windows Forms library contains several controls that can be combined in sophisticated ways to make the user experience much better and more intuitive than text-based methods.

One section showed how to implement an n-tiered architecture using the Model-View-Controller design pattern. Windows Forms components served as the client interface. There were a couple data management classes that served as the Model. The Model and View were held in coordination with a Controller class.

The last section covered menus. There was an example that enhanced the main form by adding menu support.

Although the next chapter is about a totally different subject, File I/O, the examples are implemented in Windows Forms, and you will see several controls and dialogs that weren't presented in this chapter.

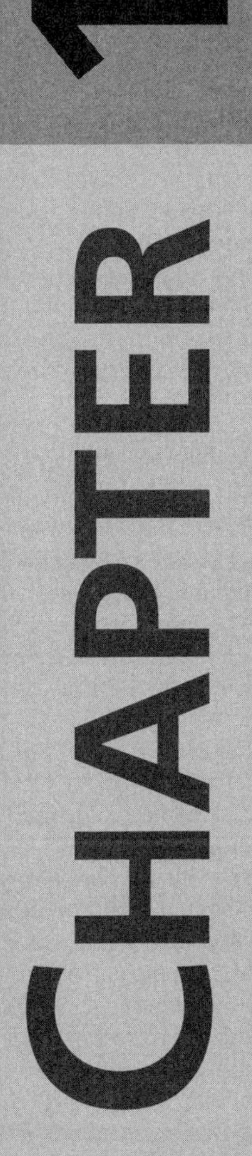

File I/O and Serialization

IN THIS CHAPTER

- **Files and Directories** *382*
- **Streams** *391*
- **Serialization** *398*

File input/output (I/O) is essential to any computer program beyond the simplest utility. The .NET framework includes extensive support for performing I/O. Additionally, there are specialized classes for working with `DirectoryInfo` and file objects at a very high level. These objects create directories and files as well as inspect and modify their attributes.

The underlying capability of file I/O resides in streams, which are mechanisms that facilitate the manipulation and movement of data through a system. C# programs can access specialized classes for working with file, memory, and network streams.

Files and Directories

The base class library (BCL) contains classes for working with files and directories: `File`, `FileInfo`, `DirectoryInfo`, and `DirectoryInfoInfo`. What's nice about these classes is that they provide a simplified, high-level interface for working with files and directories. Anyone who has had to perform low-level operating system file system manipulation in the past is likely to appreciate the ease of use that comes with using these classes. Anything that can be done to a file or DirectoryInfo can be performed with the `File` and `DirectoryInfo` classes, including viewing attributes, creation, modification, and deletion operations.

Table 17.1 shows some of the `File` and `DirectoryInfo` classes available. Notice the convention where `FileInfo` and `DirectoryInfoInfo` classes contain static methods and `File` and `DirectoryInfo` classes contain instance methods. `File` and `FileInfo` classes help create, copy, delete, move, and open files. `DirectoryInfo` and `DirectoryInfoInfo` classes help create, move, and enumerate directories. The `Path` class provides a platform-independent method of specifying a DirectoryInfo/file string. The .NET Frameworks SDK documentation has full descriptions on the many members contained in the classes in Table 17.1.

Table 17.1 File and DirectoryInfo Classes

Class Name	*Description*
`File`	Contains static methods for working with files
`DirectoryInfo`	Contains static methods for working with directories
`Path`	Cross-platform `DirectoryInfo` string management
`FileInfo`	Contains instance methods for working with files
`DirectoryInfoInfo`	Contains instance methods for working with directories

The classes in Table 17.1 have similar functionality that enables them to work with the file and directory structure of the underlying operating system. The program in Listing 17.1 demonstrates how to instantiate and use several properties of the `FileInfo` object. This is typical usage of both file and directory objects.

LISTING 17.1 The `FileInfo` class: `ViewFiles.cs`

```
using System;
using System.IO;

class ViewFiles
{
    static void Main(string[] args)
    {
        FileInfo fi = new FileInfo("ViewFiles.exe");

        string   name   = fi.Name;
        string   dir    = fi.DirectoryName;
        string   ext    = fi.Extension;
        long     length = fi.Length;
        DateTime crTime = fi.CreationTime;
        DateTime laTime = fi.LastAccessTime;
        DateTime lwTime = fi.LastWriteTime;

        Console.WriteLine("\nFile Info:");
        Console.WriteLine(  "----------\n");
        Console.WriteLine("Name:      {0}", name  );
        Console.WriteLine("Directory: {0}", dir   );
        Console.WriteLine("Extension: {0}", ext   );
        Console.WriteLine("Length:    {0}", length);
        Console.WriteLine("Created:   {0}", crTime);
        Console.WriteLine("Accessed:  {0}", laTime);
        Console.WriteLine("Written:   {0}", lwTime);
    }
}
```

And here's the output:

```
File Info:
----------

Name:      ViewFiles.exe
Directory: D:\My Documents\Visual Studio Projects\Chapter 17\FileIO\bin\Debug
Extension: .exe
Length:    4608
Created:   9/10/2001 10:12:17 PM
Accessed:  9/15/2001 3:32:21 PM
Written:   9/15/2001 3:32:04 PM
```

This program instantiates a `FileInfo` object and extracts several properties. While most of the properties generally stay the same, the time properties tend to change. When the file is compiled, its written time changes, and when it is run, its accessed time changes. `FileInfo` class properties and methods are shown in Tables 17.2 and 17.3, respectively. The program in Listing 17.1 can be compiled with the following command line:

```
csc ViewFiles.cs
```

TABLE 17.2 `FileInfo` Class Properties

Property Name	*Description*
`Attributes`	List of attributes such as `normal`, `archive`, or `hidden`
`CreationTime`	When the file was first created
`Directory`	Returns an instance of the parent directory
`DirectoryName`	The full path name of a file
`Exists`	Returns true if a file exists
`Extension`	The file's extension
`FullName`	The full path of a directory or file
`LastAccessedTime`	Last time the file was accessed
`LastWriteTime`	Last time the file was written to
`Length`	File size
`Name`	File name

TABLE 17.3 `FileInfo` Class Methods

Method Name	*Description*
`AppendText`	Enables appending text to a file
`CopyTo`	Copies one file to another
`Create`	Creates a new file
`CreateObjRef`	Creates an object reference for remoting
`CreateText`	Creates a new text file
`Delete`	Deletes a file
`GetLifetimeService`	Returns lease object for remoting
`InitializeLifetimeService`	Prepares remoting lifetime management services
`MoveTo`	Moves a file to another place
`Open`	Opens a file

TABLE 17.3 continued

Method Name	*Description*
`OpenRead`	Opens a file for reading
`OpenText`	Opens a file for text operations
`OpenWrite`	Opens a file for writing
`Refresh`	Refreshes an object's state

The `DirectoryInfo` class can be instantiated to obtain information from and perform several operations on directories. Listing 17.2 shows how to work with the `DirectoryInfo` and `Directory` classes.

LISTING 17.2 The `DirectoryInfo` Class: `ModDirs.cs`

```
using System;
using System.IO;

class ModDirs
{
    DirectoryInfo myDir;

    public ModDirs()
    {
        myDir = new DirectoryInfo(
                        @"D:\My Documents"         +
                        @"\Visual Studio Projects" +
                        @"\Chapter 17\Listing17.2" );
    }

    public void ShowDirInfo()
    {
        string        name     = myDir.Name;
        string        fullName = myDir.FullName;
        DirectoryInfo parent   = myDir.Parent;
        DirectoryInfo root     = myDir.Root;

        Console.WriteLine("\nDirectory Info:");
        Console.WriteLine(  "---------------\n");
        Console.WriteLine("Name:      {0}", name      );
        Console.WriteLine("Full Name: {0}", fullName );
        Console.WriteLine("Parent:    {0}", parent   );
        Console.WriteLine("Root:      {0}", root     );
    }

    public void PrintDirectories(string title)
    {
        Console.WriteLine("\n{0}:", title);
```

LISTING 17.2 continued

```
        for (int i=0; i < title.Length; i++)
            Console.Write("-");

        Console.WriteLine();

        DirectoryInfo[] aDirInfo = myDir.GetDirectories();

        foreach (DirectoryInfo eachDir in aDirInfo)
        {
            Console.WriteLine(eachDir.Name);
        }
    }

    static void Main(string[] args)
    {
        string mySubDir = "MySubDirectory";
        string movedDir = "MovedSubDirectory";
        ModDirs md      = new ModDirs();

        md.ShowDirInfo();
        md.PrintDirectories("Directories");
        md.myDir.CreateSubdirectory(mySubDir);
        md.PrintDirectories("After Creating " + mySubDir);

        string srcDir = md.myDir.FullName + @"\" + mySubDir;
        string dstDir = md.myDir.FullName + @"\" + movedDir;

        Directory.Move(srcDir, dstDir);
        md.PrintDirectories("After Moving" + mySubDir +
                            " to " + movedDir);

        Directory.Delete(dstDir);
        md.PrintDirectories("After Deleting " + movedDir);
    }
}
```

And here's the output:

```
Directory Info:
---------------

Name:      Listing17.2
Full Name: D:\My Documents\Visual Studio Projects\Chapter 17
➥\Listing17.2
Parent:    D:\My Documents\Visual Studio Projects\Chapter 17
Root:      D:\

Directories:
-----------
```

```
bin
obj

After Creating MySubDirectory:
------------------------------
bin
MySubDirectory
obj

After MovingMySubDirectory to MovedSubDirectory:
------------------------------------------------
bin
MovedSubDirectory
obj

After Deleting MovedSubDirectory:
---------------------------------
bin
obj
```


After printing directory information, this program uses the `DirectoryInfo` instance, `myDir`, to create a new subdirectory. Then, instead of using `myDir`, the program uses the static `Directory` class to move a directory and then delete it. `DirectoryInfo` properties and methods are listed in Tables 17.4 and 17.5, respectively. The following command line compiles the program in Listing 17.2:

```
csc ModDirs.cs
```

Tip

The static `Directory` and `File` classes are more efficient when you don't need a class instance. However, when many operations are necessary for a specific file, the `DirectoryInfo` and `FileInfo` classes are the more efficient choice.

TABLE 17.4 `DirectoryInfo` Class Properties

Property Name	*Description*
`Attributes`	List of attributes such as normal, archive, or hidden
`CreationTime`	When the directory was first created
`Exists`	Returns true if a directory exists
`Extension`	The file's extension
`FullName`	The full path of a directory or file
`LastAccessedTime`	Last time the file was accessed

TABLE 17.4 continued

Property Name	*Description*
`LastWriteTime`	Last time the file was written to
`Name`	Filename
`Parent`	Parent directory
`Root`	Root portion of a path

TABLE 17.5 `DirectoryInfo` Class Methods

Method Name	*Description*
`Create`	Creates a new file
`CreateObjRef`	Creates an object reference for remoting
`CreateSubdirectory`	Creates a new subdirectory
`Delete`	Deletes a directory
`GetDirectories`	Returns subdirectories of this directory
`GetFiles`	Returns file list in this directory
`GetFileSystemInfos`	Returns array of `FileSystemInfo` objects
`GetLifetimeService`	Returns lease object for remoting
`InitializeLifetimeService`	Prepares remoting lifetime management services
`MoveTo`	Moves a file to another place
`Refresh`	Refreshes an object's state

The System.IO namespace has another file management class with some interesting behavior. It's the `FileSystemWatcher` class, and it enables a program to keep track of changes in a file system. Listing 17.3 demonstrates how to use the `FileSystemWatcher` class to detect when a file is renamed.

LISTING 17.3 `FileSystemWatcher` Class Demonstration: `FileWatch.cs`

```
using System;
using System.IO;

public class FileWatch
{
    public FileWatch()
    {
```

LISTING 17.3 continued

```
        FileSystemWatcher fileWatch = new FileSystemWatcher(".", "*.*");

        fileWatch.Renamed += new RenamedEventHandler(this.HandleRenamedFile);
        fileWatch.EnableRaisingEvents = true;
    }

    public void HandleRenamedFile(object sender,
                                  RenamedEventArgs e)
    {
        Console.WriteLine("\nFile Renamed:\n");
        Console.WriteLine(
               "Change Type:   {0}", e.ChangeType );
        Console.WriteLine(
               "Full Path:     {0}", e.FullPath   );
        Console.WriteLine(
               "Name:          {0}", e.Name       );
        Console.WriteLine(
               "Old Full Path: {0}", e.OldFullPath);
        Console.WriteLine(
               "Old Name:      {0}", e.OldName    );
    }

    static void Main(string[] args)
    {
        FileWatch fw = new FileWatch();

        // sit and wait for file changes
        Console.ReadLine();
    }
}
```

The constructor in this program initializes the `FileSystemWatcher` object with two constructor arguments. The first argument is the current directory, indicating the file system path to be monitored. The second argument is the wildcard characters, specifying that all files with all extensions will be monitored.

The next statement in the constructor initializes the `Renamed` event of the `FileSystemWatcher` object. It uses the `RenamedEventHandler` delegate to assign the `HandleRenamedEvent()` method to the `Renamed` event. When one of the files in the current directory is modified, the `HandleRenamedEvent()` method is invoked. The following command line compiles Listing 17.3:

```
csc FileWatch.cs
```

Note

Listing 17.3 shows an excellent example of using events and delegates in a non-graphical environment.

Remember to set the `EnableRaisingEvents` property of the `FileSystemWatcher` object to `true`. Otherwise, you may be scratching your head for a while, wondering why the program doesn't work. The `EnableRaisingEvents` property allows a program to turn file change monitoring on and off at will.

When testing this program, I opened two command windows. In one window, I first started the `FileWatch` program. It sat there and looked at me because I put the `Console.ReadLine()` statement at the end of the `Main()` method to make sure it wouldn't stop before I could do something. This is the desired behavior.

In the other window, I went to the same directory where `FileWatch` was running. Then I created a file called `afile`. This didn't produce any results because the `FileWatch` program wasn't set up to look for created files. Then I changed the name of `afile` to `bfile` with the `ren` command. This action produced the following output:

```
File Renamed:

Change Type:   Renamed
Full Path:     .\bfile
Name:          bfile
Old Full Path: .\afile
Old Name:      afile
```

The values in the output come from the `RenamedEventArgs` parameter of the `HandleRenamedEvent()` method. This was so entertaining that I went for an encore performance by changing the name back from `bfile` to `afile`. The results, as expected, were

```
File Renamed:

Change Type:   Renamed
Full Path:     .\afile
Name:          afile
Old Full Path: .\bfile
Old Name:      bfile
```

Streams

In C#, streams are objects that are read from and written to. They are often associated with files but can also be used for memory storage or network communication. Streams abstract the underlying details of operating system, firmware, and hardware I/O. This lets programmers concentrate on what information needs to be processed, rather than how it's processed.

All C# streams are derived from the `Stream` class. Examples in this section focus on the `FileStream`, `BufferedStream`, `StreamReader`, `StreamWriter`, and `CryptoStream`. However, the concepts are easily translated to other streams, such as `BinaryReader`, `BinaryWriter`, `MemoryStream`, `StringReader`, and `StringWriter` classes. The `NetworkSream` is demonstrated in a later chapter. Table 17.6 lists the available stream classes.

TABLE 17.6 Stream Classes

Stream Name	*Description*
`BinaryReader`	Reads primitive data types
`BinaryWriter`	Writes primitive data types
`BufferedStream`	Provides buffering for other streams
`CryptoStream`	Performs cryptographic transformations for other streams
`FileStream`	Enables random access to files
`MemoryStream`	Provides access to a temporary memory store
`NetworkStream`	Enables I/O over a network
`StreamReader`	Reads characters with a specified encoding
`StreamWriter`	Writes characters with a specified encoding
`StringReader`	Stream read access to a string object
`StringWriter`	Stream write access to a string object

Reading and Writing with Streams

One of the most common implementation of streams is to work with files. This calls for `FileStream` class, which enables working with files in many ways. The program in Listing 17.4 wraps a `FileStream` in a `BufferedStream`, which is given to a `StreamWriter` for output to a file. The program then reads the contents of a file by instantiating a new `FileStream` and passing it directly to a `StreamReader`.

LISTING 17.4 Accessing a File with Streams: `StreamEx.cs`

```
using System;
using System.IO;

class StreamEx
{
    static void Main(string[] args)
    {
        string         fileName  = "test.txt";

        // write file
        FileStream     filStream = new FileStream(
                                    fileName,
                                    FileMode.OpenOrCreate,
                                    FileAccess.Write);
        BufferedStream bufStream = new BufferedStream(
                                    filStream);
        StreamWriter     sWriter = new StreamWriter(
                                    bufStream);

        sWriter.WriteLine("Line Number One");
        sWriter.WriteLine("Line Number Two");
        sWriter.Flush();

        sWriter.Close();

        // read file
        filStream = new FileStream(
                            fileName,
                            FileMode.Open,
                            FileAccess.Read);
        StreamReader sReader = new StreamReader(
                            filStream);

        Console.WriteLine("\nReading File: {0}\n", fileName);
        string line = sReader.ReadLine();

        while (line != null)
        {
            Console.WriteLine(line);
            line = sReader.ReadLine();
        }

        Console.WriteLine("\nSeeking File: {0}\n", fileName);

        filStream.Seek(0, SeekOrigin.Begin);
        Console.WriteLine(sReader.ReadLine());

        char[] buffer = new Char[7];
        filStream.Seek(5, SeekOrigin.Current);
```

LISTING 17.4 continued

```
            sReader.Read(buffer, 0, 4);
            Console.WriteLine(new String(buffer));

            Console.WriteLine(sReader.ReadLine());

            filStream.Seek(-12, SeekOrigin.End);
            sReader.Read(buffer, 0, 6);
            Console.WriteLine(new string(buffer));

            sReader.Close();
        }
}
```

And the output is

```
Reading File: test.txt

Line Number One
Line Number Two

Seeking File: test.txt

Line Number One
Line
 Number Two
Number
```

The `FileStream` in Listing 17.4 is instantiated by passing filename, mode, and access as parameters. The mode parameter specifies how the file will be opened and can be any of the values of the `FileMode` enums listed in Table 17.7. The access parameter identifies whether the `FileStream` is read, written, or both and can be any of the values of the `FileAccess` enums listed in Table 17.8.

TABLE 17.7 The `FileMode` Enums

Member Name	*Description*
`Append`	Opens or creates a new file and concatenates new text to the end—write only
`Create`	Creates a new file or overwrites an existing file
`CreateNew`	Creates a new file or throws IOException if file exists
`Open`	Opens an existing file
`OpenOrCreate`	Opens an existing file or creates a new one if the file doesn't exist
`Truncate`	Opens a file and deletes its contents

TABLE 17.8 The `FileAccess` Enums

Member Name	*Description*
`Read`	Readonly access to a file
`ReadWrite`	Read and write access to a file
`Write`	Writeonly access to a file

Once the `FileStream` is instantiated, it's passed as a parameter to instantiate a `BufferedStream`, which is then passed as a parameter to instantiate a `StreamWriter`. This program doesn't pass an encoding to the `StreamWriter` constructor, defaulting to `UTF8Encoding`, which handles Unicode characters correctly.

> **Tip**
>
> The `BufferedStream` class can increase program efficiency by limiting physical I/O to when the buffer becomes full. This prevents programs with many small reads and writes from eating up CPU cycles unnecessarily.

The program uses the `WriteLine()` method of the `StreamWriter` to write a couple lines of text to the file. Because the stream has a `BufferedReader`, the program uses the `Flush()` method of the `StreamWriter` to force the text out of the buffer and into the file. Closing a stream also flushes the buffer.

The `Close()` method of the `StreamWriter` closes the entire stream and the file. Therefore, it isn't necessary to close the `BufferedStream` and the `FileStream`. The rule is to close the outer stream, and all inner streams will also be closed.

> **Tip**
>
> When creating your own stream classes, remember to also close the inner stream. Otherwise, your implementation will fail if another programmer uses your custom stream class, expecting standard stream behavior.

Reading from a stream is the opposite of writing. The example opens a stream to read with read access. The program then uses the `ReadLine()` method of the `StreamReader` class to read text until the stream returns null. This is simple serial file read access.

The final code in the example demonstrates random access by using the FileStream Seek() method. The first parameter represents an offset, and the second parameter is a member of the SeekOrigin enum: Begin, Current, or End. The Seek() method manages an internal file pointer that specifies where the next operation will occur in a file.

The example begins its random access by calling Seek(0, SeekOrigin.Begin), which rewinds the file pointer to the beginning of the stream. Then the next line is read with the ReadLine() method, as shown here:

```
filStream.Seek(0, SeekOrigin.Begin);
Console.WriteLine(sReader.ReadLine());
```


After reading an entire line with the ReadLine() command, the file pointer is now at the beginning of the second line in the stream. This time, instead of reading the entire line, a char array, buffer, is set up as a buffer, and the Read() method is invoked to read four characters from the stream. The parameters to the Read() method are buffer, the beginning offset within buffer, and the number of characters to read. The result is that the first four characters of the second line are in buffer, and the file pointer is at the fifth position of the second line in the stream. The following code shows how this is performed:

```
char[] buffer = new Char[7];
filStream.Seek(5, SeekOrigin.Current);
sReader.Read(buffer, 0, 4);
Console.WriteLine(new String(buffer));
```

The program then performs a ReadLine() on the stream. This action moves the file pointer to the end of the stream as shown here:

```
Console.WriteLine(sReader.ReadLine());
```

File access may also occur relative to the end of a file. The next command uses a negative offset to adjust the file pointer to 12 characters before the end of the stream. The Read() method of the StreamReader is again invoked to extract six characters from the stream. This places the file pointer at six characters from the end of the stream. The following code shows how this is done:

```
filStream.Seek(-12, SeekOrigin.End);
sReader.Read(buffer, 0, 6);
Console.WriteLine(new string(buffer));
```

Implementing a Cryptographic Stream

Cryptographic streams enable a program to encrypt and decrypt data as a part of normal stream operations. The base class library has built-in support for several well-known encryption algorithms. The example in Listing 17.5 implements a cryptographic stream with the Rijndael symmetric encryption algorithm.

LISTING 17.5 Implementing a Cryptographic Stream

```
using System;
using System.IO;
using System.Text;
using System.Security.Cryptography;

class Crypto
{
    static void Main(string[] args)
    {
        string fileName   = "encryptedtext.txt";
        string passPhrase = "Wouldn't you like to know!";

        FileStream fStream = new FileStream(
                                fileName,
                                FileMode.OpenOrCreate,
                                FileAccess.Write);

        byte[] writeBuffer = new byte[1024];
        byte[] key         = new Byte[]
                                { 1, 2, 3, 4, 5, 6, 7, 8, 9,
                                10, 11, 12, 13, 14, 15, 16 };
        byte[] initVect    = new Byte[]
                                { 1, 2, 3, 4, 5, 6, 7, 8, 9,
                                10, 11, 12, 13, 14, 15, 16 };

        RijndaelManaged rijn = new RijndaelManaged();

        CryptoStream encStream = new CryptoStream(
                        fStream,
                        rijn.CreateEncryptor(key, initVect),
                        CryptoStreamMode.Write);

        Console.WriteLine(
            "\nEncrypting Phrase: {0} - to file: {1}\n",
            passPhrase, fileName);

        ASCIIEncoding byteConverter = new ASCIIEncoding();
        writeBuffer = byteConverter.GetBytes(passPhrase);

        encStream.Write(writeBuffer, 0, passPhrase.Length);

        fStream.Close();

        fStream = new FileStream(fileName,
                                 FileMode.Open,
                                 FileAccess.Read);

        byte[] encBuffer = new byte[100];
        fStream.Read(encBuffer, 0, passPhrase.Length);
```

LISTING 17.5 continued

```
        string readResult
            = byteConverter.GetString(encBuffer);
        Console.WriteLine(
            "Encrypted Text: {0}\n", readResult);

        fStream.Seek(0, SeekOrigin.Begin);
        CryptoStream decStream = new CryptoStream(
                        fStream,
                        rijn.CreateDecryptor(key, initVect),
                        CryptoStreamMode.Read);

        byte[] readBuffer = new byte[passPhrase.Length];
        decStream.Read(readBuffer, 0, passPhrase.Length);
        readResult = byteConverter.GetString(readBuffer);
        Console.WriteLine("Decrypted Text: {0}\n",
                           readResult);

        fStream.Close();
    }
}
```

And here's the output:

```
Encrypting Phrase: Wouldn't you like to know!
➥ - to file: encryptedtext.txt

Encrypted Text: ga/?B8[
?##$v47X¶-Odj9?t?[


Decrypted Text: Wouldn't you like to know!
```


Listing 17.5 contains several items covered in the previous section on reading and writing streams, so I'll just zero in on the cryptographic stream implementation. A `CryptoStream` works with a managed cryptographic provider. In this program it implements a `RijndaelManaged` object to implement encryption and decryption:

```
        RijndaelManaged rijn = new RijndaelManaged();
```

Next, the `CryptoStream` is set up with three arguments: a `filestream`, an `encryptor`, and an access mode. The following statement instantiates the `CryptoStream`:

```
        CryptoStream encStream = new CryptoStream(
                        fStream,
                        rijn.CreateEncryptor(key, initVect),
                        CryptoStreamMode.Write);
```

The CryptoStream accepts an encryptor argument as its second parameter. The encryptor accepts two arguments itself: the encryption key and the intitialization vector. Each of these items, shown in the following example, is passed as byte arrays. The size of these arrays can be read or set with the `KeySize` property of the managed cryptographic provider object, `RijndaelManaged`. This is similar in operation to any of the other managed cryptographic providers.

```
byte[] key          = new Byte[]
                          { 1, 2, 3, 4, 5, 6, 7, 8, 9,
                          10, 11, 12, 13, 14, 15, 16 };
byte[] initVect     = new Byte[]
                          { 1, 2, 3, 4, 5, 6, 7, 8, 9,
                          10, 11, 12, 13, 14, 15, 16 };
```

This sets up the cryptographic stream, which may then be used like any other stream. The rest of the program writes to the stream, reads the raw encrypted data through a normal file stream, and then rewinds and reads the data through a read-only cryptographic stream that decrypts the data.

Note

The `CryptoStream` uses symmetric encryption algorithms, which encrypt and decrypt with a single key. This differs from public key encryption in which there are two keys, public and private. In public key encryption, other people or programs encrypt information with your public key and their private key. You or your program then decrypts the information with your private key and their public key.

Serialization

Serialization is the capability to save the state of an object to a stream for later recovery. This is common for distributed network communications technologies such as remoting and Web services. Serialization may be performed automatically with attributes or with a customized solution.

Automatic Serialization

Automatic serialization occurs by adding C# elements, known as attributes, to a class and, optionally, its members. These are the `Serializable` and `NonSerialized` attributes as demonstrated in Listing 17.6. Attributes are discussed in detail in a later chapter.

LISTING 17.6 Automatic Serialization: `Serialized.cs`

```
using System;
using System.IO;
using System.Text;
using System.Runtime.Serialization;
using System.Runtime.Serialization.Formatters.Binary;

[Serializable]
public class Serialized
{
    string permanent;

    [NonSerialized]
    string temporary;

    public Serialized()
    {
    }

    public string Perm
    {
        get
        {
            return permanent;
        }
        set
        {
            permanent = value;
        }
    }

    public string Temp
    {
        get
        {
            return temporary;
        }
        set
        {
            temporary = value;
        }
    }
}

class Serializer
{
    static void Main(string[] args)
    {
        Serialized serOut = new Serialized();
```

LISTING 17.6 continued

```
        serOut.Perm = "I'm persistent.";
        serOut.Temp = "I'm transient.";

        Console.WriteLine("Before Serialization:\n");
        Console.WriteLine("\tPerm: '{0}'\n\tTemp: '{1}'\n",
                          serOut.Perm, serOut.Temp);

        FileStream outStream = new FileStream(
                               "Serialized.ser",
                               FileMode.OpenOrCreate,
                               FileAccess.Write);

        BinaryFormatter binWriter = new BinaryFormatter();
        binWriter.Serialize(outStream, serOut);

        outStream.Close();

        FileStream inStream = new FileStream(
                               "Serialized.ser",
                               FileMode.Open,
                               FileAccess.Read);

        StreamReader sReader = new StreamReader(inStream);
        string serializedFile = sReader.ReadToEnd();

        Console.WriteLine("Contents of Serialized File: \n");
        Console.WriteLine("\t{0}\n", serializedFile);

        inStream.Seek(0, SeekOrigin.Begin);
        Serialized serIn = new Serialized();
        BinaryFormatter binReader = new BinaryFormatter();
        serIn = (Serialized) binReader.Deserialize(inStream);

        Console.WriteLine("After Serialization:\n");
        Console.WriteLine("\tPerm: '{0}'\n\tTemp: '{1}'\n",
                          serIn.Perm, serIn.Temp);

        inStream.Close();
        Console.ReadLine();
    }
}
```

And here's the output:

```
Before Serialization:

        Perm: 'I'm persistent.'
        Temp: 'I'm transient.'
```

```
Contents of Serialized File:

        ?   ?        ??   GSerializer,
➥ Version=1.0.624.27316, Culture=neutral, P
ublicKeyToken=null??
Serialized?     permanent??   ??   ?
➥I'm persistent.?ersistent.?

After Serialization:

        Perm: 'I'm persistent.'
        Temp: ''
```


Automatic serialization is performed by adding the `Serializable` attribute to a class. This causes all fields in a class to be serialized. In Listing 17.6, the `Serialized` class has a `Serializable` attribute, indicating that it may be serialized.

It may not be desirable to serialize some fields, in which case they can be marked with the `NonSerialized` attribute. This is useful if a field was just a working variable that wasn't meant to hold any permanent object state.

This example uses a serialization formatter named `BinaryFormatter` to determine how the object should be serialized. After instantiation, the `Serialize` method of the `BinaryFormatter` is invoked with two arguments: the stream and the object to be serialized. This serializes the `Serialized` class, writing its fields, or state, to the stream.

The stream is then read back into a newly instantiated `Serialized` object. However, the `transient` field is empty when read back in. This was because it was marked as `NonSerialized`.

Custom Serialization

Sometimes you need more control over serialization. This would require custom serialization. To implement custom serialization, inherit the class to be serialized from the `ISerializable` interface and implement the `GetObjectData()` method for serialization and a special constructor for deserialization. Listing 17.7 shows how to implement custom serialization.

LISTING 17.7 Custom Serialization: `CustomSerializer.cs`

```
using System;
using System.IO;
using System.Text;
using System.Collections;
using System.Reflection;
using System.Runtime.Serialization;
```

LISTING 17.7 continued

```
using System.Runtime.Serialization.Formatters.Soap;

[assembly: AssemblyVersion("1.0.0.0")]

[Serializable]
public class Serialized : ISerializable
{
    string permanent;
    string temporary;

    public Serialized(SerializationInfo serInfo,
                      StreamingContext streamContext)
    {
        string assembly;
        string[] assemblyAttributes = new string[2];

        Console.WriteLine(
            "Inside Serialization Constructor\n");

        permanent = serInfo.GetString("permanent");
        assembly  = serInfo.AssemblyName;

        foreach(string eachAttrib
                in assembly.Split(new char[] {','}))
        {
            assemblyAttributes
                = eachAttrib.Split(new char[] {'='});
            if (assemblyAttributes[0].Trim().Equals(
                                           "Version"))
            {
                Console.WriteLine("Version: {0}",
                     assemblyAttributes[1].Trim());
            }
        }
    }

    public void GetObjectData(SerializationInfo serInfo,
                              StreamingContext streamContext)
    {
        Console.WriteLine("Inside GetObjectData\n");
        serInfo.AddValue("permanent", permanent);
    }

    public string Perm
    {
        get
        {
            return permanent;
        }
```

LISTING 17.7 continued

```
        set
        {
            permanent = value;
        }
    }

    public string Temp
    {
        get
        {
            return temporary;
        }
        set
        {
            temporary = value;
        }
    }
}

class CustomSerializer
{
    static void Main(string[] args)
    {
        string fileName = @"Custom.ser";

        Serialized serOut = new Serialized();

        serOut.Perm = "I'm persistent.";
        serOut.Temp = "I'm transient.";

        Console.WriteLine("Before Serialization:\n");
        Console.WriteLine("\tPerm: '{0}'\n\tTemp: '{1}'\n",
                          serOut.Perm, serOut.Temp);

        FileStream outStream = new FileStream(
                                   fileName,
                                   FileMode.OpenOrCreate,
                                   FileAccess.Write);

        SoapFormatter soapWriter = new SoapFormatter();
        soapWriter.Serialize(outStream, serOut);

        outStream.Close();

        FileStream inStream = new FileStream(
                                   fileName,
                                   FileMode.Open,
                                   FileAccess.Read);
```

LISTING 17.7 continued

```
        StreamReader sReader = new StreamReader(inStream);

        string serializedFile = sReader.ReadToEnd();

        Console.WriteLine("Contents of Serialized File: \n");
        Console.WriteLine("{0}\n", serializedFile);

        inStream.Seek(0, SeekOrigin.Begin);

        Serialized serIn = new Serialized();
        SoapFormatter soapReader = new SoapFormatter();

        serIn = (Serialized)soapReader.Deserialize(inStream);

        Console.WriteLine("After Serialization:\n");
        Console.WriteLine("\tPerm: '{0}'\n\tTemp: '{1}'\n",
                          serIn.Perm, serIn.Temp);

        inStream.Close();
    }
}
```

And here's the output:

```
Before Serialization:

        Perm: 'I'm persistent.'
        Temp: 'I'm transient.'

Inside GetObjectData

Contents of Serialized File:

<SOAP-ENV:Envelope xmlns:xsi="http://www.w3.org/2001
➥/XMLSchema-instance" xmlns:xsd="http://www.w3.org
➥/2001/XMLSchema" xmlns:SOAP-E
NC=http://schemas.xmlsoap.org/soap/encoding/
➥ xmlns:SOAP-ENV="http://schemas.xmlsoap.org/
➥soap/envelope/" SOAP-ENV:encodingStyle="
http://schemas.xmlsoap.org/soap/encoding/" xmlns:a1="http://
➥schemas.microsoft.com/clr/assem/CustomSerializer">
<SOAP-ENV:Body>
<a1:Serialized id="ref-1">
<permanent id="ref-3">I&#39;m persistent.</permanent>
</a1:Serialized>
</SOAP-ENV:Body>
</SOAP-ENV:Envelope>
```

```
Inside Serialization Constructor

Version: 1.0.0.0
After Serialization:

        Perm: 'I'm persistent.'
        Temp: ''
```

The body of the `Main()` method in the `CustomSerializer` class is essentially the same as what appeared in the automatic serialization example with one exception. This implementation uses a `SoapFormatter` class, a member of the System.Runtime.Serialization.Formatters.Soap namespace, which serializes object state in the Simple Object Access Protocol (SOAP) format. SOAP is a relatively new standard that enables interprocess communication over the HTTP protocol in a specialized XML format.

The primary focus of this example is in the `Serialized` class, which implements the `ISerializable` interface. There are two class members that are instrumental in custom serialization: the `GetObjectData()` to serialize to a stream and a custom constructor to deserialize from a stream.

Both the custom constructor and `GetObjectData()` method have a `SerializationInfo` parameter. The `GetObjectData()` method uses the `AddValue()` method of the `SerializationInfo` object to load data in key/value pairs. The custom constructor uses one of several methods to get the data type for each class field that should be deserialized. The example uses the `getString()` method, but there are also methods for other built-in types. For example, if the type to deserialize were `decimal` or `int`, the method to get the values would be `GetDecimal()` or `GetInt32()`, respectively.

The `SerializationInfo` object also has three properties: `AssemblyName`, `FullTypeName`, and `MemberCount`. `FullTypeName` holds the formal name of the class type for serialization purposes, and `MemberCount` holds the number of class variables that are held. `AssemblyName` holds a string indicating the class name, version, culture, and public key information.

After extracting the class fields, the custom constructor obtains the `AssemblyName` and parses the version number out of it. The version number is `1.0.0.0` because it was explicitly set with the `AssemblyVersion` attribute at the beginning of the file, just below the namespace declarations. This may come in handy when you want to begin versioning your classes and desire to implement custom serialization to make your versions compatible.

Summary

The base class library (BCL) has both `static` and `instance` classes for working with files and directories. The `File` classes help obtain information and attributes about files as well as conducting operations such as copy, delete, move, and modify. `Directory` classes also provide information and attributes for directories as well as creating, deleting, and moving directories.

Other BCL classes make it easy to work with various types of streams to read and write to various data stores. Specific stream types enable operation on binary and text data. They provide random access to information and allow operations such as buffering and cryptographic transformation.

Another form of I/O is serialization, which enables object state to be transferred to another location via streams. Programmers have the option to either use automatic serialization, which uses attributes, or implement a custom serialization scenario.

Toward the end of this chapter, I showed how to implement serialization with the `SOAPFormatter`, which uses XML to structure the data. The next chapter, "XML," gives you an idea of how the `SOAPFormatter` works to properly lay out the serialized data.

CHAPTER

XML

In This Chapter

- **Writing** ***408***
- **Reading** ***411***

Extensible Markup Language (XML) is one of the most significant advancements in information sharing today and in the future. It permeates nearly every part of the .NET Frameworks and is the essential data transport format for Web Services, a new distributed computing technology. XML enables a standardized method of passing information between programs, file saving and reading, data validation, and many other useful tasks. This chapter explains how to use C# and the XML class libraries to interact with XML data.

Writing

Writing XML documentation is greatly simplified with the `System.XML` class library. The particular class used in this section is the `XMLTextWriter` class. It has numerous convenience methods that make producing XML documents a snap. The .NET Frameworks documentation lists all the available methods for the `XMLTextWriter` class. Listing 18.1 shows how to write XML data to a file.

LISTING 18.1 Writing an XML Document

```
/// <summary>
///        write XML data to a file
/// </summary>
void WriteXML()
{
    XmlTextWriter xr = new XmlTextWriter(fileName, null);

    xr.Formatting  = Formatting.Indented;
    xr.Indentation = 4;

    xr.WriteStartDocument();

    xr.WriteComment("Holds data for the MoneyTalk program.");

    xr.WriteStartElement("MoneyTalk");

    xr.WriteElementString("Talk",
"A penny saved is too small, make it a buck.");

    xr.WriteElementString("Talk",
"Keep your wooden nickel. It'll be worth something someday.");

    xr.WriteElementString("Talk",
"It's your dime, but you're better off dialing 10-10-XXX.");

    xr.WriteEndElement();
```

LISTING 18.1 continued

```
    xr.Flush();
    xr.Close();
}
```

Writing to an XML data file is similar to writing to a normal text file. Just follow these steps:

1. Open the file stream.
2. Write XML data to file.
3. Close the file stream.

The following explanation follows those three steps. The code for each example is from Listing 18.1.

The first step in this sequence is opening the stream. This is performed at the same time as creation of the `XmlTextWriter` object:

```
XmlTextWriter xr = new XmlTextWriter(fileName, null);
```


The `XmlTextWriter` constructor in this example accepts two parameters. The first is a string denoting the name of the file to be written to. The second is the text encoding written to the file; passing a null parameter here causes the constructor to use the default encoding, `UTF8`. Possible encodings are `ASCII`, `BigEndianUnicode`, `Unicode`, `Default`, `UTF7`, or `UTF8`.

The `XmlTextWriter` class uses the `Formatting` enum to set its `Formatting` property, which specifies the way XML data is written:

```
xr.Formatting  = Formatting.Indented;
xr.Indentation = 4;
```

This example sets the Formatting and Indentation properties. The `Formatting.Indented` enum causes subordinate elements to be indented. The behavior of this indentation is controlled by the `Indentation` and `IndentChar` properties. This example sets the `Indentation` property to `4`. The default is `2`. The `IndentChar` property isn't used, because the example uses the default space character.

Once the stream is open and set up, the next step is to write the XML data to the file. The `XmlTextWriter` class has several methods for writing standard XML tags to file. The first is the standard XML v1.0 header tag:

```
xr.WriteStartDocument();
```

Tip

Since the default of the `WriteStartDocument` method is to produce a version 1.0 header, it may be necessary to derive a new class from the `XmlTextWriter` and override this method. This would provide flexibility for version changes.

Formatted comments are also easy to place into the XML document. Just use the `WriteComment()` method. It takes a single string parameter:

```
    xr.WriteComment("Holds data for the MoneyTalk program.");
```

The `XmlTextWriter` class provides a simple method of creating a hierarchical organization of tags:

```
    xr.WriteStartElement("MoneyTalk");
```

The `WriteStartElement()` method creates a start tag for a new level of organization. This example creates a start tag with the text "MoneyTalk". Following elements will be indented.

It's easy to write tags with associated data. The `XmlTextWriter` class has numerous convenience methods to create elements of any type. The following example uses strings, but it would be just as easy to write several other types of elements, including Boolean, integer, float, decimal, char, cdata, and date.

```
    xr.WriteElementString("Talk",
"A penny saved is too small, make it a buck.");

    xr.WriteElementString("Talk",
"Keep your wooden nickel. It'll be worth something someday.");

    xr.WriteElementString("Talk",
"It's your dime, but you're better off dialing 10-10-XXX.");
```

This example writes string tags to the XML file. The name of the tag surrounding the data is the first string parameter, "Talk". The second string parameter is the data within the start and end tags. There's no need for formatting, because the `WriteElement()` method calls do it automatically.

Just as there was a start element ("MoneyTalk"), there is a corresponding end element. For each `WriteStartElement()` method call, there must be a `WriteEndElement()` method call with the matching end tag to the file:

```
    xr.WriteEndElement();
```

Once all writing of XML data to the file is complete, it's time to close the file. This example flushes the stream and then closes it:

```
xr.Flush();
xr.Close();
```

Reading

The `System.Xml` namespace has several classes for making reading of XML files easy. These classes encapsulate the code necessary to parse these files and obtain data related to specific tags. Listing 18.2 shows how to read and parse pertinent data from the file that was written by the method in Listing 18.1.

LISTING 18.2 Reading an XML Document

```
/// <summary>
///       read XML data from a file
/// </summary>
void ReadXML()
{
    XmlTextReader xr = new XmlTextReader(fileName);
    string nodeName;

    while (xr.Read())
    {
        nodeName = xr.Name;

        if (nodeName == "Talk")
        {
            talk.Add(xr.ReadString());
        }
    }

    xr = new XmlTextReader(fileName);

    XmlDocument xd = new XmlDocument();

    xd.PreserveWhitespace = true;

    xd.Load(xr);

    Console.WriteLine(xd.InnerXml);

    xr.Close();
}
```

Reading from an XML data file is similar to reading from a normal text file. Just follow these steps:

1. Open the file stream.
2. Read XML data from file.
3. Close the file stream.

Let's look at these steps in more detail. The example code is from Listing 18.2.

The first step in this sequence is opening the stream. This is performed at the same time that you create the `XmlTextReader` object:

```
XmlTextReader xr = new XmlTextReader(fileName);
```

The `XmlTextReader` constructor accepts a single string parameter that designates the file to open. Once the file is open, it can be read using the `Read()` method, which sets the value of the `XmlTextReader` object to the next available node (XML tag).

```
while (xr.Read())
```

Each node has a name; the name is the text value inside the tag. To obtain this value, use the `Name` property:

```
    nodeName = xr.Name;
```

In this example, the only nodes that are of interest are the `<Talk>` tags. Therefore, the program checks to see if the name of the node is "Talk". If so, it gets the value of the string following the `<Talk>` tag. This is accomplished with the `ReadString()` method of the `XmlTextReader` class. In this example the strings from the `<Talk>` nodes are added to a collection named `talk:if (nodeName == "Talk")`

```
    {
        talk.Add(xr.ReadString());
    }
```

The next thing this program does is to grab the entire XML document for output. This example creates a new `XmlTextReader` that gets a fresh object to point at the first node in the file. Then a new `XmlDocument` object is created, which holds a copy of the XML file:

```
xr = new XmlTextReader(fileName);

XmlDocument xd = new XmlDocument();
```

The `PreserveWhitespace` property of the `XmlDocument` object makes the object maintain `whitespace` characters.

```
xd.PreserveWhitespace = true;
```

Up to this point, the `XmlDocument` has been empty. Now it loads XML data from the `XmlTextReader` object by invoking the `Load()` method of the `XmlDocument` object and providing the `XmlTextReader` object as a parameter:

```
xd.Load(xr);
```

The program needs to print the contents of the `XmlDocument` to the console. It accomplishes this by calling the `Console.WriteLine()` method and passing the `InnerXml` property of the `XmlDocument` object as a parameter:

```
Console.WriteLine(xd.InnerXml);
```

The final step in the reading process is to close the stream. This is done by simply calling the `Close()` method of the `XmlTextReader` class:

```
xr.Close();
```

To show how the previous listings are used, Listing 18.3 contains the entire program. It shows how to read and write XML data.

LISTING 18.3 The MoneyTalk Program

```
using System;
using System.Xml;
using System.Text;
using System.Collections;

/// <summary>
///    manages a list of money related
///    phrases to be obtained by a client
/// </summary>
public class MoneyTalk
{
    ArrayList talk  = new ArrayList();
    string fileName;

    public MoneyTalk(string file)
    {
        fileName = file;
    }

    /// <summary>
    ///         write XML data to a file
    /// </summary>
    void WriteXML()
    {
        XmlTextWriter xr = new XmlTextWriter(fileName, null);
```

LISTING 18.3 continued

```
        xr.Formatting  = Formatting.Indented;
        xr.Indentation = 4;

        xr.WriteStartDocument();

        xr.WriteComment(
"Holds data for the MoneyTalk program.");
        xr.WriteStartElement("MoneyTalk");

        xr.WriteElementString("Talk",
"A penny saved is too small, make it a buck.");

        xr.WriteElementString("Talk",
"Keep your wooden nickel. It'll be worth something someday.");

        xr.WriteElementString("Talk",
"It's your dime, but you're better off dialing 10-10-XXX.");

        xr.WriteEndElement();

        xr.Flush();
        xr.Close();
    }

    /// <summary>
    ///        read XML data from a file
    /// </summary>
    void ReadXML()
    {
        XmlTextReader xr = new XmlTextReader(fileName);
        string nodeName;

        while (xr.Read())
        {
            nodeName = xr.Name;

            if (nodeName == "Talk")
            {
                talk.Add(xr.ReadString());
            }
        }

        xr = new XmlTextReader(fileName);

        XmlDocument xd = new XmlDocument();

        xd.PreserveWhitespace = true;
```

LISTING 18.3 continued

```
        xd.Load(xr);

        Console.WriteLine(xd.InnerXml);

        xr.Close();
    }

    /// <summary>
    ///         get a phrase
    /// </summary>
    public string Talk
    {
        get
        {
            Random rnd = new Random();

            int index = rnd.Next(talk.Count);

            return (string)talk[index];
        }
    }

    public static int Main(string[] args)
    {
        MoneyTalk mt = new MoneyTalk(@"c:\myxml.xml");

        mt.WriteXML();
        mt.ReadXML();

        Console.WriteLine("\nMoneyTalk: {0}", mt.Talk);

        return 0;
    }
}
```


This example shows how to implement a class that performs reading and writing of XML data. The class has an `ArrayList` collection named `talk` and a string field for holding a filename. The talk field is filled during the `XMLRead()` method. The constructor initializes the filename with the passed-in parameter.

The class has a property named `Talk`—a read-only property that returns a phrase in the form of a string when called. By using a `Random` object, it makes a new decision on which element of the talk `ArrayList` to return upon each invocation.

The `Main()` method instantiates a new `MoneyTalk` object with the name of a file to use for reading and writing of XML data. It calls the `XMLWrite()` method first to create and populate the file. If the file exists, it's overwritten. Then it calls the `XMLRead()` method to get the values of the `<Talk>` nodes from the file, add them to the talk `ArrayList`, and print out the XML data file. Before returning, the program prints a new entry from the talk `ArrayList` using the `Talk` property.

Summary

This chapter showed how to use C# and the XML classes in the `System.Xml` namespace to read and write XML data. It showed how to create a file and write formatted XML data to it.

There was also an explanation of how to read from that same file. This was a greatly simplified process because the XML class libraries streamlined much of the tag parsing and data reading.

You also examined how to combine reading and writing of XML data into a working program.

CHAPTER 19

Database Programming with ADO.NET

In This Chapter

- **Making Connections** *418*
- **Viewing Data** *420*
- **Manipulating Data** *425*
- **Calling Stored Procedures** *429*
- **Retrieving DataSets** *435*

ADO.NET is the primary technology for connecting to a database with C#. It offers a high level of abstraction, hiding the low-level details of a particular database vendor's implementation. With ADO.NET, a program can view, insert, update, and delete database records. ADO.NET supports in-memory databases, stored procedures, and disconnected databases.

A significant new capability introduced with ADO.NET is in working with disconnected databases. In a traditional scenario, a program initiates a session with a database and holds that session open during the lifetime of the application. This introduces scalability issues because when too many sessions are opened simultaneously, system performance degrades. An ADO.NET disconnected database solves this problem by making an initial query from the database and disconnecting the session. The information queried from the database is then held in memory without the overhead associated with session management. The capability still exists to initiate another session later by connecting to the database, performing a transaction, and disconnecting as soon as the transaction is complete. The disconnected approach is superior in read-only scenarios, commonly found in many Internet applications.

ADO.NET is an interoperable technology. Besides data storage and retrieval, ADO.NET introduces the capability to integrate with XML. Data can be serialized directly to and from XML for file I/O or network transfer. XML is the emerging data representation format taking the computing world by storm. ADO.NET has full and extensible support for any type of XML operation.

Making Connections

Before a program can do anything with a database it must make a connection. A connection is the action that establishes a session with a database. A session is the sequence of actions to view, insert, update, delete, and perform other management commands with a database. When a program is connected, a session begins. Likewise, when a program is disconnected, a session ends.

There is an ADO.NET class that represents a connection. A connection object must be instantiated and opened to establish a database session. Connection objects have attributes that define various aspects of the session being initiated, and these attributes depend upon the requirements of the underlying database. For example, a name and location are required to indicate which database a program needs to work with. Other common attributes are the username and password to support database security. The following example instantiates a connection object, which establishes a session with an MS-Access database:

```
OleDbConnection conn      = null;

conn = new OleDbConnection(@"Provider=Microsoft.Jet.OLEDB.4.0;
    User Id=;Password=;
    Data Source=D:\My Documents\C#\Northwind.mdb");

conn.Open();
```

In this example, the connection object is called `OleDbConnection`, and it has a single string as a parameter. This string is used to specify connection attributes via semicolon-separated key/value pairs, formatted as `<key>=<value>`. There are four attributes for this connection:

- `Provider`—This is the Microsoft Jet database engine used to connect to MS-Access databases. This attribute is specific to the underlying vendor's database.
- `User Id`—Identifies the program user for security purposes. In this case the user is the program and, therefore, the database must have a security setting to allow this program (user) to access the database. In the example, the `User Id` is blank, which is not very secure in a multi-user environment.
- `Password`—A password is a secret code necessary to maintain database security. In the example, the password is blank, which is not very secure in a multi-user environment. Normally, there would be a password associated with a `User Id` that should be specified after the equal sign.
- `Data Source`—Location of the database. The example shows the place on my hard drive where I placed a copy of the Northwind Traders database. This is the database that comes with MS-Access.

Once the connection has been instantiated, it can be opened with the `Open()` method of the connection object, `OleDbConnection`.

Note

ADO.NET supports the ability for different vendors to add their own database-specific classes that conform the ADO.NET rules. These vendor-specific classes are called data providers. The standard data providers that come with the .NET frameworks are the OLE DB data provider and the SQL data provider.

The OLE DB data provider makes it easy to connect to a wide variety of databases using existing OLE DB technology. Another type of data provider, supplied with .NET, is the SQL data provider. It's built specifically for and provides optimized access to Microsoft SQL Server.

Viewing Data

An efficient means of viewing database information is through an ADO.NET `DataReader`, which is used to obtain a forward-only, read-only data stream from a database. A `DataReader` may not be written to or modified. This is a very efficient means of obtaining data when the only action required is to view information. There are three steps to create a `DataReader`:

1. Create a command object from the connection object.
2. Specify what the command object should do by initializing its `CommandText` property.
3. Create a reader based upon the command object.

The following example shows how to create an `OleDbDataReader`, the `DataReader` belonging to the OLE DB data provider.

```
OleDbDataReader dbReader  = null;

OleDbCommand cmd = conn.CreateCommand();
cmd.CommandText  = "SELECT * FROM Shippers";

dbReader = cmd.ExecuteReader();
```

The example shows how to create an `OleDbCommand` and how to use that command to create an `OleDbDataReader`. The `OleDbCommand` object is created by using the `CreateCommand()` method of the connection object. This way, the command object knows what command is to be executed and which database to work with. The actual command stored is a SQL string added to the `CommandText` property of the command object.

Note

The `OleDbDataReader` is a `sealed` class. This is an excellent example of how to use the `sealed` modifier to help optimize class performance.

The SQL string in the `CommandText` object specifies what records will be read from the database. After the command object is initialized, an `OleDbDataReader` is created by invoking the `ExecuteReader()` method of the command object.

The following example shows how to read database data with `DataReader`. It prints each of the column names, and then it prints each row of data aligned under its corresponding column name.

```
for (int i=0; i < dbReader.FieldCount; i++)
{
    Console.Write("{0}", dbReader.GetName(i).PadLeft(20, ' '));
}
Console.WriteLine("\n{0}", "".PadLeft(60, '-'));

int    index;
string companyName;
string phone;

while (dbReader.Read())
{
    index       = dbReader.GetInt32(0);
    companyName = (string)dbReader.GetValue(1);
    phone       = (string)dbReader["Phone"];

    Console.WriteLine("{0}{1}{2}",
        index.ToString().PadLeft(20, ' '),
        companyName.PadLeft(20, ' '),
        phone.PadLeft(20, ' '));
}
```

The `for` loop uses the `FieldCount` property of the `OleDbDataReader` to determine how many columns there are in the table. For each table column, the `GetName()` method of the `OleDbDataReader` is called. This returns a string with the name of the column. The column returned corresponds to the integer parameter passed, as a column index, into the `GetName()` method.

The `PadLeft()` method aligns its string to the right and fills space, to the left of the string, with the character specified in its second parameter. The first parameter specifies the entire size of the field. Within the `for` loop, the `PadLeft()` method operates on the string returned from the `GetName()` method of the `OleDbDataReader`. After the `for` loop, the `PadLeft()` method operates on a blank string literal. Since the string is blank, this prints a string of dash characters. This creates an underline effect and separates the column titles from table data.

A simple `while` loop controls access to table data. The lifetime of the `while` loop is controlled by the `Read()` method of the `OleDbDataReader`. When there are no more rows, `Read()` returns `false`. As long as there are rows to return, `Read()` returns `true`, permitting execution of the `while` loop statements.

The body of the `while` loop performs two functions: loading column data and printing each row to the console. The column data fields are `index`, `companyName`, and `phone`. To show different ways of obtaining `OleDbDataReader` data, three separate methods are used: typed retrieval by index, default typed retrieval by index, and default type retrieval by name.

The default typed retrieval by index technique uses the `GetValue()` method of the `OleDbDataReader`. It takes an index corresponding to the table column order and retrieves the data as the native type of that column. The object returned is of type `object` and requires explicit conversion for assignment to its native type. The `companyName` field is populated with the `GetValue()` method.

The default type retrieval by name method uses the indexer of the `OleDbDataReader` to obtain a column value. The index value is a string corresponding to the actual column name in the table. This is one of the column names retrieved with the previous `for` loop. The value returned is of type `object` and requires explicit conversion for assignment to its native type. Using the `OleDbDataReader` indexer populates the `phone` field.

The typed retrieval by index technique has several methods within the `OleDbDataReader` class. This technique returns a value of the type corresponding to the method used. Each of the typed methods use an index corresponding to the table column desired. The example uses the `GetInt32()` method to return an `int` type value to the `index` field. Table 19.1 shows other methods that can be used to return typed data from an `OleDbDataReader` object.

TABLE 19.1 `OleDbDataReader` Typed Methods and Return Types

Method	*Return Type*
`GetBoolean`	bool
`GetByte`	byte
`GetBytes`	array of bytes
`GetChar`	char
`GetChars`	array of chars
`GetDateTime`	DateTime object
`GetDecimal`	decimal
`GetDouble`	double
`GetFloat`	float
`GetGuid`	Guid object
`GetInt16`	short
`GetInt32`	int
`GetInt64`	long
`GetString`	string
`GetTimeSpan`	TimeSpan object

For a more comprehensive perspective, Listing 19.1 shows how the information in this section fits together. It is followed by Listing 19.2, which provides compilation instructions. Then there is an explanation of the extra elements necessary to make this program work.

LISTING 19.1 Reading Database Information: DBAccess.cs

```
using System;
using System.Data;
using System.Data.OleDb;

/// <summary>
///    A program to read database information
///    and display it on the console screen.
/// </summary>
class DBAccess
{
    static void Main(string[] args)
    {
        OleDbConnection conn      = null;
        OleDbDataReader dbReader  = null;

        try
        {
            conn = new OleDbConnection(@"
              Provider=Microsoft.Jet.OLEDB.4.0;
              User Id=;
              Password=;
              Data Source=D:\My Documents\C#\Northwind.mdb");

            conn.Open();

            OleDbCommand cmd = conn.CreateCommand();
            cmd.CommandText  = "SELECT * FROM Shippers";

            dbReader = cmd.ExecuteReader();

            for (int i=0; i < dbReader.FieldCount; i++)
            {
                Console.Write("{0}",
                    dbReader.GetName(i).PadLeft(20, ' '));
            }
            Console.WriteLine("\n{0}", "".PadLeft(60, '-'));

            int    index;
            string companyName;
            string phone;
```

LISTING 19.1 continued

```
            while (dbReader.Read())
            {
                index       = dbReader.GetInt32(0);
                companyName = (string)dbReader.GetValue(1);
                phone       = (string)dbReader["Phone"];

                Console.WriteLine("{0}{1}{2}",
                    index.ToString().PadLeft(20, ' '),
                    companyName.PadLeft(20, ' '),
                    phone.PadLeft(20, ' '));
            }
        }
        catch (OleDbException odbe)
        {
            Console.WriteLine("OleDbException: {0}",
                              odbe.Message);
        }
        finally
        {
            if (dbReader != null)
            {
                dbReader.Close();
                conn.Close();
            }
        }
    }
}
```

LISTING 19.2 Compilation Instructions for Listing 19.1

```
csc DBAccess.cs /r:System.Data.dll
```

Listing 19.1 is an example of implementing the concepts presented in this section. The main points to get from this listing are the namespaces, error handling, and database closure.

At the top of the listing are a couple using statements for database-related namespaces. The `System.Data` namespace contains the basic types needed to program with ADO.NET. The `System.Data.OleDb` namespace contains the components necessary to implement the OLE DB data provider. To ensure the program compiles properly, include a reference to the `System.Data.dll` library on the command line, as shown in Listing 19.2. The `System.Data.dll` is the assembly that contains the `System.Data` and `System.Data.OleDb` namespaces.

The majority of statements in this program are enclosed in a `try/catch/finally` block. The purpose of this is to capture database-related errors. The `catch` block accepts an exception of type `OleDbException`. It only prints the value of the exception, but this is still useful. In cases such as when the database path is specified incorrectly, the user will receive a message indicating that the database couldn't be found.

Regardless of program failure or success, certain actions must be performed. This is handled in the `finally` block. At the beginning of the program, the `dbReader` and `conn` fields are set to `null`. If instantiation of either of these objects fails, the `dbReader` will still be `null` by the time the `finally` block executes. Therefore, there is an additional check to ensure that `Close()` methods for the `DataReader` object, `dbReader`, and the connection object, `conn`, are executed only when necessary.

Tip

Listing 19.1 uses a `finally` block to close database resources. This is a good example of how to use `finally` blocks to ensure that resources are released back to the system.

Manipulating Data

Previous sections showed how to use ADO.NET to view data. However, many applications need to change or manipulate the data in the database. The data manipulation operations supported by ADO.NET are the same as the standard SQL operations used to insert, update, and delete data.

One of the primary differences between viewing data and manipulating data is the method of the command object that is invoked. Data manipulation commands are executed by calling the `ExecuteNonQuery()` method of the command object. Listing 19.3 shows how to perform four standard database commands: reading (as demonstrated in earlier sections) and manipulation commands to include insert, update, and delete.

LISTING 19.3 Manipulating Database Information: `DataManipulator.cs`

```
using System;
using System.Data;
using System.Data.OleDb;

/// <summary>
///        This class shows how to execute database
///        commands to manipulate rows in a table.
```

Listing 19.3 continued

```
/// </summary>
class DataManipulator
{
    // print shippers table to console
    void PrintReport()
    {
        OleDbDataReader dbReader  = null;
        OleDbConnection conn      = null;

        try
        {
            conn = new OleDbConnection(@"
                Provider=Microsoft.Jet.OLEDB.4.0;
                User Id=;
                Password=;
                Data Source=D:\My Documents\C#\Northwind.mdb"
            );

            conn.Open();

            OleDbCommand rcmd = conn.CreateCommand();
            rcmd.CommandText  = "SELECT * FROM Shippers";

            dbReader = rcmd.ExecuteReader();

            Console.WriteLine();

            for (int i=0; i < dbReader.FieldCount; i++)
            {
                Console.Write("{0}",
                    dbReader.GetName(i).PadLeft(20, ' '));
            }
            Console.WriteLine("\n{0}", "".PadLeft(60, '-'));

            int    index;
            string companyName;
            string phone;

            while (dbReader.Read())
            {
                index       = dbReader.GetInt32(0);
                companyName = (string)dbReader.GetValue(1);
                phone       = (string)dbReader["Phone"];
                Console.WriteLine("{0}{1}{2}",
                    index.ToString().PadLeft(20, ' '),
                    companyName.PadLeft(20, ' '),
                    phone.PadLeft(20, ' '));
            }
        }
```

LISTING 19.3 continued

```
        catch (OleDbException odbe)
        {
            Console.WriteLine("OleDbException: {0}",
                              odbe.Message);
        }
        finally
        {
            if (dbReader != null)
            {
                dbReader.Close();
                conn.Close();
            }
        }
    }

    // insert, update, or delete row in shippers table
    void ModifyTable(string modCommand)
    {
        OleDbConnection conn      = null;

        try
        {
            conn = new OleDbConnection(@"
                Provider=Microsoft.Jet.OLEDB.4.0;
                User Id=;
                Password=;
                Data Source=D:\My Documents\C#\Northwind.mdb"
            );

            conn.Open();

            OleDbCommand nqcmd = conn.CreateCommand();
            nqcmd.CommandText  = modCommand;
            nqcmd.ExecuteNonQuery();
        }
        catch (OleDbException odbe)
        {
            Console.WriteLine("OleDbException: {0}",
                              odbe.Message);
        }
        finally
        {
            if (conn != null)
            {
                conn.Close();
            }
        }
    }
```

LISTING 19.3 continued

```
    // insert, update, delete, and
    // print a database table
    static void Main(string[] args)
    {
        DataManipulator dm = new DataManipulator();

        // show original table contents
        dm.PrintReport();

        // insert row and show results
        dm.ModifyTable(@"INSERT INTO Shippers
                         (companyname, phone)
                         VALUES (""Desert Cargo"",
                                 ""480-555-1234"")
                         ");
        dm.PrintReport();

        // modify row and show results
        dm.ModifyTable(@"UPDATE Shippers
                         SET phone = ""(480) 555-1234""
                         WHERE companyname = ""Desert Cargo""
                         ");
        dm.PrintReport();

        // delete row and show results
        dm.ModifyTable(@"DELETE FROM Shippers
                         WHERE companyname = ""Desert Cargo""
                         ");
        dm.PrintReport();
    }
}
```

This example has three major sections: the `Main()` method, the `PrintReport()` method, and the `ModifyTable()` method. The `PrintReport()` method contains code from previous sections necessary to view `Shipper` table data. The `Main()` method drives the program, using the other two methods to insert, update, delete, and print `Shipper` table data. The portion of this example to concentrate on for this section is the `ModifyTable()` method.

Code within the `ModifyTable()` method is similar to what has been presented in previous sections for the connection and command objects. The primary difference is the initialization and execution of the command object. The command object is initialized with the `modCommand` string parameter. This string holds either an insert, update, or delete SQL command.

Execution of this command is accomplished by invoking the `ExecuteNonQuery()` method of the command object. Since there isn't any data to read as a result of this query, capturing its return value isn't required. The `ExecuteNonQuery()` command returns the number of rows affected for insert, update, and delete queries. Otherwise, it returns a `-1`.

The `Main()` method executes the `ModifyTable()` method with insert, update, and delete SQL commands. The arguments to the `ModifyTable()` method are verbatim string literals. Quotes within the string are specified with double quotes, and the commands are separated into lines for better formatting and readability of the code. This program can be compiled with the command line from Listing 19.4.

Tip

Listing 19.4 uses verbatim string literals for SQL commands. This is a good example of how to use verbatim string literals to format such strings for easier readability and program maintenance. The actual contents of the string depend on the underlying database management system.

LISTING 19.4 Compilation Instructions for Listing 19.3

```
csc DataManipulator.cs /r:System.Data.dll
```

Calling Stored Procedures

Stored procedures provide a degree of efficiency over the normal database calls shown so far. The program in this section uses the SQL Server data provider for working with stored procedures. Listing 19.5 shows the implementation of the SQL Server managed provider, how to create a stored procedure, and how to execute a stored procedure with parameters.

LISTING 19.5 Creating and Executing a Stored Procedure: `StoredProcedures.cs`

```
using System;
using System.Data;
using System.Data.SqlClient;

/// <summary>
///     Program demonstrating creating and
///     execution of stored procedures.
/// </summary>
class StoredProcedures
{
```

LISTING 19.5 continued

```
// print shippers table to console
void PrintReport()
{
    SqlDataReader dbReader  = null;
    SqlConnection conn = null;

    try
    {
        conn = new SqlConnection("
            Data Source=localhost;
            User Id=sa;
            Password=pwd;
            Initial Catalog=northwind
        ");

        SqlCommand cmd  = conn.CreateCommand();
        cmd.CommandText = "SELECT * FROM Shippers";

        conn.Open();

        dbReader = cmd.ExecuteReader();

        Console.WriteLine();

        for (int i=0; i < dbReader.FieldCount; i++)
        {
            Console.Write("{0}", dbReader.GetName(i).PadLeft(20, ' '));
        }

        Console.WriteLine("\n{0}", "".PadLeft(60, '-'));

        int    index;
        string companyName;
        string phone;

        while (dbReader.Read())
        {
            index       = dbReader.GetInt32(0);
            companyName = (string)dbReader.GetValue(1);
            phone       = (string)dbReader["Phone"];

            Console.WriteLine("{0}{1}{2}",
                index.ToString().PadLeft(20, ' '),
                companyName.PadLeft(20, ' '),
                phone.PadLeft(20, ' '));
        }
    }
    catch (SqlException sqle)
    {
```

LISTING 19.5 continued

```
            Console.WriteLine("SqlException: {0}", sqle.Message);
        }
        catch (Exception e)
        {
            Console.WriteLine("Generic Exception: {0}", e.Message);
        }
        finally
        {
            if (dbReader != null)
            {
                dbReader.Close();
                conn.Close();
            }
        }
    }

    // create a stored procedure in the
    // Northwind Traders database
    void CreateStoredProcedure()
    {
        SqlConnection conn = null;
        try
        {
            conn = new SqlConnection("
                Data Source=localhost;
                User Id=sa;
                Password=pwd;
                Initial Catalog=northwind
            ");

            conn.Open();

            SqlCommand nqcmd = conn.CreateCommand();
            nqcmd.CommandText  =
                @"
                    CREATE PROCEDURE GetPhoneNumber
                        @companyName nvarchar(20),
                        @phone       nvarchar(20) output
                    AS
                    SELECT @phone = phone FROM Shippers
                    WHERE companyName = @companyName
                ";

            nqcmd.ExecuteNonQuery();
        }
        catch (SqlException sqle)
        {
            Console.WriteLine(
                "CreateStoredProcedure SqlException: {0}",
```

LISTING 19.5 continued

```
                sqle.Message);
        }
        catch (Exception e)
        {
            Console.WriteLine("Generic Exception: {0}", e.Message);
        }
        finally
        {
            if (conn != null)
            {
                conn.Close();
            }
        }
    }

    // run a stored procedure
    void ExecuteStoredProcedure()
    {
        SqlConnection conn      = null;
        SqlDataReader dbReader  = null;

        try
        {
            conn = new SqlConnection("
                Data Source=localhost;
                User Id=sa;
                Password=pwd;
                Initial Catalog=northwind");

            conn.Open();

            SqlCommand cmd = new SqlCommand("GetPhoneNumber",
                                            conn);
            cmd.CommandType = CommandType.StoredProcedure;

            SqlParameter inParam  = new SqlParameter(
                                            "@companyName",
                                            SqlDbType.NChar,
                                            20);
            inParam.Direction     = ParameterDirection.Input;
            inParam.Value         = "United Package";

            SqlParameter outParam = new SqlParameter(
                                            "@phone",
                                            SqlDbType.NChar,
                                            20);
            outParam.Direction    = ParameterDirection.Output;
```

LISTING 19.5 continued

```
            cmd.Parameters.Add(inParam);
            cmd.Parameters.Add(outParam);

            dbReader = cmd.ExecuteReader();

            Console.WriteLine("United Package Phone #: {0}",
                              cmd.Parameters["@phone"].Value);

            SqlCommand nqcmd = conn.CreateCommand();
            nqcmd.CommandText  =
                "DROP PROCEDURE GetPhoneNumber";
            nqcmd.ExecuteNonQuery();
        }
        catch (SqlException sqle)
        {
            Console.WriteLine(
                "ExecuteStoredProcedure SqlException: {0}",
                sqle.Message);
        }
        catch (Exception e)
        {
            Console.WriteLine(
                "Generic Exception: {0}",
                e.Message);
        }
        finally
        {
            if (dbReader != null)
            {
                dbReader.Close();
                conn.Close();
            }
        }
    }

    // create and execute a stored procedure
    static void Main(string[] args)
    {
        StoredProcedures stProc = new StoredProcedures();

        stProc.CreateStoredProcedure();

        stProc.ExecuteStoredProcedure();

        stProc.PrintReport();
    }
}
```

Implementing the SQL Server managed provider is similar to implementing the OLE DB managed provider in previous sections. The most notable difference is the connection string. Make sure that SQL Server authentication is set for Windows and SQL Server. Also, the password for the user ID `sa` may be blank. If so, specify it as `password=;`.

The `CreateStoredProcedure()` method creates a stored procedure. The steps required to set up the command are similar to those in the "Manipulating Data" section of this chapter. The exception is that the objects belong to the SQL Server managed provider.

Executing the stored procedure is more detailed because it's a parameterized query. The execution code is in the `ExecuteStoredProcedure()` method. A command object for a stored procedure is instantiated with its first parameter set to the name of the stored procedure. In this example, the stored procedure name is `GetPhoneNumber`. The default command type for a command object is `Text`. To execute a stored procedure with parameters, the `CommandType` property of the command object must be set to the enumeration `CommandType.StoredProcedure`. Once the command object is set up, the program creates the stored procedure parameters.

The stored procedure in this program uses two parameters: an input parameter for `companyname` and an output parameter for `phone`. The `SqlParameter` constructor form in this program uses three parameters: the first is the name of the stored procedure parameter; the second is the `SqlDbType` enumeration, specifying the database type; and the third specifies the size of the field. Once each `SqlParameter` object is created, certain `SqlParameter` properties are set to further specialize the parameter.

The `ParameterDirection` properties are set with the `ParameterDirection` enumeration. The `inParam` object is set to `ParameterDirection.Input`, and the `outParam` object is set to `ParameterDirection.Output`, indicating how they are used in the stored procedure. The `Value` property of `inParam` is set to "United Package", providing the stored procedure with criteria to act upon. Once the parameters are set up, they're added to the `Parameters` collection of the command object, and the command is ready to be executed.

To execute the stored procedure, invoke the `ExecuteReader()` method of the command object. The return value of the `ExecuteReader()` isn't used. Instead, the value of the `@phone` parameter from the `Parameters` collection of the command object is extracted to obtain the query result.

To make Listing 19.5 a useful demonstration, before the `ExecuteStoredProcedure()` method exits, it creates a new command to remove the stored procedure from the database. Without this, the program would generate an exception the second time it is run because the stored procedure already exists. All listings in this chapter compile with similar command lines. Therefore, you won't find any surprises with the compilation command line in Listing 19.6.

LISTING 19.6 Compilation Instructions for Listing 19.5

```
csc StoredProcedures.cs /r:System.Data.dll
```

Retrieving DataSets

All examples in this chapter so far have made a connection to a database, performed whatever operations were pertinent, and disconnected. This is similar to what many people are comfortable and familiar with. Now the rules change. The new game in town is DataSets. A DataSet is a disconnected database. In the context of the DataSet, the term disconnected means that a connection is made to establish a session with the database, the required data is read into a DataSet, and then the session is closed by disconnecting from the database. At the point the session is closed by disconnecting from the database, the DataSet becomes a disconnected database. One of the major benefits of this is that a program doesn't hold on to connection resources, thus freeing network bandwidth and increasing database efficiency. A DataSet can hold an entire database or parts of a database in memory—whatever makes sense for the application. DataSets are made for Internet applications that require scalability supported by stateless component interaction.

Now that the program has the data, let go of the connection, and made changes, how do changes get written back to the database? The answer is the DataAdapter. A DataAdapter works hand-in-hand with a DataSet to keep track of database changes. Listing 19.7 shows how to fill a DataSet with database information, modify that information, and print the results.

LISTING 19.7 Using DataSets: `DataSetExample.cs`

```
using System;
using System.Data;
using System.Data.SqlClient;

/// <summary>
///     Summary description for Class1.
/// </summary>
class DataSetsExample
{
    static void Main(string[] args)
    {
        SqlConnection conn = null;

        try
        {
            conn = new SqlConnection("
```

LISTING 19.7 continued

```
            Data Source=localhost;
            User Id=sa;
            Password=pwd;
            Initial Catalog=northwind");

        DataSet shippersDS = new DataSet();

        SqlDataAdapter shippersAdapter =
            new SqlDataAdapter("SELECT * FROM Shippers",
                                    conn);

        shippersAdapter.Fill(shippersDS, "Shippers");

        DataTable shippersTable =
            shippersDS.Tables["Shippers"];

        DataRow newShipper = shippersTable.NewRow();
        newShipper["CompanyName"] = "Desert Cargo";
        newShipper["Phone"]       = "(480) 555-1234";

        shippersTable.Rows.Add(newShipper);

        Console.WriteLine();

        for (int i=1; i<shippersTable.Columns.Count; i++)
        {
            Console.Write("{0}",
    shippersTable.Columns[i].Caption.PadLeft(20, ' '));
        }
        Console.WriteLine("\n{0}", "".PadLeft(60, '-'));

        string companyName;
        string phone;

        foreach(DataRow shipper in shippersTable.Rows)
        {
            companyName = (string)shipper["CompanyName"];
            phone       = (string)shipper["Phone"];

            Console.WriteLine("{0}{1}",
                companyName.PadLeft(20, ' '),
                phone.PadLeft(20, ' '));
        }

        //shippersAdapter.Update(shippersDS, "Shippers");
    }
    catch (SqlException sqle)
    {
        Console.WriteLine(
```

LISTING 19.7 continued

```
                "CreateStoredProcedure SqlException: {0}",
                sqle.Message);
        }
        catch (Exception e)
        {
            Console.WriteLine(
                "Generic Exception: {0}",
                e.Message);
        }
    }
}
```

In Listing 19.7, the DataSet is declared with no arguments and is empty at the point in time that it is instantiated. The DataSet has no connection to the database and, therefore, requires a DataAdapter to fill it. The DataAdapter is instantiated with a SQL command and a connection object. To place data into the DataSet, use the `Fill()` method of the DataAdapter. The `Fill()` method accepts a DataSet object and a table name as parameters. This is how the DataSet is populated with database information. The next part of the example adds information to the DataSet.

This example adds a new record to the `Shippers` table in the DataSet. First it creates a DataTable object by specifying the Shippers table in the `Tables` collection indexer of the DataSet. Next, a DataRow object is created by invoking the `NewRow()` method of the DataTable object, `shippersTable`. The DataRow object has an indexer, which is used to fill the specified columns of the DataRow object with new values. Once the DataRow, `newShipper`, is initialized, it is added to the DataTable by calling the `Add()` method of the `Rows` collection in the `shipperTable` object. The next thing to do is show the results of this change.

The program in Listing 19.7 produces output similar to examples in earlier sections in this chapter but accesses the data in different ways. Columns are obtained by iterating through the `Columns` collection of the `shippersTable` object. The column name is obtained by reading the `Caption` property of each column.

The `Rows` collection of the `shippersTable` object can be used in a `foreach` loop to look at each row in the table. The columns of each row are read by using the DataRow object indexer.

The DataAdapter object makes connections and engages in transactions with the database. For every transaction with the database, the DataAdapter opens the connection, makes the transaction, and then closes the connection on its own. This is the reason why there are not any `Open()` or `Close()` methods invoked on the connection object in Listing 19.7. The code in Listing 19.7 can be compiled with the command line in Listing 19.8.

LISTING 19.8 Compilation Instructions for Listing 19.7

```
csc DataSetExample.cs /r:System.Data.dll
```

Summary

This chapter covered many of the main aspects of ADO.NET. It explained what managed providers were, which are available, and how to connect to each.

You saw how to database data. Before viewing data, the information to be read must be specified in the form of a command object. The command object is then executed to produce a DataReader. The DataReader object contains functionality necessary for reading database queries.

I also showed how to manipulate database data by performing insert, update, and delete operations on a database. Another section showed how to perform the same types of operations with stored procedures.

The last section showed how to retrieve database information into a DataSet. The DataSet object is a means of holding partial or full databases supporting disconnected, Web-centric scenarios. One of the primary purposes of ASP technology is to make presenting database information easier. With this in mind, the information from this chapter should be helpful when learning ASP.NET.

CHAPTER 20

Writing Web Applications with ASP.NET

In This Chapter

- A Simple Web Page *440*
- Controls *441*
- Making a Web Form *443*
- Code-Behind Web Pages *452*

ASP.NET is the latest evolution of Active Server Pages (ASP) technology. ASP.NET pages have several advantages over the earlier ASP model. One significant difference is that ASP.NET pages are compiled and execute faster. New server controls provide more options for the programmer, but they are translated into their HTML equivalents for browsing. Another addition is code-behind pages—separate programming modules that promote well-engineered Web pages.

This chapter shows how ASP.NET Web pages are programmed with C#. It's assumed that you already have some Internet experience; understand Web pages, including HTML; and have a basic knowledge of the HTTP protocol. Although knowledge of ASP certainly helps, it isn't necessary.

For further information on individual controls, I'll identify the appropriate class to reference. A good source for this information is the .NET Frameworks SDK, a freely downloadable set of software with technical documentation for the .NET libraries. These libraries are so extensive that it wouldn't be practical to list all their contents here. Complete coverage of this topic would fill a book of its own. This chapter will introduce enough ASP.NET for you to get a good start.

A Simple Web Page

ASP.NET still supports the ASP model of programming Web pages. The most striking difference a seasoned ASP programmer may notice right away is that VBScript has been replaced by Visual Basic.NET, JScript.NET, and C#. As expected, all ASP.NET code in this chapter is written in C#. Just to get started, take a look at the code in Listing 20.1. It is a very simple Web page, printing the phrase, "Howdy, Partner!" to the browser screen.

LISTING 20.1 A Simple ASP.NET Web Page: `howdy.aspx`

```
<%@ Page Language="C#" Description="Print Howdy, Partner!" %>
<html>
    <body>
        <%
            Response.Write("Howdy, Partner!");
        %>
    </body>
</html>
```

To view the page in Listing 20.1, simply point a browser at the location of the `howdy.aspx` file. The first line of this program contains the `Page` directive with `Language` and `Description` attributes. There can be only one `Page` directive in a program, and it must be enclosed with `<%@` at the beginning and `%>` at the end. The `Language` attribute specifies the programming language used as code on this page—C# in this case. The `Description` attribute is used to add documentation for the Web page.

Within the body section of the page is a block of code delimited by `<%` and `%>`. The `Response.Write()` method sends output to the browser window. In this example, the words "Howdy, Partner!" will be written in the browser window. The rest of the page is normal HTML.

Controls

There are three types of controls for ASP.NET Web pages: server, HTML, and validation. Server and HTML controls are user interface items such as buttons and textboxes that are displayed in a Web browser. The other type of control, validation, examines user input and responds accordingly, based upon whether or not the input is acceptable.

Server Controls

Server controls are graphical user interface items that a user interacts with to run a Web application. Although server controls have parallel HTML controls, such as text boxes and buttons, some of the server controls—the ad rotator and calendar, for instance—are much more sophisticated. Table 20.1 lists the ASP.NET server controls.

TABLE 20.1 ASP.NET Server Controls

Name	*Description*
AdRotator	Displays a sequence of advertisements
Button	Can be clicked for an event
Calendar	Displays a monthly calendar
CheckBox	Boolean state check box
CheckBoxList	Multi-selection check box group
DataGrid	Displays database data in multiple columns
DataList	Drop-down list with database data
DropDownList	Single selection drop-down list
HyperLink	Link to other Web sites
Image	Displays a picture
ImageButton	Button with an image
Label	Static text label
LinkButton	Button that works like a hyperlink

TABLE 20.1 continued

Name	*Description*
ListBox	Scrollable list of items
Panel	Contains other controls
RadioButton	Single option button
RadioButtonList	Group of radio buttons
Repeater	Container for each item in a data list
Table	Holds tabular data
TableRow	Single row in a table
TextBox	Free form text entry

The controls in Table 20.1 are called server controls because they're processed on the server where they reside. Server controls are translated into their HTML tag equivalents for presentation in a browser.

HTML Controls

HTML controls perform the same functions as their HTML tag equivalents. The primary difference is that HTML controls can be referenced programmatically. Table 20.2 shows the HTML controls.

TABLE 20.2 ASP.NET HTML Controls

Name	*HTML Equivalent*
HtmlAnchor	<a>
HtmlButton	<button>
HtmlForm	<form>
HtmlGenericControl	Tags such as <span>, <div>, <body>, and <font> that don't map to another HTML control
Image	<img>
HtmlInputButton	<input type = button|submit|reset>
HtmlInputCheckBox	<input type = checkbox>
HtmlInputFile	<input type = file>
HtmlInputHidden	<input type = hidden>
HtmlInputImage	<input type = image>
HtmlInputRadioButton	<input type = radio>

TABLE 20.2 continued

Name	*HTML Equivalent*
HtmlInputText	<input type = text|password>
HtmlSelect	<select>
HtmlTable	<table>
HtmlTableCell	<td> or <th>
HtmlTableRow	<tr>
HtmlTextArea	<textarea>

HTML controls are specified the same as their HTML tag equivalents except for an additional attribute. To programmatically access the HTML controls in Table 20.2, add the `runat="server"` attribute and value to the tag.

Validation Controls

Validation controls check a user's input against predefined criteria. Table 20.3 lists the available validation controls.

TABLE 20.3 ASP.NET Validation Controls

Name	*Description*
CompareValidator	Compares the entry against another value
CustomValidator	Used to create custom validators
RangeValidator	Ensures entry is between upper and lower bounds
RegularExpressionValidator	Checks entry to see if it matches a given regular expression
RequiredFieldValidator	Ensures entry exists
ValidationSummary	Shows a summary of the results of all validations for a page

Making a Web Form

Web forms are regions of an ASP.NET Web page where various controls can be placed. This establishes the user interface of a Web page. Each control can be customized for appearance and linked to events to manage Web page behavior. Let's look at a simple Web form first, and then look at the manipulation of Web form controls.

A Simple Web Form

Listing 20.2 shows how to create a simple Web form. This Web form has a few server controls with common attributes. It also has a Button server control hooked to an event method. Please see the .NET Frameworks SDK documentation for more in-depth information on individual classes.

LISTING 20.2 A Simple Web Form: `WebFormEx.aspx`

```
<%@ Page language="C#" Description="Web Form Example" %>
<HTML>
    <HEAD>
        <TITLE>
            Web Form Example
        </TITLE>
    </HEAD>
    <body>
        <form method=post runat="server">
            <P align=center>
            <asp:label
                id=titleLabel
                runat="server"
                Width="360px"
                Height="11px"
                Font-Bold="True"
                Font-Size="X-Large">
                    Shipper List Login Screen
            </asp:label>
            </P>
            <P align=center>
            <asp:label
                id=nameLabel
                runat="server">
                    Please Enter Your Name:
            </asp:label>
            <br>
            <asp:textbox
                id=nameTextBox
                runat="server">
            </asp:textbox>
            <br>
            <asp:requiredfieldvalidator
                id=nameRequiredValidator
                runat="server"
                ErrorMessage="Name is Required"
                ControlToValidate="nameTextBox">
            </asp:requiredfieldvalidator>
            </P>
            <P align=center>
```

LISTING 20.2 continued

```
            <asp:button
                id=logInButton
                onclick=logInButton_Click
                runat="server" Text="Log In">
            </asp:button>
            </P>
        </form>
        <script language=C# runat="server">
            protected void logInButton_Click(
                object sender, System.EventArgs e)
            {
                Response.Redirect(
                    "ShippersForm.aspx?nameTextBox=" +
                     nameTextBox.Text);
            }
        </script>
    </body>
</HTML>
```

For this discussion, the pertinent part of Listing 20.2 begins on the line where the `<form>` tag begins. This is the beginning of the Web form, and it has a `method` attribute with a value of `post`. All controls for this Web page are between the beginning `<form>` and ending `</form>` tags. The `method` attribute is the HTTP command method this form uses when submitted. The `runat` attribute indicates that this form is processed on the server before being sent to the requesting browser. Here are the lines from Listing 20.2 with the `<form>` tags:

```
        <form method=post runat="server">
            ...
        </form>
```

The first of three controls on this form is the `label` server control. The `asp:` prefix to the control type indicator (`label` in this case) identifies server controls. This particular `label` server control has several attributes. The `id` attribute indicates the name of this control and serves as an identifier for accessing this control programmatically. Similar to all other controls, the `runat` attribute specifies that this control be processed at the server before being sent to the browser. When processed at the server, this control is translated to its HTML equivalent. The `Width` and `Height` attributes set the size of the `label` control in pixels.

The `label` has a couple of font style attributes. If the `Font-Bold` attribute is not specified, the label font is normal. In this example, the font style is bold. Font attributes correspond to the properties of the `FontInfo` class. Appending a `FontInfo` property to `Font-` creates the relevant attribute. An appropriate value for the `Font-Size` attribute is one of 10 static field values of the FontUnit class. To find all the options available, check out the Font class. Furthermore, for a list of all attributes available for the label server control, check out the Label class. The following lines show the label server control from Listing 20.2.

```
<asp:label
    id=titleLabel
    runat="server"
    Width="360px"
    Height="11px"
    Font-Bold="True"
    Font-Size="X-Large">
        Shipper List Login Screen
</asp:label>
```

The next few lines show how simple a label control can be. It only has an id and runat attributes:

```
<asp:label
    id=nameLabel
    runat="server">
        Please Enter Your Name:
</asp:label>
```

The textbox server control is as simple to code as the label in the previous example. It only takes an id and runat attributes. Here's what the textbox server control code from Listing 20.2 looks like:

```
<asp:textbox
    id=nameTextBox
    runat="server">
</asp:textbox>
```

The final control on this form is a button server control. Like the label and textbox server controls, the button server control has id and runat attributes. However, the button server control also has an onclick attribute, which is an event attribute. Its value specifies the method to be invoked when the button server control is clicked. The logInButton_click() method will be discussed shortly. Here's the button server control code from Listing 20.2:

```
<asp:button
    id=logInButton
    onclick=logInButton_Click
    runat="server" Text="Log In">
</asp:button>
```

Following the </form> tag is the script section of the Web page. It begins with the <script> tag and ends with the </script> tag. The section between these two tags contains methods to be used for executing this Web page. The <script> tag has language and runat attributes. The language attribute indicates what language this script section is written in and helps identify which compiler to use when compiling this section of the Web page. The runat attribute has a similar meaning as controls, that this code is compiled on the server and not interpreted at the requesting browser.

The logInButton_click() method in the script section is an event handler for the button server control's onclick event. This particular example causes the requesting browser to be redirected to another Web page. Each Web page has various objects associated with it for sending and receiving information. One of these objects, Response, controls what information is sent back to the requesting browser. The Response object's Redirect() method has a string parameter that is returned to the user, directing his browser to go to a specified Web page.

An interesting fact about this string parameter is the way it passes information obtained from this Web page to the ShippersForm.aspx Web page. The id of the textbox server control, with an = sign is at the end of this string. Then the value of nameTextBox is appended to the end of this string. The string parameter for the Redirect() method of the Response object is sent via HTTP to the ShippersForm.aspx Web page. Once the ShippersForm.aspx Web page is executed, it has the capability to extract the value from the nameTextBox parameter portion of the string that was sent to it. The following example is from the script section of Listing 20.2:

```
<script language=C# runat="server">
    protected void logInButton_Click(
        object sender, System.EventArgs e)
    {
        Response.Redirect(
            "ShippersForm.aspx?nameTextBox=" +
             nameTextBox.Text);
    }
</script>
```

Figure 20.1 shows what an ASP.NET Web form should look like when viewed in a browser. The figure shows the output from the required validator control. This was produced by leaving the text box blank and pressing the Log In button. Then the name, Joe, is entered into the text box, which is what appears in the figure.

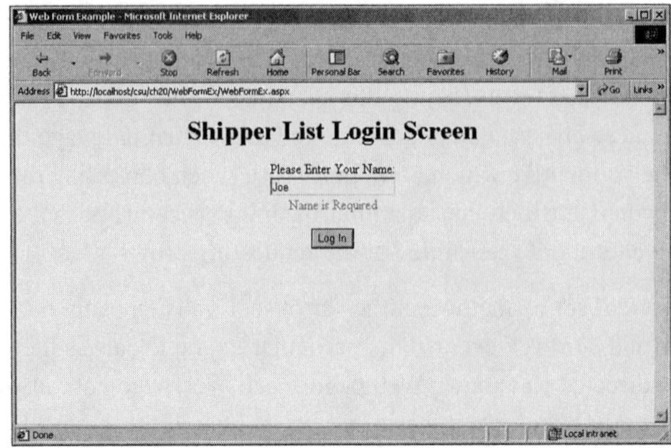

FIGURE 20.1
An ASP.NET Web form.

Manipulating Web Form Controls

Listing 20.3 shows how to manipulate Web form controls. The code performs three notable tasks: HTML control manipulation, database access, and filling a datagrid server control with data.

LISTING 20.3 Manipulating Web Form Controls: `ShippersForm.aspx`

```
<%@ Page language="c#" description="Shows the Shippers Table"%>
<%@ Import Namespace="System.Data.SqlClient" %>
<%@ Import Namespace="System.Data" %>

<HTML>
    <body>
        <script language=C# runat="server">
            private void Page_Load(object sender,
                System.EventArgs e)
            {
                userLabel.InnerHtml = "For " +
                    Request.QueryString["nameTextBox"];

                try
                {
                    SqlConnection conn = new SqlConnection(
                        "Data Source=localhost;
                        User Id=sa;
                        Password=;
                        Initial Catalog=northwind");

                    DataSet shippersDs = new DataSet();
                    SqlDataAdapter  shippersDa = new
                        SqlDataAdapter (
```

LISTING 20.3 continued

```
                    "SELECT * FROM Shippers",
                    conn);

                shippersDa.Fill(shippersDs, "Shippers");
                ShippersGrid.DataSource =
            shippersDs.Tables["Shippers"].DefaultView;
                ShippersGrid.DataBind();
            }
            catch (SqlException sqle)
            {
                Response.Write(
                    "Page_Load SqlException: " +
                    sqle.Message);
            }
            catch (Exception ge)
            {
                Response.Write(
                    "Page_Load Generic Exception: " +
                    ge.Message);
            }
        }
    </script>
    <form method=post runat="server">
        <P align=center>
            <asp:label
                id=Label1
                runat="server"
                Width="123px"
                Height="27px"
                Font-Size="Large">
                    Shipper List
            </asp:label>
        </P>
            <DIV
                align=center
                id=userLabel
                runat="server">
                <TABLE
                    height=19
                    cellSpacing=0
                    cellPadding=0
                    width=174
                    border=0
                    ms_1d_layout="TRUE">
                    <TR>
                        <TD>
                            Label
                        </TD>
                    </TR>
```

Listing 20.3 continued

```
                </TABLE>
            </DIV>
        <P align=center>
            <asp:datagrid
                id=ShippersGrid
                runat="server">
            </asp:datagrid>
        </P>
    </form>
  </body>
</HTML>
```

The most striking structural difference between the two previous listings is that the script section comes before the form section of the Web page in Listing 20.3. Within the script section is the `Page_Load()` method, a standard event method that is called automatically when the page is loaded. This method performs two primary functions: It initializes a simulated HTML label control, and it fills a datagrid server control with data.

The reason I use the term *simulated* HTML label control is because there is no HTML label control. The following example shows the code excerpt from Listing 20.3 that produces the simulated HTML label control, hereafter referred to as `label`.

```
<DIV
    align=center
    id=userLabel
    runat="server">
    <TABLE
        height=19
        cellSpacing=0
        cellPadding=0
        width=174
        border=0
        ms_1d_layout="TRUE">
        <TR>
            <TD>
                Label
            </TD>
        </TR>
    </TABLE>
</DIV>
```

The `label` is composed of an HTML `table` with a single row and a single cell. The `table` is surrounded by the `<DIV>` and `</DIV>` tags for reference and structure. The interesting aspects of the `<DIV>` tag are the `id` and `runat` attributes. The `runat` attribute allows processing of the `label` at the server, and the `id` attribute permits code to find and manipulate the label.

The `label` is modified by the following code. This code comes from the `Page_Load()` method, which means that it is executed at the server before the final HTML is rendered and sent to the requesting browser. This statement sets the `InnerHtml` property of the `userLabel` control, which is the `id` attribute of the `label` we described in the previous paragraph.

```
userLabel.InnerHtml = "For " +
    Request.QueryString["nameTextBox"];
```

The string placed into the `label` is constructed from the HTTP query string that was sent to this Web page. This task is performed by using the `Request` object, another object associated with the Web page for passing information between servers and browsers. This statement uses the string indexer of the `QueryString` collection of the `Request` object to obtain the `nameTextBox` parameter from the HTTP query string sent to this page. This is the same query string that was built for the `Redirect()` method of the `Response` object in the `logInButton_Click()` event handler in Listing 20.2.

Tip

Collections are used extensively throughout the ASP.NET class libraries. They provide intuitive access to an object's data structures, and build consistency. Chapter 26, "C# Collections," shows how to create and use collections so that you can build classes with the same benefits.

Once the label has been initialized, the next task in the `Page_Load()` method is to fill the datagrid server control with data. The datagrid server control is coded with only the `id` and `runat` attributes, which serve the same purpose as other server controls. Here's the datagrid from Listing 20.3:

```
<asp:datagrid
    id=ShippersGrid
    runat="server">
</asp:datagrid>
```

The code to fill the datagrid is in the `Page_Load()` method. This routine creates a `DataSet` object and binds the `DataSet` to the `datagrid` server control. The code to fill the `DataSet` is similar to how it was explained in Chapter 19, "Database Programming with ADO.NET." The pertinent part of this code is how the `datagrid` server control is bound to the `DataSet`. The `DefaultView` property of the `Tables` collection from the `shippersDS` `DataSet` object is assigned to the `DataSource` property of the `ShippersGrid` datagrid server control. Behind the scenes, the `DataSource` property of a datagrid server control accepts an `IEnumerable` interface object that it can use to obtain information and data. The next statement executed is the `DataBind()` method of the `ShippersGrid` datagrid object. The `DataBind` method verifies that the data source can be bound to the datagrid and performs work behind the scenes to populate the datagrid with data from the data source. There's an incredible amount of work necessary to populate a datagrid, but the following code shows how easy it is for the programmer:

```
    ShippersGrid.DataSource =
shippersDs.Tables["Shippers"].DefaultView;
    ShippersGrid.DataBind();
```

Figure 20.2 shows what the ShippersForm.aspx should look like when viewed in a browser. The label is filled with the words For Joe, where the Joe part was sent from the WebFormEx.aspx Web page. The datagrid is filled with data from the Shippers table of the Northwind database.

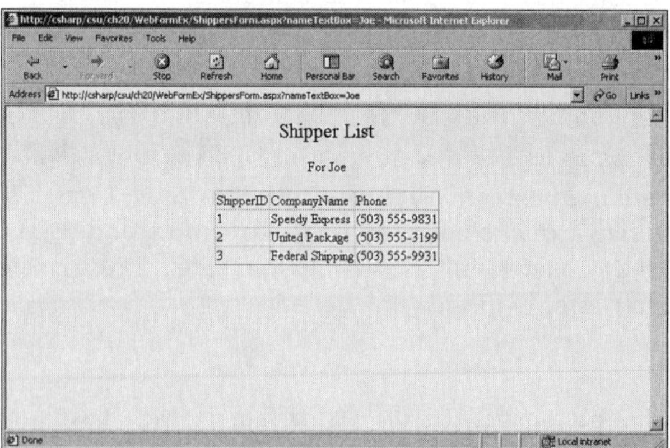

FIGURE 20.2
Programmatic manipulation of ASP.NET controls.

Code-Behind Web Pages

One of the primary benefits of ASP.NET is that it supports structured programming. The most significant contribution to this is code-behind Web pages, modules of program code that are separate from the page itself. A code-behind Web page is simply a file of C# code that is compiled and executed on the server when an ASP.NET Web page is requested. Technically the code-behind page doesn't get re-compiled unless the Web server is restarted or the code is replaced. Code-behind Web pages promote structured programming by separating control logic, which belongs with the code-behind page, from presentation logic, which is part of the main ASP.NET page. Listing 20.4 shows how to use code-behind Web pages.

LISTING 20.4 ASP.NET Web Page Supporting a Code-Behind Web Page: `CodeBehind.aspx`

```
<%@ Page language="c#" Codebehind="CodeBehind.aspx.cs"
➥Inherits="CodeBehind.WebForm1" %>

<HTML>
    <HEAD>
        <title>
            "Code Behind Example"
        </title>
    </HEAD>
    <body>
        <form method="post" runat="server">
            <H1>
                Table Selector
            </H1>
            <P>
                <asp:Label
                    id=tableLabel
                    runat="server">
                        Please Select a Database:
                </asp:Label>
            <BR>
                <asp:dropdownlist
                    id=tableDropList
                    runat="server"
                    NAME="tableDropList">
                    <asp:ListItem
                        Value="Categories"
                        Selected="True">
                            Categories
                    </asp:ListItem>
                    <asp:ListItem
                        Value="Customers">
                            Customers
                    </asp:ListItem>
                    <asp:ListItem
                        Value="Employees">
                            Employees
                    </asp:ListItem>
                    <asp:ListItem
                        Value="Orders">
                            Orders
                    </asp:ListItem>
                    <asp:ListItem
                        Value="Products">
                            Products
                    </asp:ListItem>
                </asp:dropdownlist>
            </P>
```

Listing 20.4 continued

```
            <p>
                <asp:datagrid
                    id=NwDataGrid
                    runat="server">
                </asp:datagrid>
            </p>
        </form>
    </body>
</HTML>
```

The most notable feature of Listing 20.4 is that, unlike previous listings, it doesn't have any code. The code is located in the `CodeBehind.aspx.cs` file, as indicated by the `Codebehind` attribute of the `@Page` directive. Another attribute of the `@Page` directive is `Inherits`, which tells the class name that this Web page is derived from.

This page shows how to add items to a `dropdownlist` server control. Other server controls in Listing 20.4 are similar to those in earlier listings. However, none of them has declared event attributes. All events and class methods are defined in the code-behind Web page, as shown in Listing 20.5.

Listing 20.5 ASP.NET Code-Behind Web Page: `CodeBehind.aspx.cs`

```
namespace CodeBehind
{
    using System;
    using System.Collections;
    using System.ComponentModel;
    using System.Data;
    using System.Data.SqlClient;
    using System.Drawing;
    using System.Web;
    using System.Web.SessionState;
    using System.Web.UI;
    using System.Web.UI.WebControls;
    using System.Web.UI.HtmlControls;

    public class WebForm1 : System.Web.UI.Page
    {
        protected DropDownList tableDropList;
        protected Repeater     NwRepeater;
        protected DataGrid     NwDataGrid;
        protected Label        tableLabel;

        public WebForm1()
        {
```

LISTING 20.5 continued

```
            Page.Init += new System.EventHandler(Page_Init);
        }

        protected void Page_Init(object sender, EventArgs e)
        {
            InitializeComponent();
        }

        private void InitializeComponent()
        {
            this.Load +=
                new System.EventHandler(this.Page_Load);
            this.tableDropList.SelectedIndexChanged +=
                new System.EventHandler(
                    this.tableDropList_SelectedIndexChanged);
        }

        private void LoadTableData()
        {
            string selectedTable =
                tableDropList.SelectedItem.Text;
            try
            {
                SqlConnection conn = new SqlConnection("
                    Data Source=localhost;
                    User Id=sa;
                    Password=;
                    Initial Catalog=northwind");
                DataSet nwDs = new DataSet();
                SqlDataAdapter  nwDa = new SqlDataAdapter (
                    "SELECT * FROM " + selectedTable, conn);

                nwDa.Fill(nwDs, selectedTable);

                NwDataGrid.DataSource =
                    nwDs.Tables[selectedTable].DefaultView;
                NwDataGrid.DataBind();
            }
            catch (SqlException sqle)
            {
                Response.Write("Load_Data SqlException: " +
                                sqle.Message);
            }
            catch (Exception ge)
            {
                Response.Write("Load_Data Generic Exception: " +
                                ge.Message);
            }
        }
```

Listing 20.5 continued

```
        private void Page_Load(object sender,
                               System.EventArgs e)
        {
            LoadTableData();
        }

        protected void tableDropList_SelectedIndexChanged(
            object sender, System.EventArgs e)
        {
            LoadTableData();
        }
    }
}
```

The `WebForm1` class from Listing 20.5 is derived from the `Page` class. All code-behind Web pages are derived from the `Page` class. The `WebForm1` class holds all the methods and fields for running the main Web page (Listing 20.4).

The fields of the `WebForm1` class must correspond to server controls on the main Web page. This is how the methods in the code-behind page can reference the server controls on the main page.

The WebForm1 constructor initializes the Init event of the Page class with the `Page_Init()` event handler method, as the following code shows:

```
        public WebForm1()
        {
            Page.Init += new System.EventHandler(Page_Init);
        }
```

The `Page_Init()` method is called the first time this page is started. It executes once each time this object is loaded into memory and calls the `InitializeComponent()` method, which in turn hooks up event handlers for the main Web page. The first event handler is the `Page_Load()` method, which is assigned to the inherited `Page` object's `Load` event. The `Page_Load()` method is invoked every time the main Web page is requested. The next event handler is for the `SelectedIndexChanged` event of the `tableDropList` `dropdownlist` server control. This enables the `tableDropList_SelectedIndexChanged()` event handler method to be invoked every time the value of the `dropdownlist` sever control is changed. Here's the code for `InitializeComponent()`:

```
        private void InitializeComponent()
        {
            this.Load +=
                new System.EventHandler(this.Page_Load);
```

```
            this.tableDropList.SelectedIndexChanged +=
                new System.EventHandler(
                    this.tableDropList_SelectedIndexChanged);
        }
```

For the purposes of this discussion, there isn't anything special about the rest of the code in Listing 20.5. It's normal C# code that should be familiar by now. The output from Listings 20.4 and 20.5 is shown in Figure 20.3.

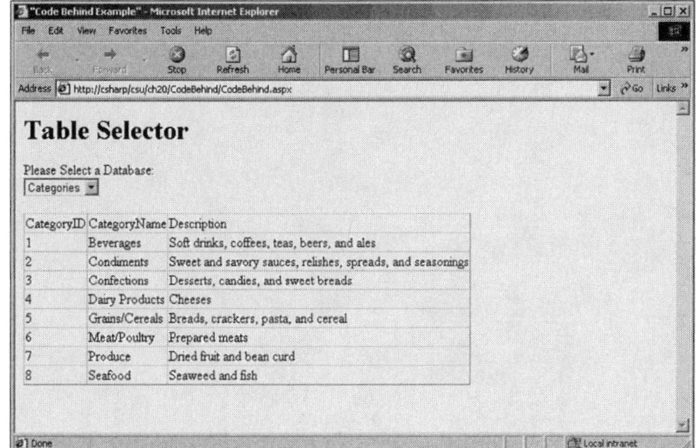

FIGURE 20.3
An ASP.NET Web page with a code-behind Web page.

Summary

This chapter introduced ASP.NET Web pages. It showed a simple Web page and demonstrated how ASP.NET still supports the traditional ASP programming model. Further, ASP.NET builds upon that model with special Web page controls and code-behind Web pages.

ASP.NET supports three different types of controls: server, validation, and HTML. Server controls correspond to HTML tags in addition to providing more sophisticated controls that can be manipulated programmatically. Validation controls permit various types of checks to be made on server controls before a Web page is posted back to the server. HTML controls mirror the HTML tags and can be manipulated at the server.

Controls may be manipulated at the server by both on-page code and code-behind Web pages. In both scenarios, this code can be written in C#. The code-behind Web page option promotes structured programming and separation of user interface from event logic.

The examples in this chapter showed how to build client/server and three-tier systems. However, as applications grow in sophistication, the need for a multi-tier architecture increases. The next chapter, "Remoting," discusses ways of extending programs to support multi-tiered distributed architectures.

CHAPTER

Remoting

In This Chapter

- **Basic Remoting** *460*
- **Proxys** *471*
- **Channels** *475*
- **Lifetime Management** *478*

Many of today's enterprise applications employ distributed applications for scalability. Remoting is a new technology supporting this goal, allowing objects to communicate across `AppDomains` with minimal overhead. The remoting architecture abstracts as much of the underlying communications plumbing associated with distributed computing. It's easy to set up communication between multiple distributed objects and communicate as if the objects were in the same process space.

Remoting can be approached at many different levels. One of the significant differences between remoting and other distributed object technologies is its architectural extensibility. The remoting architecture is very flexible, enabling the capability to extend an application by adding custom components that participate in the communication process.

An integral feature of remoting is lifetime management of remote server components through leases. Client applications communicate with a lease manager to control the lifetime of these components.

Basic Remoting

At its most basic level, remoting is the capability to communicate with components in separate `AppDomains`. Figure 21.1 shows a simplified view of two objects communicating via remoting—a client component in `AppDomain A` communicates with a server component in `AppDomain B`.

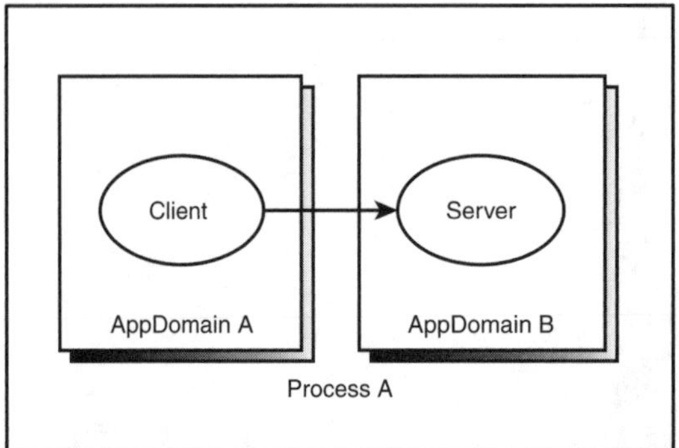

FIGURE 21.1
Basic remoting diagram.

> **Note**
>
> An `AppDomain` is an execution environment within a process. It separates managed applications during execution. This provides several benefits including reliability and security.

Since remoting supports multitiered as well as distributed architectures, the server component in AppDomain B could easily be extended to a client role, communicating with a server component in another AppDomain. Furthermore, a remote component could be located in another process on either the same or a different machine. Once a component is set up, the underlying plumbing required to maintain remote communications is hidden by the remoting architecture.

Remoting Server

A remoting server object is simply a class that inherits from MarshalByRefObject. Listing 21.1 shows how to implement a remoting server object.

LISTING 21.1 Remoting Server Demo: BasicRemotingServer.cs

```
using System;

namespace BasicServer
{
    /// <summary>
    /// Basic Remoting Server Demo.
    /// </summary>
    public class BasicRemotingServer : MarshalByRefObject
    {
        public string getServerResponse()
        {
            return
"Greetings from the BasicRemotingServer component!";
        }
    }
}
```

The BasicServer class in Listing 21.1 inherits MarshalByRefObject, which supports the basic functionality for a callable component over the remoting architecture. This class is implemented as a DLL, negating the need for a Main() method. The only method in this class is the getServerResponse() method, keeping things simple. This is the remoting server object used in the rest of the examples in this chapter.

Each remoted component requires a configuration file, named web.config, to specify necessary operating parameters. The web.config file for the remote server component in Listing 21.1 is shown in Listing 21.2.

LISTING 21.2 Remote Server Component Configuration File: web.config

```
<configuration>
    <system.runtime.remoting>
```

LISTING 21.2 continued

```
        <application>
            <service>

                <wellknown mode="SingleCall"
type="BasicServer.BasicRemotingServer, BasicServer"
objectUri="BasicRemotingServer.soap" />

            </service>
        </application>
    </system.runtime.remoting>
</configuration>
```

The configuration file in Listing 21.2 is located in the same directory in which Listing 21.1 was built. It contains a special section for remoting, marked by a tag named after the remoting namespace, `<system.runtime.remoting>`. Further down the hierarchy is an `<application>` tag, containing a `<service>` tag. The `<service>` section has a `<wellknown>` tag with three attributes that assist in making this remoted object run properly: `mode`, `type`, and `objectUri`.

A `mode` has two possible values: `SingleCall` and `Singleton`. These values identify basic lifetime issues associated with a remote object.

`SingleCall` components are activated and live for the duration of a single call from the remote client. For example, when a remote client calls the `getServerResponse()` method of the `BasicRemotingServer` class (from Listing 21.1), a new `BasicRemotingServer` object is instantiated when the call begins. When the call ends, the server object is destroyed. Furthermore, each client receives a reference to a unique server object whenever it makes a call.

`Singleton` components are the only instance of a given class. They stick around to provide service to every call of every client.

The decision to designate a remote server component depends on the nature of the application. There are a couple tradeoffs to consider. `SingleCall` components are more scalable, supporting an increasing number of clients as hardware constraints allow. A potential drawback to `SingleCall` components is that they lose state between method invocations and don't support shared state between clients. A solution to this would be to have a separate component supporting state management to a backing store such as a database or file. `Singleton` components are good for sharing information between clients and their method invocations. This also increases complexity associated with managing the integrity of state between clients. Additionally, `Singleton` components are not as scalable as `SingleCall` components. It's also conceivable that a hybrid system of remote

SingleCall and Singleton objects can be established. Just remember that a single class can't have both SingleCall and Singleton instantiations.

The type attribute of the <wellknown> tag has a quoted pair of values that identify the remote server object. The first value is the fully qualified name of the class. The second value is the executable filename of the assembly to which the class belongs.

The last attribute of the <wellknown> tag is the objectUri, which holds the Universal Resource Identifier (URI) of the server component. A URI is a unique identifier for an Internet resource.

> **Note**
>
> A URI is a more generic term for objects on the Internet, such as those objects used in remoting. A Universal Resource Locator (URL) is more specific to the Web and uniquely identifies a Web page.

Remoting Client

Writing a remoting client is just a little more involved than writing a remoting server. Basically, writing a client requires finding out the type and location of the remote server object, initializing configuration from a file, and creating an instance of the remote object with the type and location information obtained earlier. Listing 21.3 shows how to write a basic client for a remote server component.

LISTING 21.3 Basic Remoting Client: BasicRemotingClient.cs

```
using System;
using System.Runtime.Remoting;
using BasicServer;

/// <summary>
/// Basic Remoting Client Demo.
/// </summary>
class BasicRemotingClient
{
    static void Main(string[] args)
    {
        Type   type = typeof(BasicRemotingServer);
        String url  =
"http://localhost/BasicServiceDemo/BasicRemotingServer.soap";

        RemotingConfiguration.Configure(
            "BasicRemotingClient.exe.config");
```

LISTING 21.3 continued

```
        BasicRemotingServer brs =
         (BasicRemotingServer)Activator.GetObject(type, url);

        Console.WriteLine(brs.getServerResponse());
    }
}
```

And here's the output:

```
Greetings from the BasicRemotingServer component!
```

Listing 21.3 uses two additional namespaces: `System.Runtime.Remoting` and `BasicServer`. The `System.Runtime.Remoting` namespace contains all the basic remoting classes. Our remote server component that will be instantiated and called is in the `BasicServer` namespace.

Within the `Main()` method, the type of the `BasicRemotingServer` class is obtained with the `typeof` operator and stored in a `Type` object. Next, the URL of the `BasicRemotingServer` component is specified. Notice that it appends the `BasicRemotingServer.soap` URI to the full URL definition. This is the same URI specified in the `web.config` file (Listing 21.2) for the remote server. Then the client must configure itself in preparation for communication with the remoting system. It does so with the static `Configure()` method of the `RemotingConfiguration` class. The string parameter, `"BasicRemotingClient.exe.config"`, of the `Configure()` method specifies the configuration file to use. This is similar in purpose to the `web.config` file, but specialized for the needs of the client. Listing 21.4 shows the configuration file for the remoting client.

LISTING 21.4 Client Configuration File: `BasicRemotingClient.exe.config`

```
<configuration>
    <system.runtime.remoting>
        <application name="BasicRemotingClient">
            <channels>

                <channel
type="System.Runtime.Remoting.Channels.Http.HttpChannel,
➥System.Runtime.Remoting" />

            </channels>
        </application>
    </system.runtime.remoting>
</configuration>
```

A client configuration file must be named after the executable of the client with the `.config` extension. Since the executable name of the program in Listing 21.3 is `BasicRemotingClient.exe`, the configuration filename must be `BasicRemotingClient.exe.config`.

The first difference between the `web.config` file and `BasicRemotingClient.exe.config` is that the `<application>` tag has a `name` attribute defined. This is the name of the client class, `BasicRemotingClient`.

Lower in the hierarchy is the `<channels>` tag, where a channel is defined. Channels will be discussed in more detail later, so this is just a brief explanation. The `<channels>` section has a `<channel>` tag with a `type` attribute that has a string with two values. The first value specifies what type of channel will be used to communicate with the server component. The second parameter identifies the namespace associated with the channel.

Once the client is configured, it may obtain a reference to the remote object. This is accomplished by calling the static `GetObject()` method of the `Activator` class. The two parameters to the `GetObject()` method are the `type` and `url`, respectively, that were obtained earlier. Since the reference is returned as an object type, the return value is cast to `BasicRemotingServer`. Here's the code obtaining a reference to the remote server component:

```
BasicRemotingServer brs =
 (BasicRemotingServer)Activator.GetObject(type, url);
```

After the remote server component reference is obtained, it can be used just like any other reference. In the following example, the `getServerResponse()` method of the remote server component is invoked, returning a string to the `Console.WriteLine()` method for printing to the console:

```
Console.WriteLine(brs.getServerResponse());
```

Remoting Setup

There are two ways to get a remoting application up and running: via a Web server or a host utility. The first example will use Microsoft Internet Information Server (IIS) as the Web server to host the remote server component. Demonstrating the host utility requires code for a new client and server program as well as the utility itself.

Web Server Setup

The following procedures show how to set up a remote server component via the IIS Web server:

1. Before actually starting this procedure, work out a directory structure so it will be easy to follow along. Given an arbitrary path, `<path>`, to the source code files, you'll have two directories at the end of this path, `BasicServer` and `BasicClient`. Put the `BasicServer.cs` file from Listing 21.1 and `web.config` file from Listing 21.2 into the `BasicServer` directory. Then put the `BasicClient.cs` file from Listing 21.3 and the `BasicClient.exe.config` file from Listing 21.4 into the `BasicClient` directory. Next, create a directory named `bin` under the `BasicServer` directory. Here's what your directory structure should look like:

```
<path>\BasicServer
    BasicServer.cs
    Web.config
    <path>\BasicServer\bin
<path>\BasicClient
    BasicClient.cs
    BasicClient.exe.config
```

2. Compile the server component from Listing 21.1 in the `BasicServer` directory with the following command line:

```
csc /t:library BasicServer.cs
```

   This produces the `BasicServer.dll` file, which should be copied to `<path>\BasicServer\bin`. This is the location where the Web server will be looking.

3. Open the Internet Services Manager. In Windows 2000, it's located in the Administrative Tools folder of the Control Panel.

4. Expand the server node under which you want to create a virtual directory and right-click on Default Web Site. From the menu, select New and then select Virtual Directory. This opens the Virtual Directory Creation Wizard. Click Next.

5. In the text box for an Alias, type in any meaningful name for the virtual directory, such as **`BasicServerDemo`**. Click Next.

6. In the text box for the physical path that the virtual directory will refer to, **`<path>\BasicServer`** directory should be entered, where `<path>` is the actual directory you specified in step 1. I'm personally a big fan of using the Browse button because, more often than not, I'll mistype the path and end up scratching my head later when things don't work. Click Next.

7. There are several access permissions from which to choose. The Read and Run Scripts (such as ASP) options are already checked, and that's fine. Accept the defaults, click Next, and then click Finish on the last screen. IIS will use the `web.config` file in the `BasicServer` directory when it loads the server component. The remote server component is now set up.

8. Use the following command line to compile the remoting client program from Listing 21.3:

```
csc /r:..\BasicServer\BasicServer.dll BasicClient.cs
```

9. Finally, run the `BasicClient.exe` program in the `BasicClient` directory to test the system out. If all goes well, the following output will be printed to the console:

```
Greetings from the BasicRemotingServer component!
```

Host Utility Setup

The host utility setup method uses a program that configures the remote server component so clients can find it. The process isn't necessarily easier or harder than the Web server setup method—it's just different. As with the Web server setup method, an organized approach simplifies things.

Follow a similar directory-naming scheme as described in step 1 of the previous section, "Web Server Setup". Replace the `BasicServer` with `HostedServer` and the `BasicClient` with the `HostedClient` directory names. To be organized, you may want to create a new directory, at the same level as `HostedServer` and `HostedClient`, named `RemotingHost` to hold the source and executable for the host utility.

The server and client components of this example are pretty much the same as the previous listings in this section. However, for demonstration purposes, it's necessary to have unique listings to keep track of what's going on. Listing 21.5 shows the remoting server component, and Listing 21.6 is the server's `web.config` configuration file.

LISTING 21.5 Hosted Server Demo: `HostedServer.cs`

```
using System;

namespace Host
{
    /// <summary>
    /// Hosted Server Component Demo.
    /// </summary>
    public class HostedServer : MarshalByRefObject
    {
        public string getServerResponse()
        {
            return
                "Greetings from the HostedServer component!";
        }
    }
}
```

LISTING 21.6 Host Server Config File: `web.config`

```
<configuration>
    <system.runtime.remoting>
        <application>
            <service>

                <wellknown mode="SingleCall"
                    type="Host.HostedServer, HostedServer"
                    objectUri="HostedServer.soap" />

            </service>
        </application>
    </system.runtime.remoting>
</configuration>
```

No surprises in Listing 21.5: the names were changed to protect the innocent and the text of the return string from the `getServerResponse()` method is different. The same goes for the `web.config` file in Listing 21.6. The code in Listing 21.5 can be compiled with the following command line:

```
csc /t:library HostedServer.cs
```

Listing 21.7 shows the client code, which calls the server, and Listing 21.8 shows its configuration file.

LISTING 21.7 Remoting Client Demo: `HostedClient.cs`

```
using System;
using System.Runtime.Remoting;
using Host;

namespace HostedClient
{
    /// <summary>
    /// Client for a Hosted Remote Server.
    /// </summary>
    class HostedClient
    {
        static void Main(string[] args)
        {
            Type   type = typeof(HostedServer);
            String url  =
"http://localhost:8000/HostedServer/HostedServer.soap";

            RemotingConfiguration.Configure(
                "HostedClient.exe.config");
```

LISTING 21.7 continued

```
                HostedServer hostedServer =
                    (HostedServer)Activator.GetObject(type, url);

                Console.WriteLine(
                    hostedServer.getServerResponse());
            }
        }
}
```

LISTING 21.8 Remoting Client Configuration File: `HostedClient.exe.config`

```
<configuration>
    <system.runtime.remoting>
        <application name="HostedClient">
            <client url="http://localhost:8000/HostedServer">

                <wellknown
type="Host.HostedServer, HostedServer"
url="http://localhost:8000/HostedServer/HostedServer.soap" />

            </client>
            <channels>

                <channel
type="System.Runtime.Remoting.Channels.Http.HttpChannel,
➥System.Runtime.Remoting" />

            </channels>
        </application>
    </system.runtime.remoting>
</configuration>
```

Again, the code in Listing 21.7 doesn't present anything new; however, there is a difference in the configuration file in Listing 21.8. It contains a new section, represented by the `<client>` tag. The `<client>` tag has an `url` attribute, specifying the location of the server component. Within the `<client>` section is a `<wellknown>` tag with `type` and `url` attributes. The `type` indicates the fully qualified name and the `url` indicates location information for the server component.

The code for Listing 21.7 can be compiled with the following command line:

```
csc /r:..\HostedServer\HostedServer.dll HostedClient.cs
```

A host utility enables clients to find a remote server component. Its implementation is straightforward, simply configuring the remote server component and pausing for a length of time necessary for the server to be used. Listing 21.9 shows how to implement a host utility.

LISTING 21.9 Host Utility Demo: RemotingHost.cs

```
using System;
using System.Runtime.Remoting;

/// <summary>
/// Summary description for RemoteHost.
/// </summary>
public class RemoteHost
{
    public static void Main()
    {
        RemotingConfiguration.Configure(
            "RemoteHost.exe.config");

        Console.WriteLine("Press any key to exit...");
        Console.ReadLine();
    }
}
```

The `Main()` method of the `RemoteHost` class in Listing 21.9 begins by configuring the remote server component. Then it pauses, prompting the user to press a key to continue. It's necessary for the host utility to remain running while the server is being used. This guarantees that the remoting system will recognize the server and provide a path for clients to find it. Listing 21.10 is the host utility configuration file.

LISTING 21.10 Host Utility Configuration File: RemoteHost.exe.config

```
<configuration>
    <system.runtime.remoting>
        <application name="HostedServer">
            <service>

                <wellknown mode="SingleCall"
                    type="Host.HostedServer, HostedServer"
                    objectUri="HostedServer.soap" />

            </service>
            <channels>

                <channel port="8000"
type="System.Runtime.Remoting.Channels.Http.HttpChannel,
➥System.Runtime.Remoting" />
```

LISTING 21.10 continued

```
            </channels>
        </application>
    </system.runtime.remoting>
</configuration>
```

This file has both `<service>` and `<channels>` sections. These are defined pretty much the same as corresponding sections in previous configuration file listings. The difference is that port 8000 is specified in the location data. You will recall that the client configuration file in Listing 21.8 specified the same port. The following example shows how to compile the host utility in Listing 21.9:

```
csc RemotingHost.cs
```

Proxys

Proxys are the objects that hide low-level communication details from client objects, making a remote object appear local. The previous section of this chapter showed the basics of using the remoting framework. This section and the rest of the chapter show a bit of inner workings, extensibility, and management of the remoting framework.

A proxy is an object that acts on behalf of another object. When obtaining a reference to the remote server component, a client can make calls as if it had a direct reference to a local object. Actually, this is a reference to a proxy, which enables communication with the remote server component by interacting with the remoting framework. Figure 21.2 shows the proxy's role in remoting.

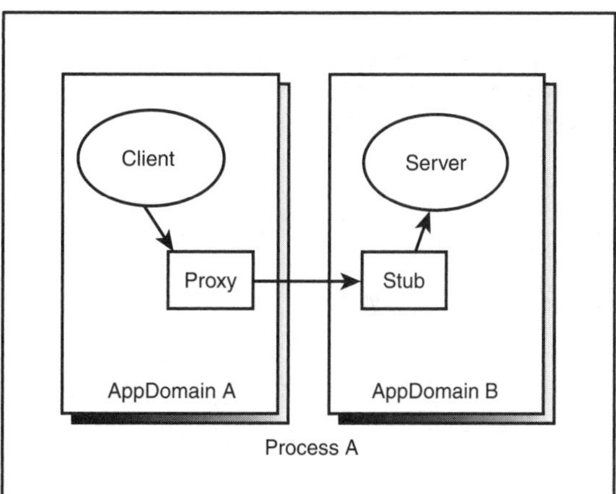

FIGURE 21.2
Remoting proxys.

In the figure, the proxy in `AppDomain A` receives requests from the client. It then communicates with the remoting framework to format and marshal the request so it can cross `AppDomain` boundaries. The stub in `AppDomain B` receives the request from the proxy in `AppDomain A`. After unmarshalling and deciphering the request format, it forwards the request to the server. The server processes the request and returns its result through the stub and proxy via the formatting and marshalling process. The proxy then returns the results to the client. The next section, "Channels," goes a little deeper into what happens between the proxy and stub.

Actually, a proxy is made up of two distinct proxies: transparent and real. A transparent proxy holds the actual interface to the remote server component. It is the reference returned from a new or `GetObject()` call when obtaining a reference to the remote server component. Since it holds the interface, a transparent proxy can't be changed, extended, or inherited from. This is what the real proxy is for.

Plugging in a custom proxy, a custom class inheriting the `RealProxy` class, can extend the proxy portion of the framework. The real proxy delivers a reference to an encapsulated transparent proxy to a requesting client. It then receives member invocation requests from the transparent proxy. When an invocation request is received from the transparent proxy, the real proxy takes responsibility for communicating with the rest of the remoting framework to deliver the request, receive a response, and forward the results back to transparent proxy and subsequently back to the client. Listing 21.11 shows how to implement a custom real proxy, and Listing 21.12 is its configuration file.

LISTING 21.11 A Custom Real Proxy: `ProxyDemo.cs`

```
using System;
using System.Collections;
using System.Runtime.Remoting;
using System.Runtime.Remoting.Channels;
using System.Runtime.Remoting.Proxies;
using System.Runtime.Remoting.Messaging;
using BasicServer;

/// <summary>
/// Custom Proxy Class.
/// </summary>
public class MyRealProxy : RealProxy
{
    Type myType;

    public MyRealProxy(Type type) : base(type)
    {
        myType = type;
    }
```

LISTING 21.11 continued

```
    public override IMessage Invoke(IMessage msg)
    {
        Console.WriteLine("IMessage Properties:\n");

        IDictionary myProps = msg.Properties;

        foreach (object key in myProps.Keys)
        {
            Console.WriteLine(
                "  Key: {0}\n           Value: {1}",
                key.ToString(), myProps[key]);
        }

        MarshalByRefObject myObject =
         (MarshalByRefObject)Activator.CreateInstance(myType);

        ObjRef myRef = RemotingServices.Marshal(myObject);

        msg.Properties["__Uri"] = myRef.URI;

        IMessage returnMsg =
            ChannelServices.SyncDispatchMessage(msg);

        return returnMsg;
    }
}

/// <summary>
/// Remoting Proxy Client.
/// </summary>
class RemotingProxyClient
{
    static void Main(string[] args)
    {
        Type   type = typeof(BasicRemotingServer);

        RemotingConfiguration.Configure(
            "RemotingProxyClient.exe.config");

        MyRealProxy myProxy = new MyRealProxy(type);

        BasicRemotingServer brs =
         (BasicRemotingServer)myProxy.GetTransparentProxy();

        Console.WriteLine("\nServer Response: {0}",
            brs.getServerResponse());
    }
}
```

And the output is

```
Greetings from the BasicRemotingServer component!
```

Within the `Main()` method of the `RemotingProxyClient` class, a custom proxy, `MyRealProxy`, is instantiated. This proxy is used to obtain a reference to a transparent proxy, which is used to make method calls on the remote server object.

The custom proxy inherits the `RealProxy` class. It implements the `Invoke()` method, which accepts a single parameter of interface type `IMessage`. An `IMessage` object contains a list of properties describing a method call.

The `Invoke()` method of the `MyRealProxy` class obtains the `Properties` collection, which is of interface type `IDictionary`, of the `IMessage` parameter. It then iterates through the collection with a `foreach` statement, printing each property and its value to the console.

The next statements create an instance of the server object. The `CreateInstance()` method accepts a `Type` parameter. This is the type of the remote server object passed to the `MyRealProxy` constructor and saved in the local `myType` field. The `BasicServer` object is returned as a reference to its parent class, `MarshalByRefObject` as shown here:

```
MarshalByRefObject myObject =
 (MarshalByRefObject)Activator.CreateInstance(myType);
```

The `MarshalByRefObject` is used to obtain an `ObjRef` for the remote server component. The `ObjRef` class is an integral component of the remoting framework, containing all the serialized information about the remote server component. Under the covers, `ObjRefs` are returned from server hosting `AppDomains` to client hosting `AppDomains` and used to construct proxies. The following example shows how to obtain the `ObjRef` for the remote server component:

```
ObjRef myRef = RemotingServices.Marshal(myObject);
```

One of the pieces of information from the `ObjRef` that's interesting for this program is the URI. This is because when `IMessage` is passed to the real proxy `Invoke()` method, its URI property value is blank. The URI is critical for the proxy to be able to locate the server object, which is why it was necessary to go through the previous steps to obtain the URI. The following code demonstrates how to load the `IMessage` `Uri` property with the `ObjRef` URI:

```
msg.Properties["__Uri"] = myRef.URI;
```

Now `IMessage` contains all the message properties it needs for the remoting system to locate and send a method call to the remote server component. The `IMessage` is used as the parameter to the static `ChannelServices.SyncDispatchMessage()` method. The return value is stored in a local field and returned to the transparent proxy, the caller of the `Invoke()` method, as shown in the following example:

```
IMessage returnMsg =
    ChannelServices.SyncDispatchMessage(msg);
```

The configuration file in Listing 21.12 identifies the client application name but doesn't differ conceptually from other client configuration files seen so far. Listing 21.11 can be compiled with the following command line:

```
csc /r:<server path>\BasicServer.dll RemotingProxyClient.cs
```

LISTING 21.12 Custom Proxy Client Configuration File: `RemotingProxyClient.exe.config`

```
<configuration>
    <system.runtime.remoting>
        <application name="RemotingProxyClient">
            <channels>

                <channel
type="System.Runtime.Remoting.Channels.Http.HttpChannel,
➥System.Runtime.Remoting" />

            </channels>
        </application>
    </system.runtime.remoting>
</configuration>
```

Channels

Channels marshal, format, and transmit messages across `AppDomains`. Each of a channel's tasks opens new opportunities for extensibility. For example, message contents can be marshaled to conform to the proper data representation using custom sinks. The message itself can be formatted via the built-in Simple Object Access Protocol (SOAP) or binary formatters. Additionally, transport protocols, such as HTTP or TCP, which are built-in, can be configured with ease. The architecture also supports customizable marshalling, formatting, and transmission components that can be plugged in as needed. Figure 21.3 shows the relationship of the channel to other remoting architecture components. The `HTTPChannel`, linking the proxy in `AppDomain A` to the stub in `AppDomain B`, is a built-in channel component supporting default marshalling, XML/SOAP Formatting, and HTTP protocol transmission.

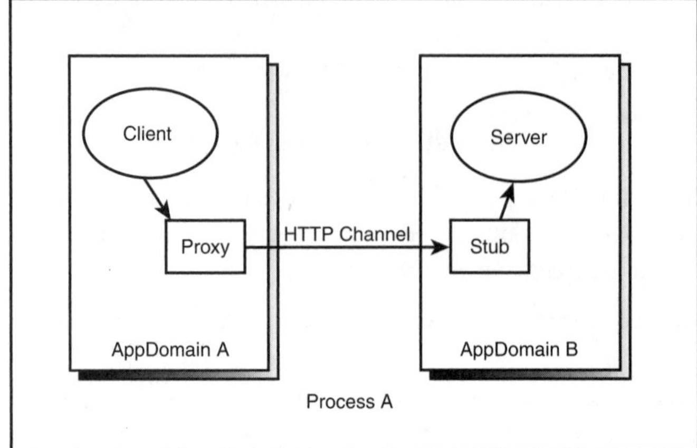

FIGURE 21.3
Remoting channels.

Previous listings in this chapter used configuration files to specify their channels. The following example is an excerpt from one of the configuration files:

```
<channels>

    <channel
type="System.Runtime.Remoting.Channels.Http.HttpChannel,
➥System.Runtime.Remoting" />

</channels>
```

The `<channels>` section in the previous example contains channel information for remoting components. When the configuration file is read by the `RemotingConfiguration.Configure()` method, the specified channel is registered with the remoting system. The `<channel>` tag has a `type` attribute, specifying the channel type to be used, as its first value and the applicable namespace as the second parameter. All of the previous programs in this chapter used these parameters, meaning that they used an `HttpChannel` as their remoting channel.

Instead of configuration files, a program may register its channels programmatically. At the most basic level, all that's required is to invoke a single registration command, and the channel is registered. Listing 21.13 shows how to register a remoting channel.

LISTING 21.13 Programatic Remoting Channel Registration: `RemotingProxyClient.cs`

```
using System;
using System.Runtime.Remoting;
using System.Runtime.Remoting.Channels;
```

LISTING 21.13 continued

```
using System.Runtime.Remoting.Channels.Http;
using BasicServer;

/// <summary>
/// Remoting Proxy Client.
/// </summary>
class RemotingProxyClient
{
    static void Main(string[] args)
    {
        ChannelServices.RegisterChannel(new HttpChannel());

        BasicRemotingServer brs = new BasicRemotingServer();

        Console.WriteLine("\nServer Response: {0}",
            brs.getServerResponse());
    }
}
```

The program in Listing 21.13 registers an `HttpChannel` with the static `ChannelServices.RegisterChannel()` method. After that, it instantiates the remote server component, just like any other object, and invokes a remote server component method. Instead of the `HttpChannel` object, the program could have just as easily created a new `TcpChannel` object, which uses the binary formatter and TCP transport protocol. The program in Listing 21.13 can be compiled with the following command line:

```
csc /r:..\BasicServer\BasicServer.dll RemotingProxyClient.cs
```

Tip

The `HttpChannel` is good for open standards communication. It uses SOAP to format messages in XML and HTTP for transport. However, XML/SOAP-formatted messages are much larger packages than a traditional binary-formatted message. The larger messages, which consume more network bandwidth, may be an issue for some projects. If standards are not a concern and your application needs speed, use the `TcpChannel`. It uses a binary formatter, leading to more compressed data, and the TCP transmission protocol, leading to faster transmission speeds.

Lifetime Management

When left alone, a remote server component exists for a default amount of time and then makes itself available for garbage collection. It's often more desirable to explicitly manage the lifetime of remote components. This is why the remoting framework provides a leasing mechanism for finer granularity of control in remote component lifetime management.

Remote leasing operates via a collaborative protocol between one or more client components, a server component, and a lease manager.

Remote server components begin life with a designated amount of time before garbage collection. Client components register with the server component's lease manager for notification of when the server's lifetime is expiring. The lease manager keeps track of server components and notifies clients of when the server will expire. Once a server has reached its expiration time, the lease manager notifies the client and waits for a designated amount of time for a reply from the client. If the client wants the server to remain alive, it returns the amount of time the server can live to the lease manager. If the designated reply time from the client to the lease renewal query expires, the lease manager marks the server object for garbage collection.

To participate in remote server component lifetime management, a client must implement the `ISponsor` interface. This interface has a single method, `Renewal()`, which the lease manager calls when a remote server component needs its lifetime updated. Listing 21.14 shows how to implement a client that uses remote leasing.

LISTING 21.14 Remote Leasing Demo: `LeasingDemo.cs`

```
using System;
using System.Runtime.Remoting;
using System.Runtime.Remoting.Channels;
using System.Runtime.Remoting.Channels.Http;
using System.Runtime.Remoting.Lifetime;
using BasicServer;

/// <summary>
/// Remoting Object Lifetime Demo.
/// </summary>
class LeasingDemo : ISponsor
{
    ILease lease;

    // implement lease logic
    public void ImplementLease()
```

LISTING 21.14 continued

```
    {
        BasicRemotingServer brs = new BasicRemotingServer();

        lease = (ILease)brs.InitializeLifetimeService();
        lease.Register(this, new TimeSpan(0, 0, 3));

        PrintLeaseInfo();

        Console.WriteLine("\nServer Response: {0}",
            brs.getServerResponse());
    }

    // ISponsor.Renewal - called to renew lease
    public TimeSpan Renewal(ILease myLease)
    {
        TimeSpan timeSpan = new TimeSpan(0, 0, 3);

        Console.WriteLine("\nLease Renewed.\n");

        PrintLeaseInfo();

        return timeSpan;
    }

    // print lease info
    void PrintLeaseInfo()
    {
        if (lease != null)
        {
            Console.WriteLine("Lease Info\n");
            Console.WriteLine("  CurrentLeaseTime: {0}", lease.CurrentLeaseTime
);
            Console.WriteLine("  InitialLeaseTime: {0}",
lease.InitialLeaseTime);
            Console.WriteLine("   RenewOnCallTime: {0}", lease.RenewOnCallTime);
            Console.WriteLine("SponsorshipTimeout: {0}",
lease.SponsorshipTimeout);
        }
    }

    // entry point
    static void Main(string[] args)
    {
        ChannelServices.RegisterChannel(new HttpChannel());

        LeasingDemo leaseDemo = new LeasingDemo();
        leaseDemo.ImplementLease();
    }
}
```

And here's the output:

```
  CurrentLeaseTime: 00:00:02.9499280
  InitialLeaseTime: 00:05:00
   RenewOnCallTime: 00:02:00
SponsorshipTimeout: 00:02:00

Server Response: Greetings from the BasicRemotingServer component!

Lease Renewed.

Lease Info

  CurrentLeaseTime: -00:00:07.1145440
  InitialLeaseTime: 00:05:00
   RenewOnCallTime: 00:02:00
SponsorshipTimeout: 00:02:00

Lease Renewed.
```

The `Main()` method of the `LeasingDemo` class in Listing 21.14 registers an `HttpChannel`, instantiates a `LeasingDemo` object, and calls the `ImplementLease()` method to run this program.

The leasing demo method initializes a lease manager for the remote server component and receives a lease manager object, which implements the `ILease` interface. The following line shows how to initialize the lease manager:

```
lease = (ILease)brs.InitializeLifetimeService();
```

With the lease manager object, the client registers itself to receive notifications of the remote server component's lifetime expiration. Additionally, the second parameter to the `Register` method provides the lease manager with the remote server components initial lifetime, using a `TimeSpan` object, as shown here:

```
lease.Register(this, new TimeSpan(0, 0, 3));
```

All the client needs to do now is invoke methods on the server component and wait for renewal requests from the lease manager. The lease manager calls the client's `Renewal()` method when the lifetime of the remote server component expires. The client in this example simply creates a new `TimeSpan` object and returns it to the lease manager to keep the remote server component alive for three more seconds. The `TimeSpan` constructor overload in the example of Listing 21.14 uses three parameters: `hours`, `minutes`, and `seconds`, respectively.

Summary

In its most basic form, remoting is a mechanism enabling communication across `AppDomains` between client and server components. Remote server components expose their methods to be consumed by one or more clients. Clients use configuration files to specify remoting parameters that help them use the remoting framework to find and invoke methods on remote server components. Remote server components can be set up via a Web server or a specialized host utility.

The remoting framework is extensible. For instance, a program can use a custom proxy. There is also a flexible channel mechanism with configurable marshalling, formatting, and transport services. These channel services can be replaced with custom components.

Remote server component lifetime can be managed via a leasing mechanism. This leasing mechanism exposes a lease manager, assisting collaboration of lifetime issues between remoting client and server components. The leasing mechanism allows clients to control the lifetime of remote server components.

The next chapter presents another distributed computing technology, Web services. While remoting and Web services are two separate technologies, the concepts from this chapter should provide insight into the inner workings of Web services.

CHAPTER 22

Web Services

In This Chapter

- Web Service Basics *484*
- Using Web Services *490*

Web Services is a distributed computing technology enabling the exposure and reuse of logical business entities over the Internet. There are all types of distributed computing technologies, but the emphasis here is on open standards. In particular, these are based upon World Wide Web Consortium (W3C) protocols and communications standards.

With open standards, businesses can deploy components on the Web to be consumed by anyone, anywhere. It does not matter what computer is being used, its operating system, or the programming language used to implement the logic. Applicable bits include the communications protocol, data formats, and registry interaction, which are defined by open W3C standards.

Web Service Basics

Creating ASP.NET Web services is incredibly easy. ASP.NET Web services are supported by the ASP.NET infrastructure. This provides an environment where all of the underlying plumbing is encapsulated. The net result is reduced complexity and more time for a developer to concentrate on business logic in lieu of plumbing.

Web Service Technologies

Several open standards technologies play a significant role in making Web services a reality. These standards can be categorized by description, discovery, and transmission.

Description

The Web Services Description Language (WSDL) is an XML-based format for describing a Web service. It describes what the Web service is, its parameters, and how to use it.

Discovery

Universal Description Discovery and Integration (UDDI) directories support discovery. These directories manage WSDL documents and provide a means for clients to find and use Web services.

Transmission

The Simple Object Access Protocol (SOAP) is a communications protocol that enables clients to interact with UDDI directories and Web services. It's an open-standard protocol that wraps a method call into an envelope for delivery between end points. SOAP rides upon other open-standard transmission protocols, such as HTTP (very common) or TCP.

A Basic Web Service

With ASP.NET Web services, hereafter referred to as Web services, the underlying technologies supporting description, discovery, and transmission are hidden with the rest of the system plumbing. To make a Web service, you should create two files. The first file is an ASP.NET header, as shown in Listing 22.1. The second is a code-behind file with business logic, as shown in Listing 22.2.

LISTING 22.1 Web Service Header: `BasicWebService.asmx`

```
<%@ WebService Language="c#"
➥Codebehind="BasicWebService.asmx.cs"
➥Class="BasicWebService.BasicWebService" %>
```

Similar to an ASP.NET Web page header, the Web Service header in Listing 22.1 communicates with the ASP.NET system to enable compilation and the underlying plumbing that supports the Web service. The `@WebService` directive tells the ASP.NET system that this is a Web service, as opposed to the `@Page` directive, which identifies an ASP.NET Web page. The `@WebService` directive has three attributes: `Language`, `Codebehind`, and `Class`.

The `Language` attribute specifies the language that this Web service will be compiled with. It could have been any .NET compatible language, but here we're only interested in C#.

The `Codebehind` attribute identifies the source code file holding the actual code. The current convention is to use `<filename>.asmx.cs`, where `<filename>` can be any name.

The `Class` attribute indicates the Web service class that clients must instantiate. In Listing 22.1, the class is shown as `BasicWebService`, which is part of the identically named namespace `BasicWebService`. The contents of the `BasicWebService` class are shown in Listing 22.2.

LISTING 22.2 Web Service Code: `BasicWebService.asmx.cs`

```
using System;
using System.Web;
using System.Web.Services;

namespace BasicWebService
{
    /// <summary>
    /// Basic Web Service Demo.
    /// </summary>
    [WebService(Namespace="http://SAMS/C#.Unleashed/WebServices")]
```

LISTING 22.2 continued

```
    public class BasicWebService : System.Web.Services.WebService
    {
        [WebMethod]
        public string Greetings(string name)
        {
            return "Hello " + name + "!";
        }
    }
}
```

The `BasicWebService` class in this listing defines a single method, `Greetings()`, which accepts a string parameter and returns a string. The only noticeable difference from any other class is the inheritance chain and attributes.

A Web service class may optionally inherit from the `WebService` class, which is part of the `System.Web.Services` namespace. Doing so provides the class with access to ASP.NET objects such as application and session state. In the case of Listing 22.2, the inheritance of the `WebService` class could have been left out with no implications.

An optional attribute, `WebService`, decorates the `BasicWebService` class. Its purpose in Listing 22.2 is to define the XML namespace in which this Web service resides. The only requirement is that the namespace be unique, unless it is supposed to be a member of an existing XML namespace. The named parameter, `Namespace`, sets the `BasicWebService` Web service into the `http://SAMS/C#.Unleashed/WebServices` namespace.

Exposed methods for Web services must be decorated with the `WebMethod` attribute. Additionally, these classes must be public, which makes sense because external components must be able to see and access the method.

You can deploy the source files in Listing 22.1 and Listing 22.2 by copying them to an appropriate Web server directory.

Viewing Web Service Info

The ASP.NET infrastructure provides the means to view information and test the operation of a Web service. To do so, point your browser to the location of the Web service on a Web server. Figure 22.1 shows the results of pointing a browser at a Web service.

The screen in Listing 22.1 shows a list of all available operations for a Web service. The `BasicWebService` Web service has only a single operation, `Greetings()`. Clicking on the `greetings` hyperlink results in the page shown in Figure 22.2.

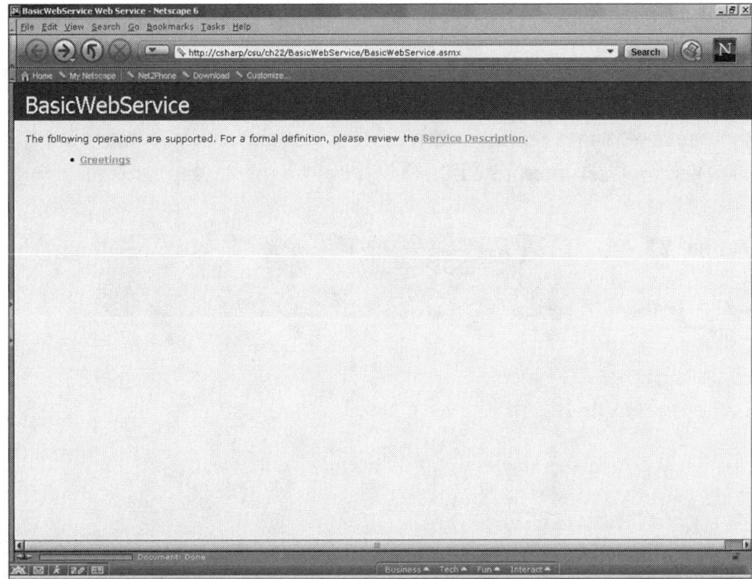

FIGURE 22.1
Locating a Web service with a browser.

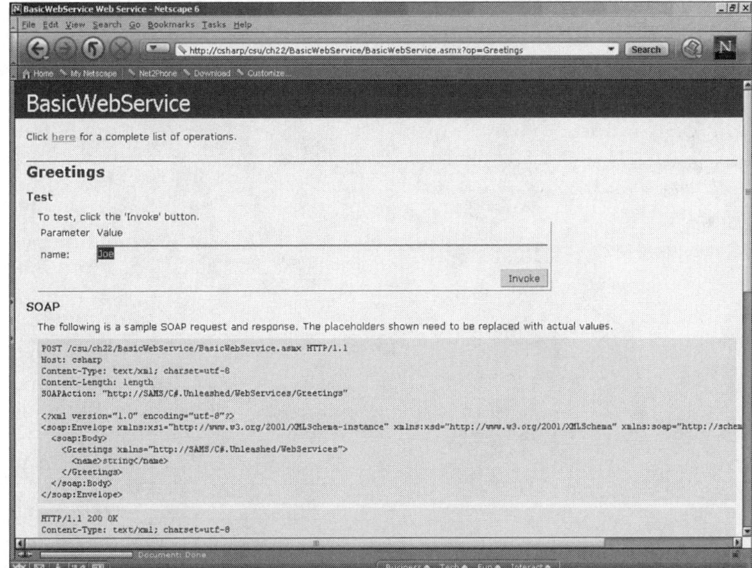

FIGURE 22.2
Testing a Web service.

The `name` parameter with the text box following it is where a string can be entered as a parameter to the `Greetings()` operation. In the example, the string "Joe" is entered as the `name` parameter. Clicking the Invoke button does what one would expect, invokes the

Greetings() method. There's more information on the test page, and I'll explain that in a little bit.

Figure 22.3 shows the text string returned from invoking the Greetings() operation on the BasicWebService Web service. However, the actual result is not this simple, because the Web browser interpreted the XML before displaying a result.

FIGURE 22.3
Web service invocation results: text reply.

The real reply that was returned is shown in Figure 22.4.

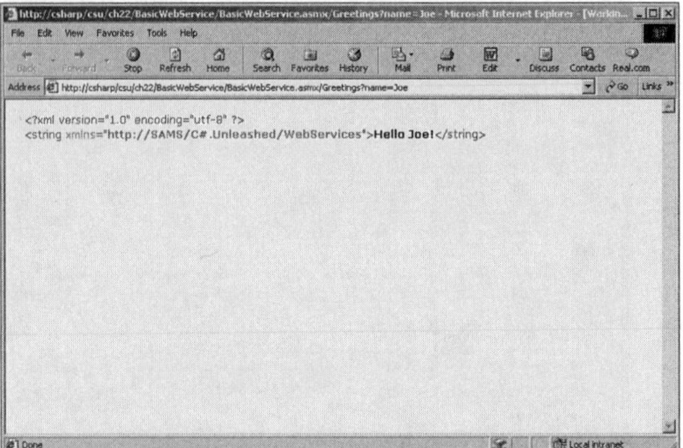

FIGURE 22.4
Web service invocation results: XML reply.

The top of the display in Figure 22.4 shows a standard XML header. What is most interesting is the next line with the <string> tag, which has an xmlns attribute. This attribute identifies the XML namespace of which this Web service is a part. The namespace is exactly the same namespace specified in the WebService attribute of the BasicWebService class definition in Listing 22.2. The value is the same string reply shown in Figure 22.3, with the difference being that Figure 22.4 shows the full XML reply. Now, looking back at the test screen, Figure 22.5 shows the message format.

FIGURE 22.5
SOAP message format.

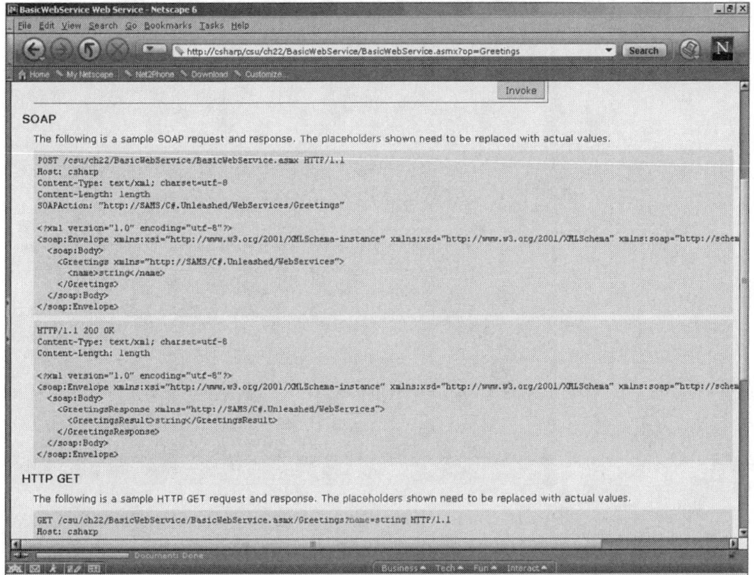

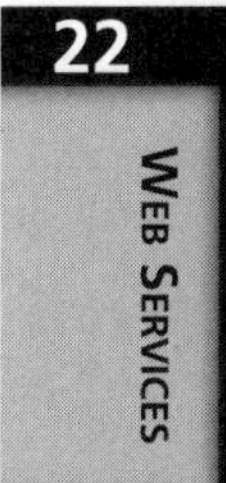

Figure 22.5 shows the format of the SOAP request and response for the `Greetings` operation of the `BasicWebService` Web service. The first code block shows the SOAP request with the first five lines being the HTTP protocol headers. After the XML header is the SOAP envelope, the outer layer of a SOAP message. Within the SOAP envelope is the SOAP body, which in turn holds the `Greetings` request. The tag of the `Greetings` request has an `xmlns` namespace attribute. This is the same namespace specified in the `WebService` attribute decorating the `BasicWebService` class in Listing 22.2. When a SOAP request is made for the `Greetings` operation, the string is entered in the `name` element when the call was invoked.

The SOAP response for the `Greetings` operation is similar to the request with three HTTP response headers, the XML header, and a SOAP envelope with a SOAP body. The difference is that the name of the operation is appended with the word `Response`, `GreetingsResponse`, and the result is the name of the operation appended with the word `Result`, `GreetingsResult`. The result will be a string returned from the `Greetings` operation of the `BasicWebService` Web service.

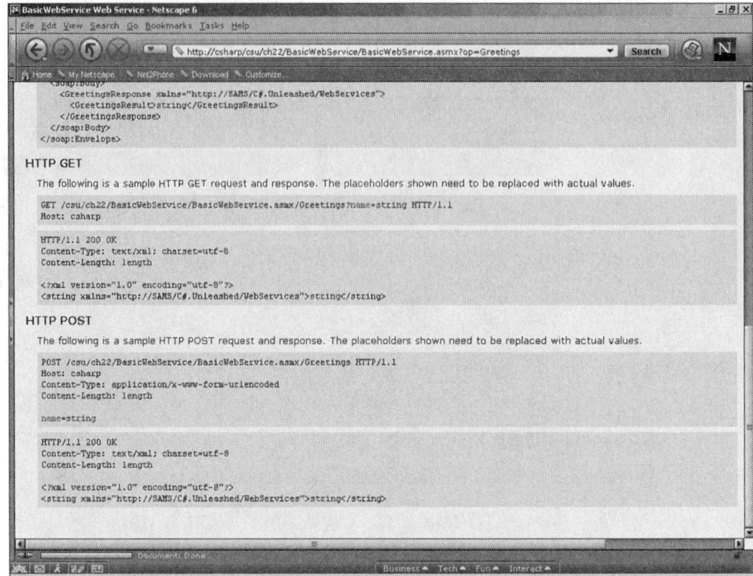

FIGURE 22.6
HTTP message formats.

A Web service may also be called with `HTTP PUT` and `GET` operations, as shown in Figure 22.6. Examining the `HTTP GET` request command and comparing it to the URL from the browser in Figure 22.4 indicates that the invoke operation from the test page in Figure 22.2 uses an `HTTP GET` operation. Comparing the XML portion of the `HTTP GET` response from Figure 22.6 to the XML output in Figure 22.4 confirms this. An `HTTP POST` message is formatted differently, according to `HTTP POST` protocol, yet returns a response in exactly the same format as the `HTTP GET` response.

Using Web Services

If an application wraps a method call into a SOAP envelope and uses the HTTP protocol, it could use the method described in Figure 22.5 to communicate with the `BasicWebService` Web service. Alternatively, the client could use one of the `HTTP GET` or `POST` methods from Figure 22.6. It's possible, but that would be a lot of work.

The .NET Framework comes with a utility called `wsdl` that frees a client from creating all this plumbing. This utility takes the URL to a Web service and creates a proxy, which is used by the client to call the Web service. The following command line creates a proxy to the `BasicWebService` Web service with the name `BasicWebService.cs`, shown in Listing 22.3:

```
wsdl http://csharp/csu/ch22/
➥BasicWebService/BasicWebService.asmx?wsdl
```

Warning

While experimentation with the code of a proxy can certainly be cool and educational, be careful. If you later try to use the code and it doesn't work, you may end up having to regenerate the proxy all over again to get things working.

LISTING 22.3 Auto-Generated Web Service Proxy: `BasicWebService.cs`

```
//------------------------------------------------------------------------------
// <autogenerated>
//     This code was generated by a tool.
//     Runtime Version: 1.0.2914.14
//
//     Changes to this file may cause incorrect behavior
➥ and will be lost if
//     the code is regenerated.
// </autogenerated>
//------------------------------------------------------------------------------

//
// This source code was auto-generated by wsdl,
➥ Version=1.0.2914.14.
//
using System.Diagnostics;
using System.Xml.Serialization;
using System;
using System.Web.Services.Protocols;
using System.Web.Services;


[System.Web.Services.WebServiceBindingAttribute(
➥Name="BasicWebServiceSoap", Namespace=
➥"http://SAMS/C#.Unleashed/WebServices")]
public class BasicWebService :
➥ System.Web.Services.Protocols.SoapHttpClientProtocol {

    [System.Diagnostics.DebuggerStepThroughAttribute()]
    public BasicWebService() {
        this.Url = "http://csharp/csu/ch22/
➥BasicWebService/BasicWebService.asmx";
    }

    [System.Diagnostics.DebuggerStepThroughAttribute()]
    [System.Web.Services.Protocols.SoapDocumentMethodAttribute
➥("http://SAMS/C#.Unleashed/WebServices/Greetings",
➥ RequestNamespace="http://SAMS/C#.Unleashed/
➥WebServices", ResponseNamespace="http://SAMS/C#.Unleashed
```

LISTING 22.3 continued

```
➥/WebServices", Use=System.Web.Services.Description
➥.SoapBindingUse.Literal, ParameterStyle=System.
➥Web.Services.Protocols.SoapParameterStyle.Wrapped)]
    public string Greetings(string name) {
        object[] results = this.Invoke("Greetings", new object[] {
                    name});
        return ((string)(results[0]));
    }

    [System.Diagnostics.DebuggerStepThroughAttribute()]
    public System.IAsyncResult BeginGreetings(string name,
➥System.AsyncCallback callback, object asyncState) {
        return this.BeginInvoke("Greetings", new object[] {
                    name}, callback, asyncState);
    }

    [System.Diagnostics.DebuggerStepThroughAttribute()]
    public string EndGreetings(System.IAsyncResult asyncResult) {
        object[] results = this.EndInvoke(asyncResult);
        return ((string)(results[0]));
    }
}
```

The `BasicWebService` class from the proxy in Listing 22.3 inherits from the `System.Web.Services.Protocols.SoapHttpClientProtocol`, indicating that the client request and response will be wrapped in the SOAP protocol, similar to that shown in Figure 22.5. Another item of interest is the `Greetings()` method, decorated with the `SoapDocumentMethod` attribute. One of the great things about this whole process is that the internals of the proxy class and other underlying plumbing can be ignored. It may be interesting to know, but not necessary to use the Web Service.

Using a Web service requires a client to declare an instance of the proxy class and then call the necessary Web service operation, defined in the proxy class. Listing 22.4 shows how to do this.

LISTING 22.4 Using a Web Service: `WebServiceClient.cs`

```
using System;

namespace WebServiceClient
{
    /// <summary>
    /// Summary description for Class1.
    /// </summary>
    class WebServiceClient
```

LISTING 22.4 continued

```
    {
        static void Main(string[] args)
        {
            BasicWebService myWebService =
                new BasicWebService();

            Console.WriteLine(myWebService.Greetings("Joe"));
        }
    }
}
```


And here's the output:

```
Hello Joe!
```

The `Main()` method of Listing 22.4 instantiates a new `BasicWebService` object. Then within a `Console.WriteLine()` statement, it calls the `Greetings()` method with a string parameter. Actually, it's calling these methods on the proxy, which is hiding all the underlying details of communicating with the Web Service.

It's evident from Listing 22.4 that using a Web Service is as easy as calling a method in any other class. The secret is the proxy, which uses several classes of the base class library to package the request and response messages into SOAP format messages and transport them via HTTP. The following command line creates the client:

```
csc WebServiceClient.cs BasicWebService.cs
```

Summary

Web services provide a platform-independent means of exposing business logic over the Internet. They are created using several open-standards technologies.

Creating ASP.NET Web services is easy and abstracts much of the complexity associated with Internet communications. This allows developers to concentrate on business logic instead of underlying plumbing.

Using a Web service involves creating a proxy class that communicates with the Web service on behalf of a client. The client application then communicates directly with the proxy to invoke necessary Web service operations.

Extreme C#

PART IV

IN THIS PART

23 Multi-Threading *497*

24 Browsing the Network Libraries *503*

25 String Manipulation *515*

26 C# Collections *545*

27 Attributes *567*

28 Reflection *581*

29 Localization and Resources *595*

30 Unsafe Code and Pinvoke *619*

31 Runtime De-Bugging *635*

32 Performance Monitoring *647*

33 Integrating C# with COM *679*

CHAPTER 23

Multi-Threading

IN THIS CHAPTER

- Creating New Threads *498*
- Synchronization *499*

Multi-threading is the capability to execute multiple threads simultaneously. As systems become more sophisticated, it's often desirable to take advantage of machine capabilities such as multi-processor architectures. Even on single processing machines, multi-threading provides performance enhancements in some applications.

Besides boosting performance, multi-threading is handy in other scenarios such as event-driven operating environments. For instance, it's often necessary to invoke a progress indicator in its own thread so it can receive updates to an ongoing operation in another thread. Multi-threaded programs allow a program to engage in simultaneous events that can provide a user with real-time feedback.

Creating New Threads

The act of creating and invoking a new thread in C# is relatively straightforward. The process involves creating a `Thread` object, instantiating a `ThreadStart` delegate with a delegate method handler, and passing the `ThreadStart` delegate to the new `Thread` object. All that's remaining is to start the thread, and off it runs. Listing 23.1 shows how to create and execute a new thread.

LISTING 23.1 Creating a New Thread: `SingleThread.cs`

```
using System;
using System.Threading;

/// <summary>
///     Shows how to create a single thread of execution.
/// </summary>
class SingleThread
{
    static void Main(string[] args)
    {
        SingleThread st = new SingleThread();

        Thread th = new Thread(new ThreadStart(st.SayHello));

        th.Start();
    }

    public void SayHello()
    {
        Console.WriteLine("Hello from a single thread.");
    }
}
```

And here's the output:

```
Hello from a single thread.
```

In Listing 23.1, an object of type `SingleThread` is instantiated within the `Main()` method. It contains the `SayHello()` method, which is executed as part of the thread in this program. All of the thread creation and initialization occurs in the following line:

```
Thread th = new Thread(new ThreadStart(st.SayHello));
```

The `Thread` object is declared as `th`. It's instantiated as a new `Thread` object with a new `ThreadStart` delegate as its parameter. The delegate method handler for the `ThreadStart` delegate is the `SayHello()` method of the `SingleThread` object, `st`.

Now the thread exists, but it's idle, waiting for directions. It's said to be in the `unstarted` state. To get this thread running, the program invokes the `Start()` method of the `Thread` object, `th`.

Synchronization

Using the techniques from Listing 23.1, it's easy to create multiple threads of execution. As long as each thread minds its own business, the program runs fine. However, in many situations, this is not practical. It's often necessary for multiple threads to share a resource. Without control, the behavior of multi-threaded programs sharing a resource yields non-deterministic results.

To provide that control, C# allocates methods to coordinate activities between threads. This coordination is properly termed *synchronization*. Correct implementation of synchronization enables programs to take advantage of performance benefits of multithreading as well as maintaining the integrity of object state and data.

This section uses the C# `lock` keyword to provide data synchronization. The code in Listing 23.2 shows how.

LISTING 23.2 Synchronized Data Access: `Synchronization.cs`

```
using System;
using System.Threading;

/// <summary>
///     Synchronized data.
/// </summary>
class SyncData
{
    int index = 0;
```

LISTING 23.2 continued

```
    string[] comment = new string[]
        { "one", "two",   "three", "four", "five",
          "six", "seven", "eight", "nine", "ten" };

    public string GetNextComment()
    {
        // allow only a single thread at a time
        lock (this)
        {
            if (index < comment.Length)
            {
                return comment[index++];
            }
            else
            {
                return "empty";
            }
        }
    }
}

/// <summary>
///    Demonstrates synchronized data access.
/// </summary>
class Synchronization
{
    SyncData sdat = new SyncData();

    static void Main(string[] args)
    {
        Synchronization sync = new Synchronization();

        Thread t1 = new Thread(new ThreadStart(sync.GetComments));
        Thread t2 = new Thread(new ThreadStart(sync.GetComments));
        Thread t3 = new Thread(new ThreadStart(sync.GetComments));

        t1.Name = "Thread 1";
        t2.Name = "Thread 2";
        t3.Name = "Thread 3";

        t1.Start();
        t2.Start();
        t3.Start();
    }

    public void GetComments()
    {
        string comment;
```

LISTING 23.2 continued

```
        do
        {
            comment = sdat.GetNextComment();

            Console.WriteLine(
                "Current Thread: {0}, comment: {1}",
                Thread.CurrentThread.Name, comment);

        } while (comment != "empty");
    }
}
```

Here's sample output from Listing 23.2:

```
Current Thread: Thread 1, comment: one
Current Thread: Thread 3, comment: two
Current Thread: Thread 2, comment: three
Current Thread: Thread 1, comment: four
Current Thread: Thread 1, comment: five
Current Thread: Thread 1, comment: six
Current Thread: Thread 1, comment: seven
Current Thread: Thread 1, comment: eight
Current Thread: Thread 1, comment: nine
Current Thread: Thread 1, comment: ten
Current Thread: Thread 1, comment: empty
Current Thread: Thread 3, comment: empty
Current Thread: Thread 2, comment: empty
```


There are three threads of execution in Listing 23.2 that obtain synchronized access to data. The construction of the threads in the `Main()` method of the `Synchronization` class is similar to how threads were created in Listing 23.1. To keep track of each thread, the program sets each thread's `Name` property.

The `GetComments()` method of the `Synchronization` class is run by each thread. This method obtains a new piece of data, `comment`, from a `SyncData` object and prints its value to the console. The loop ends when the `SyncData` object returns the string `empty`.

The `SyncData` object provides synchronized access to its data. The only way to get to the data is through the public `GetNextComment()` method. Within this method is an `if` statement, keeping data reads from going beyond the bounds of the array. Until `index` reaches the end of the array, the next comment is returned and `index` is incremented so the next thread gets the next comment. When `index` reaches the end of the array, the method returns the string `empty` to signify that there is no more data to return.

Surrounding the `if` statement in the `GetNextComment()` method is a `lock` statement. Here's a cutout of the `lock` statement from Listing 23.2:

```
lock (this)
{
    // statements
}
```

The parameter of the `lock` statement is `this`. The parameter for a `lock` statement can be any reference type expression. An invalid expression would be a value type, such as an `int` type. The `lock` statement implements mutual exclusion on the statements inside the curly braces.

Tip

Use the lock statement for mutually exclusive access to data in a multi-threaded program.

Without the lock statement, it would be possible for two or more threads to be reading the same value at the same time. In the absence of a lock statement, if the statements inside the curly braces represented an airline seat reservation or a bank account withdrawal, the results would not be nice. The `lock` statement ensures that only one thread at a time can be executing those statements.

Summary

This chapter presented multi-threaded applications in C#. The first section discussed how to create and start a thread, including declaring a thread argument and passing it a delegate with the method to be invoked, as well as executing the thread.

To keep threads from wreaking havoc with shared data, it's often necessary to use synchronization objects. Proper thread synchronization helps manage access to program data. The example program in this chapter used `lock` statements, providing a mutual exclusion access scenario to program data.

Multi-threading is common on server programs that create new threads to handle client requests. The next chapter, "Browsing the Network Libraries," shows how to create clients and servers that communicate over a network.

CHAPTER 24

Browsing the Network Libraries

IN THIS CHAPTER

- Implementing Sockets *504*
- Working with HTTP *512*

The C# language has access to an entire suite of networking libraries. Some of the capabilities range from low-level socket connections to wrappered HTTP classes.

An understanding of the TCP/IP protocol would be helpful in understanding the sockets implementation. However, I have tried to explain it in a way that most programmers will understand. The examples demonstrate a client and a server communicating with the TCP/IP protocol, using socket library classes.

It would also be advantageous to understand the HTTP protocol. The HTTP example implements a client program that requests a Web page from an Internet server. It uses special library objects to send a request for a Web page and retrieve a response.

Implementing Sockets

Although more focus is given today to distributed, n-tier concepts, there may still be a need for client/server computing. There are plenty of legacy systems out there and Internet utilities that require sockets.

This section shows how to create socket-based programs. It has two components: a client and a server. The server delivers quotes, and the client requests a quote and prints it to the console. When trying the programs out, bring up the server first and then start the client in a different process or window.

A Socket Server

The server program uses sockets to deliver information (quotes) to requesting clients. Listing 24.1 demonstrates how to create a server program with sockets:

LISTING 24.1 Creating a Socket Server: `MoneyServer.cs`

```
using System;
using System.Collections;
using System.Text;
using System.Net.Sockets;

/// <summary>
///     A TCP Server.
/// </summary>
class MoneyServer
{
    ArrayList talk  = new ArrayList();

    public MoneyServer ()
    {
        talk.Add(
```

LISTING 24.1 continued

```
"A penny saved is too small, make it a buck.");
        talk.Add(
"Keep your wooden nickel. It'll be worth something someday.");
        talk.Add(
"It's your dime, but you're better off dialing 10-10-XXX.");
    }

    static void Main(string[] args)
    {
        MoneyServer mSvr = new MoneyServer();
        ASCIIEncoding ASCII = new ASCIIEncoding();
        Byte[] inStream  = new Byte[256];
        Byte[] outStream = new Byte[256];
        Random rnd;
        string reqString = "";
        int index;

        TcpListener tcpl = new TcpListener(2010);
        tcpl.Start();
        Console.WriteLine("Server is Running...");

        do
        {
            try
            {
                Socket sock = tcpl.AcceptSocket();

                int count = sock.Receive( inStream,
                                          inStream.Length,
                                          0 );
                reqString = ASCII.GetString(inStream,
                                            0,
                                            count);
                Console.WriteLine(reqString);

                rnd = new Random();
                index = rnd.Next(mSvr.talk.Count);
                outStream = ASCII.GetBytes(
                    (string)mSvr.talk[index] );

                sock.Send( outStream, outStream.Length, 0 );
            }
            catch (Exception e)
            {
                Console.WriteLine(
                "Generic Exception Message: {0}", e.Message);
            }
```

LISTING 24.1 continued

```
        } while (reqString != "bye");

        tcpl.Stop();
    }
}
```

This server program instantiates an `ArrayList`, `talk`, and initializes it with quote strings during constructor processing. The real action for this program starts in the `Main()` method.

Socket operations are encapsulated in the TCP classes. This program uses the `TcpListener` class to create a socket connection on the local host. The example accepts a single parameter, indicating the port number. Once the `TcpListener` class is instantiated, it must be started with the `Start()` method. The following snippet from Listing 24.1 shows how to instantiate and share a `TcpListener`:

```
TcpListener tcpl = new TcpListener(2010);
tcpl.Start();
Console.WriteLine("Server is Running...");
```

Once the `TcpListener` has been started, it must listen for client connections. This happens by calling its `AcceptSocket()` method, which causes the program to remain idle, in a listening state, until it receives a connection request from a client on port 2010. When a client connects, the `AcceptSocket()` method returns a `Socket` object. The following code line shows how to accept a client connection and retrieve a `Socket` object:

```
Socket sock = tcpl.AcceptSocket();
```

After the `Socket` object is created, it's used to read the input from the client. This program uses the `Receive()` method of the `Socket` object, which has three parameters. The first parameter is a byte array to store input; the second is the maximum number of bytes to read; and the third is the offset into the byte array to begin filling. The `Receive()` method returns the number of bytes read. This command is shown in the following code lines:

```
int count = sock.Receive( inStream,
                          inStream.Length,
                          0 );
```

The client sends data in the form of a byte array, which needs to be converted to a string so the program can deal with it appropriately. This program uses an `ASCIIEncoding` object to transform a byte array to a string. The `GetString()` method of the `ASCIIEncoding` class performs this function. Its first parameter identifies the byte array to be converted. The second parameter is the byte array offset to begin at, and the third parameter is the number of bytes to read. This conversion is in the following code lines:

```
reqString = ASCII.GetString(inStream,
                            0,
                            count);
Console.WriteLine(reqString);
```

After receiving the request string from the client and printing it to the console, the program obtains a random string from the `talk` `ArrayList`. To send this string to the client, the server must convert it to a byte array. It does so by invoking the `GetBytes()` method of the `ASCIIEncoder` object, `ASCII`. The `GetBytes()` method takes a single string parameter. This task is shown in the following code:

```
rnd = new Random();
index = rnd.Next(mSvr.talk.Count);
outStream = ASCII.GetBytes(
    (string)mSvr.talk[index] );
```

To actually send the quote back to the client, the program uses the `Socket` class's `Send()` method, which takes three parameters. The first parameter is the byte array to be sent; the second is the number of bytes to send; and the third is the offset in the byte array to begin reading. The `Send()` method is shown in the following code line:

```
sock.Send( outStream, outStream.Length, 0 );
```

The client can keep sending requests for quotes as long as it wants to. When it no longer wants to interact, it sends the string "`bye`". The server ends operations when it reads this string and then closes the socket connection. The following code lines show the end of the `do` loop where a stop or go decision is made and the invocation of the `Stop()` method of the `TcpListener` class when the client breaks the connection.

```
} while (reqString != "bye");

tcpl.Stop();
```

That's all there is to implementing a TCP server. Open a socket, listen for clients, and respond to their requests. The next section shows how to build a client that talks to this server.

A Socket Client

The client program uses sockets to request information from a server. It makes a socket connection, sends a request, and receives a reply. Listing 24.2 shows how a client program is built using sockets:

LISTING 24.2 Creating a Socket Client: `EntrepreneurialClient.cs`

```
using System;
using System.IO;
using System.Text;
using System.Net.Sockets;

/// <summary>
///     tcp client
/// </summary>
class EntrepreneurialClient
{
    static void Main(string[] args)
    {
        ASCIIEncoding ASCII = new ASCIIEncoding();
        Byte[] inStream     = new Byte[256];
        Byte[] outStream    = new Byte[256];
        string freeAdvice;
        string choice       = "Q";

        do
        {
            try
            {
                Console.WriteLine("\nMoney Line\n");
                Console.WriteLine("1 - Get Advice");
                Console.WriteLine("Q - Quit");
                Console.Write("\nPlease Choose:  ");
                choice = Console.ReadLine();
                Console.WriteLine();

                TcpClient myClient  =
                    new TcpClient( "localhost", 2010 );
                Stream myStream     = myClient.GetStream();

                outStream = ASCII.GetBytes(
                    "What is the secret of making money?");

                if (choice == "1")
                {
                    // send request to server
                    myStream.Write(outStream,
                                   0,
                                   outStream.Length);

                    // clean garbage chars from byte array
                    for (int i=0; i < inStream.Length; i++)
                    {
                        inStream[i] = 0;
                    }
```

LISTING 24.2 continued

```
                // retrieve response from server
                myStream.Read(inStream,
                              0,
                              inStream.Length);
                freeAdvice = ASCII.GetString(
                                        inStream,
                                        0,
                                        inStream.Length);
                Console.WriteLine("Server Response: {0}",
                                  freeAdvice);
            }
            else
            {
                // close session with server
                outStream = ASCII.GetBytes("bye");
                myStream.Write(outStream,
                               0,
                               outStream.Length);
            }
        }
        catch( InvalidOperationException ioe )
        {
            Console.WriteLine(
               "Invalid Operation Message: {0}",
                ioe.Message);
        }
        catch ( Exception e )
        {
            Console.WriteLine(
                "Generic Exception Message: {0}",
                 e.Message);
        }
      } while (choice == "1");
   }
}
```


The client application that connects to a server, retrieves quotes, and ends a session based on user input. After presenting a menu to the user, the program opens a connection to the server with the `TcpClient` class. The `TcpClient` object, `myClient`, is instantiated with a constructor that accepts two arguments. The first argument indicates the DNS host name of the server. Since the server is on the same machine, this parameter is "`localhost`". The second argument is the port number, `2010`, which is the same port used by the server in Listing 24.1. Here's the statement that creates a `TcpClient` object and makes a connection:

```
TcpClient myClient  =
    new TcpClient( "localhost", 2010 );
```

Tip

The listings in this chapter use try/catch blocks for processing exceptions, which is especially important because of the nature of network communications. Most of the time there is no way to know what will happen on the other end of the network connection. Effective use of exception handling gives programs a way to gracefully degrade in the face of network errors.

The `TcpClient` class has an alternate constructor that accepts an `IPEndPoint` object. An `IPEndPoint` object is constructed with an `IPAddress` object, which holds a numeric IP address and a port number.

Instead of getting a `Socket` object as the server did, the `TcpClient` program obtains a stream. Here's the code line that uses the `GetStream()` method of the `TcpClient` class to obtain a stream to the server:

```
Stream myStream     = myClient.GetStream();
```

The client program converts a string to a byte array by using an object of the `ASCIIEncoding` class. The following code lines create the request stream that is sent to the server to obtain a quote and then, assuming the user chose to get a quote, sends the request to the server with the `Write()` method of the `Stream` object. The parameters for the `Write()` method are, in order, the byte array, the offset to begin reading, and the number of bytes to read.

```
outStream = ASCII.GetBytes(
    "What is the secret of making money?");

    myStream.Write(outStream,
                   0,
                   outStream.Length);
```

Between requests, the program cleans old data out of the byte array used to obtain input. Otherwise, when a shorter piece of information is retrieved, it would have garbage from the previous quote hanging off the end of the string. The `for` loop accomplishes this task:

```
// clean garbage chars from byte array
for (int i=0; i < inStream.Length; i++)
{
    inStream[i] = 0;
}
```

Obtaining the quote from the server requires reading data from the input stream and converting the bytes to a string. Reading from the server occurs through the `Read()` method of the Stream object, myStream. Its parameters are, in order, the byte array to read data into, the offset into the byte array to begin placing data, and the maximum number of bytes to read. As seen in previous explanations, the GetString() method of the ASCIIEncoding class converts the byte array to a string. The following code lines show these methods, along with the statement to print the results to the console.

```
// retrieve response from server
myStream.Read(inStream,
              0,
              inStream.Length);
freeAdvice = ASCII.GetString(
                        inStream,
                        0,
                        inStream.Length);
Console.WriteLine("Server Response: {0}",
                   freeAdvice);
```

When the user wants to quit the program, he selects the Q—or anything other than 1—option from the menu. This runs the following code lines, which send a message to the server indicating that the client wants to end its session. The GetBytes() method of the ASCIIEncoding class and the Write() method of the Stream class operate as previously described.

```
// close session with server
outStream = ASCII.GetBytes("bye");
myStream.Write(outStream,
               0,
               outStream.Length);
```

This client hooks up to the server in Listing 24.1. The next part explains how to compile and run these two programs.

Compiling and Running Server and Client

Both of these programs are easy to compile with the following command lines:

```
csc MoneyServer.cs
csc EntrepreneurialClient.cs
```

Open a separate window or begin a new process with the MoneyServer program to start the server that will listen for the client.

Open a separate window or begin a new process for the EntrepreneurialClient program to start the client and present a menu. Press 1 for a new quote or press Q to end the session.

Working with HTTP

The System.Net namespace contains several classes to make working with the HTTP protocol easier. HTTP is the standard protocol for communicating on the World Wide Web, often just called the Web. The examples in this section use the HTTP classes to create a program that obtains a Web page. Listing 24.3 uses the `HttpWebRequest`, `HttpWebResponse`, and `HttpStream` classes to obtain a Web page.

LISTING 24.3 Creating an HTTP Client: `SiteReader.cs`

```
using System;
using System.IO;
using System.Net;
using System.Text;

/// <summary>
///     Reads a Web page.
/// </summary>
class SiteReader
{
    static void Main(string[] args)
    {
        try
        {
            ASCIIEncoding ASCII = new ASCIIEncoding();
            byte[] buf          = new byte[2048];

            HttpWebRequest httpReq =
                (HttpWebRequest)WebRequest.Create(
                    "http://localhost/howdy_partner.htm");

            HttpWebResponse httpResp =
                (HttpWebResponse)httpReq.GetResponse();

            Stream httpStream = httpResp.GetResponseStream();

            int count = httpStream.Read(buf, 0, buf.Length);

            Console.WriteLine(
                ASCII.GetString(buf, 0, count));
        }
        catch (Exception e)
        {
            Console.WriteLine("Generic Exception: {0}",
                              e.Message);
        }
    }
}
```

Tip

You may want to change your Internet Information Server (IIS) authentication method to `Anonymous`. Otherwise, you may face security problems when trying to access a Web page on `localhost`.

The example in Listing 24.3 shows how to obtain a Web page by using HTTP classes. The primary classes for making an HTTP request are `HttpWebRequest` and `HttpWebResponse`. The statement that instantiates an `HttpWebRequest` class uses the static `Create()` method of the `WebRequest` class and returns a `WebRequest` object. `WebRequest` is the abstract parent class of `HttpWebRequest`. Therefore, a cast operation is necessary to convert the return value of the `Create()` method to an `HttpWebRequest` object. The `Create()` method accepts a string representation of an URL. Here's the statement:

```
HttpWebRequest httpReq =
    (HttpWebRequest)WebRequest.Create(
        "http://localhost/howdy_partner.htm");
```

Once an `HttpWebRequest` object is created, it can be used to obtain an `HttpWebResponse` object. This happens by invoking its `GetResponse` method, which returns a `WebResponse` object. The `WebResponse` object is an abstract base class of the `HttpWebResponse` class, and a cast operation is necessary for conversion. The following statement from Listing 24.3 shows how to use the `GetResponse()` method:

```
HttpWebResponse httpResp =
    (HttpWebResponse)httpReq.GetResponse();
```

The only thing left to do is get the response stream and print it to the console. Use the `GetResponseStream()` method of the `HttpWebResponse` class to obtain a `Stream` object. Then the `Read()` method of the `Stream` object fills a byte array. The method's three parameters are the byte array to fill with stream data, the offset into the byte array to begin, and the maximum number of bytes to read. The byte array is converted to a string with the `GetString()` method of the `ASCIIEncoding` class. The `GetString()` method accepts three parameters in order: a byte array to read from, the offset into the byte array to begin reading, and the number of bytes to read. The following code lines get the response stream, convert it, and print it to the console.

```
Stream httpStream = httpResp.GetResponseStream();

int count = httpStream.Read(buf, 0, buf.Length);

Console.WriteLine(
    ASCII.GetString(buf, 0, count));
```

Beyond the basic functionality explained in this section, the `HttpWebRequest` and `HttpWebResponse` classes have several methods and properties for using the HTTP protocol. This capability includes functionality such as setting and reading headers and cookies.

Summary

This chapter showed how to uses library classes for sockets and HTTP operations. Sockets are easily managed with the `TcpClient` and `TcpListener` classes. The examples used these classes to implement both a socket server and a corresponding socket client.

I also showed how to use the HTTP classes to read a Web page. Some of the same classes were used for both the HTTP and socket examples. These included encoders and streams that worked with byte arrays.

As the examples in this chapter showed, many networking programs work extensively with strings extensively. The next chapter, "String Manipulation," provides detailed explanations on how to work with strings.

CHAPTER 25

String Manipulation

IN THIS CHAPTER

- The `String` Class 516
- The `StringBuilder` Class 533
- `String` Formatting 540
- Regular Expressions 541

The base class libraries include an extensive set of APIs for working with strings. This chapter goes beyond the `string` type and introduces specialized classes that make working with strings easier.

The `String` class is similar to the `string` type, but with much more power. Although the `String` class is very robust, it is also immutable, which means that once a `String` object is created, it can't be modified.

When there is a need to manipulate strings, use the `StringBuilder` class. The `StringBuilder` class isn't as streamlined as the `String` class, but it is built especially for modifying strings in any way necessary.

A topic related to strings is regular expressions. The `String` and `StringBuilder` classes have many capabilities, but regular expressions beat them both, hands down, at searching and text matching. The following sections go into detail about `String` and `StringBuilder` types, string formatting, and regular expressions.

Tip

The `String` and `StringBuilder` classes contain `instance` and `static` methods. When a `String` or `StringBuilder` instance already exists, use the `instance` method. However, you can gain performance advantages by avoiding unnecessary instantiations and using `static` methods.

The `String` Class

The `String` class mirrors the functionality of the `string` type, plus much more. There are numerous methods that compare, read, and search a `String` object's contents.

`String`s are immutable, meaning that they can't be modified once created. All methods that appear to modify a `String` really don't. They actually return a new `String` that has been modified based on the method invoked. When heavy modification is needed, use the `StringBuilder` class, which is discussed in the next section.

The `String` class is also sealed. This means that it can't be inherited. Being immutable and sealed makes the `String` class more efficient. Now, let's check out what the `String` class has to offer by examining its methods.

`static` Methods

The `String` class has several `static` methods. These are class methods that don't need an instance of the `String` class to be invoked. The following paragraphs discuss the `static String` class methods.

The `Compare()` Method

The `static Compare()` method compares two strings, which are referred to here as `str1` (string one) and `str2` (string two). It produces the following integer results:

- `str1 < str2` = negative
- `str1 == str2` = zero
- `str1 > str2` = positive

An empty string, `""`, is always greater than null. Here's an example of how to implement the `Compare()` method:

```
int intResult;
string str1 = "string 1";
string str2 = "string 2";

intResult = String.Compare(str1, str2);

Console.WriteLine("String.Compare({0}, {1}) = {2}\n",
  str1, str2, intResult);
```

The `Compare()` method has the following overloads:

- `Compare(str1, str2, ignoreCase)`
- `Compare(str1, str2, ignoreCase, CultureInfo)`
- `Compare(str1, index1, str2, index2, length)`
- `Compare(str1, index1, str2, index2, length, ignoreCase)`
- `Compare(str1, index1, str2, index2, length, ignoreCase, CultureInfo)`

In these overloads, `str1` and `str2` are the strings to be compared, and `index1` and `index2` are the respective integer offsets into those strings to begin making the comparison. The `length` parameter is the number of characters to compare. The `ignoreCase` is a `bool` parameter where `true` means to ignore character case and `false` means to make a case-sensitive comparison. `CultureInfo` is a class for specifying localization information.

The `CompareOrdinal()` Method

The `static` `CompareOrdinal()` method compares two strings—str1 (string one) and str2 (string two)—independent of localization. It produces the following integer results:

- `str1 < str2` = negative
- `str1 == str2` = zero
- `str1 > str2` = positive

An empty string, `""`, is always greater than null. Here's an example of how to implement the `CompareOrdinal()` method:

```
int intResult;
string str1 = "string 1";
string str2 = "string 2";

intResult = String.CompareOrdinal(str2, str1);

Console.WriteLine("String.CompareOrdinal({0}, {1}) = {2}\n",
  str2, str1, intResult);
```

The `CompareOrdinal()` method has the following overload:

- `CompareOrdinal(str1, index1, str2, index2, length)`

In this overload, `str1` and `str2` are the strings to be compared, and `index1` and `index2` are the respective integer offsets into those strings to begin making the comparison. The `length` parameter is the number of characters to compare.

The `Concat()` Method

The `static` `Concat()` method creates a new string from one or more input strings or objects. Here's an example of how to implement the `Concat()` method using two strings:

```
int intResult;
string str1 = "string 1";
string str2 = "string 2";

stringResult = String.Concat(str1, str2);

Console.WriteLine("String.Concat({0}, {1}) = {2}\n",
  str1, str2, stringResult);
```

The example shows the `Concat()` method accepting two string parameters. The result is a single string with the second string concatenated to the first. The `Concat()` method has the following overloads:

- `Concat (Object)`

- `Concat (Object[])`
- `Concat (String[])`
- `Concat (Object, Object)`
- `Concat (Object, Object, Object)`
- `Concat (string, string, string)`
- `Concat (string, string, string, string)`

In these overloads, all object parameters are converted to `String` objects before concatenation. The elements of the array parameters are concatenated in order to create a single string. The other overloads, with multiple parameters, form a single `String` by concatenating each of the parameters in the order they appear.

The `Copy()` Method

The `static` `Copy()` method returns a copy of a String. Here's an example of how to implement the `Copy()` method:

```
string stringResult;
string str1 = "string 1";

stringResult = String.Copy(str1);

Console.WriteLine("String.Copy({0}) = {1}\n",
  str1, stringResult);
```

The `Copy()` method makes a copy of `str1`. The result is a copy of `str1` placed in `stringResult`.

The `Equals()` Method

The `static` `Equals()` method determines whether two strings are equal, returning a `bool` value of true when they are equal and a `bool` value of false when they're not. Here's an example of how to implement the `Equals()` method:

```
bool boolResult;
string str1 = "string 1";
string str2 = "string 2";

boolResult = String.Equals(str1, str2);

Console.WriteLine("String.Equals({0}, {1}) = {2}\n",
  str1, str2, boolResult);
```

The `Equals()` method accepts the two string parameters. The result is a `bool` that will evaluate to `false` because `str1` and `str2` are not the same value.

The `Format()` Method

The static `Format()` method returns a textual representation of an object after applying a specified format string. Here's an example of how to implement the `Format()` method:

```
string stringResult;
string str1 = "string 1";
string str2 = "string 2";

String formatString = "{0,15}";

stringResult = String.Format(formatString, str2);

Console.WriteLine("String.Format({0}, {1}) = [{2}]\n",
  formatString, str2, stringResult);
```

This example shows the `Format()` method accepting two string parameters. The first parameter is a format string that will be applied to the second parameter. The result is a 15-character string with the text right-aligned and padded to the left with spaces. The `Format()` method has the following overloads:

- `Format (string, Object[])`
- `Format (IFormatProvider, string, Object[])`
- `Format (string, Object, Object)`
- `Format (string, Object, Object, Object)`

In these overloads, the string parameter specifies the format string. Whether an array or individual object, each `Object` parameter is formatted according to its corresponding placeholder in the format string. The `IFormatProvider` is an interface that is implemented by an object for managing formatting.

The `Intern()` Method

The static `Intern()` method returns a reference to a string in the string intern pool. A C# program maintains a string intern pool where literal and constant strings are automatically placed. When strings are built on-the-fly (or programmatically), they are separate objects and are not intern pool members. The `Intern()` method will accept a parameter with a string that was programmatically constructed and return a reference to the identical string from the intern pool. Here's an example of how to implement the `Intern()` method:

```
string str1      = "string1";
String objStr1    = String.Concat("string", "1");
String internedStr1 = String.Intern(objStr1);
```

```
Console.WriteLine(
  "(object)objStr1 == (object)str1 is {0}\n",
  ((object)objStr1 == (object)str1));

Console.WriteLine(
  "(object)internedStr1 == (object)str1 is {0}\n",
  ((object)internedStr1 == (object)str1));
```

The example shows the effects of using the `Intern()` method on a programmatically constructed string. The `Concat()` method constructs a string on-the-fly, `objStr1`, that is identical in value to `str1`. `objStr1` is a separate object and not a member of the intern string pool. The `Intern()` method returns a reference to a value in the intern pool that is identical to the value of `objStr1` (values are the same, but references are still different). The first `WriteLine()` method will return the value `false` because `objStr1` refers to a separate object, and `str1` refers to a literal string that was added to the intern pool. The second `WriteLine()` method returns `true` because `internedStr1` received a reference to the intern pool, which is the same as `str1` (references are the same).

The `IsInterned()` Method

The `static` `IsInterned()` method returns a reference to an interned string if it is a member of the intern pool. Otherwise, it returns `null`. Here's an example of how to implement the `IsInterned()` method:

```
stringResult = String.IsInterned(internedStr1);

Console.WriteLine("String.IsInterned({0}) = {1}\n",
  internedStr1, stringResult);
```

The example shows the `IsInterned()` method determining whether a string is in the intern pool. Assuming that the `internedStr1` string parameter has been interned, the `IsInterned()` method will return a reference to that string in the intern pool.

> **Note**
>
> The intern pool is a system table that eliminates duplication by allowing multiple references to the same constant string when the strings are identical. This saves system memory. The intern-related methods of the string class enable a program to determine if a string is interned and to place it in the intern pool to take advantage of the associate memory optimizations.

The Join() Method

The static Join() method concatenates strings with a specified separator between them. Here's an example of how to implement the Join() method:

```
string stringResult;
string str1 = "string 1";
string str2 = "string 2";

String[] strArr = new String[] { str1, str2 };

stringResult = String.Join(",", strArr);

Console.WriteLine(
  "String.Join(\",\", [str1 and str2]) = {0}\n",
  stringResult);
```

This example shows how to create a comma-separated list of strings with the Join() method. The first parameter of the Join() method specifies the separator character, a comma in this case. The second parameter is an array of strings that will be separated, resulting in a string where each member of the array is separated by the separation character. The Join() method has the following overload:

- Join(string, stringArray, int1, int2)

In the preceding overload, string is the separator character and stringArray is an array of strings to be separated. The next two parameters are the beginning array element to start separating (that is, the first array element to be followed by the separation character) and the number of elements in the array to be separated.

Instance Methods

Instance String methods act upon an existing string object. Often referred to as this String, the instance acted upon by these methods is the same instance that is invoking the method.

The Clone() Method

The Clone() method returns this String. Here's an example of how to implement the Clone() method:

```
String stringResult;
string str1 = "string 1";

stringResult = (String)str1.Clone();

Console.WriteLine("(String){0}.Clone() = {1}\n",
  str1, stringResult);
```

The example demonstrates how the `Clone()` method returns a reference to the same instance it is invoked upon. Since the `Clone()` method returns an `Object` reference, the return value must be cast to a `String` before assignment to `stringResult`.

The `CompareTo()` Method

The `CompareTo()` method compares the value of `this` instance with a string. It produces the following integer results:

- `this < string` = negative
- `this == string` = zero
- `this > string` = positive
- `string is null` = 1

An empty string, `""`, is always greater than `null`. If both `this` and `string` are null, then they are equal (zero result). Here's an example of how to implement the `CompareTo()` method:

```
int intResult;
string str1 = "string 1";
string str2 = "string 2";

intResult = str1.CompareTo(str2);

Console.WriteLine("{0}.CompareTo({1}) = {2}\n",
  str1, str2, intResult);
```

The `CompareTo()` method has the following overload:

- `CompareTo(Object)`

In this overload, the `Object` parameter must be a `String`.

The `CopyTo()` Method

The `CopyTo()` method copies a specified number of characters from `this String` to an array of characters. Here's an example of how to implement the `CopyTo()` method:

```
string str1 = "string 1";

char[] charArr = new char[str1.Length];

str1.CopyTo(0, charArr, 0, str1.Length);

Console.WriteLine(
  "{0}.CopyTo(0, charArr, 0, str1.Length) = ",
  str1);
```

```
foreach(char character in charArr)
{
  Console.Write("{0} ", character);
}
Console.WriteLine("\n");
```

This example shows the `CopyTo()` method filling a character array. It copies each character from `str1` into `charArr`, beginning at position 0 and continuing for the length of `str1`. The `foreach` loop iterates through each element of `charArr`, printing the results.

The `EndsWith()` Method

The `EndsWith()` method determines if a String suffix matches a specified String. Here's an example of how to implement the `EndsWith()` method:

```
bool boolResult;
string str1 = "string 1";
string str2 = "string 2";

boolResult = str1.EndsWith("2");

Console.WriteLine("{0}.EndsWith(\"2\") = {1}\n",
  str1, boolResult);
```

In this case, the `EndsWith()` method checks to see if `str1` ends with the number 2. The result is `false` because `str1` ends with the number 1.

The `Equals()` Method

The `static Equals()` method determines whether two strings are equal, returning a `bool` value of true when they are equal and a `bool` value of false when they're not. Here's an example of how to implement the `Equals()` method:

```
int intResult;
string str1 = "string 1";
string str2 = "string 2";

boolResult = str1.Equals(str2);

Console.WriteLine("{0}.Equals({1}) = {2}\n",
  str1, str2, boolResult);
```

In this example the `Equals()` method accepts one string parameter. Since `str1` has a different value than `str2`, the return value is `false`. The `Equals()` method has a single instance overload:

- `Compare(Object)`

In the overload, the `Object` parameter must be a `String`.

The `GetEnumerator()` Method

The `GetEnumerator()` method returns a `CharacterEnumerator` for `this String`. The `foreach` statement uses `IEnumerator` to iterate through a collection. The `CharacterEnumerator`, returned by this method, is an `IEnumerator`. Here's an example of how to implement the `GetEnumerator()` method:

```
string str1 = "string 1";

CharEnumerator charEnum = str1.GetEnumerator();

Console.WriteLine("charEnum is IEnumerator: {0}",
  charEnum is IEnumerator);
```

The `CharacterEnumerator` inherits from the `System.Collections.IEnumerator` interface. This is why the value returned from the `charEnum is IEnumerator` expression in the `Console.WriteLine()` method will be true.

The `IndexOf()` Method

The `IndexOf()` method returns the position of a string or characters within `this String`. When the character or string is not found, `IndexOf()` returns –1. Here's an example of how to implement the `IndexOf()` method:

```
int intResult;
string str1 = "string1";

intResult = str1.IndexOf('1');

Console.WriteLine("str1.IndexOf('1'): {0}", intResult);
```

The return value of this operation is 6 because that's the zero-based position within `str1` that the character '1' occurs. The `IndexOf()` method has the following overloads:

- `IndexOf(char[])`
- `IndexOf(string)`
- `IndexOf(char, beginInt)`
- `IndexOf(char[],beginInt)`
- `IndexOf(string, beginInt)`
- `IndexOf(char, beginInt, endInt)`
- `IndexOf(char[],beginInt, endInt)`
- `IndexOf(string, beginInt, endInt)`

In these overloads, `char[]` parameters return the first instance of any character in the char array, and string parameters specify that the first instance of that string should be searched for. The `beginInt` parameter means to start searching at that index within `this String`, and the `endInt` means to stop searching at that position within `this String`.

The `Insert()` Method

The `Insert()` method returns a string where a specified string is placed in a specified position of `this String`. All characters at and to the right of the insertion point are pushed right to make room for the inserted string. Here's an example of how to implement the `Insert()` method:

```
string stringResult;
string str2 = "string2";

stringResult = str2.Insert(6, "1");

Console.WriteLine("str2.Insert(6, \"1\"): {0}",
  stringResult);
```

This example places a `"1"` into `str2`, producing `"string12"`.

The `LastIndexOf()` Method

The `LastIndexOf()` method returns the position of the last occurrence of a string or characters within `this String`. Here's an example of how to implement the `LastIndexOf()` method:

```
int intResult;
string stateString = "Mississippi";

intResult = stateString.LastIndexOf('s');

Console.WriteLine("stateString.LastIndexOf('s'): {0}",
  intResult);
```

The preceding example shows how to use the `LastIndexOf()` method to find the position of the last occurrence of the letter 's' in `stateString`. The zero-based result is 6. The `LastIndexOf()` method has the following overloads:

- `LastIndexOf(char[])`
- `LastIndexOf(string)`
- `LastIndexOf(char, beginInt)`
- `LastIndexOf(char[],beginInt)`
- `LastIndexOf(string, beginInt)`
- `LastIndexOf(char, beginInt, endInt)`
- `LastIndexOf(char[],beginInt, endInt)`
- `LastIndexOf(string, beginInt, endInt)`

In these overloads, `char[]` parameters return the last instance of any character in the `char` array, and string parameters specify that the last instance of that string should be searched for. The `beginInt` parameter means to start searching at that index within `this String`, and the `endInt` means to stop searching at that position within `this String`.

The `PadLeft()` Method

The `PadLeft()` method right aligns the characters of a string and pads on the left with spaces (by default) or a specified character. Here's an example of how to implement the `Equals()` method:

```
string stringResult;
string str1 = "string 1";

stringResult = str1.PadLeft(15);

Console.WriteLine("str1.PadLeft(15): [{0}]",
  stringResult);
```

In this example the `PadLeft()` method creates a 15-character string with the original string right aligned and filled to the left with space characters. The `PadLeft()` method has the following overload:

- `PadLeft(int, char)`

It accepts an integer specifying the number of characters for the new string and a char parameter for the padding character.

The `PadRight()` Method

The `PadRight()` method left aligns the characters of a string and pads on the right with spaces (by default) or a specified character. Here's an example of how to implement the `PadRight()` method:

```
string stringResult;
string str1 = "string 1";

stringResult = str1.PadRight(15, '*');

Console.WriteLine("str1.PadRight(15, '*'): [{0}]",
  stringResult);
```

The example shows the `PadRight()` method creating a 15-character string with the original string left aligned and filled to the right with '*' characters. The `PadRight()` method has the following overload:

- `PadRight(int)`

It accepts an integer specifying the number of characters for the new string, and it defaults to a space for the padding character.

The `Remove()` Method

The `Remove()` method deletes a specified number of characters from a position in `this String`. Here's an example of how to implement the `Remove()` method:

```
string stringResult;
string str2 = "string2";

stringResult = str2.Remove(3, 3);

Console.WriteLine("str2.Remove(3, 3): {0}",
  stringResult);
```

This example shows the `Remove()` method deleting the fourth, fifth, and sixth characters from `str2`. The first parameter is the zero-based starting position to begin deleting, and the second parameter is the number of characters to delete. The result is "str2", where the "ing" was removed from the original string.

The `Replace()` Method

The `Replace()` method replaces all occurrences of a character or string with a new character or string, respectively. Here's an example of how to implement the `Replace()` method:

```
int intResult;
string str2 = "string 2";

stringResult = str2.Replace('2', '5');

Console.WriteLine("str2.Replace('2', '5'): {0}",
stringResult);
```

In this example the `Replace()` method accepts two character parameters. The first parameter is the char to be replaced, and the second parameter is the char that will replace the first. The `Replace()` method has the following overload:

- `Replace(string, string)`

In this overload, all occurrences of the first string are replaced by the second string.

The `Split()` Method

The `Split()` method extracts individual strings separated by a specified set of characters and places each of those strings into a string array. Here's an example of how to implement the `Split()` method:

```
String csvString = "one, two, three";

string[] stringArray = csvString.Split(new char[] {','});

foreach( string strItem in stringArray )
{
  Console.WriteLine("Item: {0}", strItem);
}
```

The example shows the `Split()` method extracting strings that are separated by commas. The individual strings "one", " two", and " three" are placed into a different index of `stringArray`. Notice the spaces before the strings " two" and " three"; that is how the `Split()` method preserves white space. The `Split()` method has the following overload:

- `Split(char[], int)`

In this overload, `char[]` is an array of characters used as separators, and `int` is the number of strings to place into the resulting array.

The StartsWith() Method

The `StartsWith()` method determines if a `String` prefix matches a specified `String`. Here's an example of how to implement the `StartsWith()` method:

```
bool boolResult;
string str1 = "string 1";

boolResult = str1.StartsWith("Str");

Console.WriteLine("str1.StartsWith(\"Str\"): {0}",
  boolResult);
```

In this case, the `StartsWith()` method checks to see if `str1` begins with the "Str". The result is `false` because `str1` begins with "str", where the first character is lowercase.

The SubString() Method

The `SubString()` method retrieves a substring at a specified location from `this String`. Here's an example of how to implement the `SubString()` method:

```
string stringResult;
string str1 = "string1";

stringResult = str1.Substring(3);

Console.WriteLine("str1.Substring(3): {0}",
stringResult);
```

The result of this example is "ing1". The `SubString()` method has the following overload:

- `SubString (int, int)`

The first `int` is the zero-based position to begin extracting the substring from, and the second parameter is the number of characters to get.

The `ToCharArray()` Method

The `ToCharArray()` method copies the characters from `this String` into a character array. Here's an example of how to implement the `ToCharArray()` method:

```
int intResult;
string str1 = "string1";

char[] characterArray = str1.ToCharArray();

foreach( char character in charArr )
{
  Console.WriteLine("Char: {0}", character);
}
```

The `ToCharArray()` method has the following overload:

- `ToCharArray(int, int)`

The first int specifies the beginning of a substring to copy to the character array, and the second parameter indicates how many characters to move.

The `ToLower()` Method

The `ToLower()` method returns a copy of `this string` converted to lowercase characters. Here's an example of how to implement the `ToLower()` method:

```
string stringResult;
string ucString = "UpperCaseString";

stringResult = ucString.ToLower();

Console.WriteLine("ucString.ToLower(): {0}",
  stringResult);
```

The result of this example converts "UpperCaseString" to "uppercasestring". The `ToLower()` method has the following overload:

- `ToLower(CultureInfo)`

`CultureInfo` is a class for specifying localization information.

The ToUpper() Method

The ToUpper() method returns a copy of this String converted to uppercase characters. Here's an example of how to implement the ToUpper() method:

```
string stringResult;
string str1 = "string1";

stringResult = str1.ToUpper();

Console.WriteLine("str1.ToUpper(): {0}",
  stringResult);
```

In this example, the result converts "string1" to "STRING1". The ToUpper() method has the following overload:

- ToUpper(CultureInfo)

CultureInfo is a class for specifying localization information.

The Trim() Method

The Trim() method removes whitespace or a specified set of characters from the beginning and ending of this String. Here's an example of how to implement the Trim() method:

```
string stringResult;
string trimString = "  nonwhitespace  ";

stringResult = trimString.Trim();

Console.WriteLine("trimString.Trim(): [{0}]",
  stringResult);
```

The example shows the Trim() method being used to remove all the whitespace from the beginning and end of trimString. The result is "nonwhitespace", with no spaces on either side. The Trim() method has the following overload:

- Trim(char[])

In this overload, char[] is an array of characters that are trimmed from the beginning and end of a string.

The TrimEnd() Method

The TrimEnd() method removes a specified set of characters from the end of this String. Here's an example of how to implement the TrimEnd() method:

```
string stringResult;
string trimString = "  nonwhitespace  ";
```

```
stringResult = trimString.TrimEnd(new char[] {' '});

Console.WriteLine("trimString.TrimEnd(): [{0}]",
  stringResult);
```

In this example the `TrimEnd()` method removes all the whitespace from the end of `trimString`. The result is " nonwhitespace", with no spaces on the right side.

The `TrimStart()` Method

The `Trim()` method removes whitespace or a specified set of characters from the beginning of `this String`. Here's an example of how to implement the `Trim()` method:

```
string stringResult;
string trimString = "  nonwhitespace  ";

stringResult = trimString.TrimStart(new char[] {' '});

Console.WriteLine("trimString.TrimStart(): [{0}]",
  stringResult);
```

Here, the `TrimStart()` method removes all the whitespace from the beginning of `trimString`. The result is "nonwhitespace", with no spaces on the left side.

Properties and Indexers

The `String` class has a single property, `Length`, and an indexer.

The `Length` Property

The `Length` property returns the number of characters in a `String`. Here's an example of how to implement the `Length` property:

```
int intResult;
string str1 = "string1";

intResult = str1.Length;

Console.WriteLine("str1.Length: {0}",
  intResult);
```

The example shows the `Length` property being used to get the number of characters in `str1`. The result is 7.

The `String` Indexer

The `String` indexer returns a character within the string at a specified location. Here's an example of how to implement the `String` indexer:

```
char charResult;
string str1 = "string 1";

charResult = str1[3];

Console.WriteLine("str1[3]: {0}",
  charResult);
```

In this example, the indexer extracts the third character from a zero-based count on `str1`. The result is the character 'i'.

The `StringBuilder` Class

For direct manipulation of a string, use the `StringBuilder` class. It's the best solution when a lot of work needs to be done to change a string. It's more efficient for manipulation operations because, unlike a `String` object, it doesn't incur the overhead involved in creating a new object on every method call. The `StringBuilder` class is a member of the `System.Text` namespace.

Tip

A `String` instantiates and returns a new object when its contents are modified. It's a good idea to consider using a `StringBuilder` for string modifications to avoid the overhead associated with additional instantiations of modified string objects.

Instance Methods

The `StringBuilder` class doesn't have static methods. All of its methods operate on the instance they're invoked from. The invoking object is referred to in following sections as `this StringBuilder`.

The `Append()` Method

The `Append()` method adds a typed object to `this StringBuilder`. Here's an example of how to implement the `Append()` method:

```
StringBuilder myStringBuilder;
myStringBuilder = new StringBuilder("Original");

myStringBuilder.Append("Appended");

Console.WriteLine(
  "myStringBuilder.Append(\"Appended\"): {0}",
  myStringBuilder);
```

This example shows how to append one string to another with the `Append()` method. The result is "OriginalAppended". The `Append()` method has the following overloads:

- `Append(bool)`
- `Append(byte)`
- `Append(char)`
- `Append(char[])`
- `Append(decimal)`
- `Append(double)`
- `Append(short)`
- `Append(int)`
- `Append(long)`
- `Append(Object)`
- `Append(sbyte)`
- `Append(float)`
- `Append(ushort)`
- `Append(uint)`
- `Append(ulong)`
- `Append(char, int)`
- `Append(char[], int, int)`
- `Append(string, int, int)`

In these overloads, each type is converted to its string representation and appended to `this StringBuilder`. The `Append(char, int)` overload appends a specified number, `int`, of `char` to `this StringBuilder`. In the last two overloads, the first `int` specifies the beginning character of either the `char[]` or `string` to start appending, and the second `int` specifies the number of characters to append.

The `AppendFormat()` Method

The `AppendFormat()` method can replace multiple format specifications with a properly formatted value. Here's an example of how to implement the `AppendFormat()` method:

```
StringBuilder myStringBuilder;
myStringBuilder = new StringBuilder("Original");

myStringBuilder.AppendFormat("{0,10}", "Appended");

Console.WriteLine(
```

```
"myStringBuilder.AppendFormat(\"{0,10}\",\"Appended\"): {0}",
myStringBuilder);
```

This example uses the `AppendFormat()` method to format the `"Appended"` string to 10 characters and then append it to `myStringBuilder`. The result is “Original Appended”, with two spaces between words because “Appended” was formatted to 10 characters. The `AppendFormat()` method has the following overloads:

- `AppendFormat(string, Object[])`
- `AppendFormat(IformatProvider, string, Object)`
- `AppendFormat(string, Object, Object)`
- `AppendFormat(string, Object, Object, Object)`

In these overloads, the `string` parameter is the format specification. The `Object` parameters are the object(s) upon which to apply formatting. The `IFormatProvider` is an interface that is implemented by an object to manage formatting.

The `EnsureCapacity()` Method

The `EnsureCapacity()` method guarantees that a `StringBuilder` will have a specified minimal size. Here’s an example of how to implement the `EnsureCapacity()` method:

```
StringBuilder myStringBuilder;
int capacity;
myStringBuilder = new StringBuilder();

capacity = myStringBuilder.EnsureCapacity(129);

Console.WriteLine(
  "myStringBuilder.EnsureCapacity(129): {0}",
  capacity);
```

The example shows the `EnsureCapacity()` method guaranteeing that `myStringBuilder` will have at least a 129-character capacity. The result will have an actual capacity setting of 256, because, interestingly, the capacity is set to the lowest power of two greater than the specified capacity. Setting the minimum capacity to 258, for instance, results in an actual capacity setting of 512.

The `Equals()` Method

The `Equals()` method compares a given `StringBuilder` to `this StringBuilder`. It returns true when both `StringBuilders` are equal, and false otherwise. Here’s an example of how to implement the `EnsureCapacity ()` method:

```
StringBuilder myStringBuilder;
StringBuilder anotherStringBuilder;
```

```
bool boolResult;
myStringBuilder    = new StringBuilder("my string builder");
anotherStringBuilder = new StringBuilder("another string builder");

boolResult = myStringBuilder.Equals(anotherStringBuilder);

Console.WriteLine(
  "myStringBuilder.Equals(anotherStringBuilder): {0}",
  boolResult);
```

The `Equals()` method in this example compares two `StringBuilder` objects. Since their values are different, the `Equals()` method returns `false`.

The `Insert()` Method

The `Insert()` method places a specified object into `this StringBuilder` at a specified location. Here's an example of how to implement the `Insert()` method:

```
StringBuilder myStringBuilder;
myStringBuilder = new StringBuilder("one, three");

myStringBuilder.Insert(3, ", two");

Console.WriteLine(
  "myStringBuilder.Insert(3, \", two\"): {0}",
  myStringBuilder);
```

The example shows how to insert a string into a StringBuilder. The original string, "one, three" becomes "one, two, three". The `Insert()` method has the following overloads:

- `Insert(int, bool)`
- `Insert(int, byte)`
- `Insert(int, char)`
- `Insert(int, char[])`
- `Insert(int, decimal)`
- `Insert(int, double)`
- `Insert(int, short)`
- `Insert(int, int)`
- `Insert(int, long)`
- `Insert(int, Object)`
- `Insert(int, sbyte)`
- `Insert(int, float)`
- `Insert(int, ushort)`

- `Insert(int, uint)`
- `Insert(int, ulong)`
- `Insert(int, string, countInt)`
- `Insert(int, char[], beginInt, numberInt)`

In the overloads, each type is converted to its string representation and inserted into `this StringBuilder` at the position specified by `int`. The `countInt` specifies the number of strings to insert at `int` position. The `beginInt` and `numberInt` parameters indicate, respectively, where in `char[]` to begin using characters to insert, and `numberInt` indicates how many items from `char[]` to insert.

The `Remove()` Method

The `Remove()` method deletes a specified span of characters from `this StringBuilder`. Here's an example of how to implement the `Remove()` method:

```
StringBuilder myStringBuilder;
myStringBuilder = new StringBuilder("Jane X. Doe");

myStringBuilder.Remove(4, 3);

Console.WriteLine(
  "myStringBuilder.Remove(4, 3): {0}",
  myStringBuilder);
```

As the example shows, the first parameter is the zero-based position to begin removing characters, and the second parameter is the number of characters to remove. Removing three characters transforms "Jane X. Doe" into "Jane Doe".

The `Replace()` Method

The `Replace()` method replaces a specified set of characters with another. Here's an example of how to implement the `Replace()` method:

```
StringBuilder myStringBuilder;
myStringBuilder = new StringBuilder("Jane X. Doe");

myStringBuilder.Replace('X', 'B');

Console.WriteLine(
  "myStringBuilder.Replace('X', 'B'): {0}",
  myStringBuilder);
```

This example shows the `Replace()` method accepting two string parameters. The first is the character to be replaced, and the second parameter is the character that will replace the first. The result is that "Jane X. Doe" is transformed to "Jane B. Doe". The `Replace()` method has the following overloads:

- `Replace(string, string)`
- `Replace(char, char, beginInt, numberInt)`
- `Replace(string, string, beginInt, numberInt)`

In these overloads, a second `string` parameter will replace the first, and a second `char` parameter will replace the first `char` parameter. The `beginInt` parameter references the position in `this StringBuilder` to begin replacement, and the `numberInt` indicates the offset from `beginInt` of where to stop replacing.

The `ToString()` Method

The `ToString()` method converts `this StringBuilder` to a string. Here's an example of how to implement the `ToString()` method:

```
StringBuilder myStringBuilder;
string stringResult;
myStringBuilder = new StringBuilder("my string");

stringResult = myStringBuilder.ToString();

Console.WriteLine(
  "myStringBuilder.ToString(): {0}",
  stringResult);
```

The `ToString()` method has the following overload:

- `ToString(beginInt, numberInt)`

In the overload, `beginInt` is the starting position in `this StringBuilder` to start extracting characters, and `numberInt` is the number of characters to convert.

Properties and Indexers

The `String` class has a few properties and an indexer.

The `Capacity` Property

The `Capacity` property sets and returns the number of characters `this StringBuilder` can hold. Here's an example of how to implement the `Capacity` property:

```
StringBuilder myStringBuilder;
int intResult;
myStringBuilder = new StringBuilder("my string");

intResult = myStringBuilder.Capacity;
```

```
Console.WriteLine(
  "myStringBuilder.Capacity: {0}",
  intResult);
```

The result of this example is 16.

The `Length` Property

The `StringBuilder` `Length` property returns the number of characters in a `String`. Here's an example of how to implement the `Length` property:

```
StringBuilder myStringBuilder;
int intResult;
myStringBuilder = new StringBuilder("my string");

intResult = myStringBuilder.Length;

Console.WriteLine(
  "myStringBuilder.Length: {0}",
  intResult);
```

The result of this example is 9.

The `MaxCapacity` Property

The `MaxCapacity` property is a read-only property that returns the maximum number of characters `this` `StringBuilder` can hold. Here's an example of how to implement the `MaxCapacity` property:

```
StringBuilder myStringBuilder;
int intResult;
myStringBuilder = new StringBuilder("my string");

intResult = myStringBuilder.MaxCapacity;

Console.WriteLine(
  "myStringBuilder.MaxCapacity: {0}",
  intResult);
```

The result of this example is 2147483647.

The Indexer

The indexer permits reading and writing of a specified character at a certain position. Here's an example of how to implement the `Indexer` property:

```
StringBuilder myStringBuilder;
char charResult;
myStringBuilder = new StringBuilder("my string");

charResult = myStringBuilder[1];
```

```
Console.WriteLine(
  "myStringBuilder[1]: {0}",
  charResult);
```

The return value in this case is 'y'.

String Formatting

When performing a `Console.WriteLine()` method call, any format strings default to string type unless special formatting is applied. Often it's necessary to perform more sophisticated formatting on various types such as numbers, strings, and dates.

Numeric Formatting

C# has several formatting characters for numeric formatting. Table 25.1 shows the C# number format specifiers.

TABLE 25.1 Numeric Format Specifiers

Format Character	*Description*
`C` or `c`	Currency
`D` or `d`	Decimal
`E` or `e`	Scientific/exponential
`F` or `f`	Fixed point
`G` or `g`	General (can be E or F format)
`N` or `n`	Number
`R` or `r`	Roundtrip (convertible to string and back)
`X` or `x`	Hexadecimal

The following example shows how to use numeric formatting:

```
Console.WriteLine("Hex: {0:x}", 255);
```

This example converts the integer `255` to hexadecimal notation. The result is `hex ff`. The value is in lowercase because a lowercase format character was used. Results are in uppercase when uppercase format characters are used.

Picture Formatting

It's often necessary to have more control over the format of output beyond default formatting or a simple numeric formatting character. In these cases, picture formatting will help present output exactly as desired. Table 25.2 shows the picture formatting characters.

TABLE 25.2 Picture Format Characters

Format Character	*Description*
`0`	Zero placeholder
`#`	Display digit placeholder
`.`	Decimal point
`,`	Group separator/multiplier
`%`	Percent
`E+0`, `E-0`, `e+0`, `e-0`	Exponent notation
`\`	Literal character
`'ABC'` or "ABC"	Literal string
`;`	Section separator

The following example shows how to use picture formatting:

```
Console.WriteLine("Million: {0:$#,#.00}", 1000000);
```

This example formats the number to make it appear as currency. (The `C` number format character could have been used, but it wouldn't have served the purpose of this example.) The result of this formatting produces "$1,000,000.00". The `$` sign is placed into the output at the position it appears. The `#` symbol holds a place for a number before and after the comma. The `','` character causes a comma to be placed between every three digits of the output. The decimal point will be placed to the right of the whole number. To get the cents portion to appear, two zeros are put after the decimal point in the format specifier. Had these been `#` symbols, nothing would have appeared after the decimal point.

Regular Expressions

Regular expressions provide the capability to manipulate and search text efficiently. The `System.Text.RegularExpressions` namespace contains a set of classes that enable regular expression operations in C# programs. Listing 25.1 shows the code for a program similar to `grep` (Global Regular Expression Print) expressions:

LISTING 25.1 Regular Expressions

```
using System;
using System.Text.RegularExpressions;
using System.IO;

class lrep
{
  static int Main(string[] args)
  {
    if (args.Length < 2)
    {
      Console.WriteLine("Wrong number of args!");
      return 1;
    }

    Regex re = new Regex(args[0]);

    StreamReader sr = new StreamReader(args[1]);

    string nextLine = sr.ReadLine();

    while (nextLine != null)
    {
      Match myMatch = re.Match(nextLine);

      if (myMatch.Success)
      {
        Console.WriteLine("{0}: {1}", args[1], nextLine);
      }

      nextLine = sr.ReadLine();
    }
    sr.Close();

    return 0;
  }
}
```

Note

Global Regular Expression Print (grep), written by Doug McIlroy, is a popular Unix utility. It allows you to perform a command line search for regular expressions within the text of one or more files.

The Listing 25.1 program is called `lrep`, which stands for Limited Regular Expression Print. It may be limited in features, but because of the built-in regular expression classes, it's very powerful. Here's an example of how to use it:

```
lrep string lrep.cs
```

The first parameter, `lrep`, is the command name of the program. The second parameter, `string`, is the regular expression. It happens to be a normal string without anything special, but can also take the same set of regular expressions as the `Perl` programming language. The third parameter, `lrep.cs`, is the filename to search for the regular expression. Here's the output:

```
lrep.cs:        static int Main(string[] args)
lrep.cs:            string nextLine = sr.ReadLine();
```

Each line of output contains the name of the file that was searched. Following that is the text of the line where the regular expression matched. The next example shows how the regular expression is set in the program:

```
    Regex re = new Regex(args[0]);
```

A regular expression is created by instantiating a `Regex` object. The following example shows one way to use a regular expression object:

```
      Match myMatch = re.Match(nextLine);
```

The `Match()` method of the `Regex` class is used to determine if a given string contains text that matches a regular expression. This program opens a file, specified in the command line arguments, and reads each line to see if there is a match. By using the `Success` property of the match object, the program can figure out that a match was made. This program writes the positive matching lines to the console, as shown in the output lines.

This program used a late bound matching scheme to achieve its goals. However, a regular expression may be initialized with constants, increasing efficiency through compile time optimization.

Summary

There is a plethora of options available in the way of string manipulation with the system libraries. The `String` class provides basic string handling but has many methods available for returning new strings with various modifications.

For sophisticated string manipulation, use the `StringBuilder` class. It allows modification of the string in the same object without the overhead of creating a new object with each operation.

`Strings` need to be formatted for many processing activities. There are simple number formatting options as well as picture formatting.

A welcome feature of the system libraries is regular expressions. Regular expressions allow powerful string manipulation that is more efficient than either `String` or `StringBuilder` class operations.

`Strings` and `StringBuilders` have various features that make them work well as collection objects. The next chapter, "C# Collections," explains why this is true and provides insight to help understand the internal mechanism of collections.

CHAPTER 26

C# Collections

IN THIS CHAPTER

- Pre-Existing Collections *546*
- Collection Interfaces *552*
- Creating a Collection *553*

Collection classes are data structures in the `System.Collections` namespace. They provide various ways to manage data for a C# program. They can be used in place of arrays for more sophisticated management of a group of object. Some of the more popular collections are those that manage data as dynamically resizable arrays, hashtables, queues, and stacks.

It's easy to use collection classes because they incorporate array-like semantics. This includes indexer access to collection elements and the `IEnumerable` interface for iterating through collection elements.

Pre-Existing Collections

For the greatest amount of flexibility, the `System.Collections` namespace contains several collection classes that can be instantiated and used immediately. These pre-existing classes are designed for a wide variety of computing tasks requiring data structures.

The `ArrayList` Collection

Normal arrays have a fixed size, and once they fill up, you're either stuck or have to craft a work around. The `ArrayList` collection addresses this very problem through its ability to dynamically resize itself on-the-fly. Listing 26.1 shows how to use the `ArrayList` collection.

LISTING 26.1 `ArrayList` Collection Example

```
using System;
using System.Collections;

/// <summary>
///     ArrayList example.
/// </summary>
class ArrayListExample
{
    static void Main(string[] args)
    {
        ArrayList al = new ArrayList(2);

        for (int i=0; i < 6; i++)
        {
            al.Add(i);
            Console.WriteLine("al.Capacity: {0}, al[i]: {1}",
                al.Capacity, al[i]);
        }
    }
}
```

And here's the output:

```
al.Capacity: 2, al[i]: 0
al.Capacity: 2, al[i]: 1
al.Capacity: 4, al[i]: 2
al.Capacity: 4, al[i]: 3
al.Capacity: 8, al[i]: 4
al.Capacity: 8, al[i]: 5
```

Listing 26.1 shows how an `ArrayList` dynamically resizes itself. During instantiation, the `ArrayList` capacity is set to 2. When the `for` loop executes, it adds six new items to the `ArrayList`.

The output shows the effects on the `ArrayList` as each item is added to it. The capacity of the `ArrayList` is automatically increased when the number of items added exceeds its current capacity. Notice how the capacity increases when 2 and 4, the third and fifth items respectively, are added to the `ArrayList`. The capacity is doubled every time the number of items in the `ArrayList` exceeds its current value.

The `BitArray` Collection

C and C++ programmers may have felt cheated when reviewing the C# built-in types and didn't see a way to add bit fields to their structures. This is compensated for, to some degree, by the `BitArray` collection, which is a data structure for managing bit level data. The `BitArray` collection is used in Listing 26.2.

LISTING 26.2 `BitArray` Collection Example

```
using System;
using System.Collections;

/// <summary>
///     BitArray Example.
/// </summary>
class BitArrayExample
{
    static void Main(string[] args)
    {
        BitArray ba = new BitArray(4);

        ba[0] = true;
        ba[1] = false;
        ba[2] = true;

        Console.WriteLine("\nBefore xor...\n");
```

LISTING 26.2 continued

```
        foreach(bool bval in ba)
        {
            Console.WriteLine("BitArray: {0}", bval);
        }

        ba.Xor(new BitArray(new bool[] {true, true, true, true}));

        Console.WriteLine("\nAfter xor...\n");

        foreach(bool bval in ba)
        {
            Console.WriteLine("BitArray: {0}", bval);
        }
    }
}
```

And here's the output:

```
Before xor...

BitArray: True
BitArray: False
BitArray: True
BitArray: False

After xor...

BitArray: False
BitArray: True
BitArray: False
BitArray: True
```

Listing 26.2 shows how to initialize a `BitArray` and call its methods. The `BitArray` is instantiated with a size of `4`. The first three elements are set to `true`, `false`, and `true`, respectively. Notice that the fourth element was not initialized, and therefore is left with the default value of `false`. This is evident by viewing the first four `BitArray` elements in the output.

After initialization, the example calls the `Xor()` method of the `BitArray`. The parameter to the `Xor()` method is a new `BitArray`, and the parameter of the new `BitArray` is a new array of type `bool`. Each element of the `bool` array is set to `true`, which creates a `BitArray` with four `true` elements. When the `Xor()` method is invoked, this causes a toggle effect that flips the value of each `true` bit to `false` and each `false` bit to `true`. This effect can be seen in the last four lines in the output.

The Hashtable Collection

Hashtables are an absolute must for many programming applications. The Hashtable collection fits the bill perfectly. Hashtables work on the principle of key/value pairs. Each value must be added and retrieved with the same unique key. Listing 26.3 shows the use of a Hashtable collection where items are added as key/value pairs.

LISTING 26.3 Hashtable Collection Example

```
using System;
using System.Collections;
/// <summary>
///     Hashtable Example.
/// </summary>
class HashtableExample
{
    static void Main(string[] args)
    {
        Hashtable ht = new Hashtable();

        ht.Add("Hospital",        "555-1234");
        ht.Add("Fire Department", "555-3535");
        ht.Add("Police",          "555-7777");

        Console.WriteLine("Fire Department: {0}",
            ht["Fire Department"]);
    }
}
```

And here's the output:

```
Fire Department: 555-3535
```

The keys, the first parameter of the Add() method, are agency names that could be in a quick reference telephone list. The second parameter to the Add() method is the value, which in this case is the telephone number to the agency identified by the key.

The second argument to the Console.WriteLine() method demonstrates how to obtain values from a Hashtable collection. It uses an indexer with the key for the index. The return value is the value in the Hashtable collection corresponding to that key.

The Queue Collection

The System.collections namespace includes a Queue collection class. This allows first-in, first-out (FIFO) data management operations. The example in Listing 26.4 shows the operation of a Queue collection.

LISTING 26.4 Queue Collection Example

```
using System;
using System.Collections;

/// <summary>
///     Queue Example.
/// </summary>
class QueueExample
{
    static void Main(string[] args)
    {
        Queue q = new Queue();

        q.Enqueue("message 1");
        q.Enqueue("message 2");
        q.Enqueue("message 3");

        Console.WriteLine("First Message: {0}", q.Dequeue());
    }
}
```

And here's the output:

```
First Message: message 1
```

After instantiating the `Queue` class, the program puts three items on the `Queue` with the `Enqueue()` method.

The second parameter of the `Console.WriteLine()` method pulls an item off the `Queue`. Since a `Queue` is FIFO, the `Dequeue()` method pulls off the first item that was placed on the `Queue`, which is the output following Listing 26.4.

The `SortedList` Collection

The `SortedList` collection is much like the `ArrayList` for managing data, with the primary distinction, as its name suggests, that it keeps its data sorted. The example in Listing 26.5 shows how to implement a sorted list of items with the `SortedList` collection.

LISTING 26.5 `SortedList` Collection Example

```
using System;
using System.Collections;
/// <summary>
///     SortedList Example.
/// </summary>
class Class1
```

LISTING 26.5 continued

```
{
    static void Main(string[] args)
    {
        SortedList sl = new SortedList();

        sl.Add("Fire Department", "555-3535");
        sl.Add("Police",          "555-7777");
        sl.Add("Hospital",        "555-1234");

        for(int i=0; i < sl.Count; i++)
        {
            Console.WriteLine("{0}: {1}",
                sl.GetKey(i),
                sl.GetByIndex(i));
        }
    }
}
```

And here's the output:

```
Fire Department: 555-3535
Hospital: 555-1234
Police: 555-7777
```

Three items are added to the `SortedList`, in random order. The `for` loop prints out each item in the sorted list, in order, as the output shows.

The `Stack` Collection

For last-in, first-out (LIFO) operations, use the `Stack` collection. It permits pushing data onto a stack and popping data off the top. Listing 26.6 demonstrates how to implement a program using the `Stack` collection.

LISTING 26.6 `Stack` Collection Example

```
using System;
using System.Collections;

/// <summary>
///     Stack Collection Example.
/// </summary>
class StackExample
{
    static void Main(string[] args)
    {
        Stack st = new Stack();
```

LISTING 26.6 continued

```
        st.Push("widget 1");
        st.Push("widget 2");
        st.Push("widget 3");

        Console.WriteLine("Top of Stack: {0}", st.Pop());
    }
}
```

And here's the output:

```
Top of Stack: widget 3
```

Each item is placed on the stack with the `Push()` method. The second parameter to `Console.WriteLine()` uses the `Pop()` method to obtain the top value on the stack. The output shows that this was the last item pushed onto the stack, illustrating the LIFO nature of a stack.

Collection Interfaces

The collection classes have many methods in common, which make them more predictable and easier to program because of their consistency. This consistency is maintained by the use of specialized collection interfaces. Table 26.1 details the interfaces implemented by collection classes.

TABLE 26.1 Collection Interfaces

Interface Name	*Description*
`ICollection`	Enumerator, size, and synchronization for all collections
`IComparer`	Compares two objects
`IDictionary`	Key/value pair collection
`IDictionaryEnumerator`	Enumerator for `IDictionary`
`IEnumerable`	Gets an enumerator
`IHashCodeProvider`	Obtains a hash code
`IList`	Indexed collection

Collections implement one or more of these collection interfaces. The interface they implement will depend upon the type of collection. For example a `Hashtable` implements `IDictionary`, stating that it implements key/value pair semantics.

Creating a Collection

The predefined collections are nice for a variety of tasks, but ultimately many programmers will want to have their own data structures. For maximum benefit and integration with the language, design your C# data structures as collections.

A List Collection

The `SiteList` class used in earlier chapters had many collection-like features. It was a wannabe collection, and its perseverance throughout the book was so admirable that I decided to design it as a full-fledged collection. Listing 26.7 shows the new full-featured `SiteList` collection in action.

LISTING 26.7 The `SiteList` Collection Class: `WebSites.cs`

```
namespace WebSites
{
    using System;
    using System.Collections;

    /// <summary>
    ///     Describes a single web site.
    /// </summary>
    public class WebSite
    {
        public string siteName;
        public string url;
        public string description;

        public WebSite(string newSite,
                       string newURL,
                       string newDesc)
        {
            siteName    = newSite;
            url         = newURL;
            description = newDesc;
        }

        public override string ToString()
        {
            return siteName +
                   ", "     +
                   url      +
                   ", "     +
                   description;
        }
```

LISTING 26.7 continued

```
        public override bool Equals(object evalString)
        {
            return this.ToString() == evalString.ToString();
        }

        public override int GetHashCode()
        {
            return this.ToString().GetHashCode();
        }
    }

    /// <summary>
    ///     This object holds a collection of WebSites.
    /// </summary>
    public class SiteList : ICollection, IComparer, IEnumerable, IList
    {
        protected ArrayList sites;

        public SiteList()
        {
            sites = new ArrayList();
        }

        // ICollection.Count
        public int Count
        {
            get
            {
                return sites.Count;
            }
        }

        // ICollection.IsSynchronized
        public bool IsSynchronized
        {
            get
            {
                return sites.IsSynchronized;
            }
        }

        // ICollection.SyncRoot
        public object SyncRoot
        {
            get
            {
                return sites.SyncRoot;
            }
        }
```

LISTING 26.7 continued

```
        // ICollection.CopyTo
        public void CopyTo(Array dest, int index)
        {
            sites.CopyTo(dest, index);
        }

        // IComparer.Compare
        public int Compare(object site1, object site2)
        {
            return String.Compare(site1.ToString(),
                                  site2.ToString());
        }

        // IEnumerable.GetEnumerator
        public IEnumerator GetEnumerator()
        {
            Console.WriteLine(
                "SiteList GetEnumerator called.");
            return new SiteEnumerator(sites);
        }

        // IEnumerator class
        class SiteEnumerator : IEnumerator
        {
            ArrayList   sites;
            IEnumerator myEnumerator;

            public SiteEnumerator(ArrayList sites)
            {
                Console.WriteLine(
                    "SiteEnumerator Constructor called.");
                this.sites   = sites;
                myEnumerator = sites.GetEnumerator();
            }

            // IEnumerator.Current
            public object Current
            {
                get
                {
                    Console.WriteLine(
                        "SiteEnumerator Current called.");
                    return myEnumerator.Current;
                }
            }

            // IEnumerator.MoveNext
            public bool MoveNext()
            {
```

LISTING 26.7 continued

```
            Console.WriteLine(
                "SiteEnumerator MoveNext called.");
            return myEnumerator.MoveNext();
        }

        // IEnumerator.Reset
        public void Reset()
        {
            Console.WriteLine(
                "SiteEnumerator Reset called.");
        }
    }

    // IList.IsFixedSize
    public bool IsFixedSize
    {
        get
        {
            return true;
        }
    }

    // IList.IsReadOnly
    public bool IsReadOnly
    {
        get
        {
            return false;
        }
    }

    // IList.Item
    public object this[int index]
    {
        get
        {
            if (index > sites.Count)
                return (WebSite)null;

            return (WebSite) sites[index];
        }
        set
        {
            if ( index < 10 )
                sites.Add(value);
        }
    }

    // IList.Add
```

LISTING 26.7 continued

```
        public int Add(object webSite)
        {
            if ( sites.Count < 10 )
                return sites.Add(webSite);

            return -1;
        }

        // IList.Clear
        public void Clear()
        {
            sites.Clear();
        }

        // IList.Contains
        public bool Contains(object webSite)
        {
            return sites.Contains(webSite);
        }

        // IList.IndexOf
        public int IndexOf(object webSite)
        {
            return sites.IndexOf(webSite);
        }

        // IList.Insert
        public void Insert(int index, object webSite)
        {
            sites.Insert(index, webSite);
        }

        // IList.Remove
        public void Remove(object webSite)
        {
            sites.Remove(webSite);
        }

        // IList.RemoveAt
        public void RemoveAt(int element)
        {
            if ( element < Count )
            {
                sites.RemoveAt(element);
            }
        }
    }
}
```

Listing 26.7 is a member of the `WebSites` namespace, along with the `WebSite` class, which is the object type that the `SiteList` collection holds. As its name suggests, `SiteList` has list semantics and inherits list-related interfaces: `ICollection`, `IComparer`, and `IList`. The `SiteList` class declaration is as follows:

```
public class SiteList : ICollection, IComparer, IEnumerable, IList
```

Implementing the `ICollection` Interface

The `ICollection` interface requires three property implementations: `Count`, `IsSynchronized`, and `SyncRoot`. Each of these properties wraps the internal `sites` object, which is an `ArrayList` collection.

The `Count` property returns the actual number of items stored in the collection. The following code shows implementation of the `ICollection.Count` property:

```
// ICollection.Count
public int Count
{
    get
    {
        return sites.Count;
    }
}
```

The `IsSynchronized` property returns an indication of whether the collection is synchronized. If this property returns `true`, the object may be used safely in multithreaded applications. Here's the implementation of the `ICollection.IsSynchronized` property:

```
// ICollection.IsSynchronized
public bool IsSynchronized
{
    get
    {
        return sites.IsSynchronized;
    }
}
```

The `SyncRoot` property returns a reference to a synchronized version of this collection. Here's an implementation of the `ICollection.SyncRoot` property:

```
// ICollection.SyncRoot
public object SyncRoot
{
    get
    {
        return sites.SyncRoot;
    }
}
```

The `ICollection` interface has a single method, `CopyTo()`. This method copies the contents of this collection to a destination array, beginning at a specified index. Here's an implementation of the `ICollection.CopyTo()` method:

```
// ICollection.CopyTo
public void CopyTo(Array dest, int index)
{
    sites.CopyTo(dest, index);
}
```

Implementing the `IComparer` Interface

The `IComparer` interface has a single method, `Compare()`. The compare method returns the following results:

- `obj1 < obj2` = negative
- `obj1 == obj2` = zero
- `obj1 > obj2` = positive

The following implementation of the `IComparer.Compare()` method uses the `String` class to compare the string representation of two `WebSite` objects:

```
// IComparer.Compare
public int Compare(object site1, object site2)
{
    return String.Compare(site1.ToString(),
                          site2.ToString());
}
```

Implementing the `IEnumerable` Interface

`SiteList` also implements the `IEnumerable` interface, which supports iteration through collection elements. The `foreach` loop works on classes that support the `IEnumerable` interface. The following example shows how to implement `IEnumerable.GetEnumerator()`, the only member of the IEnumerable interface:

```
// IEnumerable.GetEnumerator
public IEnumerator GetEnumerator()
{
    Console.WriteLine(
        "SiteList GetEnumerator called.");
    return new SiteEnumerator(sites);
}
```

The `GetEnumerator()` method in the example returns a `SiteEnumerator` class, which is a nested class implementing the `IEnumerator` interface. The `GetEnumerator()` method instantiates a class implementing `IEnumerator` before returning.

Implementing the IEnumerator Interface

The IEnumerator interface defines the property and methods that are called by a foreach loop to iterate through a collection: Current, MoveNext(), and Reset(). Each of these operates via a position indicator within the collection, which is referred to in following paragraphs as a cursor. The Reset() method sets the cursor to the first element of the collection. The MoveNext() method moves the cursor to the next element in the collection. The Current property returns the object at the cursor. The following example shows the declaration of the nested SiteEnumerator class:

```
class SiteEnumerator : IEnumerator
```

The SiteEnumerator class is initialized by sending it an ArrayList collection. Its constructor keeps a reference of the ArrayList and obtains an IEnumerator by invoking the GetEnumerator() method of the ArrayList. The following example shows the SiteEnumerator constructor and class fields to initialize:

```
ArrayList   sites;
IEnumerator myEnumerator;

public SiteEnumerator(ArrayList sites)
{
    Console.WriteLine(
        "SiteEnumerator Constructor called.");
    this.sites    = sites;
    myEnumerator = sites.GetEnumerator();
}
```

The IEnumerator interface has a read-only Current property that returns a copy of the element at the cursor. Here's an example that shows how to implement the IEnumerator.Current property:

```
// IEnumerator.Current
public object Current
{
    get
    {
        Console.WriteLine(
            "SiteEnumerator Current called.");
        return myEnumerator.Current;
    }
}
```

The MoveNext() method moves the cursor to the next element in the collection. The following example shows how to implement the IEnumerator.MoveNext() method:

```
// IEnumerator.MoveNext
public bool MoveNext()
{
```

```
            Console.WriteLine(
                "SiteEnumerator MoveNext called.");
            return myEnumerator.MoveNext();
        }
```

The `Reset()` method moves the cursor to the first element in the collection. Here's an example of how to implement the `IEnumerator.Reset()` method:

```
        // IEnumerator.Reset
        public void Reset()
        {
            Console.WriteLine(
                "SiteEnumerator Reset called.");
        }
```

Implementing the `IList` Interface

The `IList` interface has several methods, properties, and an indexer, enabling a class to behave as a list collection. Understanding the methods of the `IList` interface helps when working with any type of list collection.

Lists may be a fixed size or change their size dynamically. The `IsFixedSize` property tells which of these features a list has. The following example implements `IList.IsFixedSize` by returning `true` to indicate that this is a fixed-size collection:

```
    // IList.IsFixedSize
    public bool IsFixedSize
    {
        get
        {
            return true;
        }
    }
```

A list may be read-only or read-write. The `IsReadOnly` property tells which of these features a list has. The following example implements `IList.IsReadOnly` by returning `false` to indicate that this list is a read-write collection:

```
    // IList.IsReadOnly
    public bool IsReadOnly
    {
        get
        {
            return false;
        }
    }
```

An essential list member is the indexer, which permits a collection to be used like an array. Here's an example that shows an implementation of the `IList` indexer:

```
// IList Indexer
public object this[int index]
{
    get
    {
        if (index > sites.Count)
            return (WebSite)null;

        return (WebSite) sites[index];
    }
    set
    {
        if ( index < 10 )
            sites.Add(value);
    }
}
```

The `Add()` method adds a new element to a collection. The following example shows how to implement the `IList.Add()` method:

```
// IList.Add
public int Add(object webSite)
{
    if ( sites.Count < 10 )
        return sites.Add(webSite);

    return -1;
}
```

The `Clear()` method empties a collection of all its elements. The following example shows how to implement the `IList.Clear()` method:

```
// IList.Clear
public void Clear()
{
    sites.Clear();
}
```

To determine whether an element is a member of a list, use the `Contains()` method. It returns a value of `true` if the element is a member of the list. Here's how to implement the `IList.Contains()` method:

```
// IList.Contains
public bool Contains(object webSite)
{
    return sites.Contains(webSite);
}
```

When it's necessary to find the position of an element in a list, the `IndexOf()` method can be used. The following example shows how to implement the `IList.IndexOf()` method:

```
// IList.IndexOf
public int IndexOf(object webSite)
{
    return sites.IndexOf(webSite);
}
```

The difference between the `Add()` and `Insert()` methods is that the `Insert()` method allows an element to be added to a specific position within the list. Here's an example of how to implement the `IList.Insert()` method:

```
// IList.Insert
public void Insert(int index, object webSite)
{
    sites.Insert(index, webSite);
}
```

The `Remove()` method removes a specified element from a collection, regardless of its position. The following example shows how to implement the `IList.Remove()` method:

```
// IList.Remove
public void Remove(object webSite)
{
    sites.Remove(webSite);
}
```

The `RemoveAt()` method removes an element from a specified position of a list, regardless of what the element is. Here's an example of implementing the `IList.RemoveAt()` method:

```
// IList.RemoveAt
public void RemoveAt(int element)
{
    if ( element < Count )
    {
        sites.RemoveAt(element);
    }
}
```

Using the `SiteList` Collection

The `SiteList` collection can now be used just like any other list collection, as demonstrated in Listing 26.8.

LISTING 26.8 Collection Test Driver: `SiteManager.cs`

```
using System;
using WebSites;

/// <summary>
///     Uses the SiteList Collection.
```

LISTING 26.8 continued

```
/// </summary>
class SiteManager
{
    SiteList sites = new SiteList();

    public SiteManager()
    {
        sites = new WebSites.SiteList();
        sites[sites.Count] = new WebSite(
            "Joe",
            "http://www.mysite.com",
            "Great Site!");
        sites[sites.Count] = new WebSite(
            "Don",
            "http://www.dondotnet.com",
            "okay.");
        sites[sites.Count] = new WebSite(
            "Bob",
            "www.bob.com",
            "No http://");
    }

    static void Main(string[] args)
    {
        SiteManager sm = new SiteManager();

        foreach (WebSite site in sm.sites)
        {
            Console.WriteLine("Site: {0}", site);
        }
    }
}
```

And here's the output:

```
SiteList GetEnumerator called.
SiteEnumerator Constructor called.
SiteEnumerator MoveNext called.
SiteEnumerator Current called.
Site: Joe, http://www.mysite.com, Great Site!
SiteEnumerator MoveNext called.
SiteEnumerator Current called.
Site: Don, http://www.dondotnet.com, okay.
SiteEnumerator MoveNext called.
SiteEnumerator Current called.
Site: Bob, www.bob.com, No http://
SiteEnumerator MoveNext called.
```

The important aspects of Listing 26.8 are the constructor initialization and iterating through the `SiteList` collection data in the `Main()` method. The constructor instantiates a `SiteList` object and adds new `WebSite` objects to it using an indexer, exactly as any other list collection.

The `foreach` loop in the `Main()` method shows the power of using a collection. It simply iterates through the `SiteList` collection, printing the string representation of each `WebSite` object. The significance of this is how the `foreach` loop manages this iteration behind the scenes.

Support of `foreach` is made possible through implementation of the `IEnumerable` interface and the nested `SiteEnumerator` class implementing the `IEnumerator` interface in the `SiteList` collection. The `IEnumerable.GetEnumerator()` method of `SiteList` returns a reference to the nested `SiteEnumerator` class to the `foreach` loop. This is shown in the first line of output. The second line of output is from the `SiteEnumerator` constructor, demonstrating that it was instantiated before use.

Once the `foreach` loop has a reference to an `IEnumerator`, it calls the `MoveNext()` method to set the cursor to the first element. Upon startup, the cursor must be initialized to the first element with the `MoveNext()` method. This is shown in the third line of output.

The `foreach` loop then calls the `Current` property to extract the element at the cursor as shown in the fourth line of output. This element is placed into the site field of the `foreach` loop and subsequently printed to the console as shown in the fifth line of output.

The `MoveNext()` method and `Current` property are invoked continuously until the `MoveNext()` method returns `false`, indicating that the cursor is past the last element of the collection. The `foreach` loop then exits, passing control to the next statement following the closing braces of the `foreach` loop.

Listing 26.9 provides the code for compiling both Listing 26.7 and Listing 26.8.

LISTING 26.9 Compilation Instructions for Listing 26.7 and Listing 26.8

```
csc SiteManager.cs WebSites.cs
```

Summary

There are several collection classes available in the system libraries for use in C# collections. These collection classes support array-like operations on data structures for a variety of tasks.

The collection classes implement sets of interfaces that give them an identity that can be used predictably by C# programs. These interfaces establish semantics that allow a collection to behave like a list or dictionary data structure.

Using the system collection interfaces, custom collections can be constructed, conforming to the same standards as the `System` collections. This enables custom collections to be used just like any other collection. For example, implementing the `IEnumerable` and `IEnumerator` interfaces in the appropriate manner makes a class able to be used in a `foreach` loop.

CHAPTER 27

Attributes

IN THIS CHAPTER

- Using Attributes *568*
- Using Attribute Parameters *570*
- Using Attribute Targets *572*
- Creating Your Own Attributes *574*
- Getting Attributes from a Class *578*

Attributes are program elements that decorate code to provide declarative functionality and metadata for a program. Metadata is the information about a program, its internal elements, and any other aspects of the code that may be interesting to developers. Other languages and systems use Interface Definition Language (IDL), interfaces, type libraries, and basic reflection to obtain metadata on programs.

C# uses reflection, which is a way to discover information about a program at runtime, to obtain metadata, but uses attributes to express additional metadata. Attributes provide a means for a developer to explicitly include decorations in their code for logic, reflection, and tool support.

Attributes are easy to use and have their own unique syntax. It's expected that most programs will use predefined system attributes, for which there are many in the system libraries. When the predefined libraries are not enough, you can create your own custom attributes.

For C++ and Java Programmers

C++ and Java don't have attributes. Although Java has extensive reflection capabilities, it doesn't have the customizable metadata facilities available with attributes.

Using Attributes

Using attributes is simple. They are placed on the line above the program element to which they refer and are surrounded by square brackets. Within the square brackets, there are one or more comma-separated attributes. Attribute parameters may be specified as either positional or named.

Using a Single Attribute

The simplest attribute to implement is one with no parameters. Listing 27.1 shows an example of the `Flags` attribute, which is used on the `ProblemStatus` enum.

LISTING 27.1 Using a Single Attribute

```
using System;

/// <summary>
///     Using a Single Attribute.
/// </summary>
class SingleAttribute
```

LISTING 27.1 continued

```
{
    [Flags]
    public enum ProblemStatus
    {
        Assigned  = 0x0001,
        NoProblem = 0x0002,
        Open      = 0x0004,
        Resolved  = 0x0008
    }

    static void Main(string[] args)
    {
        ProblemStatus currentStatus =
             (ProblemStatus.Open | ProblemStatus.Assigned);

        if (((currentStatus & ProblemStatus.NoProblem) != 0) |
            ((currentStatus & ProblemStatus.Resolved)  != 0) )
        {
            Console.WriteLine("Problem Closed: {0}",
                currentStatus);
        }
        else
        {
            Console.WriteLine("Problem Still Open: {0}",
                currentStatus);
        }
    }
}
```

And the output is:

```
Problem Still Open: Assigned, Open
```

The `Flags` attribute gives an `enum` the capability to be treated like a bitfield, using logical operations such as the OR (`|`) in the `Main()` method.

Using Multiple Attributes

Multiple attributes may be specified together. Listing 27.2 demonstrates the proper syntax of using multiple attributes to a single program element.

LISTING 27.2 Using Multiple Attributes

```
using System;

/// <summary>
///     Using Multiple Attributes.
```

LISTING 27.2 continued

```
/// </summary>
class MultipleAttributes
{
    [Flags, Serializable]
    public enum ProblemStatus
    {
        Assigned  = 0x0001,
        NoProblem = 0x0002,
        Open      = 0x0004,
        Resolved  = 0x0008
    }

    static void Main(string[] args)
    {
    }
}
```

Listing 27.2 demonstrates how a comma separates the `Flags` and `Serializable` attributes. The `Serializable` attribute means that a program element can be serialized. Used in a class declaration, it means the same as the `ISerializable` interface. The `Flags` and `Serializable` interface could have also been specified as follows:

```
[Flags]
[Serializable]
public enum ProblemStatus
{
    Assigned  = 0x0001,
    NoProblem = 0x0002,
    Open      = 0x0004,
    Resolved  = 0x0008
}
```

Each attribute of the example is specified in its own square brackets; however, the result is the same as that shown in Listing 27.2. This is just another way to specify the same thing.

Using Attribute Parameters

Attribute parameters enable you to initialize an attribute with information specific to the code being written. Since an attribute is really another object, the parameters act the same as parameters for instance constructors. The main difference is that it's also possible to initialize public attribute fields and parameters at the same time.

There are two types of parameters: positional and named. Parameters can include only positional, only named, or a combination of both positional and named. Positional attributes are mandatory and always come before named attributes. The following sections go into more detail on each of these attribute parameter types.

Positional Parameters

Positional parameters correspond to the parameters of an attribute's public constructors. If there's only a single public constructor, the parameters of that constructor must be used. Otherwise, positional parameters for any available public constructor of the attribute may be used. Positional parameters must be specified in total and in the proper order for the attribute constructor being implemented. Listing 27.3 shows an example of using an attribute with positional parameters.

LISTING 27.3 Positional Parameters

```
using System;

/// <summary>
///     Positional Parameter.
/// </summary>
class PositionalParameter
{
    [Obsolete("Use this method at your own risk!")]
    public static void OldMethod()
    {
    }

    static void Main(string[] args)
    {
        OldMethod();
    }
}
```

The `Obsolete` attribute in Listing 27.3 uses a positional parameter, which is a string used to display a message during compilation. By default, this displays a warning, but the `Obsolete` attribute has another positional parameter called `IsError`. Here's how the second positional parameter is used.

```
[Obsolete("Use this method at your own risk!", true)]
```

The `IsError` positional parameter generates a compile-time error, displaying the message from the first positional parameter.

Named Parameters

Named parameters correspond to the public read-write fields and properties of an attribute. It's a compiler error for named parameters to be used for static or read-only fields and properties. Listing 27.4 demonstrates proper use of an attribute with named parameters.

LISTING 27.4 Named Parameters

```
using System;
using System.Runtime.InteropServices;

/// <summary>
///     Named Parameter.
/// </summary>
///
[StructLayout(LayoutKind.Auto, CharSet=CharSet.Unicode)]
class NamedParameter
{
    static void Main(string[] args)
    {
    }
}
```

Listing 27.4 uses the `StructLayout` attribute, showing how to use a named parameter. The `StructLayout` attribute has its positional parameter, which is required, and then the named parameter. The named parameter has a name label, the equal sign, and then the value of the parameter. The `StructLayout` attribute is useful for passing `classes` and `structs` to unmanaged code where the physical layout of members must be exact.

Using Attribute Targets

Attribute targets specify to what program element an attribute is being applied. They're not always required but can sometimes help make the intent of the attribute more understandable. For example, if there were ambiguity between whether an attribute applied to a method's return value or the method itself, then an attribute target specification would resolve the ambiguity. Listing 27.5 contains an example of how to specify attribute targets.

LISTING 27.5 Attribute Targets

```
using System;

/// <summary>
///     Attribute Targets.
/// </summary>
[assembly:CLSCompliant(false)]
class AttributeTarget
{
```

LISTING 27.5 continued

```
    static void Main(string[] args)
    {
    }
}
```

The attribute in Listing 27.5 specifies that the `CLSCompliant` attribute applies to `assembly`, rather than the class it is near. It has the target, `assembly`, separated from the attribute, `CLSCompliant`, by a single colon.

Had the target not been specified, there would be no way to tell whether this attribute decorates the `class` it is over or `assembly`. Had the positional parameter been `true`, the `assembly` target would have been required before applying the `CLSCompliant` attribute to any other program element. Table 27.1 shows what targets are available when specifying attribute targets.

TABLE 27.1 Attribute Target Specifiers

Target Name	*Applicable To*
all	Any element
assembly	Entire assembly
class	A class
constructor	A constructor
delegate	A delegate
enum	An enum
event	An event
field	A field
interface	An interface
method	A method
module	Containing module
param	A parameter
property	A property
return	A return value
struct	A struct

Creating Your Own Attributes

When the predefined system library attributes are not enough for development needs, it may be desirable to customize your own. This is similar to creating a normal class, except that it is decorated with the `AttributeUsage` attribute and inherit from the `System.Attribute` class.

The `AttributeUsage` Attribute

The `AttributeUsage` attribute specifies how an attribute can be used in a program. It tells what program elements the attribute can be used on, if the attribute can be used multiple times, and whether the attribute can be inherited.

Allowed Elements

Some attributes will only make sense on certain program elements. For example, the `Flags` attribute only makes sense on an `enum` and would be illogical if applied to anything else such as a `class` or `delegate`.

The `AttributeUsage` attribute has a single positional parameter that specifies how an attribute may be used. Allowable values for this positional parameter may be one of the `AttributeTargets enum` members shown in Table 27.2.

TABLE 27.2 `AttributeTarget Enum` Members Used in the `AttributeUsage` Attribute

Target Name	*Description*
`All`	Any `AttributeTargets` member
`Assembly`	Assemblies
`Class`	Classes
`ClassMembers`	Class, constructor, delegate, enum, event, field, interface, method, parameter, property, or struct
`Constructor`	Constructors
`Delegate`	Delegates
`Enum`	Enums
`Event`	Events
`Field`	Fields
`Interface`	Interfaces
`Method`	Methods
`Module`	Modules

TABLE 27.2 continued

Target Name	*Description*
`Parameter`	Parameters
`Property`	Properties
`ReturnValue`	Return values
`Struct`	Structs

The `AttributeUsage` attribute is used just like any other attribute. It has a positional parameter, described previously, and two named parameters. Listing 27.6 has the program we'll use in both this and subsequent sections to describe the `AttributeUsage` attribute and implementation of a custom attribute. The positional parameter of the `AttributeUsage` attribute in Listing 27.6 is set to `AttributeTargets.All`, which means it can be used on any C# program element.

LISTING 27.6 Custom Attribute Example

```
using System;

/// <summary>
///     Custom Attribute Example.
/// </summary>
[
    Tracker("CR-0001",
            "some fix",
            EngineerId = "Joe",
            ChangeDate = "07/04/2001")
]
class SomeProgram
{
    static void Main(string[] args)
    {
        SomeProgram sp = new SomeProgram();
    }
}

[
    AttributeUsage(AttributeTargets.All,
                   AllowMultiple = true,
                   Inherited     = true)
]
class TrackerAttribute : Attribute
{
    public  string   ProblemId;
    public  string   EngineerId;
```

LISTING 27.6 continued

```
    private string   fixDescription;
    private DateTime changeDate;

    public string FixDescription
    {
        get
        {
            return fixDescription;
        }
        set
        {
            fixDescription = value;
        }
    }

    public string ChangeDate
    {
        get
        {
            return changeDate.ToString("d");
        }
        set
        {
            changeDate = DateTime.Parse(value);
        }
    }

    public TrackerAttribute()
    {
        ProblemId      = "UNASSIGNED";
        EngineerId     = "Unidentified Engineer";
        FixDescription = "No description provided";
        ChangeDate     = "01/01/2001";
    }

    public TrackerAttribute(string problemId, string fixDescription)
    {
        ProblemId      = problemId;
        EngineerId     = "Unidentified Engineer";
        FixDescription = fixDescription;
        ChangeDate     = "01/01/2001";
    }
}
```

In Listing 27.6, the `TrackerAttribute` class has an `AttributeUsage` attribute, showing that this attribute may be used on any type of C# Element. All attributes inherit the `System.Attribute` class. Parameters of the `AttributeUsage` attribute are discussed in following sections.

The TrackerAttribute class has two public and two private fields. The private fields are exposed through class properties. The public fields, as expected, are directly exposed to user classes.

Note

Attribute class fields and properties must be read/write and public.

There is a default constructor and a constructor with two parameters within the TrackerAttribute class. The default constructor initializes all fields and properties to default values. The two-parameter constructor sets the ProblemId field and FixDescription property, while setting the EngineerId field and ChangeDate property to default values.

The implementation of the SomeProgram class in Listing 27.6 shows how this attribute can be used. It uses the two-parameter constructor implementation and adds the EngineerId and ChangeDate named parameters.

Tip

A common naming convention for C# attributes is to add the "Attribute" suffix to the attribute class name declaration. When actually using the attribute, you can take a shortcut by leaving off the "Attribute" suffix, and C# will still recognize the appropriate attribute.

Multiplicity

Controlling the number of times an attribute may be used on a single program element is specified by the named parameter, AllowMultiple, of the AttributeUsage attribute. The AllowMultiple named parameter of the following example is set to true:

```
[
    AttributeUsage(AttributeTargets.All,
                   AllowMultiple = true,
                   Inherited     = true)
]
```

In the case of the Tracker attribute in Listing 27.6, it may be used multiple times on a program element because the AllowMultiple attribute of its AttributeUsage attribute is set to true. Other attributes, such as the Flags and Serializable attribute will have their AllowMultiple named parameter set to false because they may only be used one time, which makes sense if you think about how they're used.

The common terminology is that an attribute is "multi-use" when its AllowMultiple named parameter is set to true and "single-use" when its AllowMultiple named parameter is set to false. Attributes are single-use by default.

Inheritance

Using the Inherited named parameter of the AttributeUsage attribute controls inheritance of attributes. When set to true, the attribute may be inherited; false means that the attribute may not be inherited. The following example shows how the Inherited named parameter is used in the AttributeUsage attribute of the Tracker attribute class declaration:

```
[
    AttributeUsage(AttributeTargets.All,
                   AllowMultiple = true,
                   Inherited     = true)
]
```

The Inherited named parameter essentially is analogous in meaning to the C# sealed modifier. Attributes may be inherited by default.

Getting Attributes from a Class

Class attributes may be obtained by using the GetAttribute() and GetAttributes() methods of the Attribute class. They get a single attribute or an array of attributes, respectively. Listing 27.7 demonstrates how to get a single attribute using the GetAttribute() method.

LISTING 27.7 Getting Attributes from a Class

```
[
    Tracker("CR-0001",
    "some fix",
    EngineerId = "Joe",
    ChangeDate = "07/04/2001")
]
class SomeProgram
{
    static void Main(string[] args)
    {
        try
        {
            Type classType     = typeof(SomeProgram);
            Type attributeType = typeof(TrackerAttribute);
```

LISTING 27.7 continued

```
            TrackerAttribute attrib = (TrackerAttribute)
                Attribute.GetCustomAttribute(classType,
                                             attributeType);

            Console.WriteLine("Problem #:     {0}",
                attrib.ProblemId);
            Console.WriteLine("Engineeer ID: {0}",
                attrib.EngineerId);
            Console.WriteLine("Change Date:  {0}",
                attrib.ChangeDate);
            Console.WriteLine("Description:  {0}",
                attrib.FixDescription);
        }
        catch(Exception e)
        {
            Console.WriteLine(
                "Generic Exception: {0}\nStack Trace:\n{1}",
                e.Message, e.StackTrace);
        }
    }
}
```


The code in Listing 27.7 gets a `Type` object for the class to be examined and a `Type` object for the attribute being retrieved. These `Type` objects are passed to the `GetCustomAttribute()` method to obtain an `attribute` object, which is an attribute of the `TrackerAttribute` attribute class type. The public fields and properties of the `TrackerAttribute` are then displayed on the console.

Summary

Attributes are a special type of metadata used to decorate program elements with information the programmer chooses. There are several pre-built attributes such as the `Serializable` and `CLSCompliant` attributes that you'll use on a regular basis.

When the pre-built attributes don't meet requirements, it's possible to create custom attributes. Custom attributes are special classes derived from the `Attribute` class and can be designed to support any metadata requirement imaginable.

The `Attribute` class has special methods for obtaining attribute metadata from program elements. Single attributes or all attributes associated with a program element may be extracted and read.

The metadata extraction capabilities described are merely a fraction of what can be accomplished in C#. In the next chapter, "Reflection," you'll learn how to obtain metadata on all types of C# program elements, in addition to attributes.

CHAPTER 28

Reflection

IN THIS CHAPTER

- **Discovering Program Information** *582*
- **Dynamically Activating Code** *588*
- **`Reflection.Emit`** *590*

Reflection is the capability to inspect the metadata of a program and gather information about its types. Using reflection, it's possible to learn about program assemblies, modules, and all types of internal program elements.

This is particularly useful for design tools, supporting the automated building of code based on user selections derived from the metadata of the underlying types being used. Reflection also provides excellent support for late-bound frameworks where runtime determination is required for selecting required libraries or other functionality on-the-fly.

Discovering Program Information

The reflection API is based on a hierarchical model where higher-level items are composed of one or more lower-level items. Figure 28.1 shows this hierarchy. Assemblies, the basic unit of program distribution in C#, are at the top. Assemblies may be composed of one or more modules. Modules may have one or more types. Types are program elements such as `classes`, `structs`, `delegates`, and `enums`. Types may contain one or more `fields`, `properties`, `methods`, or `events`, depending on the type. It may be handy to think about this model as you progress through the sections of this chapter.

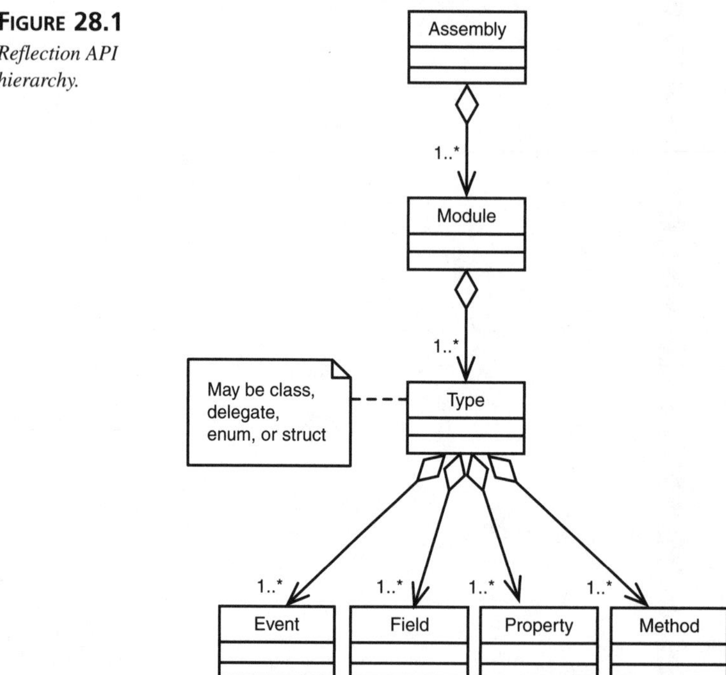

FIGURE 28.1
Reflection API hierarchy.

The primary purpose of reflection is to discover program information. The C# reflection API makes it possible to find out all information available about a program. The program elements to be searched include assemblies, modules, types, and type members. Listing 28.1 creates a class that will be reflected upon, and Listing 28.2 demonstrates how to obtain the various reflection objects and inspect their available information.

LISTING 28.1 Class to Reflect Upon: `Reflected.cs`

```
using System;
using System.Collections;

/// <summary>
///     Reflected Class
/// </summary>
public class Reflected
{
    public    int       MyField;
    protected ArrayList myArray;

    public Reflected()
    {
        myArray = new ArrayList();
        myArray.Add("Some ArrayList Entry");
    }

    public float MyProperty
    {
        get
        {
            return MyEvent();
        }
    }

    public object this[int index]
    {
        get
        {
            if (index <= index)
            {
                return myArray[index];
            }
            else
            {
                return null;
            }
        }
        set
        {
```

LISTING 28.1 continued

```
            myArray.Add(value);
        }
    }

    public float MyInstanceMethod()
    {
        Console.WriteLine("Invoking Instance MyMethod.");

        return 0.02f;
    }

    public static float MyStaticMethod()
    {
        Console.WriteLine("Invoking Static MyMethod.");

        return 0.02f;
    }

    public delegate float MyDelegate();

    public event MyDelegate MyEvent
        = new MyDelegate(MyStaticMethod);

    public enum MyEnum { valOne, valTwo, valThree };
}
```

LISTING 28.2 Performing Reflection: `Reflecting.cs`

```
using System;
using System.Reflection;

/// <summary>
///     Performing Reflection.
/// </summary>
class Reflecting
{
    static void Main(string[] args)
    {
        Reflecting reflect = new Reflecting();

        Assembly myAssembly
            = Assembly.LoadFrom("Reflecting.exe");

        reflect.GetReflectionInfo(myAssembly);
    }

    void GetReflectionInfo(Assembly myAssembly)
    {
        Type[] typeArr = myAssembly.GetTypes();
```

LISTING 28.2 continued

```
        foreach (Type type in typeArr)
        {
            Console.WriteLine("\nType: {0}\n", type.FullName);

            ConstructorInfo[] MyConstructors
                = type.GetConstructors();
            foreach (ConstructorInfo constructor
                     in MyConstructors)
            {
                Console.WriteLine("\tConstructor: {0}",
                                  constructor.ToString());
            }
            Console.WriteLine();

            FieldInfo[] MyFields = type.GetFields();
            foreach (FieldInfo field in MyFields)
            {
                Console.WriteLine("\tField: {0}",
                                  field.ToString());
            }
            Console.WriteLine();

            MethodInfo[] MyMethods = type.GetMethods();
            foreach (MethodInfo method in MyMethods)
            {
                Console.WriteLine("\tMethod: {0}",
                                  method.ToString());
            }
            Console.WriteLine();

            PropertyInfo[] MyProperties
                = type.GetProperties();

            foreach (PropertyInfo property in MyProperties)
            {
                Console.WriteLine("\tProperty: {0}",
                                  property.ToString());
            }
            Console.WriteLine();

            EventInfo[] MyEvents = type.GetEvents();
            foreach (EventInfo anEvent in MyEvents)
            {
                Console.WriteLine("\tEvent: {0}",
                                  anEvent.ToString());
            }
            Console.WriteLine();
        }
    }
}
```

And the output is:

```
Type: Reflecting

        Constructor: Void .ctor()


        Method: Int32 GetHashCode()
        Method: Boolean Equals(System.Object)
        Method: System.String ToString()
        Method: System.Type GetType()




Type: Reflected

        Constructor: Void .ctor()

        Field: Int32 MyField

        Method: Int32 GetHashCode()
        Method: Boolean Equals(System.Object)
        Method: System.String ToString()
        Method: Single get_MyProperty()
        Method: System.Object get_Item(Int32)
        Method: Void set_Item(Int32, System.Object)
        Method: Single MyInstanceMethod()
        Method: Single MyStaticMethod()
        Method: Void add_MyEvent(MyDelegate)
        Method: Void remove_MyEvent(MyDelegate)
        Method: System.Type GetType()

        Property: Single MyProperty
        Property: System.Object Item [Int32]

        Event: MyDelegate MyEvent


Type: Reflected+MyDelegate

        Constructor: Void .ctor(System.Object, UIntPtr)


        Method: Single EndInvoke(System.IAsyncResult)
        Method: System.IAsyncResult BeginInvoke(
                                        System.AsyncCallback,
                                        System.Object)
        Method: Single Invoke()
        Method: Void GetObjectData(
```

```
    System.Runtime.Serialization.SerializationInfo,
 System.Runtime.Serialization.StreamingContext)
Method: System.Object Clone()
Method: System.Delegate[] GetInvocationList()
Method: Int32 GetHashCode()
Method: Boolean Equals(System.Object)
Method: System.String ToString()
Method: System.Object DynamicInvoke(System.Object[])
Method: System.Reflection.MethodInfo get_Method()
Method: System.Object get_Target()
Method: System.Type GetType()

Property: System.Reflection.MethodInfo Method
Property: System.Object Target



Type: Reflected+MyEnum


        Field: Int32 value__
        Field: MyEnum valOne
        Field: MyEnum valTwo
        Field: MyEnum valThree

        Method: System.String ToString(System.IFormatProvider)
        Method: System.TypeCode GetTypeCode()
        Method: System.String ToString(System.String,
                                       System.IFormatProvider)
        Method: Int32 CompareTo(System.Object)
        Method: Int32 GetHashCode()
        Method: Boolean Equals(System.Object)
        Method: System.String ToString()
        Method: System.String ToString(System.String)
        Method: System.Type GetType()
```

The primary purpose of Listing 28.1 is to have a class available with all types of class members to reflect upon. It does nothing more than serve that purpose, and all of its program elements should be familiar by now.

Listing 28.2 is where the interesting bits are. The `Main()` method obtains an `assembly` object by calling the static `LoadFrom()` method of the `Assembly` class. The `LoadFrom()` method has a `string` parameter, specifying the name of the executable file, or assembly, to load.

Within the `GetReflectionInfo()` method, the `Assembly` object, `myAssembly`, invokes its `GetTypes()` method to obtain an array of all types available in the assembly.

> **Tip**
>
> The `Assembly` type has a `GetModules()` method that will get an array of modules within an assembly. From each of the modules, it's possible to use `GetTypes()` to get an array of types to work with. As a shortcut, Listing 28.2 uses the `GetTypes()` method of the `Assembly` type to get all types belonging to all modules within that assembly.

Within the `foreach` loop, each type is extracted and printed. The types are obtained with a `Get<X>()` method, and the result is an `<X>info` object where `<X>` is one of the following type members:

- Constructor
- Field
- Method
- Property (including indexer)
- Event

Each type member is printed to the console with the `ToString()` method, but this isn't the only thing that can be done with each member. Each `<X>Info` class includes numerous methods and properties that can be invoked to obtain information. A good source of information on available methods and properties is the .NET SDK Frameworks documentation. Listing 28.3 shows how to compile the programs in Listings 28.1 and 28.2.

LISTING 28.3 Compile Instructions for Listings 28.1 and 28.2

```
csc Reflecting.cs Reflected.cs
```

Dynamically Activating Code

Dynamic code activation is the capability to make a runtime determination of what code will be executed. This capability can be useful in any situation where a late-bound framework is required.

Consider the Simple Object Access Protocol (SOAP) specification, which is transport protocol independent. Although SOAP is widely used with the HTTP protocol, the specification itself was constructed to allow implementation over other protocols, such as Simple Message Transport Protocol (SMTP). With an appropriate interface, Dynamic Link Libraries (DLL) could be constructed to separate the SOAP implementation from the underlying protocol. Furthermore, with late-bound implementation, new protocols with the proper interface, packaged in their own DLLs, could be added to the framework at any time, without recompilation of the code. The late-bound capabilities of reflection could enable this scenario by assisting in the runtime determination of what transport protocol would be used for SOAP packages.

Examples in this chapter do not attempt to be this ambitious. However, Listing 28.4 shows how to perform a late-bound operation by dynamically activating the code in a specified assembly during runtime.

LISTING 28.4 Dynamically Activating Code: `Reflecting.cs`

```
using System;
using System.Reflection;

/// <summary>
///     Dynamically Activating Code.
/// </summary>
class Reflecting
{
    static void Main(string[] args)
    {
        Reflecting reflect = new Reflecting();

        Assembly myAssembly
            = Assembly.LoadFrom("Reflecting.exe");

        reflect.DynamicallyInvokeMembers(myAssembly);
    }

    void DynamicallyInvokeMembers(Assembly myAssembly)
    {
        Type classType = myAssembly.GetType("Reflected");

        PropertyInfo myProperty
            = classType.GetProperty("MyProperty");

        MethodInfo propGet = myProperty.GetGetMethod();

        object reflectedObject
            = Activator.CreateInstance(classType);

        propGet.Invoke(reflectedObject, null);

        MethodInfo myMethod
            = classType.GetMethod("MyInstanceMethod");

        myMethod.Invoke(reflectedObject, null);
    }
}
```

And the output is:

```
Invoking Static MyMethod.
Invoking Instance MyMethod.
```

The `Main()` method of Listing 28.4 gets an `Assembly` object with the static `Assembly.LoadFrom()` method. The `DynamicallyInvokeMembers()` method uses the `Assembly` object to get the `Type` object from the `Reflected` class. The `Type` object is then used to obtain the `MyProperty` property. Next, a `MethodInfo` object is obtained by calling the `GetGetMethod()` of the `PropertyInfo` object. The `GetGetMethod()` retrieves a copy of a property's `get` method, which is, for reflection purposes, treated just like a method.

> **Note**
>
> Indexer `get` and `set` accessors are obtained just like property `get` and `set` accessors, with `GetGetMethod()` and `GetSetMethod()` calls.

The `Reflected` class is instantiated by using the `Activator.CreateInstance()` method. The instantiated object is then used as the first parameter in the `Invoke()` method of the `MethodInfo` object. This identifies which object to invoke the method on. The `Invoke()` method's second parameter is the parameter list to send to the method, which would be an array of objects if there were parameters. In this case there are no parameters to send to the method, so the `Invoke()` method's second parameter is set to `null`.

The next two lines show how to dynamically invoke an instance method. The syntax is the same as just explained for the property `get` accessor. However, the intermediate step, used in properties, isn't necessary, and the method can be obtained directly with the `GetMethod()` method of the `Type` object.

The code in Listing 28.4 can be combined with Listing 28.1 to create an executable. Listing 28.5 shows how to compile them.

LISTING 28.5 Compile Instructions for Listings 28.1 and 28.4

```
csc Reflecting.cs Reflected.cs
```

Reflection.Emit

The `Reflection.Emit` API provides a means to dynamically create new assemblies. Using customized builders and generating Microsoft Intermediate Language (MSIL) or Common Intermediate Language (CIL) code enables programs to create new programs at runtime. These assemblies may be dynamically invoked or saved to file where they may be reloaded and invoked or used by other programs.

Dynamic assembly creation can be useful for back-ends to compilers or scripting engines on tools such as Web browsers. Using the `Reflection.Emit` API, any tool can be extended to dynamically support .NET or any other Common Language Infrastructure (CLI) compliant system. Listing 28.6 shows how to both generate a dynamic assembly and save it as a console program.

LISTING 28.6 Dynamic Assembly Generation

```
using System;
using System.Reflection;
using System.Reflection.Emit;

/// <summary>
///     Reflection Emit.
/// </summary>
class Emit
{
    static void Main(string[] args)
    {
        AppDomain myAppDomain = AppDomain.CurrentDomain;

        AssemblyName myAssemblyName = new AssemblyName();
        myAssemblyName.Name = "DynamicAssembly";

        AssemblyBuilder myAssemblyBuilder =
            myAppDomain.DefineDynamicAssembly(
            myAssemblyName,
            AssemblyBuilderAccess.RunAndSave);

        ModuleBuilder myModuleBuilder =
            myAssemblyBuilder.DefineDynamicModule(
            "DynamicModule",
            "emitter.netmodule");

        TypeBuilder myTypeBuilder =
            myModuleBuilder.DefineType(
            "EmitTestClass");

        MethodBuilder myMethodBuilder =
            myTypeBuilder.DefineMethod(
            "Main",
            MethodAttributes.Public|MethodAttributes.Static,
            null,
            null);
```

LISTING 28.6 continued

```
        ILGenerator myILGenerator
            = myMethodBuilder.GetILGenerator();
        myILGenerator.EmitWriteLine(
            "\n\tI must emit, reflection is pretty cool!\n");
        myILGenerator.Emit(OpCodes.Ret);

        Type myType = myTypeBuilder.CreateType();
        object myObjectInstance
            = Activator.CreateInstance(myType);

        Console.WriteLine("\nDynamic Invocation:");

        MethodInfo myMethod = myType.GetMethod("Main");
        myMethod.Invoke(myObjectInstance, null);

        myAssemblyBuilder.SetEntryPoint(myMethod);
        myAssemblyBuilder.Save("emitter.exe");
    }
}
```

Before walking through the code in Listing 28.6, you may want to refer to Figure 28.1, which shows a model of the relationships between Reflection API components. The figure may make it clearer as to why each step is necessary.

New assemblies must be created in a specific `AppDomain`. A greatly simplified definition is that `AppDomains` are memory regions where a single process executes. Invocation of members belonging to a `Type` within an assembly must be done in the current `AppDomain`. Therefore, when this program begins, it gets a new `AppDomain` object by calling the `CurrentDomain()` method of the `AppDomain` class.

To create the entire assembly in Listing 28.6, several steps are required:

1. Create an `AssemblyBuilder`.
2. Create a `ModuleBuilder`.
3. Create a `TypeBuilder`.
4. Create a `MethodBuilder`.
5. Generate IL.
6. Invoke members or persist assembly.

Each builder is created using a defining method of its parent in the hierarchy. This is another reason why the `AppDomain` object is required, to get an `AssemblyBuilder`.

The `AssemblyBuilder` object is created by calling the `DefineDynamicAssembly()` method of the `AppDomain` object. The parameters passed to `DefineDynamicAssembly()` are an `AssemblyName` object and an `AssemblyBuilderAccess enum`. The `AssemblyBuilderAccess enum` has three members: `Run`, `RunAndSave`, and `Save`. `Run` means the assembly can only be invoked in memory; `Save` means that the assembly can only be persisted (saved) to file; and `RunAndSave` means both `Run` and `Save`.

With an `AssemblyBuilder` object, a `ModuleBuilder` object is created. The parameters of the `DefineDynamicModule()` method are a `string` with name for the module and another `string` with the filename the module will be saved as. The example shows that the module filename will be "emitter.netmodule".

Tip

The `DefineDynamicModule()` method has four overloads: two are for run-only modules and the other two are for run and persist modules. To guarantee that a module is included during persistence of an assembly, ensure one of the overloads with the filename parameter of the `DefineDynamicAssembly()` method is used.

`TypeBuilder` objects are created with the `DefineType()` method of the `ModuleBuilder` object. The `DefineType()` method takes a single `string` parameter with the name of the `Type`.

The final builder object in Listing 28.6 is the `MethodBuilder`, which is created using the `DefineMethod()` method of the `TypeBuilder` object. `DefineMethod()` has four parameters: `name`, `method attributes`, `return type`, and `parameter types`.

The `name` parameter is a `string` with the name of the method. In this case, it's the `Main()` method. Since a `Main()` method must be defined as `public` and `static`, the second parameter uses the `Public` and `Static` members of the `MethodAttributes enum`. The `return type` is `null`, which defaults to `void`, and the `parameter types` is also `null` which means that this method does not accept arguments. When a method accepts arguments, the fourth parameter would be an array with the type definitions of each method parameter.

Next, the code is generated. To accomplish this, invoke the `MethodBuilder` object's `GetILGenerator()` method. This results in an `ILGenerator` class that is used to create code.

This is a very simple method that writes a line of text to the console and returns. The `EmitWriteLine()` and `Emit()` methods perform this task.

Prior to invoking code, a type instance is created by calling the `GetType()` method of the `TypeBuilder` object. The resulting `Type` object is then instantiated with the static `Activator.CreateInstance()` method.

Once an object instance is available, the program gets a `MethodInfo` object and dynamically invokes the method, just like in the last section.

What's really cool about this entire procedure is that you can save the work that was done to a file. With the `Assembly` object, the `SetEntryPoint()` method is invoked with the `MethodInfo` parameter for the dynamically generated `Main()` method. Then the file is saved with the `Save` command, which accepts a single `string` parameter specifying the assembly file name.

> **Warning**
>
> One of the goals of Listing 28.6 was to create an executable console application. For a C# program to run standalone, it must have a `Main()` method. Since the program did have a `Main()` method, it would be easy to assume that everything was good to go. However, the `SetEntryPoint()` method of the `AssemblyBuilder` must still be called or else the program will not run standalone. Remember, the system libraries are cross-language compatible, and you shouldn't make the assumption that they know C#.

The `Save()` method of the `AssemblyBuilder` object creates two files. One file is the module named `emitter.netmodule`. This file can be compiled with other modules to create an executable. The other file is the executable named `emitter.exe`. This is a standalone program that will execute when invoked from the command line.

Summary

Reflection provides the capability to discover information about a program at runtime. Pertinent program items that can be reflected upon include assemblies, modules, types, and other kinds of C# program elements.

Another feature of reflection is the capability to dynamically activate code at runtime. This is especially relevant to situations where late-bound operations are required. With reflection, any type of C# code can be loaded and invoked dynamically.

The `Reflection.Emit` API provides advanced features for dynamically creating assemblies. This feature could be used in tools such as scripting engines and compilers. Once the code is created, it can be dynamically invoked or saved to file for later use.

CHAPTER 29

Localization and Resources

IN THIS CHAPTER

- Resource Files 596
- Multiple Locales 609

If everyone were the same, this world would be a pretty boring place. With the plethora of cultures, ideas, and means of communication there needs to be a way to make applications and information accessible on the desktop and over the Internet. This is the role of localization.

Localization is the process of making computer programs accessible to a diverse set of cultures. A localized program identifies selected cultures and presents information, such as language, fonts, and graphics, in a specific manner for each culture. This way, a person in Italy, Thailand, or anywhere else can have the same user experience as a person from the United States.

Resource Files

Setting up and using resource files is the primary means of localizing programs. *Resource files* are specialized binary files that can be bound to a standalone DLL or added into a program assembly. They contain strings, graphics, and other binary resources that assist in localizing a program.

Creating a Resource File

The resource generator utility `ResGen` is a string resource creation utility that comes with the Microsoft .NET Framework SDK. Given a properly formatted `.txt` (text) file, `ResGen` converts it into a `.resources` (binary resources) file that can subsequently be added to an assembly.

> **Note**
>
> In simplistic terms, an assembly is a unit of deployment. Assemblies are covered in more detail in later chapters, but for now, it will be helpful to think of them as executable files or dynamic link libraries (DLLs).

Without a special resource creation tool, string resources begin life as a specially formatted `.txt` file. They have headers, comments, and name/value pairs as shown in Table 29.1.

TABLE 29.1 `.txt` Resource File Elements

Element	*Description*
`[header]`	Optional file header
`;`	Optional comment marker
`name = value`	Resource string declaration

Header elements must match the filename without the extension. For example if the resource file's name is `myResources.txt`, then the header contents must be `[myResources]`. Comments are useful for delimiting groups of resource strings or adding more information to the use of a string. All comments are removed from compiled resources.

Name/value pairs are the reason for the resources file. The `name` portion is used as a key in programs to identify a particular string resource. A `value` is the string itself. An example `.txt` resource file is shown in Listing 29.1.

LISTING 29.1 `.txt` Resource File: `strings.txt`

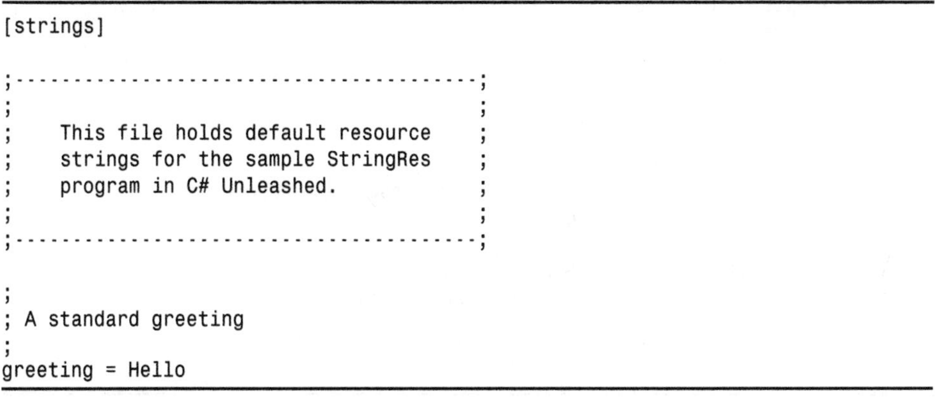

```
[strings]

;---------------------------------------;
;                                       ;
;    This file holds default resource   ;
;    strings for the sample StringRes   ;
;    program in C# Unleashed.           ;
;                                       ;
;---------------------------------------;

;
; A standard greeting
;
greeting = Hello
```

Because the filename of the code in Listing 29.1 is `strings.txt`, the header text is `[strings]`, according to the rules for the header element. There are comments describing the purpose of the resource file and a shorter comment describing the greeting string resource. The following example shows how to prepare the resources file for use:

```
resgen strings.txt
al /out:strings.resources.dll /embed:strings.resources
```

The first line uses the `ResGen` utility (discussed previously) to convert the `strings.txt` file into a `strings.resources` file. The second line uses the assembly generation tool, included in the .NET Frameworks SDK, to create a DLL. The first parameter is the `/out` option, which works the same as the `/out` option when invoking the C# compiler. The `/embed` option identifies the binary resource file. The example creates the file `strings.resources.dll`, which can be used by any application to obtain predefined resources.

There are a couple things to do when using resources. First, declare an instance of the `ResourceManager` class, which assists in using resources; then use `ResourceManager` class members to access resources. This is demonstrated in Listing 29.2.

LISTING 29.2 Using Resources: `StringRes.cs`

```
using System;
using System.Resources;

namespace StringRes
{
    /// <summary>
    /// Example of Using String Resources.
    /// </summary>
    class StringRes
    {
        static void Main(string[] args)
        {
            ResourceManager rm =
              ResourceManager.CreateFileBasedResourceManager(
              "strings", ".", null);

            Console.WriteLine("Greeting: {0}",
                              rm.GetString("greeting"));
        }
    }
}
```

And the output is

```
Greeting: Hello
```

Listing 29.2 includes the `System.Resources` namespace, which contains the `ResourceManager` class. Within the `Main()` method, an instance of the `ResourceManager` class is instantiated with the `CreateFileBasedResourceManager()` method, which takes three parameters.

The first parameter is the name of the resource file. The `.resources` extension is assumed. The second parameter specifies the directory where the `.resources` file is located. The example specifies the current directory. The third parameter is `null`, specifying that the type of `ResourceSet` is the default `ResourceSet`. A `ResourceSet` is a class that stores properties as a hash table and can be derived from, enabling the third parameter of the `CreateFileBasedResourceManager()` method to indicate the type of a customized `ResourceSet`.

Within the `Console.WriteLine()` method, there is a single parameter that obtains the greeting resource to display on the screen. This resource is obtained by using the `GetString()` method of the `ResourceManager` object. The parameter is a string with the name of the key to the resource being used. As evident in the results, the parameter is the value part of the `greeting` resource from Listing 29.1. The code in Listing 29.2 is compiled with the following command line:

```
csc StringRes.cs
```

Writing a Resource File

Resource files may be created programmatically. This is useful for automated `.resource` file generation utilities or resource tools in IDEs. The steps involved in creating a `.resource` file are to open a `ResourceWriter` stream, add whatever resources are needed, and then close the stream. This procedure is demonstrated in Listing 29.3.

LISTING 29.3 Writing a Resource File: `ResWrite.cs`

```
using System;
using System.Resources;

namespace ResWrite
{
    /// <summary>
    /// Resource Writing Example
    /// </summary>
    class ResWrite
    {
        static void Main(string[] args)
        {
            IResourceWriter resWriter =
                new ResourceWriter("strings.resources");

            resWriter.AddResource("thanks",  "Thank you.");
            resWriter.AddResource("welcome", "Your welcome.");
```

LISTING 29.3 continued

```
            resWriter.Close();
        }
    }
}
```

The default ResourceWriter class in the System.Resources namespace implements IResourceWriter. This is why it's possible to create an IResourceWriter object within the Main() method of Listing 29.3. The ResourceWriter constructor accepts a string parameter specifying the resource file to create. If a file by that name exists, it will be overwritten.

String resources are added with the AddResource method of the resWriter object. Its parameters conform to the name/value pair format of resources with the first parameter as the name and the second parameter as the value. The resWriter stream is then closed with the Close() method. This program is compiled with the following command line:

```
csc ResWrite.cs
```

Reading a Resource File

The ResourceReader class is also useful in creating resource manipulation utilities and IDE tools to manage resources. A utility uses the ResourceReader functionality to read in an existing resource file; the program performs any necessary manipulations; and then the ResourceWriter helps write the new resources back to the persistent .resources file. Listing 29.4 shows how to read resources.

LISTING 29.4 Reading a Resource File: ResRead.cs

```
using System;
using System.Resources;
using System.Collections;

namespace ResRead
{
    /// <summary>
    /// Resource Reading Example
    /// </summary>
    class ResRead
    {
        static void Main(string[] args)
        {
            IResourceReader resReader =
                new ResourceReader("strings.resources");
```

LISTING 29.4 continued

```
            IDictionaryEnumerator resEnumerator =
                resReader.GetEnumerator();

            while (resEnumerator.MoveNext())
            {
                Console.WriteLine("{0} = {1}",
                    resEnumerator.Key, resEnumerator.Value);
            }
            resReader.Close();
        }
    }
}
```

And here's the output:

```
greeting = Hello.
thanks = Thank you.
welcome = You're welcome.
```

The `IResourceReader` object is created, similar to the `IresourceWriter`, by instantiating a new `ResourceWriter` with the `.resources` file specified as its constructor parameter. The `IResourceReader` may be used as a collection of resources by obtaining an enumerator and iterating through the list of resources. This program prints each resource to screen and then closes the `ResourceReader` stream with the `Close()` method. Listing 29.4 is compiled with the following command line:

```
csc resread.cs
```

Converting a Resource File

Another use of `ResGen` is to convert between `.txt`, `.resources`, and `.resx` files. `.resx` files are XML format files used for binary resources such as graphics, fonts, icons, and cursors. For example the following command line converts the `.resources` file to a `.resx` file:

```
resgen strings.resources strings.resx
```

This produces an XML format file, as shown in Listing 29.5. The same exact file would have been generated if you had performed the following command line:

```
resgen strings.txt strings.resx
```

Alternatively, it's possible to generate `.txt` files from either `.resx` or `.resources` files. As explained earlier, it's possible to convert `.txt` and `.resx` files to `.resources` files. This is the most common scenario as `.resources` files are added to assemblies. Because of its binary format, the `.resources` file is barely readable, which can be verified by opening up a `.resources` file in Notepad.

> **Warning**
>
> If a `.resx` or `.resources` file already contains graphics, it can't be converted to a `.txt` file, which holds only strings.

LISTING 29.5 Generated `.resx` File: `strings.resx`

```
<?xml version="1.0" encoding="utf-8"?>
<root>
  <xsd:schema id="root" targetNamespace="" xmlns=""
➥xmlns:xsd="http://www.w3.org/2001/XMLSchema"
➥xmlns:msdata="urn:schemas-microsoft-com:xml-msdata">
    <xsd:element name="root" msdata:IsDataSet="true">
      <xsd:complexType>
        <xsd:choice maxOccurs="unbounded">
          <xsd:element name="data">
            <xsd:complexType>
              <xsd:sequence>
                <xsd:element name="value" type="xsd:string"
➥minOccurs="0" msdata:Ordinal="1" />
                <xsd:element name="comment"
➥type="xsd:string" minOccurs="0" msdata:Ordinal="2" />
              </xsd:sequence>
              <xsd:attribute name="name" type="xsd:string" />
              <xsd:attribute name="type" type="xsd:string" />
              <xsd:attribute name="mimetype"
➥type="xsd:string" />
            </xsd:complexType>
          </xsd:element>
          <xsd:element name="resheader">
            <xsd:complexType>
              <xsd:sequence>
                <xsd:element name="value" type="xsd:string"
➥minOccurs="0" msdata:Ordinal="1" />
              </xsd:sequence>
              <xsd:attribute name="name" type="xsd:string"
➥use="required" />
            </xsd:complexType>
          </xsd:element>
        </xsd:choice>
      </xsd:complexType>
    </xsd:element>
  </xsd:schema>
  <data name="thanks">
```

LISTING 29.5 continued

```
    <value>Thank you.</value>
  </data>
  <data name="welcome">
    <value>Your welcome.</value>
  </data>
  <resheader name="ResMimeType">
    <value>text/microsoft-resx</value>
  </resheader>
  <resheader name="Version">
    <value>1.0.0.0</value>
  </resheader>
  <resheader name="Reader">
    <value>System.Resources.ResXResourceReader</value>
  </resheader>
  <resheader name="Writer">
    <value>System.Resources.ResXResourceWriter</value>
  </resheader>
</root>
```

The header at the top of Listing 29.5 indicates that this is an XML file. There's a `<root>` element enclosing several subelements. The first of these is the XML schema definition, which defines the format, types, and constraints on the resources. The second portion of this file is the set of `<data>` elements, holding the name/value pairs used in programs. The `name` part is an attribute of the `<data>` element, and the `value` part is a `<value>` subelement of the `<data>` element. The final elements of the file are mime type information, versioning information, and reader and writer class definitions.

Creating Graphical Resources

The .NET Framework SDK includes a couple sample programs that help manage graphical resources. One is the `ResXGen` program, which adds a graphic to a `.resx` file. The other is the `ResEditor` program, which manages all types of resources for `.resources` files. An added bonus is that these two utilities come with source code, so you can examine graphical resource manipulation code in detail.

The source code is located in subdirectories at `C:\Program Files\Microsoft.Net\FrameworkSDK\Samples\tutorials\resourcesandlocalization` on my computer. If you've customized your directory structure, then search for the relative location of the `Samples` directory on your own system. Each executable can be compiled by running the `build.bat` batch file in its respective directory.

Tip

For convenience, I copied the ResEditor and ResXGen executables into my C:\Program Files\Microsoft.Net\FrameworkSDK\bin directory, which is in my PATH environment variable and makes each utility accessible from my command line without having to specify the long path.

The ResXGen Utility

The ResXGen utility generates a .resx XML formatted file for graphical resources. The actual formatting within the .resx file is done via the base class library's System.Serialization.Formatters.Binary.BinaryFormatter and then encoded to a base-64 format. To demonstrate the ResXGen utility, copy un.jpg, a JPEG picture of the United Nations Flag, from the C:\Program Files\Microsoft.Net\FrameworkSDK\Samples\tutorials\resourcesandlocalization\graphics\cs\images directory into a local working directory and run the following command line:

```
ResXGen /i:un.jpg /o:graphics.resx /n:flag
```

The /i option is the input graphic file; the /o option is the output .resx file; and the /n option is the resource key name used in programs to identify this resource. The help option, /?, explains all the other options available. Another option, /s, generates the XML schema definition of a .resx file. The result is relatively the same as the <xsd:schema> element from Listing 29.5 and a little more explanatory information. Here's how to generate the XML schema definition:

```
ResXGen /s
```

Between the ResGen and ResXGen utilities, the job of creating a .resources file gets done, but there are limitations. For instance, each of these utilities generates a brand new .resources file each time it runs. There are no options to add a .txt or .resx file to a .resources file without wiping out the existing .resources file's current content. Therefore, by using only these two utilities, ResGen and ResXGen, the only way to generate an assembly is to create separate .resources files and add them separately to an assembly, as the following example demonstrates:

```
ResXGen /i:un.jpg /o:unflag.resx /n:flag
ResGen unflag.resx unflag.resources
ResGen strings.txt strings.resources
al /out:graphics.resources.dll /embed:strings.resources
al /out:graphics.resources.dll /embed:unflag.resources
```

In this example, ResXGen creates the unflag.resx file from the un.jpg graphics file. Then the unflag.resx is converted to unflag.resources, and strings.txt is converted to strings.resources with ResGen. Finally, both .resources files just generated are added to the graphics.resources.dll library with the al utility. You could reduce the pain of all this work by modifying the source code of the ResXGen utility or use a batch or make file for automation. Another alternative is the ResEditor utility.

The ResEditor Utility

The ResEditor utility is a graphical program that enables manipulation of .resources files. The ResEditor screen is shown in Figure 29.1.

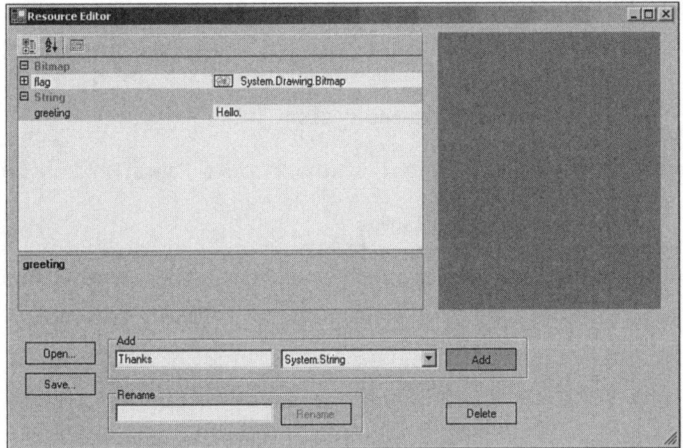

FIGURE 29.1
The ResEditor *utility.*

For Figure 29.1, I clicked the Open button to select a file and chose the unflag.resources file. I create a new string resource by making a new entry in the Add section, typing the name **greeting** in the first text box, selecting the System.String item in the drop-down list, and clicking the Add button. This created the greeting entry in the first column of the main list box under the Strings heading. Then I typed the value **Hello** into the second column of the same row in which the greeting name is entered. Figure 29.1 shows another string entry, thanks, being entered into the Add section. Finally, any changes can be made by clicking the Save button and entering a new .resources filename.

Using Graphical Resources

Using graphical resources are similar to using string resources. Just create a ResourceManager and then get the resource. In Listing 29.6, the GetObject() method of the ResourceManager obtains the binary graphics object. With the graphics object in hand, it can be manipulated according to how that type of resource would normally be manipulated in a program. Listing 29.6 shows how a JPEG image file resource is obtained and used in an application.

LISTING 29.6 Using Graphical Resources: `GraphRes.cs`

```
using System;
using System.Drawing;
using System.Collections;
using System.ComponentModel;
using System.Windows.Forms;
using System.Data;
using System.Resources;

namespace GraphicRes
{
    /// <summary>
    /// Graphics Resources Demonstration.
    /// </summary>
    public class GraphicResFrm : System.Windows.Forms.Form
    {
        private PictureBox flagPic;
        private Label      HelloLbl;
        private System.ComponentModel.Container components = null;

        public GraphicResFrm()
        {
            InitializeComponent();
        }

        /// <summary>
        /// Clean up any resources being used.
        /// </summary>
        protected override void Dispose( bool disposing )
        {
            if( disposing )
            {
                if (components != null)
                {
                    components.Dispose();
                }
            }
            base.Dispose( disposing );
        }

        private void InitializeComponent()
        {
            this.HelloLbl = new Label();
            this.flagPic  = new PictureBox();
```

LISTING 29.6 continued

```
        this.SuspendLayout();
        //
        // HelloLbl
        //
        this.HelloLbl.Font      = new Font(
            "Microsoft Sans Serif",
            14.25F,
            FontStyle.Regular,
            GraphicsUnit.Point,
            ((byte)(0)));
        this.HelloLbl.Location  = new Point(24, 136);
        this.HelloLbl.Name      = "HelloLbl";
        this.HelloLbl.Size      = new Size(240, 32);
        this.HelloLbl.TabIndex  = 1;
        this.HelloLbl.Text      = "label1";
        this.HelloLbl.TextAlign =
            ContentAlignment.MiddleCenter;
        //
        // flagPic
        //
        this.flagPic.Location = new Point(64, 24);
        this.flagPic.Name     = "flagPic";
        this.flagPic.Size     = new Size(160, 96);
        this.flagPic.SizeMode =
            PictureBoxSizeMode.StretchImage;
        this.flagPic.TabIndex = 0;
        this.flagPic.TabStop  = false;
        //
        // GraphicResFrm
        //
        this.AutoScaleBaseSize = new Size(5, 13);
        this.ClientSize        = new Size(292, 197);
        this.Controls.AddRange(new Control[] {
        this.HelloLbl,
        this.flagPic});
        this.Name  = "GraphicResFrm";
        this.Text  = "Graphical Resources Demo";
        this.Load += new
            System.EventHandler(this.GraphicResFrm_Load);
        this.ResumeLayout(false);
    }

    /// <summary>
    /// The main entry point for the application.
    /// </summary>
    static void Main()
    {
        Application.Run(new GraphicResFrm());
    }
```

LISTING 29.6 continued

```
        private void GraphicResFrm_Load(object sender,
                                        System.EventArgs e)
        {
            ResourceManager graphRes  = ResourceManager.
            CreateFileBasedResourceManager(
                "unflag", ".", null);
            ResourceManager stringRes = ResourceManager.
            CreateFileBasedResourceManager(
                "strings", ".", null);

            flagPic.Image = (System.Drawing.Image)
                graphRes.GetObject("flag");

            HelloLbl.Text = stringRes.GetString("greeting");
        }
    }
}
```

The majority of Listing 29.6 is just Windows Forms code supporting the main form and its `PictureBox` and `Label` controls. The pertinent part of the listing is the `GraphicResFrm_Load()` method that is called when the form is loaded to screen. It creates two `ResourceManager` objects, `graphRes` and `stringRes`.

The `graphRes` object is created with the `unflag.resources` file. This is where the `un.jpg` resource is stored. The `un.jpg` resource was the value with a name of `flag`. To obtain this resource, the program uses the `GetObject()` method of the `graphRes` object and stores it in the `Image` property of the `flagPic` object, which is a Windows Forms `PictureBox` control. This action displays the United Nations flag on the form.

The string resource is obtained the same way as shown earlier in this chapter. The value obtained from the GetString() method of the stringRes object is stored in the Text property of the HelloLbl object, which is a Windows Forms Label control. The form produced from Listing 29.6 is shown in Figure 29.2. Listing 29.6 was compiled with the following command line:

```
csc /t:winexe GraphRes.cs
```

FIGURE 29.2
Displaying a graphical resource.

Multiple Locales

The purpose of resource files is to support multiple locales. The official way of specifying locales is via cultures, as specified in RFC 1766, ISO 639, and ISO 6133. Cultures are denoted with four-character designations. The first two characters specify the language in lowercase, and the second two specify the country or region in uppercase. Table 29.2 contains some examples of culture designations. The total list is much too large to be included here. You can check out the RFC and ISOs listed previously for further information.

TABLE 29.2 Sample List of Cultures

Tag	*Description*
`de_CH`	Swiss German
`en`	English
`en_US`	United States English
`en_GB`	British English
`it`	Italian
`ja`	Japanese

A separate resource file must be created for each locale. There are multiple ways to deploy these resources: compiled into a program, via satellite assembly, or via a global assembly. Your choice depends on what the program is trying to accomplish. There is also a sequence of steps a program goes through to figure out which resources it should use.

Implementing Multiple Locales

Through a combination of resource files and a directory structure geared toward targeted cultures, any program can be localized. The directory structure corresponds to each culture implemented in a program. The following directory structure supports localization for a program named `MultiCulture`:

```
MultiCulture
    en
    en-US
    en-GB
    ja
```

The `MultiCulture` directory holds the executable program, and each of the subdirectories holds libraries with localized resources corresponding to the culture specified in the directory name. Each resource file contains the resources as specified in Table 29.3.

TABLE 29.3 Resource File Contents

Culture	*Flag/Greeting*
en	en-US.jpg/Hi
en-US	en-US.jpg/Hi
en-GB	en-GB.jpg/Hello
it	it.jpg/ciao
ja	ja.jpg/Konnichiwa
unspecified	un.jpg/Hello

Create each resource file in its corresponding directory with the name pattern MultiCulture.<culture>.resources. For example, the Japanese resource file would be built in the ja subdirectory with the name multiculture.ja.resources. Then create an assembly named MultiCulture.Resources.Dll in each directory with a localized resource file. The following example shows how to create the Japanese assembly:

```
al /out:MultiCulture.Resources.Dll /c:ja
➥ /embed:MultiCulture.ja.resources,
➥MultiCulture.ja.resources,Private
```

This follows the same method of creating resource files from assemblies that was explained earlier in this chapter. The only difference is the `/c` option, which specifies the culture. Remember to perform this task in each culture subdirectory, substituting culture abbreviations as appropriate.

If the appropriate culture subdirectory is present, a localized program can automatically pick up the resources corresponding to its default locale. For example, the default culture on my computer is `en-US`, resulting in the resources from the `en-US` culture subdirectory being used in the `MultiCulture` localized program. This program is shown in Listing 29.7.

LISTING 29.7 A Localized Program: MultiCulture.cs

```
using System;
using System.Drawing;
using System.Collections;
using System.ComponentModel;
using System.Windows.Forms;
using System.Data;
using System.Resources;
using System.Threading;
using System.Globalization;

namespace MultiCulture
{
    /// <summary>
    /// Summary description for MultiCulture.
    /// </summary>
    public class MultiCulture : System.Windows.Forms.Form
    {
        ResourceManager multiRes;

        private System.Windows.Forms.PictureBox flagPic;
        private System.Windows.Forms.Label greetingLbl;
        private System.Windows.Forms.ComboBox cultureCbx;

        private System.ComponentModel.Container components
            = null;

        public MultiCulture()
        {
            InitializeComponent();
            multiRes = new ResourceManager("multiculture",
                this.GetType().Assembly);
        }

        /// <summary>
        /// Clean up any resources being used.
        /// </summary>
        protected override void Dispose( bool disposing )
        {
            if( disposing )
            {
```

LISTING 29.7 continued

```
            if (components != null)
            {
                components.Dispose();
            }
        }

        base.Dispose( disposing );
    }

    private void InitializeComponent()
    {
        this.flagPic
            = new System.Windows.Forms.PictureBox();
        this.cultureCbx
            = new System.Windows.Forms.ComboBox();
        this.greetingLbl
            = new System.Windows.Forms.Label();
        this.SuspendLayout();
        //
        // flagPic
        //
        this.flagPic.Location
            = new System.Drawing.Point(64, 24);
        this.flagPic.Name = "flagPic";
        this.flagPic.Size
            = new System.Drawing.Size(168, 104);
        this.flagPic.SizeMode
= System.Windows.Forms.PictureBoxSizeMode.StretchImage;
        this.flagPic.TabIndex = 0;
        this.flagPic.TabStop = false;
        //
        // cultureCbx
        //
        this.cultureCbx.DisplayMember = "en-US";
        this.cultureCbx.DropDownWidth = 121;
        this.cultureCbx.Items.AddRange(new object[] {
                                            "en-US",
                                            "en-GB",
                                            "ja-JP",
                                            "de-CH",
                                            "it",
                                            "mars"});
        this.cultureCbx.Location
            = new System.Drawing.Point(88, 216);
        this.cultureCbx.Name = "cultureCbx";
        this.cultureCbx.Size
            = new System.Drawing.Size(121, 21);
        this.cultureCbx.TabIndex = 2;
        this.cultureCbx.Text = "en-US";
```

LISTING 29.7 continued

```
            this.cultureCbx.SelectedIndexChanged += new
                System.EventHandler(
                this.cultureCbx_SelectedIndexChanged);
            //
            // greetingLbl
            //
            this.greetingLbl.Font = new System.Drawing.Font(
                    "Microsoft Sans Serif",
                    14.25F,
                    System.Drawing.FontStyle.Regular,
                    System.Drawing.GraphicsUnit.Point,
                    ((System.Byte)(0)));
            this.greetingLbl.Location
                = new System.Drawing.Point(64, 160);
            this.greetingLbl.Name = "greetingLbl";
            this.greetingLbl.Size
                = new System.Drawing.Size(168, 23);
            this.greetingLbl.TabIndex = 1;
            this.greetingLbl.Text = "greeting";
            this.greetingLbl.TextAlign
              = System.Drawing.ContentAlignment.MiddleCenter;
            //
            // MultiCulture
            //
            this.AutoScaleBaseSize
                = new System.Drawing.Size(5, 13);
            this.ClientSize
                = new System.Drawing.Size(292, 273);
            this.Controls.AddRange(
                new System.Windows.Forms.Control[] {
                    this.cultureCbx,
                    this.greetingLbl,
                    this.flagPic});
            this.Name = "MultiCulture";
            this.Text = "Localization Demo";
            this.Load += new
                System.EventHandler(this.MultiCulture_Load);
            this.ResumeLayout(false);
        }

        /// <summary>
        /// The main entry point for the application.
        /// </summary>
        static void Main()
        {
            Application.Run(new MultiCulture());
        }
```

LISTING 29.7 continued

```
        private void SetLocalizedResources()
        {
            flagPic.Image
                = (System.Drawing.Image)
                multiRes.GetObject("flag");

            greetingLbl.Text
                = multiRes.GetString("greeting");
        }

        private void MultiCulture_Load(object sender,
                                       System.EventArgs e)
        {
            SetLocalizedResources();
        }

        private void cultureCbx_SelectedIndexChanged(
            object sender, System.EventArgs e)
        {
            Thread.CurrentThread.CurrentUICulture = new
        CultureInfo(this.cultureCbx.SelectedItem.ToString());

            SetLocalizedResources();
        }
    }
}
```

The first difference between this program and demos in earlier sections is the way the resources are used. Earlier programs declared `ResourceManager` classes that used `.resource` files directly. The `MultiCulture` program in Listing 29.7 uses the satellite assemblies located in each culture subdirectory. The manner in which it finds the appropriate assembly is hidden within the `ResourceManager` class. This program enables this functionality in the way it initializes the `ResourceManager` instance.

The ResourceManager object is declared as a class field and initialized in the MultiCulture form constructor. The ResourceManager constructor accepts two parameters. The first is the root name of the resources to read. Since each file is named multiculture.resources.dll, the root name is multiculture. The second parameter identifies the main assembly for the resources, which is the MultiCulture assembly. The MultiCulture program is compiled with default resources, in case a requested culture doesn't have a specific culture subdirectory. The following command line compiles Listing 29.7:

```
csc /t:winexe /res:multiculture.resources MultiCulture.cs
```

In this command line, the /t:winexe option keeps the pesky console window from popping up every time the program is run. The default resources file, identified in the /res option, contains resources from the unspecified column of Table 29.3 and doesn't have a culture abbreviation in the name.

The SetLocalizedResources() method sets the PictureBox and Label controls, similar to earlier examples. This method is called by the MultiCulture_Load() method, which is invoked when the form loads. It's also called by the cultureCbx_SelectedIndexChanged() method.

The cultureCbx_SelectedIndexChanged() method is instrumental in enabling dynamic localization in this program. It's called when a new item in the drop-down list is selected. The following very busy line of code changes the program's culture:

```
Thread.CurrentThread.CurrentUICulture =

    new CultureInfo(this.cultureCbx.SelectedItem.ToString());
```

This command resets the CurrentUICulture property of the CurrentThread object, which is the current thread this program is running in. The value placed into the CurrentUICulture property is a CultureInfo object. It's initialized with the culture identifier that the user selected from the drop-down list.

Warning

Thread.CurrentThread contains both CurrentCulture and CurrentUICulture properties. Be sure to use the CurrentUICulture property (with the UI in the middle) when changing locales. It might save a few hours' worth of headaches when you try to change a program's culture and nothing happens.

CultureInfo is the standard Base Class Library class for localization. It holds pertinent information for calendars, numbers, and string formatting. In its current role, it's the primary means of providing dynamic manipulation of cultures. The MultiCultures program is shown in Figure 29.3.

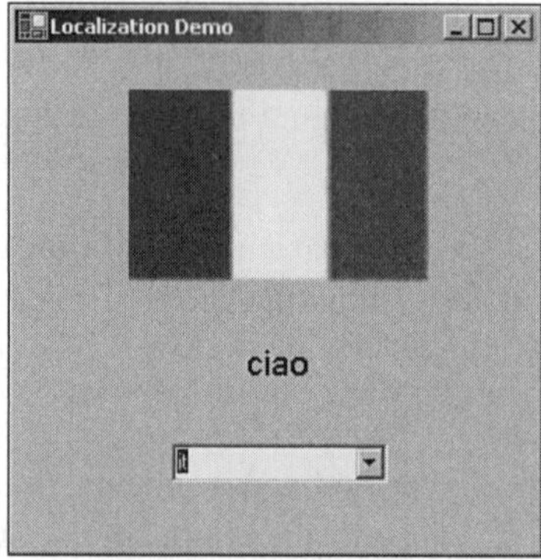

FIGURE 29.3
The MultiCultures program.

Finding Resources

A localized application follows a specific path when resolving where it obtains resources. As would be expected, this resolution strategy is based on moving from the most specific to a general source of resources. The resource resolution process follows these steps and ends whenever a resource is found or an exception is thrown:

1. Search the global assembly cache for the specific resource. The global assembly cache is discussed in detail in a later chapter, but for now think of it as a central repository for all programs on a machine to access.
2. Search culture subdirectories of the localized program.
3. Search the global assembly cache for parent resources. For instance, if the original resource selected, but not found, was `en-US`, then search the global assembly cache for `en` only.
4. Search culture subdirectories of the localized program for the parent resources.
5. Search culture subdirectories of the localized program for parent resources of the last parent resource searched. A resource has only a single parent, but the chain of parents can extend multiple levels.
6. Use the default resource. This is the unspecified resource that was compiled with the main assembly.
7. If the resource is not found, throw a `System.Argument.Exception`.

Tip

To reduce complexity, it's useful to begin localizing a program with only two cultures. Imagine what would happen if a more meaningful resource name was desired after all locales had been created. If this happens often enough during development, it would get annoying to change every resource file.

Also seriously consider having default parent culture resources for every subculture you support. This way you could do a quick modification for a new subculture, allowing the majority of resources to default to the parent, while concentrating on those resources specific to the subculture.

Experimenting with this resolution process can be done with the `MultiCultures` program. For example, selecting `en-GB`, `it`, or `ja` will use the resources from the corresponding culture subdirectories. Since `en-US` doesn't have a culture subdirectory, it defaults to its parent, `en`, which happens to have a U.S. flag and greeting. The `de-CH` culture doesn't have any resources of its own and must use the default assembly, which was compiled into the main `MultiCulture` assembly. Finally, although there has been much speculation as to whether there is life on the planet Mars, the `mars` locale is not installed on this operating system, generating an exception when selected.

Summary

Program localization is supported through resources. There are several ways to generate resources, depending on the resource type. The available formats are text files with name/value pairs of strings or XML files, which are specifically suited to binary resources. These two file types are then converted to binary resource files, which may be included in assemblies.

The `ResGen` tool, included in the .NET Frameworks SDK, enables conversion between different resource types. The `ResXGen` and `ResEditor` are sample programs included with the .NET Framework SDK that help manage resources.

Resource files are placed in specified directories so localized programs can find the right resources. `ResourceManager` is the primary class, providing management of resources for program use. Assigning `CultureInfo` objects to the `CurrentUICulture` property of the current thread may dynamically change cultures. Localized programs use a resolution process to find the most specific resources available. A combination of specialized culture subdirectories and resource files make program localization a straightforward process.

CHAPTER 30

Unsafe Code and PInvoke

In This Chapter

- Unsafe Code 620
- Platform Invoke 631

An important consideration in any project is reuse of existing code. The ability to access legacy code containing business logic or low-level system functionality could lead to significant benefits in time and cost. To meet this demand, C# provides a mechanism to access legacy systems, with a feature known as `PInvoke`, short for Platform Invoke.

Unsafe code permits a block of code to use pointers, low-level types that allow indirect access to memory and other types. This opens new opportunities for optimization and interfaces to operating system or legacy code that requires pointers. The primary reason for unsafe code blocks is to separate safe C# code from pointer-related code, which could cause problems if mixed together.

Unsafe Code

Unsafe code, as defined in the next section, permits the use of pointers, which supports certain performance optimizations and interface to legacy code and operating systems. Unsafe code is identified with a special keyword, `unsafe`, which marks either a block of code or a field. This establishes an `unsafe` context where pointer operations can be implemented.

There are special keywords associated with `unsafe` contexts, making it easier to work with pointers. The `fixed` keyword helps pin down objects in memory so the garbage collector doesn't move them in the middle of an operation. Obtaining the size of a pointer or field can be accomplished by using the `sizeof` operator. The `stackalloc` operator enables memory to be allocated on the stack. In addition to keywords, there are a few other operators that facilitate pointer operations, such as the dereferencing operator (`*`), the address of operator (`&`), and the indirection operator (`->`).

What Do You Mean My Code Is Unsafe?

A subject of much confusion and discussion, C# brings a whole new vocabulary relating whether code is safe, unsafe, managed, or unmanaged. For full understanding of the issues in this chapter, it's important to define what these terms are and why they're important.

- **Safe**—The normal mode of operation in a C# program is safe. When code is safe, it's type-safe and secure. Although there may not be a formal type of code called safe, it's illustrative to differentiate it from unsafe code.
- **Unsafe**—Unsafe code is identified by the unsafe keyword. This is code that is allowed to use pointers. It's also the only place that certain statements and operators such as fixed, sizeof, and stackalloc may be used. Unsafe code is more

complex and prone to error than normal safe code, so it requires the unsafe keyword to separate it from normal safe C# code.

Although unsafe code permits operations that are not part of normal C# practices, unsafe code is still managed. It's managed because the Common Language Runtime (CLR) or Virtual Execution System (VES) still has control over the code and still manages memory.

- **Managed**—All C# code is managed. Managed code is under control of the CLR, which has full control of all memory and security operations. Unsafe code is still managed code.

  Managed types are all reference types and value types with a nested reference type. Managed types reside on the heap and are managed by the CLR.

- **Unmanaged**—Native code, such as that accessed through Platform Invoke or COM Interop, is unmanaged. Code that is unmanaged is not controlled by the CLR.

  Unmanaged types include all value types (without nested reference types), enums, and pointers.

The Power of Pointers

A pointer is an indirect address to another object. At its most basic level, it's similar to an object reference, but much more powerful. While references provide a mechanism to refer to an object, pointers can be arithmetically manipulated to move forward and backward through a group of objects. Pointers can be set to any addressable location and even view memory locations where no object exists.

Classification-wise, a pointer type is considered a peer of value and reference types. Pointers are declared as a specific value or reference type. This means that they hold the address of the types they are declared as. For instance, a pointer to an `int` is declared like one of the following:

```
int *intPtr;
```

or

```
int* intPtr;
```

or

```
int * intPtr;
```

This creates an uninitialized integer pointer. The asterisk (`*`) means that `intPtr` is a pointer. The keyword, `int`, indicates the type of which this pointer can hold an address. This is the same as any other field declaration except it has the `*` to indicate that it is a pointer.

Pointers hold addresses of objects. Therefore, in most cases it would be illogical to assign a field value to a pointer. The address-of operator, shown in the following example, is used to load a value into a pointer:

```
int myInt = 7;
intPtr = &myInt;
```

The address-of, `&`, operator returns the memory address of a field. In this example, the address of the `myInt` variable is assigned to the `intPtr` pointer. Now `intPtr` refers to the value held by `myInt`.

Right now, the value of `myInt` is 7, and the value of `intPtr` is the address of `myInt`. This is nice, but the real benefit of `intPtr` comes when it can be used to indirectly read the value from `myInt`. The following example shows how to use the indirection operator to enable a pointer to read the value from a normal field:

```
int retrievedInt = *intPtr;
```

Now the value of `myInt`, 7, has been assigned to `retrievedInt` through the `int` pointer, `intPtr`. This was made possible by the dereferencing operator (`*`), which returns the value of the field it is pointing to.

At this point, the `*` has been used twice in the context of pointers. The first time it was used in the declaration of a pointer to specify that this is a pointer type declaration, as opposed to a reference type or value type declaration. The second time it was used as an indirection operator, returning the value of the object it pointed to. This one operator, `*`, is used for both pointer declaration and pointer indirection.

Pointers may have multiple levels of indirection, which is essentially a pointer to a pointer. Here's an example of how to declare a pointer to a pointer.

```
int **intPtrPtr = &intPtr;
```

The address of `intPtr`, which is a pointer itself, is assigned to another pointer, `intPtrPtr`. This time, two `*`'s are needed to declare `intPtrPtr` because it is a pointer to a pointer of type `int`. Although further levels of indirection are possible, it may be quite rare that they would be necessary.

An interesting relationship exists between arrays and pointers, where pointers may be represented as arrays. The following example shows how to use a pointer as an array:

```
int myInt = intPtr[0]; // myInt = 7
```

This time `intPtr` was used just like an array. Since it has only one element, the example accessed the first (zero-based) element in the array, which returned the value `7`. Pointing to just the first element of an array won't accomplish much, and hints at the need for some mechanism to get to the other elements of the array. One obvious solution is to use an index into the array to get to the elements necessary. However, there's another way to do this—with pointer arithmetic, as shown in Listing 30.1.

LISTING 30.1 Pointer Arithmetic: `PointerArithmetic.cs`

```
using System;

/// <summary>
///     Pointer Arithmetic Demonstration.
/// </summary>
class PointerArithmetic
{
    struct IntStruct
    {
        int one;
        int two;
        int three;

        public IntStruct(int first, int second, int third)
        {
            one   = first;
            two   = second;
            three = third;
        }
    }

    unsafe static void Main(string[] args)
    {
        IntStruct myIntStruct = new IntStruct(3, 5, 7);

        int *intPtr = (int *)&myIntStruct;

        Console.WriteLine(
            "\nPointer with array indexing - \n");

        for (int i=0; i < 3; i++)
        {
            Console.WriteLine("intPtr[]: {0}", intPtr[i]);
        }

        Console.WriteLine("\nPointer arithmetic - \n");

        for (int i=0; i < 3; i++)
        {
            Console.WriteLine("*intPtr: {0}", (*intPtr)++);
        }

    Console.WriteLine("\nPointer to member access
```

LISTING 30.1 continued

```
[ccc]with dereferencing (*) operator) - \n");
    IntStruct *isPtr = &myIntStruct;
    Console.WriteLine("(*isPtr).one:   {0}", (*isPtr).one);
    Console.WriteLine("(*isPtr).two:   {0}", (*isPtr).two);
    Console.WriteLine("(*isPtr).three: {0}", (*isPtr).three);
    }
}
```

And here's the output:

```
Pointer with array indexing -

intPtr[]: 3
intPtr[]: 5
intPtr[]: 7

Pointer arithmetic -

*intPtr: 3
*intPtr: 5
*intPtr: 7

Pointer member access -

isPtr->one:   3
isPtr->two:   5
isPtr->three: 7
```

The first `for` loop in Listing 30.1 uses array indexing to access each member of the `IntStruct`. Although `myIntStruct` is a `struct`, its members are sitting in a contiguous block of memory, which is accessible by a pointer. The indexer serves as an offset from the address the pointer actually points to.

The second `for` loop uses pointer arithmetic to move the pointer to the next location in memory. The actual location moved to in memory is relative to the size of the pointer type. As with any other C# expression, addition, subtraction, increment, or decrement operators may be used to arithmetically manipulate the value of a pointer.

Listing 30.2 shows how to compile this program. The `/unsafe` command line option is required.

LISTING 30.2 Compilation Instructions for Listing 30.1

```
csc /unsafe PointerArithmetic.cs
```

The last part of Listing 30.1 shows how to use the indirection operator, `->`, to reference the members of the `myIntStruct struct`. This is how pointers reference `struct` members, rather than using the dot operator.

Going back to the second `for` loop of Listing 30.1, the post-increment operator modifies the value of the pointer so that its value is now at the next address. The type of pointer determines what that next address will be. Since an `int` is four bytes long, the post-increment operator would yield an address that is four bytes beyond its current location.

The `sizeof()` Operator

Knowing the size of a type can help in several areas. For instance, if the program only had a certain amount of memory to work with, it would need to keep track of where the pointer was in a loop to make sure it didn't go too far. To help with these types of scenarios, the `sizeof()` operator is available. The `sizeof()` operator may only be used on unmanaged types. Listing 30.3 demonstrates how to use the `sizeof()` operator.

LISTING 30.3 Using the `sizeof()` Operator

```
using System;

/// <summary>
///     sizeof operator demo
/// </summary>
class SizeOfDemo
{
    unsafe static void Main(string[] args)
    {
        Console.WriteLine("\nsizeof Operator Demo\n");

        Console.WriteLine("sizeof(bool):    {0}", sizeof(bool));
        Console.WriteLine("sizeof(char):    {0}", sizeof(char));
        Console.WriteLine("sizeof(byte):    {0}", sizeof(byte));
        Console.WriteLine("sizeof(short):   {0}", sizeof(short));
        Console.WriteLine("sizeof(int):     {0}", sizeof(int));
        Console.WriteLine("sizeof(long):    {0}", sizeof(long));
        Console.WriteLine("sizeof(float):   {0}", sizeof(float));
        Console.WriteLine("sizeof(double):  {0}", sizeof(double));
        Console.WriteLine("sizeof(decimal): {0}", sizeof(decimal));
    }
}
```

And here's the output:

```
sizeof Operator Demo

sizeof(bool):    1
sizeof(char):    2
sizeof(byte):    1
sizeof(short):   2
sizeof(int):     4
sizeof(long):    8
sizeof(float):   4
sizeof(double):  8
sizeof(decimal): 16
```

The code in Listing 30.3 shows the `sizeof()` operator used with the C# primitive types. The `sizeof()` operator tells the number of bytes a pointer will move when it is incremented or decremented by one. Listing 30.4 shows how to compile Listing 30.3.

Listing 30.4 Compilation Instructions for Listing 30.3

```
csc /unsafe SizeOfDemo.cs
```

The `stackalloc` Operator

A common requirement when working with pointers is to have a pool of memory to work with to accomplish a task. The `stackalloc` operator allocates memory on the stack and may only be used on unmanaged types. There's no need to explicitly free memory obtained through `stackalloc` because it's returned to the system when the routine ends. Listing 30.5 shows how to use the `stackalloc` operator.

Listing 30.5 `stackalloc` Demonstration: `StackAllocDemo.cs`

```
using System;

/// <summary>
///     stackalloc demo.
/// </summary>
class StackAllocDemo
{
    unsafe static void Main(string[] args)
    {
        string myString = "Unsafe is still Managed!";

        char *charArr = stackalloc char[myString.Length];
        char *charPtr = charArr;
```

LISTING 30.5 continued

```
        Console.WriteLine("\nCreating String...\n");

        int count = 0;
        foreach(char character in myString)
        {
            *charPtr++ = character;
            Console.Write("{0} ", charArr[count++]);
        }
        Console.WriteLine();
    }
}
```

And the output is

```
Creating String...

U n s a f e   i s   s t i l l   M a n a g e d !
```

The example in Listing 30.5 loads a string into a block of `stackalloc` allocated memory. The memory is allocated by using array-like syntax. Instead of the `new` statement, it uses `stackalloc`. The block of memory allocated by `stackalloc` must be assigned to a pointer of the type that was allocated, which is a char `*` named `charArr`. The reason it's named `charArr` is because it will be used with array syntax later in the program. Here's the line using the `stackalloc` operator:

```
char *charArr = stackalloc char[myString.Length];
```

The `charArr` pointer needs to remain stationary, so its address is assigned to the `charPtr` character pointer. Note that the address of a pointer is assigned with the pointer type itself as opposed to a field that requires the address-of, `&`, operator. The address assignment is shown here:

```
char *charPtr = charArr;
```

Within the `foreach` loop, each character of the `string` is copied to the memory that was allocated with `stackalloc`. The indirection operator is used to assign the character value to the proper memory position. After dereferencing and assignment, the location of the `charPtr` is incremented to the next character position as shown in the following statement:

```
*charPtr++ = character;
```

After assigning each character to its corresponding position in the allocated memory block, the value of that location in memory is printed to the console. The reason we left the `charArr` character pointer alone was so it can be used with array-like syntax to reference each character. The `count` field is used to index into the allocated memory and is then incremented. The line showing element access with the `charArr` pointer is shown here:

```
Console.Write("{0} ", charArr[count++]);
```

The `stackalloc` program from Listing 30.5 can be compiled with the command line from Listing 30.6.

LISTING 30.6 Compilation Instructions for Listing 30.5

```
csc /unsafe StackAllocDemo.cs
```

Tip

The `stackalloc` operator allocates memory on the stack. If there's a need to allocate heap memory, you should create a class that uses `PInvoke` to call operating system memory allocation routines. For example, the Windows `HeapAlloc()` and `HeapFree()` functions allocate and free heap memory.

The `fixed` Statement

The `fixed` statement keeps moveable objects pinned while accessing them with a pointer. When using the `fixed` statement, you pin a variable, which is then considered pinned. Because of garbage collection and other memory optimization processes, there would be no guarantee that the object being pointed to in one operation would be the same the next time the pointer was referenced. The `fixed` statement guarantees that moveable objects stay put.

There are two categories of variables to consider when using the `fixed` statement: fixed and movable. Fixed variables include local variables and value types, values resulting from a `struct` member access where the `struct` is fixed, and pointer indirection or pointer member access.

Moveable variables include reference types, `ref` and `out` parameters, a boxed variable, and static variables. Listing 30.7 shows how to use the `fixed` statement.

LISTING 30.7 `fixed` Statement Demo: `FixedStatementDemo.cs`

```
using System;

/// <summary>
///     fixed Statement Demo.
/// </summary>
class FixedStatementDemo
{
    unsafe static int strstr(string subString,
                             string searchString)
    {
        int  pos   = 0;
        bool found = false;
        char *tmpPtr;

        fixed (char *stringPtr = searchString)
        {
            char *charPtr = stringPtr;

            for(int i=0; i < searchString.Length; i++)
            {
                if (subString[0] != *charPtr++)
                    continue;

                pos    = i;
                tmpPtr = charPtr;

                for(int j=1; j < subString.Length; j++)
                {
                    found = true;

                    if (subString[j] != *tmpPtr++)
                    {
                        found = false;
                        pos = 0;
                        break;
                    }
                }
                if (found)
                    return pos;
            }
        }
        return -1;
    }

    static void Main(string[] args)
    {
        string subString    = "an";
        string searchString = "banana";
```

LISTING 30.7 continued

```
        int pos = strstr(subString, searchString);

        if (pos == -1)
            Console.WriteLine(
                "'{0}' not found in '{1}'",
                subString, searchString);
        else
            Console.WriteLine(
                "Found '{0}' in '{1}' at position {2}",
                subString, searchString, pos+1);
    }
}
```

And here's the output:

```
Found 'an' in 'banana' at position 2
```

The first thing to notice about the example in Listing 30.7 is that the `fixed` statement is inside the `strstr()` method. It would have been easy to pin the strings before calling `strstr()` and then send in pointers, but that would have violated an important rule when using the `fixed` statement: Objects should only be pinned for the minimum amount of time necessary.

The rationale for this rule is simple when you consider the reason for pinning a variable. A pinned variable can't be garbage-collected. To prevent the pinned variable from being garbage-collected, some mechanism must be in place to recognize that this variable is pinned. This involves overhead that won't exist if the object is not pinned.

Therefore, the `fixed` statement is placed inside the `strstr()` method, and the routine is optimized to spend the minimal amount of time finding a substring within a string. The `fixed` statement assigns the moveable object to a pointer of a compatible type as shown here:

```
fixed (char *stringPtr = searchString)
```

This creates a read-only pointer. Another pointer must be created and assigned the value of `stringPtr` to read the rest of the string:

```
char *charPtr = stringPtr;
```

We want to rip through the search string in a linear fashion, so the first thing done is to keep reading until the first characters match. When the characters don't match, skip all other loop processing:

```
if (subString[0] != *charPtr++)
    continue;
```

There's similar logic throughout this routine, but the point is to do what's necessary and leave as soon as possible. Listing 30.8 shows how to compile the code in Listing 30.7, again using the `/unsafe` command-line option.

LISTING 30.8 Compilation Instructions for Listing 30.7

```
csc /unsafe FixedStatementDemo.cs
```

Platform Invoke

Platform Invoke—`PInvoke`—provides a means for C# programs to execute native code. This is of great help when there's a need to reuse legacy code or communicate with systems that don't have other readily available interfaces. Once legacy code is wrapped in a DLL, it can be called with C# through `PInvoke`.

Another use of `PInvoke` is to access existing operating system and third-party DLLs. Using `PInvoke` is as simple as declaring the method prototype as static extern and decorating it with the `DllImport` attribute. Listing 30.9 has a couple examples of how to use the `DllImport` attribute to implement `PInvoke`.

LISTING 30.9 Platform Invoke Demo: `PinvokeDemo.cs`

```
using System;
using System.Runtime.InteropServices;

/// <summary>
///     Platform Invocation Demo.
/// </summary>
class PInvokeDemo
{
    const int ABORT_RETRY_IGNORE = 2;

    [DllImport("user32.dll")]
    static extern int MessageBox(
        int hWnd, string message, string title, int options);

    [DllImport("user32.dll",
        EntryPoint="MessageBox", CharSet = CharSet.Unicode)]
    static extern int SpecialMessageBox(
        int hWnd, string message, string title, int options);

    static void Main(string[] args)
    {
        MessageBox(
            0, "Plain Message Box", "PInvoke Example #1", 0);
```

LISTING 30.9 continued

```
            SpecialMessageBox(
                0, "Special Message Box", "PInvoke Example #2",
                ABORT_RETRY_IGNORE);
        }
    }
```

Listing 30.9 has two examples of how to use the `DllImport` attribute. The first example contains positional parameter to specify which DLL has the function we want to call. It uses the `MessageBox` call to display the Windows message box on the screen, as shown in Figure 30.1.

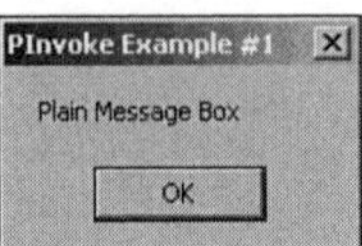

FIGURE 30.1
Plain message box.

The `DllImport` attribute in the second example is more detailed, with the `EntryPoint` and `CharSet` named parameters. The `EntryPoint` named parameter specifies the name of the method being called. This permits the method declaration being decorated to have any other name. In this example, the method is called `SpecialMessageBox()`.

The `CharSet` named parameter specifies two things: What character set to translate when marshalling strings to native code and method name mangling. Windows commonly uses a name-mangling convention for multiple versions of a method. Methods ending in `A` accept `Ansi` strings, and methods ending in `W` accept Unicode strings. When neither of these name-mangling conventions is used in either the `EntryPoint` named parameter or the method name of the declaration, `PInvoke` uses the `CharSet` named parameter to select the appropriate function.

Options for the `CharSet` named parameter include members of the `CharSet` enum: `Ansi`, `Auto`, `None`, and `Unicode`. `Ansi` and `Unicode` specify which character set to use when marshalling strings. `None` means that no `CharSet` is specified. `Auto`, the default, is platform dependent. For example, Windows NT is `Unicode` and Windows 9x is `Ansi`. Figure 30.2 shows what the second message box looks like. Listing 30.10 contains the command line for compiling the example in Listing 30.9.

LISTING 30.10 Compilation Instructions for Listing 30.9

```
csc FixedStatementDemo.cs
```

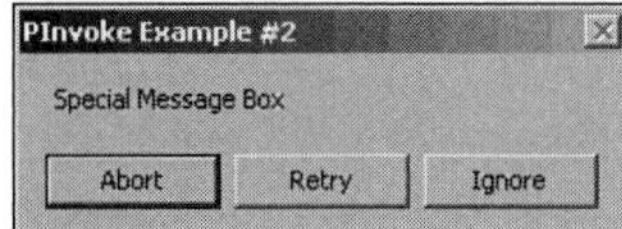

FIGURE 30.2
Special message box.

Summary

Unsafe code allows you to use pointers, a low-level mechanism designed to help optimize some routines. Pointers operate by holding the address of objects, providing indirect access to an object's value and member-wise access to `structs`. Pointers also may be manipulated arithmetically.

There are a few keywords that assist working with unsafe code. The `sizeof()` operator returns the number of bytes in a variable. Memory allocation is performed with the `stackalloc` operator. Since there's no guarantee that a moveable object in memory will stay in place, the `fixed` statement is used to pin a movable object in memory.

Platform Invoke—`PInvoke`—is a capability that allows C# programs to call native code libraries. To use `PInvoke`, methods are decorated with the `DllImport` attribute.

If you're going to be using unsafe code and invoking native libraries, it's a good idea to have some runtime support to help isolate problems when they occur. The next chapter, "Runtime Debugging," helps to do just that.

CHAPTER 31

Runtime Debugging

In This Chapter

- Simple Debugging 636
- Conditional Debugging 638
- Runtime Tracing 641
- Making Assertions 643

There are several situations where runtime debugging and tracing are desirable. Often it's easy to turn on debugging in a program, let it run, and watch a console screen for specific printouts representing the state of the program during execution. This is a quick way of isolating system failures during development.

For critical code, it may be useful to install a runtime trace facility. This provides a means to capture real-time information on production code and interact with administrators or analysts on what could be causing a problem.

The system libraries have facilities for supporting runtime debugging and tracing. This includes attributes and switches for conditional debugging and multilevel conditions for controlling trace output. It's also possible to monitor the logical implementation of code with assertions.

The `System.Diagnostics` namespace has two primary classes for runtime debugging: `Debug` and `Trace`. For the most part, their functionality is similar; the primary difference between the two comes from how they are used. The `Debug` class is strictly for development environments and requires a `DEBUG` directive or command-line option to be specified to activate its functionality. The `Trace` class is automatically activated and doesn't require any directive or command-line options. This is because the `Trace` class is for programs to be deployed with debugging capability. Debugging code introduces overhead in a program. If programs should not be deployed with debugging information, which reduces overhead, use the `Debug` class. However, if there's a need to have debugging information available in deployment and the overhead is acceptable, the `Trace` class does the trick.

Simple Debugging

In its simplest form, runtime debugging is just a matter of printing out statements to the console. The `Debug` class, a member of the `System.Diagnostics` namespace, has two methods for supporting explicit debugging: `Write()` and `WriteLine()`. These methods work similar to their `Console` class counterparts. Listing 31.1 shows an example that uses the `WriteLine()` method of the `Debug` class.

LISTING 31.1 A Simple Debugging Example: `PlainDebugDemo.cs`

```
#define DEBUG

using System;
using System.Diagnostics;

/// <summary>
///     Plain Debug Demo.
```

LISTING 31.1 continued

```
/// </summary>
class PlainDebugDemo
{
    static void DebuggedMethod()
    {
        Debug.WriteLine("Debug: Entered MyMethod()");
    }

    static void Main(string[] args)
    {
        TextWriterTraceListener myListener =
            new TextWriterTraceListener(Console.Out);

        Debug.Listeners.Add(myListener);

        DebuggedMethod();
    }
}
```

And here's the output:

```
Debug: Entered MyMethod()
```

Setting up a program for debugging requires statements to specify where debug output should be sent. The `Main()` method in Listing 31.1 creates a `TextWriterTraceListener` class that directs debugging output to the console window. It then adds the listener to the collection of Debug listeners.

Listing 31.1 used a `TextWriter` object, `Console.out`, as its output destination. However, debug output could have been just as well sent to a file by instantiating a `Stream` object and providing it as the parameter to the `TextWriterTraceListener` instantiation. The `TextWriterTraceListener` class also has methods to flush and close debug output with the `Flush()` and `Close()` methods, respectively.

The `Listeners` collection of the `Debug` class accepts any derived `TraceListener` class. Therefore, it's possible to create customized trace listeners by deriving them from either the `TraceListener` or `TextWriterTraceListener` classes.

Once an output destination is set up, the program invokes the `DebuggedMethod()` method, which calls the `WriteLine()` method of the `Debug` class. This produces the output shown following the listing.

There are a couple ways to enable debugging. At the top of Listing 31.1 is a `#define DEBUG` directive, enabling the operation of the `Debug` class. Additionally, Listing 31.2 shows how to enable debugging with the command line option, `/d:DEBUG`. One or the other of these methods, directive or compilation option, enables debugging, but they both are not required together. If neither of these, directive or compilation option, are present, the `Debug` class does not operate, and there would be no output.

LISTING 31.2 Compilation Instructions for Listing 31.1

```
csc /d:DEBUG PlainDebugDemo.cs
```

Conditional Debugging

A program's capability to turn debugging on and off as needed is called *conditional debugging*. During development, output from debugging can clutter up normal output or force paths of execution that isn't necessary on every run. The `System.Diagnostics` namespace has both attributes and switches to turn debugging on and off as necessary. Listing 31.3 shows how to use attributes to control conditional debugging.

LISTING 31.3 Debugging with Conditional Attributes: `ConditionalDebugDemo.cs`

```
#define DEBUG

using System;
using System.Diagnostics;

/// <summary>
///     Conditional Debug Demo.
/// </summary>
class ConditionalDebugDemo
{
    static bool Debugging = true;

    [Conditional("DEBUG")]
    static void SetupDebugListener()
    {
        TextWriterTraceListener myListener =
            new TextWriterTraceListener(Console.Out);

        Debug.Listeners.Add(myListener);
    }

    [Conditional("DEBUG")]
    static void CheckState()
    {
        Debug.WriteLineIf(Debugging, "Debug: Entered CheckState()");
    }
```

LISTING 31.3 continued

```
    static void Main(string[] args)
    {
        SetupDebugListener();

        CheckState();
    }
}
```

And here's the output:

```
Debug: Entered CheckState()
```

Two features of Listing 31.3 are of primary interest: the `Conditional` attribute and a Boolean condition on output. The `Conditional` attribute is placed at the beginning of a method that can be turned on and off at will. The condition causing the method to be invoked is either the `#define DEBUG` directive at the top of the listing or the command line `/d:DEBUG` option, shown in Listing 31.4. If neither of these, directive or command line option, is present, the methods with the `Conditional` attribute are invoked when called by the `Main()` method.

LISTING 31.4 Compilation Instructions for Listing 31.3

```
csc /d:DEBUG ConditionalDebugDemo.cs
```

The second item of interest in Listing 31.3 is the Boolean condition parameter of the `WriteLineIf()` method in the `CheckState()` method. The `WriteLineIf()` method of the `Debug` class has a first parameter that takes a `bool`. In the example, the static class field `Debugging` is used as an argument. It's set to `true`, but had it been set to `false`, there would have been no output.

The examples presented so far expect that the code will be recompiled to turn debugging on and off. In a development environment, this is fine. However, in production, such luxury is not likely to be available. That's why the example in Listing 31.5 uses the `BooleanSwitch` and `Trace` classes.

LISTING 31.5 Implementing Debugging with a Boolean Switch: BooleanSwitchDemo.cs

```
using System;
using System.Diagnostics;

/// <summary>
///     BooleanSwitch Demo.
```

LISTING 31.5 continued

```
/// </summary>
class BooleanSwitchDemo
{
    BooleanSwitch traceOutput = new
        BooleanSwitch("TraceOutput", "Boolean Switch Demo");

    void SetupDebugListener()
    {
        TextWriterTraceListener myListener =
            new TextWriterTraceListener(Console.Out);

        Trace.Listeners.Add(myListener);
    }

    void CheckState()
    {
        Trace.WriteLineIf(traceOutput.Enabled,
            "Debug: Entered CheckState()");
    }

    static void Main(string[] args)
    {
        BooleanSwitchDemo bsd = new BooleanSwitchDemo();

        bsd.SetupDebugListener();
        bsd.CheckState();
    }
}
```

And the output is:

```
Debug: Entered CheckState()
```

The `CheckState()` method of Listing 31.5 is similar to the same method in Listing 31.3, except that the `WriteLineIf()` method uses the `Enabled` property of a `BooleanSwitch` object as its first parameter. The `BooleanSwitch` class is instantiated with a first parameter as the display name and a second parameter as a description.

An entry must be added to the program's configuration file to turn on tracing. Listing 31.6 shows how to add the `BooleanSwitch` display name entry into the configuration file. The configuration file must have the same name as the executable with a .config extension.

LISTING 31.6 `BooleanSwitch` entry in Configuration File: `BooleanSwitchDemo.config`

```
<configuration>
    <system.diagnostics>
```

LISTING 31.6 continued

```
        <switches>
            <add name="TraceOutput" value="1" />
        </switches>
    </system.diagnostics>
</configuration>
```

LISTING 31.7 Compilation Instructions for Listing 31.5

```
csc /d:TRACE BooleanSwitchDemo.cs
```

Runtime Tracing

Runtime tracing is the capability to perform debug tracing while a program is running. Sometimes it's necessary to have more control over what debugging information is displayed. Specific types of problems often indicate what information should be displayed in trace output. The `TraceSwitch` class is similar to the `BooleanSwitch` class in that it allows you to create a configuration file or set an environment variable. However, its real value comes in being able to specify a finer degree of granularity in determining what information is displayed. The example in Listing 31.8 demonstrates how to use the `TraceSwitch` class.

LISTING 31.8 `TraceSwitch` Class Demo: `TraceSwitchDemo.cs`

```
using System;
using System.Diagnostics;

/// <summary>
///     TraceSwitch Demo.
/// </summary>
class TraceSwitchDemo
{
    public static TraceSwitch traceOutput = new
        TraceSwitch("TraceOutput", "TraceSwitch Demo");

    void SetupDebugListener()
    {
        TextWriterTraceListener myListener =
            new TextWriterTraceListener(Console.Out);

        Trace.Listeners.Add(myListener);
    }
```

LISTING 31.8 continued

```
    void CheckState()
    {
        Trace.WriteLineIf(traceOutput.TraceInfo,
            "Trace: Entered CheckState()");
    }

    static void Main(string[] args)
    {
        TraceSwitchDemo tsd = new TraceSwitchDemo();

        tsd.SetupDebugListener();
        tsd.CheckState();
    }
}
```

And here's the output:

```
Trace: Entered CheckState()
```

The implementation of the `TraceSwitch` is similar to the `BooleanSwitch`, except that the first parameter to the `WriteLineIf()` method in the `CheckState()` method is the `TraceInfo` property of the `TraceSwitch` class. This parameter can be any of the possible values corresponding to a member of the `TraceLevel` enum, shown in Table 31.1.

TABLE 31.1 `TraceLevel` Enum

`TraceLevel` *enum*	*Description*
`Verbose`	Output everything
`Info`	Output info, error, and warning
`Warning`	Output error and warning
`Error`	Output error
`Off`	Output nothing

`TraceSwitch` must be set in a configuration file. Values may be from `0` to `4` with `Verbose` equal to `4` and descending to `Off`, which is equal to `0`. It's possible to create a custom switch by inheriting the `Switch` class and defining Boolean properties with your own unique names that map to the available members of the `TraceLevel` enum. The configuration file in Listing 31.9 has `TraceOutput` set to `3`, which causes evaluation of `TraceInfo` to return `true`.

LISTING 31.9 TraceSwitch Entry in Config File: TraceSwitchDemo.config

```
<configuration>
    <system.diagnostics>
        <switches>
            <add name="TraceOutput" value="3" />
        </switches>
    </system.diagnostics>
</configuration>
```

LISTING 31.10 Compilation Instructions for Listing 31.8

```
csc /d:TRACE TraceSwitchDemo.cs
```

Making Assertions

Another common debugging task is to check the state of a program at various intervals for logical consistency. This is performed with the `Debug.Assert()` method. By sprinkling `Assert()` methods at strategic points in a routine, such as preconditions, intermediate state, and post-conditions, you can verify that routine's logical consistency. Whenever the assertion proves false, a given message is displayed in the form of a message box. Listing 31.11 has a simple program demonstrating the mechanics of the `Assert()` method.

LISTING 31.11 Assertion Demonstration: AssertDemo.cs

```
using System;
using System.Diagnostics;

/// <summary>
///     Assertion Demonstration.
/// </summary>
class AssertDemo
{
    static void Main(string[] args)
    {
        decimal profit = -0.01m;

        // do some calculations

        Debug.Assert(profit >= 0.0m,
            "Illogical Negative Profit Calculation");
    }
}
```

The example in Listing 31.11 simulates some fictitious profit calculation that should never return a negative result. The `Debug.Assert()` method takes two parameters. The first is the logical condition to check, which should evaluate to a Boolean `true` or `false`. In this case, it's making sure the profit is always zero or greater. The second parameter is the message to be displayed. The example forces the assertion to evaluate to `false`, displaying the message shown in Figure 31.1.

Assertions are designed to work only in debugging mode. Therefore, you will want to add a `/define` switch to the command-line when debugging. This program can be compiled with the command line in Listing 31.12.

LISTING 31.12 Compilation Instructions for Listing 31.11

```
csc /d:DEBUG AssertDemo.cs
```

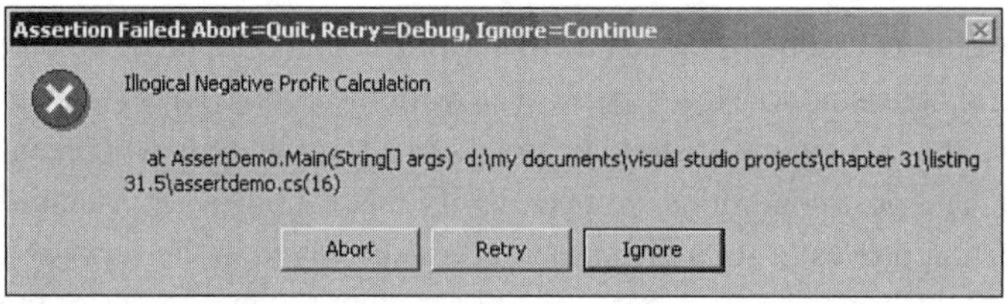

FIGURE 31.1
Assertion message box.

Summary

Once appropriate statements and methods are in place, runtime debugging can make program verification more efficient by watching console printouts of viewing log files for pertinent results. Runtime debugging can be turned on and off with conditional attributes, specialized output methods that accept Boolean parameters, command line options, and preprocessing directives.

The `Debug` class is effective in development environments where the debugging code will be removed for deployment. Alternatively, the `Trace` class would be the best decision for situations where code should be deployed with a debugging capability.

Runtime debugging in trace-enabled code can be controlled with Boolean switches or multilevel trace switches. Each option provides a means of controlling the level of debugging with less disruption to a customer.

The `Debug.Assert()` method assists in verifying the logical consistency of an application during debugging. When a specified constraint fails, the `Assert()` method notifies the user with a message box displaying information about the reason for the failure.

Runtime detection of program errors is an important capability. Similarly, it's important to monitor the performance of a program. The next chapter, "Performance Monitoring," shows how to capture runtime performance of an application.

CHAPTER 32

Performance Monitoring

IN THIS CHAPTER

- Accessing Built-in Performance Counters *648*
- Implementing Timers *656*
- Building a Customized Performance Counter *657*
- Analyzing Performance with Sampling *668*

It's agreed that a program must run correctly and produce accurate results, but in many systems this isn't enough. Enterprise-class applications are of such mass that they must also be scalable. Verifying the scalability of an application traditionally requires specialized tools and bolted-on functionality to support monitoring. Now there's help, using the performance counter capability of the `System.Diagnostics` namespace.

Performance counters present an object framework for supporting application monitoring. The framework hooks into the operating system performance counter system to access available counters. Additionally, the performance counter framework can be extended for customized counters and data sampling. Such samples may be collected efficiently with timers, which, as their name suggests, enable periodic execution of logic via specified time intervals. By using either built-in or customized performance counters, a program can be monitored under various conditions to verify its performance and scalability.

Accessing Built-in Performance Counters

The performance counter framework provides access to existing operating system counters. The help files associated with the operating system performance monitor application have more information on what counters are available.

Using a performance counter involves declaring a `PerformanceCounter` object, initializing its properties as desired and requesting the counter value at various intervals to watch performance. The program in Listings 32.1 and 32.2 comprise a fictitious ordering system that demonstrates the use of system performance counters. The program is sufficiently equipped to degrade system performance, where the effects can be observed by watching the performance counter.

LISTING 32.1 System Performance Counter Demo: `OrderClient.cs`

```
using System;
using System.Drawing;
using System.Collections;
using System.ComponentModel;
using System.Windows.Forms;
using System.Data;
using System.Threading;
using System.Diagnostics;

namespace OrderingClient
{
```

LISTING 32.1 continued

```
/// <summary>
/// Performance Counter Demo.
/// </summary>
public class OrderClient : System.Windows.Forms.Form
{
    private System.Windows.Forms.Label maxOrdLbl;
    private System.Windows.Forms.Label curOrdLbl;
    private System.Windows.Forms.TextBox maxOrdTxt;
    private System.Windows.Forms.Label curOrdResultLbl;
    private System.Windows.Forms.Button updateBtn;
    private int maxOrders;
    private int curOrders;
    private OrderProcessor orderProc;
    private System.Windows.Forms.Timer orderTimer;
    private System.Windows.Forms.Timer countTimer;
    private System.Windows.Forms.Label threadLbl;
    private System.Windows.Forms.Label threadResultLbl;

    private System.Diagnostics.PerformanceCounter
        threadCounter;

    private System.ComponentModel.IContainer components;

    public OrderClient()
    {
        InitializeComponent();
        maxOrders = 10;
        maxOrdTxt.Text = maxOrders.ToString();
        orderProc = new OrderProcessor();
        curOrders = orderProc.CurNoOrders;
        curOrdResultLbl.Text = curOrders.ToString();
    }

    /// <summary>
    /// Clean up any resources being used.
    /// </summary>
    protected override void Dispose( bool disposing )
    {
        if( disposing )
        {
            if (components != null)
            {
                components.Dispose();
            }
        }
        base.Dispose( disposing );
    }
```

LISTING 32.1 continued

```
        private void InitializeComponent()
        {
            this.components =
                new System.ComponentModel.Container();
            this.maxOrdTxt =
                new System.Windows.Forms.TextBox();
            this.updateBtn =
                new System.Windows.Forms.Button();
            this.maxOrdLbl =
                new System.Windows.Forms.Label();
            this.curOrdLbl =
                new System.Windows.Forms.Label();
            this.orderTimer =
                new System.Windows.Forms.Timer(
                    this.components);
            this.curOrdResultLbl =
                new System.Windows.Forms.Label();
            this.countTimer =
                new System.Windows.Forms.Timer(
                    this.components);
            this.threadLbl =
                new System.Windows.Forms.Label();
            this.threadResultLbl =
                new System.Windows.Forms.Label();
            this.threadCounter =
                new System.Diagnostics.PerformanceCounter();
                 ((System.ComponentModel.ISupportInitialize)
                     (this.threadCounter)).BeginInit();
            this.SuspendLayout();

            this.maxOrdTxt.Location =
                new System.Drawing.Point(152, 24);
            this.maxOrdTxt.Name = "maxOrdTxt";
            this.maxOrdTxt.TabIndex = 2;
            this.maxOrdTxt.Text = "";
            this.maxOrdTxt.TextAlign =
              System.Windows.Forms.HorizontalAlignment.Right;

            this.updateBtn.Location =
                new System.Drawing.Point(104, 152);
            this.updateBtn.Name = "updateBtn";
            this.updateBtn.TabIndex = 4;
            this.updateBtn.Text = "Update";
            this.updateBtn.Click +=
                new System.EventHandler(this.updateBtn_Click);

            this.maxOrdLbl.Location =
                new System.Drawing.Point(40, 24);
            this.maxOrdLbl.Name = "maxOrdLbl";
```

LISTING 32.1 continued

```
            this.maxOrdLbl.TabIndex = 0;
            this.maxOrdLbl.Text = "Max Orders:";
            this.maxOrdLbl.TextAlign =
                System.Drawing.ContentAlignment.MiddleRight;

            this.curOrdLbl.Location =
                new System.Drawing.Point(40, 64);
            this.curOrdLbl.Name = "curOrdLbl";
            this.curOrdLbl.TabIndex = 1;
            this.curOrdLbl.Text = "Current Orders:";
            this.curOrdLbl.TextAlign =
                System.Drawing.ContentAlignment.MiddleRight;

            this.orderTimer.Enabled = true;
            this.orderTimer.Interval = 2000;
            this.orderTimer.Tick +=
                new System.EventHandler(this.orderTimer_Tick);

            this.curOrdResultLbl.BorderStyle =
                System.Windows.Forms.BorderStyle.Fixed3D;
            this.curOrdResultLbl.Location =
                new System.Drawing.Point(152, 64);
            this.curOrdResultLbl.Name = "curOrdResultLbl";
            this.curOrdResultLbl.Size =
                new System.Drawing.Size(100, 20);
            this.curOrdResultLbl.TabIndex = 3;
            this.curOrdResultLbl.TextAlign =
                System.Drawing.ContentAlignment.MiddleRight;

            this.countTimer.Enabled = true;
            this.countTimer.Interval = 1000;
            this.countTimer.Tick +=
                new System.EventHandler(this.countTimer_Tick);

            this.threadLbl.Location =
                new System.Drawing.Point(40, 104);
            this.threadLbl.Name = "threadLbl";
            this.threadLbl.TabIndex = 1;
            this.threadLbl.Text = "Thread Count:";
            this.threadLbl.TextAlign =
                System.Drawing.ContentAlignment.MiddleRight;

            this.threadResultLbl.BorderStyle =
                System.Windows.Forms.BorderStyle.Fixed3D;
            this.threadResultLbl.Location =
                new System.Drawing.Point(152, 104);
            this.threadResultLbl.Name = "threadResultLbl";
            this.threadResultLbl.Size =
                new System.Drawing.Size(100, 20);
```

LISTING 32.1 continued

```
        this.threadResultLbl.TabIndex = 3;
        this.threadResultLbl.TextAlign =
            System.Drawing.ContentAlignment.MiddleRight;

        this.threadCounter.CategoryName =
            ".NET CLR LocksAndThreads";
        this.threadCounter.CounterName =
            "# of current physical Threads";
        this.threadCounter.InstanceName =
            "OrderingClient";

        this.AutoScaleBaseSize =
            new System.Drawing.Size(5, 13);
        this.ClientSize =
            new System.Drawing.Size(288, 197);
        this.Controls.AddRange(
            new System.Windows.Forms.Control[] {
                this.threadLbl,
                this.threadResultLbl,
                this.updateBtn,
                this.curOrdResultLbl,
                this.maxOrdTxt,
                this.curOrdLbl,
                this.maxOrdLbl});
        this.Name = "OrderClient";
        this.Text = "Order Client";
        ((System.ComponentModel.ISupportInitialize)
            (this.threadCounter)).EndInit();
        this.ResumeLayout(false);
    }

    static void Main()
    {
        Application.Run(new OrderClient());
    }

    private void updateBtn_Click(object sender, System.EventArgs e)
    {
        maxOrders = Convert.ToInt32(maxOrdTxt.Text);
    }

    private void orderTimer_Tick(object sender, System.EventArgs e)
    {
        orderTimer.Enabled = false;
        Thread th = new Thread(new ThreadStart(ProcessOrders));
        th.Start();

        orderTimer.Enabled = true;
    }
```

LISTING 32.1 continued

```
        private void countTimer_Tick(object sender, System.EventArgs e)
        {
            countTimer.Enabled = false;
            curOrdResultLbl.Text = orderProc.CurNoOrders.ToString();
            threadResultLbl.Text = threadCounter.NextValue().ToString();
            countTimer.Enabled = true;
        }

        private void ProcessOrders()
        {
            for (curOrders = orderProc.CurNoOrders;
                 curOrders <= maxOrders;
                 curOrders++)
            {
                curOrdResultLbl.Text = curOrders.ToString();
                orderProc.ProcessOrder();
            }
        }
    }
}
```


LISTING 32.2 Server Component of System Performance Counter Demo: `OrderProcessor.cs`

```
using System;
using System.Threading;

namespace OrderingClient
{
    /// <summary>
    /// Summary description for OrderProcessor.
    /// </summary>
    public class OrderProcessor
    {
        private static int curNoOrders = 0;
        private Random rand;

        public OrderProcessor()
        {
            rand = new Random();
        }

        public int ProcessOrder()
        {
            Thread th = new Thread(new ThreadStart(doOrder));
            th.Start();
```

LISTING 32.2 continued

```
            curNoOrders++;
            return 0;
        }

        public int CurNoOrders
        {
            get
            {
                return curNoOrders;
            }
            set
            {
                curNoOrders = value;
            }
        }

        private void doOrder()
        {
            for (int delay = rand.Next(10000000);
                 delay >= 0;
                 delay—)
            ;

            curNoOrders—;
        }
    }
}
```

The performance counter framework belongs to the `System.Diagnostics` namespace. Performance counters are declared like any other class as follows:

```
private System.Diagnostics.PerformanceCounter
    threadCounter;
```

This particular performance counter keeps track of the number of .NET Common Language Runtime (CLR) threads. There are three pertinent properties of a performance counter that are required: `CategoryName`, `CounterName`, and `InstanceName` as shown next.

```
this.threadCounter.CategoryName =
    ".NET CLR LocksAndThreads";
this.threadCounter.CounterName =
    "# of current physical Threads";
this.threadCounter.InstanceName =
    "OrderingClient";
```

Performance counters are broken into categories that help organize each counter into a logical related group. The preceding example sets the category for the `threadCounter` object to ".NET CLR LocksAndThreads". An examination of this category in the .NET Framework Documentation shows that this category has counters for different types of threads and other counters associated with thread synchronization. This example assigns the "# of current physical Threads" counter to the CounterName property of the threadCounter object. The InstanceName property holds the name of the executable file whose count property will be monitored.

To get the value of the counter, call the NextValue() method of the PerformanceCounter object. The following example shows how to do this:

```
threadResultLbl.Text = threadCounter.NextValue().ToString();
```


The example converts the integer value returned from the NextValue() method into a string and places it into a Windows forms label control for presentation onscreen. Figure 32.1 shows what the code from Listings 32.1 and 32.2 look like when compiled and executed. Increasing the number in the Max Orders text box stresses the system. This can be observed by watching the numbers change more sluggishly, indicating performance degradation. Here are the compilation instructions:

```
csc /t:winexe /out:OrderingClient.exe OrderClient.cs
➥ OrderProcessor.cs
```

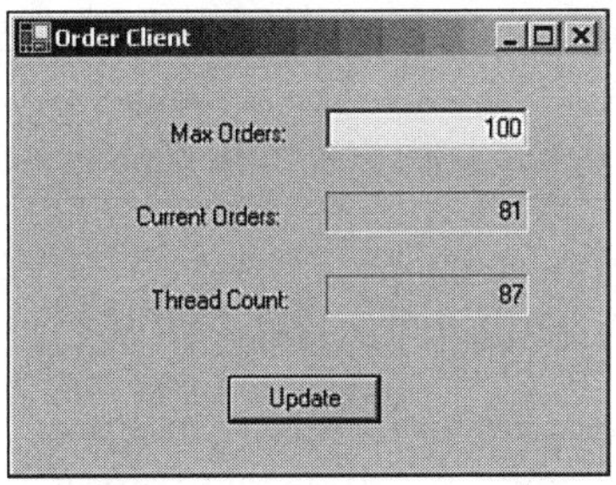

FIGURE 32.1
A system performance counter.

The program from Listings 32.1 and 32.2 use threads extensively. OrderClient uses threads to execute its loop efficiently. It finishes quickly so it doesn't hold up any other program activities, such as the ability to update Max Orders, update the count fields, and execute timers.

The OrderProcessor class uses threads so it can accept orders efficiently without making the client block for each order. Otherwise, there would be no telling how long it could take to process an order, because the program is set to take a random amount of time for each order. This simulates the nature of many ordering systems, which typically have multiple types of orders and several options or variables that make the amount of time for each order practically unpredictable.

Tip

As the world turns, Moore's law (which states that the speed of computers doubles every 18–24 months) has my faithful but inadequate computer dragging behind in performance. If you don't experience significant performance hits when incrementing `Max Orders` in this program, bump up the number of zeros in the `rand.Next()` method in the `for` loop initializer of the `doOrder()` method in Listing 32.2.

Implementing Timers

It would be easy to use existing C# constructs, such as sleeping threads or `for` and `while` loops, to control the periodic collection of performance counter data. The primary problems with these methods are their synchronous nature. Furthermore, loops like `for` and `while` deliver a significant performance hit. A better solution for performing logic via specified intervals is the timer.

A timer can be set for a specified time interval, executing a callback routine whenever that interval elapses. The primary benefit of this approach is the asynchronous behavior of the timer, which delivers much better performance than the synchronous methods discussed earlier. Just set the timer interval, assign a callback routine to execute, and then move on and process the rest of the program logic. The following example shows how timers are declared:

```
private System.Windows.Forms.Timer orderTimer;
private System.Windows.Forms.Timer countTimer;
```

These timers are members of the `System.Windows.Forms` namespace. The `orderTimer` will fire periodically to make sure the number of orders being processed go up to, but not over, the maximum number of orders. The `countTimer` fires periodically to update the number of orders being processed and to get and display the current value of the `threadCounter` performance counter. Here's an example of how the timers are set up:

```
this.orderTimer.Enabled = true;
this.orderTimer.Interval = 2000;
this.orderTimer.Tick +=
    new System.EventHandler(this.orderTimer_Tick);

this.countTimer.Enabled = true;
this.countTimer.Interval = 1000;
this.countTimer.Tick +=
    new System.EventHandler(this.countTimer_Tick);
```

Both of these timers have their `Enabled` properties set to `true`, meaning that the timers are turned on. A timer can be turned off by setting the `Enabled` property to `false`; this is necessary when a program is in the middle of a callback and doesn't want the timer firing while a previous callback based on that timer is still executing.

Setting the `Interval` property to `1000` makes the timer tick approximately every second. Thus, the `orderTimer` will tick in about two seconds, and the count timer will tick about once per second.

Warning

Being based on the underlying operating system timer, don't bet on timers having a great degree of accuracy. This is because there are various operating system events that may preclude the tick event from firing on time; therefore, the safest assumption to make with timers is that they provide an approximate timing mechanism.

Callback routines are attached to the `Tick` event of a timer with the `EventHandler` delegate. The `orderTimer` timer calls the `ordertimer_Tick()` method, and the `countTimer` timer calls the `countTimer_Tick()` method when their respective `Tick` events fire. Listing 32.1 has the full code that shows what these routines do when their `Tick` event fires.

Building a Customized Performance Counter

Often the system performance counters are enough for monitoring a system's performance. However, sometimes you need a specialized counter that gives a unique picture of what's happening in a specific program. Making customized performance counters is possible, due to the extensible nature of the performance counter framework.

Implementing a customized performance counter requires creating a new counter type and a new category to hold the new counter. The performance counter will be instantiated with the new counter and category definitions. Additional logic is also necessary to load the custom performance counter with program specific data. Listings 32.3 and 32.4 show how to implement custom performance counters.

LISTING 32.3 Client Using Data from Custom Performance Counter: CustomOrderClient.cs

```
using System;
using System.Drawing;
using System.Collections;
using System.ComponentModel;
using System.Windows.Forms;
using System.Data;
using System.Threading;
using System.Diagnostics;

namespace OrderingClient
{
    /// <summary>
    /// Summary description for Form1.
    /// </summary>
    public class CustomClient : System.Windows.Forms.Form
    {
        private System.Windows.Forms.Label maxOrdLbl;
        private System.Windows.Forms.Label curOrdLbl;
        private System.Windows.Forms.TextBox maxOrdTxt;
        private System.Windows.Forms.Label curOrdResultLbl;
        private System.Windows.Forms.Button updateBtn;
        private int maxOrders;
        private int curOrders;
        private CustomOrderProcessor orderProc;
        private System.Windows.Forms.Timer orderTimer;
        private System.Windows.Forms.Timer countTimer;
        private System.Windows.Forms.Label threadLbl;
        private System.Windows.Forms.Label threadResultLbl;
        private System.Diagnostics.PerformanceCounter
            threadCounter;
        private System.ComponentModel.IContainer components;

        public CustomClient()
        {
            InitializeComponent();
            maxOrders = 10;
            maxOrdTxt.Text = maxOrders.ToString();
            orderProc = new CustomOrderProcessor();
            curOrders = orderProc.CurNoOrders;
            curOrdResultLbl.Text = curOrders.ToString();
        }

        /// <summary>
        /// Clean up any resources being used.
        /// </summary>
        protected override void Dispose( bool disposing )
        {
            if( disposing )
```

LISTING 32.3 continued

```
            {
                if (components != null)
                {
                    components.Dispose();
                }
            }
            base.Dispose( disposing );
        }

        private void InitializeComponent()
        {
            this.components =
                new System.ComponentModel.Container();
            this.maxOrdTxt =
                new System.Windows.Forms.TextBox();
            this.threadLbl =
                new System.Windows.Forms.Label();
            this.orderTimer =
                new System.Windows.Forms.Timer(this.components);
            this.updateBtn =
                new System.Windows.Forms.Button();
            this.threadResultLbl =
                new System.Windows.Forms.Label();
            this.curOrdResultLbl =
                new System.Windows.Forms.Label();
            this.threadCounter =
                new System.Diagnostics.PerformanceCounter();
            this.curOrdLbl =
                new System.Windows.Forms.Label();
            this.countTimer =
                new System.Windows.Forms.Timer(this.components);
            this.maxOrdLbl =
                new System.Windows.Forms.Label();
            ((System.ComponentModel.ISupportInitialize)
                 (this.threadCounter)).BeginInit();
            this.SuspendLayout();

            this.maxOrdTxt.Location =
                new System.Drawing.Point(152, 24);
            this.maxOrdTxt.Name = "maxOrdTxt";
            this.maxOrdTxt.TabIndex = 2;
            this.maxOrdTxt.Text = "";
            this.maxOrdTxt.TextAlign =
              System.Windows.Forms.HorizontalAlignment.Right;

            this.threadLbl.Location =
                new System.Drawing.Point(40, 104);
            this.threadLbl.Name = "threadLbl";
            this.threadLbl.TabIndex = 1;
```

LISTING 32.3 continued

```
            this.threadLbl.Text = "Thread Count:";
            this.threadLbl.TextAlign =
                System.Drawing.ContentAlignment.MiddleRight;

            this.orderTimer.Enabled = true;
            this.orderTimer.Interval = 2000;
            this.orderTimer.Tick +=
                new System.EventHandler(this.orderTimer_Tick);

            this.updateBtn.Location =
                new System.Drawing.Point(104, 152);
            this.updateBtn.Name = "updateBtn";
            this.updateBtn.TabIndex = 4;
            this.updateBtn.Text = "Update";
            this.updateBtn.Click +=
                new System.EventHandler(this.updateBtn_Click);

            this.threadResultLbl.BorderStyle =
                System.Windows.Forms.BorderStyle.Fixed3D;
            this.threadResultLbl.Location =
                new System.Drawing.Point(152, 104);
            this.threadResultLbl.Name = "threadResultLbl";
            this.threadResultLbl.Size =
                new System.Drawing.Size(100, 20);
            this.threadResultLbl.TabIndex = 3;
            this.threadResultLbl.TextAlign =
                System.Drawing.ContentAlignment.MiddleRight;

            this.curOrdResultLbl.BorderStyle =
                System.Windows.Forms.BorderStyle.Fixed3D;
            this.curOrdResultLbl.Location =
                new System.Drawing.Point(152, 64);
            this.curOrdResultLbl.Name = "curOrdResultLbl";
            this.curOrdResultLbl.Size =
                new System.Drawing.Size(100, 20);
            this.curOrdResultLbl.TabIndex = 3;
            this.curOrdResultLbl.TextAlign =
                System.Drawing.ContentAlignment.MiddleRight;

            this.threadCounter.CategoryName =
                ".NET CLR LocksAndThreads";
            this.threadCounter.CounterName =
                "# of current physical Threads";
            this.threadCounter.InstanceName =
                "CustomClient";

            this.curOrdLbl.Location =
                new System.Drawing.Point(40, 64);
            this.curOrdLbl.Name = "curOrdLbl";
```

LISTING 32.3 continued

```
        this.curOrdLbl.TabIndex = 1;
        this.curOrdLbl.Text = "Current Orders:";
        this.curOrdLbl.TextAlign =
            System.Drawing.ContentAlignment.MiddleRight;

        this.countTimer.Enabled = true;
        this.countTimer.Interval = 1000;
        this.countTimer.Tick +=
            new System.EventHandler(this.countTimer_Tick);

        this.maxOrdLbl.Location =
            new System.Drawing.Point(40, 24);
        this.maxOrdLbl.Name = "maxOrdLbl";
        this.maxOrdLbl.TabIndex = 0;
        this.maxOrdLbl.Text = "Max Orders:";
        this.maxOrdLbl.TextAlign =
            System.Drawing.ContentAlignment.MiddleRight;

        this.AutoScaleBaseSize =
            new System.Drawing.Size(5, 13);
        this.ClientSize =
            new System.Drawing.Size(288, 197);
        this.Controls.AddRange(
            new System.Windows.Forms.Control[] {
                this.threadLbl,
                this.threadResultLbl,
                this.updateBtn,
                this.curOrdResultLbl,
                this.maxOrdTxt,
                this.curOrdLbl,
                this.maxOrdLbl});
        this.Name = "CustomClient";
        this.Text = "Custom Client";
        this.Closing +=
            new System.ComponentModel.CancelEventHandler(
                this.CustomClient_Closing);
        ((System.ComponentModel.ISupportInitialize)
            (this.threadCounter)).EndInit();
        this.ResumeLayout(false);
    }

    static void Main()
    {
        Application.Run(new CustomClient());
    }

    private void updateBtn_Click(
        object sender, System.EventArgs e)
    {
```

LISTING 32.3 continued

```
            maxOrders = Convert.ToInt32(maxOrdTxt.Text);
        }

        private void orderTimer_Tick(
            object sender, System.EventArgs e)
        {
            orderTimer.Enabled = false;

            Thread th = new Thread(
                new ThreadStart(ProcessOrders));
            th.Start();

            orderTimer.Enabled = true;
        }

        private void countTimer_Tick(
            object sender, System.EventArgs e)
        {
            countTimer.Enabled = false;

            curOrdResultLbl.Text =
                orderProc.CurNoOrders.ToString();
            threadResultLbl.Text =
                threadCounter.NextValue().ToString();

            countTimer.Enabled = true;
        }

        private void ProcessOrders()
        {
            for (curOrders = orderProc.CurNoOrders;
                 curOrders <= maxOrders;
                 curOrders++)
            {
                curOrdResultLbl.Text = curOrders.ToString();
                orderProc.ProcessOrder();
            }
        }

        private void CustomClient_Closing(object sender,
            System.ComponentModel.CancelEventArgs e)
        {
            orderProc.Dispose();
        }
    }
}
```

LISTING 32.4 Server Implementing a Custom Performance Counter: CustomOrderProcessor.cs

```
using System;
using System.Threading;
using System.Diagnostics;

namespace OrderingClient
{
    /// <summary>
    /// Summary description for CustomOrderProcessor.
    /// </summary>
    public class CustomOrderProcessor : IDisposable
    {
        private PerformanceCounter orderCounter;
        private Random rand;

        public CustomOrderProcessor()
        {
            rand = new Random();

            CounterCreationDataCollection myCounters =
                new CounterCreationDataCollection();

            CounterCreationData myCounterCreationData =
                new CounterCreationData();

            myCounterCreationData.CounterName =
                "Order Count";
            myCounterCreationData.CounterHelp =
                "Displays number of orders being processed.";
            myCounterCreationData.CounterType =
                PerformanceCounterType.NumberOfItems32;

            myCounters.Add(myCounterCreationData);

            if (PerformanceCounterCategory.Exists(
                "Order Processor"))
            {
                PerformanceCounterCategory.Delete(
                    "Order Processor");
            }

            PerformanceCounterCategory.Create(
                "Order Processor",
                "OrderProcessor class counters",
                myCounters);

            orderCounter = new PerformanceCounter(
                "Order Processor",
```

LISTING 32.4 continued

```
                "Order Count",
                false);

            orderCounter.RawValue = 0;
        }

        public int ProcessOrder()
        {
            Thread th = new Thread(new ThreadStart(doOrder));
            th.Start();

            CurNoOrders++;
            return 0;
        }

        public int CurNoOrders
        {
            get
            {
                return (int)orderCounter.NextValue();
            }
            set
            {
                orderCounter.RawValue = value;
            }
        }

        private void doOrder()
        {
            for (int delay = rand.Next(1000000);
                 delay >= 0;
                 delay—)
            ;
            CurNoOrders—;
        }

        public void Dispose()
        {
            PerformanceCounterCategory.Delete(
                "Order Processor");
        }
    }
}
```

The interesting bits of this program are in Listing 32.4. The custom counter is initialized in the constructor, and the updates are managed with the `CurNoOrders` property. The two primary classes supporting custom counters are the `CounterCreationDataCollection` and `CounterCreationData`, which are each instantiated with default constructors, as shown here:

```
CounterCreationDataCollection myCounters =
    new CounterCreationDataCollection();

CounterCreationData myCounterCreationData =
    new CounterCreationData();
```

The `CounterCreationData` class holds counter definition properties that must be set to create a new counter. The `CounterName` property is a user-defined name of a counter. The `CounterType` property may be any member of the `PerformanceCounterType` enum, which are listed in Table 32.1. The following code sets the `CounterCreationData` properties, including the `CounterHelp` property, which is a description of the custom counter:


```
myCounterCreationData.CounterName =
    "Order Count";
myCounterCreationData.CounterHelp =
    "Displays number of orders being processed.";
myCounterCreationData.CounterType =
    PerformanceCounterType.NumberOfItems32;
```

TABLE 32.1 Members of the `PerformanceCounterType` Enum

Counter Name	*Description*
`AverageBase`	Denominator for `AverageCount32` and `AverageCount64`
`AverageCount64`	64-bit average count
`AverageCount32`	32-bit average count
`AverageTimer32`	32-bit average elapsed time
`CounterDelta32`	32-bit difference between counts
`CounterDelta64`	64-bit difference between counts
`CounterMultiBase`	Denominator for `CounterMultiTimer`, `CounterMultiTimerInverse`, `CounterMultiTimer100Ns`, and `CounterMultiTimer100NsInverse`
`CounterMultiTimer`	Multiple time samplings—in use
`CounterMultiTimer100Ns`	Multiple time samplings in 100 nanosecond units
`CounterMultiTimerInverse`	Multiple time samplings—not in use
`CounterTimer`	Time sampling—in use
`CounterTimerInverse`	Time sampling—not in use
`CountPerTimeInterval32`	32-bit count per time interval
`CountPerTimeInterval64`	64-bit count per time interval

TABLE 32.1 continued

Counter Name	*Description*
`ElapsedTime`	Difference between timer start and sample
`NumberOfItems32`	32-bit count
`NumberOfItems64`	64-bit count
`NumberOfItemsHEX32`	32-bit hexadecimal count
`NumberOfItemsHEX64`	64-bit hexadecimal count
`RateOfCountsPerSecond32`	32-bit number of counts per second
`RateOfCountsPerSecond64`	64-bit number of counts per second
`RawBase`	Denominator for `RawFraction`
`RawFraction`	Numerator of a fractional count
`SampleBase`	Denominator representing number of samplings
`SampleCounter`	Number of ones returned from 0 or 1 count
`SampleFraction`	Percentage of ones returned from 0 or 1 count
`Timer100Ns`	Time in 100 nanosecond units—in use
`Timer100NsInverse`	Time in 100 nanosecond units—not in use

Once the new counter is defined, add the `CounterCreationData` object to the `CounterCreationDataCollection` object. This completes the definition of the counter, and now the counter must be added to a category. To create the `CounterCategory`, call the static `Create()` method of the `PerformanceCounterCategory` class with three parameters: category name, category description, and the `CounterCreationDataCollection` object just described. As you may suspect, multiple counters may be added to a category by just adding more `CounterCreationData` counters to the `CounterCreationDataCollection` object used as the third parameter to the `Create()` method of the `PerformanceCounterCategory` class. Here's the definition of the customized counter with a custom category:

```
myCounters.Add(myCounterCreationData);

if (PerformanceCounterCategory.Exists(
    "Order Processor"))
{
    PerformanceCounterCategory.Delete(
        "Order Processor");
}

PerformanceCounterCategory.Create(
    "Order Processor",
    "OrderProcessor class counters",
    myCounters);
```

This example also contains a check for whether the new category exists. If this is true, the category is deleted before it is recreated. If a performance counter category already exists, then it can't be recreated, throwing a runtime exception. This program could just as well have used an exception handler around this code, which may be better form. However, to be instructive, this example shows how to use the `Exists()` and `Delete()` methods of the `PerformanceCounterCategory` class. There's also a `Delete()` method call in the `Dispose()` method so the program doesn't leave counters laying around unnecessarily.

The performance counter object for this new custom performance counter is declared the same as any other performance counter. One important item to address is that a program must manage the custom counter itself, updating its value as appropriate. This performance counter value is initialized by setting its `RawValue` property to `0`, as the following code shows:

```
orderCounter = new PerformanceCounter(
    "Order Processor",
    "Order Count",
    false);

orderCounter.RawValue = 0;
```

Subsequent management of the custom performance counter resides in the `CurNoOrders` property. The `get` accessor obtains the `NextValue()`, a `float` result, and casts it to an `int` before returning the value. The `set` accessor directly sets the counter's `RawValue` property. Here's the `CurNoOrders` property:

```
public int CurNoOrders
{
    get
    {
        return (int)orderCounter.NextValue();
    }
    set
    {
        orderCounter.RawValue = value;
    }
}
```

Custom performance counters present a unique view of special conditions within a program. They provide insight not available with the generalized view of system performance counters. Figure 32.2 shows the executed program from Listings 32.3 and 32.4. Here are the compilation instructions:

```
csc /t:winexe /out:CustomClient.exe CustomClient.cs
➥ CustomOrderProcessor.cs
```

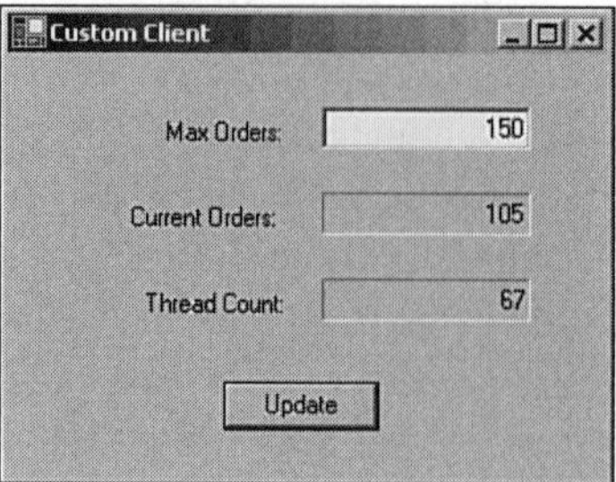

FIGURE 32.2
A custom performance counter.

Analyzing Performance with Sampling

Previous programs in this chapter provided interesting statistics to look at and even provided a general idea of what was happening with system performance. This is nice, but sometimes you really need to zero in on what's going on with a program and get a better picture of a more sophisticated scenario. Performance counter sampling does just that.

Sampling is the capability to perform specialized calculations between successive performance counter results. This is especially relevant in tracking averages and discovering trends. Listings 32.5 and 32.6 show how to create a custom performance counter that performs sampling.

LISTING 32.5 Sampling Client: `SampleClient.cs`

```
using System;
using System.Drawing;
using System.Collections;
using System.ComponentModel;
using System.Windows.Forms;
using System.Data;
using System.Threading;
using System.Diagnostics;

namespace OrderingClient
{
    /// <summary>
    /// Summary description for Form1.
    /// </summary>
    public class SampleClient : System.Windows.Forms.Form
    {
        private System.Windows.Forms.Label maxOrdLbl;
        private System.Windows.Forms.TextBox maxOrdTxt;
        private System.Windows.Forms.Button updateBtn;
```

LISTING 32.5 continued

```
        private int maxOrders;
        private int curOrders;
        private CustomSamplingProcessor orderProc;
        private System.Windows.Forms.Timer orderTimer;
        private System.Windows.Forms.Timer countTimer;
        private System.Windows.Forms.Label threadLbl;
        private System.Windows.Forms.Label threadResultLbl;
        private System.Diagnostics.PerformanceCounter
            threadCounter;
        private System.Windows.Forms.Label ordRateResultLbl;
        private System.Windows.Forms.Label ordRateLbl;
        private System.ComponentModel.IContainer components;

        public SampleClient()
        {
            InitializeComponent();
            maxOrders = 10;
            maxOrdTxt.Text = maxOrders.ToString();
            orderProc = new CustomSamplingProcessor();
            curOrders = orderProc.CurNoOrders;
            ordRateResultLbl.Text = curOrders.ToString();
        }

        /// <summary>
        /// Clean up any resources being used.
        /// </summary>
        protected override void Dispose( bool disposing )
        {
            if( disposing )
            {
                if (components != null)
                {
                    components.Dispose();
                }
            }
            base.Dispose( disposing );
        }

        private void InitializeComponent()
        {
            this.components =
                new System.ComponentModel.Container();
            this.maxOrdTxt =
                new System.Windows.Forms.TextBox();
            this.ordRateResultLbl =
                new System.Windows.Forms.Label();
            this.threadLbl =
                new System.Windows.Forms.Label();
            this.ordRateLbl =
```

LISTING 32.5 continued

```
        new System.Windows.Forms.Label();
    this.orderTimer =
        new System.Windows.Forms.Timer(
            this.components);
    this.updateBtn =
        new System.Windows.Forms.Button();
    this.threadResultLbl =
        new System.Windows.Forms.Label();
    this.threadCounter =
        new System.Diagnostics.PerformanceCounter();
    this.countTimer =
        new System.Windows.Forms.Timer(
            this.components);
    this.maxOrdLbl =
        new System.Windows.Forms.Label();
    ((System.ComponentModel.ISupportInitialize)
         (this.threadCounter)).BeginInit();
    this.SuspendLayout();

    this.maxOrdTxt.Location =
        new System.Drawing.Point(152, 24);
    this.maxOrdTxt.Name = "maxOrdTxt";
    this.maxOrdTxt.TabIndex = 2;
    this.maxOrdTxt.Text = "";
    this.maxOrdTxt.TextAlign =
      System.Windows.Forms.HorizontalAlignment.Right;

    this.ordRateResultLbl.BorderStyle =
        System.Windows.Forms.BorderStyle.Fixed3D;
    this.ordRateResultLbl.Location =
        new System.Drawing.Point(152, 64);
    this.ordRateResultLbl.Name = "ordRateResultLbl";
    this.ordRateResultLbl.Size =
        new System.Drawing.Size(100, 20);
    this.ordRateResultLbl.TabIndex = 3;
    this.ordRateResultLbl.TextAlign =
        System.Drawing.ContentAlignment.MiddleRight;

    this.threadLbl.Location =
        new System.Drawing.Point(40, 104);
    this.threadLbl.Name = "threadLbl";
    this.threadLbl.TabIndex = 1;
    this.threadLbl.Text = "Thread Count:";
    this.threadLbl.TextAlign =
        System.Drawing.ContentAlignment.MiddleRight;

    this.ordRateLbl.Location =
        new System.Drawing.Point(40, 64);
    this.ordRateLbl.Name = "ordRateLbl";
```

LISTING 32.5 continued

```
this.ordRateLbl.TabIndex = 1;
this.ordRateLbl.Text = "Orders/Sec:";
this.ordRateLbl.TextAlign =
    System.Drawing.ContentAlignment.MiddleRight;

this.orderTimer.Enabled = true;
this.orderTimer.Interval = 2000;
this.orderTimer.Tick +=
    new System.EventHandler(
        this.orderTimer_Tick);

this.updateBtn.Location =
    new System.Drawing.Point(104, 152);
this.updateBtn.Name = "updateBtn";
this.updateBtn.TabIndex = 4;
this.updateBtn.Text = "Update";
this.updateBtn.Click +=
    new System.EventHandler(
        this.updateBtn_Click);

this.threadResultLbl.BorderStyle =
    System.Windows.Forms.BorderStyle.Fixed3D;
this.threadResultLbl.Location =
    new System.Drawing.Point(152, 104);
this.threadResultLbl.Name =
    "threadResultLbl";
this.threadResultLbl.Size =
    new System.Drawing.Size(100, 20);
this.threadResultLbl.TabIndex = 3;
this.threadResultLbl.TextAlign =
    System.Drawing.ContentAlignment.MiddleRight;

this.threadCounter.CategoryName =
    ".NET CLR LocksAndThreads";
this.threadCounter.CounterName =
    "# of current physical Threads";
this.threadCounter.InstanceName =
    "SampleClient";

this.countTimer.Enabled = true;
this.countTimer.Interval = 1000;
this.countTimer.Tick +=
    new System.EventHandler(
        this.countTimer_Tick);

this.maxOrdLbl.Location =
    new System.Drawing.Point(40, 24);
this.maxOrdLbl.Name = "maxOrdLbl";
this.maxOrdLbl.TabIndex = 0;
```

LISTING 32.5 continued

```
            this.maxOrdLbl.Text = "Max Orders:";
            this.maxOrdLbl.TextAlign =
                System.Drawing.ContentAlignment.MiddleRight;

            this.AutoScaleBaseSize =
                new System.Drawing.Size(5, 13);
            this.ClientSize =
                new System.Drawing.Size(288, 197);
            this.Controls.AddRange(
                new System.Windows.Forms.Control[] {
                    this.threadLbl,
                    this.threadResultLbl,
                    this.updateBtn,
                    this.ordRateResultLbl,
                    this.maxOrdTxt,
                    this.ordRateLbl,
                    this.maxOrdLbl});
            this.Name = "SampleClient";
            this.Text = "Sample Client";
            this.Closing +=
                new System.ComponentModel.CancelEventHandler(
                    this.SampleClient_Closing);
            ((System.ComponentModel.ISupportInitialize)
                (this.threadCounter)).EndInit();
            this.ResumeLayout(false);
        }

        static void Main()
        {
            Application.Run(new SampleClient());
        }

        private void updateBtn_Click(object sender,
            System.EventArgs e)
        {
            maxOrders = Convert.ToInt32(maxOrdTxt.Text);
        }

        private void orderTimer_Tick(object sender,
            System.EventArgs e)
        {
            orderTimer.Enabled = false;

            Thread th = new Thread(
                new ThreadStart(ProcessOrders));
            th.Start();

            orderTimer.Enabled = true;
        }
```

LISTING 32.5 continued

```
        private void countTimer_Tick(object sender,
            System.EventArgs e)
        {
            countTimer.Enabled = false;

            ordRateResultLbl.Text =
                ((int)orderProc.OrderRate).ToString();
            threadResultLbl.Text =
                threadCounter.NextValue().ToString();

            countTimer.Enabled = true;
        }

        private void ProcessOrders()
        {
            for (curOrders = orderProc.CurNoOrders;
                 curOrders <= maxOrders;
                 curOrders++)
            {
                orderProc.ProcessOrder();
            }
        }

        private void SampleClient_Closing(object sender,
            System.ComponentModel.CancelEventArgs e)
        {
            orderProc.Dispose();
        }
    }
}
```

LISTING 32.6 Custom Performance Counter Sampling: `CustomSamplingProcessor.cs`

```
using System;
using System.Threading;
using System.Diagnostics;

namespace OrderingClient
{
    /// <summary>
    /// Summary description for CustomSamplingProcessor.
    /// </summary>
    public class CustomSamplingProcessor : IDisposable
    {
        private PerformanceCounter orderCounter;
        private CounterSample      orderSample;
        private static int curNoOrders = 0;
        private Random rand;
```

LISTING 32.6 continued

```
        public CustomSamplingProcessor()
        {
            rand = new Random();
            CounterCreationDataCollection myCounters =
                new CounterCreationDataCollection();
            CounterCreationData myCounterCreationData =
                new CounterCreationData();
            myCounterCreationData.CounterName =
                "Order Count";
            myCounterCreationData.CounterHelp =
                "Displays the of orders being processed.";
            myCounterCreationData.CounterType =
              PerformanceCounterType.RateOfCountsPerSecond32;
            myCounters.Add(myCounterCreationData);

            if (PerformanceCounterCategory.Exists(
                "Order Processor"))
            {
                PerformanceCounterCategory.Delete(
                    "Order Processor");
            }

            PerformanceCounterCategory.Create(
                "Order Processor",
                "OrderProcessor class counters",
                myCounters);

            orderCounter = new PerformanceCounter(
                "Order Processor",
                "Order Count",
                false);

            orderCounter.RawValue = 0;
            orderSample = new CounterSample();
            orderSample = orderCounter.NextSample();
        }

        public int ProcessOrder()
        {
            Thread th = new Thread(new ThreadStart(doOrder));
            th.Start();

            CurNoOrders++;
            return 0;
        }

        public int CurNoOrders
        {
            get
```

LISTING 32.6 continued

```
            {
                return curNoOrders;
            }
            set
            {
                curNoOrders = value;
            }
        }

        public float OrderRate
        {
            get
            {
                CounterSample tempSample
                    = new CounterSample();
                tempSample = orderCounter.NextSample();

                float sample = CounterSample.Calculate(
                    orderSample, tempSample);

                orderSample = tempSample;
                return sample;
            }
        }

        private void doOrder()
        {
            for (int delay = rand.Next(1000000);
                 delay >= 0;
                 delay—)
            ;

            CurNoOrders—;
            orderCounter.Increment();
        }

        public void Dispose()
        {
            PerformanceCounterCategory.Delete(
                "Order Processor");
        }
    }
}
```

The example program in Listings 32.5 and 32.6 is similar to the one in Listings 32.3 and 32.4, except in the way the data is collected. During creation of the `CounterCreationData` instance, the `CounterType` property is set to `RateOfCountsPerSecond32`. This enables the counter to support a count of the number of orders per second processed by the `CustomSamplingProcessor` object. Here is the property setting:

```
myCounterCreationData.CounterType =
  PerformanceCounterType.RateOfCountsPerSecond32;
```

Another difference in sampling is that the `NextSample()` method of the counter object is called instead of `NextValue()`. The `NextSample()` method returns a `CounterSample` object. Here's how to declare and collect a single counter sampling:

```
orderSample = new CounterSample();
orderSample = orderCounter.NextSample();
```

Proper sampling of a `RateOfCountsPerSecond32` type counter requires two samples. These samples are presented to the static `Calculate()` method of the `CounterSample` class. The result of the `Calculate()` method is a `float` type value representing the number of orders per second processed. The following example shows how the details of the `Calculate()` method are encapsulated in the read-only `OrderRate` property:

```
public float OrderRate
{
    get
    {
        CounterSample tempSample
            = new CounterSample();
        tempSample = orderCounter.NextSample();

        float sample = CounterSample.Calculate(
            orderSample, tempSample);

        orderSample = tempSample;
        return sample;
    }
}
```

This counter clearly provides valuable information about the performance of the program. An average on the way up shows potential for more capacity; when the average peaks, you have a good idea of what the system limits are; and a descending average indicates overload. The output from Listings 32.5 and 32.6 are shown in Figure 32.3. Here are the compilation instructions:

```
csc /t:winexe /out:SampleClient.exe SampleClient.cs
➥ CustomSamplingProcessor.cs
```

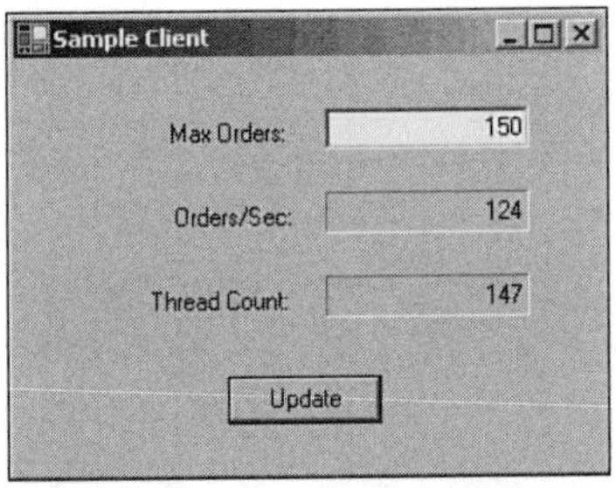

FIGURE 32.3
A custom sampling performance counter.

> **Tip**
>
> Any of the performance counters used or created in this chapter may be monitored with the Windows Performance tool. In Windows 2000, the System Monitor can be found by selecting Settings, Control Panel from the Start menu. Then open the Administrative Tools folder and run the Performance Tool.

Summary

The `System.Diagnostics` namespace includes a framework for supporting performance counters. Performance counters enable a program to be monitored for performance and scalability. At a basic level, predefined system performance counters can be used to examine a program's behavior.

The performance counter framework supports customized performance counters for situations in which it's necessary to monitor specialized behavior. Custom performance counters identify conditions specific to an application and must be explicitly managed by the application.

Sampling provides more sophisticated monitoring of program performance. This technique takes a number of samples and performs calculations on a regular basis. More so than other methods, the results of sampling can provide much more insight into a program's capability.

This chapter examined how to monitor your system to see how it performs under various circumstances. The next chapter integrates C# with COM and shows you ways to enhance performance with enterprise services, such as COM+.

CHAPTER 33

Integrating C# with COM

In This Chapter

- Communicating with COM from .NET 680
- Exposing a .NET Component as a COM Component 683
- Introduction to .NET Support for COM+ Services 685

COM has been the most successful binary reuse component framework ever. Every machine running any flavor of Windows is probably running at least one COM application, and that's in addition to the OS itself. .NET technology builds upon the successful aspects of COM through its promotion of component concepts and cross-language interoperability. Because of the tremendous base of COM applications in use today, .NET programs must have the capability to reuse existing COM components.

The .NET platform supports a method of communication between .NET and COM known as COM Interop, which supports making COM objects appear as managed objects to .NET components and making .NET components appear as COM objects to unmanaged code. Another related technology is COM+ services, which is supported extensively by .NET.

Communicating with COM from .NET

One of the most likely interop scenarios is communicating from .NET to existing COM components. This can allow preservation of existing infrastructure and reduction in overall development cost.

COM components may be called via either early or late binding. Using early binding, legacy COM components can be made to appear as managed objects in the .NET environment. This is accomplished by a utility that reads an existing type library and creates a proxy for the .NET component to interact with.

Early-bound components are those that are bound at compile time. This promotes type safety and improves a program's overall performance. However, sometimes a type library may not be available. In these cases it's necessary to use late-bound techniques. Late binding occurs at runtime. This has its drawbacks, though, because of additional overhead with the late-binding process and the possibility of exceptions raised if a method doesn't exist or is specified incorrectly.

Early-Bound COM Component Calls

Early-bound calls require the use of a .NET Framework to create a proxy for the COM component. The proxy is then compiled into the C# program where the COM component can be instantiated and called just like any other managed component. Listing 33.1 shows a method from a COM component written in C++.

LISTING 33.1 A C++ COM Component: `ComObj.dll`

```
STDMETHODIMP CCom4DotNet::GetResponseFromCom(void)
{
    printf("Hello from COM!");
    return S_OK;
}
```

This code simply prints a sentence to the console when called. The following instructions should help in creating this component in Visual Studio.NET:

1. Select File, New, Project to open the Project window; then select ALT project and immediately name it **`ComObj.dll`**. The IDE will build a skeleton with many files.
2. Right-click the Solution Explorer window, and from the pop-up menu, choose Add, Add Class to open a wizard. Select ATL Control and then name the component **`Com4DotNet`**. This creates a class named `CCom4DotNet` and an interface named `ICom4DotNet`.
3. Go to the Class View window and right-click the `ICom4DotNet` interface. Select Add, Add Method. When a wizard displays, name the method **`GetResponseFromCom`** with no parameters.
4. Go to the `CCom4DotNet` class where the `GetResponseFromCom()` method shell is defined and then add the contents shown in Listing 33.1. This completes creation of the COM component necessary for this example.

The COM component from Listing 33.1 should have an associated type library. Type libraries are input into the `TlbImp` command to create a proxy object called a Runtime Callable Wrapper (RCW). A C# program doesn't need to worry about underlying plumbing, such as reference counting, HRESULTS, and so on, because the RCW takes care of all these tasks. The following command line creates an RCW named `ComObj.dll`:

```
tlbimp _ComObj.tlb
```

The `ComObj.dll` must be referenced by a C# program, just as any other .NET library. Listing 33.2 shows a C# program calling a COM component.

LISTING 33.2 A C# Program Calling a COM Component: `TalkToCom.cs`

```
using System;
using ComObj;

namespace TalkToCom
{
    /// <summary>
    /// Calls a COM Component.
```

LISTING 33.2 continued

```
    /// </summary>
    class CallCom
    {
        static void Main(string[] args)
        {
            CCom4DotNet c4dn = new CCom4DotNet();
            c4dn.GetResponseFromCom();
        }
    }
}
```

And here's the output:

```
Hello from COM!
```

The namespace for referencing the COM component corresponds to the name of the file containing it because that's the method `TlbImp` used during creation of the RCW. Within the `Main()` method, the COM component is instantiated the same as a normal C# object. The `GetResponseFromCom()` method prints to the console from the COM component method as shown in the output.

Late-Bound COM Component Calls

For times when a type library isn't available, or there's a dynamic invocation requirement, a C# program can perform a late-bound call to a COM component. Listing 33.3 demonstrates how to do this.

LISTING 33.3 Late-Bound COM Component Invocation: `TalkToComLater.cs`

```
using System;
using System.Runtime.InteropServices;
using System.Reflection;

namespace TalkToComLater
{
    /// <summary>
    /// Makes a late bound call to a COM Component.
    /// </summary>
    class CallComLater
    {
        static void Main(string[] args)
        {
            Type lateBoundType
                = Type.GetTypeFromProgID("ComObj.Com4DotNet");
```

LISTING 33.3 continued

```
            object lateBoundObject
                = Activator.CreateInstance(lateBoundType);

            lateBoundType.InvokeMember(
                            "GetResponseFromCom",
                            BindingFlags.Default|
                            BindingFlags.InvokeMethod,
                            null,
                            lateBoundObject,
                            null);
        }
    }
}
```

And here's the output:

```
Hello from COM!
```

Late-bound COM component invocations are performed using C# reflection. The program in Listing 33.3 invokes the COM component containing the code from Listing 33.1. It first obtains a `ProgID` from the COM object, as listed in the Windows registry. Once a type object is obtained, an object is created using the static `CreateInstance()` method of the `Activator` class. The `GetResponseFromCom()` method of the COM component is then invoked with the `InvokeMember()` method of the `Type` object, `lateBoundType`.

Exposing a .NET Component as a COM Component

C# components are accessible as COM components with the use of a couple .NET Framework tools to create an unmanaged proxy and enter the proper settings in the registry. This enables unmanaged code to use .NET components as if they were COM components. Listing 33.4 shows a C# component to be exposed as a COM component.

LISTING 33.4 A C# Component Exposed as a COM Component: `CallFromCom.dll`

```
using System;

public interface ICSharp
{
    string GetResponseFromCSharp();
}

namespace CallFromCom
{
```

LISTING 33.4 continued

```
    /// <summary>
    /// C# DLL to be called as a COM object.
    /// </summary>
    public class CallCSharp: ICSharp
    {
        public string GetResponseFromCSharp()
        {
            return "Hello from C#!";
        }
    }
}
```

The code in Listing 33.4 appears as any other C# library. To expose this library as a COM object, use the `RegAsm` utility as shown on the following command line:

```
RegAsm CallFromCom.dll /tlb:CallFromCom.tlb
```

This command line registers the C# library as a COM component. Additionally, the `/tlb` option creates a type library to facilitate early binding. To generate a type library without registering the library, use the `TlbExp` program as shown in the following command line:

```
TlbExp CallFromCom.dll
```

This creates a type library named `CallFromCom.tlb`. If you needed another name you could use the `/out` command line option. For a list of all command line options for `RegAsm`, `TlbExp`, or `TlbImp`, just type the command name with the `-h` option.

Once a C# program has been registered with `RegAsm`, it can be called as a COM component by any other program. The Visual Basic program shown in Figure 33.1 calls the C# COM component when its button is clicked. The code that calls the C# COM component is shown in Listing 33.5.

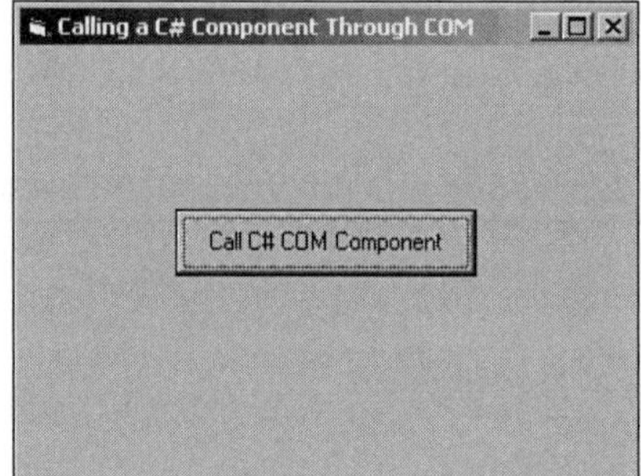

FIGURE 33.1
A VB program calling a C# COM component.

LISTING 33.5 Calling a C# Component Exposed as a COM Component

```
Private Sub Command1_Click()
    Dim myCSharp As New CallCSharp.CallCSharp
    myString = myCSharp.GetResponseFromCSharp()
    response = MsgBox(myString, vbOKOnly, "Response From C#")
End Sub
```

The `RegAsm` program automatically registered the `CallCSharp` object under the `CallCSharp` namespace. This is why the object is instantiated as `CallCSharp.CallCSharp`. Once the C# COM object is instantiated, its members can be called just like any other COM object. Figure 33.2 shows the message box that pops up when the button shown in Figure 33.1 is clicked.

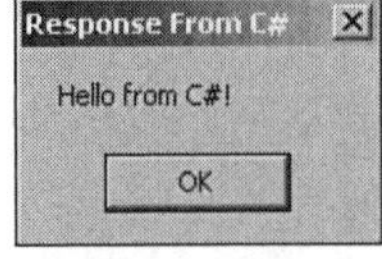

FIGURE 33.2
A message box showing the response from a C# COM component.

> **Note**
>
> The C# COM object should be copied into the same directory as the VB program or added to the Global Assembly Cache with the `gacutil /i` command.

Introduction to .NET Support for COM+ Services

The .NET Frameworks provides extensive support for COM+ services such as transactions, JIT activation, object pooling, and others. COM+ Services are activated through the use of attributes, which decorate a specific C# element as appropriate. These attributes are analogous to the COM+ concepts you may already be familiar with. To get started, let's take a look at Listing 33.6, a minimal C# program that will be registered as a COM+ component.

LISTING 33.6 A Minimal C# COM+ Component

```
using System;
using System.Reflection;
using System.EnterpriseServices;
```

LISTING 33.6 continued

```
[assembly: ApplicationName("CPSkel")]
[assembly: AssemblyKeyFileAttribute(@"..\..\CPSkel.snk")]

namespace ComPlusServices
{
    /// <summary>
    /// COM+ Service Skeleton.
    /// </summary>
    public class CPSkel : ServicedComponent
    {
        public CPSkel()
        {
        }
    }
}
```

The primary part of the code in Listing 33.6 that makes it a COM+ service is the fact that the `CPSkel` class is derived from `System.EnterpriseServices.ServicedComponent`. The other step necessary to make this C# program work as a COM+ service is to register it. The `ApplicationName` attribute identifies the COM+ name, and the `AssemblyKeyFile` attribute specifies the strong name key to register the assembly with. The following command line shows how to create a strong name key:

```
sn -k CPSkel.snk
```

The `sn` program creates a public key pair to be used when the assembly is registered. It uniquely identifies the assembly it is used with. The `RegSvcs` program registers the C# library as a COM+ service as shown here:

```
D:\My Documents\Visual Studio Projects\Chapter 33
➥\ComPlusServices\bin\Debug>RegSvcs ComPlusServices.dll
RegSvcs - .NET Services Installation Utility
➥Version 1.0.2914.16
Copyright  Microsoft Corp. 2000-2001.  All rights reserved.

Installed Assembly:
        Assembly: D:\My Documents\Visual Studio Projects
➥\Chapter 33\ComPlusServices\bin\Debug\ComPlusServices.dll
        Application: CPSkel
        TypeLib: d:\my documents\visual studio projects
➥\chapter 33\complusservices\bin\debug\ComPlusServices.tlb
```

This registers a COM+ service named `CPSkel` and generates a type library named `ComPlusServices.tlb`. Figure 33.3 shows what this new service looks like in the Component Services Explorer. The program in Listing 33.6 didn't have any class members other than a constructor. However, Figure 33.3 shows that the `CPSkel` COM+ service contains interfaces for `object`, `IDisposable`, and others, showing that it hasn't lost any of its managed behavior.

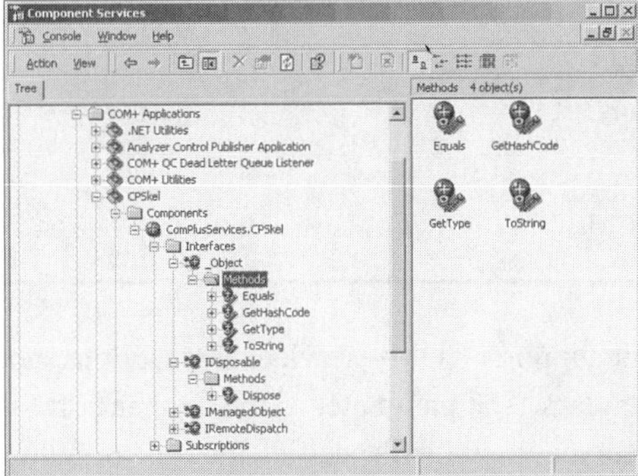

FIGURE 33.3
A C# program registered as a COM+ service.

Transactions

A transaction is a way to combine multiple actions into a single body of work to guarantee that all actions either succeed or fail together. C# programs can participate in COM+ services transactions by inheriting from the `ComPlusServices` class and marking their classes with a `Transaction` attribute. Listing 33.7 shows how to create a COM+ services transactional component in C#.

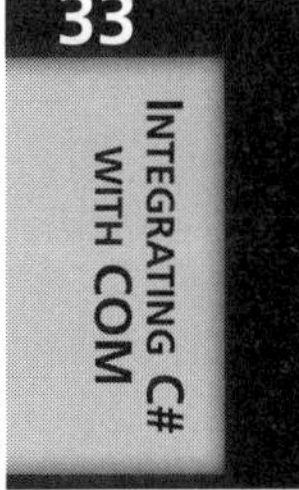

LISTING 33.7 A COM+ Transactional Component in C#: `CPTrans.cs`

```
using System;
using System.Reflection;
using System.EnterpriseServices;

[assembly: ApplicationName("CPTrans")]
[assembly: AssemblyKeyFileAttribute(@"..\..\CPTrans.snk")]

namespace ComPlusServices
{
    /// <summary>
    /// COM+ Transaction Service.
    /// </summary>
    [Transaction(TransactionOption.Required)]
    public class CPTrans : ServicedComponent
    {
        public CPTrans()
        {
        }
```

LISTING 33.7 continued

```
        [AutoComplete]
        public bool PayBill()
        {
            // debit from account
            // send amount to creditor
            // record transaction
            return true;
        }
    }
}
```

To indicate that a component supports COM+ services transactions, apply the `Transaction` attribute to the class. The parameter to the `Transaction` attribute is a member of the `TransactionOption` enum, which specifies the type of automatic transaction to execute.

Another transaction-related attribute is `AutoComplete`. `AutoComplete` enables a transaction to commit automatically if all items succeed. However, if an exception is raised, `AutoComplete` causes the transaction to abort.

JIT Activation

Just-in-time (JIT) activation is the capability to instantiate a new component when it's needed and have that component go away automatically when it's no longer needed. By using COM+ services and associated attributes, a C# component can participate in JIT activation. Listing 33.8 shows a C# component implemented to use COM+ services JIT activation.

LISTING 33.8 A C# Component Configured for JIT Activation: `CPJit.cs`

```
using System;
using System.Reflection;
using System.EnterpriseServices;

[assembly: ApplicationName("CPJit")]
[assembly: AssemblyKeyFileAttribute(@"..\..\CPJit.snk")]

namespace ComPlusServices
{
    /// <summary>
    /// COM+ Transaction Service.
    /// </summary>
    [JustInTimeActivation]
    public class CPJit : ServicedComponent
    {
```

LISTING 33.8 continued

```
        public CPJit()
        {
        }
    }
}
```

Implementing JIT activation only requires specifying the `JustInTimeActivation` attribute. JIT activation is `true` by default, but if you want to turn it off, just specify `false` as the first attribute parameter.

Object Pooling

Another COM+ service enabling efficient use of resources is object pooling. An object pool is a group of components that stay activated and ready for connections at all times. This reduces the overhead associated with activation and deactivation of components. Listing 33.9 shows how to implement COM+ services object pooling.

LISTING 33.9 COM+ Services Object Pooling Implemented in C#: `CPPool.cs`

```
using System;
using System.Reflection;
using System.EnterpriseServices;

[assembly: ApplicationName("CPPool")]
[assembly: AssemblyKeyFileAttribute(@"..\..\CPPool.snk")]

namespace ComPlusServices
{
    /// <summary>
    /// COM+ Transaction Service.
    /// </summary>
    [ObjectPooling(Enabled=true,
    MinPoolSize=5, MaxPoolSize=11)]
    public class CPPool : ServicedComponent
    {
        public CPPool()
        {
        }

        public override void Activate()
        {
        }

        public override void Deactivate()
        {
        }
```

Listing 33.9 continued

```
        public override bool CanBePooled()
        {
            return true;
        }
    }
}
```

The `ObjectPooling` attribute has three parameters: `Enabled`, `MinPoolSize`, and `MaxPoolSize`. The `Enabled` parameter turns object pooling on. The `MinPoolSize` parameter specifies the minimum number of objects held in the pool, and the `MaxPoolSize` parameter specifies the maximum number of objects to be held in the pool.

There are three methods associated with object pooling: `Activate()`, `Deactivate()`, and `CanBePooled()`. The `Activate()` method is invoked when an object is pulled from the pool for use. When the object is returned to the pool, its `Deactivate()` method is invoked. The `CanBePooled()` method informs a requester about whether the object can be pooled.

Other Services

COM+ services include several other technologies not listed in this chapter, such as roles, security, and message queuing. Using the techniques described in other sections and examining the applicable attributes in the `System.EnterpriseServices` namespace, you can implement these other COM+ services in C#.

> **Note**
>
> C# and COM+ services security are mutually exclusive. That is, you can use either one or the other, but not both in the same program. This book focuses on how to use C# with .NET; Chapter 38 covers security in the managed environment.

Summary

The ability to communicate with legacy COM applications is absolutely essential for some C# development projects. Through COM Interop, a C# program can call methods of any COM component. The process of making this happen involves both early and late binding techniques.

A .NET component may also be exposed as a COM component. The C# component doesn't need anything special within the code. However, there are utilities that register the C# component and generate a type library.

C# provides full support for COM+ services. By inheriting from the `System.EnterpriseServices.ComPlusServices` class, a C# program inherits all functionality necessary to operate as a COM+ service. Specific COM+ services are implemented by adding appropriate attributes to C# program elements. Special utilities are available to register a C# program as a COM+ service.

One of the things near and dear to a COM programmer's heart is object lifetime management, especially for C and C++ programmers. The next chapter, "Garbage Collection," addresses this issue directly. It provides the theory and operation of memory management and object destruction in .NET.

The C# Environment

PART V

IN THIS PART

34 Garbage Collection *695*

35 Cross Language Programming with C# *711*

36 The Common Language Runtime *725*

37 Versioning and Assemblies *733*

38 Securing Code *745*

CHAPTER 34

Garbage Collection

In This Chapter

- **Automatic Memory Management** *696*
- **Finalizing Your Code Properly** *699*
- **Controlling Garbage Collection** *703*

C# has automatic garbage collection. This means that the memory allocated for objects is automatically tracked and cleaned up by the common language runtime. This is a welcome addition for people who have suffered through numerous memory management bugs throughout the years in other languages.

It would be nice if all we needed to do were program business logic without worrying about memory management. However, this is not yet the case. There are resource management issues also associated with memory management. Yes, the problems have decreased, but it is still necessary to understand the garbage collection process to ensure that a program runs properly and is a good citizen with resources.

Automatic Memory Management

Objects are initially allocated on the heap when they are instantiated with the new keyword. Memory allocation is very efficient because objects are created sequentially on the heap. The heap has a special pointer that begins at position 0 on the heap and is incremented for the size of the allocated object. This establishes the beginning point for the next object to be allocated. The process continues until memory is full.

Figure 34.1 is a graphical representation of the heap after four objects—A, B, C, and D—have been allocated on the heap. After each allocation, the Next Object Pointer points to the top of the last allocated object, marking the location of the beginning of the next object to be allocated.

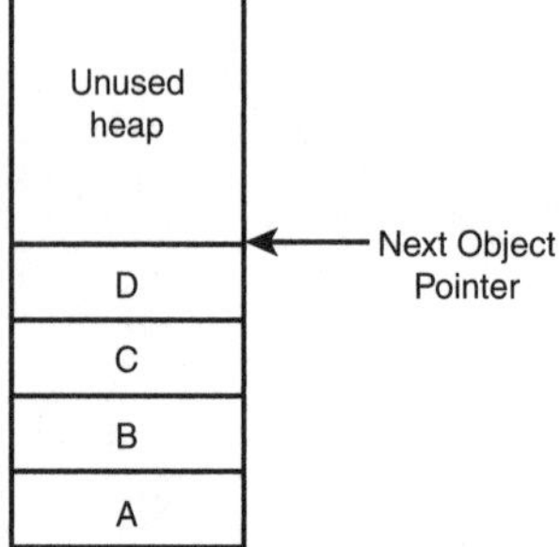

FIGURE 34.1
Memory allocation.

When the heap is full, two things can happen. If all allocated objects are live and in-use, an OutOfMemory<check> exception is thrown, and your program must free some objects before allocating any more. The more likely case is that there are unused objects in memory, and the garbage collector can kick in and clean up these objects, freeing heap space for the new allocations.

Inside the Garbage Collector

The purpose of the garbage collector is to clean up unused objects on the heap. When an object goes out of scope or all references to it are set to null, that object becomes available for garbage collection.

Determining what objects are collectable involves a process of creating a graph of live objects and, once all objects have been visited, cleaning up objects that are not in the graph. This graph begins with a set of roots, such as global and static objects. Following each object reference from each root and adding each referenced object creates the graph. Circularities are avoided by first checking to see if an object already belongs to the graph.

The garbage collector then goes to work, clearing the objects that aren't in the graph. The remaining objects are then compacted on the heap, and the pointer to the next available heap memory location is set to the position past the last object in the compacted heap.

Figure 34.2 shows the garbage collection process in three stages:

Beginning GC: This stage shows the status of objects in memory as the garbage collector constructs the active-object graph. Object A is the root, pointing to objects B and D. Further object visitation discovers that object B contains a reference to object F, which is then added to the graph.

During DC: Since objects C and E are no longer referenced by any other objects, they're cleaned up. This leaves gaps in memory as you can see in the second stage.

After GC: The last stage shows how heap objects are compacted and the Next Object Pointer is reset, ready for the next object to be allocated.

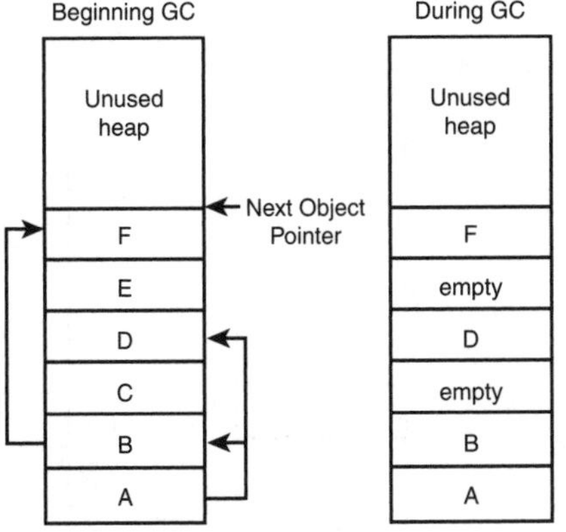

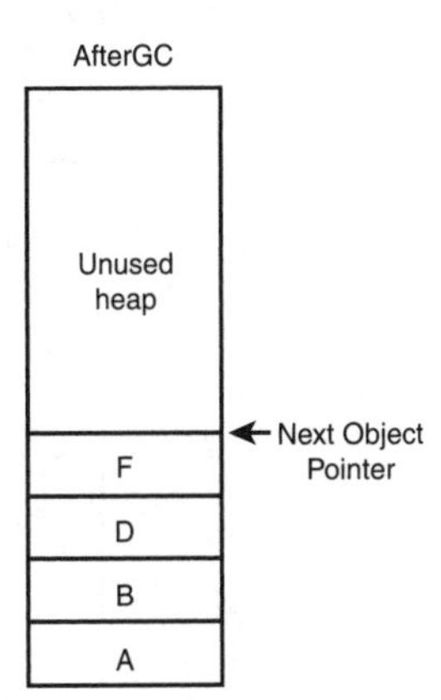

FIGURE 34.2
The garbage collection process.

Garbage Collector Optimization

The garbage collector has several optimizations that increase its execution speed. According to Microsoft, the current execution time for a garbage collection on .NET approximates a typical page fault. While other optimizations would be interesting to discuss at a theoretical level, the generations optimization is the only one that directly affects you as a programmer. Generations are based on research that has revealed the fact that the older an object is, the more likely it is to stick around.

The garbage collector manages three generations, numbered 0 to 2. All objects begin life at generation 0. Objects that live through a garbage collection are promoted to the next generation, up to level 2. For example, generation 0 objects become generation 1 objects after the first garbage collection occurring after their creation. If generation 1 objects are still alive during the next garbage collection, they're moved to generation 2, which is the highest they can go.

Figure 34.3 shows an example of the three-stage generational optimization:

Initial Heap: The first stage shows objects A, B, and C after they are initialized and their generation is set to 0.

1st GC: After the first garbage collection, objects A and C are moved up to generation 1. Object B has been removed because it was determined to be unused. Objects D and E were instantiated and set to generation 0, as all newly instantiated objects are.

2nd GC: Before the second garbage collection occurs, object D is determined to be unused. Therefore the second garbage collection moves objects A and C to generation 2, removes object D, and moves object E to generation 1. After the garbage collection, object F is instantiated and becomes a generation 0 object.

FIGURE 34.3
The generations optimization.

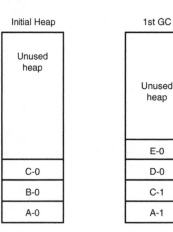

Initial Heap
Unused heap
C-0
B-0
A-0

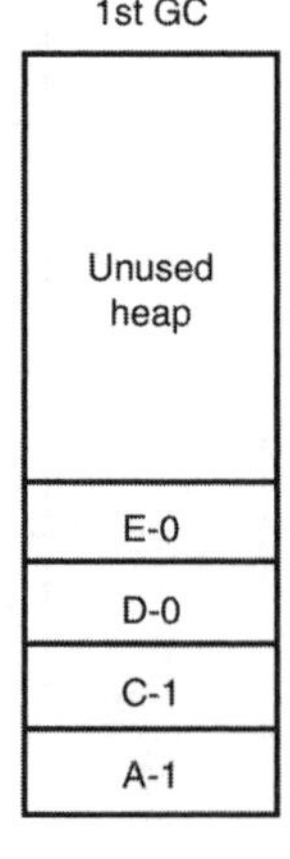

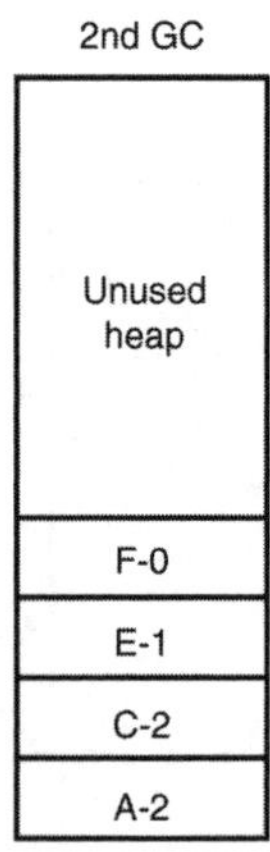

Finalizing Your Code Properly

Classes with finalizers or destructors are more expensive to clean up than objects without destructors. This is because the garbage collector has to make two passes for objects with destructors: the first pass executes the destructor, and the second pass cleans up the object.

The garbage collector has two structures to manage objects with destructors: a finalization queue and a F-reachable queue. When an object with a destructor becomes unusable, a pointer to it is added to the finalization queue. This indicates that the object must have its destructor called before it's cleaned up. During a garbage collection, all entries in the finalization queue are moved to the F-reachable queue; their destructors are called; and their objects are moved to the live-object graph. This means that their objects are not cleaned up on the first pass. On the next garbage collection, all objects pointed to in the F-reachable queue are cleaned up.

The Problems with Destructors

The preceding discussion about garbage collector management of objects with destructors brings up some immediately obvious problems. First of all, garbage collection on objects with destructors is expensive. With two collections per object, the amount of time to clean up an object is doubled.

Another set of problems derives from the non-deterministic nature of garbage collection. There is no way to tell when the garbage collection will happen. There are some garbage collection methods that provide information and allow you to force a garbage collection, but the benefit-to-effort ratio is so small that they would be a waste of time.

Non-deterministic finalization also means that a program has no way to control the release of resources with destructors alone. There's also no guarantee of the order in which destructors will be called by the garbage collector. Therefore, sequential dependencies between object destructors should be avoided at all cost.

Tip

Destructors should be avoided unless absolutely necessary. This chapter presents alternatives to destructors, such as the `IDisposable` interface and the `using` directive, which provide a deterministic means of releasing system resources.

The Dispose Pattern

An alternative to destructors for releasing resources is use the Dispose pattern, which declares `Close()` or `Dispose()` methods. A controlling object calls one of these methods to give the called object an opportunity to release resources before it becomes unusable. The `Close()` method is normally defined for objects with resources that can be reopened, such as file streams. The `Dispose()` method is a good general-purpose method for releasing resources in any case.

A common interface supporting the Dispose pattern is `IDisposable`, which defines the `Dispose()` method. This is convenient because an object can be checked to see whether it supports the `IDisposable` interface and, if it does, have its `Dispose()` method called. Listing 34.1 shows how to implement the Dispose pattern.

LISTING 34.1 The Dispose Pattern: `DisposePattern.cs`

```
using System;

class DisposePattern
{
    static void Main(string[] args)
    {
        DisposableClass dc = new DisposableClass();

        try
        {
            if (dc is IDisposable)
            {
                Console.WriteLine(
                    "DisposableClass is IDisposable");
            }
        }
        finally
        {
            dc.Dispose();
        }
    }
}

public class DisposableClass: IDisposable
{
    public void Dispose()
    {
        Console.WriteLine(
            "DisposableClass is being disposed.");
    }
}
```

And here's the output:

```
DisposableClass is IDisposable
DisposableClass is being disposed.
```

The Dispose pattern is implemented by making a class that needs to release resources to implement the `IDisposable` interface. In Listing 34.1, this class is `DisposableClass`, which implements `IDisposable` by declaring the `Dispose()` method.

The `DisposePattern` class instantiates an object of type `DisposableClass`. By performing actions in a `try/finally` block, the program guarantees that the `Dispose()` method will always be called, thus releasing resources immediately when they are no longer needed.

The `using` Statement

Hand-in-hand with the `IDisposable` interface is the `using` statement. The parameter to the `using` statement must be an `IDisposable` object, otherwise a compile-time error will occur. Listing 34.2 shows how to implement the `using` statement.

> **Note**
>
> The `using` statement should not be confused with the `using` declaration, the latter supporting declaration of external namespaces. The `using` statement supports deterministic resource release through the Dispose pattern.

LISTING 34.2 The `using` Statement: `UsingStatement.cs`

```
using System;

class UsingStatement
{
    static void Main(string[] args)
    {
        DisposableClass dc = new DisposableClass();

        using (dc)
        {
            if (dc is IDisposable)
            {
                Console.WriteLine(
                    "DisposableClass is IDisposable");
            }
        }
    }
}
```

LISTING 34.2 continued

```
public class DisposableClass: IDisposable
{
    public void Dispose()
    {
        Console.WriteLine(
            "DisposableClass is being disposed.");

        GC.SuppressFinalize(this);
    }

    ~DisposableClass()
    {
        Dispose();
    }
}
```

And here's the output:

```
DisposableClass is IDisposable
DisposableClass is being disposed.
```

The `using` statement in the `Main()` method ensures the `Dispose()` method of the `DisposableClass` instance is called after the code in the enclosing block is executed. The effect is essentially the same as that in Listing 34.1. The following example shows how to implement a single block for multiple `IDisposable` objects by adding multiple `using` statements before the block:

```
DisposableClass dc1 = new DisposableClass();
DisposableClass dc2 = new DisposableClass();

using (dc1)
using (dc2)
{
    // some operation
}
```

In this example the `Disposable` class has a destructor, which calls the `Dispose()` method. For performance, it's also a good idea to call the `SuppressFinalize()` method of the `GC` class. This removes the pointer to the object from the finalization queue and prevents the `Dispose()` method from being called twice.

Controlling Garbage Collection

For most applications, interacting with the garbage collector will not be necessary. However, there may be times when it's desirable to invoke a garbage collection or inspect the status of some objects. For example, during program idle time or during an I/O might be good opportunities to force a garbage collection. This may minimize the possibility of a garbage collection during times when the program needs CPU cycles for higher priority tasks.

Controlling Objects

The `GC` class has several class members for working with the garbage collector; these are shown in Table 34.1. For an example of how to force a garbage collection and observe its effects, see Listing 34.3.

TABLE 34.1 `GC` Class Members

Member Name	*Description*
`MaxGeneration`	Specifies the maximum number of generations the garbage collector supports.
`Collect`	Forces a garbage collection.
`GetGeneration`	Tells what generation an object belongs to.
`GetTotalMemory`	Returns the amount of allocated memory.
`KeepAlive`	Prevents an object from being finalized.
`ReRegisterForFinalize`	Adds a reference to an object back to the finalization queue.
`SuppressFinalize`	Removes reference to an object from the finalization queue.
`WaitForPendingFinalizers`	Waits for all finalizers for objects referenced in the finalization queue to complete.

LISTING 34.3 Interacting with the Garbage Collector: `CollectGenerations.cs`

```
using System;
using System.Collections;

class CollectGenerations
{
    static void Main(string[] args)
    {
        int maxGenerations = GC.MaxGeneration;
```

LISTING 34.3 continued

```
        ArrayList heapObjects = new ArrayList();
        string[] IDs = new string[]
            {"A", "B", "C", "D", "E", "F", "G",
             "H", "I", "J", "K", "L", "M", "N"};

        for (int i=0, j=0; i <= maxGenerations; i++, j+=2)
        {
            Console.WriteLine(
                "\nGarbage Collection #{0}: \n", i);

            heapObjects.Add(new AllocatedObject(IDs[j]));
            heapObjects.Add(new AllocatedObject(IDs[j+1]));

            foreach (AllocatedObject obj in heapObjects)
            {
                obj.TellGeneration();
            }

            GC.Collect();
        }
    }
}

class AllocatedObject
{
    string name;

    public AllocatedObject(string name)
    {
        this.name = name;
    }

    public void TellGeneration()
    {
        Console.WriteLine("Object {0} is Generation {1}.",
            name, GC.GetGeneration(this));
    }
}
```

And here's the output:

```

Garbage Collection #0:

Object A is Generation 0.
Object B is Generation 0.

Garbage Collection #1:
```

LISTING 34.3 continued

```
Object A is Generation 1.
Object B is Generation 1.
Object C is Generation 0.
Object D is Generation 0.

Garbage Collection #2:

Object A is Generation 2.
Object B is Generation 2.
Object C is Generation 1.
Object D is Generation 1.
Object E is Generation 0.
Object F is Generation 0.
```

The first statement in the `Main()` method of Listing 34.3 uses the `GC` class to get the maximum number of generations supported by the garbage collector. Then it uses a loop to allocate objects and perform garbage collections. Each of the objects is from the class `AllocatedObject`, which has a `TellGeneration()` method. On every pass through the `for` loop, the `TellGeneration()` method is called on each `AllocatedObject` object. Within the `TellGeneration()` method is a `Console.WriteLine()` method that takes a second parameter telling which generation the object belongs to. The result for the second parameter is produced by a call to the `GetGeneration()` method of the `GC` class. The parameter to the `GetGeneration()` method specifies the object whose generation will be returned.

Weak References

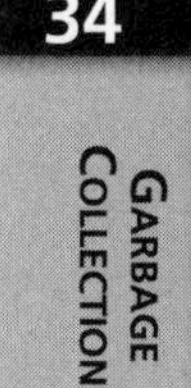

Weak references provide a compromise between marking objects as unusable and having them available for possible future use. The benefit of this is that when memory is full, a garbage collection can take place and free up resources without running out of memory. At the same time, if an object is marked as a weak reference and hasn't been garbage collected, it could be reclaimed by the program and used again.

A possible application of weak references would be a text editor. Some documents are so long that keeping the entire text in memory would be extremely inefficient and introduce the potential to run out of heap space. This is the role of strong references, where an object must go out of scope or be explicitly set to null before the memory is released. However, it would be more efficient to allow parts of the document, perhaps the beginning, that may or may not be looked at again, to be set as a weak reference and leave only the current working part of the document assigned to strong references. This way if the user scrolls back to the beginning of the document, there is a good chance that the weak reference hasn't been garbage collected, and the memory can be reset to a strong reference and used again. However, if the garbage collector has already cleaned up the weak referenced objects, no big deal—just recreate the object from scratch. Sometimes the potential for performance gains through the weak references far outweigh the drawbacks of recreating the objects if they've been garbage collected. Listing 34.4 demonstrates how to use weak references.

LISTING 34.4 Weak References: `WeakestLink.cs`

```
using System;

class WeakestLink
{
    static void Main(string[] args)
    {
        Console.WriteLine("Strong References Created:");

        LinkA la = new LinkA();
        LinkB lb = new LinkB();

        Console.WriteLine("Weak References Created:");

        WeakReference wra = new WeakReference(la);
        WeakReference wrb = new WeakReference(lb, true);

        la = null;
        lb = null;

        Console.WriteLine("First Collection:");

        GC.Collect();

        la = (LinkA)wra.Target;
        lb = (LinkB)wrb.Target;

        if (la == null)
            Console.WriteLine("LinkA has been collected.");
        else
            Console.WriteLine("LinkA has been revived.");

        if (lb == null)
            Console.WriteLine("LinkB has been collected.");
        else
            Console.WriteLine("LinkB has been revived.");

        Console.WriteLine("Making LinkB Weak Again:");
```

LISTING 34.4 continued

```
        WeakReference wrb2 = new WeakReference(lb);
        GC.ReRegisterForFinalize(lb);
        lb = null;

        Console.WriteLine("Second Collection:");
        GC.Collect();

        Console.WriteLine("Third Collection:");
        GC.Collect();

        lb = (LinkB)wrb.Target;

        if (lb == null)
            Console.WriteLine("LinkB has been collected.");
        else
            Console.WriteLine("LinkB has been revived.");
    }
}

class LinkA
{
    public LinkA()
    {
        Console.WriteLine("LinkA initialized.");
    }
}

class LinkB
{
    public LinkB()
    {
        Console.WriteLine("LinkB initialized.");
    }

    ~LinkB()
    {
        Console.WriteLine("I am the weakest link, G'dby!");
    }
}
```

And the output is

```
Strong References Created:
LinkA initialized.
LinkB initialized.
Weak References Created:
First Collection:
I am the weakest link, G'dby!
LinkA has been collected.
```

```
LinkB has been revived.
Making LinkB Weak Again:
Second Collection:
I am the weakest link, G'dby!
Third Collection:
LinkB has been collected.
```

The example in Listing 34.4 instantiates a couple of objects, turns them into weak references, and invokes garbage collections to show the behavior of weak references. The classes used as weak references, `LinkA` and `LinkB`, differ only in that `LinkB` has a destructor.

Instances of the `WeakReference` class are created with their constructor parameters set to live objects. Thereafter, the object reference may be set to `null`. The following example shows how to declare a `WeakReference` object:

```
WeakReference wra = new WeakReference(la);
WeakReference wrb = new WeakReference(lb, true);

la = null;
lb = null;
```

The `WeakReference` constructor has an overloaded constructor with a second `Boolean` parameter for tracking resurrection, which defaults to `false` if not specified. Since `LinkA` doesn't have a destructor, its `WeakReference` object doesn't have the tracking resurrection parameter. Specifying the tracking resurrection parameter for an object without a destructor makes no difference in the handling of that weak reference, as it will be ignored. Since the `LinkB` class has a destructor, setting the resurrection tracking parameter to `true` makes sense. This ensures that the object can be revived after its destructor has been called, but before the actual object is removed from memory (while it still has an entry in the F-reachable queue).

Once a `WeakReference` object has been created, the program forces a garbage collection. The output shows that the `LinkB` destructor is called immediately after the first garbage collection. Since `LinkA` doesn't have a destructor, its object has been removed from memory. However, `LinkB` still has an entry in the F-reachable queue because a second garbage collection hasn't taken place yet. If you recall, objects with destructors require two garbage collections before the objects are removed from memory. The following example shows how to revive a weak reference:

```
la = (LinkA)wra.Target;
lb = (LinkB)wrb.Target;
```

That's how to turn a weak reference back into a strong reference. The `WeakReference` object holds a pointer to the object in its `Target` property. The garbage collector ignores pointers in the `Target` property of `WeakReference` objects when building the live object graph, enabling weak references to work as expected. In the preceding example, `la` is set to `null` because its object has been collected. However, `lb` is set to the pointer of its original object and can now be used again.

The `LinkB` object's destructor has already been called. Therefore, when the `LinkB` object was revived, its entry in the finalization queue no longer existed. This means that if the `LinkB` object is garbage collected, its destructor will not be called again. Under normal circumstances, a class with a destructor has that destructor for a good reason, normally to release resources. This means that a `LinkB` object will not release resources unless some other special action is taken. The recommended method of releasing resources is to use the Dispose pattern. Another alternative is to invoke the `ReRegisterForFinalize()` method of the `GC` class as shown in the following example:

```
WeakReference wrb2 = new WeakReference(lb);
GC.ReRegisterForFinalize(lb);
lb = null;
```

The call to `ReRegisterForFinalize()` method adds a new entry to the finalization queue so a destructor will be called as expected. When the second garbage collection is forced, the `LinkB` destructor is called again as shown in the program output. After the third garbage collection, the `LinkB` object is finally removed from memory.

Summary

C# runs in an environment that includes an automatic garbage collector. Although this eliminates many of the problems associated with memory management in other languages, it introduces other concerns.

One of the primary issues is non-deterministic destruction. To resolve this problem, a good understanding of finalization is necessary to ensure resources are properly released.

The base class library includes a `GC` class designed to help work with the garbage collector. In most situations it's best to allow the garbage collector to run without intervention, but the `GC` class is there to help when necessary.

Weak references provide the ability to make objects available for garbage collection, yet give the program an opportunity to take the objects back as strong references before they're collected. They enable opportunities for certain programs to optimize program performance, while being good citizens with heap memory.

CHAPTER 35

Cross-Language Programming with C#

In This Chapter

- The Common Type System (CTS) *712*
- The Common Language Specification (CLS) *713*
- Tips for Making Your Code CLS-Compatible *713*
- Writing a Cross-Language Program *721*

The Common Language Specification (CLS) is a standard for assemblies to be written in the developer's language of choice, yet the compiled assemblies can be used by any other language. For example, if a DLL is written in Visual Basic.NET and follows the rules of the CLS, the types in that library can be used by any C# program. An important element supporting the CLS is the Common Type System (CTS), which provides a set of types that are common for all CLS-compatible languages.

This essentially means that programmers can use any CTS/CLS–compliant language they want and still create types and libraries that are compatible with any other CTS/CLS–compliant language. The results are much larger reusable code bases for a wider variety of programmers. The .NET Frameworks, written in Managed C++ (C++), Visual Basic (VB), JScript, and of course C#, are a testament to the reality that this works.

The Common Type System (CTS)

The Common Type System (CTS) is an infrastructure supporting strong code and type verification. It also is the key to ensuring that managed code is self-describing.

The CTS is the foundation of cross-language programming. For example, an `int` in C# is the same as an `int` in Managed C++. The name doesn't need to be the same, as long as there is a 1-to-1 mapping between types, such as a C# `float` and a VB `single`. Regarding C# intrinsic types, unsigned integral types are not CLS-compliant, but all other C# intrinsic types are CLS-compliant.

Many of the typing principles in C# have been presented in earlier chapters. For example, you should already know the difference between value and reference types, which intrinsic types fall into each category, and how to create user-defined types that fall into each category. Table 35.1 has a comparison of types among four languages that support the CTS: C#, Visual Basic.NET (VB), Managed C++ (MCPP), and JScript.NET (JS).

TABLE 35.1 CTS Compatible Language Type Comparison

C#	*VB*	*MCPP*	*JS*
byte	Byte	char	byte
sbyte	Sbyte	signed char	Sbyte
short	Short	short	short
int	Integer	int or long	int
long	Long	__int64	long
ushort	UInt16	unsigned short	UInt16

TABLE 35.1 continued

C#	*VB*	*MCPP*	*JS*
uint	Uint32	unsigned int or unsigned long	UInt32
ulong	UInt64	unsigned __int64	UInt64
float	Single	float	float
double	Double	double	double
bool	Boolean	bool	bool
char	Char	wchar_t	char
decimal	Decimal	Decimal	Decimal
IntPtr	IntPtr	IntPtr	IntPtr
object	Object	Object	Object
string	String	String	String

The Common Language Specification (CLS)

At this point a lot of people are thinking, "Get real! All languages are not the same." I'd have to agree because C# is definitely the best of them all (as the author dodges a tomato for utterly terrible comedy). The reality is that there are several differences between languages that would make it impossible for modules written with language-specific extensions to communicate.

This is where the Common Language Specification (CLS) comes in. There must be a set of rules for languages to follow to be cross-language compatible. The CLS is the intersection of all .NET languages and enables code to be shared equally among all CLS-compliant languages.

Tips for Making Your Code CLS-Compatible

The CLS is generic in that it accounts for what any CLS-compliant language needs. Because most of the C# language specification follows CLS-compliance rules, many applications written in C# are CLS-compliant. However, there are still a few items to consider.

When the `CLSCompliant` attribute is applied to an assembly, the C# compiler checks code for CLS compliance and generates an error or warning on violations. The assembly-level `CLSCompliant` attribute is declared after `using` statements and before any code as follows:

```
[assembly: CLSCompliant(true)]
```

The `CLSCompliant` attribute may also be applied to any type or its members. The `CLSCompliant` attribute may decorate a type without a type specification as the following example shows:

```
[CLSCompliant(true)]
```

So far, all `CLSCompliant` examples have had a true parameter, indicating that the compiler should check types and members for CLS compliance. However, the `CLSCompliant` attribute parameter may also be set to `false`, indicating that the type or member should not be checked for CLS compliance. The following example shows a `CLSCompliant` attribute that directs the compiler to not check for CLS compliance:

```
[assembly: CLSCompliant(false)]
```

Most of the examples in the following sections set the `CLSCompliant` attribute to `true`. By causing the compiler to generate a warning or error, you can see first-hand what to avoid when creating CLS-compliant applications.

General

Private members don't participate in the CLS compliance of an assembly. This is an important point because it is often necessary to use non–CLS-compliant features in your code. You can use all the non–CLS-compliant features you want, just as long as they are not a part of an application's public interface. Listing 35.1 shows a private method that is not CLS-compliant.

LISTING 35.1 A Private Non–CLS-Compliant Method: `General.cs`

```
using System;

[assembly: CLSCompliant(true)]

public class General
{
    private void myUnsignedInt(uint myInt) {}
    public void myUnsignedLong(ulong myLong) {}

    static void Main(string[] args)
    {
    }
}
```

When this program is compiled, it will generate a compiler error because the public `myUnsignedLong()` method has an unsigned long as its parameter. However, the `myUnsignedInt()` method is also non–CLS-compliant because of its unsigned `int` parameter. The `myUnsignedInt()` method doesn't generate a compiler error because it has private visibility and is not exposed outside the assembly.

Naming

Two type members cannot have the same name. The C# compiler returns an error if you use the same name twice. Listing 35.2 shows a class with a field and a method that have the same name:

LISTING 35.2 Using the Same Name for Different Members: `Naming.cs`

```
using System;

[assembly: CLSCompliant(true)]

class Naming
{
    public int ambiguous;

    public void ambiguous() {}

    static void Main(string[] args)
    {
    }
}
```

Since the C# language specification already prohibits using the same name for different members, it generates a compiler error rather than a CLS-compliance warning.

Another naming rule is that the return type and parameters of a method must be CLS-compliant. Listing 35.1 demonstrated this: the `ulong` parameter generated a CLS compliance warning.

Types

Unsigned types are not CLS-compliant. This was also shown in Listing 35.1.

A program can overload constructors, indexers, and methods, but it can't overload fields or events. Listing 35.3 shows a program that won't compile because of improper overloading.

LISTING 35.3 Improper Overloading: `Types.cs`

```
using System;

[assembly: CLSCompliant(true)]

public delegate void myDelegate1();
public delegate void myDelegate2();

class Types
{
    public event myDelegate1 myEvent;
    public event myDelegate2 myEvent;

    short myField;
    float myField;
}
```

The C# language specification won't allow overloading of events, fields, or non-indexed properties. These CLS violations will generate compiler errors, rather than CLS non-compliance warnings.

Methods

The accessibility of an overriding method must be the same as its base class virtual method. Listing 35.4 shows an override of a virtual method where both declarations have different accessibility.

LISTING 35.4 An Override and Virtual Method with Different Accessibility: `Methods.cs`

```
using System;

[assembly: CLSCompliant(true)]

public class Super
{
    protected virtual void MyMethod() {}
}

public class Methods : Super
{
    public override void MyMethod() {}
}
```

You'll notice that the accessibility of `MyMethod()` in the `Methods` class in Listing 35.4 is public, whereas the accessibility of `MyMethod()` in the `Super` class is protected.

MyMethod() in the Methods class overrides MyMethod() in the Super class, so a compile-time error will be generated because the accessibility between an overriding method and a virtual method are different.

Indexers and Properties

Accessors of both indexers and properties must have the same accessibility as the indexer or property itself. Listing 35.5 shows a program that has a property containing accessors with different accessibility.

LISTING 35.5 Accessibility of Indexers and Properties: PropIndex.cs

```
using System;

public class PropIndex
{
    int myInt;

    public int MyProperty
    {
        private get
        {
            return 1;
        }
        protected set
        {
            myInt = value;
        }
    }
}
```

A C# program is always compliant in this regard because modifiers on indexer and property accessors aren't allowed. For this same reason, accessors may not be modified as static or virtual. The code in Listing 35.5 generates compiler errors because there are accessibility modifiers on the MyProperty property's accessors.

Events

The same standards that apply to indexer and property accessors apply to event accessors as well. If there is an add accessor, there must be a remove accessor and vice versa. Both accessors must have the same accessibility. Likewise, accessors must have the same modifiers (such as static or virtual).

Pointers

Pointers are not CLS compliant because pointers are unique to C#. They're used in what is called `unsafe` code, allowing a C# program to perform actions that would never be allowed in any other language. Because of the uniqueness of pointers, they are not considered something that should be common across multiple languages. Therefore, pointers have been left out of the CLS.

Interfaces

Interfaces can't force a class to implement a non–CLS-compliant method. Listing 35.6 shows a non–CLS-compliant interface.

LISTING 35.6 A Non–CLS-Compliant Interface: `Interfaces.cs`

```
using System;

[assembly: CLSCompliant(true)]

public interface Interfaces
{
    void MethodToImplement(ulong lparam);
}
```

The code in listing 35.6 generates a compiler error because the interface `Interfaces` has a non–CLS-compliant method specification. The `MethodToImplement()` method has an unsigned long parameter that is not CLS-compliant. Any class that implements the `Interfaces` interface is forced to implement `MethodToImplement()` and is, therefore, implementing a non–CLS-compliant member.

Inheritance

All inherited classes must be CLS-compliant. Listing 35.7 shows a class, `NonClsCompliant`, that is non–CLS-compliant, and Listing 35.8 shows another class that inherits the `NonClsCompliant` class.

LISTING 35.7 A Non–CLS-Compliant Base Class: `NonClsCompliant.cs`

```
using System;

public class NonClsCompliant
{
    public void NonCompliantMethod(ulong NonCompliantParam) {}
}
```

LISTING 35.8 A CLS-Compliant Derived Class Inheriting from a Non–CLS-Compliant Base Class: `Inheritance.cs`

```
using System;

[assembly: CLSCompliant(true)]

public class Inheritance : NonClsCompliant
{
}
```

This generates an error because the NonClsCompliant class is not CLS-compliant.

Arrays

Array elements must be CLS-compliant. The class in Listing 35.9 contains an array that is not CLS-compliant.

LISTING 35.9 A Non–CLS-Compliant Array: `Arrays.cs`

```
using System;

[assembly: CLSCompliant(true)]

namespace Arrays
{
    public class Arrays
    {
        ulong[] arUlong  = new ulong[5];

        public Arrays()
        {
            arUlong[0] = 1977;
        }
    }
}
```

The `arUlong` array in Listing 35.9 holds unsigned long (`ulong`) types, which are not CLS-compliant. The code in the listing should, therefore, generate a compiler error.

Enums

The underlying type of an enum must be CLS-compliant. Listing 35.10 shows an enum that is not CLS-compliant.

LISTING 35.10 A Non–CLS-Compliant Enum: `enum.cs`

```
using System;

[assembly: CLSCompliant(true)]

public enum Test: ulong {one, two, three};
```

The enum in Listing 35.10 generates a compiler error because it is not CLS-compliant. The underlying type of the `Test` enum is `ulong`, which is not CLS-compliant. Since the underlying type of the enum is non–CLS-compliant, the enum is also non–CLS-compliant.

Attributes

Attributes must be CLS-compliant. Listing 35.11 shows a non–CLS-compliant attribute.

LISTING 35.11 A Non–CLS-Compliant Custom Attribute: `Attributes.cs`

```
using System;

[assembly: CLSCompliant(true)]

[AttributeUsage(AttributeTargets.All)]
public class CustomAttributes : Attribute
{
    public CustomAttributes(ulong lparam)
    {
    }
}
```

The attribute in Listing 35.11 is non–CLS-compliant because it has a non–CLS-compliant positional parameter, `ulong lparam`. It will generate an error.

Assemblies

Sometimes an assembly may have separate types with different CLS compliance. For example, ClassA may be CLS-compliant, but ClassB may not be. Since their CLS compliance is different, both ClassA and ClassB must have a `CLSCompliant` attribute. Furthermore, any assembly that has types with different compliance must decorate each type with a `CLSCompliant` attribute. Another way to put this rule is that if all types in an assembly are CLS-compliant or all types in an assembly are non–CLS-compliant, then every type does not have to be decorated with a CLS compliant attribute. However, if there is any difference in the CLS compliance between any two types in an assembly, then every type in that assembly must be decorated with the CLS compliant attribute. Listing 35.12 shows an assembly containing types with opposite CLS compliance.

LISTING 35.12 Assembly Containing Types with Different CLS Compliance: `Assembly.cs`

```
using System;

[assembly: CLSCompliant(true)]

[CLSCompliant(false)]
public class NonClsCompliant
{
    public void NonCompliantMethod(ulong NonCompliantParam) {}
}

public class ClsCompliant
{
    public void CompliantMethod() {}
}
```

The assembly in Listing 35.10 has an assembly-level `CLSCompliant` attribute set to `true`. The `NonClsCompliant` class also has a `CLSCompliant` attribute, but its value is set to `false`. This is the only way to get this assembly to compile, because the CLS compliance of the `NonClsCompliant` class is different from every other type in the assembly. Commenting out the `CLSCompliant` attribute on the `NonClsCompliant` class generates a compiler error.

Additionally, members must have the same CLS compliance as their type.

Writing a Cross-Language Program

The whole purpose of CLS compliance is to create a common specification for multiple languages to interoperate. According to the CLS standard, any CLS-compliant program can be compiled into a `dll` and used by any other CLS-compliant language. The base class libraries, written in different languages, prove that this works. To demonstrate the cross-language interoperability features, I've provided a program composed of objects from JScript.NET, Managed C++, Visual Basic.NET, and C#. Listings 35.13, 35.14, 35.15, 35.16, and 35.17 show objects written in each of these languages.

LISTING 35.13 A Jscript Class: `clJS.js`

```
// JScript class to be used in C#
public class clJS
{
    public var Greeting : String;
```

LISTING 35.13 continued

```
    function clJS()
    {
        this.Greeting = "Hello From JScript";
    }
}
```

LISTING 35.14 A C++ Class Definition: `clCPP.h`

```
#pragma once

using namespace System;

namespace CrossLangCPP
{
    public __gc class clCPP
    {
    public:
        // Virtual C++ method to be overriden in C#
        virtual int CppMethod(int intParam);
    };
}
```

LISTING 35.15 A C++ Class Implementation: `clCPP.cpp`

```
#include "stdafx.h"

#include "CrossLangCPP.h"

// Virtual C++ method to be overriden in C#
int CrossLangCPP::clCPP::CppMethod(int intParam)
{
    return 0;
}
```

LISTING 35.16 A VB.NET Interface Definition: `clVB.vb`

```
Public Interface clVB

    Function VBInterfaceMethod() As Int32

End Interface
```

LISTING 35.17 A C# Program Using Objects Written in Other Languages: `clCS.cs`

```
using System;
using CrossLangCPP;
using CrossLangVB;

namespace CrossLangCS
{
    /// <summary>
    /// Cross Language Program Implementation
    /// </summary>
    class clCS: clCPP, clVB
    {
        clJS myJScriptObj = new clJS();

        static void Main(string[] args)
        {
            clCS myCrossLangObj = new clCS();
            Console.WriteLine(myCrossLangObj.myJScriptObj.Greeting);
        }

        /// <summary>
        /// Overrides a C++ virtual method
        /// </summary>
        public override int CppMethod(int intParam)
        {
            return 0;
        }

        /// <summary>
        /// Implements a VB interface method
        /// </summary>
        public int VBInterfaceMethod()
        {
            return 0;
        }
    }
}
```

The C# program in Listing 35.17 uses three objects defined in other languages. First, it contains the JScript object defined in Listing 35.13. The JScript object has a public string variable, which the C# program accesses and prints its value to the console screen.

Next, the C# program inherits the C++ base class from Listings 35.14 and 35.15. The C++ class defines a virtual method, which is overridden in the C# derived class.

The C# program also inherits the VB.NET interface defined in Listing 35.16. As Listing 35.17 shows, the C# program provides an implementation for the VB.NET interface.

Summary

The Common Type System (CTS) defines a set of standard types for .NET languages to implement. A well-defined CTS enables the Common Language Specification (CLS), the set of rules for enabling cross-language programming.

There are several rules to follow when creating a CLS-compliant application. Most of the CLS compliance rules are also part of the C# language specification. In C#, the majority of non–CLS-compliant syntax is flagged as compiler errors rather than as warnings.

The CLS enables types to be written in any compliant language and reused in other CLS-compliant languages. The example in this chapter demonstrated a C# program that encapsulated a JScript object, inherited from a Managed C++ base class, and inherited a Visual Basic.NET interface.

36

The Common Language Runtime

IN THIS CHAPTER

- Managed Execution 726
- Metadata 728
- Managed Services 729

The Common Language Runtime (CLR) is the virtual machine environment that all .NET languages run in. It is a managed execution environment, which provides several services for running programs.

The specific services include security, type system safety, memory management, a common language environment, managed and unmanaged code interoperability, just-in-time (JIT) code activation, and the capability to be hosted within other environments.

Most of the topics associated with the CLR have been discussed in other chapters. The subjects in this chapter flesh out the remaining subject matter that doesn't fit well anywhere else.

Managed Execution

A primary feature of the CLR is managed execution. Supporting its role in managing security, providing a type-safe environment, and managing memory, the CLR has a well-defined managed execution process. This process has similarities to other language execution processes. However, there are also significant differences. The following sequence of events summarizes the CLR managed execution process:

1. Create source code.
2. Compile to intermediate language (IL).
3. Compile to native.
4. Execute.

Figure 36.1 takes this sequence one step further, showing what happens during runtime. The first step is taken by the Assembly Resolver, which locates the assembly. Referenced types are located, and the Assembly Loader brings those types into memory for compilation. Once in memory, the IL from the assembly is JIT compiled to native code. During compilation of a type, the JIT Compiler calls upon the Assembly Loader if a referenced type is not already compiled into memory. If the type being compiled references an assembly that hasn't been compiled yet, the JIT Compiler sends a request to the Assembly Resolver. The JIT Compiler produces managed native code, which is transferred to a machine CPU and executed. The CLR calls the JIT Compiler to compile and deliver any methods that aren't in memory during execution. The cycle continues as necessary until the program is finished.

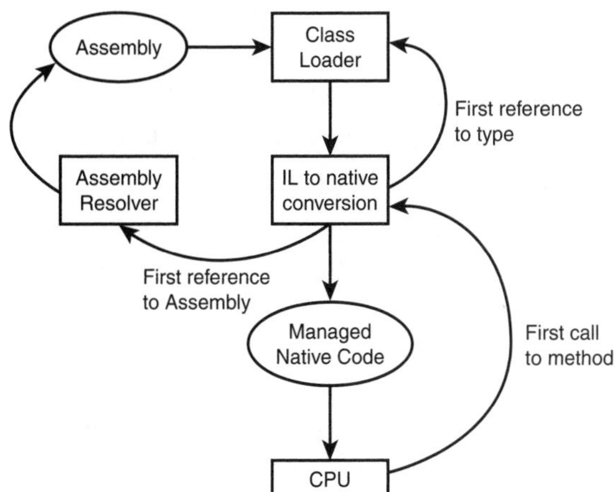

FIGURE 36.1
The runtime execution model.

Creating Source Code

This is what we've done throughout this entire book—write source code. No surprises, but it's listed here for completeness of the process.

Compiling to Intermediate Code

When C# code is compiled with the `csc` compiler, it produces an assembly language-like code called intermediate language. Microsoft calls its intermediate language Microsoft Intermediate Language (MSIL), and the ECMA standard is called Common Intermediate Language (CIL).

Compiling to Native Code

Prior to execution, IL code must be compiled to the native machine language for the computer on which it's running. This is performed with a just-in-time (JIT) compiler. There are a few different types of JIT compilers (or Jitters, as they are affectionately named): Econo-JIT, Pre-JIT, and Standard-JIT.

Econo-JIT

The Econo-JIT is characterized by fast compilation times and portability. Its speed helps in cases where program load time is important. Also, segments of code can be discarded from memory and reloaded later very efficiently.

The Econo-JIT is also more portable because of the more generic code it generates, targeting multiple CPUs or operating systems. For example, an Econo-JIT could produce code for a Pentium II class computer, running Windows 98, but that same code could be generated on Windows NT/2000/XP systems running on later model Athalon or Pentium computers.

The primary tradeoff with the Econo-JIT is the lack of optimization. It could levy a large performance hit on algorithms requiring the quickest execution speed.

Pre-JIT

A Pre-JIT compiles code completely sometime before the first execution, normally during installation. This results in fast load times and execution. The CLR still makes version checks and will revert to Standard-JIT when these checks fail.

Standard-JIT

Standard-JIT is the normal execution mode for managed code. This is the process described in Figure 36.1. The advantages of Standard-JIT are dynamic late-bound code execution, high optimization, and improved code verification. The primary drawback to this approach is slow start-up due to the load and optimization processes.

Executing the Program

Once code has been JIT compiled, it can execute in the CLR's managed environment. During execution, the CLR provides security, memory management, interoperability with unmanaged code, cross-language debugging, and enhanced support for deployment and versioning.

Metadata

Metadata is information that describes every piece of information managed by the CLR. It is automatically generated as a part of the compilation process. Elements of metadata include information on assemblies, types, and attributes:

Assemblies. Metadata provides identity by expressing assembly name, version, culture, and/or public key. It tells what types are exported and which types are referenced. Assembly security is also described through meta-data.

Types. Type information includes the type name, visibility, base classes, and implemented interfaces. There is metadata for type members, such as methods, fields, properties, indexers, events, and nested types.

Attributes. Attribute metadata comes from user-defined custom attributes, compiler-defined attributes (such as `const`), and system-defined attributes (such as `CLSCompliant` and `WebMethod`).

Uses of Metadata

The role of metadata is ubiquitous in the managed execution process. The classes of the `System.Reflection` namespace allow a program to view the metadata of an assembly. Here's a list of many of the ways metadata is utilized:

Serialization	Reflection
Type library exporter	Designers
Compilers	Debugger
Type browsers	Profiler
Schema generator	Proxy generator

Managed Services

The Common Language Runtime (CLR) provides several managed services including exception handling, security, automatic lifetime management, debugging and profiling, and interoperability. The reason these services are called managed services is to differentiate them from how these tasks are handled in other languages. For example, the C programming language can be considered an unmanaged environment because of its comparatively low type safety and capability to wreak havoc throughout a system with pointers. The term *managed* indicates that the CLR has much more control over how a program is executed and what it is allowed to do.

Exception Handling

CLR exception handling services include both typed and filtered exceptions. C# allows custom exception types and uses the try/catch mechanism to filter exceptions.

During compilation, exception handler tables are created. When an exception is generated, the handler follows a two-pass algorithm for dealing with it. The first pass locates the exception in the table, and the second pass handles the exception.

CLR optimizes its exception-handling model to minimize overhead in normal running code. The greatest performance hit occurs when an exception is actually generated. This behavior recognizes that exceptions will not be thrown if a program is operating normally. Most programs operate normally, without generating exceptions, and there should not be system overhead associated with declaring exceptions. Therefore, the CLR is designed to utilize a greater amount of system resources at the time an exception is raised.

Automatic Lifetime Management

The CLR's automatic lifetime management capability focuses on an efficient garbage collector. The garbage collector eliminates memory fragmentation and reduces the working set of objects that require management. This process is extremely efficient and estimated to be no more intrusive than a normal page fault.

Although object references may be moved during collection, the garbage collector ensures that all C# references are updated accordingly. This movement is one of the reasons why it's necessary to pin down objects with the `fixed` statement when implementing unsafe code.

Interoperability

CLR provides a bridge between itself and COM, which preserves programming models on each side of the boundary. Interoperability services strive to abstract the inconsistencies between the two models. Some of these inconsistencies include data types, methods, exceptions, activation models, and object discovery.

Another CLR interoperability feature is Platform Invocation (P/Invoke) services. This feature enables C# programs to access static entry points in unmanaged libraries. Marshalling between C# and the unmanaged library is performed via the same interoperability mechanism used with COM.

Security

The CLR provides both code- and role-based security for executing code. This process is enabled through application of metadata and security policy.

Profiling and Debugging

Profiling and debugging tools make extensive use of metadata. The CLR provides the necessary services to assist these tools during the execution process.

Summary

The Common Language Runtime (CLR) provides several services for a managed execution environment. Its managed execution process includes steps for code design, intermediate language (IL) code creation, native code generation via just-in-time (JIT) compilation, and execution. The execution model has a few JIT compilation options that vary by level of optimization, execution speed, and availability of CLR services.

Metadata enables the CLR to provide managed execution services. The metadata used includes information on assemblies, types, and attributes. Managed services include exception handling, security, automatic lifetime management, debugging and profiling, and interoperability.

CHAPTER 37

Versioning and Assemblies

IN THIS CHAPTER

- Inside Assemblies *734*
- Assembly Features *738*
- Configuration *740*
- Deployment *743*

Assemblies are the Common Language Infrastructure (CLI) logical units of functionality, providing identity, scope, security, and version management. Composed of one or more files, assemblies solve several problems that plague executable and library files on other platforms.

Some of the more prominent aspects of assemblies are side-by-side deployment, full containment and self-description, and security. Some of these aspects are reminiscent of earlier programming methodologies but are much improved with unique approaches to avoiding known problems.

Inside Assemblies

Assemblies can be made up of one or more files. Each file can be either a module or another assembly. The contents of an assembly could include a manifest, type metadata, IL code, and/or resources. One of the files in the assembly must contain a manifest. Figure 37.1 shows a possible assembly configuration.

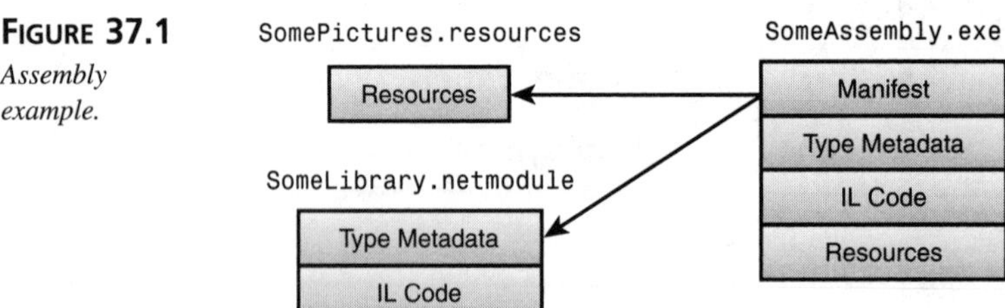

FIGURE 37.1
Assembly example.

The example in Figure 37.1 shows three different files that make up an assembly. The main file, `SomeAssembly.exe`, contains all four elements of an assembly, including the assembly manifest. The other files, `SomePictures.resources` and `SomeLibrary.netmodule`, contain additions to the assembly.

Resources are files that hold various types of reusable data. Possible contents include strings, icons, pictures, or sound files. An earlier chapter discussed creation of resource files to support localization.

Modules are always deployed as part of an assembly, because they are not meant to be separate executable entities. One benefit is modularization: the capability to separate code into logical entities, providing another way to group and manage code. Another benefit is multi-language integration: the ability to pull code written in multiple languages into a single assembly. For example, if ModuleA contains code written in

Managed C++ and ModuleB contains code written in VB, then both of these modules can be compiled into an assembly with a C# source file that uses code in both modules. The following command line creates a module:

```
csc /target:module SomeLibrary.cs
```

This example creates the file `SomeLibrary.netmodule`. Use the following command line to add the module to an assembly:

```
csc SomeAssembly.cs /addmodule:SomeLibrary.netmodule
```

That command line creates a new assembly `SomeAssembly.exe`, which includes a reference to the module `SomeLibrary.netmodule`. The `/addmodule` command-line option makes the resulting `SomeAssembly.exe` assembly reference the `SomeLibrary.netmodule` file. Therefore, the `SomeLibrary.netmodule` file must be in the same directory as the `SomeAssembly.exe`, otherwise a `FileNotFoundException` exception is generated.

Manifests

As mentioned earlier, every assembly must have a manifest. The manifest may reside in its own file or within another file with other assembly elements. Manifests contain metadata about the assembly. Table 37.1 lists manifest contents.

TABLE 37.1 Manifest Contents

Content Type	*Description*
Culture	Localization info
Files	List of files inside assembly
Name	Name of assembly
References	Referenced assemblies
Strong Name	Public key info
Types	List of types inside assembly
Version	Version number of assembly

Attributes

Several attributes decorate assemblies for various purposes. These attributes can be categorized as identity, informational, manifest, and strong name.

Identity

Identity attributes provide uniqueness to distinguish one assembly from another. The benefits of this are that different versions of an assembly may be running at the same time, and there must be a way to tell each version apart. Programs also have the option to call the assembly they want to use by specifying culture and/or version requirements in their configuration files. Table 37.2 outlines assembly identity attributes.

TABLE 37.2 Identity Attributes

Attribute Name	*Description*
`AssemblyCulture`	Localization Info
`AssemblyVersion`	Version number of assembly
`AssemblyFlags`	Controls side-by-side execution

Here are a couple examples of identity attributes:

```
[assembly: AssemblyCulture("en_US")]
```

```
[assembly: AssemblyVersion("1.0.*")]
```

Informational

The informational attributes impart knowledge about the origin of an assembly. These attributes tell which company created the assembly, and copyright, trademark, and other proprietary information about the assembly. Table 37.3 outlines informational attributes of assemblies.

TABLE 37.3 Informational Attributes

Attribute Name	*Description*
`AssemblyCompany`	Company name
`AssemblyCopyright`	Copyright Info
`AssemblyFileVersion`	Win32 file version, defaults to assembly version
`AssemblyInformationalVersion`	Product version number, not used by runtime
`AssemblyProduct`	Product information
`AssemblyTrademark`	Trademark information

Here are some examples of identity attributes:

```
[assembly: AssemblyCompany("MyCompany")]

[assembly: AssemblyProduct("My Product Name")]

[assembly: AssemblyCopyright("Copyright 2001")]

[assembly: AssemblyTrademark("TM Product Name")]
```

Manifest

The manifest attributes explain what an assembly is and how it should be used. With a short name, full name, and description, a user can get a good idea of how to use the assembly. The configuration can provide insights into what environment an assembly can be used. Table 37.4 outlines assembly manifest attributes.

TABLE 37.4 Manifest Attributes

Attribute Name	*Description*
`AssemblyConfiguration`	Config info such as `Release` or `Debug`
`AssemblyDefaultAlias`	Short friendly name of assembly
`AssemblyDescription`	Summary of what assembly is
`AssemblyTitle`	Full friendly name of assembly

Here are a few examples of identity attributes:

```
[assembly: AssemblyTitle("My Assembly")]

[assembly: AssemblyDescription("Provides extensive widget support.")]

[assembly: AssemblyConfiguration("Release")]
```

Strong Name

The strong name attributes primarily support security. They identify the key, key file, and timing associated with various security issues. An assembly can have what is called a strong name, which consists of a combination of identity, manifest, and strong name attributes. How to create a strong name for an assembly is discussed later in this chapter. Table 37.5 outlines strong name attributes for assemblies.

TABLE 37.5 Strong Name Attributes

Attribute Name	*Description*
`AssemblyDelaySign`	Indicates if delayed signing is used
`AssemblyKeyFile`	Name of key file
`AssemblyKeyName`	Name of key container

Here are a couple examples of identity attributes:

```
[assembly: AssemblyDelaySign(false)]

[assembly: AssemblyKeyFile("MyKey.snk")]

[assembly: AssemblyKeyName("MyKeyContainer")]
```

Assembly Features

Besides being just another executable program or library, an assembly offers several features that enhance program management and execution. The features of identity, scope, versioning, and security form a basis for assigning a strong name to an assembly.

Identity

An assembly is a unit of identity. For instance, a class named `MyClass` in an assembly named `AssemblyOne` is different from a class named `MyClass` in an assembly named `AssemblyTwo`.

Scope

Through proper use of the `internal` modifier, assembly types are visible only within that assembly. External assemblies won't be able to see or access any types marked as `internal`.

Versioning

The ability to version assemblies allows a few key capabilities, such as automatic upgrades, enhanced deployment, and side-by-side execution. An assembly version is a 4-tuple separated by dots with the following format:

```
<major>.<minor>.<build>.<revision>
```

Table 37.6 shows the meaning of each position and a suggested method of implementation.

TABLE 37.6 Assembly Version Numbers

Position	*Description*
major	Major release number
minor	Minor release number
build	Intermediate build
revision	Hot fix number

The version may be specifically stated in the `AssemblyVersion` attribute, or defaults may be accepted. In the following `AssemblyVersion` attribute, the major version is `1`, the minor version is `0`, and the build and revision version numbers will be assigned during compilation:

```
[assembly: AssemblyVersion("1.0.*")]
```

Security

Public keys and certificates make assemblies inherently more reliable and secure than the libraries and executables developed in traditional machine-compiled languages. There are two ways to secure your assemblies: strong names and digital signatures.

Strong Names

Strong names consist of assembly name, version, culture, and public key. The following command line generates a key file to be used in applying a strong name to an assembly:

```
sn -k Mykey.snk
```

Once a key file is generated, it may be referenced in an assembly by specifying the generated key file name in an `AssemblyKeyFile` attribute as follows:

```
[assembly: AssemblyKeyFile("MyKey.snk")]
```

Certificates

Certificates provide proof of code identity and are the secure compliment to strong names. More specifically, a strong name alone does not guarantee authenticity of code. You need a certificate to prove identity.

Normally, certificates are obtained through certification authorities such as Verisign and Thawte. However, for testing purposes there are a couple tools in the .NET Frameworks SDK that make it easy to create a test certificate. The `makecert` utility creates an X.509 certificate as the following example shows:

```
makecert mycert.cer -sk mykey
```

This command line creates an X.509 certificate named `mycert.cer` and a registry key named `mykey`. The certificate must be translated into a Software Publisher Certificate (SPC):

```
cert2spc mycert.cer mycert.spc
```

The `cert2spc` utility created a new SPC named `mycert.spc`, which contains the X.509 certificate specified in `mycert.cer`. Now that we finally have a certificate, the assembly may be signed as follows:

```
signcode /spc mycert.spc /v mykey SomeAssembly.exe
```

The `signcode` utility added the `mycert.spc` SPC, identified with the `/spc` switch, to the `SomeAssembly.exe` assembly. The key was the `mykey` registry key, which was created with the `makecert`.

Now the `SomeAssembly.exe` assembly is signed and secure.

The utilities in this section have many options to customize their functionality. Just use the `-h` option for help. Additionally, executing the `signcode` utility without command-line options opens a wizard application that steps you through the certification process.

Configuration

Another benefit of assemblies is that they can be configured dynamically through configuration files. These files are written in XML, providing human readable access to program configuration.

There are basically two types of configuration files: machine and application. Machine configuration files hold configuration information for all applications running on a machine. In this light, they are intended to be more generic and applicable to multiple applications. Machine configuration files are located at `%runtime install path%\Config\Machine.config`. When running applications, the machine configuration file is consulted first, and then the application configuration file settings are applied.

Executable application configuration files have the same name as the executable file name with the extension `.config` appended. For example if a program were named `MyApp.exe`, its configuration file would be named `MyApp.exe.config`. ASP.NET and Web Service configuration files are named `web.config`.

All configuration files have a `<configuration>` root element. Subsections are divided into startup, runtime, remoting, crypto, class api, and security settings. This chapter focuses specifically on assemblies, so I'll discuss startup and runtime settings in the next couple sections.

Startup Configuration

Startup configuration options are specified within the <startup> section of a configuration file. Presently, there is only one option, the <runtime> element, which specifies which Common Language Runtime (CLR) version to use. The following code shows the <runtime> section:

```
<configuration>
   <startup>
      <requiredRuntime version="1.0.2914.0" safeMode="true"/>
   </startup>
</configuration>
```

According to this configuration file, a program must run with CLR version 1.0.2914.0. Setting the safeMode attribute to true enables a registry search to see if this assembly was redirected to run against another version of the CLR. The sequence of operations in determining which CLR to use is as follows:

1. Check the CLR for which the assembly was.
2. Check the <requiredRuntime> configuration element.
3. Check the registry.

Runtime Configuration

There are three possible options for runtime configuration: concurrent garbage collection, assembly version redirection, and assembly location. All are sub-elements of the <runtime> section.

Concurrent Garbage Collection

Concurrent garbage collection occurs when the garbage collector runs in a separate thread from the application. This is good for performance when an application has a lot of user interaction. However, you would want to disable it to optimize performance for server-bound operations. The following example shows how to disable concurrent garbage collection:

```
<configuration>
   <runtime>
       <gcConcurrent enabled="false"/>
   </runtime>
</configuration>
```

Concurrent garbage collection is disabled by setting the enabled attribute of the <gcConcurrent> element to false. The default for concurrent garbage collection is true.

Assembly Version Redirection

Normally, assemblies run against other specified assemblies as specified at compile time. However, configuration files enable redirection from one assembly to another at runtime. This is useful when a third-party library is upgraded and is also backward compatible with the older version. The following example shows how to redirect an assembly:

```
<configuration>
    <runtime>
        <assemblyBinding xmlns="urn:schemas-microsoft-com:asm.v1">
            <dependentAssembly>
                <assemblyIdentity name="SomeAssembly"
                           publickeytoken="fa3a9d02dc01aa10"
                           culture="en-us" />
                <bindingRedirect oldVersion="1.0.0.0"
                           newVersion="2.0.0.0"/>
            </dependentAssembly>
        </assemblyBinding>
    </runtime>
</configuration>
```

The `<assemblyBinding>` section contains the details for redirecting an assembly's binding. It contains an `xmlns` attribute set to `"urn:schemas-microsoft-com:asm.v1"`, which is a mandatory entry. The two elements within the `<assemblyBinding>` section are `<assemblyIdentity>` and `<bindingRedirect>`.

The `<assemblyIdentity>` element identifies the assembly to redirect. Its first parameter, `name`, is the name of the assembly. The `publickeytoken` and `culture` attributes are optional. However, if you wanted to add the `publickeytoken`, an easy way to obtain it is by using the strong name utility with the `-T` option, as follows:

```
sn -T SomeAssembly.dll
```

The `<bindingRedirect>` element has an `oldVersion` attribute, which specifies the preexisting version of the assembly, and a `newVersion` attribute, which specifies the new assembly to redirect to.

Assembly Location

There are two assembly location elements to find where a given assembly resides: `<codeBase>` and `<probing>`. The `<codeBase>` element specifies where the runtime can find a shared assembly. The following example demonstrates the `<codeBase>` element:

```
<configuration>
  <runtime>
    <assemblyBinding xmlns="urn:schemas-microsoft-com:asm.v1">
      <dependentAssembly>
        <assemblyIdentity name="SomeAssembly"
```

```
➥publicKeyToken="b77a5c561934e089" />
        <codeBase version="1.0.0.0"
➥href="file:///C:\Program Files\Some Application" />
      </dependentAssembly>
    </assemblyBinding>
  </runtime>
</configuration>
```

The version attribute of the `<codeBase>` element is optional, and version ranges are not allowed. The `href` attribute is mandatory and must include the protocol in the URI.

The other method of locating an assembly is via probing, which specifies which subdirectories of an application may be searched. The following example shows how to configure probing:

```
<configuration>
   <runtime>
      <assemblyBinding xmlns="urn:schemas-microsoft-com:asm.v1">
         <probing privatePath="subdir1;subdir2\subsubdir;subdir2"/>
      </assemblyBinding>
   </runtime>
</configuration>
```

The private attribute of the `<probing>` element specifies the subdirectories to search. A semicolon separates each subdirectory.

MMC Configuration Tool

This section shows how to create the text-based XML configuration files. For those who prefer a graphical tool with wizards, there is an easier way to produce configuration files: the MMC snap-in called the .NET Admin Tool at `%windir%\Microsoft.NET\Framework\v1.0.xxxx` (where *%windir%* is the environment variable for your Windows directory, and *xxxx* is the most current build). With the knowledge gained from this section, using the .NET Admin Tool should be quite easy.

Deployment

Assemblies can be deployed as either private or shared. A private assembly resides in the same directory, or a subdirectory, as its main program. Private directories don't need any special configuration or handling to work with a program. Just copy them where they go and they work.

Shared assemblies are another matter. As the name suggests, multiple programs may execute a shared assembly. Special preparation is required to give the assembly a strong name and deploy it to a central repository called the global assembly cache (GAC). The following command line demonstrates how to add an assembly to the GAC:

```
gacutil -i SomeAssembly.dll
```

The `gacutil` utility has several other options that can be viewed with the `-h` option. All assemblies added to the GAC must have a strong name. Please refer to the "Assembly Features/Strong Names" section earlier in this chapter for information on adding strong names to an assembly.

Summary

Assemblies can be composed of several elements including manifests, type catalogs, IL code, and resources. These elements may be in separate files. A manifest is required.

Features of assemblies include identity, scope, versioning, and security. These features are combined to form the strong name of an assembly.

The runtime behavior of an assembly can be altered with configuration files. These behaviors include concurrent garbage collection, binding, and location.

Simply copying assemblies to where they need to be and executing them is all that is required for private assemblies. Shared assemblies require an extra step of assigning a strong name and adding them to the global assembly cache. They're self-contained entities that don't require external catalogs or registries to enable their execution.

CHAPTER 38

Securing Code

In This Chapter

- **Code-Based Security** *746*
- **Role-Based Security** *755*
- **Security Utilities** *757*

The .NET security model introduces a significant security enhancement, referred to as *code-based security*. The need for code-based security has grown out of recent years' experience in which foreign code is accessible and downloadable to computers from diverse sources throughout the Internet. Code-based security makes a system more secure by limiting the ability of code to perform specified actions.

Traditional role-based security is also a major component of the .NET security model. *Role-based security* controls the capability of agents or individuals to perform actions on a computing system. The security types are managed by specific policies, which guide their implementation. Tools, such as public key signatures, encryption, and security certificates, assist in implementation of the security policy, for both code- and role-based security.

Code-Based Security

Code-based security is implemented via a multifaceted approach that pulls together cooperative security mechanisms to determine what an assembly is allowed to do in a system. Through the security mechanisms of evidence, code groups, security levels, and security policy, an assembly is assigned permissions in a computer system.

A code-based security policy is constructed by use of evidence, permissions, code groups, and security policy levels. Each assembly contains evidence, which is used to categorize it into a code group. Each code group has permissions that are assigned to an assembly belonging to that code group. The union of all the permissions from the code group to which the assembly belongs is then given to the assembly. Finally, there are security policy levels, each with its own set of code groups, which the assembly is evaluated against. The final set of permissions for an assembly is based upon the intersection of the permissions from each security policy level. The following sections go into more detail about how these pieces fit together.

Evidence

The information that is examined to determine an assembly's permissions is called *evidence*. There are seven primary types of evidence, as shown in Table 38.1.

TABLE 38.1 Types of Evidence

Type	*Description*
Application Directory	Where the application is installed
Hash	MD5 or SHA1 cryptographic hash

TABLE 38.1 continued

Type	*Description*
Publisher	Software publisher's signature
Site	Web or Internet site where software came from
Strong Name	Assembly's cryptographic strong name
URL	URL where software came from
Zone	Zone where software originated

In a couple more sections, you'll see how evidence is used to classify assemblies into code groups. Each code group has criteria upon which to compare evidence to see if an assembly belongs to that group.

Permissions

The .NET Framework includes named permission sets that define sets of permissions that can be granted to assemblies. Table 38.2 lists the available named permission sets. Only three of the permission sets may be modified: `Internet`, `LocalIntranet`, and `Everything`.

TABLE 38.2 Named Permission Sets

Permission	*Description*
`Nothing`	No Permissions
`Execution`	Can run, but has no access to system resources
`Internet`	Has permissions for when origin is unknown
`LocalIntranet`	Code has enterprise permissions
`Everything`	All permissions except security verification
`FullTrust`	No limits

The code groups to which an assembly belongs determine the set of permissions that can be granted. The next section, "Code Groups," goes into greater detail on the relationship between code groups and assemblies.

Code Groups

Assemblies are classified into code groups based upon the evidence presented by the assembly. A code group is a member of a hierarchical structure that is used to logically classify types of assemblies. As an intermediate step to full determination of permissions, assemblies are granted permissions based on the code groups to which they belong. Later sections on security policy level and security requests explain how the final permissions are granted to an assembly. Figure 38.1 shows a code group hierarchy that could be implemented on a system.

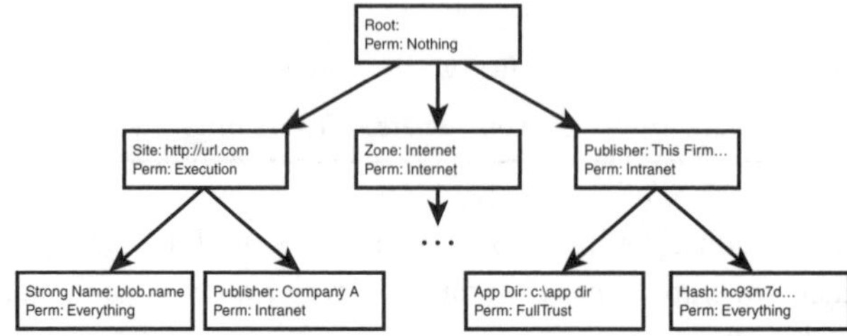

FIGURE 38.1
A code group hierarchy.

Every hierarchy has a `Root` group, which represents all code. Child groups represent specializations that help categorize code. In Figure 38.1, each group is represented by a rectangle with a group name, membership condition, and permission. The first line shows the group name and membership condition, separated by a colon. Except for the `Root` group, each group name is one of the types of evidence from Table 38.1. The second line shows the permission associated with that group, after the word `Perm` and a colon. Permissions correspond to entries in Table 38.2. The code group hierarchy may be shaped and extended as far as necessary. Also, evidence may be repeated throughout the hierarchy.

It is expected that an assembly will be a member of multiple code groups. Membership determination begins at the `Root` group and continues to child groups. If an assembly matches the membership criteria for a group, then it may be evaluated for membership in that group's children (if any). An assembly must have membership in all parents of a group before it may be evaluated with that group.

To trace how permissions are assigned with code groups, consider an assembly with a publisher certificate for `This Firm` and located at `c:\appdir`. As shown in Figure 38.2, this assembly automatically belongs to the `Root` group, which has a membership condition of all code. The assembly doesn't come from the `Internet`, and its `Url` is not `http://url.com`, so it doesn't belong the `Site` or `Zone` groups on the second level. However, it does have a publisher certificate from `This Firm`, and therefore belongs to the `Publisher` group. Since this assembly does not belong to the `Site` group on the second level, it won't be evaluated against the `Strong Name` and `Publisher` child groups on the third level. Similarly, this assembly will not be evaluated for membership in any child groups of the `Zone` group on the second level. However, the assembly will be evaluated for membership in the children, on the third level, of the `Publisher` group, on the second level. As it turns out, the assembly is located in `c:\appdir` and is a member of the `Application Directory` group. In this example, I make the assumption that the hash code for this assembly doesn't match the one in the `Hash` group.

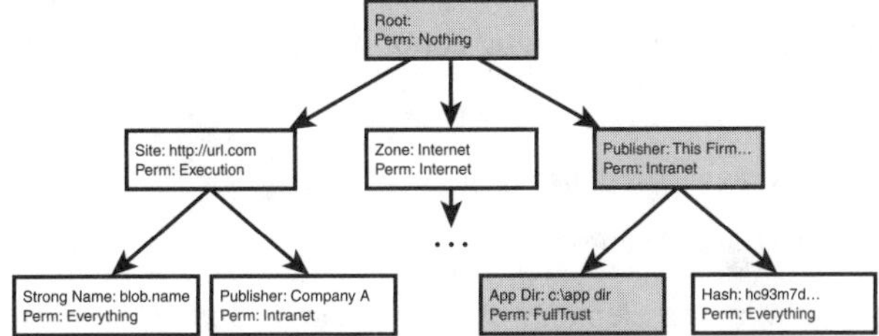

FIGURE 38.2
Code group membership.

Permissions for this assembly are determined by taking the union of all code groups to which it belongs. Therefore, this assembly has the permissions contained in the `Root` + `Publisher` + `Application Directory`, which are `Nothing` + `Intranet` + `FullTrust`.

This is not the final word in the allowable permissions for this assembly. You see, code groups belong to security policy levels, and the assembly must be evaluated with the code group of each security policy level, which is the subject of the next section.

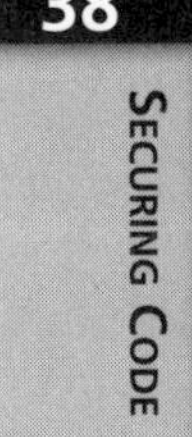

Security Policy Levels

After classification into code groups and accumulating allowable permissions, an assembly is then evaluated according to the four security policy levels: `Enterprise`, `Machine`, `User`, and `Application Domain`. The security policy level evaluation grants the intersection of the results of the code level permissions with each security level. This is different from the code group permission determination, which grants the union of all permissions to an assembly. Table 38.3 lists the security policy levels.

TABLE 38.3 Security Policy Levels

Level	*Description*
`Enterprise`	Managed code belonging to the enterprise
`Machine`	Managed code on the computer
`User`	Managed code belonging to the operating system user when the CLR starts
`Application Domain`	Managed code in the application domain

A host, such as a browser or other application that can host the CLR, sets the application domain policy level. The System Administrator sets `Enterprise`, `Machine`, and `User` policy levels. Additionally, a user may set the `User` policy level.

When determining permissions, the code group membership of each security policy level is evaluated, and permissions are assigned for each security policy level. Then the intersection of the permissions from each policy level is taken to get the next set of permissions. For example, review the following set of permissions for a given assembly:

- `Enterprise`: `Execution` + `Intranet`
- `Machine`: `Intranet` + `Internet`
- `User`: `FullTrust` + `Intranet`

The intersection, or common element, of these security policy levels is the `Intranet` named permission set. Therefore, the security policy has granted the `intranet` permission to this assembly.

Although the security policy has granted permission to this assembly, it is not the final word in what permissions the assembly will have. That's because the assembly itself must specify what permissions it wants.

Permission Requests

The final permissions an assembly receives are always a subset of the permissions granted by security policy. In other words, an assembly may have permissions that are equal to or less than the permissions specified in the security policy. This final set of permissions depends upon what the assembly requests.

There are two ways for assemblies to request permissions: declarative and imperative. Declarative requests are performed using C# attributes and are evaluated at assembly load time. Imperative requests are made by instantiating a permission object and invoking the appropriate request method. Imperative requests are evaluated at runtime. Listing 38.1 shows how to make a declarative security request.

LISTING 38.1 A Declarative Security Request

```
using System;
using System.Security.Permissions;

[assembly:ReflectionPermissionAttribute(
SecurityAction.RequestMinimum, ReflectionEmit=false)]

class CodeGroups
{
```

LISTING 38.1 continued

```
    static void Main(string[] args)
    {
    }
}
```

Declarative security requests may be applied at the assembly, class, or member level. The declarative security request in Listing 38.1 applies to the entire assembly. The particular request is for the `ReflectionPermission`. This requests asks for reflection to be given as a minimum requirement, and the request does not include reflection emit capabilities.

There are three types of permission requests that can be made with a declarative request: `RequestMinimum`, `RequestOptional`, and `RequestRefused`. Minimal permissions are ones that an assembly must have to operate. Optional permissions are nice to have, but the assembly can find a way to deal with the situation if they're not available. Refused permissions are those that the assembly doesn't want. These permission requests are members of the `SecurityAction` enum. When determining permissions for declarative requests, the following steps are taken by the CLR:

1. Take the union of minimal and optional permissions.
2. Remove the refused permissions from the results of step 1.
3. Take the intersection of the security policy permissions and the results of step 2.

The `System.Security.Permissions` namespace contains specifications for the reflection permission and others. Table 38.4 provides a quick list of what permissions are available.

TABLE 38.4 Individual Permissions

Permission	*Description*
`Environment`	Read and write environment variables
`FileDialog`	Read access to a file
`FileIO`	Append, read, or write to a file
`IsolatedStorageFile`	Control access and amount of virtual file system
`IsolatedStorage`	Control access and amount of generic isolated storage
`Principal`	Role-based security checks
`PublisherIdentity`	Access for a software publisher
`Reflection`	Can use C# reflection
`Registry`	Access operating system registry
`Security`	Security permissions that can be invoked

TABLE 38.4 continued

Permission	*Description*
`SiteIdentity`	Access to software from a specific Web site
`StrongName`	Access to assembly with a specific strong name
`UI`	User interface and clipboard
`URL`	Access to software from a location on the Internet
`Zone`	Access to specified zones

Imperative security requests are a part of the code. They're performed by instantiating an object of the appropriate permission type and calling the `Demand()` method. Listing 38.2 shows how to use imperative security requests.

LISTING 38.2 An Imperative Security Request

```
using System;
using System.Security;
using System.Security.Permissions;

class CodeGroups
{
    static void Main(string[] args)
    {
        CodeGroups cg = new CodeGroups();
        cg.MakeDemand();
    }

    public void MakeDemand()
    {
        try
        {
            UIPermission uip = new UIPermission(
                UIPermissionWindow.AllWindows,
                UIPermissionClipboard.AllClipboard);

            uip.Demand();
        }
        catch(SecurityException se)
        {
            Console.WriteLine("UI Permission Refused");
        }
    }
}
```

Within the `MakeDemand()` method a `UIPermission` object is instantiated. A `UIPermission` allows code to create windows and access the clipboard. The `UIPermission` object in Listing 38.2 is instantiated with parameters that request permissions for performing all types of window operations and performing all actions with the clipboard. The request is made by invoking the permission object's `Demand()` method. If the request succeeds, all is well, and the program continues. However, a `SecurityException` exception will be raised if the assembly is not allowed the `UIPermission` permission.

Implementing Security Policy

The creation of permissions associated with code groups and security policy levels forms the security policy of a computer system. Fortunately, the CLR comes configured with a default security policy that provides some protection against the wilds of the Web. With knowledge of how permissions are granted, you're ready to create security policies to meet the needs of your code and computer system.

Security policy can be viewed and changed with the `caspol.exe` utility. For example, the following command line prints the current security policy:

```
caspol -l
```

The output of this command would fill a few pages with the default security policy that comes with the .NET Frameworks installation. For a more focused view involving code groups, use the `-lg` option as follows:

```
caspol -lg
```

And here's the output:

```
Security is ON
Execution checking is ON
Policy change prompt is ON

Level = Machine

Code Groups:

1.  All code: Nothing
   1.1.  Zone - MyComputer: FullTrust
   1.2.  Zone - Intranet: LocalIntranet
      1.2.1.  All code: Same site Web.
      1.2.2.  All code: Same directory FileIO -
➥Read, PathDiscovery
   1.3.  Zone - Internet: Internet
      1.3.1.  All code: Same site Web.
   1.4.  Zone - Untrusted: Nothing
```

```
   1.5.  Zone - Trusted: Internet
      1.5.1.  All code: Same site Web.
   1.6.  StrongName -
➥002400000480000094000000060200000024000052534131000400000001000
➥10007D1FA57C4AED9F0A32E84AA0FAEFD0DE9E8FD6AEC8F87FB03766C834C
➥99921EB23BE79AD9D5DCC1DD9AD236132102900B723CF980957FC4E177108
➥FC607774F29E8320E92EA05ECE4E821C0A5EFE8F1645C4C0C93C1AB99285D
➥622CAA652C1DFAD63D745D6F2DE5F17E5EAF0FC4963D261C8A12436518206
➥DC093344D5AD293: FullTrust
   1.7.  StrongName -
➥00000000000000000400000000000000: FullTrust
Success
```

As you can see, the default security policy is composed of `Zone`, `All Code`, and `Strong Name` evidence. The most often used option for developers may be the `-u` option, to configure the `User` security policy level. To target a specific policy level, such as `User`, specify its option on the command line as follows:

```
caspol -u -lg
```

And here's the output:

```
Security is ON
Execution checking is ON
Policy change prompt is ON

Level = User

Code Groups:

1.  All code: FullTrust
Success
```

This example performs a group listing on the `User` security policy level. The default policy level without an option is the `Machine` policy level. The following commands show how to add a code group to the security policy:

```
caspol -ag 1.1 -appdir FullTrust
caspol -lg
```

And here's the output:

```
Security is ON
Execution checking is ON
Policy change prompt is ON

Level = Machine

Code Groups:
```

```
1.  All code: Nothing
   1.1.  Zone - MyComputer: FullTrust
      1.1.1.  ApplicationDirectory: FullTrust
   1.2.  Zone - Intranet: LocalIntranet
      1.2.1.  All code: Same site Web.
      1.2.2.  All code: Same directory FileIO -
➥Read, PathDiscovery
   1.3.  Zone - Internet: Internet
      1.3.1.  All code: Same site Web.
   1.4.  Zone - Untrusted: Nothing
   1.5.  Zone - Trusted: Internet
      1.5.1.  All code: Same site Web.
   1.6.  StrongName -
➥00240000048000009400000006020000002400005253413100040000001000
➥10007D1FA57C4AED9F0A32E84AA0FAEFD0DE9E8FD6AEC8F87FB03766C834C
➥99921EB23BE79AD9D5DCC1DD9AD236132102900B723CF980957FC4E177108
➥FC607774F29E8320E92EA05ECE4E821C0A5EFE8F1645C4C0C93C1AB99285D
➥622CAA652C1DFAD63D745D6F2DE5F17E5EAF0FC4963D261C8A12436518206
➥DC093344D5AD293: FullTrust
   1.7.  StrongName -
➥00000000000000000400000000000000: FullTrust
Success
```

The -ag option performs an add group operation. In the example a new code group was added below the parent, specified by the number `1.1`. The new group, added at location `1.1.1`, was for `ApplicationDirectory` membership and was given `FullTrust` permissions. The new ApplicationDirectory group was shown in the output. To remove this group, type the following command line:

```
caspol -rg 1.1.1
```

This removes the group we just added, which was at location `1.1.1` in the policy. For more help on how to configure security policy, use the `-h` option.

Role-Based Security

The .NET framework includes a suite of classes specialized for traditional role-based security. These classes permit code to grant and restrict access to specified agents and users to support a security policy. The primary object in role-based security is the `Principal` object. It contains both a user identity and a role.

The .NET framework contains two methods of managing role-based security: Windows and Generic. The first is through the native Windows security system, and the other is a more general and independent mechanism. Listing 38.3 shows how to find a given role using the native Windows security system.

LISTING 38.3 Role-Based Security with `WindowsPrincipal`

```
using System;
using System.Threading;
using System.Security.Principal;

class WinPerm
{
    static void Main(string[] args)
    {
        AppDomain.CurrentDomain.SetPrincipalPolicy(
                PrincipalPolicy.WindowsPrincipal);

        WindowsPrincipal wp
                = (WindowsPrincipal) Thread.CurrentPrincipal;

        if (wp.IsInRole(WindowsBuiltInRole.PowerUser))
        {
            Console.WriteLine("Access Granted!");
        }
        else
        {
            Console.WriteLine("Access Denied!");
        }
    }
}
```

The call to `AppDomain.CurrentDomain.SetPrincipalPolicy()` method initializes the current thread with `WindowsPrincipal` representing the current user. The `WindowsPrincipal` object is extracted from the `CurrentPrincipal` property of the current thread. Listing 38.3 uses the `IsInRole()` method of the `WindowsPrincipal` object to determine if the current user is in the `PowerUser` role. The parameter to the `IsInRole()` method is a member of the `WindowBuiltInRole` enum.

The more general method of implementing role-based security is through the `GenericPrinicpal` and `GenericIdentity` objects. Listing 38.4 shows how to use general role-based security.

LISTING 38.4 Role-Based Security with `GenericPrincipal`

```
using System;
using System.Threading;
using System.Security.Principal;

class GenPerm
{
    static void Main(string[] args)
    {
```

LISTING 38.4 continued

```
        GenericIdentity gid
                = new GenericIdentity("Administrator");

        String[] Roles = {"Administrator", "Developer"};

        GenericPrincipal gp
                = new GenericPrincipal(gid, Roles);

        Thread.CurrentPrincipal = gp;

        if (gp.Identity.Name == "Administrator")
        {
            Console.WriteLine("Good to go!");
        }
        else
        {
            Console.WriteLine("Not in this lifetime!");
        }
    }
}
```


Listing 38.4 creates a `GenericIdentity` object with a username. It then passes the `GenericIdentity` and an array of roles as parameters to create a new `GenericPrincipal` object. The flexibility of the `GenericIdentity` and `GenericPrincipal` objects makes it easy to create permissions infrastructures independent of the underlying operating system.

Security Utilities

The .NET Framework comes with several security-related utilities. Some will be familiar from this and previous chapters. Although I won't go into detail on all of them, they're listed in Table 38.5 to give you an idea about what is available. Remember to use the `-h` option on the command line for help on how to use each utility.

TABLE 38.5 .NET Security Utilities

Name	*Description*
`Makecert.exe`	Creates test X.509 certificates
`Certmgr.exe`	Manages certificate trust and revocation lists
`Chktrust.exe`	Checks validity of a file signed with a certificate
`Caspol.exe`	Manages security policy
`Signcode.exe`	Signs an assembly

TABLE 38.5 continued

Name	*Description*
`Storeadm.exe`	Isolated storage management
`Permview.exe`	View an assembly's permissions
`Peverify.exe`	Checks whether an assembly can be verified during JIT compilation
`Secutil.exe`	Extracts keys and certificates from an assembly
`Setreg.exe`	Sets signatures and certificates in the registry
`Cert2spc.exe`	Creates test software publisher certificates
`Sn.exe`	Strong name tool that generates keys for assemblies

Summary

Creating a security policy for code-based security includes combining evidence, code groups, permissions, and security policy levels. The evidence is the information revealed about an assembly. Code groups use evidence to categorize assemblies and grant permissions. Through a process of unions of the code groups and intersections of security policy levels, a security policy is applied to an assembly.

Assemblies can request permissions at load time and runtime. Imperative requests are made in code, and declarative requests are made with C# attributes.

Role-based security includes native Windows and Generic request mechanisms. The native Windows `Principal` and `Identity` objects interoperate with the operating system to provide role and identity security. The Generic `Principal` and `Identity` objects are more flexible for working with other security systems.

Several security utilities are available for working with certificates, keys, signatures, and other security issues.

Finally, here we are at the last chapter of *C# Unleashed*. However, this is not really an end, but a very exciting beginning to a bright new future in computing. You now have a brand new set of tools in your software engineering backpack. I hope they help you create many wonderful technologies, and I wish you well and the best of luck in all your endeavors.

Sincerely,

Joe Mayo

Appendixes

Part VI

In This Part

A Compiling Programs 761

B The .NET Frameworks Class Library 767

C Online Resources 773

APPENDIX A

Compiling Programs

IN THIS APPENDIX

- **Assemblies** *762*
- **Debug** *762*
- **Miscellaneous** *763*
- **Optimization** *764*
- **Preprocessing** *765*

Throughout *C# Unleashed* are numerous examples of how to compile libraries and programs. Many of the compiler options are covered in one form or another. However, there are still several other options that are useful. The following sections group and present each option of the C# compiler.

Assemblies

- **/addmodule:<filename>[;<filename>[. . .]]** Adds a module to an assembly. Semicolons separate multiple modules. Module must not contain a manifest.

  `csc /addmodule:mod1.netmodule;mod2.netmodule aprog.cs`

- **/lib:<filename>[,<filename>[. . .]]** Specifies a directory to search for library references. Commas separate multiple directories.

  `csc /lib:dir1,dir2 /reference:alib.dll aprog.cs`

- **/nostdlib[+|-]** Prevents `mscorlib.dll`, library for the `System` namespace, from being imported automatically. Allows implementation of a custom System namespace.

  `csc /nostdlib /reference:customstdlib.dll aprog.cs`

- **/reference:<filename>[;<filename>[. . .]]** Imports assembly metadata so types of the referenced assembly may be used in a program. Semicolons separate multiple directories. Referenced assembly must have a manifest.

  `csc /reference:alib.dll aprog.cs`

Debug

- **/bugreport:<filename>** Produces a file with information that can be submitted as a bug report. Information includes source code, command-line options, system information, and compiler output. The system will also prompt you for information, such as a bug description and advice on how to fix the bug.

  `csc /bugreport:myreport.txt aprog.cs`

- **/checked[+|-]** Controls runtime overflow checking.

  `csc /checked- aprog.cs`

- **/debug[+|-]** Generates debugging information in output files.

  `csc /debug aprog.cs`

- **/fullpaths** Shows the full path of files where errors and warnings occur.

  `csc /fullpaths aprog.cs`

- **/nowarn:<error#>[,<error#>[. . .]]** Turns off warning reporting on specified warning messages. Commas separate warning numbers.

  ```
  csc /nowarn:108,109 aprog.cs
  ```
- **/warn:<0|1|2|3|4>** Turns on warning levels. There are five levels of warnings with level 0 showing no warnings and level 4 showing all warnings.

  ```
  csc /warn:3 aprog.cs
  ```
- **/warnaserror[+|-]** Makes all warnings appear as errors. `/warnaserror` and `/warnaserror+` (with plus) turn warnings into errors, and `/warnaserror-`, the default, leaves warnings as they would normally be.

  ```
  csc /warnaserror+ aprog.cs
  ```

Miscellaneous

- `@` Uses a response file, which contains a list of compilation commands. Given the following response file named `respfile.rsp`:

  ```
  /target:exe aProg.cs
  ```

  You may use that response file with the following command:

  ```
  csc @rspfile.rsp
  ```
- **`/?`** Prints a list of help options to the console.

  ```
  csc /?
  ```
- **/baseaddress:<address>** Specifies the base address of a library.

  ```
  csc /target:library /baseaddress:0x11110000 aLib.cs
  ```
- **/codepage:<id>** Indicates the code page to compile programs with (for instance, the id 1252 specifies the ANSI character set).

  ```
  csc /codepage:1252 aProg.cs
  ```
- **/help** Prints a list of help options to the console. Same as `/?`.

  ```
  csc /help
  ```
- **/incremental[+|-]** Performs a partial build on a program. Only those files that have changed will be recompiled.

  ```
  csc /incremental aProg1.cs aProg2.cs
  ```
- **/main:<classname>** Specifies type containing the desired entry point when multiple `Main()` methods are defined in an assembly.

  ```
  csc /main:aClass aProg1.cs aProg2.cs
  ```
- **/noconfig** Prevents reading global and local `csc.rsp` files. The `csc.rsp` files contain response file entries that are always invoked by default.

  ```
  csc /noconfig aProg.cs
  ```

- **/nologo** Doesn't show the compiler banner.

```
csc /nologo aProg.cs
```

- **/recurse:[<dir>\]file** Searches subdirectories for files. No directory defaults to the current directory.

```
csc /recurse:*.cs aProg1.cs aProg2.cs
```

- **/unsafe** Allows the use of unsafe code.

```
csc /unsafe aProg.cs
```

- **/utf8output** Converts compiler output to utf8 encoding. Some locales aren't able to support default encoding and use this option with redirection to an output file.

```
csc /utf8output aProg.cs > compilerOutput.txt
```

Optimization

- **/filealign:<size>** Specifies the size of sections written to an output file. Can make efficient use of space on smaller devices.

```
csc /filealign:512 aProg.cs
```

- **/optimize[+|-]** Turns optimization on or off. Optimization is on by default.

```
csc /optimize- /debug+ aProg.cs
```

Output

- **/doc:<filename>** Produces XML documentation for appropriately formatted XML comments in the code.

```
csc /doc:aProgDocs.xml aProg.cs
```

- **/out:<filename>** Specifies the name of an output file.

```
csc /out:greatprogram.exe aProg.cs
```

- **/target:<exe|library|module|winexe>** Specifies the type of file to be generated. Options are `exe` for an executable, `library` for a dll, `module` for a non-executable module, and `winexe` for a windows forms program. The default is `exe`.

```
csc /target:library /out:musthaveutils.dll aLib.cs
```

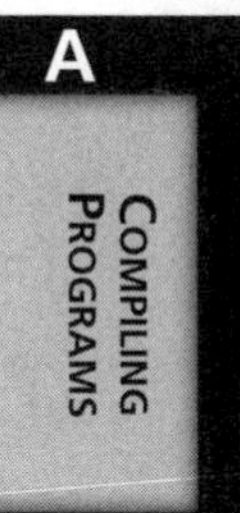

Preprocessing

- **/define:<name>[,<name>]** Declares a preprocessing #DEFINE statement through the command line.

```
csc /define:DEBUG aProg.cs
```

Resources

- **/linkresource:<filename>[,<identifier>]** Links an external resource to an assembly. Can have an optional identifier, which contains the logical name of the resource.

```
csc /linkresource:aResource.resource aProg.cs
```

- **/resource:<filename>** Embeds a resource into an assembly.

```
csc /resource:aResource.resource aProg.cs
```

- **/win32icon:<filename>** Embeds a Windows icon into an assembly.

```
csc /target:winexe /win32icon:anIcon.ico aProg.cs
```

- **/win32res:<filename>** Adds a Win32 resource to an assembly.

```
csc /target:winexe /win32res:aResource.res aProg.cs
```

The .NET Frameworks Class Libraries

The .NET Framework includes a huge library of reusable code, which is essential to developing C# programs. Complete coverage would fill volumes and is, of course, not possible here. The table that follows presents the .NET Frameworks class libraries by identifying namespaces and a general description of the contents of each namespace.

Namespace	*Description*
`Microsoft.CSharp`	Support for C# code compilation and generation
`Microsoft.JScript`	Support for JScript code compilation and generation
`Microsoft.VisualBasic`	Support for Visual Basic code compilation and generation
`Microsoft.Vsa`	Support for Visual Studio for Applications scripting engine
`Microsoft.Win32`	Handles OS events and registry manipulation
`System`	Fundamental classes for commonly used types
`System.CodeDom`	Represents elements and structure of a source code document
`System.CodeDom.Compiler`	Manages generation and compilation of source code
`System.Collections`	Interfaces and classes that define collections of objects
`System.Collections.Specialized`	Strongly typed collections
`System.ComponentModel`	Helps manage runtime and design time component behavior
`System.ComponentModel.Design`	Assists in development of custom design time logic and behavior of components
`System.ComponentModel.Design.Serialization`	Supports designers with component serialization
`System.Configuration`	Allows programmatic access to configuration files
`System.Configuration.Assemblies`	Used to configure assemblies
`System.Configuration.Install`	Enables building custom installers for components

Namespace	Description
System.Data	ADO.NET architecture classes
System.Data.Common	Classes shared by .NET data providers
System.Data.OleDb	OLE DB .NET data provider
System.Data.SqlClient	SQL Server .NET data provider
System.Data.SqlTypes	Native SQL Server type access
System.Diagnostics	Assists with debugging and tracing
System.Diagnostics.SymbolStore	Allows reading and writing of debug symbol information
System.DirectoryServices	Accesses Active Directory
System.Drawing	Basic GDI+ graphics library
System.Drawing.Design	Supports design-time GUI logic
System.Drawing.Drawing2D	Supports two-dimensional and vector drawing
System.Drawing.Imaging	Advanced GDI+ graphics library
System.Drawing.Printing	Customized printing
System.Drawing.Text	Text drawing functionality
System.EnterpriseServices	Provides COM+ services
System.EnterpriseServices.CompensatingResourceManager	Compensating Resource Manager functionality
System.Globalization	Culture-related information management
System.IO	Read/write capability to data streams
System.IO.IsolatedStorage	I/O to isolated storage
System.Management	Assists in working with Windows Management Instrumentation (WMI)
System.Management.Instrumentation	More types for the Windows Management Instrumentation (WMI)
System.Messaging	Accesses message queue functionality
System.Net	Networking classes
System.Net.Sockets	Windows Sockets Interface
System.Reflection	Performs operations with reflection services
System.Reflection.Emit	Dynamically creates assemblies
System.Resources	Works with resource files

Namespace	*Description*
`System.Runtime.CompilerServices`	Compiler development support
`System.Runtime.InteropServices`	Accesses native APIs and COM
`System.Runtime.InteropServices.CustomMarshalers`	Helps marshal types during Interop
`System.Runtime.InteropServices.Expando`	Interface for working with types
`System.Runtime.Remoting`	Supports distributed applications
`System.Runtime.Remoting.Activation`	Supports activation of remote objects
`System.Runtime.Remoting.Channels`	Handles channels and channel sinks
`System.Runtime.Remoting.Channels.Http`	Handles HTTP channels
`System.Runtime.Remoting.Channels.Tcp`	Handles TCP channels
`System.Runtime.Remoting.Contexts`	Environment management
`System.Runtime.Remoting.Lifetime`	Controls object lifetimes and leasing
`System.Runtime.Remoting.Messaging`	Manages messages between objects
`System.Runtime.Remoting.Metadata`	Assists in SOAP serialization
`System.Runtime.Remoting.MetadataServices`	Helps in converting metadata to XML schema
`System.Runtime.Remoting.Proxies`	Manages proxy creation and functionality
`System.Runtime.Remoting.Services`	Provides tracking services for receipt and disconnect of remoting objects and services
`System.Runtime.Serialization`	Supports for object serialization
`System.Runtime.Serialization.Formatters`	Specialized classes to support creating serialization formatters
`System.Runtime.Serialization.Formatters.Binary`	Binary serialization formatter
`System.Runtime.Serialization.Formatters.Soap`	Soap serialization formatter
`System.Security`	Underlying classes for the .NET security system
`System.Security.Cryptography`	Cryptographic services
`System.Security.Cryptography.X509Certificates`	X509 certificate management
`System.Security.Cryptography.Xml`	Integrates XML and the security system

Namespace	*Description*
`System.Security.Permission`	Security access and controls
`System.Security.Policy`	Manages code groups, membership conditions, and evidence
`System.Security.Principal`	Manages a security context
`System.ServiceProcess`	Helps run OS services
`System.Text`	Assists in managing various text encodings
`System.Text.RegularExpressions`	The .NET regular expression library
`System.Threading`	Enables multithreaded programming
`System.Timers`	Allows a program to raise events at specified time intervals
`System.Web`	Basic classes for Web browser/server communication
`System.Web.Caching`	Helps cache information on a Web server
`System.Web.Configuration`	ASP.NET configuration support
`System.Web.Hosting`	ASP.NET hosting services
`System.Web.Mail`	Internet smtp mail services
`System.Web.Security`	ASP.NET security classes
`System.Web.Services`	Classes for building Web services
`System.Web.Services.Description`	Assists with the Web Service Description Language (WSDL)
`System.Web.Services.Discovery`	Helps use the Web services discovery process
`System.Web.Services.Protocols`	Various classes to assist in protocols communicating with Web services
`System.Web.SessionState`	Assistance with session management
`System.Web.UI`	Support for controls and Web pages
`System.Web.UI.Design`	Design-time support for Web applications
`System.Web.UI.Design.WebControls`	Design-time support specific to Web controls
`System.Web.UI.HtmlControls`	Support for HTML related controls
`System.Web.UI.WebControls`	Support for more abstract Web controls

Namespace	*Description*
`System.Windows.Forms`	Helps create Windows GUI applications
`System.Windows.Forms.Design`	Design-time support for Windows GUI applications
`System.Xml`	Base class for standardized XML support
`System.Xml.Schema`	Standardized XML schema support
`System.Xml.Serialization`	Assists in XML formatted serialization of objects
`System.Xml.XPath`	XPath support
`System.Xml.Xsl`	XSL/T transformation support

APPENDIX C

Online Resources

IN THIS APPENDIX

- C# Sites 774
- .NET Sites 774

C# Sites

- **C# Corner**

  `http://www.c-sharpcorner.com/`

- **C# Help**

  `http://www.csharphelp.com/`

- **C# Station**

  `http://www.csharp-station.com/`

- **csharpindex**

  `http://www.csharpindex.com/`

- **Sharp Develop**

  `http://www.icsharpcode.net/`

.NET Sites

- **DEV/X Links**

  `http://www.devx.com/dotnet/resources/`

- **GotDotNet**

  `http://www.gotdotnet.com/`

- **MSDN**

  `http://msdn.microsoft.com/`

INDEX

A

abstract classes, 115, 217
interfaces and vs., 302
polymorphism and, 200–217
abstract methods, 205–209
abstract modifier, in events and event handling, 271
abstraction, 114–115
structs and, 293
accessibility modifiers, 131–132
accessors, 157–160
in events and event handling, modification of, 269–275
Active Server Pages (ASP), ASP.NET and, 440
adapters (Java) (*See* delegates)
Add( ), even/in events and event handling, 269
Add( ), 562
addition operator, 52
address of operator, unsafe code and, 620
ADO.NET, 5, 16, 417–438
accessing table data using, 421
aligning table data using, 421
calling stored procedures using, 429–434
columns of database and, 421, 437
connections to database with, 418–419
data source and, 419
DataAdapter and, 437–438
dataset retrieval using, 435–438
default type retrieval in, 422
deleting data using, 425–429
error handling in, 425
ExecuteNonQuery( ) in, 425
inserting data using, 425–429
manipulating data using, 425–429
namespaces and, 424
parameterized queries and, 434
passwords and, 418–419
Provider attribute of connection in, 419
security and, 418
SQL and, 419, 429–434
try/catch and finally blocks in, 425
typed retrieval by index technique in, 422
updating data using, 425–429
User ID attribute of connection in, 419
usernames and, 418
vendor specific class support in, 419
viewing data using DataReader of, 420–425
XML and, 418
AdRotator control, 441
advanced topics, 5–6
alias directive, 281–282
allowed attribute elements, 574–577
anchoring of controls, graphical user interfaces (GUIs) and, 347
AND operator, 55–57
AppDomains
reflection and, 592
remoting and, 460
Append( ) method, 533–534
AppendFormat( ) method, 534–535
application configuration files, 740
architecture (*See* NET architecture)
args, 45
arguments, command-line, 45
arithmetic expressions, conversion and, 331–335
arithmetic operators, 51–53, 68
array expressions, 63
ArrayList, 546–547
arrays, 5, 34–35, 40–43, 46, 63, 68, 203
array expressions and, 63–65
ArrayList, 546–547
BitArray, 547–548
cross-language programming and, 719
indexers and, 162–164
initialization of, 41
Length property of, 64
methods and properties of, 64–65
params parameters and, 152–155
pointers and 622–625
size of, 41
as operator, 60, 68, 203
ASCII, 25
ASP.NET for Web applications, 5, 16, 439–458
Active Server Pages (ASP) in, 440
button in, 446
code-behind web pages using, 452–457
collections and, 451
controls in, 441–443
database access for web form using, 448–452
DataGrid control in, 448–452
DataSource for, 451–452
event handling and, 447
form for web page using, 443–452
<form> tags for, 445, 447
HTML controls in, 440, 442–443, 450
HTTP and, 440, 445, 451
labels in, 445–446, 450–451
manipulating form controls in, 448–452
<script> tags for, 447
server controls in, 441–442
simple web page design using, 440–441
textbox in, 446
validation controls in, 443, 447
viewing Web service info using, 486–490
Web service creation using, 485–486
Web services and, 484
assemblies, 7, 596, 733–744
attributes in, 735–738
certificates for, 739–740
Common Language Infrastructure (CLI) and, 734

compiler, 762
configuration of, 740–743
cross-language programming and, 714, 720–721
deployment of, 743–744
files in, 734–738
garbage collection and, concurrent, 741–743
Global Assembly Cache (GAC) and, 744
identity attributes in, 736, 738
informational attributes of, 736–737
location of, 742–743
manifests in, 735, 737
metadata in, 728, 735
MMC snap in configuration tool for, 743
modules and, 734
private, 743
resources in, 734
runtime configuration of, 741
scope of, 738
security and, 739
shared, 743
startup configuration of, 741
strong name attribute of, 737–738, 739, 744
version redirection in, 742
versioning in, 738–739

Assembly type, 588

AssemblyBuilder object, 593–594

assertions, in debugging, 643–644

assignment operators, 58–59

associativity, 66–67

@ symbol, 25

attaching to processes for debugging, 101–106

attributes, 5, 20, 34, 110–112, 567–580
allowed elements in, 574–577
assemblies and, 735–738
AttributeUsage, 574–578
brackets to delimit, 568
comma as separator for, 570
component properties and, 123–125
conditional debugging, 638–641
constructors and, 577
creating, 574–578
cross-language programming and, 714, 720
GetAttribute( ), 578–579
getting, from a class, 578–579
inheritance and, 113–114, 578
Interface Definition Language (IDL) and, 568
metadata and, 568, 729
multiple, use of, 569–570, 577–578
named parameters for, 568, 570–572
parameters for, 568, 570–572
positional parameters for, 568, 570–572
private properties for, 577
public properties for, 577
serialization and, 398–405
single, use of, 568–569
specifiers for targets of, 573
targets for, 572–573

AttributeUsage, 574–578

automatic expression conversions, 331

automatic lifetime management, CLR and, 730

automatic memory management in, 696–699

automatic serialization, 398–401

B

Base Class Library (BCL), 12–14, 382

base classes, 4–5, 178–180, 217
calling members of, 188–191
conversion and, 338–339
hiding members of, 191–192
Object class as, 182–188
versioning of, 193–197

behaviors, 20, 34, 110–112, 116–120
inheritance and, 113–114
interfaces and, 302
methods and (*See* methods), 143–156
polymorphism in, 116–120

binary expressions, 3

binary operators, 48, 51–59, 68
overloading, 228, 233

binding
Component Object Model (COM/COM+) and, 680, 682–683
late bound object creation and properties in, 161–162

BitArray, 547–548

bitwise AND operator, 55–56

bitwise complement operator, 50–51

bitwise exclusive OR operator, 56

bitwise inclusive OR operator, 56

bitwise logic, 55–58

blocks of code, 21, 37, 65–66, 68, 286

body, method, 147

bool, 46, 294

boolean AND operator, 56

boolean exclusive OR operator, 57

boolean expressions, 50

boolean inclusive OR operator, 56–57

boolean logic, 55–58
do loops in,78–79
for loops in, 79–80
if else if else statement in, 71–73
if statement and, 70–73
if then else statement in, 71
side effects of, 58
while loop in, 77–78

Boolean types, 29

BooleanSwitch, 640

boxing
conversion and, 332
type, 295

braces as block code delimiters, 21, 65–66

brackets as attribute delimiters, 568

branching, 2, 88–89
goto statements in, 81–82
break statement, 73–74, 83, 88
breakpoints, debugging, 99, 103–106
browsing network libraries, 503–514
HTTP and, 512–514
sockets implementation for, 504–511
buffers, streams and, 394
built-in operators, 48
built-in performance counters, 648–656
buttons, 348, 354–355, 441, 446
byte, 30, 31, 32, 35, 294
conversion and, 331–335

C

C ++, 2, 17, 21, 24, 30, 32, 36, 37, 40, 712
Calendar, 441
calling base class members, 188–191
camel casing, 27
Cancel buttons, 363
Capacity property, string manipulation and, 538–539
capitalization, 27
case fall-through, 73–75
case sensitivity, 21, 27
case statement, 74–75
default case in switch statements for, 76
casting conversion, 30
catch (*See* try/catch blocks)
certificates, assemblies and, 739–740
channels, remoting and, 465, 475–477
char, 30, 32, 294
conversion and, 332
CheckBox, 348, 441
CheckBoxList, 441
checked statement, 251–253
checked( ) operator, 61, 68
CheckListBox, 349
child objects, 113–114
class, 3–4
CLASS declaration, 20
class keyword, 24, 26
class libraries, 4–5, 767–772
class variables, 37–38
classes, 34, 111–112, 129–176
abstract, 180–188
attributes and, retrieval of, 578–579
base, 178–180
calling base class members in, 188–191
constructors for, 135–142, 190–191
conversion and, 338–339
derived, 178, 182, 189–190, 205
encapsulation and, 116, 198–200
exception, predefined, 241
explicit implementation of interface in, 315–321
implicit implementation of interface, 304–315
indexers for, 162–164
inheritance in, 292
initialization order in, 139
interfaces and, 302
loaded, 141–142
namespaces and, accessing, 284
Object class as, 182–188
overloading members in (*See also* overloading), 218–236
polymorphism in, 200–217
properties and (*See also* properties), 156–162
re-declaring members of, 287–288
reference types and, 291–292
reflection and, 582, 587
resolving overloaded members of, 234–235
sealed, 197–198
static methods and, 155–156
structs and, 290–294
versioning of, 193–197
Clear( ), 562
client/server systems, 1
remoting and, 461–465, 478–480
sockets and, 504–511
clients
remoting and, 463–465, 478–480
sockets and, 507–511
Clone( ), 187, 522–523
CLS compliant code, 713–721
COBOL, 2
code-based security, 745–755
code-behind web pages, 452–457
Web services and, 485
code groups, 747–749
collections, 5, 35, 545–566
Add( ), 562
ArrayList, 546–547
ASP.NET and, 451
BitArray, 547–548
Clear( ), 562
Compare( ), 559
Contains( ), 562
creating, 553–565
HashTable, 549
ICollection interface implementation for, 558–559
IComparer interface implementation for, 559
IEnumerable interface implementation for, 559
IEnumerator interface implementation for, 560–561
IList interface implementation for, 561–563
IndexOf( ), 562–563
Insert( ), 563
interfaces for, 552
MoveNext( ), 560
pre-existing, 546–552
Queue, 549–550
Remove( ), 563
RemoveAt( ), 563
Reset( ), 561
SiteList example, creating, 553–565
SortedList, 550–551
Stack, 551–552
use of, SiteList example, 563–565

columns, 373
COM+ services (*See also* Component Object Model)
just-in-time (JIT) activation and, 688–689
object pooling in, 689–690
registration of COM+ services in, 686–687
transactions and, 687–688
ComboBox, 349, 366, 369, 370
comma as array element separator, 41
comma attribute separator, 570
command-line utility, 43–46
comments, 22–24, 46, 94
pre-processing and, 94
XML (*See also* XML comments), 135, 156, 162, 164, 165–176, 410
Common Intermediate Language (CIL), 13, 590, 727
Common Language Infrastructure (CLI), 12–17
assemblies and, 734
reflection and, 591
Windows Forms and, 344
Common Language Runtime (CLR), 16, 725–731
automatic lifetime management in, 730
Common Intermediate Language (CIL) and, 727
compiling to intermediate code in, 727
compiling to native code in, 727
debugging in, 730
Econo-JIT in, 727–728
exception handling using,729–730
executing programs in, 728
interoperability and, 730
managed execution in, 762–728
managed services in, 729–730
metadata and, 728–729
Microsoft Intermediate Language (MSIL) and, 727
namespaces and, 279
performance monitoring and, 654
Pre JIT in, 728
profiling in, 730
security and, 730
source code creation in, 727
Standard JIT in, 728
Common Language Specification (CLS), 6, 12–13, 17, 712–713
Common Type System (CTS), 12–13, 17, 712–713
communications, 5
compact profile, 14
Compare( ), 517, 559
CompareOrdinal( ) method, 518
CompareTo ( ) method, 523
comparisons (*See* relational operators)
compiler warning, 101, 194
compilers, 7, 27–28
assemblies options, 762
Common Language Runtime (CLR) and, 727
cross-language programming and, 714–715
debug options, 762
definite assignment in, 133–134
miscellaneous options, 763–764
optimization, 764
options for, 761–765
output options, 764
preprocessing, 765
resource options for, 765
sockets and, 511
warnings for, during debugging, 101, 194
complete profile, 15
component-based programming, 1, 3
component events, 125–127
component interfaces, 120–123
Component Object Model (COM/COM+), 6, 677, 679–691
binding and, 680
communicating with, from NET, 680
copying, 685
dynamic invocation and, 682
early binding in, 680–682
exposing NET component as a, 683–685
Global Assembly Cache for, 685
just-in-time (JIT) activation and, 688–689
late binding in, 680, 682–683
NET programs and, 680
NET support for COM+ services, 685–690
object pooling in, 689–690
registration of COM+ services in, 686–687
reuse of, 680
Runtime Callable Wrapper (RCW) in, 681
security and, 690
transactions and, 687–688
component properties, 123–125
compound operators, 58–59
computer speed, 656
Concat( ) method, 518–519
conditional AND operator, 57
conditional debugging, 638–641
conditional logic, 55–58
conditional operator, 59, 92–93, 228
conditional OR operator, 57–58
constant fields, 134
constructors, 3, 135–142, 190–191
attributes and, 577
declaring, 136
default, 140, 190–191
derived class and, 189–190
initialization order in, 139, 190–191

instance, 136–141
Java and, 140
methods and, 146–147
multiple use of, 138–140
parameters in, 139
private vs. public, 140–141
serialization and, 405
static, 141–142
structs and, 293, 296–297
this keyword and, 137, 139

containment, 115–116, 200
Contains( ), 562
ContextMenu, 374
continue statements, 84, 88
controls
ASP.NET and, 441
graphical user interfaces (GUIs) and, 347, 348–351
conversions, 38–40, 46, 329–340
automatic expression, 331
boxing, 332
class, base and derived, 338–339
implicit vs. explicit, 330–335
inheritance and, 339
reference type, 338–339
struct, 336–337
toType and fromType in, 335–337
unboxing, 332–333
value type 335–337
converting a resource file, 601–603
Copy( ) method, 519
CopyTo( ) method, 523–524
count, 49
counters of performance
customized, 657–668
performance monitoring and, 648–656
sampling performance with, 668–677
cross-environment support, 15–16
cross-language programming, 6, 15–17, 711–724
arrays in, 719
assemblies, 714, 720–721
attributes in, 714, 720
C++ and, 712
Common Language Specification (CLS) and, 712–713
Common Type System (CTS) and, 712–713
compilers, 714, 715
enums in, 719–720
events in, 717
indexers in, 717
inheritance in, 718–719
interfaces in, 718
JScript and, 712, 721–723
making code CLS compatible for, 713–721
Managed C++ (MCPP) and, 712, 721–723
methods in, 716–717
naming conventions in, 715
overriding methods in, 716
pointers in, 718
private methods, 714
properties in, 717
types and typing, 714–716
Visual Basic and, 712, 721–723
writing a program using, 721–723, 721
cryptographic streams, 395–398
cultures, resource files, 609–611, 616–617
curly braces, 70, 112
custom serialization, 401–405
customized performance counter for, 657–668

D

data hiding, 198, 217
data source
ADO.NET and, 419
ASP.NET and, 451–452
DataAdapter, ADO.NET and, 437–438
databases, ADO.NET and (*See* ADO.NET), 417–438
DataGrid, 349, 441, 448–452
DataList, 441
DataReader, ADO.NET, 420–425
dataset retrieval, ADO.NET and, 435–438
DateTimePicker, 349
Debug class, 636–638
Debugger for, NET Frameworks SDK, 96–101, 106
debugging, 3, 6, 91, 94–106, 635–645
approaches to, 95–96
assertions in, 643–644
attaching to processes for, 101–106
BooleanSwitch in, 640
breakpoints in, 99, 103–106
Common Language Runtime (CLR) and, 730
compilation option for, 638, 762–763
compiler warnings in, 101
conditional 638–641
Debug class for, 636–638
debug+ option in, 98
Debugger for, NET Frameworks SDK, 96–101, 106
directive option for, 638
enabling, 637–638
iterations to run through, 103
optimize option in, 98
output from, 637–638
runtime tracing, 641–643
runtime, 635–645
simple form of, 636–638
stepping through code in, 99–100
trace listeners in, 637
tracing, 640–643
decimal, 32–34, 46, 49, 295
declarations, 66, 68
declarative permission requests, 750–753
declaring data, 286–288
declaring objects, 20
decrement operator, 50
default case in switch statements, 76
default constructors, 140, 190–191

define directive, 92–93, 106
definite assignment, 37–38, 133–134
delegates, 4, 34, 256–261
defining, 256
equality of, 261
in events and event handling, 263, 265
invoking methods using, 258
method handler for, 257–258
multicast, 258–261
thread creation using, 498–499
dereferencing operator, unsafe code and, 620
derived classes, 178, 182
abstract and virtual methods in, 205–209
constructors called from, 189–190
conversion and, 338–339
hiding base class members in, 191–192
interfaces and, 302
sealed classes vs., 197–198
versioning of, 193–197
description technologies, Web services and, 484
destructors, 3, 142–143
garbage collection and, 699
structs and, 293, 296–297
dialog boxes, 356
modal vs. modeless, 355
directives, namespaces and, 280–282
directories, namespaces and, 285
DirectoryInfo class (*See* files and directories)
disambiguation of interface, 315, 319–320
discovering program information using reflection, 582–588
discovery technologies, Web services and, 484
Dispose method, 700–702
distributed applications, remoting, 458–481
division operator, 51
do loops, 78–79, 88
docking of controls, graphical user interfaces (GUIs) and, 347
documentation comments (XML), 23–24, 46, 408–416
DomainUpDown, 349
dot operator, in namespace, 284–285
double, 32–34, 295
conversion and, 334
DropDownList, 369, 441
dynamic invocation, Component Object Model (COM/COM+) and, 682
dynamic link libraries (DLL), 588–589
PInvoke and, 631–633
dynamic referencing, 34–35
dynamically activating code using reflection, 588–590
dynamically invoking methods, 203

E

early binding, Component Object Model (COM/COM+) and, 680–682
Econo-JIT, Common Language Runtime (CLR) and, 727–728
elif directive, 93, 106
else directive, 93, 106
e-mail, 5
embedded devices, 14
encapsulation, 115–116, 124, 198–200, 217
containment and, 200
data hiding and, 198
inheritance and, 200
interfaces and, 303–304
internal access modifier for, 199
modifiers for, 199
namespaces and, 286
private access modifier for, 199
protected access modifier for, 199
protected internal access modifier for, 199
public access modifier for, 199
sockets and, 506
structs and, 293, 297
encryption, 398
cryptographic streams and, 395–398
HashTable collection, 549
endif directive, 93, 106
EndsWith( ) method, 524
EnsureCapacity( ) method, 535
enum, 35–36, 46, 61–63
conversion and, 333
cross-language programming and, 719–720
enumeration expressions and, 61–63
Enum class, 61–63
enumeration expressions, 61–63, 68
environment for C#, 6–7
equal operator, 53
Equals( ), 183, 187–188, 519, 524, 535–536
error directive, 94, 106
errors (*See* exception and error handling)
escape characters/sequences, 24–25, 30–31
European Computer Manufacturers Association (ECMA), 15, 344
events and event handling, 4, 262–274, 389–390
abstract modifier for, 271
ASP.NET and, 447
callback method modification for, 269–275
calling multiple events in, 314
component events and, 125–127
cross-language programming and, 717
declaring an event for, 262–263
defining handlers for, 262–263

delegates for, 256–261, 263, 265
firing, 267–269
graphical user interfaces (GUIs) and, 344, 355
implementing, 265–267
interfaces and, 304
menus in GUIs, 379
modifying add/remove accessors in, 269–275
overrides modifier for, 271
publisher/subscriber pattern for registration of, 264–265
re-declaring, 287–288
registering for, 264–265
static modifier for, 271
virtual modifier for, 271

evidence, 745–746

exception and error handling, 4, 237–254
ADO.NET and, 425
checked statement in, 251–253
checked( ) operator and, 61
Common Language Runtime (CLR) and, 729–730
error directive in, 94, 106
exceptions defined, 238
explicit conversion and, 39–40
finally blocks in, 240–241, 248
GenerateException( ) for, 250–251
graceful degradation in, 246–248
multiple, 242–243
overflow of arithmetic operations and, 251–253
passing of, to calling program, 243–246
predefined classes for, 241
pre-processing errors and, 93–94
recovery from, 246–248
sequence of events in, 245–246
sockets and, 510
techniques for, 241–248
throw clause in, 243–246
try/catch blocks for, 238–240, 242–243, 248, 252–253
unchecked statement in, 251–253
user-designed exceptions in, 249–251

exclusive OR operator, 56, 57

executable files, 740

executing programs, Common Language Runtime (CLR) and, 728

execution environment, 726

explicit conversion, 38–40, 46, 330–335

explicit implementation of interface, 315–321

exponential notation, 33

exposing NET component as COM component, 683–685

expressions, 2, 3, 28, 47–68
arithmetic operators and, 51–53, 68
array, 63–65, 68
as operator and, 60, 68
assignment operators and, 58–59
binary operators and, 48, 51–59, 68
blocks of code and, 65–66, 68
built-in operators and, 48
checked( ) operator and, 61, 68
declarations and, 66, 68
enumeration, 61–63, 68
is operator and, 60, 68
labels and, 66, 68
logical operators and, 55–58
operator precedence and associativity in, 66–67
relational operators and, 53–55, 68
sizeof( ) operator and, 60, 68
statements and, 65, 68
ternary operators and, 48, 59, 68
typeof( ) operator and, 60–61, 68
unary operators and, 48–51, 68
unchecked( ) operator and, 61, 68

Extensible Markup Language (*See* XML)

extern methods, PInvoke and, 631–633

F

F-reachable queue, 699

fall-through, case, 73–74, 75

fields, 3, 111–112, 132–135
constant, 134
definite assignment in, 133–134
initialization in, 132–133
methods and, 147–148
properties vs., 159–160
readonly, 135
XML comments and, 135

File class (*See* files and directories)

FileInfo class (*See* files and directories)

files and directories, 382–390
assemblies and, 734–738
base class library (BCL) and, 382
classes for, 382
Directory class for, 385
DirectoryInfo class for, 382, 385–388
File class for, 382
FileInfo class for, 383–385
FileSystemWatcher class in, 388–390
namespaces and, 285
streams to manipulate, 391–398
Universal Description Discovery and Integration (UDDI) directories, 484

FileSystemWatcher class (*See also* files and directories), 388–390

filters, 84

Finalize( ), 183, 188

finalizing code, 699–702

finally block, 240–241, 248
ADO.NET and, 425

firing events, 267–269
first in first out (FIFO) processing, 549–550
fixed keyword, unsafe code and, 620, 628–631
float, 28–29, 32–34, 295
conversion and, 333, 334, 337
floating point, 32–34, 46, 49, 54
flow control, 3, 69–89
branching in, 88–89
break statement and, 74, 83, 88
case fall-through in, 75
case statement and, 74, 75
continue statements in, 84, 88
default case in switch statements for, 76
do loops in,78–79, 88
for loops in, 79–80, 88
foreach loops in, 80–81, 88
goto statements in, 81–82
if else if else statement in, 71–73, 88
if else in, 88
if statements in, 70–73, 88
if then else statement in, 71
loops in,76–81, 88
return statements in, 84–88
switch statement in, 73–76, 83, 88
while loop in, 77–78, 88
for loop, 3, 79–80, 88
foreach, 3, 80–81, 88, 203
Form, 349
form, for web page, using ASP.NET, 443–452, 443
Format( ), 62, 520
formatting, string manipulation and, 540–541
FromString( ), 62
fromType, 335–337
fully qualified names, 285
function pointers (C language) (*See* delegates)

G

garbage collection, 6, 34, 147, 695–709
assemblies and, 741–743
automatic memory management in, 696–699
concurrent, 741–743
control of, 703–709
destructors and, 142, 699
Dispose method for, 700–702
finalizing code and, 699–702
F-reachable queue and, 699
GC class for, 703–709
internal workings of, 697
live object graph and, 699
object control in,703–705
optimization of, 698
pinned variables, 630
remoting and, 478
stages of, 697–698
unsafe code and, 620, 630
using statement and, 701–702
weak references and, 706–709
GenerateException( ), 250–251
get accessor, 157–158, 215
GET, HTTP operation, 490, 513
GetAttribute( ), 578–579
GetEnumerator( ) method, 525
GetHashCode( ), 183, 187
GetModules( ), 588
GetName( ), 62
GetType( ), 183, 188, 588
GetValues( ), 63
Global Assembly Cache (GAC), 685, 744
Global Regular Expression Print (GREP), 542
goto, 3, 66, 81–82
graceful degradation, 246–248
graphical user interfaces (GUIs), 262, 343–380
adding a Web site listing, example of, 361–363
alignment of objects in, 347, 363
anchoring of controls in, 347
building a simple Windows type, 344–348
buttons in, 354–355
Cancel buttons in, 363
columns in, 373
ComboBox in, 366, 369, 370
command-line compilation of, 378
Common Language Infrastructure (CLI), 344
container object in, 346
controls in, 347–351
dialog boxes in, 356
docking of controls in, 347
drop-down list in, 369
event handling in, 355
events and event handling in, 344
Group controls in, 366
GroupBox in, 370
Labels in, 346–347, 355
ListView in, 372
menus for, 373–379
MessageBox, 379
modal dialog boxes in, 355
Model View Controller (MVC) in, 351
modeless dialog boxes, 355
n-tier architecture in, 351–373
namespaces in, 345–346
NET Framework, 344
OK buttons in, 363
Panel in, 366
separators in, 366
Text properties for, 348, 354–355
TextBox in, 363
Windows Forms library and, 344
windows within, 344–348
graphics, resource files, 603
conversion and, 602
greater than operator, 54
greater than or equal operator, 55
Group controls, 366
GroupBox, 349, 370

H

handlers event, 262–263
has a relationships, 116
HashTable collection, 549
headers, Web services and, 485
heap allocation, 34, 147
automatic memory management in, 696–699
structs and, 291–292
unsafe code and, 628
Hewlett Packard, 15
hexadecimal notation, 30
hiding base class members, 191–192
hiding data (*See* data hiding)
hierarchies of objects, 113–114
hierarchy of interfaces, 324–327
hierarchy of menu items, 379
host, sockets, 509
host utility setup, remoting and, 467–471
hosting, 726
HTML, ASP.NET and, 440, 442–443, 450
HTTP, 5, 15, 512–514
ASP.NET and, 440, 445, 451
GET in, 513
reflection and, 588
remoting and, 475, 477
request and response in, 513
Web services and, 484, 489–490
HyperLink, 441

I

ICollection interface implementation, 558–559
IComparer interface implementation, 559
identifiers, 24–25, 27, 46, 66
errors in, 93–94
identity attributes, assemblies and, 736, 738
IEnumerable interface implementation, 559
IEnumerator interface implementation, 560–561
if else if else statement, 71–73, 88
if else statement, 88
if statement, 3, 70–73, 88, 93, 106
if then else statement, 71
IList interface implementation, 561–563
Image, 441
ImageButton, 441
imperative permission requests, 750–753
implicit conversion, 38–40, 46, 330–335
implicit implementation of interface, 304–315
in/out parameters (*See* reference parameters)
inclusive OR operator, 56–57
increment operator, 49–50
index expression, 49
indexers, 3, 50, 162–164, 217, 561–562
cross-language programming and, 717
interfaces and, 304, 307
overloading, 223–227
pointers and 623–625
polymorphism in, 215–217
re-declaring, 287–288
string manipulation and, 532–533, 538–540
XML comments and, 164
IndexOf( ), 84, 525–526, 562–563
indirection
pointers and 622–625
unsafe code and, 620
informational attributes, assemblies and, 736–737
inheritance, 113–114, 178–198, 217
abstract classes and, 180–188
attributes and, 578
base classes and, 178–180
component interfaces vs., 121–123
containment vs., 200
conversion and, 339
cross-language programming and, 718–719
derived classes and, 178, 182, 189–190
encapsulation and, 200
interfaces and, 303, 322–327
multiple, 200
polymorphism and, 194
sealed classes vs., 197–198
string manipulation and, 516
structs and, 290, 292, 296–297
versioning and, 193–197
initialization, 37
arrays and, 41
constructors for, 135–142, 190–191
declaration and, 66
definite assignment and, 37–38, 133–134
field, 132–133
structs and, 298
input/output (I/O), 4
Insert( ) method, 526, 536–537, 563
instance constructors, 136–141
instance fields, constructors for, 136–141
instance members, 131
instance methods, 144
string manipulation and, 522–532, 533–538
instance objects, 21
instances, 115
instantiation of abstract class, 180
int/integer, 28–32, 35, 49, 52, 294
conversion and, 331–335, 331
integral, 30–32, 46
Intel, 15
interactive programs, 43–46
interface-based programming, 4
Interface Definition Language (IDL), 568
interfaces, 34, 301–327
abstract class vs., 302
behaviors and, 302

classes and, 302
collection type, 552
component type, 120–123
cross-language programming and, 718
declaring, 302–304
derived classes, 302
disambiguation of, 315, 319–320
encapsulation and, 303–304
events and, 304
explicit implementation of, 315–321
graphical user (*See* graphical user interfaces)
hiding implementation of, 317
hierarchy of, 324–327
ICollection, 558–559
IComparer, 559
IEnumerable, 559
IEnumerator, 560–561
IList, 561–563
implicit implementation of, 304–315
indexers and, 304, 307
inheritance and, 303, 322–327
internal modifier for, 303
mapping, 321–324
members of, 302–304
methods and, 303
modifiers for, 303
new modifier for, 303
polymorphism and, simulation of, 309–315
private modifier for, 303
properties and, 303–304
protected modifier for, 303
public modifier for, 303
single class, implementation of, 305–309
struct and, 304
virtual methods and, 302

intermediate code, Common Language Runtime (CLR) and, 727
intermediate language (IL), 731
intern pool, string manipulation and, 520–521
Intern( ) method, 520–521
internal access modifier, 199
internal accessor, 132
internal modifier, interfaces and, 303
Internet Information Server (IIS), 513
remoting and, 465–467
interoperability, Common Language Runtime (CLR) and, 730
is a relationships, 113, 178, 338
is operator, 60, 68
IsDefined( ), 63
IsInterned( ) method, 521
iteration, 2

J

jagged arrays, 42–43
params parameters and, 152–155
Java, 2, 21, 25, 32, 37, 40
constructor use and, 140
Join( ) method, 522
JScript, 17, 712, 721–723
just-in-time (JIT) activation, 726, 731
COM+ services and, 688–689

K

kernel profile, 13, 14
keyword, class, 21
keywords, 24–27, 46
unsafe code and, 620

L

labels, 66, 68, 83, 349, 355, 441
ASP.NET and, 445–446, 450–451
graphical user interfaces (GUIs) and, 346–347
language support, 17
last-in first-out (LIFO) processing, 551–552
LastIndexOf( ) method, 526–527
late binding, Component Object Model (COM/COM+) and, 680, 682–683
late bound object creation, 161–162
leasing, remote, 478
least significant bit, 28
left shift operator, 52
legacy systems
PInvoke and, 631–633
unsafe code and PInvoke in, 620–633
Length property, string manipulation and, 532, 539
less than operator, 54
less than or equal operator, 54–55
libraries, 16
browsing, 503–514, 503
lifetime management
Common Language Runtime (CLR) and, 730
remoting and, 478–480
Limited Regular Expression Print (LREP), 543
line directive, 94, 106
line numbers, in pre-processing, 94
LinkButton, 441
LinkLabel, 349
List View, 349
ListBox, 349, 442
lists
Add( ), 562
Clear( ), 562
Contains( ), 562
IList interface implementation for, 561–563
indexer for, 561
IndexOf( ), 562–563
Insert( ), 563
read only/write only for, 561
Remove( ), 563
RemoveAt( ), 563
size of, 561
SortedList, 550–551

ListView, 372
literals, 29, 31, 46
suffixes for, 34
verbatim string literals, 429
live-object graph, 699
loaded classes, static constructors and, 141–142
local fields, methods and, 147–148
local variables, 37, 147, 286
localhost, sockets, 509
localization and resources, 6, 595–617
assemblies and, 596
converting a resource file for, 601–603
cultures in, 609–611, 616–617
finding resources for, 616–617
graphical resources and, 603–609
multiple locales and, 609–617
ResEditor utility for, 604–605
resource files in, 596–609
ResourceManager in, 614
ResXGen utility for, 604–605
threading in, 615
lock statement, multi-threading, 502
logical complement operator, 50
logical operators, 55–58, 228
long, 30– 32, 35, 52, 295
loops, 3, 76–81, 88
continue statements in, 84

M

machine configuration files, 740
Main ( ), 21–22, 44–46
return statement in, 84–88, 84
MainMenu, 374
Managed C++ (MCPP), 17, 712, 721–723
managed code, 6, 13, 621, 726
managed execution, Common Language Runtime (CLR) and, 762–728
managed services, Common Language Runtime (CLR) and, 729–730
manifests, assemblies and, 735, 737
mapping interfaces, 321–324
marshalling, remoting and, 472
MaxCapacity property, string manipulation and, 539
McIlroy, Doug, 542
members of class, 130–131
MemberwiseClone( ), 183, 187
memory allocation and management, 291–292, 726
automatic memory management in, 696–699
streams, 391–398
MenuItem, 374
menus, GUI, 373–379
ContextMenu in, 374
event handlers for, 379
hierarchy of items in, 379
implementing,378–379
MainMenu in, 374
MenuItem in, 374
Text property in, 379
MessageBox, 379
messaging, methods and, 143
metadata, 12, 13, 17, 568, 580
assemblies and, 735
Common Language Runtime (CLR) and, 728–729
reflection, 581–594
method handlers, delegate, 257–258
methods, 3, 21, 37, 38, 112, 143–156
abstract, 205–209
accessibility modifiers for, 131–132
body of, 147
calling, 145–146
component events and, 125–127
constructors and, 146–147
cross-language programming and, 716–717
delegates for, 256–261
dynamic invocation of, 203
dynamic reference to, 35
fields in, 132–135
indexers and, 162–164
instance member of, 131
instance, 144
interfaces and, 303
invoking, from another class, 146
local fields in, 147–148
members of, 130–131
modifiers for, 144–147
most derived implementation of, 210–213
Object class, 183
output parameters for, 151–152
overloading, 4, 220–223
overriding, 182–183, 205–209
parameters for, 148–155
params parameters for, 152–155
re-declaring, 287–288
reference parameters for, 149–150
signatures for, 144–147
skeleton of, 130
static member of, 131, 155–156
string manipulation and, 516
value parameters for, 148–149
virtual, 205–213, 302
Web services and, 486
XML comments and, 156
Microsoft, 15
Microsoft Intermediate Language (MSIL), 590
Common Language Runtime (CLR) and, 727
Minus operator, 48–49
MMC snap in configuration tool, assemblies and, 743
modal dialog boxes, 355
Model View Controller (MVC), graphical user interfaces (GUIs) and, 351
modeless dialog boxes, 355

modifiers,
encapsulation, 199
interfaces and, 303
method, 144–147
modules, 588
assemblies and, 734
Moore's law, 656
most-derived implementations of method, 210–213
most significant bit, 28
MoveNext( ), 560
multicast delegates, 258–261
multidimensional arrays, 42
multiline comments, 22–23, 46
multiple locale resource files, 609–617
multiplication operator, 51
multithreading, 5, 497–502
delegates for, 498
localization and resources in, 615
lock statement in, 502
synchronization in, 499–502
thread creation for, 498–499

N

n-dimensional arrays, 42
n-tier architecture
graphical user interfaces (GUIs) and, 351–373
name of class, 21, 112
name/value pairs, in resource files, 596–597
named parameters, attributes and, 568, 570–572
namespaces, 4, 277–288
accessing class from other, 284
ADO.NET and, for database, 424
alias directive for, 281–282
Common Language Runtime (CLR) and, 279
creating, 282–286
directives for, 280–282
dot operator in, 284–285
encapsulation of, 286
file and directory structure for, 285
fully qualified names in, 285
graphical user interfaces (GUIs) and, 345–346
hierarchy of, 278–279, 284
members of, 286
naming conflict vs., 279–280, 284
nested, 279, 284
organization of code using, 278–270
planning for, 286
using directive for, 280–281
naming conventions, 27, 46
cross-language programming and, 715
dot operator in, 284–285
namespaces and, 279–280, 284
NaN values, 49
native code, Common Language Runtime (CLR) and, 727
negative values, 49
nested namespaces, 279, 284
NET architecture, 14, 16–17
NET Framework, 281, 281
class libraries for, 767–772
graphical user interfaces (GUIs) and, 344
Web services and, wsdl utility for, 490–493
NET Frameworks SDK, 27, 96–101, 106
NET utilities, 5, 7
new modifier, 303
newline, 44
not equal operator, 53–54
numeric data (*See also* int/integer), 28, 29
string formatting of, 540
NumericUpDown, 350

O

Object class, 182–188
object-oriented programming (OOP), 1, 3, 20, 177–217
object pooling, 689–690
objects, 20, 110–112, 115–116
abstraction and, 114–115
classification of, 112–113
component interfaces and, 120–123
component properties and, 123–125
constructors for, 135–142
containment in, 115–116
conversion of, 329–340
definition or creating an object definition for, 111–112
encapsulation and, 115–116
hierarchies of, 113–114
inheritance and, 113–114
instances and, 115
late bound creation of, properties and, 161–162
objects within, 115–116
polymorphism in, 116–120, 116
relationships between, 113, 115–116
serialization and, 398–405
OK buttons, 363
online resources, 773–774
operating system
streams, 391–398
PInvoke and, 631–633
operator precedence and associativity, 66–67
operators (*See* binary operators; built-in operators; ternary operators; unary operators)
overloading (*See also* overloading), 4, 227–234
unsafe code and, 620
user defined vs. system defined, 233
optimization, compiler, 764
OR operator, 56–58
output parameters, 151–152
overflow, 251–253
unchecked( ) operator and, 61
overloading, 4, 218–236
indexers, 223–227
methods, 220–223

operators, 227–234
resolving members of, 234–235
overrides modifier, in events and event handling, 271
overriding methods, 182–183, 205–209
cross-language programming and, 716
virtual methods vs., 205–209

P

packages (Java) (*See* namespaces)
PadLeft/PadRight( ) methods, 527–528
Panel, 350, 366, 442
parameterized queries, ADO.NET and, 434
parameters, attributes and, 568, 570–572
parameters, method, 148–155
params parameters, 152–155
pascal casing, 27
passing exceptions to calling program, 243–246
passwords, ADO.NET and, 418–419
performance counters, 6, 648–656
customized, 657–668
sampling with, 668–677
performance monitoring, 647–677
accessing built-in performance counters for, 648–656
building customized performance counter for, 657–668
Common Language Runtime (CLR) threads and, 654
management of counters in, 667
Moore's law of computer speed and, 656
sampling in, 668–677
System Monitor and, 677
threading in, 654, 655
timer implementation for, 656–657
Windows Performance tool and, 677
Performance tool, 677
permissions, 747, 750–753
picture formatting, strings, 541
PictureBox, 350
pinned variables, 630
Platform Invoke (PInvoke), 619–633
Plus operator, 48–49
pointers
cross-language programming and, 718
unsafe code and, 621–625
policies, security, 753–755
policy levels, security, 749–750
polymorphism, 116–120, 194, 200–217
abstract and virtual methods in, 205–209
dynamic operations using, 204
hiding data using, 206–209
implementing, 201–206
indexers and, 215–217
interfaces and, 309–315
most derived implementation of methods and, 210–213
properties and, 213–215
structs and, 294
pooling, object, 689–690
port numbers, socket, 509
positional parameters, attributes and, 568, 570–572
post-decrement operator, 50
post-increment operator, 49
postfix operators, 228
pre-decrement operator, 50
pre-existing collections, 546–552
pre-increment operator, 50
Pre JIT, Common Language Runtime (CLR) and, 728
pre-processing, 91–94, 106
precedence of operators, 66–67
precision of values, 33
predefined exception classes, 241
predefined types, 294–295
prefix operators, 228
preprocessing, 765
primitive data types, conversion for, 330
Principal object, 755–757
printing XML documentation, 413
private accessors, 131–132, 199
constructors and, 140–141
private assemblies, 743
private attributes, 577
private fields, 131
private key encryption, 398
private methods, cross-language programming and, 714
private modifier, interfaces and, 303
profiling, Common Language Runtime (CLR) and, 730
ProgressBar, 350
PROLOG, 2
properties, 3, 156–162, 217
accessors of, 157–159
component, 123–125
cross-language programming and, 717
fields vs., 159–160
get accessor for, 157–158
Get and Set accessor reference to, 215
indexers and, 162–164
interfaces and, 303–304
late bound object creation in, 161–162
polymorphism in, 213–215
re-declaring, 287–288
set accessor for, 157–159
side effects of, 188
static, 160
string manipulation and, 532–533, 538–540
transparent access to, 159–160
XML comments and, 162

PropertyGrid, 350
protected accessor, 132, 199
protected internal access modifier, 132, 199
protected modifier, 182, 303
Provider attribute, ADO.NET and, 419
proxies
remoting and, 471–475
Web services and, 490–493
public access modifier, 24, 131–132, 199, 577
constructors and, 140–141
interfaces and, 303
public key encryption, 398
publisher/subscriber pattern for event registration, 264–265
PUT, HTTP operation, 490

Q

queries, parameterized, 434
Queue collection, 549–550
quotation marks as string delimiters, 36

R

RadioButton, 350, 442
RadioButtonList, 442
rational numbers, 28
re-declaring data, 287–288
reading XML documentation, 411–416
reading, using streams, 391–395
ReadLine( ), 44
read-only fields, 135
real proxy, 472
recovery from exceptions, 246–248
Red Beans, 140
redirection, assemblies and, 742
reference parameters, method, 149–150
reference types, 34–35, 40, 46
as operator and, 60
classes and, 291–292
conversion and, 338–339
pointers and 621–625
readonly fields and, 135
structs and, 290, 291–292
weak references and, 706–709
referencing data, 287–288
remoting and, 465
reflection, 6, 581–594
AppDomains and, 592
AssemblyBuilder object for, 593–594
classes and, 582, 587
Common Intermediate Language (CIL) and, 590
Common Language Infrastructure (CLI) and, 591
discovering program information using, 582–588
Dynamic Link Libraries (DLL) and, 588, 589
dynamically activating code using, 588–590
HTTP, 588
instance method, dynamic invocation of, 590
metadata and, 582
Microsoft Intermediate Language (MSIL) and, 590
Reflection.Emit API for, 590–594
Simple Message Transport Protocol (SMTP), 588
Simple Object Access Protocol (SOAP) and, 588, 589
TypeBuilder object for, 593
types and, 582
Reflection.Emit API, 590–594
registering for events, 264–265
registration of COM+ services, 686–687
regular expressions, 5, 541–543
relational operators, 68
relational operators, 53–55
relationships between objects (*See also* is a), 113, 115–116, 178
remainder operator, 51–52
remoting, 5, 458–481
AppDomains in, 460
basic level of, 460–471
channels for, 465, 475–477
client for, 463–465, 478–480
distributed applications and, 460
formatting in, 472
garbage collection and, 478
host utility setup for, 467–471
HTTP and, 475, 477
Internet Information Server (IIS) and, 465–467
leasing in, 478
lifetime management for, 478–480
marshalling in, 472
proxies for, 471–475
referencing in, 465
server for, 461–463, 478–480
setup for, 465–467
Simple Object Access Protocol (SOAP) and, 475, 477
single call components in, 462–463
singleton components in, 462–463
stub in, 472
TCP and, 475, 477
Universal Resource Identifier (URI) and, 463–464, 474
Universal Resource Locator (URL) and, 463–464
Web server setup for, 465–467
Remove( ), even/in events and event handling, 269
Remove( ) method, 528, 537, 563
RemoveAt( ), 563
Repeater, 442
Replace( ) method, 528, 537–538
replies, in sockets, 510–511
request, in sockets, 507–511

ResEditor utility, 604–605
reserved keywords, 26
Reset( ), 561
resolving overloaded class members, 234–235
resource files, 596–609
assemblies and, 596, 734
converting, 601–603
creating, 596–599
cultures in, 609–611, 616–617
finding, 616–617
graphics in, 602–609
multiple locales and, 609–617
name/value pairs in, 596–597
naming, 599
reading, 600–601
ResEditor utility for, 604–605
ResourceManager in, 614
ResXGen utility for, 604–605
threading, 615
writing, 599–600
ResourceManager, 614
ResXGen utility, 604–605
return statements, 84–88
reuse of software/code, 1, 6, 15, 680
RichTextBox, 350
right shift operator, 52–53
Rijndael symmetric encryption, 395–398
role-based security, 746, 755–757
Runtime Callable Wrapper (RCW), Component Object Model (COM/COM+) and, 681
runtime debugging (*See also* debugging), 6, 635–645
runtime tracing, 641–643

S

safe code, unsafe code vs., 620
sampling for performance monitoring, 668–677
sbyte, 30, 32, 294
conversion and, 331–335
scope, 286–288
assemblies and, 738
variables, 80
<script> tags, ASP.NET and, 447
ScrollBar, 350
sealed classes, 197–198, 217
string manipulation and, 516
security, 7, 726, 745–758
ADO.NET and, 418
assemblies and, 739
code-based, 745–755
code groups in, 747–749
Common Language Runtime (CLR) and, 730
Component Object Model (COM/COM+) and, 690
declarative permission requests in, 750–753
evidence in, 745–746
imperative permission requests in, 750–753
permission requests in, 750–753
permissions in, 747
policy implementation for, 753–755
policy levels for, 749–750
Principal object and, 755–757
role-based, 746, 755–757
sealed classes and, 197–198
utilities for, 757–758
select, 3
semicolon as statement delimiter, 65, 78, 101
separators, graphical user interfaces (GUIs) and, 366
serialization, 398–405
automatic, 398–401
constructors and, 405
custom, 401–405
formatter for, 401
GetObjectData ( ) in, 401
ISerializable interface, 401
server controls, ASP.NET and, 441–442
servers, 15
host utility setup, for remoting467–471, 467
HTTP, 513
Internet Information Server (IIS) and, 465–467, 513
remoting and, 461–463, 465–467, 478–480
sockets and, 504–507
Set accessor, 157–159, 215
shared assemblies, 743
shift operators, 52–53
short, 30–32, 35, 294
conversion and, 331–335
short circuit operators, 58
signatures, method, 144–147
simple if statements, 70
Simple Message Transport Protocol (SMTP), 5, 588
Simple Object Access Protocol (SOAP), 15
reflection and, 588–589
remoting and, 475, 477
Web services and, 484, 489–490
simple types, 29
single call components, remoting and, 462–463
single-dimension array, 40–41, 152–155
single-line comments, 23, 46
singleton components, remoting and, 462–463
Site Manager Program, XML documentation using, 171–175
SiteList collection creation example, 553–565
sizeof ( ) operator, 60, 68
unsafe code and, 620, 625–626
skeleton of class, 130
slash asterisk comment delimiters, 22–23
slash comment delimiters, 23
sockets, 5, 504–511
client for, 507–511
compiling and running server and client using, 511
encapsulation of, 506
host and localhost for, 509
port numbers for, 509
reply from server through, 510–511

- requests through, 507–511
- server for, 504–507
- TCP class for, 506
- try/catch blocks for exception handling in, 510

Software Publisher Certificate (SPC), 740
SortedList, 550–551
source code creation, Common Language Runtime (CLR) and, 727
Split( ) method, 528–529
Splitter, 350
SQL, ADO.NET and, 419, 429–434
stack allocation
- Stack collection for, 551–552
- structs and, 291–293
- unsafe code and, 620, 626–628

Stack collection 551–552
stackalloc operator, unsafe code and, 620, 626–628
Standard JIT, Common Language Runtime (CLR) and, 728
standardization, 15–16
StartsWith( ) method, 529
statements, 2, 22, 65, 68
static constructors, 141–142
static extern methods, PInvoke and, 631–633
static fields, constructors for, 141–142
static members, 131
static methods, 155–156
- string manipulation and, 517

static modifier, in events and event handling, 271
static objects, 21
static properties, 160
statistics, sampling performance and, 668–677
StatusBar, 350
stepping through code, 99–100
storage, using streams, 391–398
stored procedures, ADO.NET and, 429–434
streams, 4, 391–398
- accessing a file using, 391–393
- buffers and, 394
- closing, 394
- creating, 394
- cryptographic, implementation of, 395–398
- instantiation of, 393–394
- opening, 394–395
- reading and writing using, 391–395
- serialization in, 398–405

string, 36–37, 44, 295
- verbatim string literals and, 429

String class, 5, 516–533
String indexer, 532–533
string manipulation, 5, 515–544
- Append( ) method for, 533–534
- AppendFormat( ) method for, 534–535
- Capacity property for, 538–539
- Clone( ) method for, 522–523
- compare( ) method for, 517
- CompareOrdinal( ) method for, 518
- CompareTo ( ) method for, 523
- Concat( ) method for, 518–519
- Copy( ) method for, 519
- CopyTo( ) method for, 523–524
- EndsWith( ) method for, 524
- EnsureCapacity( ) method for, 535
- Equals( ) method for, 519, 524, 535–536
- Format( ) method for, 520
- formatting for, 540–541
- GetEnumerator( ) method for, 525
- immutability of, 516
- indexers for, 532–533, 538–540
- IndexOf( ) method for, 525–526
- inheritance and, 516
- Insert( ) method for, 526, 536–537
- instance methods for, 522–538
- intern pool in, 520–521
- Intern( ) method for, 520–521
- IsInterned( ) method for, 521
- Join( ) method for, 522
- LastIndexOf( ) method for, 526–527
- Length property for, 532, 539
- MaxCapacity property for, 539
- methods and, 516
- multiple references to string in, using intern pool, 521
- numeric formatting in, 540
- PadLeft/PadRight( ) methods for, 527–528
- picture formatting in, 541
- properties for, 532–533, 538–540
- regular expressions and, 541–543
- Remove( ) method for, 528, 537
- Replace( ) method for, 528, 537–538
- sealed class and, 516
- Split( ) method for, 528–529
- StartsWith( ) method for, 529
- static methods and, 517
- String class for, 516–533
- String indexer for, 532–533
- StringBuilder class for, 516, 533–540
- SubString( ) method for, 529–530
- ToCharArray( ) method for, 530
- ToLower( ) method for, 530
- ToString( ) method for, 538
- ToUpper( ) method for, 531
- Trim( ) method for, 531
- TrimEnd( ) method for, 531–532
- TrimStart( ) method for, 532

String.Compare( ), 80
StringBuilder class, 5, 516, 533–540
strong name attribute, assemblies and, 737–739, 744
strong typing, 28
structs, 4, 34, 40, 46, 289–299
abstraction and, 293
assignment of, 293
boxing and unboxing of, 295
classes and, 290–294
constructors for, 293, 296–297
conversion and, 336–337
creating, 290–291
destructors for, 293, 296–297
encapsulation and, 293, 297
heap allocation of, 291–292
implementing, 297–298
inheritance and, 290, 292, 296–297
initialization of, 298
interfaces and, 304
polymorphism and, 294
pre-defined types as, 294–295
reference types and, 290–292
stack allocation of, 291–293
trade-offs in performance, vs. classes, 293–294
type system unification for, 294–295
user-created types for, 295–298
value vs. reference in, 291–292
stub, remoting and, 472
style, 26–27
SubString( ) method, 529–530
subtraction operator, 52
suffixes, literal, 34
switch statement, 73–76, 83, 88
switch statements
default case in, 76
symmetric encryption algorithms, 398
synchronization in multithreading, 5, 499–502
syntax, 2–3
System Monitor, 677
System statement, 44

T

TabControl, 350
Table, 442
TableRow, 442
tags, XML, 410
targets, attribute, 572–573
TCP/IP, 5
ternary operators, 3, 48, 59, 68
text editors, weak references and, 706–709
Text property
graphical user interfaces (GUIs) and, 354–355
menu item, 379
TextBox, 350, 363, 442, 446
Thawte, 739
this keyword, 137, 139
threads (*See also* multithreading)
creation of, for multithreading, 498–499
localization and resources in, 615
multithreading and, 497–502
performance monitoring and, 654, 655
synchronization in, 499–502
throw clause, 243–246
tilde as destructor indicator, 143
Timer, 350
timers, for performance monitoring, 656–657
ToCharArray( ) method, 530
ToLower( ) method, 530
ToObject( ), 63
ToolBar, 350
ToolTip, 351
ToString( ), 183, 187–188, 538
toType, 335–337
ToUpper( ) method, 531
trace listeners, 637
tracing, 6, 640–643
TrackBar, 351
transactions, COM+ services and, 687–688
Transmission Control Protocol (TCP)
remoting and, 475, 477
sockets and, 506
Web services and, 484
transmission technologies, Web services and, 484
transparent access to properties, 159–160
transparent proxy, 472
TrayIcon, 351
TreeView, 351
Trim( ) method, 531
TrimEnd( ) method, 531–532
TrimStart( ) method, 532
true/false, 29, 50, 54–56
conditionals, 92–93
if else if else statement in, 71–73
if statements, 70
if then else statement in, 71
try/catch block, 238–240, 242–243, 248, 252–253
ADO.NET and, 425
sockets and, 510
Type object, typeof( ) operator and, 60–61
type system unification, 294–295
TypeBuilder object, 593
typedef, 32
typeof( ) operator, 60–62, 68
types and typing, 4, 28–37, 46, 66, 726
ADO.NET and, 422
boxing and unboxing in, 295
Common Type System (CTS) and, 712–713
constants in, 134
conversion in, 329–340
cross-language programming and, 714, 715–716
is operator and, 60
metadata, 728
predefined types, 294–295
reflection and, 582

toType and fromType in, 335–337
type system unification for, 294–295
user-created, 295–298

U

uint, 30–32, 52, 294
conversion and, 331–335
ulong, 30–32, 52, 295
conversion and, 331–335
unary operators, 3, 48–51, 68
overloading, 228, 233
unboxing
conversion and, 332–333
type, 295
unchecked statement, 251–253
unchecked( ) operator, 61
unconditional branching, goto statements in, 81–82
undef directive, 92, 106
Unicode characters, 24–25, 30, 36, 632
Uniform Resource Locator (URL), 463–464, 490–493
Universal Description Discovery and Integration (UDDI) directories, 484
Universal Resource Identifier (URI), 463–464, 474
unmanaged code, 621, 726
unsafe code, 13, 619–633
address of operator for, 620
definition of, 620
dereferencing operator for, 620
fixed keyword for, 620, 628–631
garbage collector and, 620
indirection operator for, 620
keywords associated with, 620
managed code vs., 621
operators for, 620
PInvoke and, 631–633
pointers and 621–625
safe code vs., 620
sizeof operator for, 60, 620, 625–626
stackalloc operator for, 620, 626–628
unmanaged code vs., 621
user-created types, 295–298
user-designed exceptions, 249–251
User ID attribute, ADO.NET and, 419
user interfaces, 131
usernames, ADO.NET and, 418
ushort, 30–32, 294
conversion and, 331–335
using declaration, 701
using directive, 280–281
using statement, garbage collection and, 701–702
utilities, security, 757–758

V

validation controls, ASP.NET and, 443, 447
value parameters, method, 148–149
value types
conversion and, 335–337
pointers and 621–625
variables, 28, 29
class, 37–38
conversions for, 38–40
definite assignment of, 37–38
explicit conversions, 38–40
implicit conversions, 38–40
initialization of, 37
local, 37, 147, 286
pinned, 630
readonly fields and, 135
scope of, 80, 286–288
verbatim string literal, 36–37, 429
Verisign, 739
version redirection, assemblies and, 742
versioning, 193–197, 217, 733–744
Virtual Execution System (VES), 2, 12–13, 16, 17
virtual machine, 726
virtual methods, 205–209
interfaces and, 302
most derived implementation of, 210–213
virtual modifier, in events and event handling, 271
visibility, 286–288
Visual Basic, 14, 17, 712, 721–723
Visual C++.NET, 14
Visual Jscrip.NET, 14
void, 21, 24, 26

W

warning directive, 94
warning directive in, 106
weak references, 705–709
Web applications (*See* ASP.NET)
Web pages (*See also* ASP.NET)
code-behind, using ASP.NET, 452–457
form for, using ASP.NET, 443–452
Web servers, remoting and, 465–467
Web services, 1, 4–5, 15–16, 483–493
ASP.NET and, 484–485
class for, 486
code-behind web pages in, 485
creating, 485–486
description technologies in, 484
discovery technologies in, 484
header for, 485
HTTP and, 484, 489–490
methods in, 486
proxies and, 490–493
Simple Object Access Protocol (SOAP) in, 484, 489, 490

TCP and, 484
transmission technologies in, 484
Universal Description Discovery and Integration (UDDI) directories in, 484
use of, 490–493
viewing information on, 486–490
Web Services Description Language (WSDL) and, 484
World Wide Web Consortium (W3C) and, 484
wsdl utility for, 490–493
Web Services Description Language (WSDL), 484
Web sites of interest, 7, 773–774
WebSites library, XML documentation using, sample code, 165–171
while loop, 3, 77–78, 88
whitespace, 27, 46
Windows Forms library, 4, 16, 344
Windows Performance tool, 677
windows within GUIs, 344–348
World Wide Web Consortium (W3C), 484
Write( ), 44
WriteLine( ), 44–45, 62, 84
writing a simple C# program, 20–22
writing XML documentation, 408–411
writing, using streams, 391–395
wsdl utility, 490–493

X–Z

X.509 certification, 739–740
XML, 1, 4, 15, 407–416
ADO.NET and, 418
comments in, 23–24, 410
Formatting in, 409
Indentation in, 409
printing, 413
reading, 411–416
tags for, 410
writing documentation using, 408–411
XMLTextWriter class, 408–411
XML comments
fields and, 135
indexers and, 164
methods and, 156
properties and, 162
sample code for, 165–175
Site Manager Program with XML documentation using, 171–175
WebSites library with XML documentation using, sample code, 165–171